THE LAW AND PRACTICE
OF TRADEMARK TRANSACTIONS

ELGAR INTELLECTUAL PROPERTY LAW AND PRACTICE

Series Editors: Trevor Cook, *Partner, WilmerHale* and Johanna Gibson, *Herchel Smith Professor of Intellectual Property Law, Queen Mary University of London*

The Elgar Intellectual Property Law and Practice series is a library of works by leading practitioners and scholars covering discrete areas of law in the field of intellectual property. Each title will describe the law in detail, but will also be deeply analytical, highlighting and unpicking the legal issues that are most critical and relevant to practice. Designed to be detailed, focused reference works, the books in this series aim to offer an authoritative statement on the law and practice in key topics within the field, from *Trade Marks* to *Pharmaceuticals*, from *Patent Standards* to *Trade Secrecy* and from *IP Licensing* to *IP Valuation*.

Titles in this series include:

The Law and Regulation of Franchising in the EU
Mark Abell

The Protection of Geographical Indications
Law and Practice
Michael Blakeney

Patent Law in Greater China
Edited by Stefan Luginbuehl and Peter Ganea

Trade Secrecy and International Transactions
Law and Practice
Elizabeth A. Rowe and Sharon K. Sandeen

The Law and Practice of Trademark Transactions
A Global and Local Outlook
Edited by Irene Calboli and Jacques de Werra

THE LAW AND PRACTICE OF TRADEMARK TRANSACTIONS

A Global and Local Outlook

Edited by

IRENE CALBOLI

Deputy Director of the Applied Research Centre for Intellectual Assets and the Law in Asia and Visiting Professor at the School of Law, Singapore Management University, Singapore; Professor of Law at Texas A&M University School of Law, USA

JACQUES DE WERRA

Professor of Contract Law and Intellectual Property Law, Law School, University of Geneva, Switzerland

ELGAR INTELLECTUAL PROPERTY LAW AND PRACTICE

Cheltenham, UK • Northampton, MA, USA

© The Editors and Contributors Severally 2016

All rights reserved. No part of this publication may be reproduced, stored in a retrieval system or transmitted in any form or by any means, electronic, mechanical or photocopying, recording, or otherwise without the prior permission of the publisher.

Published by
Edward Elgar Publishing Limited
The Lypiatts
15 Lansdown Road
Cheltenham
Glos GL50 2JA
UK

Edward Elgar Publishing, Inc.
William Pratt House
9 Dewey Court
Northampton
Massachusetts 01060
USA

A catalogue record for this book
is available from the British Library

Library of Congress Control Number: 2015913904

This book is available electronically in the Elgaronline
Law subject collection
DOI 10.4337/9781783472130

ISBN 978 1 78347 212 3 (cased)
ISBN 978 1 78347 213 0 (eBook)

Typeset by Columns Design XML Ltd, Reading
Printed and bound in Great Britain by TJ International Ltd, Padstow

CONTENTS

List of figures   xx
List of tables   xxi
Editors and Contributors   xxii
Foreword Sir Robin Jacob   xxviii
Introduction Irene Calboli and Jacques de Werra   xxx
Table of cases   xxxiv
Table of legislation   xlvii

PART I   TRADEMARK TRANSACTIONS IN THE GLOBAL MARKETPLACE

Section A   International Framework

1. TRIPS, trademarks, and trademark transactions: a forced reconciliation?   5
   Daniel J. Gervais
2. Trademark transactions and the normative framework of the World Intellectual Property Organization   29
   Marcus Höpperger

Section B   Strategic Considerations

3. Licensing commercial value: from copyright to trademarks and back   53
   Jane C. Ginsburg
4. The complexities of domain names transactions: contracts for a market where value increases with time   82
   Cédric Manara
5. How to make two out of one: the ins and outs of trademark portfolio splitting transactions   98
   Gregor Bühler and Luca Dal Molin
6. Competition, markets, and trademark transactions   121
   Shubha Ghosh

Section C   Valuation, Taxation, Security Interests and Bankruptcy

7. Brand differentiation and industry segmentation: drivers for trademark valuation in corporate transactions   149
   Roy P. D'Souza

8. Trademark transactions and international tax strategies 171
Jean-Frédéric Maraia
9. Registering security interests over trademarks in Australia: theory and practice 197
Robert Burrell and Michael Handler
10. The intersection of trademarks, licenses and bankruptcy: ending uncertainties in the law 220
Xuan-Thao Nguyen

Section D Dispute Prevention and Settlement Mechanisms

11. Out of the shadows: the unique world of trademark consent agreements 255
Neil Wilkof
12. Choice-of-court and choice-of-law clauses in international trademark transactions 276
Dai Yokomizo
13. Alternative dispute resolution mechanisms for solving trademark disputes (mediation, UDRP, arbitration) 293
Jacques de Werra

PART II TRADEMARK TRANSACTIONS AT THE REGIONAL AND NATIONAL LEVEL

Section A Trademark Transactions in Europe

14. Trademark transactions in EU law: refining the approach to selective distribution networks and national unfair competition law 327
Martin Senftleben
15. UK perspectives on trademark transactions: a liberal approach 358
Laura Anderson
16. Trademark transactions in Germany: a continental European system moves towards common understanding with the US 387
Axel Nordemann and Christian Czychowski
17. French perspectives on trademark transactions: from the Civil Code to the business law? 410
Nicolas Binctin

Section B Trademark Transactions in North and South America

18. Trademark transactions in the United States: towards a de facto acceptance of trading in gross? 439
Irene Calboli

19. New dress code for business transactions in Brazil: essentials and peculiarities of trademarks in the spotlight 462
José Carlos Vaz e Dias

Section C   Trademark Transactions in Asia

20. Chinese trademark law and trademark transactions: a law in transition in the global economy 485
He Guo
21. Japanese perspectives on trademark transactions: is expansive trademark practice prevailing over the conservative stoicism? 511
Shinto Teramoto
22. Trademark transactions in ASEAN: convergences and divergences in emerging markets 537
Susanna H. S. Leong
23. Trademark transactions in India: exploring the genre, scope and consequence 558
Raman Mittal

Index 587

EXTENDED TABLE OF CONTENTS

List of figures   xx
List of tables   xxi
Editors and Contributors   xxii
Foreword Sir Robin Jacob   xxviii
Introduction Irene Calboli and Jacques de Werra   xxx
Table of cases   xxxiv
Table of legislation   xlvii

PART I   TRADEMARK TRANSACTIONS IN THE GLOBAL MARKETPLACE

Section A   International Framework

1. **TRIPS, TRADEMARKS, AND TRADEMARK TRANSACTIONS: A FORCED RECONCILIATION?**
   Daniel J. Gervais
   - A. INTRODUCTION   1.01
   - B. THE ORIGIN OF THE TRADEMARK PROVISIONS IN THE TRIPS AGREEMENT   1.03
     1. The battle between common and civil law   1.03
     2. Trademarks in major legal systems and the TRIPS Agreement   1.08
     3. The TRIPS Agreement and the Paris Convention   1.14
   - C. THE TRADEMARK PROVISIONS IN THE TRIPS AGREEMENT   1.17
     1. Article 15 of the TRIPS Agreement   1.18
     2. The function(s) of trademarks   1.20
     3. Recordal of transfers and licenses under Article 19.2 of the TRIPS Agreement   1.29
     4. Article 20 of the TRIPS Agreement   1.36
   - D. THE TRADEMARK TRANSACTIONS PROVISION: ARTICLE 21 OF THE TRIPS AGREEMENT   1.43
     1. Drafting history   1.44
     2. Compulsory licenses of trademarks   1.49
     3. Conditions on transfers and licenses and the enforcement of marks   1.54
     4. A role for competition law?   1.62
   - E. CONCLUSION   1.70

2. **TRADEMARK TRANSACTIONS AND THE NORMATIVE FRAMEWORK OF THE WORLD INTELLECTUAL PROPERTY ORGANIZATION**
   Marcus Höpperger
   - A. INTRODUCTION   2.01
   - B. THE NORMATIVE FRAMEWORK OF WIPO   2.04
     1. The Paris Convention   2.06
     2. The Singapore Treaty   2.07
     3. The Joint Recommendation   2.08
     4. The Madrid Protocol   2.09
   - C. CHANGE IN OWNERSHIP   2.10
     1. The Paris Convention   2.10
     2. The TLT and Singapore Treaty   2.14
     3. The Madrid System   2.25

D.	LICENSES	2.30
	1. The Singapore Treaty and Joint Recommendation	2.30
	2. The Madrid System	2.44
E.	RESTRICTIONS OF THE RIGHT OF DISPOSAL	2.47
F.	CONCLUSION	2.53

Section B Strategic Considerations

3. LICENSING COMMERCIAL VALUE: FROM COPYRIGHT TO TRADEMARKS AND BACK
Jane C. Ginsburg

A.	INTRODUCTION	3.01
B.	WHEN THE TRADEMARK OWNER IS NO LONGER A COPYRIGHT OWNER: TRADEMARK LICENSING IN THE SHADOW OF *DASTAR*	3.05
	1. Distinguishing trademark goodwill from works of authorship	3.07
	2. Trademark and copyright: in fact inseparable?	3.11
	3. Keeping characters out of the copyright public domain: the impact on trademarks	3.16
C.	EXPLOITING CHARACTERS WHEN THE TRADEMARK CLAIMANT WAS NOT ORIGINALLY OR IS NO LONGER THE COPYRIGHT OWNER	3.19
	1. Adopting copyright-expired characters	3.19
	2. Reversion of copyright in a trademarked character	3.25
D.	WHEN THE TRADEMARK OWNER BECOMES A COPYRIGHT OWNER: TRADEMARKS AS COPYRIGHTED WORKS	3.30
E.	CONCLUSION	3.39

4. THE COMPLEXITIES OF DOMAIN NAMES TRANSACTIONS: CONTRACTS FOR A MARKET WHERE VALUE INCREASES WITH TIME
Cédric Manara

A.	INTRODUCTION	4.01
B.	'WHICH' OBJECT FOR THE TRANSACTION?	4.06
	1. A top level domain	4.07
	(a) Private auctions	4.07
	(b) Sale of a top level domain	4.08
	(c) Lease of a top level domain	4.09
	2. A third level domain	4.10
	3. A second level domain	4.13
C.	'WHERE' WILL THE NAME BE USED?	4.14
D.	'WHO' WILL HOLD OR USE THE NAME?	4.18
	1. The case of a transfer	4.19
	(a) Eligibility	4.19
	(b) Contact information	4.24
	(c) Joint registration	4.25
	2. The case of agreements on use	4.26
	(a) General principles	4.26
	(b) Situations of joint use	4.30
E.	'WHAT' IS THE NATURE OF THE TRANSACTION?	4.31
	1. 'Sale' of a domain name	4.31
	2. License of a domain name	4.32
F.	CONCLUSION	4.33

5. HOW TO MAKE TWO OUT OF ONE: THE INS AND OUTS OF TRADEMARK PORTFOLIO SPLITTING TRANSACTIONS
Gregor Bühler and Luca Dal Molin

A.	INTRODUCTION	5.01
B.	PRELIMINARY NOTE ON APPLICABLE LAW	5.05

EXTENDED TABLE OF CONTENTS

	C.	BUILDING BLOCKS OF TRADEMARK PORTFOLIO SPLITTING			5.09
		1.	Overview		5.09
		2.	Free assignability as international standard		5.10
		3.	Partial assignment		5.12
			(a) Overview		5.12
			(b) Effect of the partial assignment		5.14
			(c) Limitations		5.16
			(d) Technicalities under a Swiss law focus		5.19
		4.	Trademark license		5.23
			(a) Overview		5.23
			(b) Limitations		5.26
			(c) Technicalities under Swiss law focus		5.28
		5.	Partial assignment and license grant compared in practice		5.31
			(a) In general: ownership v. contractual rights		5.31
			(b) Affected goods and services		5.33
			(c) Duration of the post-transactional arrangement		5.35
			(d) Flexibility of license grants v. restrictions on partial assignments		5.36
			(e) License to register new trademarks		5.37
	D.	TRADEMARK PORTFOLIO SPLITTING AGREEMENTS			5.39
		1.	Overview		5.39
		2.	Typical provisions in trademark portfolio splitting agreements		5.42
			(a) Trademark delimitation and allocation		5.42
			(b) Implementation of the allocation		5.46
			(c) Coexistence, non-compete and mutual support		5.51
			(d) Scope		5.52
			(e) Trademark maintenance		5.53
			(f) Duration and termination		5.55
			(g) Conflict resolution, governing law, jurisdiction		5.56
	E.	OTHER POSSIBLE OPTIONS AND CONSIDERATIONS			5.57
		1.	Shared ownership		5.57
		2.	Joint ventures		5.60
		3.	Rebranding		5.61
	F.	CONCLUSION			5.62

6. COMPETITION, MARKETS, AND TRADEMARK TRANSACTIONS
Shubha Ghosh

A.	INTRODUCTION	6.01
B.	COMPETITION, INTELLECTUAL PROPERTY, AND TRADEMARKS	6.15
C.	CONCEPTS, MODELS, AND TRADEMARK LAW	6.38
D.	TRADEMARK TRANSACTIONS: TYING, TRANSFERS IN GROSS AND COVENANTS NOT TO SUE	6.71
E.	CONCLUSION	6.77

Section C   Valuation, Taxation, Security Interests and Bankruptcy

7. BRAND DIFFERENTIATION AND INDUSTRY SEGMENTATION: DRIVERS FOR TRADEMARK VALUATION IN CORPORATE TRANSACTIONS
Roy P. D'Souza

A.	INTRODUCTION		7.01
B.	BRAND MANAGEMENT PRINCIPLES		7.06
C.	COMMON APPROACHES TO VALUE BRANDS		7.09
	1. Income approach		7.10
	(a) Relief from royalty		7.13
	(b) Excess earnings		7.18
	2. Market approach		7.20
D.	HISTORICAL TRANSACTIONS INVOLVING BRANDS		7.22
	1. Distressed vs. going concern (brand-only vs. business enterprise with brand)		7.23

xi

		(a) Distressed business enterprise (liquidation/brand only scenario)	7.24
		(b) Distressed enterprise key transactions	7.25
		(c) Going concern business enterprise	7.31
		(d) Going concern business enterprise key transactions	7.32
	2.	Valuation of the brands transacted	7.37
		(a) Strategic vs. Financial Target	7.37
		(b) Summary	7.38
	3.	Asset purchase agreements containing trademarks	7.39
E.	PURCHASE PRICE ALLOCATION		7.40
F.	WHY INDUSTRY MATTERS		7.41
G.	ADDITIONAL BRAND VALUATION METHODS		7.45
H.	THE WORLD'S MOST VALUABLE BRANDS		7.46
I.	CONCLUSION		7.47

8. TRADEMARK TRANSACTIONS AND INTERNATIONAL TAX STRATEGIES
Jean-Frédéric Maraia

A.	INTRODUCTION		8.01
B.	OECD – BEPS: GENERAL PRESENTATION		8.05
C.	TRADEMARK TRANSACTIONS BETWEEN THIRD PARTIES		8.10
	1.	Licensing	8.12
		(a) Tax treatment of royalties	8.14
		(b) Impact of double tax treaties in an international context	8.18
	2.	Assignment	8.27
		(a) Royalties or capital gains?	8.27
		(b) Tax treatment of capital gains	8.33
		(c) Impact of double tax treaties in an international context	8.36
	3.	Tax treatment of expenses	8.38
D.	TRADEMARK TRANSACTIONS BETWEEN RELATED PARTIES		8.41
	1.	Arm's length principle	8.43
	2.	Arm's length price	8.47
	3.	Domestic restructuring	8.54
E.	INTERNATIONAL TAX STRATEGIES		8.57
	1.	Residence of companies	8.59
	2.	Ownership	8.64
	3.	Tax status	8.69
		(a) Auxiliary status (intellectual property companies)	8.70
		(b) Licence box	8.76
F.	CONCLUSION		8.87

9. REGISTERING SECURITY INTERESTS OVER TRADEMARKS IN AUSTRALIA: THEORY AND PRACTICE
Robert Burrell and Michael Handler

A.	INTRODUCTION		9.01
B.	THE PRE-PPSA POSITION		9.03
C.	THE PPSA REFORMS		9.08
D.	TENSIONS BETWEEN THE TRADEMARK AND PPSA SYSTEMS		9.14
	1.	Imperfect information and transition costs	9.16
	2.	Ongoing role of recording claims in the Trade Marks Register	9.23
	3.	Problems caused when title in property passes to the secured party	9.25
E.	CONCLUSIONS AND OPTIONS FOR REFORM		9.32

10. THE INTERSECTION OF TRADEMARKS, LICENSES AND BANKRUPTCY: ENDING UNCERTAINTIES IN THE LAW
Xuan-Thao Nguyen

A.	INTRODUCTION	10.01
B.	TRADEMARK IN ORDINARY LICENSES	10.12

	C.	TRADEMARKS IN CORPORATE TRANSACTIONS	10.18
		1. *Chain v. Tropodyne*: sale of assets and trademark use within the acquired division	10.21
		2. *Seattle Brewing & Malting Co. v. Commissioner*: sale of assets and trademark use restricted to field of use and geographical territory	10.24
	D.	CORPORATE DIVISION SALE OF ASSETS AND TRADEMARK USE IN IN RE *EXIDE TECHNOLOGIES*	10.33
		1. In re *Exide Technologies*	10.34
		2. Causing uncertainties	10.44
		3. Adding uncertainties: In re *Interstate Bakeries* and In re *Lakewood (Sunbeam Prods., Inc. v. Chicago Am. Mfg, LLC)*	10.57
	E.	ENDING THE UNCERTAINTIES	10.68
		1. Looking beyond form, facing the substance	10.68
		2. Sales, not licenses	10.75
		3. Concurrent use – assignment of trademark rights in different fields of use	10.79
		(a) Concurrent use doctrine	10.80
		(b) Co-existence separately	10.91
		(c) Imperfect coexistence, but do not touch the license	10.94
	F.	CONCLUSION	10.95

Section D Dispute Prevention and Settlement Mechanisms

11. OUT OF THE SHADOWS: THE UNIQUE WORLD OF TRADEMARK CONSENT AGREEMENTS
Neil Wilkof

A.	INTRODUCTION	11.01
B.	THE LEGAL FOUNDATION	11.02
	1. Assignment	11.03
	2. License	11.04
	3. Consent agreement	11.06
C.	THE VARIOUS CIRCUMSTANCES IN WHICH A CONSENT AGREEMENT MAY ARISE	11.13
D.	TYPES OF CONSENT AGREEMENT	11.20
E.	IMPACT ON THE BEHAVIOUR OF THE PARTIES BY VIRTUE OF THE UNDERTAKINGS IN A CONSENT AGREEMENT	11.25
F.	THE ROLE OF LIKELIHOOD OF CONFUSION	11.31
G.	PUBLIC AND PRIVATE CONSIDERATIONS	11.35
H.	CONCLUSION	11.42
	APPENDIX	

12. CHOICE-OF-COURT AND CHOICE-OF-LAW CLAUSES IN INTERNATIONAL TRADEMARK TRANSACTIONS
Dai Yokomizo

A.	INTRODUCTION	12.01
B.	CHOICE-OF-COURT CLAUSE	12.04
	1. Practice	12.05
	(a) Which country's court is chosen?	12.05
	(b) Is a choice-of-court clause exclusive or not?	12.06
	(c) Choice-of-court clause or arbitration clause?	12.07
	(d) Summary	12.08
	2. Legal issues	12.09
	(a) Validity	12.13
	(b) Limitation	12.20
	(c) Summary	12.25
	3. Summary	12.29
C.	CHOICE-OF-LAW CLAUSE	12.31
	1. Practice	12.32
	2. Legal issues	12.34
	(a) Validity	12.35
	(b) Scope	12.39

		3.	Summary	12.41
	D.	CONCLUSION		12.42

13. ALTERNATIVE DISPUTE RESOLUTION MECHANISMS FOR SOLVING TRADEMARK DISPUTES (MEDIATION, UDRP, ARBITRATION)
Jacques de Werra

	A.	INTRODUCTION		13.01
	B.	ADR METHODS FOR SOLVING TRADEMARK DISPUTES		13.02
		1.	Mediation	13.03
		2.	The UDRP	13.06
		3.	UDRP as a model for other ADR systems for trademark-related domain name disputes	13.12
	C.	ARBITRATION OF (INTERNATIONAL) TRADEMARK DISPUTES		13.27
		1.	Introduction	13.27
		2.	Conditions and features	13.29
			(a) Objective arbitrability of intellectual property disputes	13.30
			(b) Consent of parties to submit to arbitration: the scope of the arbitration clause	13.34
		3.	Governing law	13.61
		4.	Provisional measures	13.66
	D.	CONCLUSION		13.69

PART II TRADEMARK TRANSACTIONS AT THE REGIONAL AND NATIONAL LEVEL

Section A   Trademark Transactions in Europe

14. TRADEMARK TRANSACTIONS IN EU LAW: REFINING THE APPROACH TO SELECTIVE DISTRIBUTION NETWORKS AND NATIONAL UNFAIR COMPETITION LAW
Martin Senftleben

A.	INTRODUCTION		14.01
B.	OVERVIEW OF HARMONIZED EU RULES		14.03
	1.	Community Trade Mark Regulation	14.03
	2.	Trade Mark Directive	14.10
	3.	Reform plans	14.11
C.	SELECTIVE DISTRIBUTION NETWORKS		14.14
	1.	The *Copad/Dior* case	14.14
	2.	Expansion of the concept of product quality	14.17
	3.	Impact on exhaustion of rights	14.19
	4.	Open questions	14.23
	5.	Rights against the licensee	14.29
	6.	Rights against outside traders	14.37
	7.	A more nuanced approach	14.40
D.	ROOM FOR NATIONAL UNFAIR COMPETITION LAW		14.43
	1.	The *Martin Y Paz/Depuydt* case	14.43
	2.	Mantra of complete harmonization	14.48
	3.	Function theory unsatisfactory	14.52
	4.	No pre-emption of national doctrines	14.57
E.	CONCLUSION		14.59

15. UK PERSPECTIVES ON TRADEMARK TRANSACTIONS: A LIBERAL APPROACH
Laura Anderson

A.	INTRODUCTION	15.01

B.	UK LAW AND TRADEMARK TRANSACTIONS	15.05
C.	ASSIGNMENTS OF UK TRADEMARKS	15.11
	1. Assignment of part	15.16
	2. Unregistered trademarks	15.19
	3. Requirements for valid assignment	15.20
	4. Language	15.21
	5. Identification of the intellectual property rights being assigned	15.22
	6. Consideration	15.23
	7. Assignment of the right to sue prior infringers	15.24
	8. Implied covenants as to title	15.25
	9. Registration	15.30
	10. Trusts and equitable assignments of trademarks	15.32
	11. What is required for an equitable assignment?	15.35
	12. Confirmatory assignments	15.37
D.	LICENSES OF UK TRADEMARKS	15.40
	1. The nature of a trademark license	15.42
	2. Formalities	15.44
	3. Key terms	15.47
	4. Grant and exclusivity	15.50
	5. Sublicensing	15.52
	6. Quality control	15.54
	7. Liabilities and indemnity	15.62
	8. Rights of licensees to bring infringement proceedings	15.65
	9. Warranties	15.71
	10. Term and termination	15.72
	11. Assignment of licenses	15.77
	12. Contracts Rights of Third Parties Act	15.81
	13. Registration	15.83
	14. Licensing of unregistered trademarks	15.85
E.	SECURITY INTERESTS	15.86
F.	UK COMPETITION LAW	15.91
G.	CONCLUSIONS	15.93

16. TRADEMARK TRANSACTIONS IN GERMANY: A CONTINENTAL EUROPEAN SYSTEM MOVES TOWARDS COMMON UNDERSTANDING WITH THE US
Axel Nordemann and Christian Czychowski

A.	INTRODUCTION	16.01
B.	EXISTING LEGAL RULES ON TRADEMARK TRANSACTIONS IN GERMAN LAW	16.02
	1. The legal framework – overview	16.02
	2. Relations between European Union law and German trademark law	16.11
	3. Sections 27–31 of the MarkenG	16.19
	4. The difference between transactions with regard to registered trademarks, company symbols, and titles of works	16.26
C.	TRADEMARK TRANSACTIONS IN PRACTICE	16.33
	1. Purchase agreements	16.33
	2. License agreements	16.36
	(a) General	16.36
	(b) Restrictions imposed by antitrust law	16.40
	(c) License agreements and insolvency proceedings	16.46
	(d) Trademark infringements	16.47
	(e) Registration of a license	16.49
	3. Coexistence agreements	16.50
	(a) General	16.50
	(b) Restrictions imposed by antitrust law	16.51
	(c) Applicable law	16.53
	4. Trademarks in mergers and acquisitions transactions	16.58

	5.	Trademarks as securities	16.61
D.	CONCLUSION		16.64

17. FRENCH PERSPECTIVES ON TRADEMARK TRANSACTIONS: FROM THE CIVIL CODE TO THE BUSINESS LAW?
Nicolas Binctin

A.	INTRODUCTION		17.01
B.	CONTRACTUAL FREEDOM		17.06
	1.	General principles of contract law	17.07
		(a) Trademark assignment	17.08
		(b) Trademark licensing	17.13
	2.	Specific dispositions	17.23
C.	THE TRADEMARK AS AN ELEMENT OF THE *FONDS DE COMMERCE*		17.32
	1.	Trademark and securities	17.33
	2.	Transfer of trademark	17.42
D.	TAX CONSIDERATIONS AND TRADEMARK TRANSACTIONS		17.46
	1.	Trademark operations for free	17.49
	2.	The tax qualification of a trademark license as an asset	17.52
	3.	Tax influence on merger and acquisition qualification	17.54
E.	CONCLUSION		17.57

Section B Trademark Transactions in North and South America

18. TRADEMARK TRANSACTIONS IN THE UNITED STATES: TOWARDS A DE FACTO ACCEPTANCE OF TRADING IN GROSS?
Irene Calboli

A.	INTRODUCTION		18.01
B.	A BRIEF PRIMER OF TRADEMARK LAW		18.03
C.	TRADEMARK ASSIGNMENT		18.06
	1.	The current rule on trademark assignment 'with goodwill'	18.06
		(a) Rationale of the rule	18.10
		(b) Origin of the rule	18.12
	2.	Judicial developments	18.16
		(a) Early (conservative) decisions	18.17
		(b) Shifting towards trademark assignment 'in gross'?	18.19
D.	TRADEMARK LICENSING		18.21
	1.	The current rule on trademark licensing 'with control'	18.21
		(a) Rationale of the rule	18.27
		(b) Origin of the rule	18.29
	2. Judicial developments		18.32
		(a) The evolution of the standard	18.33
		(b) Recent developments	18.36
E.	STRATEGIC TRADEMARK TRANSACTIONS		18.38
	1.	Trademark assignment and license-back	18.39
	2.	Security interests in trademarks	18.42
F.	CONCLUSION		18.45

19. NEW DRESS CODE FOR BUSINESS TRANSACTIONS IN BRAZIL: ESSENTIALS AND PECULIARITIES OF TRADEMARKS IN THE SPOTLIGHT
José Carlos Vaz e Dias

A.	INTRODUCTION	19.01
B.	THE LEGAL NATURE OF TRADEMARKS: OPPORTUNITIES AND LIMITS	19.06
C.	TRADEMARKS LICENSING	19.13
D.	TRADEMARK AND FRANCHISING IN BRAZIL	19.22
E.	TRADEMARK AS COLLATERAL AND SECURITY INTEREST	19.35

F.	ASSIGNMENT OF THE TRADEMARK APPLICATION AND/OR REGISTRATION	19.46
G.	CONCLUSION	19.63

Section C Trademark Transactions in Asia

20. CHINESE TRADEMARK LAW AND TRADEMARK TRANSACTIONS: A LAW IN TRANSITION IN THE GLOBAL ECONOMY
He Guo

A.	INTRODUCTION	20.01
B.	EVOLUTION OF THE CHINESE TRADEMARK LAW	20.03
C.	ESTABLISHING TRADEMARK RIGHTS	20.12
	1. Registered trademarks	20.13
	(a) Application for trademark registration	20.13
	(b) Examination of the application for trademark registration	20.16
	2. Unregistered trademarks	20.20
D.	ASSIGNMENT OF TRADEMARKS	20.26
	1. Concept and formalities for trademark assignment	20.26
	2. Procedures and regulations on trademark assignment	20.34
E.	TRADEMARK LICENSING	20.37
	1. Type of trademark licenses	20.40
	2. Obligations of the trademark owners and licensees	20.42
	(a) Supervision of the quality of the marked goods	20.43
	(b) Maintenance of trademark rights	20.48
	3. Ownership of the goodwill and legal responsibilities after a trademark license contract is terminated	20.50
	(a) Ownership of the goodwill	20.50
	(b) Legal responsibilities after a trademark license contract is terminated	20.51
F.	PLEDGE OF TRADEMARKS	20.53
	1. Definition and legal basis of trademark pledge	20.53
	2. Procedural requirements for the pledge of the trademark rights	20.60
	3. Effects of the pledge contract of trademark rights	20.65
G.	CONCLUSION	20.67

21. JAPANESE PERSPECTIVES ON TRADEMARK TRANSACTIONS: IS EXPANSIVE TRADEMARK PRACTICE PREVAILING OVER THE CONSERVATIVE STOICISM?
Shinto Teramoto

A.	INTRODUCTION	21.01
B.	WHAT IS A 'TRADEMARK'?	21.03
	1. Scope of 'trademarks' in the context of trademark transactions	21.03
	2. 'Trademarks' under the Trademark Act	21.05
	3. What has changed and what has not in the legal definition of trademarks	21.07
	4. Laws to be considered when negotiating trademark transactions	21.11
C.	LICENSES	21.12
	1. Definition of 'license'	21.12
	2. 'Right to use' trademarks provided under the Trademark Act	21.13
	3. Non-exclusive right to use	21.17
	4. Proprietary right to use	21.24
	5. Licensing agreements for marks not registered under the Trademark Act	21.29
	6. Governing laws of licensing agreements	21.38
	7. Japanese taxes imposed on royalties	21.39
	8. Termination of licensing agreements	21.48
	9. Application of the Anti-Monopoly Act	21.51
D.	TRADEMARK ASSIGNMENTS AND SECURITY INTERESTS	21.53
	1. General principles	21.53
	2. Trademarks that simultaneously represent the goodwill of diversified suppliers	21.56

	3.	Marks that represent the collective goodwill of multiple suppliers	21.58
	4.	Non-assignability of regional collective trademark rights	21.61
	5.	Security interests in trademark rights	21.63
E.	CONCLUSION		21.67

22. TRADEMARK TRANSACTIONS IN ASEAN: CONVERGENCES AND DIVERGENCES IN EMERGING MARKETS
Susanna H. S. Leong

A.	INTRODUCTION		22.01
B.	TRADEMARKS AS PROPERTY		22.05
C.	ASSIGNMENT OF REGISTERED TRADEMARKS		22.12
	1.	Assignment of registered trademarks with or without goodwill/business	22.14
	2.	Assignment of an application for registration of a trademark	22.21
	3.	Formalities: assignments must be in writing	22.22
	4.	Assignment of unregistered trademarks	22.23
D.	LICENSING OF REGISTERED TRADEMARKS		22.27
	1.	Singapore	22.30
	2.	Vietnam	22.35
	3.	Thailand	22.38
	4.	Philippines	22.45
	5.	Cambodia	22.46
	6.	Myanmar	22.47
	7.	Brunei	22.48
	8.	Malaysia	22.50
	9.	Laos	22.53
	10.	Indonesia	22.55
E.	REGISTRATION OF TRANSACTIONS		22.57
	1.	Singapore	22.58
	2.	Vietnam	22.60
	3.	Thailand	22.62
	4.	Philippines	22.64
	5.	Cambodia	22.65
	6.	Myanmar	22.67
	7.	Brunei	22.68
	8.	Malaysia	22.69
	9.	Laos	22.72
	10.	Indonesia	22.73
F.	CONCLUSION		22.74

23. TRADEMARK TRANSACTIONS IN INDIA: EXPLORING THE GENRE, SCOPE AND CONSEQUENCE
Raman Mittal

A.	INTRODUCTION		23.01
B.	LICENSING OF REGISTERED TRADEMARKS UNDER THE TRADE MARKS ACT OF 1999		23.04
	1.	Scope of trademark licensing	23.05
	2.	Term and territorial scope of license	23.11
	3.	Conditions for and extent of use of mark by licensee	23.13
	4.	Procedure for registration, variation, and cancellation of registration	23.18
	5.	Rights and obligations of licensor	23.23
		(a) Liability for acts of licensee	23.25
		(b) Right to sue infringers and right to be impleaded	23.26
		(c) Right to keep licensing details secret	23.27
		(d) Obligation to furnish information to the Registrar	23.28
	6.	Rights and obligations of licensee	23.29
		(a) Use of mark under accompanying legend	23.30
		(b) Assignment and sublicensing by licensee	23.31
		(c) Right to initiate infringement proceedings	23.32

		(d) Right to be impleaded	23.35
		(e) Right to be notified in case of new license or cancellation	23.36
		(f) Right over goodwill generated	23.37
		(g) Proprietorship over the mark	23.38
		(h) Right to challenge the mark	23.39
	7.	Quality control over the use of the licensed trademark	23.40
	8.	Trafficking under Trade and Merchandise Marks Act of 1958	23.43
	9.	Character merchandising and trademark licensing	23.46
	10.	Licensing and hybridization of trademarks	23.48
C.	LICENSING OF UNREGISTERED TRADEMARKS		23.49
D.	BREACH OF TRADEMARK LICENSE AND CONSEQUENCES		23.51
E.	ASSIGNMENT OF TRADEMARKS		23.55
	1.	Relation between trademark assignment and assignment of goodwill	23.59
	2.	Restrictions on assignment	23.60
	3.	Assignment resulting in splitting of trademark on territorial basis	23.62
	4.	Registration of the assignee of a registered trademark	23.63
	5.	Assignment of unregistered trademarks	23.69
	6.	Assignment of certification and associated trademarks and discretion of registrar	23.70
F.	ROYALTY FOR TRADEMARK TRANSACTIONS AND TREATMENT UNDER TAXATION LAWS		23.71
G.	CONCLUSION		23.73

Index   587

FIGURES

3.1	Steamboat Willie: From Character to Brand?	60
3.2	Steamboat Willie: The Character as Mascot (Brand)	61
3.3	The Cat in the Hat: The Brand	62
3.4	Bibendum in 1898 (public domain)	64
3.5	Bibendum today	64
3.6	Bibendum now and then	65
3.7	The 'Yellow Kid'	67
3.8	Buster Brown shoes advertisement (1950s)	69
3.9	7Up Dot: 'Coolspot'	74
3.10	M&Ms 'Spokescandy'	75
7.1	Interbrand PLC (S Curve)	152
7.2	Brand value over time	169
11.1	A, B, explicit 'no man's land'	274
11.2	A, B, no explicit 'no man's land'	274
11.3	A, not Ā	274
11.4	A, not Ā, explicit no man's land	275
11.5	A, B, with explicit exclusions to A, or vice versa	275
19.1	Revenue from franchising (BR$)	471
21.1	The concept of a 'trademark'	513
21.2	The 'Google' logo displayed on the web page of Google Inc. that provides a search engine service	515
21.3	Example of a snippet containing a trademark displayed by a search engine	515
21.4	Example of a registered trademark in a three-dimensional shape	516
21.5	Example of a registered trademark in a three-dimensional shape used as a product container	516
21.6	Example of a registered trademark using an illustrated portrait of a person (Japan Trademark Registration No. 4582803)	525
21.7	The shape of Dogo Onsen (hot-spring spa in the Dogo area) and the trademark in Chinese characters pronounced as 'dogo onsen'	534
23.1	Licensees of trademarks	560

TABLES

4.1	Example of transactions on the Domain Name Secondary Market	83
7.1	Interbrand PLC brand strength analysis	151
7.2	ktMINE license agreement search criteria	154
7.3	ktMINE license agreement royalty rate summary	155
7.4	Hostess brand transaction activity	157
7.5	Selected details of American Airlines merger with US Airways	161
7.6	ktMINE asset agreement search criteria	163
7.7	ktMINE asset agreement royalty rate summary	164
7.8	Summary allocation percentages	166
7.9	The world's most valuable brands	168

EDITORS AND CONTRIBUTORS

Laura Anderson is a Partner at Bristows LLP specializing in intellectual property transactions. She advises on a broad range of commercial transactions relating to intellectual property rights, their development, and their exploitation. Her practice covers a number of industry sectors including food and drink, consumer products, pharmaceuticals, and biotechnology. She advises leading brand owners on transactions for the exploitation of their trademark assets including licensing, franchising, strategic collaborations, and the establishment of holding structures.

Nicolas Binctin is a Professor at the Faculty of Law of the University of Poitiers. He teaches Business and Intellectual Property Law in its various components at the University of Poitiers, the University of Paris XII-UPEC, and the School of Law and Management of the University Paris II Assas-Panthéon. In 2015, he was invited as a visiting professor by the Academy of OAPI, Cameroun. He is the author of a thesis entitled *Le Capital Intellectuel* (LexisNexis 2007) and has published many articles in French and English. The 3rd edition of his book on French and European Intellectual Property Law was published in September 2014 by Lextenso-LGDJ.

Gregor Bühler is a Partner in the Intellectual Property/Information Technology practice group of Homburger AG, Switzerland. He graduated from the University of St. Gallen in 1990, receiving his doctorate in 1995. He was a visiting scholar at the Max Planck Institute for Intellectual Property in Munich and earned an LL.M. degree from Georgetown University in Washington D.C. His practice focuses on intellectual property, information technology, and privacy law, as well as on commercial litigation and arbitration. He is co-editor of a leading commentary on Swiss trademark law.

Robert Burrell is a Professor of Law at the University of Sheffield and a Professor of Law at the University of Western Australia. His research interests lie in the fields of copyright law, trademark law, and innovation policy, and he has published widely in these areas. He is the co-author of AUSTRALIAN TRADE MARK LAW (2010, with Michael Handler, 2nd ed. forthcoming 2016) and COPYRIGHT EXCEPTIONS: THE DIGITAL IMPACT (2005, with Allison Coleman). He consults regularly on trademark matters, particularly in Australia.

Irene Calboli is the Deputy Director of the Applied Research Centre for Intellectual Assets and the Law in Asia, School of Law, Singapore Management University, where she is currently Visiting Professor and Lee Kong Chian Fellow. She is also a Professor of Law at Texas A&M University School of Law, and a Transatlantic Technology Law Forum Fellow at Stanford Law School. She teaches and writes in the areas of intellectual property and international trade law. Her recent publications include

TRADEMARK PROTECTION AND TERRITORIALITY CHALLENGES IN A GLOBAL ECONOMY (2014, edited with E. Lee) and DIVERSITY IN INTELLECTUAL PROPERTY: IDENTITIES, INTERESTS, AND INTERSECTIONS (2015, edited with S. Ragavan). She is an elected member of the American Law Institute.

Christian Czychowski studied law and musicology at the University of Bonn subsequently obtaining his doctorate in the field of copyright contract law. He joined Boehmert & Boehmert in Berlin in 1997 and became a partner in 2002. His specialist areas are new media, copyright law, information technology law, trademark law as well as patent and licensing contract law. The University of Potsdam appointed him Honorary Professor in 2014. He is a contributor to HANDBOOK OF COPYRIGHT LAW (2010, Loewenheim ed.), MUNICH ATTORNEYS' HANDBOOK ON INTELLECTUAL PROPERTY (2012), and the COMMENTARY ON COPYRIGHT LAW (2014, Fromm & Nordemann eds.).

Luca Dal Molin is an Associate in the Intellectual Property/Information Technology practice group of Homburger AG, Switzerland. He advises and represents clients in all areas of intellectual property and information technology law, with a special focus on technology transactions, information technology, and software matters as well as on privacy law. He earned his law degree from University of Zurich, Switzerland, and an LL.M. in Law, Science and Technology from Stanford Law School, USA.

Roy P. D'Souza is a Managing Director responsible for leading Ocean Tomo's Valuation practice. Mr. D'Souza's work has focused on valuations of intangible, intellectual property, and tangible assets for acquisitions and divestitures, bankruptcy and restructuring, and establishment of intellectual property monetization strategies. He has served as an expert witness in intellectual property, intangible asset, business enterprise, and equity valuation disputes, having testified in Delaware Chancery Court and the Circuit Court of Cook County, Illinois. He is a frequent speaker as well as an instructor on intellectual property valuation matters.

Daniel J. Gervais is a Professor of Law at Vanderbilt University and the Editor-in-Chief of the Journal of World Intellectual Property. Prior to joining Vanderbilt, he was the Acting Dean of the Common Law Section at the University of Ottawa, a Legal Officer at the General Agreement on Tariffs and Trade, and Head of Section at the World Intellectual Property Organization. He studied computer science and law at McGill University and the University of Montreal, where he also obtained LL.B. and LL.M. degrees. He received a Diploma *summa cum laude* from the Institute of Advanced International Studies and a doctorate *magna cum laude* from the University of Nantes. He is an elected member of the Academy of Europe and the American Law Institute.

Shubha Ghosh is the Vilas Research Fellow and the George Young Bascom Professor of Intellectual Property and Business Law at the University of Wisconsin Law School. His scholarship focuses on competition policy and intellectual property, innovation and the scope of intellectual property rights, freedom of expression and data access, and legal and economic analysis of the exhaustion doctrine. He has published articles in the many leading journals and authored several casebooks. He is the author of the book IDENTITY, INVENTION, AND THE CULTURE OF PERSONALIZED MEDICINE PATENTING (2012). In 2014–2015, he was the inaugural AAAS Law & Science Fellow at the Federal Judicial Center in Washington, D.C. Since 1 January 2016, he is also Crandall Melvin Professor of Law and Director of Technology Commercialization Law Program at Syracuse University College of Law.

Jane C. Ginsburg is the Morton L. Janklow Professor of Literary and Artistic Property Law at Columbia University School of Law. She teaches Legal Methods, Copyright Law, and Trademarks Law, and is either the author or co-author of casebooks in all three subjects. A graduate of the University of Chicago (BA 1976, MA 1977), she received a JD in 1980 from Harvard, a DEA in 1985, and a Doctorate of Law in 1995 from the University of Paris II. She has been elected to several learned societies, including the British Academy and the American Academy of Arts and Sciences.

He Guo is a Professor of Law at Renmin University of China (RUC). He is currently the Deputy Dean of the Intellectual Property Academy, and the Curator of Law Library, RUC. He was elected the Secretary General of China Intellectual Property Law Society in 2012. He is also a panelist of the Asian Domain Name Dispute Resolution Center, a member of the panel of neutrals in the Domain Name Dispute Resolution Center of China International Economic and Trade Arbitration Commission, a member of the National Product Defects and Safety Management Standardization Technology Commission, a member of the Technology Commission of Auto Repairing, Renewal, and Refunding of China, and the Honorable Advisor of the Hong Kong Brand Protection Alliance.

Michael Handler is an Associate Professor in the Faculty of Law at the University of New South Wales, Australia. His main field of research is domestic and international trademark law. Michael is the co-author of AUSTRALIAN TRADE MARK LAW (2010, with Robert Burrell, 2nd ed. forthcoming 2016). He has also written numerous journal articles and book chapters on various aspects of trademark law, theory, and practice over the past decade, which have been published in Australia, Europe, and the United States.

Marcus Höpperger is the Director of the Law and Legislative Advice Division, Brands and Designs Sector of the World Intellectual Property Organization (WIPO). He is the Secretary to the WIPO Standing Committee on the Law of Trademarks, Industrial Designs and Geographical Indications (SCT). He was responsible for the holding of the 2006 Diplomatic Conference for the Adoption of the Singapore Treaty on the Law of Trademarks and the 2015 Diplomatic Conference for the Adoption of a New Act of the Lisbon Agreement for the Protection of Appellations of Origin and their International Registration.

Sir Robin Jacob joined University College London as the Hugh Laddie Professor of Intellectual Property Law and the Director of the Institute of Brand and Innovation Law in 2011. He formally retired from Court of Appeal of England and Wales to do so. After reading Natural Sciences at Cambridge, he read for the Bar (Grays Inn) and was made a Queen's Counsel in 1981. Amongst many other honours, he is an

Honorary Fellow of the London School of Economics and St Peter's College, Oxford, and a Governor of the London School of Economics. He is also the Honorary President of the United Kingdom branch of the Licensing Executive Society and the Association of Law Teachers, a member of the Advisory Board of the European Law Centre of King's College London, and a Member of the Advisory Panel of the Unified Patent Court. In 2012, he was awarded the Outstanding Achievement in intellectual property award by MIP.

Susanna H. S. Leong is an Associate Professor at the NUS Business School where she is also the Vice-Dean, Graduate Studies Office. She received her LL.B (Hons) from the National University of Singapore and her LL.M (with Merit) from University College London. Her research interests are in intellectual property and technology-related laws. She has published articles and chapters in several international and local academic journals. She is the author of INTELLECTUAL PROPERTY LAW OF SINGAPORE (2013). She is also a Senior Fellow at the Intellectual Property Academy of Singapore, and a member of the Singapore Copyright Tribunal, the World Intellectual Property Organization Domain Name Panel, and the Regional Centre for Arbitration, Kuala Lumpur (RCAKL) Panel.

Cédric Manara was a full time law professor at EDHEC Business School (France) until 2013, when he joined a startup company. He has published books, articles, comments on cases on intellectual property and internet legal issues, and was a visiting professor or researcher at several institutions in Finland, Italy, Japan, and the United States. He has been a consultant for e-commerce companies or law firms. He is also a domain dispute resolution panelist (Arbitration Center for .eu Disputes, Prague, Czech Republic, Regional Center for Arbitration, Kuala-Lumpur, Malaysia, and CEPANI, Brussels, Belgium). Cédric holds an LL.B and Masters degree from the University of Lille (France) and a Doctorate degree from the University of Versaille (France).

Jean-Frédéric Maraia was admitted to the Geneva bar in 2002 and has been a tax partner at Schellenberg Wittmer SA (Tax Department, Geneva) since 2010. He is a lecturer at the Faculty of Law, University of Geneva, where he also co-heads the LL.M. Tax program. He has published two books and several articles in the area of Swiss and international tax law, covering topics such as taxation of intellectual property, lump-sum taxation, residence of companies, exchange of information, etc.

Raman Mittal teaches Law at University of Delhi. He previously worked at the Indian Law Institute, New Delhi. He holds LL.M. and Ph.D. degrees from Panjab University, Chandigarh together with a M.S.S. from International Space University, France. His research interests include Intellectual Property, Contract, Cyber, and International Law. He has published in national and international journals and has also authored/edited books on intellectual property and cyberlaw. Dr. Mittal has advised the Government of India in international treaty negotiations and has been a member of the Drafting Committee that was tasked with drafting of Copyright Rules, 2013.

EDITORS AND CONTRIBUTORS

Xuan-Thao Nguyen is the Gerald L. Bepko Chair in Law, Indiana University McKinney School of Law. She is also the Director of the Center for Intellectual Property & Innovation at Indiana University. She is the author of the IP TAXATION treatise (Bloomberg BNA) and casebook (Carolina Academic Press) with Professor Jeff Maine. She is also the author of the treatise IP LICENSING (Bloomberg BNA), the casebook LICENSING INTELLECTUAL PROPERTY (2008, 2nd ed., with D. Conway and R. Gomulkiewicz), and the book TRANSNATIONAL INTELLECTUAL PROPERTY (2015, with D. Conway and L. Mtima). She is currently working with Professot Jeff Maine on the book IP HOLDING COMPANY (forthcoming).

Axel Nordemann studied law at the Universities of Göttingen and Munich and wrote his doctoral thesis on the law of copyright in photography. In 1993, he joined Boehmert & Boehmert, and became a partner in Berlin in 1996. The focus of his work is in trademark law, copyright law, and competition law. Since 1999, he has taught copyright law at the University of Constance where he is an Honorary Professor. He is a co-author of the text book, NORDEMANN: COMPETITION LAW – TRADE MARK LAW (2012), co-editor and co-author of the GERMAN COMMENTARY: COPYRIGHT LAW (2014, Fromm & Nordermann eds.), and contributor to the book OVERLAPPING INTELLECTUAL PROPERTY RIGHTS (2012, Wilkof & Basheer eds.), the COMMENTARY ON COMMUNITY TRADE MARK REGULATION (2015, Hasselblatt ed.), and the COMMENTARY ON COMMUNITY DESIGN REGULATION (2015, Hasselblatt ed.).

Martin Senftleben is Professor of Intellectual Property and Director of the Kooijmans Institute for Law and Governance at the Vrije Universiteit Amsterdam, and Of Counsel at Bird & Bird, The Hague. His activities focus on trademark law and the preservation of the public domain, the harmonization of trademark law in the EU and the enforcement of intellectual property rights in the digital environment. Prior to his appointment at the Vrije Universiteit, he worked in the trademarks department of WIPO. His publications include the WIPO-commissioned *Study on Misappropriation of Signs* (WIPO Doc. CDIP/9/INF/5) and the *Recommendations on Measures to Safeguard Freedom of Expression and Undistorted Competition in the EU Trademark Law*.

Shinto Teramoto is a Professor of Law at Kyushu University in Fukuoka, Japan where he teaches intellectual property law. Prior to joining Kyushu University in 2010, he was a lawyer specializing in venture capital finance and intellectual property law for about 20 years. Currently, he is Of Counsel at the intellectual property firm SHUWA in Tokyo. His recent articles include *Intellectual Property Licensing in Japan*, RESEARCH HANDBOOK ON INTELLECTUAL PROPERTY LICENSING (2013, J. de Werra ed.) and *Intermediaries, Trust and Efficiency of Communication: A Social Network Perspective*, NETWORKED GOVERNANCE, TRANSNATIONAL BUSINESS AND THE LAW (2014, M. Fenwick, S. Van Uytsel, and S. Wrbka eds.).

José Carlos Vaz e Dias is a Professor of Intellectual Property Rights at the State University of Rio de Janeiro (UERJ) where he teaches Theory of Intellectual Property Rights and Foreign Investments Laws and Technology Transfer. He is also a senior attorney at the firm Vaz e Dias Advogados & Associados. His activities are focused on trademark prosecution and litigation and matters related to foreign investment and business transactions, including foreign exchange control laws, technology transfer, and taxation. Most recently, his research and practice are focused on open innovation and the Brazilian Innovation Law.

Jacques de Werra is a Professor of Intellectual Property Law and Contract Law at the Faculty of Law of the University of Geneva, Switzerland, where he also acts as Vice-Rector since July 2015. Jacques researches, publishes, and speaks on topics related to various aspects of intellectual property law, contract law, particularly on the commercialization of intellectual property assets by way of transfer of technology, licensing and franchising, information technology and Internet law, as well as on alternative dispute resolution mechanisms for intellectual property and technology disputes. He is the organizer of the University of Geneva Internet l@w summer school (www.internetlaw-geneva.ch) and the coordinator for the University of Geneva of the World Intellectual Property Organization – University of Geneva Summer School on Intellectual Property.

Neil Wilkof is a member of Dr. Eyal Bressler and Co., Ramat-Gan, Israel, where he is engaged in both contentious and non-contentious intellectual property matters. He has served as a lecturer in various universities in the United States, Israel, and India. He has also published widely in the field of intellectual property law, including INTELLECTUAL PROPERTY IN THE GLOBAL MARKETPLACE (1999, 2nd ed., edited M. Simensky and L. Bryer), TRADE MARK LICENSING (2004, 2nd ed. with D. Burkitt), and OVERLAPPING INTELLECTUAL PROPERTY RIGHTS (2012, edited with S. Basheer). Mr. Wilkof is a graduate of Yale University, the University of Chicago, and the University of Illinois.

Dai Yokomizo is a Professor of Law at the Graduate School of Law of Nagoya University, Nagoya, Japan. His main area of interest for research and teaching is private international law. He is a member at the Committee on Intellectual Property and Private International Law of the International Law Association and an Associate Editor of the JAPANESE YEARBOOK OF INTERNATIONAL LAW. His recent articles include *Patent Infringement by Multiple Parties and Conflict of Laws*, NAGOYA UNIVERSITY JOURNAL OF LAW AND POLITICS, 199 (2013), and *Intellectual Property Infringement on the Internet and Conflict of Laws*, 36 AIPPI JOURNAL 104 (No. 3, 2011).

FOREWORD

The Rt. Hon Professor Sir Robin Jacob[*]

If you think about it, you will realise that intellectual property law really has three important divisions, or foundations: substantive law, procedural law and transactional law. Most talk and debate is about substantive law. Sadly, procedural law – how substantive law can as a practical matter be enforced – gets little discussion yet is perhaps the Queen of the game. And transactional law hardly gets a look-in. It is amazing really, since so much of the practical working of the intellectual property system depends on transactions (licences or assignments) about intellectual property rights.

Some academic institutions (including University College London) and trademark scholars have recognised this situation, and try to do something about it. So it was with particular honour and pleasure that I accepted Irene Calboli and Jacques de Werra's request to write this Foreword.

Of course, I could not fairly do it without sight of the book itself. So they sent the chapters of the book to me. I thought I would just do a quick skim. But I found, chapter by chapter, that the constellation of star authors that contributed to this book had produced what can only be described as a compelling work. In many cases the authors have extended beyond strict transactional law to deeper considerations of what really is involved. Anyone who read this book properly would gain an understanding of many facets of trademark transactions, for instance of what can and cannot be done transactionally, of how a trade mark transaction requires particular care given the inherent nature of trademark rights themselves (can there be a bare licence?), of how competition law may get in the way of commercial agreement and many other things. The book further offers original developments on international (TRIPS and WIPO) and comparative aspects of trademark transactions in various countries and regions (from Asia, Europe, South and North America, and so on). It goes even further by exploring areas outside of the intellectual property/contract interface, which play a significant role in trademark transactions, such as tax and accounting issues, security interests, domain name transactions and conflict of law issues.

---

[*] Hugh Laddie, Professor of Intellectual Property Law, University College London; former Lord Justice of Appeal of the Court of Appeal of England and Wales.

Deep down the reader of this unique compendium will emerge from reading it not only as a better trademark transactional lawyer but also as a better trademark lawyer. The reader will also enjoy it, as I did. We at UCL will certainly be putting it on our reading list for our intellectual property transactional course.

Bentham House, University College London,
October 2015

INTRODUCTION

I. TRADEMARK TRANSACTIONS: PERSPECTIVES AND CHALLENGES IN THE GLOBAL MARKETPLACE

The importance of intellectual property transactions has grown exponentially in the past decades as a result of the increasing financial value of intellectual property assets. For many companies, including those operating in high technology and patent-heavy industries, trademarks are often among the, if not *the* most important assets of the business. Moreover, the importance of trademarks generally transcends national boundaries. The continuous growth of cross-border and intercontinental trade (which is further fostered by ever expanding online e-commerce activities) increasingly implies that trademarks are used (and infringed) simultaneously in several countries. This has resulted in contractual agreements relating to trademarks becoming more and more international in the sense that they cover or relate to trademarks registered in different countries and regions. In other words, trademark transactions have gone global.

However, the rules that apply to trademark transactions (and to trademarks in general) remain largely national. Accordingly, relevant variations between national laws continue to exist even after the adoption of the Agreement of Trade-Related Aspects to Intellectual Property Rights (TRIPS) in 1994. For example, while TRIPS does establish that trademarks can be assigned with minimal formalities – i.e. without any associated business assets – it remains that a number of countries continue to require that trademarks be assigned with the associated "goodwill." Similarly, TRIPS clarifies that trademark licensing constitutes a legitimate trademark practice – this includes licensing for non-similar goods and services, an ongoing point of contention in some jurisdictions – and that countries cannot provide for compulsory licensing of trademarks. TRIPS, however, does not prescribe how trademark transactions shall be structured and what shall be permissible. As a result, countries remain largely free to set national requirements for the validity of licensing, and some countries impose a stricter "quality control" requirement on licensors compared to other jurisdictions. Individual jurisdictions also remain free to set national rules for the use of trademarks as collaterals for loans, or in bankruptcy proceedings. In addition, national procedural laws continue to vary with respect to a host of formalities to be followed for trademark transactions, even though several of these procedures have been partially harmonized with ad hoc international agreements.

The existing differences in the rules applicable to trademark transactions create territorially-based challenges for trademark owners and practitioners, who more and more frequently operate in multiple jurisdictions. In view of this situation, the objective of this book is to explore these differences and to contribute to the discussion about the potential avenues that could be followed on the way to a global harmonization of the rules applicable to trademark transactions.

II. METHODOLOGY AND STRUCTURE OF THE BOOK

This book explores the key aspects of the law governing trademark transactions in a variety of contexts and from several international and comparative perspectives. To date, no other book has offered a comprehensive analysis of these issues. This book attempts to fill this vacuum and offers to the readers a unique collection of chapters authored by distinguished academics and renowned practitioners coming from different jurisdictions and backgrounds.

As scientific editors of this book, we take pride in presenting this combination of authors and perspectives. The diversity of opinions that is reflected in the book offer to the readers a unique blend of doctrinal and critical interpretation of the rules related to trademark transactions, as well as a detailed analysis of these rules in practice. The result is a comprehensive overview of the policy-related, legal, and strategic aspects of trademark transactions, which highlight the international framework, as well as several types of trademark transactions in specific strategic contexts and under the lens of several national legal systems.

The book is structured in two main parts, which are further divided into several subparts. The first part addresses themes that relate to general aspects of trademark transactions, including the analysis of the international legislative framework under the international agreements administered by the World Intellectual Property Organization (WIPO) and under TRIPS. This part also includes several strategic perspectives on trademark transactions. For example, trademark transactions related to trademark rights attaching to copyrighted or formerly copyrighted works, and challenges therein; domain names transactions; instances of transactions resulting in splitting trademark portfolios; and the impact of transactions, and transactions strategies, on market competition. Additionally, this part addresses the use of trademarks as collaterals in secured transactions and in transactions related to bankruptcy proceedings and in tax planning. The final subsection in this part focuses on the methods of prevention and of settlement of trademark disputes – for instance, on the basis of trademark co-existence agreements. It also includes a chapter on choice of law and choice of court, which are a crucial component of any international trademark transaction, as well as a chapter on alternative dispute resolution mechanisms including mediation and arbitration.

The second part of the book focuses on selected national laws. This country-by-country analysis is essential since, as previously indicated, trademark laws remain based on the principle of territoriality. Moreover, as the relevant chapters in this part of the book indicate, national rules applicable to trademark transactions generally involve the application of national rules resulting from other legal fields, and specifically from contract law – an area that is far less harmonized than trademark law at the international or even regional level. Accordingly, important differences remain with respect to both substantive and procedural rules applicable to trademark transactions. The chapters in this part of the book highlight these differences, while also addressing the process of international and regional harmonization of laws in this area.

We are, of course, fully aware that the number of issues and countries that could be explored on the topic of trademark transactions is wider than the number of contributions that can be published in one single volume. However, we are confident that the book offers a careful and comprehensive analysis of the major legal issues that affect trademark transactions today. We also hope that more research will be done on this topic in the future. The level of international harmonization in this area will certainly increase, and this will impact the law and practice of trademark transactions both internationally and nationally. Ultimately, we hope that this book can contribute to the policy debate about the regulation of trademark transactions (and even about intellectual property transactions in general) now and in the future, and can become a useful source of reference for future developments and international cooperation on these issues.

III. ACKNOWLEDGMENTS

A collective work is the result of joint and intensive efforts of many people. While the undersigned conceived the theme and the structure of the book, the publication of this book was possible only thanks to our contributors. We express our deepest gratitude to these distinguished scholars and practitioners for their excellent chapters. The readers will appreciate the depth of their analysis, and benefit from the wealth of information that is offered in every chapter of the book. The completion of this project is also an example of the possibility of international cooperation of authors from different parts of the world and from different backgrounds. We are also very honored that the Rt. Honorable Jacob J., today Professor Robin Jacob, accepted to write the Foreword to this book.

In addition to our contributors, we thank our research assistants, who collaborated with us in the editing process of the manuscript. We particularly thank Pierre Heuzé, Elizabeth Kendall, Yanbing Li, Andrew Minten, Molly Madonia, Lori Shaw, Ashley Swick, and Jia Wang for their excellent work. We additionally thank Edward Elgar for supporting this project, and Johanna Gibson and Trevor Cook, the academic editors of the series on *Intellectual Property Law and Practice*, for publishing the book in the series. We also express our gratitude to the members of the Elgar editorial team who assisted us, with patience and professionalism, during the final stages of production.

We first discussed the possibility of editing a collective work on trademark transactions during an academic trip to Hong Kong in December 2012. Three years, several meetings, many emails and phone calls later, the book has become a reality thanks to our contributors and many other colleagues. We now welcome the publication of this book and hope that it will be useful and will be able to serve as a source of valuable guidance and reference for scholars and practitioners alike who will venture in the fascinating, but complex, world of trademark transactions.

Irene Calboli and Jacques de Werra
October 2015

TABLE OF CASES

International Cases

Court of Justice of the European Union

Adam Opel AG v. Autec AG, Case C-48/05 [2007] E.C.R. I-1017 .... 14.48
Anheuser-Busch v. Budejovicky Budvar, Case C-245/02 [2004] E.C.R. I-10989 .... 14.48
Ansul BV v. Ajax Brandbeveiliging BV, Case C-40/01 [2003] E.C.R. I-2439 .... 16.15
Arsenal Football Club plc v. Matthew Reed, Case C-206/01 [2002] E.C.R. I-10273 .... 14.48
BAT v. Commission, Case 35/83 [1985] 2 C.M.L.R. 470, 491 .... 11.37
Budějovický Budvar v. Anheuser-Busch, Case C-482/09, Judgment of 22 September 2011 .... 16.16
Canon Kabushiki Kaisha v. Metro-Goldwyn-Mayer Inc., Case C-39/97 [1998] E.C.R. I-5507, I-5531 .... 16.17
Cartel Damages Claims (CDC) Hydrogen Peroxide SA v. Akzo Nobel NV et al, Case C-352/13, decision of 21 May 2015 .... 13.35
Copad SA v. Christian Dior Couture SA and Others, Case C-59/08 [2008] E.C.R. I-03421 .... 14.02, 14.14–14.16, 14.17, 14.18, 14.19, 14.20, 14.21, 14.22, 14.23, 14.24, 14.25, 14.27, 14.28, 14.29, 14.30, 14.31, 14.32, 14.35, 14.36, 14.37, 14.38, 14.59
DHL Express France SAS v. Chronopost SA, Case C-235/09 [2011] E.C.R. I-02801 .... 14.55
Eco Swiss China Time Ltd v. Benetton International NV, Case C-126/97 [1999] E.C.R. I-03055 .... 13.65
Emanuel (Elizabeth Florence) v. Continental Shelf 128, Case C-259/04 [2006] E.C.R. I-3089 .... 14.05, 15.14
Football Association Premier League and Others v. QC Leisure and Others, Case C-403/08 and C-429/08 [2011] ECR I-09083 .... 17.15
Genentech Inc. v. Hoechst GmbH, formerly Hoechst AG, Sanofi-Aventis Deutschland GmbH, Case C- 567/14, 2015 O.J. (C 73) 12 .... 13.65
Gesellshaft fur Antriebstechnik mbH & Co.KG v. Lamellen und Kupplungsbau Beteligungs KG, Case C-4/03 [2006] E.C.R. I-06509 .... 12.21
Google France and Google et al. v. Louis Vuitton et al., Joined Cases C-236, 237 & 238/08 [2010] E.C.R. I-02417 .... 14.36, 14.53
Hauck GmbH & Co. KG v. Stokke A/S, opinion of A.G. Szpunar (14 May 2014), Case C-205/13, decision of 18 September 2014 .... 3.02
Interflora Inc. and Interflora British Unit v. Marks & Spencer plc and Flowers Direct Online Ltd., Case C-323/09 [2011] E.C.R. I-08625 .... 14.36, 14.52, 14.53, 14.55
Koninklijke Philips Electronics NV v. Remington Consumer Products Ltd., Case C-299/99 [2002] E.C.R. I-5475 .... 16.17
L'Oreal SA, et al v. Bellure et al, Case C-487/07 [2009] E.C.R. I-05185 .... 14.36, 14.48, 14.53
Leidseplein Beheer v. Red Bull, Case C-65/12 .... 14.52, 14.55
Loendersloot Internationale Expeditie v. George Ballantine & Son Ltd and others, Case C-349/95 [1997] E.C.R. I-6227 .... 16.17

Martin Y Paz Diffusion SA v. David Depuydt and Fabriek van Maroquinerie Gauquie NV,
    Case C-661/11 .... 14.02, 14.43–14.47, 14.48, 14.49, 14.50, 14.52, 14.53, 14.54, 14.57,
                                                                                      14.58, 14.59
Parfums Christian Dior SA and Parfums Christian Dior BV v. Evora BV, Case C-337/95
    [1997] E.C.R. I-6013 .... 14.17, 14.21, 14.36, 14.37, 14.38
Pie Optiek SPRL v. Bureau Gevers SA and European Registry for Internet Domains ASBL,
    Case C-376/11, ECLI:EU:C:2012:502 (2012) 4.23, 14.06
Toltecs/Dorcet II, CJEU, 399, GRUR Int. (1985) 16.51
UPC Telekabel Wien, Case C-314/12 [2014] 4.15
Viking Gas A/S v. Kosan Gas A/S Case C-46/10, [2011] E.C.R. I-06161 .... 14.56
Windsurfing International Inc. v. Commission, Case 193/83 [1986] ECR 611 .... 17.16

General Court of the European Union
The Cartoon Network, Inc. v. OHIM and Boomerang TV (Case T-285/12), (Seventh
    Chamber) October 2, 2013 .... 11.31

Commission Decision
78/253/EEC, Campari, 1978 O.J. (L 70) 69 .... 16.44

International Chamber of Commerce (ICC)
Case 4491 .... 13.42

Office for Harmonization in the Internal Market (Trademarks and Designs) (OHIM)
Decision No. 2011–1 Presidium of the Boards of Appeal, 2011 O.J. 3.10 .... 13.03

World Intellectual Property Organization (WIPO)
Case No. D2001–1484, J. C. Bamford Excavators Ltd. v. MSD (Darlington) Ltd. (WIPO 20
    March 2002) 4.12
Case No. D2002–0895, AVENTIS v. S. Priost c/o Lark Computer Ltd., (WIPO
    2002) 4.12
Case No. D2004–0206, Covance, Inc. v. Covance Campaign, Administrative Panel Decision
    (WIPO 30 April 2004) 13.07
Case No. D2004–0749, Deutsche Telekom AG v. Oded Zucker, Administrative Panel
    Decision (WIPO 2004) 13.26
Case No. D2007–1461, 1066 Housing Ass'n, Ltd. v. Mr. D. Morgan, Administrative Panel
    Decision (WIPO 18 January 2008) 13.07

World Trade Organisation (WTO) Appellate Body Report
United States – Continued Existence and Application of Zeroing Methodology, 269,
    WT/DS350/AB/R (4 February 2009) 1.64

World Trade Organisation (WTO) Dispute Settlement Panel
Indonesia – Certain Measures Affecting The Automobile Industry Case, WT/DS54/R (2
    July 1998) 1.39

TABLE OF CASES

National Cases

Australia
Advantage Rent-A-Car Inc v. Advantage Car Rental Pty Ltd (2001) 52 IPR 24 .... 9.36
Crossmark Asia v. Retail Adventures [2013] NSWSC 55 .... 9.10
Health World Ltd v. Shin-Sun Australia Pty Ltd (2010) 240 CLR 590, 597–9 .... 9.29
Mediaquest Communications LLC v. Registrar of Trade Marks (2012) 205 FCR 205 ..... 9.27
Services WA Pty. Ltd. v. ATCO Gas Australia Pty. Ltd. (2014)WA SC 10 (S) 13.41
SFS Projects Australia Pty Ltd v. Registrar of Personal Property Securities (2014) 226 FCR
    188 .... 9.28
White v. Spiers Earthworks Pty Ltd (2014) 99 ACSR 214, 221–3 .... 9.11
Woolworths Ltd v. BP Plc (2006) 150 FCR 134 .... 9.28

Canada
Bad Ass Coffee Company of Hawaii Inc. v. Bad Ass Enterprises Inc., 2008 ABQB 404
    (CanLII) 13.58
Heintzman v. 751056 Ontario Ltd, [1990] F.C.1033 (Can.), 34 C.P.R. (3d) 1
    (F.C.T.D.) 1.24
Jean Patou Inc. v. Luxo Laboratories Ltd., [2001] 67 F.C.1419 (F.C.A.) 1.24

China
Interpretation of Several Questions on the Application of Law in Trial of Trademark Civil
    Dispute Cases (promulgated by Adjudication Comm. of the Supreme People's Court,
    12 October 2002, effective 16 October 2002) 32 Sup. People's Ct. Gaz. (Interpretation
    of Trademark Disputes)
    Art 3 .... 20.40
    Art 4 .... 20.41
    Art 4, § 2 .... 20.47
Interpretation of Several Questions on the Application of the Guaranty Law of PRC
    (promulgated by Judicial Comm. Supreme People's Court, 29 September 2000, effective
    13 December 2000) 44 Sup. People's Ct. Gaz.
    Art 105 .... 20.66

Denmark
IFPI Danmark v. DMT2 A/S (Frederiksberg Court, 29 October 2008) 4.15

France
Cour de Cassation (Supreme Court)
13 May 1980, Bull. civ. IV, No. 78–15666 .... 17.54
June 24, 1986, Bull. civ. IV, No. 84–14379 .... 17.27
18 June 1996, Bull. civ. IV, No. 94–44654 .... 17.09
23 October 2007, Bull. civ. IV, No. 06–18570 .... 17.44
8 April 2008, Bull. 2008, Case 06–10961, Greenpeace v. Esso 14.52
8 April 2008, Bull. 2008, Case 07–11251, Greenpeace v. Areva 14.52
29 January 2013, Bull. civ. IV, No. 11–24713 .... 17.54

Cours d'appel (CA) (Regional Court of Appeal)
Paris, 11 May 1987, JCP E. 1988, No. 69 .... 17.09
Lyon, com., 11 February 1999, Bull. Civ. IV, No.96LY00297 .... 17.27
Le Mans Court of First Instance, Microcaz v. Oceanet (29 June 1999) 4.30
Paris Court of First Instance Mobimedia France v BDLG Sofiges and Mediaplazza.com
 (No. 05/05413, 2006) 4.12
Strasbourg Court of First Instance, Puma France v. France Telecom E-Commerce,
 Brandalley, and Vanam (2008) 4.11
Versailles Court of First Instance, EuroDNS and Laurent Nunenthal v. AFNIC (2004) 4.23
Versailles Court of First Instance, France Printemps, Somewhere, Redcats, Free v. KLTE Ltd,
 AFNIC (2006) 4.23
Conseil Constitutionnel (CC) (Constitutional Council)
Decision No. 2013–685DC, 29 December 2013, Rec. 1127 .... 17.47
Conseil d'Etat (CE) (Council of State)
No. 43573, CE, 5 November 1984, Rec. Lebon 17.52
No. 64092, CE, 24 July 1987 .... 17.52
No. 189904, CE, 18 May 1998, Rec. Lebon 17.52
No. 262219, CE Sect., 14 October 2005, Rec. Lebon 17.52
No. 308494, CE Sect., 16 October 2009, Rec. Lebon 17.53
No. 328762, CE Sect., 26 September 2011 Rec. Lebon 17.51
Tribunal Administratif de Montreuil, 1ère Chambre, Judgment of 9 February 2012 .... 4.32

Germany
Federal Court of Justice (BGH)
BGH, Altenburger Spielkarten, GRUR 754, 757 (1995) 16.27
BGH, Baader, GRUR 363 (1973) 16.19
BGH, Beta Layout, 500, GRUR mn. 25 (2009) 16.29
BGH, Buendgens, GRUR 1164, 1165 (2001) 16.30, 16.31
BGH, Cambridge Institute, GRUR 884 (2007) 16.27
BGH, City Hotel, GRUR 507, 508 (1995) 16.27
BGH, DB Immobilienfonds, GRUR 344, 345 (2001) 16.29
BGH, FROMMIA, GRUR 972, 975 (2002) 16.30, 16.31
BGH, Heilquelle, WUW/E 1385 (1975) 16.51
BGH, Hotel Krone, GRUR 378, 379 (1984) 16.27
BGH, hufeland.de, GRUR 159 (2006) 16.27
BGH, Im Namen Des Volkes Urteil, I ZR 317/99 (April 2002) 4.30
BGH, 11 March 2008, NJW 2110, 2008 .... 14.52
BGH, Jette Joop, GRUR 641–7, Case KZR 71/08 (7 December 2010),
 (2011) 11.38, 16.51
BGH, Lila Postkarte, 3 February 2005, Case I ZR 159/02, Gewerblicher Rechtsschutz und
 Urheberrecht 2005, 583 .... 14.52
BGH, Micky-Maus-Orangen, GRUR 485, 488 (1963) 16.20
BGH, Peters, GRUR 325 (1986) 16.19
BGH, Pic Nic, GRUR 923, 924 (1993) 16.27
BGH, Rialto, GRUR 155, 156 (1991) 16.27
BGH, soco.de, GRUR 262, 263 (2005) 16.27
BGH, Torres, GRUR 825, 827 (1995) 16.29

TABLE OF CASES

BGH, Verschenktexte I, GRUR 218, 220 (1990) 16.32
BGH, Windsurfing Chiemsee, BGH Bl. 210, 212 (2001) 16.29
BverfG (Federal Constitutional Court)
Weinbergsrolle, 51, BVerfGE 193 .... 16.23
Esslinger Neckarhalde II, 78, BVerfGE 58 .... 16.23
OLG Koblenz 935, 936 RIW (1993) 16.55
OLG Saarbrücken, Bierstraße, 62 NJWE-WettbR (1998) 16.27
OLG Stuttgart 260, 261 NJWE-WettbR (1999) 16.22
CAC, Kraftwerk GbR Ralf Hütter/Florian Schneider v. EURid (11 November 2006) 4.25

India
Antox v. State Drug Controller of Tamil Nadu, MANU/TN/0067/1990: 1991 IPRL
 264 .... 23.10
Babul Products Private Ltd. v. Zen Products, MANU/GJ/0346/2005: 2005 (31) PTC
 135 .... 23.32, 23.34, 23.37
Baker Hughes Limited and Another v. Hiroo Khushalani and Another,
 MANU/DE/0411/1998: I.L.R. 1999 (Del.) 41 .... 23.14, 23.54
Bawa Jagmohan Singh v. Registrar of Trade Marks, MANU/DE/2053/2001: 2002 (24) PTC
 417 (Del) 23.63
Brakes International v. Tilak Raj Bagga, 1998 A.I.R. (Del.) 146 .... 23.63
Chorion Rights Ltd. v. Ishan Apparel & Others, MANU/DE/1071/2010 .... 23.47
CIT v. Ciba of India Ltd., MANU/SC/0125/1967 .... 23.71
Classic Equipments (P) Ltd. v. Johnson Enterprises, MANU/DE/4819/2009: 2009 (41)
 PTC 385 (Del) 23.68
Cycle Corporation of India Ltd. v. T.I. Raleigh Industries Pvt. Ltd., 1995 A.I.R. (Cal.)
 73 .... 23.09, 23.23
D.M. Entertainment Pvt. Ltd. v. Baby Gift House and Ors, MANU/DE/2043/2010 ... 23.47
Eaton Corporation v. BCH Electric Ltd MANU/DE/1836/2013: 2013 (55) PTC 417
 (Del) 23.38
Fatima Tile Works v. Sudarsan Trading Company Ltd., 1992 A.I.R. (Mad.) 12 .... 23.23
Fedders North American v. Show Line and Ors. MANU/DE/1938/2006: 2006 (32) PTC
 573 .... 23.51
Forward Auto Industries v. Brakes International, 1999 PTC 787 (Del) 23.63
Himalaya Drug Co. v. Arya Aushadhi Pharmaceutical Works, 1999 A.I.R.(M.P.) 110 ... 23.33
ITO v. Sylvania and Laxaman (P) Ltd,, MANU/ID/5047/2007 .... 23.72
J.K. Jain v. Ziff Davies Inc., MANU/DE/1334/2000: 2000 PTC 244 (Del) 23.23
J.L. Morison (India) Ltd. v. Deputy Commissioner of Income Tax,
 MANU/IK/0181/2014 .... 23.71
JMA Industries v. Union of India, 1980 A.I.R. (Del.) 200 .... 23.26
Kohinoor Paints v. Paramveer Singh, MANU/DE/0713/1995: 1996 PTC 69 .... 23.63
M/s. Modi Threads Ltd. v. M/s. Som Soot Gola Factory and Anr., 1992A.I.R.
 (Del.) 4 .... 23.67
Motilal Padampat Sugar Mills v. State of UP (1979) 2 S.C.R. 641 .... 23.54
Nico Quality Products v. N.C. Arya Snuff and Cigar Co, MANU/TN/2680/2013 .... 23.61
Pepsi Foods Ltd. v. Collector of Central Excise, 2004 (28) PTC 186 (SC) 23.72
Pioneer Hi-Bred International Inc USA v. Pioneer Seed Co. Ltd, LAWS (DLH) 1988 (5)
 36: 1988 (2) ArbLR 340: 1988 (1) Del Law 136 .... 23.41, 23.54

Prestige Housewares India Ltd. and Anr. v.Gupta Light House and Anr.,
MANU/IC/5032/2007: 2007 (35) PTC 876 (IPAB) 23.09
Riverdale School Society v. Riverdale High School and Ors, MANU/IC/5034/2007: 2008
(36) PTC 131 .... 23.50, 23.56, 23.57
Rob Mathys India Pvt. Ltd. v. Synthes Ag Chur, MANU/DE/0308/1997 .... 23.49
SKOL Breweries Ltd. v. Som Distilleries and Breweries Ltd. and Anr.,
MANU/MH/1194/2009: 2009 Indlaw Mum 1764 .... 23.66, 23.67
Sun Pharmaceuticals Industries Limited v. Cipla Limited, MANU/DE/1527/2008: 2009 (39)
PTC 347 (Del) 23.65, 23.67
Synthes A.G. Chur v. Rob Mathys India, 1996 MANU/DE/1103/1996: PTC 401
(Del) 23.16
Texmo Industries, Coimbatore and others v. Aqua Pump Industries and others,
MANU/IC/0072/2004: (2005) (31) P.T.C. 335 .... 23.10
Thukral Mechanical Works v. Nitin Machine Tools, (1998) P.T.C. 18 (Del) 23.04
Velcro Industries v. Velcro India Ltd., 1992 Indlaw Mum 6333: 1993(1) Arb.LR 465 ... 23.37
Vishnudas Trading v. Vazir Sultan Tobacco Co. Ltd. (1997) 4 S.C.C. 201 .... 23.43
Ziff-Davies Inc. v. Dr. J.K. Jain and Others, MANU/DE/0215/1998: 1998 PTC (18)
739 .... 23.38

Italy
Bergamo Public Prosecutor's Officer v. Kolmisappi (Supreme Court of Cassation, 29
September 2009) 4.15

Japan
Supreme Court
28 November 1975, 29 Minshu 1554 .... 12.17
27 February 2003, Heisei 14 (ju) no. 1100, 57 SAIKŌ SAIBANSHO MINJI HANREISHŪ
[MINSHŪ] 125 .... 21.08
13 February 2004, Heisei 13 (ju) nos. 866, 867, 58 SAIKŌ SAIBANSHO MINJI
HANREISHŪ [MINSHŪ] 311 .... 21.36
17 June 2005, Heisei 16 (ju) no. 997, 59 SAIKŌ SAIBANSHO MINJI HANREISHŪ
[MINSHŪ] 21.28
2 February 2012, Heisei 21 (ju) no. 2056, 66 SAIKŌ SAIBANSHO MINJI HANREISHŪ
[MINSHŪ] 21.32
Osaka Dist. Ct. Dec. 9, 1987, Showa 59 (wa) no. 6274, Showa 62 (wa) no. 3283 .... 21.50
Osaka Dist. Ct. 8 December 2005, Heisei 16 (wa) no. 12032 .... 21.05
Osaka Dist. Ct. Sept. 12, 2013, Heisei 24 (wa) no. 12967 .... 21.66
Tokyo Dist. Court, Judgment, 28 January 1999, 995 Hanrei Taimuzu [Judicial Times] 242;
1670 Hanrei Jiho [Judicial Reports] 75 .... 12.05, 12.06, 12.32
Tokyo Dist. Court, 29 June 1999, Heisei 7 (wa) no. 13557 .... 21.32
Tokyo Dist. Court, Sonybank 2001, 2001(wa) no. 5603 .... 4.31
Tokyo Dist. Court, Judgment, 26 September 2003, 1156 Hanrei Taimuzu 268 .... 12.05, 12.32
Tokyo Dist. Court, Coral Sand Case, Judgment, 16 October 2003, 1874 Hanrei Jiho
23 .... 12.21
Tokyo Dist. Court, Judgment, 26 January 2004, 1157 Hanrei Taimuzu 267; 1847 Hanrei Jiho
123 .... 12.07
Tokyo Dist. Court Judgment, 26 October 2007 (unpublished) 12.40

TABLE OF CASES

Tokyo Dist. Court, Judgment, 30 April 2009 (unpublished) 12.40
Tokyo Dist. Court, Unpublished Judgment, 23 July 2009 .... 12.03
Tokyo Dist. Court, Judgment, 31 March 2010 .... 12.05, 12.32
Tokyo Dist. Court, 30 July 2010, Heisei 17 (wa) no. 25703 .... 21.48
Tokyo Dist. Court, Judgment, 26 March 2014 .... 12.05, 12.06, 12.32
IP High Court, Judgment, 27 March 2008 (unpublished) 12.40
IP High Court, Judgment, 29 September 2010 .... 12.02
Osaka High Ct. 29 September 2004, Heisei 14 (ne) no. 3283 .... 21.60
Tokyo High Court Judgment, 30 May 2001, 1797 Hanrei Jiho 111 .... 12.40
Tokyo High Court, 28 May 2003, 1831 Hanrei Jiho 135 .... 12.40

Netherlands
Mercis and Bruna v. Punt, Court of Appeals of Amsterdam, Case LJN BS7825, 3 September 2011 .... 14.52

Singapore
Guy Neale and others v. Ku de Ta SG Pte Ltd [2013] SGHC 250 .... 22.05
Kickapoo (Malaysia) Sdn Bhd v. The Monarch Beverage Co (Europe) Ltd [2009] SGCA 63 .... 22.32
Kickapoo (Malaysia) Sdn Bhd v. The Monarch Beverage Co (Europe) Ltd [2010] 1 SLR 1212 .... 22.27
Weir Warman Ltd v. Research & Development Pty Ltd [2007] 2 SLR 1073 .... 22.31

Sweden
Columbia Pictures Industries Inc. v. Portlane AB (Swedish Court of Appeal, 4 May 2010) 4.15

Switzerland
Federal Supreme Court (Tribunal Fédéral, TF)
TF, 119 ATF Suisse I 436 .... 8.16
TF, 2A.588/2006 .... 8.45
TF, 119 ATF Suisse Ib 116 .... 8.45
TF, 2 September 1993, ATF 119 II 380 .... 13.38
TF 115 ATF Suisse Ia 157; RDAF 1993, 407 .... 8.45
TF, 2A.346/1992 du 9 mai 1995 in Archives 65 p. 51/57, StE 1995 B 72.11 no 3 .... 8.45
TF, 4 December 2003, 2004 [StR] 524 .... 8.60
TF, 19 May 2003, 4C.40/2003 .... 13.41
TF, 13 April 2010, ATF 136 III 200 .... 13.66
TF, Feb. 27, 2014, ATF 140 III 134 .... 13.37, 13.38, 13.41
TF, BGE 133 III 360 .... 5.35
TF, Decision 4A_553/2014 of 17 February 2015 – von Roll 5.17, 13.61

Thailand
Dika.No. 10207/2553, Bangchak Petroleum Public Company Limited v. Sanpatong SR Petroleum Limited Partnership et al. (2010) Supreme Court 22.63

United Kingdom

American Greetings Corporation's Application, in re [1984] 1 W.L.R. 189 .... 23.09
Apple Corps. Limited v. Apple Computer, Inc. [2006] EWHC 996 (Ch) 13.61
Bristol Groundschool Ltd. v. Intelligent Data Capture et. al. [2014] EWHC 2145
    (Ch) 15.10
Compass Group UK and Ireland Ltd. (trading as Medirest) v. Mid Essex Hospital Services
    NHSTrust [2013] EWCA (Civ) 200, [2012] EWHC 781 (QB) 15.10
Crosstown Music Co. v. Rive Droite Music Ltd. & Ors [2010] EWCA (Civ) 1222 ...... 15.75
Don King Productions Inc. v. Warren et. al. [1998] 2 All E.R. 608 (D) 114 .... 15.08
Doosan Power Systems Ltd. v. Babcock International Group plc and another company
    [2013] EWHC (Ch) 1364 .... 15.48
Dunlop Pneumatic Tyre Co. Ltd. v. Selfridge & Co. Ltd., [1915] A.C. 847 (H.L.) 15.81
GE Trade Mark, [1972] 1 W.L.R. 729 .... 22.14
Hamsard 3147 Ltd. (trading as Mini Mode Childrenswear) & Anor v. Boots UK Ltd. [2013]
    EWHC (Pat.) 3251 .... 15.73
Harrods Ltd. v. Harrods (Buenos Aires) and Harrods (South America) Ltd. [1999] F.S.R.
    187 .... 15.85
Holly Hobbie Trade Mark [1984] R.P.C. 101 .... 15.54
Hongkong Fir Shipping Co. Ltd. v. Kawasaki Kisen Kaisha Ltd. [1962] 2 Q.B. 26 .... 15.29
Investors Compensation Scheme Ltd. v. West Bromwich Building Society and Others [1998]
    1 All E.R. 98 .... 15.21
Kijowski v. New Capital Properties Ltd. [1987] 15 Con. L.R. 1 .... 15.35
Lawson v. Donald Macpherson & Co. Ltd., [1897] 14 R.P.C. 696 .... 15.10
Leofelis SA & Anor v. Lonsdale Sports Ltd. [2012] EWHC (Ch) 485 .... 15.43
Lucasfilm Ltd. v. Ainsworth [2011] UKSC 39, [2011] 3 W.L.R 487 .... 12.11
Morley v. Boothby (1825) 130 Eng. Rep. 455; 3 Bing. 107, 111–12 .... 15.23
National Power plc v. United Gas Co. Ltd. and Another [1998] All E.R. (Q.B.) 321 .... 15.75
Northern & Shell plc v. Conde Nast and National Magazines Distributors Ltd. [1995]
    R.P.C. 117 .... 15.42
Omega SA v. Omega Engineering Inc. [2011] EWCA Civ. 645 .... 13.61
Phelps v. Spon-Smith and Co. (a firm) [1999] All E.R. (D) 1268 (Ch) 15.35
R. Griggs Group Ltd. & Ors v. Evans & Ors [2003] EWHC (Ch) 2914, [2003] 1 Ch.
    153 .... 15.32
Reckitt & Colman Products Ltd. v. Borden Inc. [1990] 1 All E.R. 873 .... 15.08
Reuter v. Mulhens, (1953) 70 RPC 235 .... 23.59
Saunders v. Vautier [1841] EWHC (Ch) J82, (1841) 41 E.R. 482 .... 15.33
Scandecor Development AB v. Scandecor Marketing AB and Another [1999] F.S.R.
    26 .... 15.13, 15.56
Scandecor Development AB v. Scandecor Marketing AB and Others and One Other Appeal
    [2001] UKHL 21, [34], [2001] All E.R. 29 (H.L.) 15.13, 15.56, 22.32
Sirdar/Phildar [1975] 1 C.M.L.R. D 93 .... 11.37
Tinsley v. Milligan [1994] 1 A.C. 340 (H.L.) 15.36
Twentieth Century Fox Film Corp & Ors v. British Telecommunications plc [2011] EWHC
    1981 (Ch) 4.15
Williams, re [1917] 1 Ch. 1 .... 15.35
Yam Seng Pte v. ITC Ltd. [2013] EWHC 111 (QB) 15.10

TABLE OF CASES

United States of America

A. Bourjois & Co. v. Katzel, 260 U.S. 689, 691 (1923) 10.75
Already, LLC v. Nike, Inc., 133 S. Ct. 721, 184 L. Ed. 2d 553 (2013) 6.35, 6.75, 6.76
Apple v. Samsung, 920 F.Supp.2d 1079 (N.D. Cal. 2013) 3.36
Apple Comp., Inc. v. Formula Intern. Inc., 725 F.2d 521 (9th Cir. 1984) 3.20
Archer Daniels Midland Co. v. Narula, 2001 WL 804025 (N.D. Ill. 12 July 2001) 18.18
Bach v. Forever Living Products U.S., Inc., 473 F. Supp. 2d 1110, 1114 (W.D. Wash. 2007) 3.01, 18.35
Barcamerica Int'l USA Trust v. Tyfield Imps., Inc., 289 F.3d 589, 597–98 (9th Cir. 2002) 18.22, 18.31. 18.35
Benihana, Inc. v. Benihana of Tokyo, LLC, 784 F.3d 887 (2d Cir. 2015) 13.45
BLT Restaurant Group LLC v. Tourondel, 855 F. Supp. 2d 4, 21 (S.D. N.Y. 2012) 18.20
Bodum USA, Inc. v. La Cafetiere, Inc., 621 F.3d 624, 631 (7th Cir. Ill. 2010) 13.56
Boston Professional Hockey Ass'n v. Dallas Cap & Emblem Mfg., 360 F. Supp. 459 (N.D. Tex. 1973), rev'd in part 510 F.2d 1004 (5th Cir. 1975) 3.03, 3.32, 18.36
Boyle v. U.S., 200 F.3d 1369 (Fed. Cir. 2000) 3.02
Bradlees Stores, In re Nos. 00–16033 (BRL), 00–16035(BRL), 00–16036(BRL), 01-CV-3934 (SAS), 2001 WL 1112308 (S.D.N.Y. 20 September 2001) 10.40
Brewski Beer Co. v. Brewski Bros., 47 U.S.P.Q.2d (BNA) 1281, 1288–9 (T.T.A.B. 1998) 18.41
Brown Bar II, L.P. v. Dixie Mills, LLC, 732 F.Supp.2d 1353, 4 (N.D. Ga. 2010) 18.20
Bulte v. Iglehart Bros., 137 F. 492, 499 (7th Cir. 1905) 18.17
Burgess v. Gilman, 316 Fed. Appx. 542 (9th Cir. 2008) 18.20
Campbell v. Acuff-Rose Music, 510 U.S. 569 (1994) 6.34
Carroll v. Duluth Superior Milling Co., 232 F. 675, 680 (8th Cir. 1916) 18.17
CDS, Inc. v. I.C.E.D. Mgmt., Inc., 80 U.S.P.Q. 2d 1572, 1585 (T.T.A.B. 2006) 10.90
CFLC, Inc., In re 89 F.3d 673, 677 (9th Cir. 1996) 10.44
Chain v. Tropodyne Corp., 93 Fed. Appx. 880, 881 (6th Cir. 2004) 10.21–10.23, 10.32, 10.73
Clorox Co. v. Chem. Bank, 40 U.S.P.Q.2d (BNA) 1098, 1103–04 (T.T.A.B. 1996) 18.43
Coca-Cola Bottling Co. v. Coca-Cola Co., 269 F. 796, 806 (D. Del. 1920) 10.45
Crescent Publ'g Group, Inc. v. Playboy Enters., 246 F.3d 142, 151 (2nd Cir. 2001) 3.38
Cumulus Media, Inc. v. Clear Channel Communications, 304 F.3d 1167 (11th Cir. 2002) 3.18
Dastar Corp. v. Twentieth Century Fox Film Corp. 539 U.S. 23 (2003) 3.05, 3.06, 3.07, 3.09, 3.15
Dawn Donut Co. v. Hart's Food Stores, Inc., 267 F.2d 358, 369 (1959) 121 U.S.P.Q. 430 (2d Cir. 1959) 1.22, 18.10, 18.27, 18.34
DC Comics v. Pacific Pictures Corp., 2012 WL 4936588 (C.D. Cal. 2012) 3.26
DC Comics v. Towle, 2015 U.S. App. LEXIS 16837 (9th Cir. 2015) 3.01
De Beers LV Trademark Ltd. v. DeBeers Diamond Syndicate, Inc., 440 F.Supp.2d 249 (S.D.N.Y. 2006) 1.40
Dep't. of Parks & Recreation v. Bazaar Del Mundo, Inc., 448 F.3d 1118, 1131 (9th Cir. 2006) 18.35
E.& J. GalloWinery v. Gallo Cattle Co., 967 F.2d 1280, 1290 (9th Cir. 1992) 18.41
Embedded Moments, Inc. v. Int'l Silver Co., 648 F. Supp. 187, 194 (E.D.N.Y. 1986) 18.34, 18.35

Eva's Bridal Ltd. v. Halanick Enterprises, Inc., 639 F.3d 788 (7th Cir. 2011) 18.35
Exide Techs., in re 340 B.R. 222 (Bankr. D. Del. 2006) 10.09, 10.10, 10.33, 10.34–10.43,
10.44, 10.45, 10.46, 10.48, 10.49, 10.51, 10.53, 10.54, 10.59, 10.71, 10.78,
10.79, 10.93, 10.94
Exide Techs, in re 607 F.3d 957 (3rd Cir. 2010) 10.09, 10.43, 10.55, 10.56, 10.59,
10.64, 10.67
Express Media Group, LLC, et al.& DVD.com v. Express Corp.& Gregory Ricks, 2007 WL 1394163 (N.D. Cal., 2007) 4.24
Exxon Corp. v. Humble Exploration Co., 592 F.Supp. 1226 (N.D. Tex. 1984), on remand from 695 F.2d 96 (5th Cir. 1983) 3.18
Fairchild Semiconductors Corp. v. Third Dimension Semiconductor, 564 F.Supp.2d 63 (D. Maine, 12 December 2008) 13.66
Faiveley Transport Malmo AB, in re 522 F. Supp. 2d 639 (S.D.N.Y. 2007) 13.67
Fitzpatrick v. Sony-BMG Music Entm't Inc., 99 U.S.P.Q.2d 1052 (S.D.N.Y. 2010) 18.20
Fogerty v. Fantasy, Inc., 510 U.S. 517, 534 (1994) 3.38
FTC v. Actavis, Inc., 133 S.Ct. 2223 (2013) 6.40, 6.67
Geisel v. Poynter Prods., 283 F.Supp. 261 (S.D.N.Y. 1968) 3.14
Geisel v. Poynter Prods., 295 F.Supp. 331 (S.D.N.Y. 1968) 3.14
Glover v. Ampak, Inc., 74 F.3d 57 (4th Cir. 1996) 1.51
Glow Indus., Inc. v. Lopez, 273 F. Supp. 2d 1095, 1107 (C.D. Cal. 2003) 18.10, 18.19,
18.39, 18.41, 18.44
Goldsmith v. Comm'r, 143 F.2d 466, 468 .... 10.78
Green River Bottling Co. v. Green River Corp., 997 F.2d 359, 361–62 (7th Cir.1993) 6.74
Griggs, Cooper & Co. v. Erie Pres. Co., 131 F. 359, 361–2 (W.D.N.Y. 1904) 10.45
Hanover Star Milling Co. v. Metcalf, 240 U.S. 403 (1916) ... 10.80, 10.81, 10.83, 10.88, 18.30
Haymaker Sports, Inc. v. Turian, 581 F.2d 257, 262 (C.C.P.A. 1978) 18.35, 18.41, 18.43
Herwig v. United States, 105 F. Supp. 384 (Ct. Cl. 1952) 10.75
Hicks v. Anchor Packing Co., 16 F.2d 723, 725 (3d Cir. 1926) 18.30
Hokto Kinoko Co. v. Concord Farms, Inc., 738 F.3d 1085, 1098 (9th Cir. 2013) 6.74
Hormel Foods Corp. v. Jim Henson Prods., Inc., 73 F.3d 497 (2d Cir. 1996) 6.74
Hy-Cross Hatchery, Inc. v. Osborne, 303 F.2d 947 (C.C.P.A. 1962) 18.18
Illinois Tool Works Inc. v. Independent Ink, Inc., 547 U.S. 28 (2006) 6.72
Institut Pasteur v. Cambridge Biotech Corp., 104 F.3d 489, 493 (1st Cir. 1997) 10.44
International Cosmetics Exchanges, Inc. v. Gapardis Health & Beauty, Inc., 303 F.3d 1242 (11th Cir. 2002) 18.19
Interstate Bakeries Corp., In re 690 F.3d 1069 (8th Cir. 2012) 10.57–10.67
InterState Netbank v. Netb@nk, 348 F. Supp. 2d 340 (D.N.J. 2004) 18.19
Int'l Order of Job's Daughters v. Lindeburg & Co., 633 F.2d 912, 919 (9th Cir. 1980) 6.74
Jefferson Parish Hospital District No. 2 v. Hyde, 466 U.S. 2 (1984) 6.72
Jews For Jesus v. Google, Inc., 2005 WL 377582 (2005) (No. 05 CV 10684) (case terminated) 4.12
KeeblerWeyl Baking Co. v. J. S Ivins' Son, Inc., 7 F. Supp. 211, 214 (E.D. Pa. 1934) 18.30
Keener v. Sizzler Family Steak Houses, 597 F.2d 453, 456 (5th Cir.1979) 6.73
Kellogg Co. v. National Biscuit Co., 305 U.S. 111 (1938) 3.14
Kentucky Fried Chicken Corp. v. Diversified Packaging Corp., 549 F.2d 368, 387 (5th Cir. 1977) 5.26, 6.74, 18.34
Kidd v. Johnson, 100 U.S. 617 (1879) 18.30

TABLE OF CASES

Klinger v. Conan Doyle Estate, 755 F.3d 496 (2014) 3.16
KP Permanent Make-Up, Inc. v. Lasting Impression I, Inc., 543 U.S. 111 (2004) 11.32
Krebs Chrysler-Plymouth, Inc. v. Valley Motors, Inc., 141 F.3d 490, 498 (3d Cir. 1998) 10.44
Kremen v. Cohen, 337 F.3d 1024, 1030 (9th Cir. 2003) 4.31
Lakewood Eng'g & Mfg. Co., Inc., 459 B.R. 306, 310 (Bankr. N.D. Ill. 2011), In re aff'd sub nom. Sunbeam Prods., Inc. v. Chi. Am.Mfg., LLC, 686 F.3d 372 (7th Cir. 2012) 10.61–10.67
Land O'Lakes Creameries, Inc. v. Oconomowoc Canning Co., 221 F. Supp. 576 (D.Wis. 1963), aff'd, 330 F.2d 667 (7th Cir. 1964) 18.10, 18.35
Laurent's Est. v. Comm'r, 34 T.C. 385 (1960) 10.75
McGraw-Hill Compensation Inc. v. Vanguard Index Trust, 139 F. Supp. 2d 544 (S.D.N.Y., 2001), aff'd 27 Fed. Appx. 23 (2d Cir. 2001) 18.18
McKesson Corp., et al. v. Health Robotics, s.r.l,. 2011 WL 3157044 (N.D.Cal.) 13.58
MacMahan Pharmacal Co. v. Denver Chem. Mfg. Co., 113 F.2d 468, 474–5 (8th Cir. 1901) 18.17, 18.29
Marshak v. Green, 746 F.2d 927, 930 (2d Cir. 1984) 18.10
Med. Creative Techs. v. Dexterity Surgical, Inc., 2004 U.S. Dist. LEXIS 11304, (E.D.Pa. 24 February 2005) 13.58
MedImmune, Inc. v. Genentech, Inc., 549 U.S. 118 (2007) 6.35
Meijer, Inc. v. Purple Cow Pancake House, 226 U.S.P.Q. 280, 280–81 (T.T.A.B. 1985) 10.90
Merck & Co. v. Smith, 261 F.2d 162 (3d Cir. 1958) 10.75
MGM Studios, Inc. v. Grokster, Ltd., 545 U.S. 913 (2005) 6.34
Mister Donut of Am., Inc. v. Mr. Donut, Inc., 418 F.2d 838 (9th Cir. 1969) 18.18
Money Store v. Harriscorp Fin., Inc., 689 F.2d 666, 678 (7th Cir. 1982) 18.18
Morse-Starrett Prods. Co. v. Steccone, 86 F. Supp. 796, 805 (N.D. Cal. 1949) 18.33
Mulhens & Kropff, Inc. v. Ferd. Muelhens, Inc., 43 F.2d 937 (2d Cir. 1930) 18.17
Nat'l Lampoon, Inc. v. Am. Broad. Cos., 376 F. Supp. 733, 737 (S.D.N.Y. 1974), aff'd per curiam, 497 F.2d 1343 (2d Cir.1974) 18.34
National Trailways Bus System v. Trailway Van Lines, Inc., 269 F. Supp. 352, 155 U.S.P.Q. 507 (E.D.N.Y. 1965) 1.22
Nelson v. J. H. Winchell & Co., 89 N.E. 180, 183–4 (Mass. 1909) 18.30
Nova Wines, Inc. v. Adler FelsWinery LLC, 467 F.Supp.2d 965, 983 (N.D. Cal. 2006) 3.02, 3.39
Oracle America, Inc. v. Myriad Group AG, 2011 U.S. Dist. LEXIS 98830, 2011 WL 3862027, 20 (N.D. Cal. 1 September 2011) 13.47, 13.49, 13.52, 13.53
Oracle America, Inc. v. Myriad Group A.G., 724 F.3d 1069 (9th Cir. 2013) 13.47, 13.54
Original Rex v. Beautiful Brands International, 792 F. Supp. 2d 2442(N.D. Okla 2011) 18.35
Panavision Int'l v.Toeppen, 141 F.3d 1316 (9th Cir. 1998) 3.03
Patterson Labs., Inc. v. Roman Cleanser Co. (in re Roman Cleanser Co.), 802 F.2d 207 (6th Cir. 1986) 18.42, 18.43
PepsiCo, Inc. v. Graphette Co., 416 F.2d 285, 290 (8th Cir. 1969) 18.10, 18.11, 18.18
Performance Unlimited, Inc. v. Questar Publishers, Inc., 52 F.3d 1373 (6th Cir. 1995) 13.66
Phillips v. Audio Active Ltd., 494 F.3d 378 (2nd Cir. 2007) 13.35

TABLE OF CASES

Pilates, Inc. v. Current Concepts, Inc. 120 F. Supp. 2d 286 (S.D.N.Y. 2002) 18.18
Prof'l Golfers Ass'n of Am. v. Bankers Life & Cas. Co., 514 F.2d 665 (5th Cir. 1975) 18.37
Pure Imagination v. Pure Imagination Studios, No. 03 C 6070. 2004 WL 2222269 (N.D. Ill. Sept. 30, 2004) 18.19
Queen City Pizza, Inc. v Domino's Pizza, Inc., 124 F.3d 430 (3d Cir. 1997) 6.73
Raufast S.A. v. Kicker's Pizzazz, Ltd., 208 U.S.P.Q. (BNA) 699, 702 (E.D.N.Y. 1980) 18.41
Reid v. Comm'r, 26 T.C. 622, 632 (1956) 10.75
Rhône-Poulenc Spécialités Chimiques v. SCM Corp., 769 F.2d 1569 (Fed. Cir. 1985) 13.35
Robinson Co. v. Plastics Research & Dev. Corp., 264 F. Supp. 852, 864 (W.D. Ark. 1967) 18.34
Rock and Roll Hall of Fame and Museum v. Gentile, 134 F.3d 749 (6th Cir. 1998) 3.12
Russell v. Price, 612 F.2d 1123 (9th Cir. 1979) 3.16
Sands, Taylor & Wood v. Quaker Oats Co., 18 U.S.P.Q.2d (BNA) 1457, 1467–68 (N.D. Ill. 1990), aff'd in part and rev'd in part, 978 F.2d 947 (7th Cir. 1992) 18.41
Sauer-Getriebe KG v.White Hydraulics, Inc., 715 F.2d 348 (7th Cir. 1983) 13.67
Sauers Milling Co. v. Kehlor Flour Mills, Co., 39 App. D.C. 535, 542 (D.C. Cir. 1913) 18.17
Scherk v. Alberto-Culver Co., 417 U.S. 506, 527 (1974) 13.31, 13.55, 13.56
Seattle Brewing & Malting Co. v. Comm'r, 6 T.C. 856, 873 (1946) 10.24–10.32, 10.46, 10.69, 10.76, 10.78
Sexton Mfg. Co. v. Chesterfield Shirt Co., 24 F.2d 288 (D.C. Cir. 1928) 18.17
Shoney's, Inc. v. Schoenbaum, 894 F.2d 92, 97–98 (4th Cir. 1990) 10.71, 10.72
Siegel v. Chicken Delight, Inc., 448 F.2d 43, 48–49 (9th Cir. 1971) 18.33
Siegel v. Warner Bros. Entertainment Inc., 542 F.Supp.2d 1098 (C.D. Cal. 2008) 3.26
Simula, Inc. v. Autoliv, Inc., 175 F.3d 716, 720–21, 723 (9th Cir. 1999) 13.35, 13.56, 13.67
Sony Corp. of America v. Universal City Studios, Inc., 464 U.S. 417 (1984) 6.34
Sporty's Farm L.L.C. v. Sportsman's Market, Inc., 202 F.3d 489 (2d Cir. 2000) 3.37
Ste. Pierre Smirnoff, Fls, Inc. v. Hirsch, 109 F. Supp. 10, 12 (S.D. Ca. 1952) 10.47, 10.75
Steelworkers v. American Mfg. Co., 363 U.S. 564, 569 (1960) 13.34
Steward v. Abend, 495 U.S. 207 (1990) 3.27
Sugar Busters LLC v. Brennan, 177 F.3d 258 (5th Cir. 1999) 18.18
Sunbeam Prods., Inc. v. Chicago Am. Mfg., LLC, 686 F.3d 372 (7th Cir. 2012) 10.61–10.67
Sunstar, Inc. v. Alberto-Culver Co., 2009 U.S. Lexis 23759 (7th Cir. 28 October 2009) 21.25, 21.38
Sunterra Corp., In re 361 F.3d 257, 264 (4th Cir. 2004) 10.44
Susser v. Carvel Corp., 206 F. Supp. 636, 641 (S.D.N.Y. 1962), aff'd, 332 F.2d 505 (2d Cir. 1964) 18.33
Syntex Labs, Inc. v. Norwich Pharmacal Co., 315 F. Supp. 45, 55–56 (S.D.N.Y. 1970), aff'd, 437 F.2d 566 (2d Cir. 1971) 18.41
T & T Mfg. Co. v. A.T. Cross Co, 449 F.Supp. 819, aff'd in 587 F.2d 533, cert. denied, 441 U.S. 60 (1978) 11.33
TMT N. Am., Inc. v. Magic Touch GmbH, 124 F.3d 876, 885–86 (7th Cir. 1997) 18.33
TR-3 Industries, in re 41 B.R. 128 (Bankr. C.D. Cal. 1984) 18.42

TABLE OF CASES

Transgo, Inc. v. Ajac Transmission Parts Corp., 768 F.2d 1001, 1017–18 (9th Cir. 1985) 18.34

United Drug Co. v. Theodore Rectanus Co., 248 U.S. 90, 96–97, 39 S.Ct. 48, 63 L.Ed. 141 (1918) 6.74, 10.80, 10.84, 10.85, 10.86, 10.87, 18.17

United States v. Carruthers, 219 F.2d 21 (9th Cir. 1955) 10.75

United States v. Giles, 213 F.3d 1247 (10th Cir. 2000) 3.03

United States v. Line Materials Company, 333 U.S. 287 (1947) 6.40

Visa U.S.A. Inc. v. Birmingham Trust Nat'l Bank, 696 F.2d 1371, 1375 (Fed. Cir. 1982) 18.18, 18.40, 18.41

Vittoria North America L.L.C. v. Euro-Asia Imports Inc., 278 F.3d 1076 (10th Cir. 2011) 18.19, 18.44

Waltham Watch Co. v. FTC, 318 F.2d 28, 29 (7th Cir. 1963), cert. denied, 375 U.S. 944 (1963) 18.22

Warne (Frederick) & Co. v. Book Sales, Inc. 481 F.Supp. 1191 (S.D.N.Y. 1979) 3.07, 3.08, 3.09, 3.10, 3.12, 3.23

Waukesha Hygiene Mineral Springs Co. v. Hygeia Sparkling Distilled Water Co., 63 F. 438 (7th Cir. 1894) 11.31, 11.35

Wexler v. Greenberg160 A.2d 430 (1960) 6.57

Williams v. Roberto Cavalli S.p.A, 113 U.S.P.Q.2d (BNA) 1944 (C.D. Cal. 2015) 3.01

XMH Corp., in re 647 F.3d 690, 696 (7th Cir. 2011) 6.74

Yamamoto & Co. (America), Inc. v. Victor United, Inc., 219 U.S.P.Q. 968 (C.D. Cal. 1982) 1.22

TABLE OF LEGISLATION

Treaties, Conventions and other International Instruments

ALI Principles: American Law Institute, Intellectual Property: Principles Governing Jurisdiction, Choice of Law, and Judgments in Transnational Disputes (2008) 12.10, 12.11, 12.24, 12.26, 12.36
    Art 202(3)(a) 12.13, 12.16
    Art 202(3)(b) 12.19
    Art 302(1) 12.35
    Art 302(4)(a) 12.36
    Art 302(5)(a) 12.36
    Art 315(1) 12.38, 12.40
Berne Convention for the Protection of Literary and Artistic Works 1.04
CLIP Principles: European Max-Planck Group on Conflict of Laws in Intellectual Property – CLIP Principles and Commentary (2013) 12.10, 12.11, 12.13, 12.19, 12.21, 12.22, 12.24, 12.26, 12.36, 12.38, 12.40
    Art 2:301(2) 12.16
    Art 2:301(3) 12.13
    Art 2:301(4) 12.20
    Art 3:501 .... 12.38
    Art 3:501(1) 12.35, 12.38
    Art 3:501(4) 12.36
    Art 3:504 .... 12.37
    Art 3:505(2) 12.36
    Art 3:506(1) 12.39
Common Regulations under the Madrid Agreement and the Madrid Protocol, as in force on 1 January 2013 .... 2.05, 2.09, 2.28, 2.46, 2.52
    r 20 .... 2.48, 2.49, 2.51
    r 20(1) 2.49
    r 20(1)(c) 2.51
    r 20(2) 2.50
    r 20(3) 2.50
    r 20bis 2.44, 2.46
    r 20bis(6)(a) 2.46
    r 20bis(6)(b) 2.46
    r 25(b) 2.27
    r 25(3) 2.26
    r 27(4) 2.29
Convention on Jurisdiction and Foreign Judgments in Civil and Commercial Matters 12.28
DSU: Understanding on Rules and Procedures Governing the Settlement of Disputes, 15 April 1994, Marrakesh Agreement Establishing the World Trade Organization, Annex 21869 U.N.T.S. 401, 33 I.L.M. 1226 (1994) 1.01
    Art 3(2) 1.07
    Art 19(2) 1.07
Free Exchange Agreement between the EU/Switzerland, 22 July 1972 ...... 8.73
Hague Convention: Convention on Choice of Court Agreements, Hague Conference on Private International Law (30 June 2005) 12.10, 12.26, 12.28
    Art 2(1) 12.22
    Art 2(3) 12.21
    Art 3(c) 12.13
    Art 6 .... 12.24
    Art 6(b) 12.19
    Art 6(c) 12.24
Havana Charter
    Ch V 1.67
IBA (International Bar Association), Guidelines for Drafting International Arbitration Clauses (2010)
    Guideline 3 .... 13.57
ICANN, Rules for Uniform Domain Name Dispute Resolution Policy

Art 1 .... 13.08
Art 3(b)(xiii) 13.08
ICC Rules of Arbitration (2012)
Art 29 .... 13.68
ILA Guidelines on Intellectual Property and Private International Law (as modified and adopted in the Washington Conference 2014) 12.29
Joint Recommendations concerning Provisions on the Protection of Well-Known Marks 1999, WIPO Pub. No. 833 .... 2.08
Joint Recommendations concerning Provisions on the Protection of Marks, and Other Industrial Property Rights in Signs, on the Internet 2001, WIPO Pub. No. 845 .... 2.08
Joint Recommendation Concerning Trademark Licenses 2000, WIPO Pub. No. 835 ...... 2.05, 2.07, 2.08, 2.30–2.43
Art 4(1) 2.37
Art 4(2) 2.38
Art 4(2)(a) 2.39
Art 4(2)(b) 2.39
Art 5 .... 2.41, 2.42
Art 6 .... 2.43
Lisbon Agreement on the Protection of Appellations of Origins, WIPO ... 1.06, 1.30
Art 22.3 .... 1.06
Art 23.2 .... 1.06
Art 24.5 .... 1.06
Madrid Agreement Concerning the International Registration of Marks 1891 (MMA) (as revised and amended), 828 U.N.T.S. 389 .... 2.05, 2.09, 2.10, 2.25, 5.08, 20.11, 20.21
Art 1(2) 2.25
Art 1(3) 2.25
Art 4 .... 2.09
Art 9*bis*(2) 2.25
Art 9ter(1) 5.18, 5.33
Art 21 .... 20.31
Madrid Protocol 1989 (MMP) 2.05, 2.09, 2.10, 2.26, 2.28, 2.44, 2.46, 20.11
Art 2(1) 2.25
Art 4 .... 2.09

Art 6(2) 2.10
Art 9 .... 2.25, 2.27
New York Convention 1958
Art 5 para 1 .... 13.58
Nice Agreement Concerning the International Classification of Goods and Services for the Purposes of the Registration of Marks, 5 May 1994, 1154 U.N.T.S. 89 .... 20.15
OECD Model Tax Convention (OECD Model) 8.04, 8.21
Art 4 .... 8.61
Art 4 § 2 .... 8.61
Art 9 .... 8.44
Art 9 § 1 .... 8.43
Art 12 .... 8.29
Art 12 §1 .... 8.18, 8.19
Art 12 § 2 .... 8.79
OECD Transfer Pricing Guidelines for Multinational Enterprises and Tax Administrations (2010) 8.07, 8.42
§ 1.2 .... 8.43
§ 2.12 .... 8.48
§ 2.56 .... 8.51
§ 6.32 .... 8.68
§ 6.89 .... 8.47
§ 6.91 .... 8.47
§ 6.92 .... 8.47
§ 6.95 .... 8.47
§ 6.108 .... 8.47
§ 6.138 .... 8.52
§ 6.139 .... 8.50
§ 6.142 .... 8.53
§ 6.150 .... 8.53
§ 6.151 .... 8.53
Paris Convention for the Protection of Industrial Property, as last revised at the Stockholm Revision Conference, 14 July 1967, 21 U.S.T. 1583, 828 U.N.T.S. 303 ...... 1.14, 1.15, 1.25, 2.05, 2.06, 2.10–2.13, 20.11, 20.21
Art 4 .... 2.12
Art 5A(4) 1.61
Art 5C(1) 2.40
Art 6 .... 2.10
Art 6*bis* 1.40, 2.12, 20.21

Art 6*quater* 1.60, 2.10, 2.11, 2.12, 2.13, 20.31
Art 6*quater*(1) 1.59
Art 6quater(2) 2.12
Art 6quinqies(1) 2.10
Art 6*quinquies*(B) 1.25
Art 6*quinquies*(B)(ii) 1.25
Art 6*quinquies*(C) 1.26
Art 6septies 14.05
Art 10*bis* 1.16, 20.21
Singapore Treaty on the Law of Trademarks 2006 (STLT), DOC. No. 110–2 (2007) 2.05, 2.07, 2.12, 2.14–2.24, 2.28, 2.30–2.43, 2.47, 5.08, 20.11
Art 7 .... 5.22
Art 7(1)(a) 5.14
Art 11 ... 2.15, 2.17, 2.21, 2.22, 2.24, 2.32, 2.33, 5.10
Art 11(1)(a) 2.17
Art 11(1)(b) 2.17
Art 11(1)(c) 2.17, 2.18
Art 11(1)(e) 2.17, 2.19
Art 11(3) 2.20
Art 11(4) 2.20
Art 11(4)(iv) 2.24
Art 16 .... 2.12
Art 17 .... 2.31, 2.32
Art 17(4) 2.34
Art 17(4)(a) 2.34
Art 17(4)(a)(i)–(iii) 2.34
Art 17(4)(b) 2.34
Art 18 .... 2.31, 2.35
Arts 19–20 .... 2.57
Art 19 .... 2.31
Art 19(1) 2.37
Art 19(2) 2.38
Art 19(3) 2.42
Art 20 .... 2.31, 2.43
Art 23(2)(ii) 2.33
Art 29(4) 2.39
Singapore Treaty Regulations, as in force on November 1, 2011 .... 2.05, 2.17
reg 10 .... 2.33
reg 10(1)(a) 2.33
reg 10(2)(a)(i) 2.34
reg 10(2)(a)(ii) 2.34

reg 10(3) 2.35
reg 10(3)(a)(i) 2.35
reg 10(3)(a)(ii) 2.35
reg 10(4) 2.35
reg 10(4)(i) 2.35
reg 10(4)(ii) 2.35
TLT: Trademark Law Treaty 1994, 2034 U.N.T.S. 298 .... 1.61, 2.07, 2.12, 2.14–2.24, 2.31, 2.47, 5.08, 18.13, 20.11
Art 7 .... 5.22
Art 7(1)(a) 5.14
Art 11 .... 2.17, 2.21, 5.10
Art 11(4)(iv) 1.61
Art 16 .... 2.12
Treaty Supplementing the Paris Convention for the Protection of Industrial Property as far as Patents Are Concerned, WIPO Doc. PLT/DC/3
rr 16–17 .... 2.53
TRIPS Agreement: Agreement on Trade-Related Aspects of Intellectual Property Rights, 15 April 1994, Marrakesh Agreement Establishing the World Trade Organization (WTO), Annex 1C, 1869 U.N.T.S. 299, 33 I.L.M. 1197 (1994) 1.01, 1.02, 1.03, 1.04, 1.05, 1.07, 1.13, 1.14, 1.16, 1.22, 1.24, 1.26, 1.56, 1.57, 1.61, 1.64, 1.66, 1.67, 1.69, 1.70, 5.08, 13.61, 18.15, 20.08, 20.11, 22.04
Part II 1.02, 1.66
Art 2.1 .... 1.60, 2.06
Art 8 .... 1.65
Art 8.2 .... 1.62, 1.63
Art 15 .... 1.02, 1.18–1.19, 1.25, 1.51
Art 15.1 .... 1.16, 1.19, 1.27, 21.10
Art 16 .... 11.08
Art 16.1 .... 1.27, 11.08
Art 16.2 .... 2.12
Art 16.3 .... 20.21
Art 17 .... 1.07
Art 19 .... 1.02, 1.28
Art 19.1 .... 2.40, 5.27
Art 19.2 .... 1.29–1.35, 1.54, 2.41
Art 20 .... 1.02, 1.36–1.42, 23.48

Art 21 ... 1.02, 1.43–1.53, 1.59, 1.60, 2.13, 2.24, 5.10, 5.11, 11.04, 16.20, 17.04, 18.15, 20.31, 23.05, 23.59
Arts 22–24 .... 1.06
Art 22 .... 11.03
Art 27.1 .... 1.05
Art 28 .... 11.08
Art 31(e) 1.61
Art 39 .... 11.08
Art 40.2 .... 1.62, 1.65, 1.66, 1.68
Art 62.3 .... 2.12
Art 64 .... 1.01
UNCITRAL Rules (1976, 2010) 13.50, 13.54
Art 23(1) 13.55
Unidroit Principles of International Commercial Contracts
Art 7.3.5 .... 13.43
United Nations Convention on the Recognition and Enforcement of Foreign Arbitral Awards 13.31
VCLT: Vienna Convention on the Law of Treaties, May 23, 1969, 1155 U.N.T.S. 331 (entered into force 27 January 1980) 1.13, 8.26
Arts 31–32 .... 1.64
Art 31 .... 1.64
Art 31.3(b) 1.38
WIPO Arbitration Rules, WIPO (2014) 13.67
Art 48d 13.67
Art 49 .... 13.68
WIPO Convention 2.01

European Union

Treaty Establishing the European Community (Consolidated Version), 2006 O.J. (C 321) E/37
Art 3 .... 16.13
Treaty on the Functioning of the European Union TFEU
Art 26(2) 16.16
Art 101 (ex Art 81 EC (ex art 85)) 13.35, 13.65, 15.91, 16.09, 17.15
Art 101(1) 16.43

Art 101(3) 16.43, 16.45
Art 102 .... 16.09, 17.02
Agreement on the European Economic Area of 2 May 1992
Art 53 .... 13.35

Regulations

Brussels I Regulation: Jurisdiction and the Recognition and Enforcement of Judgments in Civil and Commercial Matters, Reg 44/2001, 2000 O.J. (L 12) 12.16
Art 5(3) 13.35
Art 6(1) 13.35
Art 23(1) 13.35
Brussels I Regulation (Recast), Reg 1215/2012, 2012 O.J. (L351) 1 (EU)
Art 20 .... 12.16
Art 24(4) 12.21
Community Trademark Regulation (CTR/CTMR), Reg 207/2009, O.J. 2009 L 78/1 .... 5.08, 11.31, 16.03, 16.29, 17.35, 17.39
Rec 5 .... 16.16
Rec 6 .... 16.16
Art 1(2) 5.17, 16.14
Art 9(1) 11.09
Art 13(1) 11.09
Art 15 .... 5.26
Arts 16–24 .... 14.01
Art 16 .... 14.01, 14.03
Art 16(1) 14.01
Art 16(1)(a) 14.01
Art 16(1)(b) 14.01
Art 16(2) 14.01
Art 17 .... 14.04
Art 17(1) 5.10, 14.06
Art 17(2) 14.04, 16.22
Art 17(3) 14.04
Art 17(4) 14.05
Art 17(5) 14.05, 14.09
Art 18 .... 14.04, 14.05
Art 19(1) 14.09
Art 19(2) 14.09
Art 20(1) 14.09
Art 20(2) 14.03
Art 20(3) 14.09

Art 21(1)	14.03
Art 21(3)	14.09
Art 22	14.04
Art 22(1)	5.36, 14.06
Art 22(2)	14.08, 14.10, 16.47
Art 22(3)	14.08
Art 22(4)	14.08
Art 22(5)	14.09, 16.49
Art 22(3)	5.24
Art 23(1)	14.09
Art 23(3)	14.03
Art 33	17.36
Art 42(4)	11.09
Art 44(1)	5.16
Art 44(7)	5.14
Art 49(1)	5.16
Art 49(7)	5.14
Art 51(1)(c)	11.09
Art 52(2)	11.09
Art 100(3)	14.08

Implementation of the .eu Top Level Domain, Reg 733/2002, 2002 O.J. (L 113) 5

Art 1	13.14
Art 4	4.23

Public Policy Rules Concerning the Implementation and Functions of the .eu Top Level Domain and the Principles Governing Registration, Reg 874/2004, 2004 O.J. (L 162) 40 (EU)

Art 2	4.30

Rome I Regulation on the Law applicable to contractual obligations, Reg 593/2008, O.J. 2008 L 177/6 ...... 12.38, 13.64, 16.54

Art 2	16.54
Art 3(1)	5.06
Art 3(4)	12.36
Art 4(4)	16.56
Art 9	16.57
Art 28	16.54

Rome II Regulation on the Law applicable to non-contractual obligations, Reg 864/2007, O.J. 2007 L 199/40 (EC) 13.64

Art 8	13.64
Art 8(1)	5.06, 13.64
Art 8(3)	13.64
Art 14	13.64

Commission Regulation 2868/95 implementing Council Regulation (EC) No. 40/94 on the Community Trademark, [1995] O.J. L 303/1 (also amended by [2005] O.J. L 172/4)

r 18(2)	11.09

Commission Regulation 874/2004 Laying Down Public Policy Rules Concerning the Implementation and Functions of the .eu Top Level Domain and the Principles Governing Registration, 2004 O.J. (L 162) 40 (EC) 13.14

rec 16	13.14
rec 17	13.14
Art 10	13.19
Art 21	13.16, 13.19
Art 22(2)	13.17
Art 22(11)	13.18

Commission Regulation 772/2004 on the application of Article 81(3) of the Treaty to Categories of Technology Transfer Agreements, 2004 O.J. (L 123) 11 .... 16.09, 16.41

Commission Regulation 1217/2010 on the Application of Article 101(3) of the Treaty to Categories of Research and Development Agreements, 2010 O.J. (L 335) 36 .... 16.09

Commission Regulation 316/2014 on the Application of Article 101(3) of the Treaty to Categories of Technology Transfer Agreements, 2014 O.J. (L 93) 17 (TTBER) 16.41, 16.42

rec 5	16.42
Art 1(f)	16.44
Art 1(1)(b)	16.44
Art 1(2)	16.45

Directives

Consumer Rights Directive, Dir. 2011/83/EU (amending Council Directive 93/13/EEC and Directive 1999/44/EC and repealing Council Directive 85/577/EEC and Directive 97/7/EC), 2011 O.J. (L 304) 64, 73 (EC)

Art 3 .... 13.26
Product Liability Directive, Dir. 85/374,
　　1985 O.J. (L 210) 29 .... 15.62, 17.19
Reinsurance Directive, Dir. 2005/68/EC
　　(amending Council Directives
　　73/239/EEC, 92/49/EEC and
　　Directives 98/78/EC and 2002/83/EC)
　　2005 O.J. (L 323) 1 .... 17.40
Taxation of Savings Income in the Form of
　　Interest Payments (Savings Agreement)
　　Directive, Dir. 2003/48 2003 O.J.
　　(L 157) 38 (EC) 8.20, 8.21, 8.22
Art 15(1) 8.20
Trademark Directive (TD/TMD): Dir.
　　2008/95/EC, 2008 O.J. (L 299) 25
　　(EC) (replacing Council Directive
　　89/104) 5.08, 15.05, 15.93, 16.16,
　　17.02
rec 2 .... 16.16
Art 4(5) 11.09
Arts 5–7 .... 14.48, 14.49, 14.51
Art 5 .... 11.09, 14.27, 14.47, 14.48
Art 5(1) 14.23, 14.25, 14.29, 14.31,
　　14.34, 14.35
Art 5(1)(a) 14.52, 14.53, 14.55
Art 5(2) 14.23, 14.25, 14.29, 14.31,
　　14.34, 14.35, 14.52, 14.55
Art 5(3) 14.23, 14.25, 14.29, 14.31,
　　14.34, 14.35
Art 6 .... 14.48, 14.52
Art 7 .... 14.23, 14.48, 14.52
Art 7(1) 11.09, 14.19, 14.20, 14.21,
　　14.22, 14.25, 14.37, 14.38, 14.39,
　　14.52
Art 7(2) 14.16, 14.21, 14.22, 14.30,
　　14.31, 14.37
Art 8 .... 14.01, 14.10, 14.22, 14.32, 14.47,
　　14.48, 14.49, 14.50, 14.51
Art 8(1) 5.36, 14.10, 14.11, 15.41
Art 8(2) 14.10, 14.11, 14.15, 14.16,
　　14.17, 14.18, 14.19, 14.20, 14.21,
　　14.22, 14.23, 14.25, 14.26, 14.27,
　　14.28, 14.29, 14.30, 14.31, 14.32,
　　14.33, 14.34, 14.35, 14.36, 14.37,
　　14.38, 14.39, 14.40, 14.41
Art 8(2)(e) 14.17, 14.27, 14.35, 14.39
Art 9 .... 14.50

Art 10 .... 5.26
Art 12(20)(b) 11.09
Unfair Terms in Consumer Contracts
　　Directive, Dir. 93/13/EEC, 1993 O.J.
　　(L 095) 29 (EC)
Art 3 .... 13.26

National Legislation

Australia
Constitution
　s 51(xxxi) 9.11
Corporations Act 2001 (Cth) 9.04, 9.07,
　　9.08
　ss 280–282 .... 9.06
Intellectual Property Laws Amendment Act
　　2006 (Cth)
　Sch 1 item 7 .... 9.36
Patents Act 1990 (Cth) 9.07
Personal Property Securities Act 2009 (Cth)
　　(PPSA) 9.01, 9.03, 9.04, 9.05, 9.08,
　　9.12, 9.13, 9.14, 9.15, 9.16, 9.17, 9.20,
　　9.21, 9.22, 9.26, 9.31, 9.32, 9.33, 9.35
　Pt 2.6 .... 9.11
　s 10 .... 9.09, 9.10
　s 10(c) 9.09
　s 12(1) 9.09
　s 12(2)(a)–(c) 9.09
　s 12(2)(j) 9.09
　s 12(2)(k) 9.09
　s 19(2) 9.09
　s 20(1)–(2) 9.10
　s 21(1)–(2) 9.10
　s 43 .... 9.11
　s 43(1) 9.11, 9.18, 9.25, 9.27, 9.28,
　　9.29, 9.30
　s 44(1) 9.11
　s 44(2) 9.11
　s 44(2)(b) 9.11
　s 46 .... 9.11
　s 55(2)–(6) 9.12
　s 105(1) 9.10
　s 105(2) 9.10
　s 106(1) 9.11
　s 150 .... 9.10
　s 153(1) item 4 .... 9.10
　s 153(1) item 5(b) 9.10

s 155(a) 9.34
s 156 .... 9.34
s 160 .... 9.10
s 163 .... 9.10
ss 164–165 .... 9.10
s 267(2) 9.11
s 308(a) 9.10
s 310(b) 9.10
s 311 .... 9.10
s 313 .... 9.11
s 322(2) 9.18
s 322(2)(f) 9.18
Personal Property Securities (Consequential Amendments) Act 2009 (Cth) 9.05
Sch 2 .... 9.14
Personal Property Securities (Corporations and Other Amendments) Act 2010 (Cth) 9.04, 9.06
Sch 1 item 18 .... 9.08
Sch 2 item 43 .... 9.11
Proceeds of Crime Act 2002 (Cth)
s 142 .... 9.07
Trade Marks Act 1995 (Cth) (TMA) 9.03, 9.14, 9.33, 9.34, 9.36
Pt 8, div 2 .... 9.36
s 6(1) 9.13
s 22 .... 9.06, 9.07, 9.12, 9.13, 9.18
s 22(1) 9.07, 9.12, 9.18
ss 22(2)–(3) 9.07
s 22(2) 9.07
s 22(2)(b) 9.07
s 22(2A) 9.12, 9.18
s 22(3) 9.18
s 22(4) 9.12, 9.18
s 42(b) 9.36
s 72(3) 9.19
s 75 .... 9.19
s 84(2) 9.23
s 84A 9.36
s 84A(4) 9.23
s 84A(5) 9.23
s 84D 9.23
ss 85–88 .... 9.28
s 85 .... 9.28, 9.29
s 85(b) 9.28
s 88 .... 9.28
s 88(1)(b) 9.28

s 88(2) 9.28
s 95(1) 9.23, 9.33
ss 109–110 .... 9.27
s 109(1) 9.26
s 109(1)(b) 9.27
s 111 .... 9.23
s 113 .... 9.05, 9.14
s 114(1) 9.05
s 114(2) 9.05
s 116 .... 9.05
s 117 .... 9.05, 9.14
s 118 .... 9.05
s 123 .... 9.10
s 123(1) 9.10
s 190 .... 9.27
Personal Property Securities Regulations 2010 (Cth)
Sch 1 cls 2.2(1)(c)(iii)(E)–(2) 9.10
Sch 1 cls 2.2(3)(h) 9.10
Trade Marks Regulations 1995 (Cth) (TMR) 9.36
reg 8.1 .... 9.23
reg 8.1(3)(b) 9.23
reg 9.6 .... 9.23, 9.33
reg 10.1(a) 9.27
reg 10.4(1)(b) 9.23
reg 10.4(4) 9.23
reg 10.5 .... 9.23
Pesticides Act 1999 (NSW)
s 31 .... 9.07
Real Property Act 1900 (NSW)
s 43(1) 9.11
Land Title Act 1994 (Qld)
s 184(3)(b) 9.11
Transfer of Land Act 1958 (Vic)
s 43 .... 9.11

Brazil

Civil Code, Law 10,406 (Jan. 10, 2002) 19.42
Art 126 .... 19.08
Art 179 .... 19.32
Arts 186–188 .... 19.27
Art 205 .... 19.32
Art 481 .... 19.46
Art 502 .... 19.51
Arts 565–578 .... 19.16

TABLE OF LEGISLATION

Arts 579–592 .... 19.16
Art 884 .... 19.27
Art 1098 .... 19.17
Arts 1143–1149 .... 19.58
Art 1145 .... 19.58
Art 1146 .... 19.58
Art 1147 .... 19.59
Art 1215 .... 19.08
Art 1225 .... 19.08
Art 1228 .... 19.09, 19.10
Art 1424 .... 19.44
Arts 1431–1472 .... 19.41
Art 1432 .... 19.36
Art 1437 .... 19.36
Civil Procedural Code 19.09
Consumer Code (Law 8,078 of 11
 September 1990)
 Art 12 .... 19.12, 19.19
Constitution
 Art V, subsection XXIX 19.08
Franchise Law (Law 8,955 of 15 December
 1994) 19.25
 Art 3 .... 19.31
 Art 4 .... 19.12, 19.32
 Art 6 .... 19.30
 Art 8 .... 19.30, 19.32
Industrial Property Law (Law 9,279 of 14
 May 1996) 19.09
 Art 5 .... 19.08, 19.16
 Art 122 .... 19.07
 Art 123 .... 19.07
 Art 129 .... 19.09, 19.11
 Art 129(2) 19.57
 Art 130 .... 19.11, 19.12
 Art 135 .... 19.52
 Art 136 .... 19.36, 19.38
 Art 137 .... 19.36
 Arts 143–5 .... 19.10
 Art 144 .... 19.54
 Art 195 .... 19.27
Intellectual Property Law
 Art 134 .... 19.47
 Art 135 .... 19.47
 Art 137 .... 19.47
Law 4,131 of 3 September 1962 .... 19.17
Law 4,506 of 30 November 1964 .... 19.17
Law 8,383 of 31 December 1991 .... 19.17

Ministerial Ordinance 436/58 .... 19.17

Brunei
Trade Marks Act (BTMA) (Chapter 98
 Laws of Brunei, Revised Edition 2000)
 (BN008) 22.10
 § 25 .... 22.15, 22.68
 § 25(2) 22.13
 § 25(3) 22.22
 § 25(6) 22.25
 S 28(1) 22.21
 § 29(2) 22.48
Interpretation and General Clauses Act,
 Laws of Brunei
 Ch 4, s 3(1) 22.10

Cambodia
Law concerning Marks, Trade Names and
 Acts of Unfair Competition (TMA),
 NS/RKM/0202/006 (2002)
 (KH001) 22.11
 Art 11 .... 22.11
 Art 19 .... 22.46
 Art 48 .... 22.22, 22.65
 Art 52 .... 22.66

China
Anti-Unfair Competition Law, 1993 ... 20.34
 Art 5, § 2 .... 20.25
Contract Law of PRC
 Art 60, § 2 .... 20.48
 Art 97 .... 20.51
Exclusive Rights Registration Procedures
 2009 .... 20.59, 20.62
 Art 4 .... 20.64
 Art 5 .... 20.63
 Art 8 .... 20.62
Experimental Regulations on Chinese and
 Foreign Trademark Registration,
 1904 .... 20.04
General Principles of the Civil Law
 Art 15 .... 20.51
Guaranty Law 20.55
 Art 63 .... 20.53
 Art 75, § 3 .... 20.54
 Art 79 .... 20.57
 Art 80 .... 20.65

Product Quality Law
  Art 26 .... 20.44
  Art 41, § 4 .... 20.44
Property Law
  Art 79 .... 20.60, 20.61
  Art 223, § 5 .... 20.54, 20.55
  Art 227, § 2 .... 20.65
Provisional Regulations for Trademark
  Registration, 1949 .... 20.05
  Art 1 .... 20.05
Regulations on the Management of
  Trademark 1963 .... 20.05
  Art 1 .... 20.05
  Art 2 .... 20.05
  Art 3 .... 20.05
Trademark Law (23 August 1982, effective
  30 August 2013) ... 20.06, 20.07, 20.08,
             20.09, 20.10, 20.11, 20.15, 20.20,
                          20.21, 20.34, 20.67
  Art 3, § 1 .... 20.12
  Art 7, § 1 .... 20.22
  Art 7, § 2 .... 20.43
  Art 9, § 1 .... 20.16, 20.17, 20.21
  Art 10 .... 20.17
  Art 10, § 1 .... 20.18
  Art 13, § 1 .... 20.23
  Art 15, § 2 .... 20.12, 20.21
  Art 20 .... 20.15
  Art 31 .... 20.16
  Art 32 .... 20.24
  Art 33 .... 20.19
  Art 42 .... 20.36
  Art 42, § 1 .... 20.30, 20.31
  Art 42, §§ 2–3 .... 20.33
  Art 42, § 2 .... 20.32, 20.59
  Art 42, § 3 .... 20.33
  Art 42, § 4 .... 20.35
  Art 43, § 1 .... 20.45, 20.46
  Art 43, § 2 .... 20.45
  Art 43, § 3 .... 20.39, 20.47
  Art 47 .... 20.52
  Art 47, § 2 .... 20.52
  Art 47, § 3 .... 20.52
  Art 48 .... 20.24
  Art 58 .... 20.25
  Art 59, § 3 .... 20.22

Regulation of PRC Trademark Law
  2002 .... 20.13
  Art 5, § 1 .... 20.13
  Art 13, §§ 3–7 .... 20.14
  Art 14, § 1 .... 20.13
  Art 18, § 2 .... 20.16
  Art 19 .... 20.16
  Art 20, § 1 .... 20.13
  Art 22, § 2 .... 20.15
  Art 31, § 2 .... 20.32

France
Code Civil (FCC) 17.03
  Title II, Ch II, s 1 .... 17.35
  Title III 17.03
  Title VI 17.07, 17.08
  Title II, Art 1123 .... 17.08
  Art 1142 .... 17.20
  Art 1237 .... 17.18
  Art 1382 .... 1.12
  Art 1386–6 .... 17.20
  Title VI, art 1583 .... 17.08
  Art 1641 .... 17.12
  Art 1645 .... 17.17
  Title VIII, art 1692 .... 17.09
  Art 1708 .... 17.13
  Arts 2284–2285 .... 17.33
  Art 2286 .... 17.33
  Art 2329 .... 17.34
  Art 2344 .... 17.35
  Art 2346 .... 17.35
  Art 2348 .... 17.35
  Art 2355 .... 17.35, 17.37
Code Générale des Impôts (CGI)
  Art 210A 17.54
  Art 210B 17.54
  Art 719 .... 17.44
Code of Posts and Electronic
  Communications
  Art L. 45–3 (26 July 2013) 4.23
Code of Intellectual Property (Code de la
  Propriété Intellectuelle) (CPI)
  Bk VII, Title 1 .... 17.23
  Bk VII, Ch II 17.25
  Art L713–1 .... 17.31
  Art L714–1 ...... 17.04, 17.07, 17.24, 17.35
  Art L714–5 .... 17.20

Art L714–6 .... 17.17
Art L714–7 .... 17.24, 17.26
Art L715–2–4 .... 17.35
Art L716–2 .... 17.26
Art R712–2 .... 17.28
Art R714–1 .... 17.32
Art R714–4 .... 17.28
Art R714–5 .... 17.28
Art R714–6 .... 17.25
Art R714–7 .... 17.30
Art R714–8 .... 17.31
Commercial Code (Code de Commerce), March 20, 2006
  Art L 141–1 .... 17.44
  Art L 141–5 .... 17.40
  Art L142–2 .... 17.39
  Art L214–42–1 .... 17.40
  Art L 214–43 .... 17.40
Decree No. 2008–711, 17 July 2008 amending the provisions applicable to securitization funds (fonds communs de créances), Journal Officiel de la République Française (J.O.) 11554 (19 July 2008) 17.40
Law No. 2008–776, 4 August 2008, on the Modernisation de l'Economie, Journal Officiel de la République Française (J.O.) (4 August 2008)
  Art 18 .... 17.39
Law No. 94–665 of 4 August 1994, Journal Officiel de la République Française (J.O.), 5 August 1994 .... 17.28
2014 Finances Law 17.47

Germany

Aktiengesetz (AktienG) (Stock Corporation Act) 16.04
Bürgerliches Gesetzbuch (BGB) (Civil Code) 16.05, 16.64
  s 226 .... 16.05
  s 241(2) 16.05, 16.47
  s 242 .... 16.05, 16.47
  s 301 .... 16.20
  s 305 et seq 16.20
  s 389 .... 16.22
  s 398 .... 16.07, 16.34, 16.48
  s 413 .... 16.05, 16.07, 16.22
  s 705 .... 4.25, 16.06
  s 718 .... 16.06
  s 741 .... 4.25, 16.06
  s 826 .... 16.05
  s 1068(1) 16.24
  s 1030 .... 16.24
  s 1085 .... 16.24
  s 1228 .... 16.24
  s1235 .... 16.24
  s 1247 .... 16.24
  s 1273 .... 16.24
Einführungsgesetz zum Bürgerlichen Gesetzbuch (EGBGB) Introductory Act to the German Civil Code, BGBl I p. 2494 (1994)
  Art 3 .... 16.54
  Art 4 .... 16.54
  Art 27 .... 16.54
  Art 28 .... 16.54
  Art 28(1) 16.56
Gesetz gegen Wettbewerbsbeschränkungen) (GWB) (Act Against Restraints of Competition) 16.09
Gesetz gegen den unlauteren Wettbewerb (UWG) (Law on Unfair Competition), RGB 1. 499 (1909)
  s 16 .... 16.26
GG (Basic Law)
  Art 14(1) 16.23
Handelsgesetzbuch (HGB), §§ 30, 37 (2) (1897) 16.31
Handelsgesetzbuch (HGB) (Commercial Law Code) 16.04
Insolvency Act
  s 101 .... 16.46
Markengesetz, BGB1. I, 3082 (1994) (MarkenG) (Trade Mark Act) 16.03, 16.15, 16.33
  s 1 no 1 .... 16.26
  s 1 no 2 .... 16.26
  s 1 no 3 .... 16.26
  s 4 no 1–3 .... 16.19
  s 4 no 2 .... 16.15
  s 5 .... 16.15, 16.26
  s 5(2) 16.26
  s 5(3) 16.26
  s 14 .... 16.30

s 15	16.26, 16.30
s 18 et seq	16.30
s 20 et seq	16.30
ss 27–30	16.25
ss 27–31	16.19–16.25
s 27	16.30, 16.31
s 27(1)	16.19, 16.32
s 27(2)	16.21
s 28	16.21
s 28(1)	16.21
s 29	16.24, 16.61
s 29(2)	16.24, 16.49, 16.61, 16.63
s 30	16.20, 16.36
s 30(1)	16.20, 16.37
s 30(2) nos 1–5	16.38
s 30(3)	16.47
s 30(4)	16.48
s 31	16.25
s 48(2)	16.24, 16.63

Urheberrechtsgesetz (UrhG) (Copyright Act)
s 31(1) 16.23

Warenzeichengesetz, vom 5. Mai, RGBl. II S. 134 (1936) (WZG)
s 8 .... 16.19

Ordinance Concerning the German Patent and Trade Mark Office (DPMAV)
s 28 .... 16.25

MarkenV (Trademark Regulation)
Ss 33–36 .... 16.25

India

Competition Act 2002, Act No. 12 of 2003 .... 23.39
Contract Act, No. 9 of 1872 .... 23.02, 23.49, 23.51, 23.52, 23.74
Drugs and Cosmetics Act, No. 23 of 1940
  S 17B 23.10
Income Tax Act, No. 43 of 1961 .... 23.02
Specific Relief Act, No. 47 of 1963 .... 23.02, 23.51, 23.52, 23.74
Trade and Merchandise Marks Act, No. 43 of 1958 .... 23.44
  § 48 .... 23.43
  § 48(1) 23.44

Trade Marks Act, No. 47 of 1999 ...... 23.02, 23.04–23.48, 23.49, 23.51, 23.53, 23.58, 23.74, 23.75

§ 2(1)(b)	23.55, 23.57
§ 2(1)(e)	23.70
§ 2(1)(r)	23.04
§ 9	23.41
§ 12	23.38
§ 38	23.55, 23.59
§ 39	23.57, 23.59, 23.69
§ 40	23.60, 23.62
§ 40(1)	23.69
§ 41	23.62, 23.70
§ 42	23.61, 23.70
§ 43	23.70
§ 44	23.70
§ 45	23.63, 23.66, 23.67, 23.68
§ 45(1)	23.65, 23.68
§ 45(2)	23.64
§ 47(1)(b)	23.23
§ 48(1)	23.05, 23.44
§ 48(2)	23.23, 23.37
§ 49(1)	23.18
§ 49(1)(a)	23.06, 23.28
§ 49(1)(b)	23.41, 23.42
§ 49(1)(b)(i)	23.07, 23.10
§ 49(1)(b)(iii)	23.12
§ 49(1)(b)(iv)	23.11
§ 49(3)	23.19, 23.36
§ 49(4)	23.27
§ 50	23.20, 23.22, 23.36, 23.54
§ 50(1)(c)(i)	23.13, 23.17
§ 50(1)(d)	23.41, 23.42
§ 50(2)	23.36
§ 50(3)	23.21
§ 51	23.11, 23.28
§ 52	23.26, 23.32
§ 52(1)	23.08
§ 53	23.33
§ 54	23.31
§ 56(2)	23.17
§ 57	23.41
§ 57(1)	23.41
§ 69(c)	23.70
§ 136	23.35

Trade Mark Rules, 1959
  r 85 .... 23.44
Trade Mark Rules, 2002 .... 23.44

Indonesia

Law No. 15 of 1 August 2001, regarding Marks (LM) (ID046)
  Art 1(13) 22.13
  Art 40 .... 22.22
  § 40(1) 22.73
  §§ 40(1)–40(2) 22.73
  § 40(5) 22.73
  Art 41 .... 22.22
  Art 41(1) 22.15
  Art 47(1) 22.56

Israel

Trade Marks Ordinance (New Version), 5732–1972
  § 29 .... 11.10

Japan

Act Concerning the Protection of the Indications of Specific Products of Agriculture, Forestry and Fisheries, Law No. 84 of 2014 .... 21.11
Act for Partial Revision of the Trademark Act, Law No. 68 of 1996 .... 21.05
Act on General Rules for Application of Laws, Act No. 78 of 2006
  Art 4(1) 12.19
Act on Special Measures Concerning the Securing of the Necessary Sources of Revenue to Implement Measures for Reconstruction from the Great East Japan Earthquake, Law No. 117 of 2011 .... 21.41
Anti-Monopoly Act: Act on Prohibition of Private Monopolization and Maintenance of Fair Trade of Japan, Law No. 54 of 1947, as amended 21.51–21.52
  Art 21 .... 21.52
Bankruptcy Act, Law No. 75 of 2004
  Art 53, paras. 1–2 .... 21.21
  Art 56 .... 21.21

Code of Civil Procedure Law No. 89 of 1896 as amended 21.09, 21.12, 21.13, 21.32
  Art 3–7(4) 12.24
  Art 3–7(5) 12.22
  Art 3–7(6) 12.22
Commercial Code, Law No. 48 of 1899, as amended 21.11
Companies Act, Law No. 86 of 2005, as amended 21.11
Consumption Tax Act, Law No. 108 of 1985, as amended
  Art 4, para. 1 .... 21.44
  Art 29 .... 21.44
Consumption Tax Act Enforcement Ordinance, Law No. 360 of 1988, as amended
  Art 6, para. 1, item 5 .... 21.44, 21.45
  Art 6, para. 1, item 7 .... 21.46
  Art 7, para. 1, item 5 .... 21.45
  Art 8, para. 1 .... 21.45
  Art 17, para. 2, item 6 .... 21.45, 21.46
Copyright Act Law No. 48 of 1970, as amended 21.09, 21.11, 21.52
Corporation Tax Act, Law No. 34 of 1965 as amended
  Art 138, item 7(a) 21.40
  Art 141 .... 21.40
  Art 141, items 1–3 .... 21.39
Design Act 21.52
Income Tax Act], Law No. 33 of 1965, as amended
  Art 161, item 7(b) 21.41
  Art 212, para. 1 .... 21.41
  Art 213, para. 1, item 1 .... 21.41
Local Tax Act, Law No. 226 of 1950, as amended
  Art 72–83 .... 21.44
Patent Act, Law No. 121 of 1959 .... 21.52
  Art 98 para 1 .... 21.24, 21.54
  Art 98, Para 1, Items 1 and 3 .... 21.64
  Art 99 .... 21.21
Trademark Act, Law No. 127 of 1959, as amended 21.03, 21.04, 21.09, 21.11, 21.13–21.16, 21.25, 21.29, 21.30, 21.31, 21.32, 21.38, 21.44, 21.52, 21.67
  Art 2, paras 1–4 .... 21.05

Art 2 para 1 .... 21.06
Art 2, para 3 .... 21.05
Art 5 para 2 .... 21.06
Art 7–2 .... 21.61
Art 24–2, para 1 .... 21.54, 21.56
Art 24–2, para 4 .... 21.62
Art 24–4 .... 21.57
Art 30, para 1 .... 21.24
Art 30, para 4 .... 21.24
Art 31, para 1 .... 21.17
Art 31, para 2 .... 21.18
Art 31, para 4 .... 21.20
Art 32 .... 21.15
Art 34, para 3 .... 21.64
Trademark Act (amendment) Law No. 26 of
 2014 .... 21.05, 21.06, 21.37
Unfair Competition Prevention Act, Law
 No. 47 of 1993, as amended 21.09,
 21.11, 21.31
Art 2, para 1, item 1 .... 21.32
Utility Model Act 21.52
Patent Registration Order (Cabinet Order
 No. 39 of 1960, as amended)
 Art 18 .... 21.26
Trademark Registration Order (Cabinet
 Order No. 42 of 1960, as amended
 Art 10 .... 21.26

Laos
Law No. 01/NA of 20 December 2011, on
 Intellectual Property (LA025) 22.53
 Pt 4, art 47 .... 22.54

Malaysia
Trade Marks Act (TMA) (Act 175 of 1976,
 as last amended by Act A1138 of
 2002) (MY044) 22.11
§ 3(1) 22.51
§ 35 .... 22.22
§ 36 .... 22.11, 22.70
§ 47 .... 22.22
§ 48 .... 22.50
§ 48(1) 22.51, 22.52
§ 48(5) 22.51
§ 55(1) 22.13, 22.15
§ 55(1A) 22.26
§ 55(5) 22.18

Philippines
Intellectual Property Code (IPC) (Republic
 Act No. 8293)(1997)(PH001) (as
 amended Implementing Rules and
 Regulations of the Republic Act No.
 9502 of 2008, July 4, 2008, WIPO
 Lex. No. PH048 (Phil.) as amended
 Republic Act No. 10372, entitled 'An
 Act Amending Certain Provisions of
 Republic Act No. 8293', Feb. 28, 2013,
 WIPO Lex. No. PH100) 22.11
Pt III 22.11
§ 106.1 .... 22.64
§ 138 .... 22.11
§ 149.1 .... 22.15, 22.21
§ 149.2 .... 22.19
§ 149.3 .... 22.22

Singapore
Trade Marks Act (Cap 332, 2005 Rev Ed)
 (TMA)
§ 22(1)(d) 22.32
§ 36 .... 22.06
§ 38(1) 22.14
§ 38(2) 22.13
§ 38(3) 22.22
§ 38(7) 22.24
§ 39(1) 22.58
§ 39(3) 22.59
§ 39(4) 22.59
§ 41 .... 22.06
§ 42(1) 22.33
§ 42(2) 22.33
§ 42(3) 22.33
§ 42(8) 22.34
§ 43(1) 22.33
§ 43 .... 22.27

Switzerland
Federal Act on International Private Law
 (IPLA) of 18 December 1987, SR 291
Ch XII 13.31
Art 110(1) 5.06
Art 122(2) 5.06
Art 187 para 1 .... 13.61
Art 190(2)(b) 13.39

Federal Council Decree on Measures against the Improper Use of Tax Treaties concluded by the Swiss Confederation, 14 December 1962, SR 62.202 (1962 Abuse Decree) 8.23, 8.25
Art 1, para. 2(a)–(b) 8.23
Art 2, para. 1(a) 8.23
Federal Direct Tax Law (DTL), 14 December 1990, SR 642.11
Art 16 .... 8.33
Art 18 .... 8.33
Art 18, para 1 .... 8.15
Art 20, para 1(f) 8.15
Art 19 .... 8.55
Art 27, para 1 .... 8.16
Art 50 .... 8.59
Art 58 .... 8.35
Art 58, para 1 .... 8.16
Art 58, para 1(a) 8.15
Art 61 .... 8.55
Art 61, para 1(b) 8.56
Art 61, para 3 .... 8.56
Art 61, para 4 .... 8.56
Federal Trademark Protection Act (TPA/TMPA) of 28 August 1992, SR 232.11 .... 5.08
Art 11f 5.27
Art 17(1) 5.10, 5.19
Art 17a(1) 5.22
Art 17a(2) 5.16
Art 17a(3) 5.14
Art 18 .... 8.12
Art 18(1) 5.36
Art 18(2) 5.29
Art 55(4) 5.24, 5.30
Federal Tax Harmonization Law (StHG) (Harmonization Law), 14 December 1990, SR 642.14 .... 8.04
Art 7, para 1 .... 8.15
Art 7, para 4(b) 8.33
Art 8 .... 8.33, 8.55
Art 8, para 1 .... 8.15
Art 10, para 1 .... 8.16
Art 20, para 1 .... 8.59
Art 24 .... 8.35, 8.55
Art 24, para 1 .... 8.16
Art 24, para. 1(a) 8.15

Art 24, para 3(b) 8.56
Art 24, para 3–4 .... 8.56
Art 24, para 3–5 .... 8.56
Art 24(b), para 3 .... 8.80
Federal Withholding Tax Act (VStG), 13 October 1965, SR 642.21
Art 4, para. 1 .... 8.17
Law on Therapeutic Products
Art 12 .... 8.80
Ordinance on Trademark Protection of December 23, 1992 (TPO)
Art 4(1) 5.58
Art 28(2) 5.14
Art 29(1)(a) 5.29

Thailand
Trademark Act (TMA), B.E. 2543 (1991) (consolidated as of 2000) (TH004) 22.62
§ 44 .... 22.11
§ 48 .... 22.21
§ 49 .... 22.15
§ 51 .... 22.62
§§ 68–79 (Pt 5) 22.38
§ 68 .... 22.39
§ 69 .... 22.40
§ 70 .... 22.42
§ 72 .... 22.43
§ 76 .... 22.43
§ 77 .... 22.44
§ 78 .... 22.44
§ 79 .... 22.44

United Kingdom
Competition Act 1998 .... 15.92
Ch I 15.91
Consumer Protection Act 1987 .... 15.62
s 1(2) 15.62
s 2(2)(b) 15.63
Contract (Rights of Third Parties) Act 1999 (CROTPA) 15.81
s 1(1) 15.81
s 1(2) 15.82
Law of Property (Miscellaneous Provisions) Act 1994 .... 15.71
s 1 .... 15.25
ss 2–3 .... 15.27

s 3(1) 15.25
s 3(3) 15.26
Trade Marks Act 1938 .... 15.06, 15.54
   s 22(7) 15.06
   s 28 .... 15.06
Trade Marks Act 1994 .... 15.05, 15.06,
        15.08, 15.49, 15.54, 15.56, 15.60
   s 2 .... 15.39
   s 10 .... 15.40, 15.43, 15.45
   s 17 .... 15.24
   s 23 .... 15.36
   s 24 .... 15.19, 15.30, 15.78, 15.87
   s 24(1) 15.07, 15.12, 15.13, 15.15
   s 24(2) 15.16
   s 24(3) 15.20
   s 24(4) 15.87
   s 24(6) 15.19
   ss 25–31 .... 15.41
   s 25(2) 15.86, 15.87
   s 25(3) 15.83, 15.84, 15.84, 15.90
   s 25(3)(a) 15.31
   s 25(4) 15.31
   s 26 .... 15.36
   s 26(1) 15.32
   ss 28–31 .... 15.46, 15.47, 15.83
   s 28 .... 15.41
   s 28(1) 15.50
   s 28(2) 15.44, 15.45, 15.46
   s 28(3) 15.84
   s 28(4) 15.52
   s 29(1) 15.51
   ss 30–31 .... 15.65, 15.70
   s 30 ...... 15.65, 15.66, 15.67, 15.69, 15.70,
        15.74
   s 31 .... 15.65, 15.66, 15.67, 15.69, 15.70
   s 46 .... 15.13, 15.15, 15.55

United States of America
Anti-Cybersquatting Consumer Protection
    Act, 15 U.S.C. § 1125(d) (2013) ... 3.32
Bankruptcy Code 11 U.S.C. § 365 (2000 &
    Supp. V 2005) 10.38, 10.65
   s 365(n) 10.66
Constitution
   Art I, § 8, cl. 8 .... 3.01
Copyright Act 3.01

17 U.S.C. § 103(b) 3.16
17 U.S.C. § 203 .... 3.25
17 U.S.C. § 203(a) 3.25
17 U.S.C. § 203(a)(5) 3.26, 3.29
17 U.S.C. § 203(b)(1) 3.26
17 U.S.C. § 203(b)(5) 3.26, 3.29
17 U.S.C. § 302(c) 3.16
17 U.S.C. § 304 .... 3.16
17 U.S.C. § 304(c)–(d) 3.25
17 U.S.C. § 412 .... 3.38
17 U.S.C. § 501 .... 3.01
17 U.S.C. § 504(b) 3.38
17 U.S.C. § 504(c)(2) 3.38
Federal Trade Commission Act 18.22
Lanham Act (Trademark Act) 15 U.S.C.
    §§ 1051–1141, 15 U.S.C.
    (1946) 1.09, 1.22, 3.01, 10.89,
        13.52, 18.04, 18.17, 18.29, 18.31,
        18.33, 18.45
§ 1, 15 U.S.C. § 1051(a)(1)–(2) 18.07
§ 5, 15 U.S.C. § 1055 (2014) 18.21,
        18.32
§ 9(a), 15 U.S.C. § 1059(a) 3.01
§ 10, 15 U.S.C. § 1060 .... 18.09, 18.13,
        18.42, 18.44
§ 10, 15 U.S.C. § 1060(a)(1) 5.11,
        18.06, 18.07
§ 10, 15 U.S.C. § 1060(a)(2) 18.08,
        18.12
§ 10, 15 U.S.C. § 1060(a)(3) 18.09
§ 10, 15 U.S.C. §1060(a)(5) 18.09
§ 14, 15 U.S.C. § 1064(3) 18.06, 18.13
§ 22 .... 18.30
§ 32, 15 U.S.C. § 1114 .... 3.01, 3.31
§ 32, 15 U.S.C. § 1114(1) 18.25
§ 34, 15 U.S.C. § 1116 .... 3.36
§ 35(a), 15 U.S.C. § 1117(a) 3.36, 3.38
§ 43, 15 U.S.C. § 1125(a) 18.25
§ 43(a), 15 U.S.C. § 1125(a) 3.01, 3.31,
        18.05
§ 43(c), 15 U.S.C. § 1125(c) 3.01, 3.31,
        3.10
§ 43(c)(A) 3.23
§ 43(c)(1), 15 U.S.C. § 1125(c)(1) 3.37
§ 43(c)(2) 3.36
§ 43(c)(5) 3.36

§ 45, 15 U.S.C. § 1127 .... 1.09, 3.19,
        18.06, 18.21, 18.22, 18.25, 18.27,
        18.32
Trademark Act 1905 .... 18.29
    s 10 .... 18.12, 18.13, 18.17
Trademark Dilution Act (FTDA) 1995,
    Pub. L No. 104–98, §§ 3(a) & 4, 109
    Stat. 985 (effective 16 January 1996)
    (codified as amended at 15 U.S.C.
    §§ 1125, 1127) 18.05
Trademark Dilution Revision Act (TDRA)
    2006, Pub. L 109–312 (2006), 120
    Stat. 1730 (codified as amended at 15
    U.S.C. §§ 1125, 1127) 3.32, 3.37
    §§ 2, 3(e) 18.05
Trademark Law Treaty Implementation Act
    Pub. L. No. 105–330, 112 Stat. 3064
    (1998) 18.13
Trademark Revision Act of 1988, Pub. L.
    No. 100–667, Sec. 112, § 1060, 102
    Stat. 3935 .... 18.13, 18.22
    s 10(b) 18.42
    s 112, § 1060 .... 18.13
Trading with the Enemy Act 1918, Pub. L.
    No. 65–233, 40 Stat. 1020 (codified as
    amended at 50 U.S.C. app. § 7(c)
    (2000))
    s 7(c) 18.30
37 C.F.R. § 3.56 .... 18.43
Uniform Commercial Code (UCC)
    Art 9 .... 18.42

§ 9–108 .... 18.43
§ 9–109(c) 18.42
§ 9–301 .... 18.42
§9–502 .... 18.42
Restatement Third, Unfair Competition
    § 25(2) 3.23
    § 33 cmt b (1995) 5.26, 18.21, 18.44
    § 33 cmt c 18.39
    § 33 cmt d 18.37
Trademark Manual of Examination
    Procedure (TMEP)
    s 500 .... 18.09
    s 501.06 .... 18.08
    s 503.02 .... 18.26, 18.42

Vietnam
Intellectual Property Law, Law No.
    50/205/QH11 of 29 November 2005
    (promulgated by the Order No.
    28/2005/L-CTN of 12 December
    2005) (VN003) (as amended by Law
    No. 36/2009/QH12) 22.09
Art 6(3)(a) 22.09
Art 7(2) 22.09
Art 87(6) 22.21
Art 138(2) 22.22
Art 139 .... 22.20, 22.22
Art 141 .... 22.35
Art 143 .... 22.27, 22.35
Art 144 .... 22.37
Art 220 .... 22.60

Part I

TRADEMARK TRANSACTIONS IN THE GLOBAL MARKETPLACE

Section A

INTERNATIONAL FRAMEWORK

1

TRIPS, TRADEMARKS, AND TRADEMARK TRANSACTIONS: A FORCED RECONCILIATION?

Daniel J. Gervais[*]

A.	INTRODUCTION	1.01	3. Recordal of transfers and licenses under Article 19.2 of the TRIPS Agreement	1.29
B.	THE ORIGIN OF THE TRADEMARK PROVISIONS IN THE TRIPS AGREEMENT	1.03	4. Article 20 of the TRIPS Agreement	1.36
	1. The battle between common and civil law	1.03	D. THE TRADEMARK TRANSACTIONS PROVISION: ARTICLE 21 OF THE TRIPS AGREEMENT	1.43
	2. Trademarks in major legal systems and the TRIPS Agreement	1.08	1. Drafting history	1.44
	3. The TRIPS Agreement and the Paris Convention	1.14	2. Compulsory licenses of trademarks	1.49
			3. Conditions on transfers and licenses and the enforcement of marks	1.54
C.	THE TRADEMARK PROVISIONS IN THE TRIPS AGREEMENT	1.17	4. A role for competition law?	1.62
	1. Article 15 of the TRIPS Agreement	1.18		
	2. The function(s) of trademarks	1.20	E. CONCLUSION	1.70

A. INTRODUCTION

The World Trade Organization's (WTO) Agreement on Trade-Related Aspects of Intellectual Property Rights (TRIPS Agreement)[1] imposes limits to, and certain parameters for, the regulation by WTO Members of trademark transactions, such as licenses and assignments. WTO Members can challenge each other's measures implementing these provisions if they believe another Member's trademark rules violates the TRIPS Agreement using the WTO dispute-settlement system.[2]

1.01

---

[*] Professor of Law, Vanderbilt Law School.
[1] Agreement on Trade-Related Aspects of Intellectual Property Rights, 15 April 1994, Marrakesh Agreement Establishing the World Trade Organization, Annex 1C, 1869 U.N.T.S. 299, 33 I.L.M. 1197 (1994) [hereinafter TRIPS Agreement].
[2] TRIPS Agreement, *supra* note 1, Art. 64; Understanding on Rules and Procedures Governing the Settlement of Disputes, 15 April 1994, Marrakesh Agreement Establishing the World Trade Organization, Annex 21869 U.N.T.S. 401, 33 I.L.M. 1226 (1994) [hereinafter DSU].

1.02 This Chapter examines, first, the source of trademark provisions in the TRIPS Agreement and specifically whether they accord with common law or civil law trademark law and practice. It then considers the TRIPS Agreement provisions that are most likely to impact trademark transactions. After a review of Articles 15, 19 and 20 of the TRIPS Agreement, which at least indirectly impact trademark transactions, the Chapter devotes a separate part to Article 21, which provides rules applicable to licenses, transfers and assignments of trademarks.

B. THE ORIGIN OF THE TRADEMARK PROVISIONS IN THE TRIPS AGREEMENT

1. The battle between common and civil law

1.03 Like most other sections of the TRIPS Agreement, the trademark section is a compromise. While that compromise was not always between the same two positions, the differences between the two major legal systems, namely common law and civil law, do emerge rather frequently in the text. Indeed, one could attribute a score to determine which 'side' won the debate on each section of Part II of the TRIPS Agreement (that is, the part that contains the norms concerning substantive IP rights, including trademarks).

1.04 For example, common law 'scored' a major win in copyright. The TRIPS Agreement's incorporation, by reference, of the substantive provisions of the Berne Convention for the Protection of Literary and Artistic Works (Berne Convention), whose origins are deeply rooted in the soil of continental Europe, may not seem like a win.[3] However, by the time the TRIPS Agreement was signed in Marrakesh on 15 April 1994, the Berne Convention had become an unavoidable point of reference, with 107 Member States at the time,[4] especially with the addition of the United States in 1989.[5] Short of rewriting the Berne Convention *ex nihilo*, which would have implied huge transition costs, the acceptance of the Berne Convention was unavoidable.[6] Of course, the victory of common law was not in accepting the reference to the

---

3 Sam Ricketson & Jane C. Ginsburg, *The Berne Convention – Historical and Institutional Aspects*, in INTERNATIONAL INTELLECTUAL PROPERTY: A HANDBOOK OF CONTEMPORARY RESEARCH 3 (Daniel J. Gervais ed., 2015).
4 Berne Convention Member List, *available 14 September 2015 at* http://www.wipo.int/export/sites/www/treaties/en/documents/pdf/berne.pdf. As of December 2014, the Convention has 167 Member States.
5 The United States became a party to the Berne Convention with effect from 1 March 1989. See *id.* at 13.
6 DANIEL GERVAIS, THE TRIPS AGREEMENT: DRAFTING HISTORY AND ANALYSIS 143–147 (4th ed. 2012) [hereinafter GERVAIS, TRIPS AGREEMENT].

B. THE ORIGIN OF THE TRADEMARK PROVISIONS IN THE TRIPS AGREEMENT

Berne Convention. The success was in getting the countries Members of the WTO to agree to the following: (a) to remove the notion of 'author' and replace it with the more economic and utilitarian notion of 'right holder': and (b) to eviscerate the moral right by making it impossible to enforce at the WTO.

The patent section of the TRIPS Agreement is a more complex analysis owing in large part to the fact there was no unified front of common law jurisdictions. In fact, the majority of such jurisdictions though definitions in domestic law varied considerably identified patentability criteria using terminology similar to that used in civil law countries. Hence, the patentability criteria found in Article 27.1 of the TRIPS Agreement are named (but not defined) as 'inventive step' and 'industrial applicability' and not as the North American concepts of non-obviousness and utility, which are merely identified in a footnote as possible deemed synonyms.[7] The patent section of the TRIPS Agreement is thus perhaps best seen as a draw.[8] **1.05**

As we get closer to trademarks, one could mark the section on geographical indications (Articles 22 to 24) as a victory for civil law. That would be incorrect, or at least an oversimplification. The number of countries interested in a higher level of protection of geographical indications has increased over the past few years, as the renewed interest in the Lisbon Agreement on the Protection of Appellations of Origins (Lisbon Agreement) at the World Intellectual Property Organization (WIPO) has shown.[9] The debate has not been between common law and civil law as much as it has been between the 'Old World' and 'New World'.[10] Now a path forward is emerging as 'New World' nations recognize the value of geographical identifiers, from Napa (U.S.) or Marlborough (New Zealand) wines to Colombian coffee to Mexican crafts and tequila.[11] In fact, a Diplomatic Conference which should adopt a revised version of the Lisbon Agreement is scheduled to be held in 2015.[12] **1.06**

---

7   In other words Canada and the United States did not have to modify their national law because the notions of utility and non-obviousness 'may be deemed to be synonymous' with industrial application and inventive step, respectively.
8   It is no surprise that the terms used by a vast majority of countries are in the main article and the Canada/US version relegated to the footnote.
9   World Intellectual Property Organization [WIPO], *Draft Revised Lisbon Agreement on Appellations of Origin and Geographical Indications*, LI/WG/DEV/8/2 (2011), *available* 14 September 2014 at http://www.wipo.int/meetings/en/doc_details.jsp?doc_id=252459.
10 *See* Daniel Gervais, *Reinventing Lisbon: The Case for a Protocol to the Lisbon Agreement*, 11 CHI. J. INT'L L. 67, 67–126 (2010) (discussing the delineation of the border between geographical indications and existing trademarks in Articles 22.3, 23.2 and 24.5).
11 *See id.*
12 *Preparation of the Final Stages of the Negotiation of a Revised Lisbon Agreement*, WIPO (14 July 2014), *available* 14 September 2014 at http://www.wipo.int/lisbon/en/news/2014/news_0004.html.

1.07 Independently of which side 'scored' higher in the negotiation of any section of the TRIPS Agreement, the exact measure of the victory sometimes remains unclear. WTO Members run the risk of having the TRIPS Agreement interpreted in ways that were not entirely foreseen during the negotiation. For example, the panel that examined the European Union's (EU) regime for the protection of geographical indications seemed to confirm that maintaining a 'first in time, first in right' approach to the interface between trademark rights and geographical indications was acceptable in most cases.[13] The dispute-settlement panel found that the EU regime that accords higher protection to geographical indications where there was a conflict with a (non famous) pre-existing trademark was an acceptable exception to trademark rights under the TRIPS Agreement's Article 17. The rule that applies to the interpretation of the TRIPS Agreement and other WTO instruments is, however, that one should not add non-negotiated concessions to its text.[14]

2. Trademarks in major legal systems and the TRIPS Agreement

1.08 Against the backdrop of a conflict or forced reconciliation between the two major legal systems, what then can one say of the trademark section in the TRIPS Agreement? Does it reconcile civil and common law notions? To a certain extent, it tries to achieve that objective.

1.09 It is well-known that there are two different worldviews when it comes to trademark law, which one could broadly describe here again as civil law and common law approaches. Painting with a very broad brush, one could say that in common law jurisdictions trademark law is derived from the tort of 'passing off'. That is, rights in a trademark typically stem from use in commerce of a symbol to distinguish goods or services from one undertaking from those of a competitor.[15] Common law would then prevent, under tort doctrines, the use of a confusing mark by a competitor. Unregistered marks are protected at common law, typically only in the geographic area in which they were used and then only against later users.[16]

---

13 GERVAIS, TRIPS AGREEMENT, *supra* note 6, at 338–40.
14 DSU, *supra* note 2, Arts. 3(2) and 19(2).
15 This typically means one or (generally) more arms-length commercial transactions on a product or service in which the mark is featured as a distinctive symbol identifying the supplier or origin of the product or service. For the United States, *see* Lanham Act § 45, 15 U.S.C. § 1127 (1946), which defines 'Use in Commerce' as follows: 'Use in Commerce. The term "use in commerce" means the bona fide use of a mark in the ordinary course of trade, and not made merely to reserve a right in a mark.'
16 CHRISTOPHER WADLOW, THE LAW OF PASSING-OFF 6–12 (3rd ed. 2004).

B. THE ORIGIN OF THE TRADEMARK PROVISIONS IN THE TRIPS AGREEMENT

The original tort of 'passing off' prevented a merchant from putting another's mark on his wares.[17] At common law, the existence of protection depended on use in commerce by the plaintiff.[18] Modern trademark theory has recognized that trademarks protect not only the owners of marks, but also benefit consumers, especially by reducing search costs.[19] Trademarks allow consumers to identify lawful products that they wish to purchase and to expect a certain quality that they associate with a given trademark. This is an incentive for the trademark owner to maintain its brand.

1.10

Various statutes and legal doctrines have added to the arsenal of common law trademark holders over the years, including notions such as 'dilution' in the United States (U.S.) trademark law or protection outside the area where a trademark is actually used.[20] In spite of the add-ons, however, the notion that basic trademark rights arise from use, not from an act of government, still remains central to all common law systems. Consequently, in most common law jurisdictions obtaining registration of a trademark that is not in use in commerce is not possible.[21] One may *apply* for registration but may not complete the registration process without providing adequate evidence of use.

1.11

In civil law systems, by contrast, one may apply and obtain registration of a trademark that is not (yet) in use. Trademark rights arise from the administrative act of registration of the trademark.[22] Unregistered marks are not protected *as such*, although remedies are often available under general rules concerning unfair or parasitic competition.[23] This *ex ante* approach in the role of government in civil law systems is in marked contrast to the approach in common law jurisdictions where the government only intervenes *ex post*, that

1.12

---

17 Xuan-Thao N. Nguyen, *The Digital Trademark Right: A Troubling New Extraterritorial Reach of United States Law*, 81 N.C. L. REV. 483, 542–3 (2003).
18 *See* Aneta Ferguson, *The Trademark Filing Trap*, 49 IDEA 197, 224 (2009).
19 WILLIAM M. LANDES & RICHARD A. POSNER, THE ECONOMIC STRUCTURE OF INTELLECTUAL PROPERTY LAW 185–6 (2003).
20 4 J. THOMAS MCCARTHY, MCCARTHY ON TRADEMARKS AND UNFAIR COMPETITION, § 24:67 (4th ed, 2014). For example, registration of trademark at the United States Patent and Trademark office provides protection throughout the United States even if the mark is not actually used in all 50 States. *Id.* at §26:31 ('[I]n the absence of special statutory defenses, or a defect in the registration itself, the owner of a Principal Register registration has superior rights throughout the United States.'). Consonant with common law principles, however, registration is only possible after use in commerce and, for federal registration, use in interstate commerce. *Id.* at § 25:56.
21 *See generally id.*
22 It is true, however, that if a trademark is not used, it will be usually possible to obtain its removal from the register after a certain number of years.
23 In France, such protection is based upon CODE CIVIL [C. CIV.] art. 1382 (Fr.). *See* ANSELM KAMPERMAN SANDERS, UNFAIR COMPETITION LAW 28 (1997). For Germany, *see* Christian Schertz & Susanne Bergmann, *Germany*, *in* CHARACTER MERCHANDISING IN EUROPE, 136–7 (Heijo Ruijsenaars ed., 2003).

is, after use in commerce has begun. The registration process in common law jurisdictions thus recognizes a trademark that is already in existence and use.

1.13 That said, it is worth noting that the purpose of the registration of trademarks is typically not simply for the sake of registration. Trademarks are typically registered so that they can be used.[24] Put differently, it is relevant in an analysis guided by the object and purpose of the TRIPS Agreement as directed by the application of the Vienna Convention on the Law of Treaties (VCLT)[25] to ask *why* the TRIPS Agreement gives trademark owners a right to access a registration system and rights against use by third parties to understand the relevant trademark provisions.

3. The TRIPS Agreement and the Paris Convention

1.14 With its heavy emphasis on registration, the Paris Convention for the Protection of Industrial Property (Paris Convention)[26] is arguably a reflection of the civil law approach to trademark protection. Then again, providing rules to simplify registration of marks internationally was the most natural subject matter for an international instrument on trademarks in the 19th century context of World Fairs and emerging international trade, short of specifying uniform minimum substantive trademark rules as happened in the TRIPS Agreement.

1.15 The Paris Convention affords a six-month priority period for trademark owners based in a Paris Member country to apply for registration in a foreign country that is also party to the Paris Convention. The system thus presupposes that a trademark holder will have registered her trademark in country A (typically her country of origin) and then apply for registration in other jurisdictions party to the Paris Convention. Common law jurisdictions had to adapt to this system in a variety of ways. For example, the United States uses a Supplemental Register to register trademarks that are not going to be used in the United States so that they can be 'exported' to other countries under the Paris Convention system.[27]

---

[24] Trademarks are occasionally registered in some jurisdictions for other so-called defensive purposes, but those instances are minimal and also subject to challenge for non-use. *See* Yasuhiro H. Suzuki, *Navigating The 'Land of Harmony' and Finding 'Harmonization' for Foreign Trademark Applicants and Owners: A Japanese Practitioner's Perspective*, 103 TRADEMARK REP. 519, 562 (2013).

[25] Vienna Convention on the Law of Treaties, 23 May 1969, 1155 U.N.T.S. 331 (entered into force 27 January 1980) [hereinafter VCLT].

[26] Paris Convention for the Protection of Industrial Property, as last revised at the Stockholm Revision Conference, 14 July 1967, 21 U.S.T. 1583, 828 U.N.T.S. 303 [hereinafter Paris Convention].

[27] 4 MCCARTHY, *supra* note 20, at § 19:33.

C. THE TRADEMARK PROVISIONS IN THE TRIPS AGREEMENT

The TRIPS Agreement went further than the Paris Convention in several respects. The Paris Convention does not define what may constitute a trademark nor does it provide for much in terms of trademark rights or exceptions, other than Article 10*bis*, which provides substantial protection against various forms of unfair competition.[28] In contrast, the TRIPS Agreement defines the signs that may constitute trademarks, though it also reflects some level of disagreement about certain types of trademarks, in particular sound and olfactory marks. In such cases, WTO Members are free to determine that only visually perceptible marks can be protected in their country.[29]

1.16

C. THE TRADEMARK PROVISIONS IN THE TRIPS AGREEMENT

The Chapter now turns to the provisions in the TRIPS Agreement most likely to impact trademark transaction rules.

1.17

1. Article 15 of the TRIPS Agreement

While the TRIPS Agreement does not provide a full trademark code, if read as an entire document while taking its object and purpose into account, it does provide guidance as to WTO Members' shared understandings of the policies and norms relevant to trademarks.[30]

1.18

For instance, the function of trademarks can be understood by reference to the TRIPS Agreement Article 15.1, especially its first sentence, which refers to distinguishing goods and services of undertakings in the course of trade. Article 15.1 provides specifically that:

1.19

> Any sign, or any combination of signs, capable of distinguishing the goods or services of one undertaking from those of other undertakings, shall be capable of constituting a trademark. Such signs, in particular words including personal names, letters, numerals, figurative elements and combinations of colours as well as any combination of such signs, shall be eligible for registration as trademarks. Where signs are not inherently

---

28 Paris Convention, *supra* note 26, Art. 10*bis*.
29 TRIPS Agreement, *supra* note 1, Art. 15.1. In earlier drafts, the exclusion was applicable to trademarks not capable of 'graphical representation', which might not have excluded certain sound marks and perhaps even some olfactory marks, which are capable of representation using musical notations, descriptions, or chemical formulas.
30 WTO Members' shared understanding might also be described as the intention of the parties to the agreement.

capable of distinguishing the relevant goods or services, Members may make registrability depend on distinctiveness acquired through use. Members may require, as a condition of registration, that signs be visually perceptible.[31]

Civil and common law systems meet without much effort in the definition of the basic function of a trademark, as explicated in Article 15.1, namely the ability to distinguish the goods or services of one undertaking from those of other undertakings or, simply put, distinctiveness.

2. The function(s) of trademarks

1.20 An argument has been made that the purpose of trademarks are merely to separate goods or services in the market place and not to indicate a source or origin.[32] One can readily agree that trademarks should be capable of performing this distinguishing function. It does not necessarily follow that that is all that a trademark does, however. When one sees the Coca-Cola® trademark on a bottle, it does certainly mean to the average consumer that the product is not Pepsi® or some other competing soft drink. It would seem fair to add that it performs the function of ensuring to the consumer that the product in the bottle will have the taste and perceived quality that one expects from previous experience, advertising or both. While not specifying a geographic origin (whether the product was made and/or bottled at Coca-Cola Company's headquarters in Atlanta or not is not the point), the trademark also signifies that a well-known company stands behind the product.

1.21 As a commentator explained with respect to U.S. law:

> A trademark owner is free to license use of the mark for goods or services, but the licensor must ensure, in some way, that the goods or services with which the mark is used meet the licensor's quality standards. In other words, 'a trademark owner's duty under the Lanham Act not to use the mark in a manner that deceives the public entails a duty to control the quality of its licensees' products.' Reliance on the 'quality assurance' function of trademarks relieves the trademark owner of the burden of active participation, substituting the lesser obligation of quality control.[33]

1.22 Licenses without quality control are sometimes referred to as 'naked licenses' in the U.S. and other legal systems. Under the TRIPS Agreement, WTO

---

31 TRIPS Agreement, *supra* note 1, Art. 15.1.
32 NUNO PIRES DE CARVALHO, THE TRIPS REGIME OF TRADEMARKS AND DESIGNS 354 (2006). ('Trademarks are not intended to designate the source of goods and services or any other characteristic thereof. They are merely intended to distinguish goods and services.')
33 Michelle S. Friedman, *Naked Trademark Licenses in Business Format Franchising: The Quality Control Requirement and The Role Of Local Culture*, 10 J. TECH. L. & POL'Y 353, 359–60 (2005).

C. THE TRADEMARK PROVISIONS IN THE TRIPS AGREEMENT

Members may legitimately consider naked licensing as a possible cause to find a trademark is not or is no longer protected in their territory. A U.S. court described the applicable law as follows in a well-known court opinion:

> We are all agreed that the Lanham Act places an affirmative duty upon a licensor of a registered trademark to take reasonable measures to detect and prevent misleading uses of his mark by his licensees or suffer cancellation of his federal registration. The Act, 15 U.S.C.A. § 1064, provides that a trademark registration may be cancelled because the Trademark has been 'abandoned.' And 'abandoned' is defined in 15 U.S.C.A. § 1127 to include any act or omission by the registrant which causes the trademark to lose its significance as an indication of origin.[34]

1.23 In other words, trademarks can be seen as performing a distinguishing function that reduces search costs and what one might call a 'trust function', which one could define allowing 'buyers to trust and rely upon the signals conveyed by sellers as guarantees for quality, thus helping to prevent the lemonization of markets for goods with experience and credence attributes'.[35] For instance, the name of the Coca-Cola company on a product other than the well-known cola (the company sells drinks such as purified water and orange juice) and even bearing prominently another trademark (here, Dasani® and Minute Maid®) might reassure a consumer familiar with Coke® but not Dasani® that it comes from what one might call, to simplify, a 'known or reputable source'.

1.24 The melding of the two major legal systems in the TRIPS Agreement admittedly leaves room for substantive trademark law to grow in various directions on this dual function issue (distinguishing and source/quality assurance). What is the impact on the protection of a mark if the owner changes the quality of the goods? Does it lead to a loss of distinctiveness and possibly of the exclusive use of the mark? This is the law in a number of WTO Member countries.[36] Other WTO Members may decide to deal with such situations primarily as a matter of consumer protection.

---

[34] Dawn Donut Co. v. Hart's Food Stores, Inc., 267 F.2d 358, 369 (1959) 121 U.S.P.Q. 430 (2d Cir. 1959). *See also* Yamamoto & Co. (America), Inc. v. Victor United, Inc., 219 U.S.P.Q. 968 (C.D. Cal. 1982) and National Trailways Bus System v. Trailway Van Lines, Inc., 269 F. Supp. 352, 155 U.S.P.Q. 507 (E.D.N.Y. 1965). Courts in the U.S. have made it plain that the quality control mechanism need not be specified in the contract. It may just be derived from actual practice.

[35] Ariel Katz, *Beyond Search Costs: The Linguistic and Trust Functions of Trademarks*, 2010 BYU L. REV 1555, 1563 (2010).

[36] For example, in Canada, an Ontario piano manufacturer had outsourced production to Asia without informing consumers. The judge stated that '[t]he function and purpose of a trademark is to indicate the source from which goods emanate. If a mark is associated with a high quality product, its presence will assure the purchaser that the goods are likely to be of that quality. The mark, at least, allows a purchaser to tell whether or not the goods have come from a source in which he or she has confidence ... Not only were the efforts to notify the public virtually non-existent, there was clearly a deliberate attempt by the respondents to

1.25 The fact that use is required in certain (common law) systems is recognized in Article 15 of the TRIPS Agreement, which also provides that WTO Members may make registrability dependent on use,[37] but adds that actual use of a trademark shall not be a condition for *filing an application* for registration. Where signs are not inherently capable of distinguishing the relevant goods or services (for example, the shape or packaging of certain products), registrability may be made dependent on distinctiveness acquired through use. This is consonant with the Paris Convention system described in the previous section of the Chapter. It allows for registration of distinctive signs if registered in their country of origin, but also reflects the flexibility left to WTO and the Paris Convention Members to calibrate rules concerning the distinctiveness of trademarks. Article 6*quinquies*(B)(ii) of the Paris Convention allows registrability to be denied when a mark is devoid of any distinctive character, which WTO Members may base on acquisition through use if the mark is inherently incapable of distinguishing the relevant goods or services.[38]

1.26 In comparing the TRIPS Agreement with Article 6*quinquies*(B) of the Paris Convention, and recognising the principle that a mark duly registered in its country of origin should be registered, a mark should be examined on its individual merits, and proper instructions given accordingly to examiners (particularly regarding countries not party to the Paris Convention that are or will become WTO Members). This is reinforced by Article 6*quinquies*(C) of the Paris Convention, which requires that all factual circumstances be taken into consideration.[39]

1.27 The adaptation of the TRIPS Agreement to the common law world is not limited to the recognition of the validity of a requirement of use.[40] The definition contained in the first sentence of Article 15.1 of the TRIPS Agreement is not limited to registrable marks.[41] Thus, especially when read in conjunction with Article 16.1[42] *in fine*, the TRIPS Agreement contemplates also rights (for example, the common law tort of 'passing off') in respect of

---

camouflage the fact that a change of source had occurred.' Heintzman v. 751056 Ontario Ltd, [1990] F.C.1033 (Can.), 34 C.P.R. (3d) 1 (F.C.T.D.). There must be such a difference that the cheaper version must not be of a comparable quality. Jean Patou Inc. v. Luxo Laboratories Ltd., [2001] 67 F.C.1419 (F.C.A.).

37 This applies also to inherently distinctive marks and should thus not be confused with use leading to the acquisition of distinctiveness/secondary meaning of otherwise descriptive marks.
38 Paris Convention, *supra* note 26, Art. 6*quinquies*(b)(ii).
39 *Id.* at Art. 6*quinquies*(C).
40 E. K. Meltzer, *TRIPS and Trademarks, or – GATT Got Your Tongue?* 83 TRADEMARK REP. 18, 37 (1993) (TRIPS 'incorporates almost every significant concept of United States trademark law').
41 TRIPS Agreement, *supra* note 1, Art. 15.1.
42 *Id.*, Art. 16.1.

C. THE TRADEMARK PROVISIONS IN THE TRIPS AGREEMENT

unregistered marks and provides a framework for such protection, but without mandating their protection in all WTO Members.

1.28 The requirement of use and consequences of non-use are impacted also by Article 19 of the TRIPS Agreement, which limits cancellation for non-use after an 'uninterrupted period of at least three years' if 'valid reasons based on the existence of obstacles to such use are shown by the trademark owner. Circumstances arising independently of the will of the owner of the trademark which constitute an obstacle to the use of the trademark, such as import restrictions on or other government requirements for goods or services protected by the trademark, shall be recognized as valid reasons for non-use.'[43]

3. Recordal of transfers and licenses under Article 19.2 of the TRIPS Agreement

1.29 The importance of the transactional aspect of Article 19.2 of the TRIPS Agreement seems self-evident. It provides that 'When subject to the control of its owner, use of a trademark by another person shall be recognized as use of the trademark for the purpose of maintaining the registration.'[44]

1.30 Article 19.2 fills a gap left by the 1958 International Patent and Trademark Conference in Lisbon, Portugal (Lisbon Conference), which was unable to deal effectively only with concurrent use by enterprises that are co-proprietors of a mark (and not licensor and licensee, a much more common situation). The drafting history provides some guidance on the meaning of this provision. There is, however, an interesting nuance in that the term control was chosen to replace consent, the draft was modified as follows during the TRIPS Agreement negotiations (changes shown):

> Use of a trademark by another person ~~with~~ subject to the ~~consent~~ control of the owner shall be ~~recognized~~ recognised as use of the trademark for the purpose of maintaining the registration.[45]

Article 19.2 implies that a WTO Member must also accept use by a person other than the owner but subject to his control as use that qualifies to maintain the trademark.[46] Control is often effected by a licensing arrangement enumerating specific conditions under which the mark may be used by the licensee.

---

43 *Id.*, Art. 19.
44 *Id.*, Art. 19.2.
45 For a more complete description of the drafting history, see GERVAIS, TRIPS AGREEMENT, *supra* note 6, at 342–5.
46 TRIPS Agreement, *supra* note 1, Art. 19.2.

This puts the spotlight on the control that can and perhaps should be effected by the trademark owner in any licensing transaction and the key role of the specifications (or '*cahier des charge*s') that a complete trademark license, including franchising arrangement, should comprise. Under Article 19.2 of the TRIPS Agreement, WTO Members have flexibility to require control of the licensee's use by the trademark owner. Control is not the same as consent.

1.31 As WIPO noted in its *Joint Recommendation Concerning Trademark Licenses*:

> Certain national or regional laws, however, provide that use by persons other than the holder may be held to constitute use of the mark by the holder only if certain conditions are fulfilled, such as the conclusion of a formal license contract containing quality control clauses or such as the recordal of such a contract. In that respect, it is to be noted that *Article 19.2 of the TRIPS Agreement expressly allows a requirement that there be control of a licensee's use* of a mark by the holder in order to consider such use valid for maintaining the registration of a mark.[47]

1.32 While the existence of an optional recordal system for licenses and transfers seems acceptable under the TRIPS Agreement rules, there is some disagreement about whether WTO Members may *require* that a license be registered or 'recorded'. Such registration or recordal may be required under applicable corporate or business licensing laws, tax laws, or other financial regulations not related to intellectual property. Would a WTO Member be allowed not to consider use by an authorized licensee under control of the trademark owner as not sufficient to maintain registration? The text of Article 19.2 of the TRIPS Agreement does not seem to support this conclusion, by making it clear that such use 'shall be recognized' for that purpose.

1.33 The matter was debated during the negotiations, that is, prior to the adoption of the TRIPS Agreement text, at least up to a point. A need to 'control' the use of foreign trademarks by local licensees was felt and justified, during the negotiations, as follows:

> It is well recognised that foreign trademarks tend to encourage the production and consumption of non-essential and luxury goods in poorer societies, thereby distorting their socio-cultural objectives and values. Perceptive commentators have drawn attention to the typical and strong tendency in developing countries to imitate the

---

47 *Joint Recommendation Concerning Trademark Licenses*, adopted by the Assembly of the Paris Union for the Protection of Industrial Property and the General Assembly of the World Intellectual Property Organization (WIPO) at the Thirty-Fifth Series of Meetings of the Assemblies of the Member States of WIPO 25 September to 3 October 2000, Notes, pp. 6–7, *available 14 September 2014 at* http://www.wipo.int/edocs/pubdocs/en/marks/835/pub835.pdf (emphasis added) [hereinafter Joint Recommendation].

C. THE TRADEMARK PROVISIONS IN THE TRIPS AGREEMENT

consumption patterns and life styles of affluent countries, although they may be ill-suited to their own conditions and circumstances.[48]

This control was effected by a number of countries using 'registered user' requirements. As India noted:

> The mere authorisation of the use of the trademark by a third party through a private sanction, without the third party being registered as a 'Registered User', shall not constitute use.[49]

1.34 The fact that this was raised during the negotiations and that no provision was made in the TRIPS Agreement for the survival of this requirement as a condition to maintain registration is a strong argument against a mandatory requirement to register. This does not mean that registration or recordation of licenses would not be desirable and cannot be effected through other means, however. What it does mean is that sanctions for failure to do so should likely focus not on the validity of the registration or license per se but rather be in the form of administrative measures or adequate fines. This is also WIPO's view on the matter:

> The non-recordal of a license with the Office or with any other authority of the Member State shall not affect the validity of the registration of the mark which is the subject of the license, or the protection of that mark.[50]

1.35 Some enforcement and evidentiary rules could also be contingent on the recordation of licenses.[51] Finally, the TRIPS Agreement does not prevent the application of competition law where applicable.

4. Article 20 of the TRIPS Agreement[52]

1.36 Article 20 of the TRIPS Agreement provides as follows:

---

48 GATT Secretariat, *Standards and Principles Concerning the Availability Scope and Use of Trade-Related Intellectual Property Rights: Communication from India*, ¶32, MTN.GNG/NG11/W/37 (10 July 1989).
49 *Id.* at 42. Brazil also made the point around the same time that a 'licensing agreement per se is not evidence of the use of a mark.'. GATT Secretariat, *Communication from Brazil*, 43, MTN.GNG/NG11/W/57 (11 December 1989). As stated, that seems right, but use by the licensee under the control of the owner would be evidence of use. Brazil then also insisted that 'evidence of use by third parties requires the registration with the relevant government authority of the license granted by the owner of the mark'. *Id.*
50 Joint Recommendation, *supra* note 47, Art. 4(1).
51 *But see id.*, Art. 4(2).
52 This section is drawn in part from Susy Frankel & Daniel Gervais, Plain Packaging and the Interpretation of the TRIPS Agreement 46:5 VAND. J. TRANSNAT'L L. 1149 (2013).

> The use of a trademark in the course of trade shall not be unjustifiably encumbered by special requirements, such as use with another trademark, use in a special form or use in a manner detrimental to its capability to distinguish the goods or services of one undertaking from those of other undertakings. This will not preclude a requirement prescribing the use of the trademark identifying the undertaking producing the goods or services along with, but without linking it to, the trademark distinguishing the specific goods or services in question of that undertaking.[53]

1.37 Article 20 is relevant in trademark transactions in preventing some requirements of use of a trademark with another mark, for example. Whether its prohibition on encumbrances allows WTO Members to completely ban the use of marks is a matter before a WTO Dispute-Settlement Panel at the time of writing.[54]

1.38 Article 20 reflects the function of trademarks in the course of trade, a concept with strong origins in common law trademark doctrines. When interpreting Article 20, the domestic law traditions of any one party to the TRIPS Agreement will not necessarily be determinative. State practice, however, may be relevant to determining the ordinary meaning of terms incorporated in the Agreement when those terms were known to have an agreed meaning, and even an object and purpose, reflective of domestic law.[55]

1.39 The forced combination of a trademark with another by government regulation was examined in an early WTO Dispute-Settlement Panel report. In *Indonesia – Certain Measures Affecting the Automobile Industry* case,[56] the United States claimed, inter alia, on the basis of Article 20 that Indonesia had violated its TRIPS Agreement obligations. Its first argument was that:

> [a] foreign company that enters into an arrangement with a Pioneer company would be encumbered in using the trademark that it used elsewhere for the model that was adopted by the National Car Programme.[57]

The Panel did not accept this argument for the reason that:

> [I]f a foreign company *enters into an arrangement* with a Pioneer company it does so voluntarily and in the knowledge of any consequent implications for its ability to use any pre-existing trademark. In these circumstances, we do not consider the provisions

---

53 TRIPS Agreement, *supra* note 1, Art. 20.
54 For a fuller discussion, see Frankel & Gervais, *supra* note 52, at 1149.
55 VCLT, *supra* note 25, Art. 31.3(b).
56 Panel Report, *Indonesia – Certain Measures Affecting The Automobile Industry Case*, WT/DS54/R (2 July 1998).
57 *Id.* at para 14.277.

C. THE TRADEMARK PROVISIONS IN THE TRIPS AGREEMENT

of the National Car Programme as they relate to trademarks can be construed as 'requirements', in the sense of Art. 20.[58]

1.40 One argument against this position is that trademark rights are essentially territorial.[59] One could argue that Article 6*bis* of the Paris Convention (incorporated into the TRIPS Agreement) supports the U.S. point in respect of well-known marks, however. This opens the door to the question of whether trademark rights as protected under the Paris Convention and the TRIPS Agreement are mere negative nights (to prevent others from using the mark), or whether there are positive rights or privileges to use that are also relevant under such instruments. This issue requires a detailed explanation which the reader may find elsewhere.[60]

1.41 Essentially, because participating in the National Car Programme was seen as voluntary – and hence, trademark owners arguably 'accepted' use of the imposed Indonesian mark – the encroachment upon trademark owners' rights was considered not to violate Article 20. This means that the issue of forced use of trademark with another (imposed by regulation) has not been fully explored by a dispute-settlement panel. One may venture that if the function of the trademark was impaired as a result, a WTO Member may have to defend its measure under the justifiability test contained in Article 20.[61]

1.42 At the meeting of the Dispute-Settlement Body discussing adoption of the Panel report, the United States did not object to the adoption (having obtained a favourable ruling on other aspects), but it found the Panel's conclusions on Article 20 'disturbing' and incorrect:

---

58   *Id.* at para.14.278 (emphasis added).
59   *See* Geri L. Haight & Philip Catanzano, *The Effects of Global Priority of Trademark Rights*, 91 MASS. L. REV. 18, 25–26 (2007):

> While both the Paris Convention and TRIPs recognize the territoriality principle, both create potentially significant exceptions to the doctrine for famous marks. For example, both doctrines contemplate a scenario where a foreign, non-U.S.-based user is given priority rights to a mark, regardless of the level (or absence) of use in the United States. To date, however, there is scant case law in which a U.S. court discussed or applied the provisions of any treaty to a trademark dispute, and it is unclear how much weight U.S. judges will accord to foreign treaties and protocols ... Although most U.S. courts characterize the principle of territoriality as basic to trademark law, some U.S. courts – along with the treaties outlined above – have discussed (although few have applied) a potential exception to this general rule: the 'well known' or 'famous' mark doctrine.

Id. For a U.S. case on point, see De Beers LV Trademark Ltd. v. DeBeers Diamond Syndicate, Inc., 440 F.Supp.2d 249 (S.D.N.Y. 2006).
60   *See* Frankel & Gervais, *supra* note 52.
61   *Id.* (exploring in detail this test).

In addressing the U.S. claim under the TRIPS Agreement with respect to Indonesia's National Car Programme, the Panel had relied heavily on its conclusions that it was permissible for a government to confer a benefit on condition of a foreign company's relinquishment of the rights afforded under the TRIPS Agreement. [...] In the United States' view, the Panel's conclusions on this point were incorrect, short and devoid of any detailed analysis or discussion of precedent. In particular, the Panel had failed to discuss the GATT and WTO precedents supporting the proposition that there was a requirement in situations where a company had voluntarily accepted conditions in order to receive a benefit.[62]

D. THE TRADEMARK TRANSACTIONS PROVISION: ARTICLE 21 OF THE TRIPS AGREEMENT

1.43 The key provision on trademark transactions in the TRIPS Agreement is Article 21. It provides as follows:

> Members may determine conditions on the licensing and assignment of trademarks, it being understood that the compulsory licensing of trademarks shall not be permitted and that the owner of a registered trademark shall have the right to assign the trademark with or without the transfer of the business to which the trademark belongs.[63]

1. Drafting history

1.44 Let us consider, first, the drafting history. The early draft of 23 July 1990, contained inter alia the following texts:

- Compulsory licensing of trademarks shall not be permitted.
- The right to a [registered] trademark may be assigned with or without the transfer of the undertaking to which the trademark belongs. [PARTIES may require that the goodwill to which the trademark belongs be transferred with the right to the trademark.] [PARTIES may prohibit the assignment of a registered trademark which is identical with, or similar to, a famous mark indicating a state or a local public entity or an agency thereof or a non-profit organisation or enterprise working in the public interest.]
- It will be a matter for national legislation to determine the conditions for the use or assignment of a mark.

---

62 Dispute Settlement Body, *Minutes of Meeting held on 23 July 1998*, p. 13, WT/DSB/M/47 (18 September 1998).
63 TRIPS Agreement, *supra* note 1, Art. 21.

D. THE TRADEMARK TRANSACTIONS PROVISION: ARTICLE 21 OF THE TRIPS AGREEMENT

In October 1990, the text was changed twice, first to this version: **1.45**

- Compulsory licensing of trademarks shall not be permitted.
- ~~The right to a [registered]~~ The owner of a registered trademark shall have the right to assign his trademark ~~may be assigned~~ with or without the transfer of the undertaking to which the trademark belongs.
- It ~~will~~ shall be a matter for national legislation to determine the conditions for the use ~~or assignment~~ of a mark.

Then to this: **1.46**

- ~~Compulsory~~ PARTIES may determine conditions on the licensing and assignment of trademarks, it being understood that the compulsory licensing of trademarks shall not be permitted and that the owner of a registered trademark shall have the right to assign his trademark with or without the transfer of the undertaking to which the trademark belongs.
- ~~It shall be a matter for national legislation to determine the conditions for the use of a mark.~~

In November 1990, the texts were 'combined' as follows to give a text similar to the final (adopted) version: **1.47**

> PARTIES may determine conditions on the licensing and assignment of trademarks, it being understood that the compulsory licensing of trademarks shall not be permitted and that the owner of a registered trademark shall have the right to assign his trademark with or without the transfer of the ~~undertaking~~ business to which the trademark belongs.

How should one interpret the text? Let us begin with the rule concerning compulsory licenses. **1.48**

2. Compulsory licenses of trademarks

One of the purposes is clear: compulsory licensing of trademarks is prohibited. It is true that, while cases where compulsory licensing of patents may be justifiable in the public interest, it is typically not so with trademarks. Why would a WTO Member want to allow a third party not authorized by the Coca-Cola Company to sell Coke? Local consumers would be 'fooled' into believing that they are purchasing 'the real thing'. Any problem with the product could tarnish the Coca-Cola mark (and company). There is, therefore, no welfare gain for the public nor (obviously) for the trademark owner in allowing this type of free-riding. **1.49**

1.50 Since the purpose of trademark is its ability to distinguish the goods or services of one undertaking from those of another, it would be nonsensical to let a third party use that link as identifying the product or service without the consent of (and control by) the trademark owner. Other matters of possible public interest, such as eliminating unused marks from the register, are dealt with in previous Articles. If the use of a patented product is allowed under a compulsory license (say, under the Paragraph 6 System), use of the trademark of the patent holder as an indication could be misleading.[64]

1.51 Under a compulsory licensing regime, how would the licensee not working in cooperation with the trademark owner achieve the level of quality control required to maintain the distinctiveness of the mark? Trademarks perform a distinguishing function from which in many legal systems follows a quality control function: consumers rightly expect consistency of the quality (with variations for items such as food products because the materials used necessarily vary). To say that a trademark compulsory license can or should be issued because a third party (such as a government agency) is regulating the quality of a product ignores the source component of the function. That component is indicated by the direction of Article 15 of the TRIPS Agreement that a mark's purpose is to distinguish the goods or services of one undertaking from those of other undertakings.[65] As the U.S. Court of Appeals for the Fourth Circuit noted, it is precisely that function that makes a symbol a protected trademark:

> When a trademark ceases to identify in the public's mind the particular source of a product or service but rather identifies a class of product or service, regardless of source, that mark has become generic and is lost as an enforceable trademark. See 15 U.S.C. § 1064(3). To become generic, the primary significance of the mark must be its indication of the nature or class of the product or service, rather than an indication of source.[66]

1.52 While in the case of geographical indications the origin-indicating function is fully intertwined with the quality assurance function, as noted above, this often includes trademarks as well.[67] Even if third party controls are likely to maintain consistency of the goods, the welfare gains of allowing a product not manufactured by A or with A's consent to be sold as A's product are unclear at best. Consumers can be informed that the product manufactured by B is

---

[64] That would not prevent nominative use of that trademark.
[65] TRIPS Agreement, *supra* note 1, Art. 15.
[66] Glover v. Ampak, Inc., 74 F.3d 57 (4th Cir. 1996).
[67] *See generally* the discussion, *supra* notes 34 to 36. On the function of assuring perceived quality that geographical indications perform, see Gervais, *supra* note 10.

D. THE TRADEMARK TRANSACTIONS PROVISION: ARTICLE 21 OF THE TRIPS AGREEMENT

similar to the product made by A if nominative (or another similar non-confusing fair) use of A's mark is allowed.

The TRIPS Agreement ban on compulsory licensing is arguably reinforced by Article 20's prohibition.[68] The TRIPS Agreement restricts conditions that would be 'detrimental to its capability to distinguish the goods or services of one undertaking from those of other undertakings', and a compulsory license would be likely to do so unless very specific precautions were taken. Fortunately, this is not or no longer a significant issue. Even at the time of the TRIPS negotiation, very few countries allowed the compulsory licensing of trademarks.[69]

1.53

3. Conditions on transfers and licenses and the enforcement of marks

WTO Members retain the right to determine conditions of transfer and assignment. This would include contract provisions requiring, for example, that an assignment be in writing. Can registration or recordal be made mandatory? Not as a condition to maintain registration of the mark, as explained above in relation to Article 19.2 of the TRIPS Agreement.[70]

1.54

How does that affect enforcement after (the grant of a) license? As far as enforcement by a licensee is concerned, WIPO notes that whether 'a licensee should be allowed to join proceedings initiated by the licensor, or whether it would be entitled to damages resulting from an infringement of the licensed mark',[71] a matter left to national law, is not the same as asking whether 'a licensee has the right under the law of a Member State to join infringement proceedings initiated by the holder and to obtain damages resulting from an infringement of the licensed mark'.[72] In answering the second question, the answer is clear: the licensee should be able to exercise those rights independently of whether the license is recorded or registered.

1.55

This debate about enforcement by a licensee against unauthorized use by a third party continued after the adoption of the TRIPS Agreement. At a 1999 meeting at WIPO, '[s]everal delegations and the representative of an observer

1.56

---

68 *See supra* Part C.4.
69 GATT Secretariat, *Existence, Scope and Form of Generally Internationally Accepted and Applied Standards/Norms for the Protection of Intellectual Property – Note prepared by the International Bureau of WIPO*, P. 37, MTN.GNG/NGll/W/24/Rev.l (15 September 1988).
70 *See supra* Part C.3.
71 GATT Secretariat, *supra* note 69 at Note to Article 4. *See also* Committee of Experts on Trademark Licenses, 70–74, TML/CE/I/3 (30 September 1999).
72 GATT Secretariat, *supra* note 69 at Note to Article 4.

organization [...] held that the rights of third parties could depend on recordal and that the licensee could not join in infringement proceedings unless the license was recorded'.[73] Indeed the Notes to the Joint Recommendation mention that the 'question whether the non-recorded licensee should have the right to join infringement proceedings initiated by the holder and to recover damages was the subject of an intensive debate'.[74]

1.57 Subject to other provisions of the TRIPS Agreement, Members may also allow nominative uses of protected marks.

1.58 It should be noted that the first part of this Article seems to apply to all trademarks (including unregistered marks where they are protected), while the latter part (right to assign) clearly applies only to registered marks.

1.59 Article 21 goes beyond Article 6*quater*(1) of the Paris Convention which deemed that, in cases where the goodwill or business to which the mark belongs had to be transferred at the same time as the transfer of the mark, transfer of the portion of the goodwill or business located in the country concerned was sufficient. This was fully justified under the principle of independence of rights in different territories.[75] A number of countries did (some still do) require the transfer of the goodwill or business and in some cases, in spite of Article 6*quater*, required the transfer of the entire business, even if parts of it were located in foreign territories. This is also potentially in conflict with the 'trend' to develop marks as *brands* with value and existence independently of the goods or services they are associated with.

1.60 The TRIPS Agreement eliminated requirements concerning transfer of the business together with the mark. Business may be defined as 'the industrial or commercial establishment,' that is, the material basis of the activities.[76] However, contrary to Article 6*quater* of the Paris Convention, Article 21 does not refer to the 'goodwill'. Bodenhausen, in the well-known *Guide to the Paris Convention*, defines goodwill as the 'customer base'.[77] It is difficult to imagine that this element was left out unintentionally. The conclusion that follows from such a choice is that while WTO Members are not permitted to require transfer of the business, as regards transfers of the goodwill only Article

---

73 Standing Committee on the Law of Trademarks Industrial Designs and Geographical Indications (SCT), *Third Session Geneva, 8 to 12 November 1999*, 122, SCT/3/10 (26 November 1999).
74 Joint Recommendation, *supra* note 47, at Notes para 4.4.
75 G.H.C. BODENHAUSEN, GUIDE TO THE PARIS CONVENTION FOR THE PROTECTION OF INDUSTRIAL PROPERTY, 104 (WIPO Publ'n, 1969).
76 *Id.* at 105.
77 *Id.*

D. THE TRADEMARK TRANSACTIONS PROVISION: ARTICLE 21 OF THE TRIPS AGREEMENT

6*quater* of the Paris Convention applies (through Article 2.1 of the TRIPS Agreement, which incorporated the substantive provisions of the Paris Convention, including Article 6*quater*).

1.61 This conclusion is reinforced by other expressions used in various texts known to negotiators. For example, Article 5A(4) of the Paris Convention speaks of 'enterprise or goodwill', the former probably a synonym of 'undertaking', a term also used in Article 31(e) of the TRIPS Agreement.[78] The 1994 Trademark Law Treaty (TLT) is relevant as a contemporaneous instrument negotiated among many of the same parties, though it was concluded a few months after the signing of the WTO Agreement (and the TRIPS Agreement).[79] Article 11(4)(iv) of the TLT refers to the 'business or the relevant goodwill' and does not allow contracting parties, in determining the requirements to be met to record a change of ownership in a trademark, to request that evidence be furnished that the business or relevant goodwill has been transferred with the mark.[80]

4. A role for competition law?

1.62 Competition law in the TRIPS Agreement, as limited as it is, may also affect trademark transactions. Articles 8.2 and 40.2 of the TRIPS Agreement are relevant in this context. The first one provides that:

> Appropriate measures, provided that they are consistent with the provisions of this Agreement, may be needed to prevent the abuse of intellectual property rights by right holders or the resort to practices which unreasonably restrain trade or adversely affect the international transfer of technology.[81]

Article 40.2 reads as follows:

> Nothing in this Agreement shall prevent Members from specifying in their legislation licensing practices or conditions that may *in particular cases* constitute an abuse of intellectual property rights having an adverse effect on competition in the relevant market. As provided above, a Member may adopt, consistently with the other provisions of this Agreement, appropriate measures to prevent or control such practices, which may include for example exclusive grantback conditions, conditions

---

78   Paris Convention, *supra* note 26, Art. 5A(4).
79   Trademark Law Treaty, Oct. 27, 1994, *available 14 September 2015 at* http://www.wipo.int/treaties/en/ip/tlt/ [hereinafter TLT].
80   *Id*. at Art. 11(4)(iv).
81   TRIPS Agreement, *supra* note 1, Art. 8.2.

preventing challenges to validity and coercive package licensing, in the light of the relevant laws and regulations of that Member.[82]

1.63 Article 8.2, in part because the Article is titled 'Principles' and in part because of the 'provided that they are consistent with the provisions of this Agreement' may be seen as a 'policy statement with active force; that is part of the object and purpose of the TRIPS Agreement'.[83]

1.64 Object and purpose is of course of cardinal importance here. The central rule of interpretation and key part of Article 31 of the VCLT requires that a 'treaty shall be interpreted in good faith in accordance with the ordinary meaning to be given to the terms of the treaty in their context and in the light of its object and purpose'.[84] The VCLT is applicable to the interpretation of the TRIPS Agreement and other WTO instruments.[85]

1.65 Article 40.2 has direct operational force. It establishes the right of WTO Members to specify, on a case-by-case basis (thus excluding a priori determination that a particular practice or licensing condition is anti-competitive leading to the automatic imposition of a remedial measure), practices which must (a) constitute an abuse of intellectual property rights and (b) have an adverse effect on competition (using wording similar but not identical to that used in Article 8 of the TRIPS Agreement).

1.66 A broad definition of 'abuse' without a determination of adverse effect would thus not be consistent with Article 40.2. Indeed, during the negotiation, the possibility of separating these two criteria by an 'or' was discussed at length, but in the end, the wording retained seems to require that both be met simultaneously. In those cases that meet the two required criteria, measures to control or prevent such practices may be taken but only as provided in previous Articles ('as provided above' juxtaposed to 'consistently with the other provisions of this Agreement'). This means that a measure affecting contractual abusive anti-competitive practices may not be taken if it is incompatible with another provision of the TRIPS Agreement, in particular of previous sections of Part II. This requires a balance of the obligation to protect right holders with the need to protect the public from abuses of rights such as coercive package licensing and imposing an obligation to buy goods and services made or distributed by the trademark owner beyond the requirements of the licensee

---

82 *Id.*, Art. 40.2.
83 Frankel & Gervais, *supra* note 52 at 1203.
84 VCLT, *supra* note 25 Arts. 31–32.
85 Appellate Body Report, *United States – Continued Existence and Application of Zeroing Methodology*, 269, WT/DS350/AB/R (4 February 2009).

D. THE TRADEMARK TRANSACTIONS PROVISION: ARTICLE 21 OF THE TRIPS AGREEMENT

(for example off-patent goods). But competition law may be applied more broadly to ensure the proper functioning of markets. Clauses that limit a licensee's ability to research on or improve the trademark owner's product (more typical in a patent context) could come under this type of scrutiny, as WTO Members try to calibrate their IP regime to optimize local innovation.[86] Countries should carefully weigh the possible application of investment treaties in this context, especially when legislating rules that apply to existing arrangements. Case-by-case determinations that an existing arrangement violates existing competition law seems less likely to come under the type of scrutiny possible under investment protection schemes. The TRIPS Agreement and the instruments adopted since its implementation clearly favour having fewer (if any) horizontal or per se rules in this context, and point towards greater case-by-case determinations accompanied by adequate due process.

1.67 The provisions in the TRIPS Agreement suggest that consultations are to be held between the Member that believes that a contractual practice in a particular case is abusive and anti-competitive and the Member of which the right holder concerned is a national or domiciliary. To explain the role of consultations in this field, it may be useful to recall that practices not unlike those mentioned in this section were discussed in the General Agreement on Tariffs and Trade (GATT) Panels before the Uruguay Round. The emphasis on consultations may reflect the approach taken in those previous attempts to deal with what was termed 'restrictive business practices'. During the GATT Review Session held in 1954 to 1955, a proposal to add a Chapter on 'cartels' (which was Chapter V of the Havana Charter) was rejected.[87] However, a Group of Experts on 'Arrangements for Consultation' appointed in 1958 to study this matter recommended in a 1960 report that CONTRACTING PARTIES should undertake to deal with restrictive business practices.[88] That Report, adopted by the CONTRACTING PARTIES, stated that:

> [T]he CONTRACTING PARTIES should now be regarded as an appropriate and competent body to initiate action in this field [...] and should encourage direct consultations between contracting parties with a view to the elimination of the harmful effects of particular restrictive practices.[89]

---

[86] DANIEL GERVAIS, *Calibration*, in INTELLECTUAL PROPERTY, TRADE AND DEVELOPMENT, (2nd ed. Daniel Gervais ed, 2015).
[87] World Trade Organization, GATT Analytical Index, Vol.I, at p. 486 and Vol.II, at p. 879. B.I.S.D. 3S/51.
[88] Report of Experts, Restrictive Business Practices: Arrangement for Consultations, Adopted 2 June 1960, Report L/1015, B.I.S.D. 9S/170.
[89] *Id.*

1.68 Competition law is not uniform among WTO Members. Indeed, efforts to make it more uniform have so far failed. This provides a significant degree of policy flexibility to WTO Members. For instance, procedurally, it may be applied as *ex ante* regulation (clearance) of certain transactions. It can be applied *ex post* by a specialized (typically quasi-judicial) agency or by regular courts. WTO Members may, however, be more cautious in applying remedies that amount to the removal of intellectual property rights as opposed to limits on enforcement or other penalties. More importantly, as noted above, the TRIPS Agreement points to case-by-case determinations, with due process, as signalled by the 'particular cases' clause in Article 40.2.

1.69 The TRIPS Agreement is flexible on substantive conditions on transfers and licensing. The idea that the trademark owner should control uses by the licensee, for example, can be enforced as matter of trademark law, as in the Canadian example above. Because the normative pillars of trademark law in several jurisdictions focus first or at least as much on consumer interests, any license or transfer may be subjected to scrutiny to a test to see whether the transaction led to a loss of distinctiveness. We find an example in a U.S. case, where lack of quality control was described as a cause (if established) to find a mark had been 'abandoned', e.g. via naked licensing.[90]

E. CONCLUSION

1.70 The TRIPS Agreement impacts trademark transactions by limiting the flexibility of WTO Members in defining what constitutes a trademark, prohibiting compulsory licensing, and restricting conditions on transfers and licenses and possible rules on mandatory use of a trademark with another mark or use in a special form. Disagreements over past disputes and a dispute on plain packaging of tobacco in Australia, which was pending at the time of writing, mean that the exact scope of the obligations imposed on WTO Members in that respect is not entirely clear. The Agreement does, however, leave room for use of trademark law to preserve a quality assurance function and to apply competition law in appropriate cases.

---

90 *See* case law cited, *supra* note 34.

2

TRADEMARK TRANSACTIONS AND THE NORMATIVE FRAMEWORK OF THE WORLD INTELLECTUAL PROPERTY ORGANIZATION

Marcus Höpperger[*]

A. INTRODUCTION	2.01	3. The Madrid System	2.25
B. THE NORMATIVE FRAMEWORK OF WIPO	2.04	D. LICENSES	2.30
1. The Paris Convention	2.06	1. The Singapore Treaty and Joint Recommendation	2.30
2. The Singapore Treaty	2.07		
3. The Joint Recommendation	2.08	2. The Madrid System	2.44
4. The Madrid Protocol	2.09		
		E. RESTRICTIONS OF THE RIGHT OF DISPOSAL	2.47
C. CHANGE IN OWNERSHIP	2.10		
1. The Paris Convention	2.10		
2. The TLT and Singapore Treaty	2.14	F. CONCLUSION	2.53

A. INTRODUCTION

The World Intellectual Property Organization (WIPO) is the global forum for intellectual property services, policy, information and cooperation.[1] One important function of WIPO is to ensure the administration of a number of intellectual property treaties, some going back to the late 19th century.[2] Moreover, WIPO provides various fora for the development of international norms in intellectual property,[3] such as the Standing Committee on the Law of Trademarks, Industrial Designs and Geographical Indications (SCT).[4]

2.01

---

[*] Director, Law and Legislative Advice Division, Brands and Designs Sector, World Intellectual Property Organization. The views expressed by the author are strictly personal and do not constitute an official position of the World Intellectual Property Organization (WIPO). The author would like to thank Dr. J. C. Wichard for his comments on the manuscript.
[1] *Inside WIPO*, WIPO, *available 14 September 2015 at* http://www.wipo.int/about-wipo/en.
[2] WIPO administers 26 treaties including the WIPO Convention. *WIPO-Administered Treaties*, WIPO, *available 14 September 2015 at* http://www.wipo.int/treaties/en.
[3] *Policy*, WIPO, *available 14 September 2015 at* http://www.wipo.int/policy/en.
[4] *Standing Committee on the Law of Trademarks, Industrial Designs and Geographical Indications (SCT)*, WIPO, *available 14 September 2015 at* http://www.wipo.int/policy/en/sct.

2.02 This chapter offers an overview on various legal instruments administered by WIPO or negotiated under its aegis and the provisions contained in those instruments that are relevant for trademark transactions, in particular provisions relating to the assignment or transfer of trademarks, the licensing of trademarks and to restrictions of the right to dispose of trademarks.

2.03 The importance of trademark transactions was highlighted in the World Intellectual Property Report 2013, entitled *Brands – Reputation and Image in the Global Marketplace*.[5] Admitting the scarcity of economic data available on markets for brands – characterized as trademark transactions in the form of licenses, franchise agreements and transfers of rights[6] – the Report concludes that markets for brands are large and growing.[7]

B. THE NORMATIVE FRAMEWORK OF WIPO

2.04 The normative framework for intellectual property rights created and administered by WIPO can be broken down into legal norms at different levels of the hierarchy for international law. This includes international registration services for industrial property rights that produce legal effects in participating countries and organizations.

2.05 Rather than providing exhaustive descriptions of the legal instruments concerned, consideration will be given to the provisions applicable to specific types of trademark transactions – namely changes in ownership, licenses and restrictions of the right of disposal. This will be done with respect to the following legal instruments: The Paris Convention for the Protection of Industrial Property of 1883 as revised and amended (Paris Convention), the Singapore Treaty on the Law of Trademarks of 2006 and the Regulations under that Treaty as in force on 1 November 2011 (Singapore Treaty and Singapore Treaty Regulations), the Joint Recommendation Concerning Trademark Licenses of 2000 (Joint Recommendation) and the Madrid Agreement Concerning the International Registration of Marks of 1891 as revised and amended (Madrid Agreement), the Protocol thereunder of 1989 as amended (Madrid Protocol) and the Common Regulations under the Madrid Agreement and the Madrid Protocol as in force on 1 January 2013 (Common Regulations). In order to provide a context for the better appreciation of the

---

5   WIPO, Pub. No. 944/2013, 2013 WORLD INTELLECTUAL PROPERTY REPORT 61 [hereinafter 2013 WORLD IP REPORT], *available 14 September 2015 at* http://www.wipo.int/edocs/pubdocs/en/intproperty/944/wipo_pub_944_2013.pdf.
6   *Id.* at 62.
7   *Id.* at 75.

specific provisions described hereunder, this description is preceded by a short general introduction of the various instruments that will be looked at.

1. The Paris Convention

2.06 The Paris Convention can be safely described as a cornerstone of the international legal framework for industrial property rights. It stipulates a number of basic rules for the acquisition, maintenance and protection of such rights – patents, trademarks, industrial designs, appellations of origin and indications of source – in multiple jurisdictions. Those rules are being applied by the Contracting Parties to the Paris Convention through implementation into national law.[8] The Paris Convention is applicable beyond its Contracting Parties,[9] since by virtue of a reference in Article 2.1 of the Agreement of Trade Related Aspects of Intellectual Property Rights (TRIPS) of 1994,[10] its substantive provisions are also applicable to Members of the World Trade Organization (WTO) not party to the Paris Convention.

2. The Singapore Treaty

2.07 The Singapore Treaty on the Law of Trademarks of 2006[11] and the Regulations Under the Singapore Treaty on the Law of Trademarks constitutes in essence a revision of the Trademark Law Treaty of 1994 (TLT).[12] Both Treaties provide provisions for the harmonization and simplification of trademark office procedures relating to the application for the registration of trademarks, the maintenance of such registration and their management, in particular the recordal[13] of certain changes and transactions in trademark registers. Contracting Parties to both Treaties are bound to apply the treaty

---

8 Paris Convention for the Protection of Industrial Property, 20 March 1883, 21 U.S.T. 1583, 828 U.N.T.S. 305 [hereinafter Paris Convention]. For the full text of the Paris Convention and a list of Contracting Parties, visit http://www.wipo.int/treaties/en/ip/paris, *available 14 September 2015*.
9 For the list of Contracting Parties to the Paris Convention as of 15 January 2015, see http://www.wipo.int/export/sites/www/treaties/en/documents/pdf/paris.pdf, *available 14 September 2015*.
10 Agreement on Trade-Related Aspects of Intellectual Property Rights, 15 April 1994, Marrakesh Agreement Establishing the World Trade Organization, Annex 1C, LEGAL INSTRUMENTS – RESULT OF THE URUGUAY ROUNDS vol. 31, 33 I.L.M. 81 (1994) [hereinafter TRIPS].
11 Singapore Treaty on the Law of Trademarks, *opened for signature* 28 March 2006, S. TREATY DOC. No. 110–2 (2007) [hereinafter Singapore Treaty]. For the full text of the Singapore Treaty and a list of Contracting Parties, visit http://www.wipo.int/treaties/en/ip/singapore, *available 14 September 2015*.
12 Trademark Law Treaty, adopted on 27 October 1994, 2034 U.N.T.S. 298 [hereinafter TLT]. For the full text of the Trademark Law Treaty and a list of Contracting Parties, visit http://www.wipo.int/treaties/en/ip/tlt, *available 14 September 2015*.
13 The terminology used in WIPO instruments for describing the recordation of changes or transactions in a register is not uniform. The Singapore Treaty, the TLT and the Joint Recommendation use the term 'recordal', the Madrid System uses the term 'recording'. In the interest of clarity, this text uses the term 'recordal' throughout.

provisions through implementation into their national trademark laws. The text body of the Singapore Treaty is largely identical with the TLT, but the former adds an additional layer of provisions concerning, in particular, procedures for the recordal and cancellation of licenses, the effects of non-recordal of licenses and the indication of licenses on products. With regard to those latter features, the Singapore Treaty builds to some extent on the provisions of the Joint Recommendation Concerning Trademark Licenses of 2000.

3. The Joint Recommendation

2.08 The Joint Recommendation Concerning Trademark Licenses of 2000[14] is one of three recommendations adopted jointly by the WIPO General Assembly and the Assembly of the Paris Union between the years 1999 and 2001. The other two Joint Recommendations concern Provisions on the Protection of Well-Known Marks (1999)[15] and Provisions on the Protection of Marks, and Other Industrial Property Rights in Signs, on the Internet (of 2001).[16] Different from the Paris Convention and the Singapore Treaty, the Joint Recommendations are considered soft law instruments and do not foresee procedures for ratification or accession. They have been adopted by the two highest instances of WIPO in the area of industrial property and are thus endorsed by the membership of the Organization as a whole.[17]

4. The Madrid Protocol

2.09 The Madrid System Concerning the International Registration of Marks is based on the Madrid Agreement Concerning the International Registration of Marks of 1891, the Protocol Relating to the Madrid Agreement Concerning the International Registration of Marks of 1989, and the Common Regulations under the Madrid Agreement and the Protocol as in force on 1 January

---

14 WIPO, Pub. No. 835, JOINT RECOMMENDATION CONCERNING TRADEMARK LICENSES (2000) [hereinafter JOINT RECOMMENDATION], *available 14 September 2015 at* http://www.wipo.int/edocs/pubdocs/en/marks/835/pub835.pdf.

15 WIPO, Pub. No. 833, JOINT RECOMMENDATION CONCERNING PROVISIONS ON THE PROTECTION OF WELL-KNOWN MARKS (1999), *available 14 September 2015 at* http://www.wipo.int/edocs/pubdocs/en/marks/833/pub833.pdf.

16 WIPO, Pub. No. 845, JOINT RECOMMENDATION CONCERNING PROVISIONS ON THE PROTECTION OF MARKS, AND OTHER INDUSTRIAL PROPERTY RIGHTS IN SIGNS, ON THE INTERNET (2001), *available 14 September 2015 at* http://www.wipo.int/edocs/pubdocs/en/marks/845/pub845.pdf. *Cf.* J. Christian Wichard, *The Joint Recommendation Concerning Protection of Marks, and Other Industrial Property Rights in Signs, on the Internet, in* INTELLECTUAL PROPERTY AND PRIVATE INTERNATIONAL LAW, 257, 257–64 (Josef Drexl & Annette Kur eds., 2005).

17 For a more general description of soft law as a means of norm creation, see Edward Kwakwa, *Some Comments on Rulemaking at the World Intellectual Property Organization*, 12 DUKE J. COMPARATIVE & INT'L L. 179 (2002) ('[T]he term "soft law" generally is used to refer to certain categories of norms, technically non-binding in nature, that States nonetheless follow in practice or to which they at least subscribe.').

2013.[18] The Madrid Agreement and Protocol provide for the registration of trademarks in the international register kept by WIPO. A trademark thus registered has legal effects in all Contracting Parties to the Madrid Agreement or Protocol designated to that effect in the international application, except the Contracting Party from which the application for registration in the international register originates. The effect of an international registration in so-called designated Contracting Parties is the same as if the mark had been filed directly with the trademark offices of those designated Contracting Parties.[19] Unless the competent authority of a designated Contracting Party refuses – fully or in part – the effect of an international registration on its territory, the trademark right acquired through an international registration is identical in scope and effect with the right issued under a national trademark registration procedure.[20] The international registration thus constitutes a bundle of national and regional trademark rights embodied in the form of one single international record in one language. This centralized record offers numerous possibilities for the pre- and post-registration management of internationally registered trademarks. The Contracting Parties to the Madrid Agreement and the Madrid Protocol are Members of the Madrid Union. On 31 October 2015, the Madrid Protocol entered into force for Algeria, the only Contracting Party of the Madrid Agreement that had not acceded to the Madrid Protocol.[21] With this accession, all transactions under the Madrid System are governed by the Protocol. Therefore, only relevant provisions of the Madrid Protocol and the Common Regulations will be considered.

---

18   Madrid Agreement Concerning the International Registration of Marks, 14 April 1891, 828 U.N.T.S. 389 [hereinafter Madrid Agreement]; Protocol Relating to the Madrid Agreement Concerning the International Registration of Marks, 28 June 1989 [hereinafter Madrid Protocol], *available 14 September 2015 at* http://wipo.int/madrid/en/legal_texts/trtdocs_wo016.html; Common Regulations under the Madrid Agreement Concerning the International Registration of Marks and the Protocol Relating to that Agreement, *in force* 1 January 2015 [hereinafter Common Regulations], *available 14 September 2015 at* http://www.wipo.int/treaties/en/text.jsp?file_id=355319. For the full texts of the Madrid Agreement, the Madrid Protocol and the Common Regulations, as well as a list of the Contracting Parties, visit http://www.wipo.int/madrid/en/legal_texts, *available 14 September 2015.*

19   For a general description of the Madrid System, visit http://www.wipo.int/madrid/en/general, *available 14 September 2015.*

20   *See* Madrid Agreement, *supra* note 18, Article 4; Madrid Protocol, *supra* note 18, Article 4.

21   *See* http://www.wipo.int/madrid/en/news/2015/news_0020.htmlee

C. CHANGE IN OWNERSHIP

1. The Paris Convention

2.10 The provision of the Paris Convention that concerns assignments of trademarks is Article 6*quater*.[22] This article is principally dealing with the question under which conditions a trademark that is owned by one and the same enterprise in different countries can be assigned independently in different countries. The scenario that this provision addresses has to be considered in the context of the evolution of trademark protection within the early days of the Paris Union at the end of the 19th and beginning of the 20th century. Under the earlier versions of the Paris Convention, trademark registration in multiple countries of the Paris Union could be dependent on the existence of the registration for that mark in its country of origin.[23] This principle of dependence of a registration of a trademark registration abroad on the registration in the country considered its country of origin continues to live on in the Madrid Agreement and Protocol in the form of the dependence of the international registration from the registration or application on which the international trademark registration is based.[24] Nevertheless, Article 6 of the Paris Convention, which was introduced by the Revision Conference of Lisbon in 1958, clearly sets forth the principle of independence of trademark registrations, for which the conditions of filing and registrations are determined by the national law of each country of the Paris Union.[25]

---

22   Paris Convention, *supra* note 8, Article 6*quater*:

(1) When, in accordance with the law of a country of the Union, the assignment of a mark is valid only if it takes place at the same time as the transfer of the business or goodwill to which the mark belongs, it shall suffice for the recognition of such validity that the portion of the business or goodwill located in that country be transferred to the assignee, together with the exclusive right to manufacture in the said country, or to sell therein, the goods bearing the mark assigned. (2) The foregoing provision does not impose upon the countries of the Union any obligation to regard as valid the assignment of any mark the use of which by the assignee would, in fact, be of such a nature as to mislead the public, particularly as regards the origin, nature, or essential qualities, of the goods to which the mark is applied.

23   *See* G.H.C. BODENHAUSEN, GUIDE TO THE APPLICATION OF THE PARIS CONVENTION FOR THE PROTECTION OF INDUSTRIAL PROPERTY 87 (WIPO Pub No. 611, 1967), *available 14 September 2015 at* http://www.wipo.int/edocs/pubdocs/en/intproperty/611/wipo_pub_611.pdf.

24   *See* Madrid Protocol, *supra* note 18, Article 6(2).

25   One notable exception to the principle of independence of trademark registrations is contained in Article 6*quinqies*(1) of the Paris Convention, the so-called *telle quelle* clause. It is beyond the ambit of this chapter to describe and comment on Article 6*quinquies*. *See* BODENHAUSEN, *supra* note 23, at 107. Suffice to say that, because of the specific situation at hand where an application for the registration of a trademark in a member of the Paris Union other than the country of origin of the applicant invokes the registration in the country of origin, the trademark is to be accepted for filing and protected *as is* – or *telle quelle* – registered in the country of origin. Since the subsequent application invokes the registration in the country of origin, it is not independent from the latter and, for example, proof of registration of the mark in the country of origin may be requested in countries where this registration is invoked. *See* WIPO, Pub. No. 329, RECORDS OF THE DIPLOMATIC CONFERENCE FOR THE ADOPTION OF A REVISED TRADEMARK LAW TREATY 244 (2006)

2.11 Article 6*quater* does not attempt to regulate whether or not the validity of the assignment of a trademark is dependent on the simultaneous transfer of the business or goodwill to which the trademark belongs, and leaves this question to the national law of the countries of the Paris Union. However, if the law of a country member of the Paris Union requires the transfer of the business to which the trademark belongs or the goodwill attached to that trademark, then the transfer of the relevant business or goodwill must be restricted to the part of the business or goodwill located in the country in which the transfer of the trademark takes place. In other words, the national law of a country member of the Paris Union cannot require the transfer of the business or goodwill attached to a trademark outside its own jurisdiction for the transfer to be recognized domestically.[26]

2.12 Nevertheless, paragraph (2) of Article 6*quater* allows members of the Paris Union to derogate from the obligation to allow the assignment of trademarks – always under the condition mentioned in the previous paragraph – if such an assignment would be likely to mislead the public. Such a situation could be envisaged, for example in situations where a trademark that is registered for a number of goods or services[27] is transferred only partially and in respect of goods or services that are either identical or similar to those for which the assignor retains rights.[28]

2.13 The question as to the entitlement of trademark owners to assign their trademarks independently from the associated business or goodwill is also addressed in TRIPS Article 21, stating explicitly that 'the owner of a trademark shall have the right to assign the trademark with or without the

---

[hereinafter RECORDS OF TLT], *available* 14 September 2015 *at* http://www.wipo.int/edocs/pubdocs/en/marks/329/wipo_pub_329.pdf.

26 BODENHAUSEN, *supra* note 23, at 105.

27 Article 6*quater* is only applicable to trademarks registered for goods, but not trademarks registered for services. With the exception of the general provision of Article 6*sexies* providing for an undertaking of members of the Paris Union to protect service marks without an obligation to register service marks, provisions of the Paris Convention concerning marks are applicable to marks registered for goods, but not to marks registered for services. Bearing in mind the ever increasing importance of trade in services today this situation is definitively anachronistic. According to the OECD, for example, the service industry is the largest sector within domestic economies of the OECD countries (*see Services Trade*, OECD, *available* 14 September 2015 *at* http://www.oecd.org/trade/servicestrade.htm). *See also* 2013 WORLD IP REPORT, *supra* note 5, at 53, according to which the service sector now accounts for about 60–70% of economic activity in high income countries. This is remedied partially in TRIPS, which provides for the explicit application of certain provisions of the Paris Convention concerning trademarks for products to service marks (in particular TRIPS Article 16.2 making Article 6*bis* of the Paris Convention applicable to service marks, and TRIPS 62.3 making Article 4 of the Paris Convention on Convention Priority applicable to Service Marks). The Singapore Treaty as well as the TLT go further in this respect, as they provide for a general obligation for Contracting Parties to register service marks and to apply to such marks the provisions of the Paris Convention which concern trademarks. *See* Singapore Treaty, *supra* note 11, Article 16; TLT, *supra* note 12, Article 16.

28 BODENHAUSEN, *supra* note 23, at 106.

transfer of the business to which the trademark belongs'. It has been pointed out that the omission of a reference to 'goodwill' along with the relevant business, as it appears in Article 6*quater* of the Paris Convention, may not have been completely unintentional.[29] Thus, Members of the WTO may require the transfer of the goodwill attached to a trademark as a condition for accepting the assignment of the trademark.

2. The TLT and Singapore Treaty

2.14 Later adopted norms under the aegis of WIPO, such as the TLT 1994 and the Singapore Treaty, deal with the conditions for requesting the recordal of assignments in trademark registers, without attempting to regulate the substantive law underlying this type of property transfer.

2.15 Article 11 of the Singapore Treaty provides for the details of a request for the recordal of a change in ownership of a trademark registration. It is recalled that the Singapore Treaty does not establish rights for individuals in Contracting Parties. Rather, it creates an obligation for Contracting Parties to adapt their national legislation so as to conform with the standards applicable under the Treaty. In the case of the Article concerning the recordal of changes in ownership, Contracting Parties have to implement the relevant provision into national law respecting the boundaries inherent to that norm, in particular as concerns the maximum list of permitted indications and supporting documents.

2.16 The basic concept behind this provision, as with the other provisions of this type contained in the Singapore Treaty, is the establishment of an exhaustive list of indications and supporting documentary evidence that a trademark office may require from a party who requests the recordal of a change in ownership of a registration. This inventory of allowed requirements is 'capped' by a provision prohibiting expressly Contracting Parties to go beyond the stipulated maximum and 'blacklisting' certain types of information, which, under no circumstances can be required as part of the request for recordal of the assignment.[30]

---

[29] *See* DANIEL GERVAIS, THE TRIPS AGREEMENT: DRAFTING HISTORY AND ANALYSIS 356 (4th ed. 2012).

[30] The general principle underlying this approach to norm development is to create international harmonization in trademark office procedures through the definition of maximum standards. Since Contracting Parties are not allowed to go beyond these procedural maximum standards, a certain degree of uniformity is introduced among the national (and regional) laws of Contracting Parties, although Contracting Parties are free to require less than what is provided for in the Treaty.

C. CHANGE IN OWNERSHIP

2.17 As a general rule, Article 11 of the Singapore Treaty allows the assignor (referred to as 'the holder') as well as the assignee (referred to as 'the new holder') to present a request for the recordal of a change in ownership.[31] The Article then goes on and identifies different grounds for the assignment, namely a contract,[32] a merger,[33] or 'another ground'.[34] Depending on the basis for the transaction, Article 11 of the TLT envisages different kinds of documentary evidence which the requesting party – sometimes at its own choice – has to file with the Office. Where the change of ownership is based on a contract, the requesting party has the choice to either submit a copy of that contract, certified by a notary public or other public authority as being in conformity with the original contract; or an extract of the contract showing the change in ownership, again certified as being a true extract of the contract; or an uncertified certificate of transfer drawn up in accordance with a model provided for by the Regulations under the Singapore Treaty and signed by both the assignor and the assignee; or an uncertified transfer document drawn up in accordance with a model provided for the Regulations under the Singapore Treaty and signed by the assignor and the assignee.[35]

2.18 If the change in ownership results from a merger, the Singapore Treaty provides that a trademark office may require the requesting party to file the copy of an official document evidencing the merger, such as an extract from a register of commerce, and that such a document be certified by either the issuing authority or by a notary public or other competent public authority, as being in conformity with the original document.[36]

2.19 Finally, in case the change of ownership results from a ground of law other than a contract or a merger, such as, for example, from operation of law or a court decision, the trademark office may again require the requesting party to file the copy of an official document evidencing the change of ownership, and that such a document be certified by either the issuing authority or by a notary public or other competent public authority, as being in conformity with the original.[37]

2.20 Article 11(4) of the Singapore Treaty puts a cap on the various elements of information and documents that a trademark office is allowed to require as

---

31 Singapore Treaty, *supra* note 11, Article 11(1)(a).
32 *Id.* at Article 11(1)(b).
33 *Id.* at Article 11(1)(c).
34 *Id.* at Article 11(1)(e).
35 *Id.* at 11(b)(i)–(iv); Model International Forms Nos. 5, 6 under the Singapore Treaty.
36 Singapore Treaty, *supra* note 11, Article 11(1)(c).
37 *Id.* at Article 11(1)(e).

Chapter 2 TRADEMARK TRANSACTIONS AND THE NORMATIVE FRAMEWORK OF THE WIPO

part of a request for an assignment and thus renders the list of elements under that provision exhaustive. It also singles out or 'blacklists' four types of indications or documents, which never have to be produced as part of a request for recordal of an assignment. Those are a certificate of or an extract from a register of commerce (with the exception of such an extract evidencing a merger); an indication of the assignee's carrying out of an industrial or commercial activity or evidence to that effect; an indication of the assignee's carrying on an activity corresponding to the goods or services in respect of which the trademark was assigned, as well as evidence to either effect; and an indication that the assignor transferred entirely or in part its business or the relevant goodwill to the new owner as well as evidence to this effect.[38]

2.21 The main thrust that emerges from those detailed provisions is to simplify and streamline the administrative recordal procedure of trademark assignments by eliminating the obligation for requesting parties to produce certain forms of documentary evidence as part of such procedures. In doing so, the negotiators of the TLT 1994[39] and the Singapore Treaty of 2006 had to strike a balance between the interests of brand industries to be able to record assignments in a swift and straightforward manner, often in multiple jurisdictions, without having to comply with voluminous document validation and certification procedures, and the interest of the public in reliable public registries as well as in the prevention of fraud.

2.22 Looking at the various types of documentary evidence permitted by Article 11 of the Singapore Treaty, the requirement of certification, by a notary public or other competent public authority, of certain types of documents – or the absence of such a requirement, as the case may be – stands out. Thus, assignments based on contracts can be recorded in the register upon the presentation of an uncertified certificate of transfer or an uncertified transfer document, as long as they are signed by both the assignor and the assignee. However, where the request for the recordal of a transfer of ownership is based on a merger or an operation of law, the presentation of documents certified by a notary public or another competent public authority as being in conformity with the original can be required.

2.23 Among the various requirements that requests for the recordal of changes of ownership – and for that matter of other types of requests for recordals in trademark registers – have to comply with are the notarization or certification of legal documents. If the transfer of rights in trademarks concerns multiple

---

38 *Id.* at Article 11(3).
39 Article 11 of the Singapore Treaty reproduces in essence Article 11 of the TLT of 1994.

jurisdictions, the production of these types of certifications, which often have to be performed repeatedly, can bind considerable administrative and financial resources. For that reason, the form of documentary evidence to be produced in support of requests for the recordal of transactions other than changes in ownership, in particular the recordal of licenses and the recordal of restrictions of the right to dispose of a trademark, will be looked at in further detail below.

Independent from the issue whether or not and if yes, what type of certified documents need to accompany requests for the recordal of a change in ownership in application of Article 11 of the Singapore Treaty, Article 11(4)(iv) does prevent offices of Contracting Parties to require an indication that the assignor has transferred entirely or in part its business or the relevant goodwill to the assignee, as well as the furnishing of evidence to either effect. The Records of the 2006 Singapore Diplomatic Conference make it clear that this provision is not intended to deal with the validity of the transfer of a mark in relation to the transfer or assignment of the relevant business or goodwill.[40] Nevertheless, the clear prohibition to require such an indication as part of the recordal of a trademark assignment procedure can be interpreted as willingness of the Diplomatic Conference to go beyond TRIPS Article 21 by facilitating the assignment of trademarks without simultaneous transfer of part of the business or the relevant goodwill. 2.24

3. The Madrid System

The ownership of trademarks internationally registered under the Madrid System may be transferred, and it is indeed one of the big advantages of the Madrid System that this procedure can be completed in one single administrative act with legal effect for as many Contracting Parties as the international registration has effect.[41] Probably the most important restriction to the assignments of international trademarks under the Madrid System is that such trademarks can only be validly transferred to persons who are entitled, by virtue of Article 1(2) of the Madrid Agreement and Article 2(1) of the Madrid 2.25

---

40 RECORDS OF TLT, *supra* note 25, at 254.
41 Article 9 of the Madrid Protocol reads:
> At the request of the person in whose name the international registration stands, or at the request of an interested Office made ex officio or at the request of an interested person, the International Bureau shall record in the International Register any change in the ownership of that registration, in respect of all or some of the Contracting Parties in whose territories the said registration has effect and in respect of all or some of the goods and services listed in the registration, provided that the new holder is a person who, under Article 2(1), is entitled to file international applications.

Protocol, to be holders of international registrations.[42] This limitation stems from the overriding principle of the Madrid Agreement and Protocol to limit access to the Madrid System to parties that have a 'connection' to a Contracting Party and, thus, entitlement to use the Madrid System.[43] The exclusion of nationals from non-Contracting Parties or applicants not having their domicile or an establishment in a Contracting Party from the use of the Madrid System, results in the prevention of such persons from using the Madrid System and from benefiting from its advantages. In turn, this creates an incentive for States that are not party to the System to adhere to it.

2.26 Another important feature of the change in ownership procedure for international registrations is that the new holder of the international registration (or assignee) has to derive its entitlement to use the System from the same Treaty (Agreement of Protocol) as the one under which a given Contracting Party is designated – failing which the assignment cannot be recorded for that Contracting Party.[44] This latter restriction was of greater significance at a time when the number of Contracting Parties that were only bound by one Treaty (that is, either the Agreement or the Protocol) was important. However, given that at the time of writing all members but one of the Madrid System are bound by the Madrid Protocol, this specificity has already lost its relevance to a very large extent.

2.27 Assignments of international registrations can be recorded for one or several designated Contracting Parties in respect of some or all goods and services.[45] In practical terms, a request for assignment has to be presented to the International Bureau of WIPO on an official form designed to that effect by either the holder of the international registration (assignor) or the office of the Contracting Party of the holder (which is the office of the Contracting Party

---

42 *See* Madrid Protocol, *supra* note 18, Article 9; Madrid Agreement, *supra* note 18, Article 9*bis*(2). ('No transfer of a mark registered in the International Register for the benefit of a person who is not entitled to file an international mark shall be recorded.')
43 Entitlement to use the Madrid System derives from either having the nationality of one of the Contracting Parties, being domiciled in or having a real and effective industrial or commercial establishment in a Contracting Party. Under the Madrid Protocol Article 2(1), any of the three points of attachment giving entitlement to use the system can be invoked at the choice of the applicant. The Madrid Agreement Articles 1(2) and (3) provide for a hierarchy of the three points of attachment and obliges an applicant who has several such points of attachment in different Contracting Parties, for example the nationality of one and a commercial establishment in another, to invoke its nationality and, thus, file an international application with the office of the Contracting Party of which it is a national rather than with the office of the Contracting Party in which it has a commercial establishment. This so-called 'cascade' principle, however, is applicable to the Madrid Agreement only and given that, as of 31 October 2015, all members of the Madrid system are bound by the Madrid Protocol, is practically no longer applicable and more of historic significance.
44 Common Regulations, *supra* note 18, Rule 25(3).
45 Madrid Protocol, *supra* note 18, Article 9.

from which the holder derives its entitlement to use the Madrid System).[46] However, it is also possible for the transferee to present the request for the recordal of a change in ownership through the office of the Contracting Party from which it derives the entitlement to use the Madrid System – which is not necessarily the same Contracting Party as the Contracting Party of the assignor.[47]

The request for the recordal of a change of ownership does not have to be certified or notarized, nor need it be accompanied by any form of supporting document. If the request is presented by the holder of the international registration, the signature of the holder is sufficient. Where it is presented by an office, the request must be signed by the office – which in turn may request the signature of the holder, but does not have to. Compared to many national procedures and the international norms for such procedures as defined by the Singapore Treaty, the requirements for the recordal of a change of ownership of an international registration are of disarming simplicity. Best use of such simplicity is made where the holder of the international registration requests itself the recordal of the change in ownership. In case the request is presented through an office of a Contracting Party, and due to the absence of specific rules for that situation, that office may require the production of specific documents before it will sign the request for recordal a change of ownership – although the relevant provisions under the Madrid Protocol and the Common Regulations are silent on that matter. **2.28**

Following the recordal of a change of ownership, the International Bureau of WIPO will notify all designated Contracting Parties concerned, which in turn may declare that a change in ownership has no effect in their territory. Such declaration must be made within 18 months from the date of sending the notification of the recorded change in ownership. In case such a declaration is made, the change in ownership will not be recorded for the Contracting Party that refused the validity of the change and the registration will remain in the name of the assignor.[48] **2.29**

---

46 *Madrid Form MM5*, WIPO, *available 14 September 2015 at* http://www.wipo.int/madrid/en/forms.
47 Common Regulations, *supra* note 18, Rule 25(b).
48 *Id.* at Rule 27(4).

D. LICENSES

1. The Singapore Treaty and Joint Recommendation

2.30 The Singapore Treaty deals with trademark licenses from two different perspectives. One concerns the administrative requirements defined by the Treaty for trademark office procedures concerning the recordal of trademark licenses. The other is the prescription of certain legal effects attached to the recordal – or non-recordal – as the case may be, of trademark licenses.

2.31 As regards the former aspect, Articles 17 and 18 of the Singapore Treaty prescribe procedural details concerning requests for the recordal of a license (Article 17) and requests for the amendment or cancellation of the recordal of a license (Article 18). Those two articles, together with Article 19 (effects of the non-recordal of a license) and Article 20 (indication of the license) were adopted by the Diplomatic Conference and were originally not part of the TLT 1994. The former two provisions follow very closely the structure and logic of similar provisions concerning the recordal of various changes in the trademark registers as prescribed in the TLT 1994 and the Singapore Treaty. The latter two provisions are of a more substantive legal nature. All four articles are based on provisions adopted by the Assembly of the Paris Union and the WIPO General Assembly in the form of the Joint Recommendation Concerning Trademark Licenses of 2000.

2.32 As regards the request for the recordal of a license, Article 17 of the Singapore Treaty follows the same approach as Article 11. It defines a maximum list of elements or indications which can be required by Contracting Parties to the Treaty. Moreover, the provision 'blacklists' in an exemplary manner certain formal requirements which cannot be demanded as part of a request for the recordal of a license.

2.33 Different from Article 11 on the recordal of a change in ownership, the maximum list is contained in Rule 10 of the Regulations under the Singapore Treaty. Dealing with those details in the Regulations rather than in the Treaty itself introduces a degree of flexibility, as the Regulations can be amended by a decision of the Assembly of the Singapore Treaty Assembly.[49] Rule 10(1)(a) sets out in detail the various indications that may be required in a request for the recordal of a license. They are pretty much of a standard nature and will not be commented upon. Again, attention is drawn to the fact that the catalogue of indications contained in Rule 10(1)(a) is a maximum list. In other

---

49   Singapore Treaty, *supra* note 11, Article 23(2)(ii).

words, offices of Contracting Parties are allowed to require the production of all those indications, but are not required to do so, and can require fewer than all indications.

Probably of greater interest in this context is the nature of the supporting documents which offices of Contracting Parties are allowed to request from parties filing for the recordal of a license. In case a Contracting Party requires such supporting documents, the requesting party has the choice of either producing an extract of the license contract indicating the parties and the rights being licensed, certified by a notary public or any other competent public authority as being a true extract of the contract;[50] or an uncertified statement of license, the content of which corresponds to the statement of license Form provided for in the Regulations under the Singapore Treaty and signed by both the licensor and the licensee.[51] Most notably, an office of a Contracting Party must not request the presentation of an entire licensing contract as part of the request for the recordal of a license. This is explicitly stipulated by Article 17(4), which 'blacklists' certain types of indication that must not be requested by an office as part of the recordal procedure. Those are, in particular, the registration certificate of the mark which is the subject of the license, the license contract or a translation of it, and an indication of the financial terms of the license contract.[52] An identical provision is already contained in the 2000 Joint Recommendation Concerning Trademark Licenses. It is noteworthy that the 2006 Diplomatic Conference for the adoption of the Singapore Treaty added a subparagraph (b) to Article 17(4), stating that the 'blacklist' in Article 17(4)(a) is without prejudice to any obligations existing under the law of a Contracting Party concerning the disclosure of information for purposes other than the recordal of the license in the register of marks. The Records of the Singapore Diplomatic Conference state in this context that this provision makes it clear that Article 17(4)(a) does not prevent authorities of Contracting Parties other than trademark registration offices from requiring information in accordance with the applicable law, and cites as examples of such authorities tax authorities or authorities establishing statistics.[53]

2.34

Concerning requests for the cancellation or amendment of the recordal of a license, Article 18 of the Singapore Treaty refers *mutatis mutandis* to the provision applicable to the request concerning the recordal of a license. Regarding the necessary documentation supporting such a request, Singapore

2.35

---

50   *Id.* at Rule 10(2)(a)(i).
51   *Id.* at Rule 10(2)(a)(ii).
52   *Id.* at Article 17(4)(a)(i)–(iii).
53   RECORDS OF TLT, *supra* note 25, at 260.

Rule 10(3) and (4) is less detailed than the equivalent Rule concerning the request for the recordal of a license and leaves a requesting party the choice to accompany such a request by either a document substantiating the requested amendment or cancellation (without further specifying the nature of such a document);[54] or an uncertified statement of amendment or cancellation of licenses using the forms provided in the Rules for that purpose.[55]

2.36 In addition to regulating the details of requests for the recordal of licenses as well as their amendment and cancellation, the 2000 Joint Recommendation and the Singapore Treaty contain provisions regarding the effects of the non-recordal of a license, the use of a mark by persons other than the registered holder, and the indication of the license.

2.37 Article 19(1) (as well as Article 4(1) of the Joint Recommendation) set out the general principle that the non-recordal of a license – even where recordal is compulsory – should not affect the validity of the trademark registration itself or the protection of that mark. In that way, the validity and protection of the registered trademark are separated from the question of whether or not the license has to be registered with the trademark office.[56] This provision, however, is without prejudice to the effects the non-recordal of a license may have on the validity of the license in Contracting Parties where such a recordal is mandatory.

2.38 Countries that provide for the recordal of trademark licenses often require that a trademark license be recorded as a condition for the licensee to initiate infringement procedures in its own name. The Singapore Treaty as well as the Joint Recommendation do not derogate from this principle. However, they stipulate a provision in favour of the non-registered licensee in that they provide that the recordal of the license shall not be a condition for the licensee to join infringement procedures initiated by the owner of the trademark (where such a possibility exists) and to obtain damages resulting from an infringement of the mark which is the subject of the license.[57] The rationale that underlies these two provisions is that an infringer should not benefit from the omission of an administrative procedure, namely the recordal of the trademark license, in particular in situations where the economic damage accrues with the licensee and the infringer will care very little whether the infringement concerns a trademark that was legitimately used by a non-registered user. However, it should be noted that both provisions do not

---

54 Singapore Treaty, *supra* note 11, Rules 10(3)(a)(i), 10(4)(i).
55 *Id.* at Rules 10(3)(a)(ii), 10(4)(ii).
56 RECORDS OF TLT, *supra* note 25, at 260.
57 Singapore Treaty, *supra* note 11, Article 19(2); JOINT RECOMMENDATION, *supra* note 14, Article 4(2).

stipulate an entitlement for unregistered trademark licensees to initiate infringement proceedings in their own name in jurisdictions where this is subject to the recordal of the license.

2.39 It should also be mentioned that this provision was not unanimously acceptable to the Paris Union Assembly and the General Assembly of WIPO adopting the Joint Recommendation, as well as to the Singapore Diplomatic Conference, as all bodies expressed reservations to that provision.[58]

2.40 Another important question that arises out of the use of a trademark by a licensee is to determine whether such use will be considered to accrue to the registered holder of the trademark and thus have the effect to maintain the registration. In this respect, reference can be made to Article 5(C)(1) of the Paris Convention, which prescribes that trademark registrations can only be cancelled for non-use (in countries in which use of the trademark is compulsory) after 'a reasonable period' and only if the non-use cannot be justified.[59] TRIPS Article 19.1 also addresses the issue of use of the trademark and stipulates a period of at least three years of permissible non-use together with examples of valid reasons for non-use.[60]

2.41 TRIPS Article 19.2 deals with the issue of use of a trademark by a person other than the owner and explicitly recognizes such use as use of the trademark for maintaining the registration if that use is subject to the control of its owner. Such control is most regularly exercised in the form of a license agreement. This provision can be contrasted to Joint Recommendation Article 5, which goes one important step further in this regard in that it stipulates that use of a mark by a person other than the holder shall be deemed to constitute use by the holder if such use is made with the holder's consent. Article 5 of the Joint Recommendation is a very forward looking and progressive provision, as it decouples the use of a trademark by a person other than the registered owner from a specific requirement to control such a use.[61] According to the Explanatory Notes to Article 5 of the Joint Recommendation the effect of this provision is that, whenever the question of use becomes relevant, any use of a mark by any person other than the holder should be considered to be use by the holder, as long as the latter consents to such a use. Such third-party use

---

58 Article 4(2)(b) of the Joint Recommendation states that if Article 4(2)(a) is not compatible with the national law of a Member State, that subparagraph shall not apply in respect of that Member State. Singapore Treaty Article 29(4) allows Contracting Parties to make a reservation in respect of Article 19(2) of the Treaty.
59 Paris Convention, *supra* note 8, Article 5(C)(1).
60 TRIPS, *supra* note 10, Article 19.1.
61 For example through specific quality control clauses in a licensing agreement.

may go beyond the use that is generally required for maintaining the trademark registration, and can become relevant in the context of use of the trademark that is necessary in order for the trademark to acquire distinctive character or well-known mark status. Nevertheless, this provision does not address the validity of licensing agreements and the question whether or not such agreements need to contain quality control clauses for their validity.[62]

2.42   In contrast to Joint Recommendation Article 5, Article 19(3) of the Singapore Treaty is more limited and simply prevents Contracting Parties from requiring the recordal of a license as a condition for the use of the trademark by the licensee to accrue to the licensor in proceedings relating to the acquisition, maintenance and enforcement of the trademark.[63] In other words, this provision is more circumscribed than the parallel provision in the Joint Recommendation, as it limits the benefit of non-recorded trademark use to such use by the licensee (as opposed to any person other than the holder) and to situations concerning the acquisition, maintenance and enforcement of the trademark.[64]

2.43   Finally, Joint Recommendation Article 6 and Article 20 of the Singapore Treaty deal with the indication of a license. Both provisions are identical and stipulate that the non-compliance with a requirement to indicate a trademark license in jurisdictions where such obligations exist shall not affect the validity of the registration of the licensed trademark and shall be without prejudice to the possibility of the licensee to join infringement proceedings initiated by the licensor, where such a possibility exists. These provisions[65] leave it in essence to the applicable law to determine whether or not goods which are commercialized under a trademark license have to indicate that fact on their packaging. Nevertheless, non-compliance with such an obligation – where it exists – should not affect the validity of the trademark that is the subject of the license.

2. The Madrid System

2.44   The possibility of recording licenses granted for international trademark registration is not foreseen directly by the Madrid Protocol but emanates from the Common Regulations.[66] This possibility is in line with the logic of the Madrid System, namely that an international registration represents a bundle of national rights in Contracting Parties and that those individual national

---

62   *See* JOINT RECOMMENDATION, *supra* note 14, at 35.
63   Singapore Treaty, *supra* note 11, Article 19(3).
64   *Id.*
65   JOINT RECOMMENDATION, *supra* note 14, at 37.
66   *See* Common Regulations, *supra* note 18, Rule 20*bis*.

rights can be managed, that is, renewed, transferred, etc., through one administrative act to be completed with the International Bureau of WIPO.

2.45 The request for the recordal of a license can be filed by the holder of the international registration (licensor) or – if this is possible under the law of the relevant Contracting Party – through the office of the Contracting Party of the holder or the office of a Contracting Party in respect of which a license is granted. The request must be filed on an official form.[67] The form needs to be signed either by the holder of the international registration (the licensor) or, where the form is filed via one of the above-mentioned offices, by that office. As with requests for the recordal of a change in ownership of the international registration, the request for the recordal of a license does not have to be accompanied by any form of supporting documents, such as copies of the licensing agreement, and the International Bureau will disregard such documents, if submitted.

2.46 The Common Regulations do not explicitly regulate the effect of the recordal of a license for an international registration. However, Common Regulation 20*bis* provides for two types of declarations by Contracting Parties to the effect that the recordal of a license will have no effect. The first is available for Contracting Parties whose law does not provide for the recordal of a license – and therefore the recordal of a license in the international register has no effect.[68] The second type of declaration can be made by Contracting Parties whose law provides for the recordal of a license, but for which the recordal of a license in the international register shall not produce any effect. However, the latter declaration can only be made by a Contracting Party prior to the date on which it becomes bound by the Madrid Protocol – but not thereafter.[69]

E. RESTRICTIONS OF THE RIGHT OF DISPOSAL

2.47 Trademark rights are property rights that exist independently from the businesses that use them although, as was described above, it could be argued

---

67 *Madrid Form MM13*, WIPO, *available 14 September 2015 at* http://www.wipo.int/madrid/en/forms.
68 Common Regulations, *supra* note 18, Rule 20*bis*(6)(a). Australia, Germany and New Zealand have made such a declaration.
69 *Id.* at Rule 20*bis*(6)(b). China, Colombia, Georgia, Greece, India, Japan, Kyrgyzstan, Lithuania, Mexico, the Republic of Korea, the Republic of Moldova, the Russian Federation and Singapore have made a declaration that their respective laws provide for the recordal of a license, but that the recordal of a license in the international register shall not have effect in their territories. In other words, the international recordal will not substitute the necessity – where it exists – to record the license in a national register (also if it concerns an international trademark registration).

that they are intrinsically linked to the goodwill of the relevant business.[70] This opens the possibility of using trademarks as collateral for securing financial transactions.[71] If the trademark is registered, it makes sense to record the fact that this trademark is used as collateral in order to prevent good faith acquisition by a third party. The WIPO legal instruments under consideration do not provide for general norms concerning the recordal of restrictions of the right of the holder of the trademark registration to dispose of the registered trademark, and both the TLT 1994 and the Singapore Treaty of 2006 are silent on this matter.

2.48 Nevertheless, the Common Regulations under the Madrid Agreement and Protocol contain a Rule stipulating a procedure for the recordal of a restriction of the holder's right to dispose of the international registration.[72]

2.49 Contrary to other requests for the recordal of changes in the international register, Common Regulation Rule 20 does not prescribe the use of a form for the purpose of filing such a request. Common Regulation Rule 20(1) merely offers the possibility for the holder of an international registration, or the office of the Contracting Party of the holder, to inform the International Bureau of the fact that the right of the holder to dispose of the international registration has been restricted.[73] Owing to the nature of an international registration as a bundle of national rights, this restriction may be expressed in respect of one or several designated Contracting Parties. Likewise, this 'information' can be furnished by the office of a designated Contracting Party. The option to have this information forwarded by an office of a Contracting Party rather than by the holder may be interesting in cases where security rights in an internationally registered trademark were acquired by a third party, for example a creditor, but the holder of the registration is unable or unwilling to inform the International Bureau accordingly.[74]

2.50 According to Common Regulation Rule 20(3), the International Bureau records the information communicated and informs the holder, the office of the Contracting Party of the holder and the offices of the Contracting Parties concerned by the restriction. The restriction of the holder's right of disposal can be withdrawn and the withdrawal is recorded by the International Bureau

---

70 *See* DANIEL GERVAIS, THE TRIPS AGREEMENT: DRAFTING HISTORY AND ANALYSIS 356 (4th ed. 2012).
71 *See generally* UN, Pub. No. E.11.V.6, *UNCITRAL Legislative Guide on Secured Transactions, Supplement on Security Rights in IP*.
72 Common Regulations, *supra* note 18, Rule 20.
73 *Id.* Rule 20(1).
74 *Id.*

if information to that effect is communicated by the same party that had communicated the information concerning the restriction in the first place.[75]

2.51 As mentioned above, Common Regulation Rule 20 does not require the use of a form and the relevant information describing the fact that the holder's right to dispose of the international registration is to be furnished in the form of a summary statement of the main facts concerning the restriction.[76] In particular, the International Bureau does not require any documentary evidence supporting the restriction of the right. Nevertheless, the International Bureau offers an unofficial form for communicating information concerning the restriction of rights in the international registration (Form MM 19).[77]

2.52 The Common Regulations are entirely silent on the effect of the recordal of the restriction of the holder's right of disposal. In the absence of any provision to that effect, the legal effect of such a recordal is to be determined under the national law of the Contracting Party or Parties concerned.

F. CONCLUSION

2.53 The 2013 World Intellectual Property Report offers some interesting insights into brands and branding in a modern economy.[78] Against this background, the legal rules for transactions in trademarks (as the main category of IP rights that are underlying brands) gain increasing importance. This is well understood by the World Intellectual Property Organization, which has provided the institutional setting to develop the international legal framework applicable to trademark transactions. If there is one common thread across the body of WIPO norms in that area (and in related fields of industrial property),[79] it is the attempt to render the administrative procedures for trademark transactions simpler and more straightforward – in particular through abolishing requirements for the standard production of supporting documentation and the legalization or notarization of such documents or their translations.

---

75 *Id.* Rule 20(2).
76 *Id.* Rule 20(1)(c).
77 *Madrid Form MM19*, WIPO, *available 14 September 2015 at* http://www.wipo.int/madrid/en/forms.
78 *See, e.g.*, 2013 WORLD IP REPORT, *supra* note 5, (estimating that global branding investments by companies stood at US$466 billion in 2011).
79 *See, e.g.*, Treaty Supplementing the Paris Convention for the Protection of Industrial Property as far as Patents Are Concerned, WIPO Doc. PLT/DC/3, Rules 16–17 (21 December 1990), *available 14 September 2015 at* http://www.wipo.int/treaties/en/text.jsp?file_id=289512.

2.54 In doing so, a balance has to be struck between the interest of trademark owners in modern, lean and predictable administrative procedures on the one hand, and the public interest in maintaining reliable public records for the ownership of trademarks and the rights granted by the owners of trademarks to third parties.

2.55 Work in technical WIPO Committees very often reveals a certain hesitation by Member States to depart from traditional concepts of maintaining public records, and the relevant provisions of the Singapore Treaty described above provide good examples for the type of compromise that can be reached in negotiations in the multilateral arena.

2.56 This stands in contrast with the respective rules of the Madrid System for recording transactions in international trademark registrations, which are regularly more lenient and less cumbersome – in particular as regards the production of supporting documentation – than corresponding national procedures in many of its Member States. Despite the important number of such recordals,[80] the procedure does not appear to have given rise to concern or criticism.

2.57 The vast majority of rules presented in this chapter concern administrative recordal procedures. While they may have in themselves an important effect on the substantive rights that can depend on the completion of such procedures, they do not purport – save some exceptions[81] – to regulate applicable substantive national law. In view of the ever increasing importance of trademark transactions as illustrated by the WIPO 2013 World IP Report, it can be argued that this field of law would benefit from further study and work by WIPO.

---

80 The yearly number of recorded changes in ownership in the Madrid Register is around 14,000 for the years 2009 to 2013. *See General Statistics*, WIPO, *available 14 September 2015 at* http://www.wipo.int/madrid/en/statistics/general_stats.jsp.

81 *See, e.g.*, Singapore Treaty, *supra* note 11, Articles 19–20.

Section B

STRATEGIC CONSIDERATIONS

3

LICENSING COMMERCIAL VALUE: FROM COPYRIGHT TO TRADEMARKS AND BACK

Jane C. Ginsburg[*]

A. INTRODUCTION	3.01	TRADEMARK CLAIMANT WAS NOT ORIGINALLY OR IS NO LONGER THE COPYRIGHT OWNER	3.19
B. WHEN THE TRADEMARK OWNER IS NO LONGER A COPYRIGHT OWNER: TRADEMARK LICENSING IN THE SHADOW OF *DASTAR*	3.05	1. Adopting copyright-expired characters	3.19
1. Distinguishing trademark goodwill from works of authorship	3.07	2. Reversion of copyright in a trademarked character	3.25
2. Trademark and copyright: in fact inseparable?	3.11	D. WHEN THE TRADEMARK OWNER BECOMES A COPYRIGHT OWNER: TRADEMARKS AS COPYRIGHTED WORKS	3.30
3. Keeping characters out of the copyright public domain: the impact on trademarks	3.16		
C. EXPLOITING CHARACTERS WHEN THE		E. CONCLUSION	3.39

A. INTRODUCTION

Every U.S. intellectual property practitioner knows that copyright and trademarks often overlap, particularly in visual characters. The same figure may qualify as a pictorial, graphic or sculptural work on the one hand, and as a registered (or at least used) trademark on the other. The two rights, though resting on distinct foundations,[1] tend to be licensed together.[2] Trademarks **3.01**

---

[*] Jane C. Ginsburg, Morton L. Janklow Professor of Literary and Artistic Property Law, Columbia University School of Law. Many thanks to William M. Borchard, Esq., and for research assistance to Matthew Weiss, Columbia Law School class of 2015 and to Alisha Turak, Columbia Law School class of 2014.

[1] WILLIAM M. BORCHARD, A TRADEMARK IS NOT A COPYRIGHT OR A PATENT (2013), *available* 14 September 2015 *at* http://www.cll.com/clientuploads/pdfs/2013%20WMB%20PTC%20Article.pdf; 1 J. THOMAS MCCARTHY, MCCARTHY ON TRADEMARKS AND UNFAIR COMPETITION § 6:5.A (4th ed. 2014) ('The attorney must keep separate in his or her own mind the distinctions between patent, trademark and copyright law. One must be familiar with the similarities and the differences … Complex? Perhaps, but it is the attorney's stock in trade at least to be aware of the possibilities of all kinds of legal protection and the pros and cons of each.').

[2] *See, e.g.*, Craig S. Mende & Belinda Isaac, *When Copyright and Trademark Rights Overlap*, *in* OVERLAPPING INTELLECTUAL PROPERTY RIGHTS para. 7.95 (Neil Wilkof & Shamnad Basheer eds., 2012). For an example of licensing of copyright and trademark rights in Disney characters, see Exhibit 4.3, Consumer

symbolize the goodwill of the producer, and are protected insofar as copying that symbol is likely to confuse consumers as to the source or approval of the goods or services in connection with which the mark is used.[3] For famous marks, the dilution action grants a right against uses of the mark that are likely to 'blur' or 'tarnish' the distinctiveness of the mark, even in the absence of confusion.[4] In either event, the object of protection is the producer's goodwill (in theory, as a proxy for consumer source identification), not (again, in theory) the mark *per se*. Copyright, by contrast, is a right 'in gross' allowing its owner to prohibit the copying of the work without regard to source confusion.[5] Copyright protects the work of authorship itself, not the identification of that work with a single, if anonymous, source of origin.[6] Pursuant to the Constitutional grant to Congress of power to secure authors' exclusive rights 'for limited times',[7] copyright lasts for a term of years; trademarks are protected for so long as they continue to represent a single producer's goodwill. Subject to that prerequisite, registered trademarks may be renewed indefinitely.[8]

3.02 The durational disparity prompts the question whether a trademark owner may effectively perpetuate the life of the copyright in, and thus control the

---

Products License – Disney (4 June 2002), *available 14 September 2015 at* http://www.sec.gov/Archives/edgar/data/55698/000095013502005035/b44497fyexv4w3.txt. By the same token, unauthorized reproduction of a copyrighted work may also violate trademark rights, *see, e.g.* Williams v. Roberto Cavalli S.p.A, 113 U.S.P.Q.2d (BNA) 1944 (C.D. Cal. 2015) (rejecting defense that street artists' claim of copyright infringement by fashion designer's copying of their designs precluded any trademark action regarding the alleged source-identifying features of the designs):

> Moving Defendants point to no authority that supports their proposition that a design may not be protected by both the Lanham Act and copyright law. In fact, caselaw supports to the opposite conclusion. For example, in Bach v. Forever Living Products U.S., Inc., 473 F. Supp. 2d 1110, 1114 (W.D. Wash. 2007), creators of a popular book brought both a copyright infringement claim and a Lanham Act claim alleging, among other things, that the defendant used an image from the front cover of their book as its corporate logo. The plaintiffs claimed that the cover was an original design protected by copyright law. Id. at 1118. They also claimed that the design on the cover functioned as a trade dress that identified them as the creators of the book. Id. The court agreed. Id. While the copyright claim and the Lanham Act claim referred to the same facts, the two claims addressed distinct wrongs. Id. The copyright claim protected the plaintiffs' creative work, and the Lanham Act claim protected the plaintiffs' rights in their source-identifying trade dress. Id. The Court is persuaded by Bach's finding that a defendant can simultaneously violate the Lanham Act and copyright law. [Other citations omitted.]

> Id., at 13–14. *See also* DC Comics v. Towle, 2015 U.S. App. LEXIS 16837 (9th Cir. 2015) (holding the "Batmobile" both a copyrightable character and a protected trademark).

3 Lanham Act §§ 32, 43(a), 15 U.S.C. §§ 1114, 1125(a) (2013).
4 Lanham Act § 43(c), 15 U.S.C. § 1125(c) (2013).
5 *See* 17 U.S.C. § 501 (2013) (listing the elements of an infringement claim).
6 Aside from the narrow category of Works of Visual Art, the U.S. Copyright Act imposes no obligation to credit the author as the creator of the work.
7 U.S. CONST. art. I, § 8, cl. 8.
8 Lanham Act § 9(a), 15 U.S.C. § 1059(a) (2013) ('Subject to the provisions of section 8, each registration may be renewed for periods of 10 years at the end of each successive 10-year period following the date of registration upon payment of the prescribed fee and filing of a written application …'). The statute imposes no limit as to the number of times the registrant may renew.

licensing of, a visual character by controlling the use of the trademark in the same image(s).[9] For example, once the copyright in Mickey Mouse – or more accurately, in Steamboat Willie, Mickey's forebear – expires, can Disney successfully invoke its trademark rights in various depictions of The Mouse to prevent third parties from exploiting the now public domain Steamboat Willie to designate the source or sponsorship of unauthorized goods or services?[10] The difference in the rights' purpose gives rise to another problem: if the trademark owner is not also the copyright owner, for example, because of a limited grant of copyright from the artist, or because rights granted may have reverted to the artist, can the holder of one kind of right exercise that right, for example, through licensing, without infringing the rights of the holder of the other kind of right?[11]

3.03 While those questions address trademarks and copyright as potential antagonists where exercise of trademark rights threatens to frustrate copyright

---

[9] The issue is confined neither to the overlap between trademarks and copyright nor to U.S. copyright law. The Advocate General of the Court of Justice of the European Union (CJEU) recently summarized the broader problem, in a controversy concerning trademark registration for the design of a children's high chair:

> 35 However, it should be recalled that the purpose of the system of trade mark protection, which serves to provide the bases for fair competition by enhancing market transparency, differs from the premises underlying certain other intellectual property rights which serve, in essence, to promote innovation and creativity.
>
> 36 That difference in purposes explains why the protection conferred by marks is indefinite but the protection conferred by other intellectual property rights is subject to a time-limit imposed by the legislature. That limit results from the balance which is struck between the public interest in protecting innovation and creativity, on the one hand, and the economic interest based on the possibility of exploiting the intellectual achievements of other persons to promote future socio-economic development, on the other.
>
> 37 Exercise of a trade mark right in order to extend an exclusive right to immaterial assets protected by other intellectual property rights could – after those rights have expired – jeopardise the balance of interests which the legislature established inter alia by limiting the scope of protection conferred by those other rights.
>
> 38 This problem is dealt with differently in different legal systems. The EU legislature resolved it by laying down the legislative criteria which can constitute an absolute ground for refusing a trade mark which is the shape of the goods.
>
> 39 Those criteria … prevent a trade mark right from being exercised for a purpose which is incompatible with it … In particular, they also serve to maintain the balance of interests which the legislature established by placing a time-limit on the protection conferred by certain other intellectual property rights.

Case C-205/13, Hauck GmbH & Co. KG v. Stokke A/S, opinion of A.G. Szpunar (14 May 2014). The CJEU rendered its decision on 18 September 2014.

[10] *See generally* Joseph P. Liu, *The New Public Domain*, 2013 U. ILL. L. REV. 1395, 1427–40.

[11] *See* Boyle v. U.S., 200 F.3d 1369 (Fed. Cir. 2000) ('[T]he grant of a service mark registration entitles the registrant to certain rights … the right to infringe another's copyright is not one of those …'); Nova Wines, Inc. v. Adler Fels Winery LLC, 467 F.Supp.2d 965, 983 (N.D. Cal. 2006). ('[V]alid copyright does not entitle the copyright holder to infringe another's trade dress rights.')

policies (and perhaps vice versa),[12] there is another side of the coin. To an increasing extent, we are seeing trademark symbols become characters and acquire value not only as source-indicators, but also as artistic (or audiovisual) works. Recent examples include the M&Ms candies, who, now anthropomorphized, appear in promotional videos and even videogames, and the Lego figures who recently starred in the Lego Movie. The phenomenon, however, is not altogether new, since some characters (for example, Strawberry Shortcake) were created to serve both as copyrighted works and as trademarks. The strategy seems the logical endpoint of the progression, since at least the 1970s, which recognizes that the thing of value is the trademark, independently of any particular goods or services with which the mark has been associated.[13] How does turning the trademark into a copyright add to the value of the object of the license?

3.04 This Chapter will first consider the exercise of trademark rights in copyrighted works, which either have fallen into the public domain or for which the trademark owner no longer owns the copyright. It also will consider adoption as a trademark of a public domain character in which the trademark claimant never held a copyright interest or for which it was a licensee for uses ancillary to the principal entertainment-related uses of the character. Finally, the Chapter will turn to the exploitation of trademarks as works of authorship.

---

12   For further examination of trademark-copyright antagonism, see Irene Calboli, *Overlapping Rights: The Negative Effects of Trademarking Creative Works*, in THE EVOLUTION AND EQUILIBRIUM OF COPYRIGHT IN THE DIGITAL AGE 52 (Susy Frankel & Daniel Gervais eds., 2014). *See also* authorities cited *infra* note 51.

13   *See, e.g.*, Boston Professional Hockey Ass'n v. Dallas Cap & Emblem Mfg., 510 F.2d 1004 (5th Cir. 1975) (acknowledging that protecting the trademark in itself (on patches to be sewn on clothing) is a shift, '[a]lthough our decision here may slightly tilt the trademark laws from the purpose of protecting the public to the protection of the business interests of plaintiffs, we think that the two become so intermeshed when viewed against the backdrop of the common law of unfair competition that both the public and plaintiffs are better served by granting the relief sought by plaintiffs.'); Panavision Int'l v. Toeppen, 141 F.3d 1316 (9th Cir. 1998) ('Toeppen made a commercial use of Panavision's trademarks. It does not matter that he did not attach the marks to a product. Toeppen's commercial use was his attempt to sell the trademarks themselves.'). At least one circuit has viewed the 'patch case' with skepticism. See U.S. v. Giles, 213 F.3d 1247 (10th Cir. 2000) ('We believe [Boston Professional] to be of limited value for several reasons ... it dealt with civil liability, while Mr. Giles was convicted of violating the criminal version of the statute, which we must construe narrowly ... Moreover, the Fifth Circuit specifically confined its opinion to the product at hand ... the court relied upon a novel and overly broad conception of the rights that a trademark entails. In deciding that the emblems should be protected goods despite the fact that the plaintiffs had not registered their marks for use on patches, the court essentially gave the plaintiffs a monopoly over use of the trademark in commercial merchandising.'); Liu, *supra* note 10.

B. WHEN THE TRADEMARK OWNER IS NO LONGER A COPYRIGHT OWNER: TRADEMARK LICENSING IN THE SHADOW OF *DASTAR*

3.05 The U.S. Supreme Court in *Dastar Corp. v. Twentieth Century Fox Film Corp.*,[14] made clear that producers may not leverage trademark rights effectively to revive expired copyrights. In that case, the copyright in a pre-1978 motion picture had expired through non-renewal.[15] The producer nonetheless endeavoured to prevent a third party from making and distributing videocassettes of the film by claiming that purveying the videocassettes under the defendant's name rather than as a production by 20th Century Fox constituted 'reverse passing off' in violation of the federal Lanham (Trademark) Act.[16] Limiting the statutory trademark concept of a work's 'origin' to the source of the material copies of a work of authorship, the Court ruled that trademark law did not address the creator of the intellectual goods.[17] Because Dastar had made (or authorized the making of) the videocassettes that it distributed, it was the 'source or origin' of the material copies.[18] It was irrelevant that Dastar had not produced the audiovisual work. The intellectual source remained outside the trademark law's scope.[19]

3.06 If trademark law cannot bootstrap a work of authorship out of the copyright public domain, does that mean that a visual character whose copyright has expired cannot be the object of trademark licensing? *Dastar* does not foreclose the inquiry. In that case, the former copyright holder clearly sought to make an end-run around the copyright law; under the court's analysis, the plaintiff had no trademark rights to assert because the defendant's use did not involve falsely designating itself as the origin of the goods. But suppose the trademark owner seeks to license a copyright-expired visual character as a trademark, that is, as a designation of (material) origin for the goods or services on which the character appears as a distinctive sign? In other words, to exploit the character as a brand, not as a work. Can the law, and business practice, effectively distinguish between the character as a literary and artistic work, and the character as the symbol of the goodwill of a single source of origin? But if the character can be an enforceable trademark, how can third parties exploit the character as a copyright-expired work?

---

14   539 U.S. 23 (2003).
15   *Id.* at 26.
16   *Id.* at 23.
17   *Id.* at 36.
18   *Id.*
19   *Id.* at 31.

1. Distinguishing trademark goodwill from works of authorship

3.07 The Southern District of New York addressed these questions in a pre-*Dastar* decision that should still be good law. In *Frederick Warne & Co. v. Book Sales, Inc.*,[20] the original publisher of Beatrix Potter's *Peter Rabbit* illustrated stories, whose copyrights had expired, brought an action for false designation of origin against another publisher who had not only reprinted the stories, including the depictions of the characters, but also mimicked the placement on certain pages of the books of a particular illustration, the 'Sitting Rabbit,' that Warne claimed to have adopted and used as a trademark to symbolize its publications. Book Sales countered that the expiration of the *Peter Rabbit* copyrights entitled it freely to copy all the images appearing in the books, including the Sitting Rabbit. Warne did not contest Book Sales' entitlement to exploit all the images, including the Sitting Rabbit, as characters in the stories, but contended that Book Sales was not merely reprinting the image in connection with the story, but by removing that image from its context within the story in which it initially appeared and by using it as a colophon to introduce other stories, Book Sales was infringing Warne's trademark rights in the image.

3.08 In denying summary judgment to Book Sales, the court recognized that Warne would have to establish that its use of the Sitting Rabbit on the inside covers of its editions and as a colophon had come to be recognized by the public not merely as identifying the stories as *Peter Rabbit* stories, but also as *Peter Rabbit* stories *as published by Frederick Warne*. If Warne could establish such secondary meaning, then it would also need to show that Book Sales' use of the Sitting Rabbit was likely to confuse consumers into believing that the Book Sales editions were produced or authorized by Warne. The court distinguished between Book Sales' copyright entitlement to publish *Peter Rabbit* stories and Warne's trademark right to prevent Book Sales from publishing the stories as if their publisher had been Warne.

3.09 In *Dastar* terms, Warne was not seeking to deploy trademark law as a kind of 'mutant copyright,'[21] but rather was invoking trademark protection for precisely the kind of source-identifier *Dastar* envisioned: Warne was arguing that the Sitting Rabbit designated Warne as the publisher – that is, as the producer of the material copies of the books. Book Sales' use of that image in the same

---

20   481 F.Supp. 1191 (S.D.N.Y. 1979).
21   *Dastar*, 539 U.S. at 34 ('Assuming for the sake of argument that Dastar's representation of itself as the "Producer" of its videos amounted to a representation that it originated the creative work conveyed by the videos, allowing a cause of action under § 43(a) for that representation would create a species of mutant copyright law that limits the public's federal right to "copy and to use" expired copyrights ...').

B. WHEN THE TRADEMARK OWNER IS NO LONGER A COPYRIGHT OWNER

ways (divorced from the story in which it originally appeared)[22] was likely to confuse the public as to who made the books. The Sitting Rabbit might also serve to indicate the intellectual source of the stories – that is, that Beatrix Potter wrote the stories and drew their characters – but that kind of (non-trademark) 'source' identification was not at issue in the case. Nor, the court emphasized, was it necessary, in freely exploiting the stories, to employ the Sitting Rabbit in the same out-of-context ways as Warne had.

Warne suggests a way out of a potential impasse between the copyright public domain and trademark protection for visual characters vested with secondary meaning as source indicators. Returning to Mickey Mouse/Steamboat Willie, when the copyright in the 1928 original iteration of the character expires, anyone should be free not only to reissue cartoons and/or comic books (if any) in which Steamboat Willie appeared, but also to create new works starring the original, rather rat-like, incarnation of the softer, rounder Mouse we know today. Those exploiters could not, however, market Steamboat Willie as Mickey Mouse (apart, perhaps, from conveying the factual information that Willie is Mickey's immediate forebear),[23] nor could they brand their versions with any of the current Disney trademarks, for those uses both exceed the exploitation of merely the public domain pictorial or audiovisual work and might be likely to confuse consumers as to the purveyor (not the creator) of the recycled or reimagined Steamboat Willie cartoons or other works. **3.10**

2. Trademark and copyright: in fact inseparable?

But the observation that Disney continues to control the licensing of its current trademarks invites a re-vesting of secondary meaning in Steamboat Willie as a symbol of Disney productions in general before its copyright expires. And Disney does in fact appear to be dusting off that character to convert it into a source indicator: A video included at the introduction of recent Disney films begins with the current image of Mickey Mouse and travels back in time to the early depictions of Steamboat Willie (see Figure 3.1). The object of this flashback would appear to associate Steamboat Willie with the Disney output in general, rather than merely as a character in some early cartoons. **3.11**

---

22 Professor McCarthy also underscores the trademark significance of taking an image or character out of its original context. *See* MCCARTHY, *supra* note 1, at § 6:31. ('It is more likely that a court will recognize that there is a federal right to reproduce a work on which copyright has ended, so long as the user does not take the images or characters out of their original context and use them in a way that causes confusion of source or affiliation.')
23 Such references should constitute nominative fair use under Lanham Act § 43(c).

Chapter 3 LICENSING COMMERCIAL VALUE

Source: Disney Production Logo, Meet the Robinsons (2007).

Figure 3.1 Steamboat Willie: From Character to Brand?

3.12 Would that course of action now put the Steamboat Willie character off-limits to all but those who take a license from Disney? If Steamboat Willie becomes a brand in its own right, would it not follow that its unlicensed appearance would confuse the public as to the source of the copies or transmissions of the work containing an incarnation of the character? There are two answers: First, under *Warne*, the trademark consists of a particular instantiation of the character in a particular source-identifying guise divorced from its storytelling context. The court took pains to ensure that the first publisher could not bootstrap all Peter Rabbit images to the single images used in the colophon and inside book covers. Warne's use of the Sitting Rabbit in ways distinct from that image's role in the story from which Warne extracted it signaled that this incarnation of the character was source-identifying rather than narrative.[24]

3.13 By the same token, Steamboat Willie, the brand (see Figure 3.2), should remain distinct from Steamboat Willie, the character. Dr. Seuss' *The Cat in the Hat* offers an example of the distinction. The Cat, the character, stars in two eponymous children's stories. The Cat, the brand (a single image of the grinning Cat in his striped stovepipe hat), adorns the spines and front and back covers of the books in the Beginner Books 'I Can Read It All By Myself'

---

[24] *Cf.* Rock and Roll Hall of Fame and Museum v. Gentile, 134 F.3d 749 (6th Cir. 1998) (rejecting claims to trademark protection for the general appearance of the building, but acknowledging that the museum might acquire secondary meaning in a particular view of the building. The court distinguished the building's fame as a work of architecture from public perception of the building *as a trademark*).

B. WHEN THE TRADEMARK OWNER IS NO LONGER A COPYRIGHT OWNER

Source: Disney Production Logo, Tangled (2010).

Figure 3.2 Steamboat Willie: The Character as Mascot (Brand)

series of children's books (including *The Cat in the Hat* and *The Cat in the Hat Comes Back*) (see Figure 3.3).[25]

3.14 When the Dr. Seuss books fall into the public domain, anyone may republish them, but the subsistence of trademark rights in the Cat as part of the trade dress of the Random House book series (assuming it remains in print) means that any unlicensed versions of that image of the Cat, and perhaps similar images of the Cat, may not appear on the spines, back covers, or upper right-hand corners of the front covers of those republications (or on any new Cat in the Hat stories that the work's public domain status entitles anyone to create). Similarly, post-copyright expiration, a producer who seeks to merchandize images of Steamboat Willie as ornamentation on T-shirts or to sell Steamboat Willie plush toys may do so, and may lawfully identify the character as Steamboat Willie,[26] but the label must forgo all Disney insignia,

---

25 *See Beginner Books*, PENGUIN RANDOM HOUSE, *available* 14 September 2015 at http://www.penguinrandomhouse.com/series/BBK/beginner-booksr.
26 *Cf* Kellogg Co. v. National Biscuit Co., 305 U.S. 111 (1938) (finding that an expired patent entitled third parties to manufacture product and to call the product by the name by which the public had come to know the goods; but third parties must not pass off their versions as the products of the original patent owner).

Source: Dr. Seuss, *Green Eggs and Ham* (Special Edition 1960).

Figure 3.3 The Cat in the Hat: The Brand

whether of modern-day Mickey Mouse or of Steamboat Willie (assuming Disney succeeds in converting the character into a brand).[27]

3.15 One might respond that, given the close association of the character with Disney, *any* incarnation, as a label or as a good, is bound to confuse the public as to the source. This objection, if borne out by facts, brings us to the second answer: In that event, copyright and trademark policies clash, and, as *Dastar* implies, the public domain principle of copyright trumps. The public domain

---

27 *Cf.* Geisel v. Poynter Prods., 283 F.Supp. 261 (S.D.N.Y. 1968); Geisel v. Poynter Prods., 295 F.Supp. 331 (S.D.N.Y. 1968) (finding that a purchaser of copyrights in pre-Cat in the Hat cartoons by Dr. Seuss may produce plush toys in the forms of those characters, and may identify them as having been created by Theodore Geisel/Dr. Seuss, but may not market them as 'Dr. Seuss' creations and using characteristic Dr. Seuss signature on the labels).

makes the character free for competition. Assuming the character has also served as a trademark, trademark law enables the former copyright owner to ensure that free competition be fair competition. But remedies short of full injunctions may achieve 'fairness': A court should decline to grant the trademark owner any relief other than the clear labeling of disclaimers as to the source of the competing goods.[28] As a result, copyright policies significantly circumscribe any program of licensing of exclusive trademark rights in a public domain character; a licensee's 'exclusivity' will not preclude third-party exploitations of the character *qua* character.

3. Keeping characters out of the copyright public domain: the impact on trademarks

3.16 An additional consideration complicates the analysis, however. The copyright lives of visual characters may in fact last far longer than the copyright term of the character's initial incarnation. Many characters evolve over time, and later manifestations may depart sufficiently from the original version to qualify as copyright-protected derivative works.[29] The new matter added to the underlying work cannot prolong the copyright in the pre-existing material,[30] but neither does the public domain status of the underlying material deprive the new matter of its own copyright. If the term of protection is calculated from the date of publication, rather than from the life of the author, as would be the case for works published before 1978 and for works made for hire,[31] the copyright in the new matter will subsist past the term of the copyright in the underlying work. These rules mean that third parties who may freely reproduce copyright-expired characters may exploit the character as it originally appeared; however, they may not copy the appearance of the character as it has developed over time, assuming that evolution incorporates sufficient distinguishable variations from the original to warrant protection as a derivative work. Similarly, while third parties may newly vary the character's visual appearance, those variations must not resemble those introduced by the owner of the copyright in the derivative work. As a result, the commercial value of reviving the original appearance of the character may be too insignificant to attract a mass-market audience.

---

28 See Liu, *supra* note 10, at 1433 ('[A]t most the appropriate remedy would be a disclaimer, which would address the confusion without limiting the ability of a third party to use the underlying work.').
29 See *id.* at 1443–7 (discussing level of originality required to warrant derivative works protection for new versions or attributes of artistic and literary characters).
30 See 17 U.S.C. § 103(b). *Cf.* Klinger v. Conan Doyle Estate, 755 F.3d 496 (2014) (holding that a copyright subsisting in last Sherlock Holmes stories does not affect the public domain status of pre-1923 Sherlock Holmes works). *See also* Russell v. Price, 612 F.2d 1123 (9th Cir. 1979) (finding that the non-renewal of copyright in derivative work does not cast copyright-renewed underlying work into the public domain).
31 17 U.S.C. §§ 302(c), 304 (2013).

Chapter 3 LICENSING COMMERCIAL VALUE

3.17 Consider the following example: The Michelin Man, 'Bibendum,' having first appeared in Michelin advertisements in the late 19th century, has long been in the copyright public domain (at least in the U.S.). But just as the spindly and snout-nosed Steamboat Willie's contours have over time taken on a more friendly and reassuring roundness, so has Bibendum evolved from a *bon vivant* blob,[32] an almost featureless stack of narrow tubular shapes, into a still-robust but more *sportif* assemblage of thicker forms showing greater differentiation in torso, limbs, and especially facial characteristics (see Figures 3.4–3.6).

Figure 3.4   Bibendum in 1898 (public domain)

Figure 3.5   Bibendum today

---

32   The name 'Bibendum' evokes the adage (that appeared in an early Michelin advertisement, see above) 'nunc est Bibendum!' – 'Now is the time for drinking!'

B. WHEN THE TRADEMARK OWNER IS NO LONGER A COPYRIGHT OWNER

Figure 3.6   Bibendum now and then

Anyone may republish the nineteenth-century advertising posters (for which there may well be a market), but the merchandising opportunities for the original Bibendum do not seem promising. One might imagine (carefully labeled) throw pillows in the shape of the original Bibendum, but a third party would be ill-advised to enter the market for a restaurant or tour guides featuring images of the 19th century version of the Michelin mascot, for those uses are not exploiting the character *qua* character; they embrace the goodwill of the publishing arm of Michelin, and would be likely to confuse consumers as to the source of the guide books. In other words, the original Bibendum may be freely exploitable as a matter of copyright law, but it does not follow that the original character may be used by third parties as a trademark. Indeed, so long as Bibendum continues to evoke Michelin as the source of the goods, then even if there were no trademark registrations for the original version of the character, or any registrations have not been renewed, or were deemed abandoned for non-use, a third party's use as a trademark of Bibendum in his original guise would be likely to confuse consumers or to dilute the distinctiveness of the mark.[33] Nonetheless, to avoid disputes over the availability of the trademark in its original form and to ensure continued trademark protection for the copyright-expired version of character depicted in the mark, it would be desirable for the trademark owner to renew its registrations of the original Bibendum, and forestall a finding of non-use by some form of continued bona

3.18

---

[33]   There are several versions of Bibendum for which there are U.S. trademark registrations. The earliest appears to be in 1970 and lists its first use in commerce as 1950. This registration is currently in force. *See* U.S. Trademark Registration No. 888,288 (filed 5 June 1969). The registration refers to earlier versions of Bibendum ('used in another form at least as early as 1907 as to the design in different displays'), but it is not clear that the original 1898 Bibendum character was ever used in the U.S. as a mark.

fide use with a portion of the business, such as using the original version on promotional goods.[34]

C. EXPLOITING CHARACTERS WHEN THE TRADEMARK CLAIMANT WAS NOT ORIGINALLY OR IS NO LONGER THE COPYRIGHT OWNER

1. Adopting copyright-expired characters

3.19 Consider a different variation on the problem just addressed: Suppose a producer adopted as a trademark a public domain visual character that has fallen out of use and that therefore lacks pre-existing source association, or even residual goodwill. Consider, for example, the late 19th century cartoon figure, the 'Yellow Kid,' who appeared in Pulitzer newspapers during the 1890s and may have been the first successful comic strip character (see Figure 3.7).[35] Despite great popularity at the end of the 19th century, the character seems to have fallen into obscurity. Any copyright has long expired, and any trademark (were there one) would have been abandoned through non-use.[36]

3.20 Adoption of such a character should be treated like any appropriation of a generic term. Abandonment of any trademark in the character returns the name and image to the trademark public domain from which anyone may adopt them and endeavour to instill independent goodwill. Absent goodwill, the name and image should be analogized to generic terms, since the name and image are the name and the necessary representation of a thing (the character). A generic term does not cease to partake of the common lexicon even if a trademark claimant has succeeded in rendering a non-lexicographical

---

34 MCCARTHY, *supra* note 1, at § 17:26 ('In general, neither abandonment nor loss of the ability to tack-on to achieve priority will occur if the new form of the mark creates the same commercial impression as did the old form ... Trademark rights inure in the basic commercial impression created by a mark, not in any particular format or style ... '); Cumulus Media, Inc. v. Clear Channel Communications, 304 F.3d 1167 (11th Cir. 2002) (holding that the continuous low level use on business cards and an office sign held to constitute sufficient use to prevent a finding of abandonment at the preliminary injunction stage); Exxon Corp. v. Humble Exploration Co., 592 F.Supp. 1226 (N.D. Tex. 1984), *on remand from* 695 F.2d 96 (5th Cir. 1983) (holding that, after the company names and marks HUMBLE, ESSO and ENCO had been changed to EXXON nationwide, the resumed use of HUMBLE, after three years of almost complete non-use, on all 55 gallon drums of oil from one refinery was sufficient evidence of an intention to resume use of that mark and avoided a finding of abandonment). *But see*, 3 J. THOMAS MCCARTHY, MCCARTHY ON TRADEMARKS AND UNFAIR COMPETITION § 17:9 (4th ed. 2015) (casting doubt on effectiveness of trademark maintenance programs to keep alive a mark no longer actually used as a symbol of the producer's goods or services).

35 *The Yellow Kid*, OSU LIBRARIES, *available 14 September 2015 at* http://cartoons.osu.edu/digital_albums/yellowkid/. ('*Hogan's Alley* ... is considered the first commercially successful comic strip. It featured Mickey Dugan, better known as the Yellow Kid ... [in] the *New York World* from 5 May 1895 to 4 October 1896 ... moved to ... Hearst's *New York Journal* where the Yellow Kid appeared in three series.').

36 Lanham Act § 45, 15 U.S.C. § 1127 (three years non-use is presumptive abandonment).

Figure 3.7   The 'Yellow Kid'

use of the term distinctive of its goods or services. For example, 'Apple' is a trademark for digital devices; it is the generic name for a fruit. The goodwill in 'Apple' gives the mark's proprietor no claim on the fruit, though the proprietor may have an action against a rival producer of digital devices who adopts the same or similar name for its goods.[37]

That a producer might today adopt the Yellow Kid to symbolize its entertainment services, and may also create new works of authorship incorporating the public domain character, does not preclude third parties from creating their own Yellow Kid works of authorship, whether as new comic strips, audiovisual works, or other merchandising properties. Even if the first re-adopter of the character acquires secondary meaning in the character as a trademark for its entertainment services, the trademark right protects only against passing off   **3.21**

---

37   Apple Comp., Inc. v. Formula Intern., Inc., 725 F.2d 521 (9th Cir. 1984) (holding that it was not an abuse of discretion for the district court to grant a preliminary injunction in favor of Apple against the use on computer hardware of the mark 'Pineapple' or any other mark or name confusingly similar to the trademarks used by Apple).

the other goods as having been produced by the trademark proprietor; it confers no exclusive right to merchandise or otherwise exploit the character as such. As a result, any entrepreneur who revives a public domain character must appreciate the risks it incurs: The entrepreneur may succeed in re-popularizing the character, and even in making the character a symbol of its goods or services, but it will not be able completely to ward off the competition that the character's new-found commercial appeal may attract. Because the trademark does not protect the character *qua* character, the value of any trademark licensing program in the revived character will likely correspondingly diminish.

3.22 That said, the value of a character trademark need not be nonexistent. But the greatest prospects for strong trademark protection probably lie outside the core entertainment context that gave rise to the character. If the trademark owner can build up goodwill in goods or services unrelated to the literary, artistic, and audiovisual uses, the case for trademark coverage becomes more convincing (and less threatening to the copyright public domain). For example, the character Buster Brown – originally featured in a comic strip by Richard F. Outcault (the same author as the creator of the Yellow Kid) and debuted in 1902[38] (hence no longer under copyright) – has long served as a trademark for a line of children's shoes (see Figure 3.8).[39] Brown Shoe has held trademark registrations in the Buster Brown word mark and boy-and-dog logo since at least the 1980s, with first use of the word mark alleged in 1903,[40] and of the logo in 1954.[41] Many who grew up in the 1960s (including this author) may

---

[38] *Buster Brown*, ENCYCLOPEDIA BRITANNICA, *available 14 September 2015 at* http://www.britannica.com/EBchecked/topic/81484/Buster-Brown.

[39] *See Buster Brown*, FAMOUS FOOTWEAR, *available 14 September 2015 at* http://www.famousfootwear.com/buster_brown. Famous Footwear is one of the brands owned by Brown Shoe company.

[40] U.S. Trademark Registration No. 3,593,936 (word mark registered for footwear 24 March 2009, alleging first use in commerce 4 August 1903).

[41] U.S. Trademark Registration No. 176,970 (filed 11 December 1923) (depicting the boy and his dog – an earlier version of the logo that appears in the advertisement in Figure 3.8 – and identifying Brown Shoe Co. as the registrant, the goods as 'Boys' and Girls' Leather, Canvas, and Cloth Shoes', and date of first use in commerce as 4 August 1903; the registration was renewed for the second time on 4 May 2004). U.S. Trademark Registration No. 1,232,853 (filed 29 March 1983) (depicting the boy and his dog – the same logo as appears in the advertisement in Figure 3.8 – and identifying Brown Shoe Co. as the registrant, the goods as 'shoes', and date of first use in commerce as 8 February 1954. The registration was renewed on 23 November 2003.). Brown Shoe Co. also registered the Buster Brown word mark and stylized script for shoes on 28 September 1943, alleging first use in commerce 4 August 1903. *See* U.S. Trademark Registration No. 403,506 (third renewal, 30 May 2003). Brown Shoe Co. has registered updated Buster Brown logos for footwear. *See* U.S. Trademark Registration No. 3,692,537 (6 October 2009; first use in commerce 15 October 2000); U.S. Trademark Registration No. 4,354,716 (16 July 2013; first use in commerce 31 August 2012); U.S. Trademark Registration No. 4,369,261 (16 July 2013; first use in commerce 31 August 2012). Trademark ownership of Buster Brown is complicated and appears to be unrelated to any ownership of copyright in the comic strip. An apparent second-comer to the use of the mark, the Buster Brown Stocking Company of New York City first registered the Buster Brown mark, for 'hosiery' in 1906. *See* U.S. Trademark Registration No. 51,981 (1 May

Figure 3.8   Buster Brown shoes advertisement (1950s)

remember Buster Brown as a famous trademark for shoes (indeed, *de rigueur* for the annual back-to-school footwear shopping excursion) and may recall the logo depicting the boy and his dog, yet may be completely unaware that Buster Brown had been a comic strip character.[42]

As the holder of a valid trademark, the Brown Shoe Company may invoke the trademark laws to prevent competitors from selling footwear under the character name or logo, but should have no claim against a third party's revival **3.23**

1906) (The registration lists first use in commerce on 4 April 1904. The registration is still in force, having been renewed for the fifth time on 3 August 2006; it was assigned to Buster Acquisition LLC in 2013.) Another registration for hosiery, *see* U.S. Trademark Registration No. 505,225, of Buster Brown and a boy-and-dog logo different from the logo in the Brown Shoe Co. registration, was made in 1948 by United Hosiery Mills Corp. of Chattanooga, Tn. and later assigned to Buster Acquisition LLC. The registration, listing first use in commerce on 4 April 1904, was renewed for the third time on 17 July 2009. In 1965, the Buster Brown Textile Co. of Wilmington, Delaware registered the Buster Brown word mark and the same boy-and-dog logo as appears in the United Hosiery Mills registration, for children's clothing (not including shoes); the registration lists first use in commerce 4 April 1904. *See* U.S. Trademark Registration No. 800,744 (This registration has also been assigned to Buster Acquisitions, and is currently in force, having been renewed for the second time on 14 April 2006.).

42 Most contemporary consumers are probably similarly unaware that Skippy peanut butter, whose trademark dates from the 1930s, may have appropriated (without license) the name of a then-popular comic strip character. *See* SKIPPY.COM, http://www.skippy.com/ (website operated by heirs of Percy Crosby, the creator of the Skippy character).

of the copyright public domain character in a comic strip or other entertainment product. If Buster Brown is still a famous mark, its owner could avail itself of an anti-dilution claim against unrelated uses, for example as a trademark for furniture. However, the owner's rights would still encounter two important limitations: First, as *Frederick Warne* teaches us, the trademark attaches to the name and to the particular depiction of the character in the logo, not to the visual appearance of the character in general. Second, a third party's revival of the character *qua* character is not a use of the character *as a trademark* and should be either non-infringing *ab initio*[43] or at least excused under sec. 43(c)(A), which excludes '[a]ny fair use, including a nominative or descriptive fair use, or facilitation of such fair use, of a famous mark by another person other than as a designation of source for the person's own goods or services.'

3.24 The trademark owner could, under copyright law, acquire rights in gross for updated versions of the character, but the scope of those rights would be limited to the authorial value-added, as discussed earlier. We will see in Part D, however, that the additional layer of intellectual property protection that may flow from converting a trademark to a copyright may warrant the endeavor. Without such an effort, the commercial value of the character and logo primarily inheres in their association with the brand of shoes.

2. Reversion of copyright in a trademarked character

3.25 We have seen that a trademark owner cannot completely preclude third parties from exploiting characters once their copyrights have expired. However, as a practical matter, the limited scope of the public domain entitlement – particularly with respect to a character whose depiction has varied over the years – may sufficiently circumscribe third-party exploitation so as not significantly to compromise the commercial value of licensing trademark (and copyright) rights in the current version of the character. So far, we have considered the rights of the trademark owner who no longer owns the copyright because there is no longer a copyright to own. What of the trademark owner who no longer owns the copyright because those rights have

---

[43] *See, e.g.*, McCarthy, *supra* note 1, at § 24:99 ('[N]on-trademark use does not and cannot dilute by blurring.'); Restatement Third, Unfair Competition, § 25(2), comment I (1995) ('Non-trademark uses, because they do not create an association with a different user's goods, services or business, are unlikely to dilute the distinctiveness of a mark.'); Stacey Dogan & Mark Lemley, *The Trademark Use Requirement in Dilution Cases*, 24 Santa Clara Computer & High Tech. L.J. 541, 555 (2007).

reverted to the author, notably, because the author has exercised her inalienable right to terminate the grant of rights in the work of authorship?[44]

3.26 Consider, for example, the Superman character. While the heirs of Superman's creators ultimately failed in their attempts to terminate the original 1 March 1938 copyright grants,[45] suppose that they had succeeded. Suppose further that the creators' contracts assigned all trademark as well as copyright interests in the character. The Copyright Act clearly states that 'termination of a grant under this section affects only those rights covered by the grants that arise under this title, and in no way affects rights arising under any other Federal, State, or foreign laws'.[46] Any trademark assignment to Warner Bros. (successor in title to Action Comics, the original grantee) would therefore remain in force despite the termination of the assignment of copyright.

3.27 Before we consider the implications of divided ownership of the trademark and the copyright, it is important to understand that, as a matter of copyright law, rights do not fully revert to the author or her heirs: 'A derivative work prepared under authority of the grant before its termination may continue to be utilized under the terms of the grant after its termination, but this privilege does not extend to the preparation after the termination of other derivative works based upon the copyrighted work covered by the terminated grant.'[47] Thus, Warner Bros. could continue to exploit all derivative works based on the original Superman character, but could not, absent the heirs' authorization, create new derivative works. That would mean that Warner Bros. could not further update Superman's appearance (though it could continue to exploit the character's currently-evolved appearance). It would also mean that Warner Bros. could not create or license new products, including merchandising properties, depicting the current iteration of Superman if the new products (for example, a new plush toy or action figure) would constitute new derivative works. By contrast, affixing an image of the current version of Superman to a variety of merchandising properties (such as T-shirts and bedsheets) would likely remain within the scope of the terminated grantee's statutory permission to exploit extant derivative works created during the now-terminated grant.

---

44 17 U.S.C. §§ 203, 304(c)-(d) (2009) (However, as seen in § 203(a), there is no termination of grants in works made for hire.).
45 Siegel v. Warner Bros. Entertainment Inc., 542 F.Supp.2d 1098 (C.D. Cal. 2008); DC Comics v. Pacific Pictures Corp., 2012 WL 4936588 (C.D. Cal. 2012).
46 17 U.S.C. § 203(b)(5) (2009).
47 17 U.S.C. § 203(b)(1) (2009). By contrast, under the prior (1909 Act) copyright law, if the author renewed the copyright registration for the work (and had not assigned the rights for the renewal term), then all rights would revert, including as to derivative works prepared during the first term of copyright. *See* Steward v. Abend, 495 U.S. 207 (1990).

3.28 In addition to this significant carve-out from the scope of the reverted rights, we should recall that the rights that revert to the author (or her heirs) will not entitle her (or them) to exploit the new matter contributed by her terminated grantees. She retrieves rights in the original work of authorship, but, under the same principles explored earlier, she cannot herself exploit, nor grant to others, rights in the character as further elaborated by the terminated grantee (assuming those elaborations are sufficient to support their own copyrights). Had the Superman heirs succeeded in their attempts to terminate the grant of rights, they would have retrieved the Superman character as he appeared in 1938, not as he appeared in 2009, when the court decided the case.[48]

3.29 Suppose, however, that the heirs (had their terminations succeeded) now sought to license third parties to produce a variety of merchandizing properties depicting Superman in his 1938 guise. Assume also that the goods would carry disclaimers as to any connection with Warner Bros. Would the Copyright Act's specification that reversion of rights under copyright 'in no way affects' trademark rights allow Warner Bros. successfully to assert that the heirs' carefully labeled exploitations violate Warner Bros.' trademarks because the public would be confused as to the source or sponsorship of the goods? Just as trademark rights should not trump the copyright public domain when third parties exploit copyright-expired characters (as characters, not as source-identifiers), so too should the terminated grantee's retention of trademark rights not frustrate the author's or heirs' exercise of the reverted copyright interests. Moreover, the Copyright Act's provision that '[t]ermination of the grant may be effected notwithstanding any agreement to the contrary',[49] should serve to prevent the terminated grantee's subsisting trademark rights from encroaching on the author's or heirs' exercise of the reverted copyright rights. Copyright termination may not 'affect' trademark rights, but trademark rights should not 'affect' reverted copyright rights either; both regimes train on the same visual characters, but the nature of the rights should remain distinct. Even acknowledging the availability of anti-dilution protection for famous marks (surely including Superman), a trademark is not a right in gross; protecting the goodwill that the mark symbolizes should not override the copyright policy that grants authors a (rather circumscribed) right to benefit

---

48 With respect to Superman as a literary character, the heirs would have recovered all the plot elements of the initial story, and accordingly could license new stories, films, and television series, so long as the new works did not incorporate plot elements or characters later introduced by or under the authority of the terminated grantee.
49 17 U.S.C. § 203(a)(5) (2009).

from the success of their works by reclaiming – and relicensing – the copyright in their works.[50]

D. WHEN THE TRADEMARK OWNER BECOMES A COPYRIGHT OWNER: TRADEMARKS AS COPYRIGHTED WORKS

Most of the commentary on copyright/trademark overlaps focuses (generally, unfavorably) on attempts to extend the copyright monopoly through trademark protection.[51] But there is another side of the coin: the development of trademarks into copyrightable characters and other visual goods. Perhaps because a trademark may lack sufficient authorship to qualify as a 'work'[52] and, in theory, does not confer a right in gross to exploit the symbol as an independent object of property, we recently see the adaptation of trademarks into the object of copyrights through the endowment of images not only with brand significance, but also with personalities and other attributes that convert the source-identifier into a literary, artistic, or (most often) audiovisual character. The creation of characters designed pervasively to permeate children's media environment through a combination of branding consumer goods (such as breakfast cereal) and producing animated television shows and associated toys, all featuring the characters, is a familiar strategy at least since the advent of 'Strawberry Shortcake' character and brand in the mid-1980s.[53] Nonetheless, the current evolution of trademarks into copyrighted works is different because in their commercial lives these trademarks were not born as

3.30

---

50 As discussed in the text, the rights that revert to the author or her heirs are unlikely to enable her to block the trademark owner's exploitation of the image as a trademark. If the trademark is a later representation of the character, the derivative works carve-out will preclude the author's claim. If the trademark is the original image, in which copyright rights have reverted, 17 U.S.C. § 203(b)(5) indicates that reversion will not terminate the right to license the image *as a trademark*; to the extent that copyright reproduction rights necessarily accompany the licensing of trademark rights, the statutory direction that copyright termination does not 'affect' other rights, would mean that the trademark license incorporated in the copyright license survives.
51 *See, e.g.*, Calboli, *supra* note 12; Viva R. Moffat, *Mutant Copyrights and Backdoor Patents: The Problem of Overlapping Intellectual Property Protection*, 19 BERKELEY TECH. L.J. 1473 (2004); ESTELLE DERCLAYE & MATTHIAS LEISTNER, INTELLECTUAL PROPERTY OVERLAPS: A EUROPEAN PERSPECTIVE 12–15, 47–60, 130–338, 200–05, 237–54, 290–92, 295–303, 306–33, and authorities cited therein (2011) (surveying copyright/trademark overlaps in the EU and member states); Mende & Isaac, *When Copyright and Trademark Rights Overlap*, *supra* note 2.
52 The Copyright Office will not register a print or label consisting solely of trademark subject matter and lacking copyrightable expression. But it will register a trademark consisting of a logo or other visual image, if the image manifests sufficient original authorship. *See* Compendium of Copyright Office Practices, Chapter 900, Section 913.1 & 913.2 (3rd ed. 2014).
53 *See generally* Tom Engelhardt, *The Shortcake Strategy*, *in* WATCHING TELEVISION: A PANTHEON GUIDE TO POPULAR CULTURE 70 (Todd Gitlin, ed. 1986); Stephen Kline, OUT OF THE GARDEN: TOYS, TV, AND CHILDREN'S CULTURE IN THE AGE OF MARKETING 138–42 (1995) (discussing Strawberry Shortcake and other licensed character tie-in programming).

characters, but rather had the anthropomorphizing touches that turned them into characters later thrust upon them. Moreover, without those flourishes, the trademarks might have lacked sufficient authorship to warrant copyright protection. The red disk of the 7-UP dot, for example, seems too basic to survive even a cursory Copyright Office examination for originality. But accessorize it with arms and legs and coif it with a pair of sunglasses, and a banal form blossoms into the 'Cool Spot' character (see Figure 3.9).

Figure 3.9   7Up Dot: 'Coolspot'

3.31   Or take the rudimentary, single-coloured shapes of M&Ms candies, endow them with arms and legs and a range of highly expressive (if rather gender-stereotyped) facial features, and they become 'spokescandies' with pre-packaged personalities and backstories (see Figure 3.10).[54] Moreover, trademarks-as-characters star not only in advertising for the trademarked goods, but also in independent works such as videogames and even feature films (for example, the *Lego Movie*).[55]

---

54   See generally Characters, MMS, *available 14 September 2015 at* http://www.mms.com/us/characters (presenting the characters). For examples of the characters' personalities and backstories, see *M&M'S® Spokescandies to Pursue Solo Careers – Over One and a Half Million Dollars in Rewards Offered to Help Reunite 'M'*, MARS (May 2011), *available 14 September 2015 at* http://www.mars.com/global/press-center/press-list/news-releases.aspx?siteid=94&id=2973; *M&M'S® Spokescandies Reunited After Four-Month Split*, MARS (September 2011), *available 14 September 2015 at* http://www.mars.com/global/press-center/press-list/news-releases.aspx?siteid=94&id=3177.

55   For examples of videogames incorporating M&Ms characters, see *M&M's: The Lost Formula*, IGN, http://www.ign.com/games/mms-the-lost-formulas/pc-15279; *M&M's: Minis Madness*, IGN, http://www.ign.com/games/mms-mini-madness/gbc-15407; *M&M's: Shell Shocked*, IGN, http://www.ign.com/games/mms-shell-shocked/ps-16461; *M&M's: Kart Racing*, IGN, http://www.ign.com/games/mms-kart-racing/wii-909133; *M&M's: Adventure*, IGN, http://www.ign.com/games/mms-adventure/wii-14268625. Other brand examples include *7 UP: Spot: The Video Game*, MOBY GAMES, http://www.mobygames.com/game/spot; *Cool Spot*, MOBY GAMES, http://www.mobygames.com/game/cool-spot; *Spot: The Cool Adventure*, MOBY GAMES, http://www.mobygames.com/game/gameboy/spot-the-cool-adventure; *Spot Goes to Hollywood*, MOBY GAMES, http://www.mobygames.com/game/spot-goes-to-hollywood; *Burger King's Burger King character: Big*

D. WHEN THE TRADEMARK OWNER BECOMES A COPYRIGHT OWNER

Figure 3.10   M&Ms 'Spokescandy'

We have seen what copyright owners have to gain (or hope to gain) from claiming trademark protection for visual characters. What can copyright contribute to the protection of trademarks, and hence to the value of a trademark licensing program? First, because copyright is a right in gross, it strengthens the coverage available even to marks sufficiently famous to qualify for anti-dilution protection. Copyright is infringed by copying; trademark infringement requires a showing that the copying causes a likelihood of confusion or of association that is likely to 'blur' or 'tarnish' the mark.[56] It is true that in recent years, at least since the mid-1970s, trademark protection has increasingly come to bear on brand symbols in their own right, independent of the goods or services in connection with which they initially appeared.[57] Trademark law thus has been adapting to the reality, well established in the world of marketing, that the thing of value is the trademark; particularly for

3.32

Bumpin', Sneak King, and Pocketbike Racer, MOBY GAMES, http://www.ign.com/articles/2006/10/02/burger-king-and-xbox-team-up; *Cheetos: Chester Cheetah: Too Cool to Fool*, MOBY GAMES, http://www.mobygames.com/game/chester-cheetah-too-cool-to-fool; *Chester Cheetah: Wild Wild Quest*, MOBY GAMES, http://www.mobygames.com/game/chester-cheetah-wild-wild-quest. The California Raisins have a number of television spots and even a mockumentary and also sold four music albums. *See Meet the Raisins!*, IMDB, http://www.imdb.com/title/tt0261062/; *Discography*, CALIFORNIA RAISINS, http://thecaliforniaraisins.com/pages/discography.html (*all available 14 September 2015*).

56   Lanham Act, §§ 32, 43(a), 43(c), 15 U.S.C. §§ 1114, 1125(a), 1125(c) (2013).
57   *See* Boston Professional Hockey Ass'n v. Dallas Cap & Emblem Mfg., 510 F.2d 1004 (5th Cir. 1975); Anti-Cybersquatting Consumer Protection Act, 15 U.S.C. § 1125(d) (2013); Trademark Dilution Revision Act of 2006, PL 109–312 (2006). *See also* authorities cited *infra* nn. 61–63.

famous marks, the goods to which the brand applies are increasingly ancillary.[58] If in the past trademark goodwill symbolized the business, in many instances today, the goodwill *is* the business. As Jessica Litman has written:

> [T]he descriptive proposition that trade symbols have no intrinsic value has come to seem demonstrably inaccurate. The use of trademarks on promotional products has evolved from an advertising device for the underlying product line to an independent justification for bringing a so-called underlying product to market. ... The worth of such valuable trade symbols lies less in their designation of product source than in their power to imbue a product line with desirable atmospherics.

Indeed, in the new orthodoxy, marketing *is* value.[59]

3.33 But however reflective of business practice the detachment of the trademark from particular goods or services may be, its legal recognition distorts fundamental precepts of trademark law and invites doctrinal incoherence.[60] Trademark law evolved from the action of deceit; its common law antecedent is the tort of passing off. In theory, trademarks protect consumers against market place misinformation; free-riding off a producer's or a mark's goodwill, standing alone, should not suffice to support a claim of infringement. In fact, however, trademark law increasingly reprimands free-riding. Robert Bone has distinguished the traditional trademark function of 'information transmission'

---

58 *See, e.g.*, Katya Assaf, *Brand Fetishism*, 43 CONN. L. REV. 83 (2010) ('[M]any consumers who are loyal to a certain brand of soft drinks or cigarettes, ostensibly because of the superior taste of the product, actually cannot distinguish their favorite brand in a blind taste-test.'); Barton Beebe, *The Semiotic Analysis of Trademark Law*, 51 UCLA L. Rev. 621 (2004) ('In asserting that trademarks do no more than facilitate search and encourage quality, the Chicago School has long declined to acknowledge what is obvious: that firms produce trademarks as status goods, that consumers consume trademarks to signal status, and that courts routinely invest trademarks with legal protection in an effort to preserve this status-signaling function. The culture industries ... have long sold trademarks as commodities in their own right. Entire areas of trademark doctrine cannot be understood except as systems of rules designed to facilitate the commodification – indeed, the "industrial production" – of social distinction ... [I]n modern culture, the trademark need no longer identify any particular commodity (other than itself) in order to receive protection ... The modern trademark is dyadic in structure.').

59 Jessica Litman, *Breakfast With Batman: The Public Interest in the Advertising Age*, 108 YALE L.J. 1717, 1726 (1999).

60 *See, e.g.*, Litman, *supra* note 59; Robert G. Bone, *Hunting Goodwill: A History of the Concept of Goodwill in Trademark Law*, 86 B.U. L. REV. 547 (2006); Mark A. Lemley, *The Modern Lanham Act and the Death of Common Sense*, 108 YALE L.J. 1687 (1999) ('[T]here has been a gradual but fundamental shift in trademark law. Commentators and even courts increasingly talk about trademarks as property rights; as things valuable in and of themselves, rather than for the product goodwill they embody. Courts protect trademark owners against uses that would not have been infringements even a few years ago and protect as trademarks things that would not have received such protection in the past. And they are well on their way to divorcing trademarks entirely from the goods they are supposed to represent.'); Glynn S. Lunney, Jr., *Trademark Monopolies*, 48 EMORY L.J. 367 (1999) (commenting on the changes in trademark law since the 1950s, 'This expansion has encompassed both the recognition of a new trademark subject matter and a more complete bundle of ownership rights, and despite some pretense on the issue, has been only tenuously connected to concerns over material consumer deception. Instead, the expansion has focused on a trademark's value not merely as a device for conveying otherwise indiscernible information concerning a product ... but as valuable product in itself ... .').

from newer claims to protection of the trademark owner's goodwill, and has criticized the latter:

> The core of trademark law, as it is understood today, is based on a model which I shall call the 'information transmission model.' This model views trademarks as devices for communicating information to the market and sees the goal of trademark law as preventing others from using similar marks to deceive or confuse consumers.
>
> The idea of protecting goodwill fits this model rather poorly. Goodwill protection has nothing directly to do with facilitating consumer choice or safeguarding the quality of market information. It has to do instead with protecting sellers from misappropriation. Goodwill on this view denotes the special value that attaches to a mark when the seller's advertising and investments in quality generate consumer loyalty – a capacity to attract consumers over time. Trademarks are repositories or symbols of this goodwill, and trademark law prevents others from appropriating it by using a similar mark.
>
> [...] Characterizing trademark law in terms of goodwill protection ultimately conflicts with the well-recognized consumer-oriented goals of trademark law. The resulting conflict frustrates efforts to achieve doctrinal coherence, misleads judges, and pushes trademark law in troubling directions [...][61]

3.34 While trademark law traditionally derives from the action for deceit, misappropriation claims assert property rights grounded in the action for trespass. The critique of the expansion of trademark law essentially laments the passage of trademark law from a public-regarding claim to prevent misleading market information to one advancing the trademark owner's private property rights in gross in all but name. Set against this backdrop, one can view the conversion of certain trademarks into copyrighted characters as the logical next step in the progression: from property rights *de facto* (if uneasily) in gross, to rights *de jure* (and comfortably) in gross under copyright.

3.35 Nor, from the trademark owner's perspective, is there much of a downside to the conversion. While the fair use doctrine limits the scope of copyright protection – particularly for parody, criticism, and commentary – the last 20 years of trademark case law and legislation have given rise to the 'nominative fair use' defense and have imported copyright fair use concepts to excuse parodies and other critical uses of trademarks.[62] As a result, whether they are the objects of trademarks or of copyrights, visual characters seem equally susceptible to legally-privileged copying for purposes of mockery or social

---

61 Bone, *supra* note 60, at 549.
62 *See generally* Rebecca Tushnet, *Make Me Walk, Make Me Talk, Do Whatever You Please: Barbie and Exceptions*, in INTELLECTUAL PROPERTY AT THE EDGE: THE CONTESTED CONTOURS OF IP 405–26 (Rochelle Cooper Dreyfuss & Jane C. Ginsburg, eds. 2014); Jane C. Ginsburg, *Of Mutant Copyrights, Mangled Trademarks, and Barbie's Beneficence: The Influence of Copyright on Trademark Law*, in TRADEMARK LAW AND THEORY: A HANDBOOK OF CONTEMPORARY RESEARCH 481 (Graeme B. Dinwoodie & Mark D. Janis, eds. 2008).

commentary. Copyright therefore does not diminish the protection the characters would enjoy as a matter of trademark law. Admittedly, the copyrights will expire 95 years from the first publication of the trademarks-as-characters (assuming they are works made for hire), but during that very long stretch, the trademark owner will have ample time to update the character and start another 95-year clock rolling.

3.36 Finally, in addition to doctrinal coherence – about which trademark owners and their licensees are little likely to care – copyright offers significant remedial advantages over trademarks. The principal remedy for trademark infringement is injunctive relief.[63] Damages require a showing of actual confusion;[64] a trademark owner would be disinclined to wait to seek relief until consumers can be shown to have been confused in fact. On the other hand, in dilution actions, where confusion need not be proved, damages up to three times the amount proved as actual damages[65] may be available, though the claimant must prove that the defendant 'willfully intended to trade on the recognition of the famous mark.'[66]

3.37 It is not at all clear, however, how one would demonstrate actual dilution through 'blurring,' since the nature of the harm is essentially prospective. Indeed, because actual dilution is something of an oxymoron, Congress in 2006 amended the Trademark Act to clarify that a defendant is liable if its use of a famous mark 'is *likely to cause* dilution by blurring or dilution by tarnishment of the famous mark, regardless of the presence or absence of actual or likely confusion, of competition, or of actual economic injury'; plaintiffs do not have to demonstrate actual dilution.[67] The amendments,

---

63 Lanham Act § 34, 15 U.S.C. § 1116 (2013); 5 J. THOMAS MCCARTHY, MCCARTHY ON TRADEMARKS AND UNFAIR COMPETITION § 30:1 (4th ed. 2014) ('A permanent injunction is the usual and normal remedy once trademark infringement has been found in a final judgment.'); 4 J. THOMAS MCCARTHY, MCCARTHY ON TRADEMARKS AND UNFAIR COMPETITION § 24:132 (4th ed. 2014) ('The usual remedy where a violation of anti-dilution law is proven under the Federal Act is an injunction against the offending use.') (citing H.R. Rep. No. 104–374, at 7 (1995) ('With respect to relief, a new Section 43(c)(2) of the Lanham Act would provide that, normally, the owner of a famous mark will only be entitled to injunctive relief upon a finding of liability.').

64 Lanham Act § 35(a), 15 U.S.C. § 1117(a) (relief for 'any damages sustained' indicates that the trademark owner would in fact have had to have lost sales).

65 *Id.* ('In assessing damages the court may enter judgment, according to the circumstances of the case, for any sum above the amount found as actual damages, not exceeding three times such amount.')

66 *Id.* § 43(c)(5). For an example of proof of willfulness, see Apple v. Samsung, 920 F.Supp.2d 1079 (N.D. Cal. 2013) ('Samsung argues that Apple has not submitted evidence that could support the jury's verdict of willful dilution. However, Apple has submitted evidence that Samsung viewed the iPhone as revolutionary, and that Samsung attempted to create similar products. This constitutes substantial evidence in the record to support the jury's finding that Samsung willfully intended to trade on the recognition of Apple's trade dresses.'); Sporty's Farm L.L.C. v. Sportsman's Market, Inc., 202 F.3d 489 (2d Cir. 2000).

67 Lanham Act § 43(c)(1), 15 U.S.C. § 1125(c)(1) (emphasis added); 4 J. THOMAS MCCARTHY, MCCARTHY ON TRADEMARKS AND UNFAIR COMPETITION § 24:132 (4th ed. 2014) ('Since enactment of the 2006

D. WHEN THE TRADEMARK OWNER BECOMES A COPYRIGHT OWNER

however, do not affect the amount of monetary relief which remains based on the plaintiff's actual damages or on the defendant's profits. Thus, while the wrongful act may be willful intention 'to trade on the recognition of the famous mark,' an award of damages would seem to require that the bad intent result in actual harm.[68] As a practical matter then, trademark plaintiffs generally do not recover damages in non-counterfeiting cases.[69]

3.38 By contrast, in copyright law, damages are a traditional remedy. Moreover, in lieu of actual damages and profits[70] and if the work was registered with the Copyright Office prior to the commission of the infringing acts, the plaintiff may elect to receive statutory damages (and therefore does not have to prove actual damages) ranging from $750–$30,000 per work infringed as the court considers just; in the case of willful infringement, the range jumps to a maximum of $150,000 per work infringed.[71] In addition, where in trademark infringement cases attorneys fees are to be awarded only in 'exceptional cases,'[72] the Copyright Act grants the judge discretion to award attorneys fees to the prevailing copyright owner if the work was registered with the Copyright Office prior to the infringement.[73] The prospect of statutory damages and attorneys fees may serve as an additional deterrent to unlicensed exploitations of trademarks that also are the objects of copyright registrations.[74]

TDRA, a "likelihood" or probability of dilution is sufficient to violate the statute.'); Clarisa Long, *Dilution*, 106 COLUM. L. REV. 1029, n. 199 (2006) ('The proposed bill also would overturn Moseley, 537 U.S. 418, by allowing trademark holders to prove merely that a third party's use is "likely to cause dilution" rather than having to prove actual dilution.'); H.R. Rep. 109–23, at 4 (2005) ('The purpose of the FTDA is to protect famous trademarks, whether registered or unregistered, from subsequent uses that blur the distinctiveness of the mark or tarnish or disparage it, even in the absence of a likelihood of confusion.').

68   *See* MCCARTHY, *supra* note 67, at § 24:132 ('Some proof of actual impairment or harm to the famous mark is required … in the author's view, monetary recovery for dilution requires some proof that the famous mark was in fact injured or harmed by the defendant's conduct … the plaintiff needs to present some reasonable method of measuring that damage.').

69   *See* 5 MCCARTHY, *supra* note 67, at § 30:1; 4 MCCARTHY, *supra* note 67, at § 24:132 ('Monetary awards for violation for an anti-dilution statute are rare indeed.').

70   17 U.S.C. § 504(b) (2009).

71   *Id.*, § 504(c)(2) (2009).

72   Lanham Act § 35(a), 15 U.S.C. § 1117(a) (2013).

73   17 U.S.C. § 412 (2009). *See, e.g.*, Crescent Publ'g Group, Inc. v. Playboy Enters., 246 F.3d 142, 151 (2nd Cir. 2001) (referring to 'district courts' broad discretion in awarding fees'); Fogerty v. Fantasy, Inc., 510 U.S. 517, 534 (1994) ('attorney's fees are to be awarded to prevailing parties only as a matter of the court's discretion. "There is no precise rule or formula for making these determination," but instead equitable discretion should be exercised …').

74   For examples of visual character trademarks discussed in this chapter that are also the subjects of copyright registrations, see U.S. Copyright No. VAu000223219 (6 April 1992) ('M' character (plain)); U.S. Copyright No. VAu000232083 (16 July 1992) (M&M's almond 'M' character); U.S. Copyright No. VA0001729343 (23 July 2010) (M&M's pretzel 'M' character); U.S. Copyright No. VA0001841440 (19 September 2012) (M&M's Ms. Brown character).

E. CONCLUSION

3.39 This review of trademark/copyright overlaps regarding visual characters offers the following lessons for trademark licensing:

- Where the character has fallen into the copyright public domain, the trademark owner may nonetheless retain (or create) enforceable trademark rights in particular representations of the character, but should not be able to prevent third parties from exploiting the character itself and in general.
    - In the event of conflict between the copyright public domain and trademark rights in the character, the former prevails; any remedies for trademark infringement should be limited to accurate labeling (disclaimers) of the source of the third-party goods.
    - The trademark may be more likely to be enforced (and pose less risk of conflict with the copyright public domain) if it has acquired secondary meaning as a source-designation for goods or services distinct from the character's original literary, artistic, or entertainment context.
- Updating the visual appearance of the character will diminish conflicts with the copyright public domain because the modifications, if sufficiently original, will create a derivative work which (if a work made for hire) will enjoy its own 95-year copyright term; but neither the derivative work copyright owner nor the trademark licensee can prevent copyright exploitation of the copyright-expired character in its original guise.
    - To ensure continued trademark protection for the copyright-expired version of the character depicted in the mark, it would be desirable for the trademark owner to renew its registrations of the original character and forestall a finding of non-use of the original visual mark by some form of continued bona fide use, such as using the original version on promotional goods.
- If the copyright in the visual character (as a pictorial or graphic work) reverts to the author (work must not be 'for hire'), the use rights of licensees under trademark licenses granted by the terminated copyright grantee will not be affected, nor will the author acquire ownership of trademark rights built up by the terminated copyright grantee's exploitation of the trademark on its own or through trademark licensing. If the trademark consists of a later depiction (derivative work) of the character, the author's termination of the original grant will not prevent the continued copyright or trademark exploitation of derivative works prepared before termination, but new derivative works will require the author's authorization.

- o The trademark owner's subsisting rights should not frustrate the author's exercise of the reverted rights in the pictorial or graphic work; accurate labeling may provide the trademark owner the only appropriate intellectual property remedy.[75]
- At least some visual trademarks can be redesigned as copyrightable characters (for example, by adding limbs and facial features) and registered with the Copyright Office. Copyright confers protection against copying *per se*; likelihood of confusion or of dilution are not elements of the claim. Copyright protection is not absolute; the fair use doctrine permits reasonable copying particularly for purposes of criticism, commentary, or parody (but trademark law now allows these kinds of uses too). Copyright remedies for works registered prior to the infringements may be more extensive than trademark remedies, particularly with respect to damages and attorneys' fees.

---

[75] The trademark licensee may have a contract claim against a trademark licensor author whose copyright interests revert due to termination. Exploitation of the reverted copyright in a way that is inconsistent with the trademark license may violate the implied covenant of good faith and fair dealing under which the licensor should not take away the contract benefit conferred on the licensee by licensing a competitor. *Cf.* Nova Wines v. Adler Fells Winery LLC, 467 F.Supp.2d 965 (N.D. Cal. 2006) (not having to decide the contract issue because the licensee was found to have established its trademark rights before the copyright license was issued).

4

THE COMPLEXITIES OF DOMAIN NAMES TRANSACTIONS: CONTRACTS FOR A MARKET WHERE VALUE INCREASES WITH TIME

Cédric Manara[*]

A. INTRODUCTION	4.01	1. The case of a transfer	4.19
		(a) Eligibility	4.19
B. 'WHICH' OBJECT FOR THE		(b) Contact information	4.24
TRANSACTION?	4.06	(c) Joint registration	4.25
1. A top level domain	4.07	2. The case of agreements on use	4.26
(a) Private auctions	4.07	(a) General principles	4.26
(b) Sale of a top level domain	4.08	(b) Situations of joint use	4.30
(c) Lease of a top level domain	4.09		
2. A third level domain	4.10	E. 'WHAT' IS THE NATURE OF THE	
3. A second level domain	4.13	TRANSACTION?	4.31
		1. 'Sale' of a domain name	4.31
C. 'WHERE' WILL THE NAME BE USED?	4.14	2. License of a domain name	4.32
D. 'WHO' WILL HOLD OR USE THE NAME?	4.18	F. CONCLUSION	4.33

A. INTRODUCTION

4.01 There were 284 million domain names registered in October 2014.[1] There is also an active secondary market[2] where companies or investors[3] are looking for domain names to buy or to lease. On platforms dedicated to this secondary market, the transactions are usually simple: parties obey to the terms of use and/or use a template provided by the platform, with the intermediary

---

[*] Affiliate Researcher, Legal EDHEC, EDHEC Business School. The opinions expressed are solely those of the author.
[1] VERISIGN, THE DOMAIN NAME INDUSTRY BRIEF, 11 THE VERISIGN DOMAIN REPORT 4 (2015), *available 14 September 2015 at* http://www.verisigninc.com/assets/domain-name-report-january2015.pdf.
[2] ORGANIZATION FOR ECONOMIC CO-OPERATION AND DEVELOPMENT, THE SECONDARY MARKET FOR DOMAIN NAMES (2006), *available 14 September 2015 at* http://www.oecd.org/internet/broadband/36471569.pdf [hereinafter OECD].
[3] OECD, GENERIC TOP LEVEL DOMAIN NAMES: MARKET DEVELOPMENT AND ALLOCATION ISSUES (2004), *available 14 September 2015 at* http://www.oecd.org/internet/ieconomy/32996948.pdf (describing this lucrative activity for companies and investors).

sometimes offering the additional service of escrowing the payment. Practice shows that the percentage of agreements drafted by lawyers is very low compared to the overall number of domain names that change hands or are licensed through these platforms.

Table 4.1 lists significant domain name resales in the past.[4]

Table 4.1   Example of transactions on the Domain Name Secondary Market

sex.com : 13 million dollars
fund.com : 10 million dollars
porn.com : 9 million dollars
fb.com : 8 million dollars
business.com : 7.5 million dollars
diamond.com : 7.5 million dollars
beers.com : 7 million dollars
casino.com : 5.5 million dollars
asseenontv.com : 5 million dollars
korea.com : 5 million dollars
cars.com : 4 million dollars
shop.com : 3.5 million dollars
vodka.com : 3 million dollars
pizza.com : 2.6 million dollars

4.02   A domain is usually defined as a set of addresses which are managed in common. All the names ending in '.us,' for example, form a domain. All the blogs hosted on the WordPress platform have a common Uniform Resource Locator (URL) that ends with '.wordpress.com,' which also forms a domain. The allocation of a domain name to a user is a naming operation.[5]

4.03   A domain is usually managed by an entity from which the creation of a name must be obtained. This entity creates a new entry in a database, which is a technical condition for the name to exist. In some cases the entity creates names for itself; generally, names are born after a third party asks the naming entity to be granted a domain name. This is the first step in a domain name transaction, which involves the formation of a contract between the namespace

---

4   Several industry sites, such as dnjournal.com, inventory transactions. The phenomenon was first documented 15 years ago. *See* David Streitfeld, *On the Web, Simplest Names Can Become Priciest Addresses*, WASHINGTON POST, 15 July 1999, *available 14 September 2015 at* http://www.highbeam.com/doc/1P2–614236.html; *see also* Greg Johnson, *The Costly Game for Net Names*, L.A.Times, 10 April 2000, *available 14 September 2015 at* http://articles.latimes.com/2000/apr/10/news/mn-18112.

5   Stefan Bechtold, *Governance in Namespaces*, 36 LOY. L.A. L. REV. 1239 (2003).

manager and the new domain name holder, resulting in the immediate creation of the name. This contract, which has historically been verbal,[6] incorporates one or several registration rules defined or incorporated by the naming entity. The transactions that will be studied here are those that are not concomitant to the birth of the domain name, but are made during its existence. This chapter will not cover these initial contracts between the domain name holder and the registry directly[7] (that is the entity that manages a namespace, for example VeriSign for the '.com' domain or EURid for the '.eu') or the registrar (an entity accredited by a registry). Nevertheless, these registration and/or renewal agreements form at the same time as the background and the foundation of the subsequent transactions that deal with domain names, as they contain rules that may affect those transactions.

4.04 In particular, this chapter will focus on transactions that relate to the economic life of a domain name after it is registered. These transactions reveal the value that the name acquires after registration, which results in transactions at a higher price than the nominal fee paid for the registration of the name. A domain name transaction's aim is to change the holder of the name (transfer), to let someone else use it (lease), and sometimes to agree on a common use of the name.[8] Mortgages will not be studied, due to a lack of information on the practice and its extent, but many aspects of this chapter remain relevant to the drafting of a contract where a name is used as a security.

4.05 Looking at the elements that practitioners must take into account when drafting a transaction is indirectly a study of the legal regime of domain names, because this regime has a direct effect on what can or cannot be done when drafting transactions. For example, some registries prevent, or have a duty to forbid, transactions on a domain name. This is the case for '.edu,' a domain which a holder cannot sell, exchange, rent, lend, license or transfer its name to another organization.

---

6 Peter K. Yu, *The Neverending ccTLD Story*, in ADDRESSING THE WORLD: NATIONAL IDENTITY AND INTERNET COUNTRY CODE DOMAINS (Erica Schlesinger Wass ed., 2003) [hereinafter Wass]; MILTON L. MUELLER, RULING THE ROOT: INTERNET GOVERNANCE AND THE TAMING OF CYBERSPACE (MIT Press, 2002).

7 It is the case of names in the '.ch' space for example, which can be registered directly from registry SWITCH or through one of its accredited registrars. *Internet Domains, Domain Names*, SWITCH (2015), *available 14 September 2015 at* https://www.nic.ch/reg/index/view.html?lid=en.

8 The author does not remember reading registration rules which would order the use to be personal to the user. The developments that follow will not emphasize that the user may not be the registrant, they must be read keeping this in mind. It is precisely because ownership can be separated from use that transactions such as a license on a domain name can occur.

B. 'WHICH' OBJECT FOR THE TRANSACTION?

There are different levels of domain names. For example, in the address 'calboli.de-werra.com,' the '.com' is the first or top level, the 'de-werra' the second, and the 'calboli' is the third. Each of the three parts of this syntagm is a domain name. Still, in practice, when one refers to a domain name, one has in mind the combination formed by the top and second levels, 'de-werra.com' in our example. Though the immense majority of transactions on domain names are about second level domain names, there are a few on other levels, which will be addressed briefly in this section. **4.06**

1. A top level domain

(a) Private auctions

There were roughly 250 to 300 Top Level Domains (TLD) between 1998 and 2008.[9] In June 2008, during its meeting in Paris, the Internet Corporation for Assigned Names and Numbers (ICANN) decided to 'open' this level and allow applications for the creation of new domains. By the end of October 2014, 426 new TLDs had already been added to the root.[10] One thousand more may follow in the coming months and potentially even more later if ICANN launches a second round of applications. After ICANN officially accepted registrations for new domains, several entities applied for the same chain of characters. Although ICANN's Application Guidelines provided that an auction could be used to decide between applicants who were equally eligible to registration, a few candidates decided to organize their own private auctions where financial conditions were more beneficial for all participants than under ICANN terms.[11] This is the first type of transactions over the sale of a new TLD, or, more precisely, on the right to become the sole applicant for a given extension. **4.07**

(b) Sale of a top level domain

One can also predict that, with the growth of new TLDs and the participation of several investors in the cycle opened by ICANN, there will be domains that **4.08**

---

9 *See* the full list at http://www.iana.org/domains/root/db (*accessed 14 September 2015*).
10 Loïc Damilaville, *Volume de nTLDs : l'ICANN Revoit ses Prévisions à la Baisse*, DNS NEWS (25 October 2014), *available 14 September 2015 at* http://www.wmaker.net/DNSNEWS/Edito-Octobre-2014-volume-de-nTLDs-l-ICANN-revoit-ses-previsions-a-la-baisse_a343.html.
11 *See, e.g.*, Andrew Alleman, *Amazon.com Buys .spot Domain Name for $2.2 Million, .Realty Sells for $5.6 Million*, DOMAIN NAME WIRE (22 October 2014), *available 14 September 2015 at* http://domainnamewire.com/2014/10/22/amazon-dot-spot-auction/.

(c) Lease of a top level domain

4.09 One can also imagine that a TLD manager might 'lease' it to a third-party. An example of such an agreement, possibly the first one, is the contract between an American company and the State of Tuvalu. The American company operates the domain '.tv,' which is the country code TLD (ccTLD) of the State of Tuvalu, a micro-country located in the Pacific Ocean. Similarly, until September 2013, the '.nu' (Niue) had been managed by another American company[12] before switching to a Swedish foundation.

2. A third level domain

4.10 Transactions can also involve names at the third[13] level. With the saturation of the most popular namespace, that is, the '.com' domain, there are companies that have based their business model on the license of third level domains.[14] This activity is similar to any domain name registrar's and will not be studied here. Among other exploitations of third level names can be co-branding, which involves the addition of a trademark before an existing name, for example, 'thistrademark.thatname.com'. One can also imagine the use of one or several third level generic names to promote products or services on a third-party website accessible by these domains, like 'cheap-product.platform.com'. The holder of a second level domain is generally[15] free to create whatever third level name she wishes and have it used by someone else.

4.11 These contracts are not without risks. In France, the company operating the Alapage website entered into an original contract with Brand Alley. Under their agreement, the former had to promote the sales of the latter and send users to its sites through a link. After clicking on that link Alapage clients

---

12 Wass, *supra* note 6. It is said that the revenues for Tuvalu represent a quarter of the GDP of that two square kilometers State.
13 Or higher, but the author is not aware of such situations.
14 *CentralNic Dispute Resolution Policy*, CentralNic (2015), *available* 14 September 2015 at www.centralnic.com/support/dispute/policy (offering names in .eu.com, .us.com, or .cn.com); *see also* Czech Arbitration Court, *CAC to Provide UDRP Services for .co.nl Domain Names*, UDRP DISPUTES, NEWS (6 May 2009), *available* 14 September 2015 at http://udrp.adr.eu/arbitration_platform/news.php [hereinafter CAC] (providing a similar service for .co.nl by EuroDNS).
15 Still one should check whether rules governing the first level domain do not prevent or hinder operations at the third level. *See, e.g.,* NIC.TM, RULES FOR THE .TM DOMAIN AND SUB-DOMAINS, art. 4, § 1 (2011), *available* 14 September 2015 at http://www.nic.tm/rules.html (stating that an applicant must be resident in the country of Turkmenistan).

could land on a page within Brand Alley's site built in application of the agreement, which URL was <alapage.brandalley.fr>. After a third company realized that its goods were offered for sale on Brand Alley in violation of its distribution agreement, it sued not only Brand Alley, but also Alapage! In itself, this shows the risk that can exist within such deals; others can believe that a commercial offer made at a page that has two domain names, one contained in the second level and the other in the third, is actually emanating from the two companies designated by these names and not just one. In this dispute, after reviewing the agreement between Brand Alley and Alapage, the court found[16] that its goal was purely promotional and that Alapage could not be liable for illegal sales.

The person who rents a third level domain name is not the only one to bear risks. In the United States, Google was sued after having let a Blogger user create a blog on its platform with the address 'jewsforjesus.blogspot.com.' To the owner of a similar trademark, it was not only the blogger, but also the platform manager, who should be found liable for trademark infringement.[17] Though under general intermediary liability rules applicable in a wide range of countries, this is typically not a case in which the platform can be liable for content created by a user. The user alone decides to combine content with a name, an action which can lead to trademark infringement if this combination is a source of confusion with the trademark, and the holder of the second level domain name may want to protect itself by warning its users of legal risks. Lawyers will have to draft clauses that will provide for this protection. At a minimum, it is advised to remind the user of a third level domain that she has to respect the rules applicable to the use of the second level name to which this domain is attached, as several Uniform Domain Name Dispute Resolution Policy (UDRP) decisions have shown.[18]

4.12

---

16 Puma France v. France Telecom E-Commerce, Brandalley, and Vanam (Strasbourg Court of First Instance, 2008), *available 14 September 2015 at* www.legalis.net/spip.php?page=jurisprudence-decision&id_article=2174.

17 Complaint, Jews For Jesus v. Google, Inc., 2005 WL 377582- (2005) (No. 05 CV 10684) (case terminated); *see also Mobimedia France v BDLG Sofiges and Mediaplazza.com* (No. 05/05413, Paris Court of First Instance, 2006) (finding 10,000 partners of an affiliation program whose names were attached to 'sonnerie.net' or 'forfaitsms.com'. A few of them had an illegal behaviour, which resulted in a sanction not against them, but against the company that managed the affiliation network).

18 J. C. Bamford Excavators Limited v. MSD (Darlington) Ltd., World Intellectual Property Organization Case No. D2001–1484 (20 March 2002) (deciding on the similarity of complainant's trademarks and the domain names 'jcbequipment.uk.com,' 'jcb-equipment.uk.com,' 'jcbfinance.uk.com,' 'jcb-parts.uk.com,' 'jcbplant.uk.com,' 'jcb-plant.uk.com,' 'jcbs.uk.com,' 'jcbsales.uk.com,' 'jcb-sales.uk.com,' 'jcbspares.uk.com,' and 'jcb-spares.uk.com.') [hereinafter WIPO]; *see also* AVENTIS v. S. Priost c/o Lark Computer Ltd., WIPO Case No. D2002–0895 [2002] (determining whether the domain name 'aventis.eu.com' is subject to the ICANN Uniform Domain Name Dispute Resolution Policy).

3. A second level domain

4.13 The transactions over first and third level domains remain rare compared to those on second level. It is worth noting that the later would not exist if they were not attached to a TLD, each convention that deals with a domain name implicitly provides that the holder can use this TLD.

C. 'WHERE' WILL THE NAME BE USED?

4.14 The question of where the party to a transaction intends to use a domain name seems irrelevant at first sight. Because domain names are transnational by nature, and because they can be accessed everywhere there is an internet connection, any name is mechanically used globally – even in North Korea where there would be clandestine connections. Still, there are elements pertaining to the name itself that may restrict the geographic zone in which it can be used. Because of these geographic restrictions, a practitioner should advise his or her client or inform the other party of these restrictions. In case of a dispute following the transaction, the question of the appropriate jurisdiction can become tricky; thus, lawyers drafting these contracts should include a provision designating the appropriate forum as agreed to by the parties.

4.15 There may be geographical restrictions on the use of a name that is the subject of a transaction. Although a domain name is supposed to have a global reach, situations arise when it will not be accessible in a given place, usually because of a technical restriction put in place in this location, which equates to a use restriction on its holder. A court could have issued an order to block a domain name at the State level, under which access providers in this State must implement a Domain Name System (DNS)-blocking measure to prevent their users from visiting the content normally accessible under this name. The High Court of England and Wales, for example, has ordered that 'newzbin.com' must be blocked by British internet access providers.[19] In other countries, several jurisdictions[20] have taken a similar decision against 'thepiratebay.com'. In March 2014, the Court of Justice of the European Union accepted the principle of such measures, paving the way for more blocking orders in

---

[19] Twentieth Century Fox Film Corp & Ors v. British Telecommunications plc [2011] EWHC 1981 (Ch), *available 14 September 2015 at* http://www.bailii.org/ew/cases/EWHC/Ch/2011/1981.html.

[20] *See, e.g.,* Bergamo Public Prosecutor's Officer v. Kolmisappi (Italian Supreme Court of Cassation, 29 September 2009); Columbia Pictures Industries Inc. v. Portlane AB (Swedish Court of Appeal, 4 May 2010); IFPI Danmark v. DMT2 A/S (Frederiksberg Court, 29 October 2008).

Member States.[21] There are blocking orders usually that are not limited in time, meaning that the domain name will be permanently blocked, regardless of any change in the content associated with this name. To the reader who would ask why one would be interested in buying a notorious name that has been subject to blocking, it is worth a reminder of the example of 'napster-.com,' which was once a platform that allowed exchange of files and used to share infringing copies of music, but later became a legal music streaming website.

4.16 There can also be situations where a name is not blocked *per se*, but the TLD to which it is attached is blocked. When ICANN gave the green light to the launch of the '.xxx' TLD, the registration rules provide that it can only be used for adult content.[22] Following this determination, a State in the Middle East said it would block in its territory all requests to access names using that extension. With the rise of the balkanization of the internet, due diligence should extend to the checking the accessibility of the name and its capacity to be used without restriction.

4.17 Under its registration rules, which bind the user of a name even though she acquired it through a transaction and not directly from a registrar or the registry, there can be restrictions on the use of a domain name. One such restriction is that it must target a specific community. For example, all domain names registered in the '.cat' zone must open to content in Catalan or target the Catalan community.[23] Although this entire community does not live in the territory of Catalonia, it is mostly based in this area. In these circumstances, this contractual condition equates to a geographic use restriction and can lead to the deletion of the name if it is not followed by the domain name holder.

D. 'WHO' WILL HOLD OR USE THE NAME?

4.18 This section deals primarily with the person who will become the new owner, or the licensee, of the name, and only implicitly relates to the other party to the transaction. In the case of a transfer, the new owner is required to meet the criteria set out in the registration rules applicable to the domain name being

---

21 Case C-314/12, *UPC Telekabel Wien* [2014], *available 14 September 2015 at* http://curia.europa.eu/juris/liste.jsf?language=fr&num=C-314/12.
22 INTERNET CORPORATION FOR ASSIGNED NAMES AND NUMBERS, .XXX REGISTRY AGREEMENT (31 March 2011), *available 14 September 2015 at* https://www.icann.org/resources/unthemed-pages/xxx-2012-02-25-en.
23 ICANN, .CAT TLD SPONSORSHIP AGREEMENT (23 May 2005), *available 14 September 2015 at* https://www.icann.org/resources/unthemed-pages/cat-2012-02-25-en.

transferred. Even though it is not an absolute requirement, it is preferable that the seller meet these criteria at the time the contract takes place and at the time the name is transferred. What matters most in these transactions is the capacity of the future holder for the transaction to be valid. If the former holder does not fully comply with the registration rules, this is a contractual issue between that person and the registry – except, of course, in the case of fraud. In the event where the name is not transferred, but is being leased to a third-party, it is of the utmost importance that the owner of the domain name respects the terms of the registration at the date of the convention and for its entire duration, otherwise the licensee may see the name it uses being lost due to the negligence of the owner. For this reason, it can be useful to provide an audit clause or any other provision that grants the licensor the power to verify that the licensee does not put the licensor's ownership at risk by not complying with the registration rules.

1. The case of a transfer

(a) Eligibility

4.19 When the effect of the transaction is to have a new party substitute for the former, following a re-sale or a donation of the name, it is a requirement, or at least preferable, that the new holder comply with the eligibility rules that the registry stated.

(i) Capacity

4.20 There are domain names whose registration is reserved only for natural persons.[24] There are others that are restricted to companies only, and sometimes the companies of a given State,[25] or to specific entities. For example, '.museum' is only for museums[26] while '.edu' is reserved to universities accredited by the US agency Educause.[27] The '.pro' namespace was originally meant to address the needs of professionals who could give evidence that they

---

24 L'Afnic, *Ouverture du Domaine .nom.fr*, afnic (26 July 1999), *available 14 September 2015 at* http://www.afnic.fr/fr/l-afnic-en-bref/actualites/actualites-generales/2476/show/ouverture-du-domaine-nom-fr.html (requiring, for example, that the '.nom.fr' domain name be reserved for individuals).

25 The '.mc' is for example only for the 'legal commercial entities or public or private organizations.' *See* GOVERNMENT OF MONACO, DIRECTION DES COMMUNICATIONS ELECTRONIQUES DE MONACO, INFORMATION, *available 14 September 2015 at* http://nic.mc/information/mcNicInformation-us.html.

26 ICANN, .MUSEUM TLD SPONSORSHIP AGREEMENT (3 November 2007), *available 14 September 2015 at* https://www.icann.org/resources/unthemed-pages/museum-2012-02-25-en.

27 In application of the RFC 1591, which also provides, along with the RFC 2146, that the '.gov' will only be open to federal agencies. FEDERAL NETWORK COUNCIL, U.S. GOVERNMENT INTERNET DOMAIN NAMES (May 1997), *available 14 September 2015 at* ftp.rfc-editor.org/in-notes/rfc2146.txt.

are registered to a professional association.[28] The '.int' is available for registration exclusively by intergovernmental organizations and each organization can get just one name.[29]

4.21 Do these special rules prevent a potential seller from entering into a negotiation with a potential buyer when one or both know that the acquirer does not meet the contractual conditions set by the registry? This must be answered in the negative; that the candidate to the registration does not respect the registration criteria during the negotiation does not mean that this candidate will not be fully compliant on the day when the transfer of the name takes place, or on the day when the registry checks whether the relevant conditions are met. A cautious seller will add in the contract a clause stating that the buyer guarantees it has or will meet all the conditions for the registration to become valid.

(ii) Conditions of establishment

4.22 Several ccTLD registries require that the names they allocate reflect the nexus their holders have with the territory represented by the ccTLD or the larger region in which the territory is located. The '.fr' space, for example, was long restricted to legal entities which seat was in France or to natural persons who could provide an address in the French territory.[30] The '.us' is similarly reserved to local actors[31] in the U.S. Any registration within the '.asia' domain must have an administrative, technical or billing contact in the Asian, Australian or Pacific zone, which includes Israel, Kazakhstan, China and New Zealand according to the rules.[32]

4.23 Interestingly, the condition that the domain names have a nexus with the territory represented by the ccTLD is not only set out in the contractual registration rules, but is also required by law in these territories. For example,

---

28 ICANN, UNSPONSORED TLD AGREEMENT: APPENDIX C (.PRO), 'CERTIFIED PROFESSIONALS' (30 September 2004), *available 14 September 2015 at* www.icann.org/tlds/agreements/pro/registry-agmt-appc-30sep04.htm.
29 Internet Assigned Numbers Authority, *.INT Zone Management*, *available 14 September 2015 at* https://www.iana.org/domains/int.
30 Now all persons having a domicile or residence in the European Union can apply. The rule has changed for purely legal reasons – compliance with European law that forbids restrictions to the freedom of movement of persons and services – rather than to reflect an evolution of the original management principle of this domain.
31 .US, *The usTLD Nexus Requirements Policy* (2015), *available 14 September 2015 at* http://www.neustar.us/the-ustld-nexus-requirements/.
32 .Asia, *ASIA Charter Eligibility Requirement Policies* (15 August 2007), *available 14 September 2015 at* http://www.dot.asia/policies/DotAsia-Charter-Eligibility–COMPLETE-2007–08–15.pdf; *see also* Domain.com, *ASIA* (2015), *available 14 September 2015 at* https://www.domain.com/domains/tlds/asia.bml.

the European Union domain '.eu'[33] and the Norwegian domain '.no'[34] both require a nexus to the territory where they are being used. For domains such as these, where the law of the corresponding country requires a presence in the territory, is it possible to elect a proxy to circumvent the application of these rules? A U.S. company tried to circumvent the rules by granting a license to a Belgium-based practitioner. The CJEU ruled that this was a clear violation of the Regulation laying down public policy rules concerning the implementation and functions of the '.eu' TLD and the principles governing registration.[35] To the Court, these provisions, which granted a priority to trademark owners or to their licensees for the registration of a '.eu' name, must be interpreted as meaning that the word 'licensees' does not refer to a person who has been authorized by the proprietor of a trademark concerned solely to register, in his own name but on behalf of that proprietor, a domain name identical or similar to that trade mark, but without that person being authorized to use the trademark commercially in a manner consistent with its functions. In other words, the Court finds it is a fraud to designate a local trustee that would just hold a domain name when the person who has a real interest in this name does not have a local presence.[36]

(b) Contact information

4.24 A contract that is aimed at transferring a domain name will not reach its full effect if there is no change in the information recorded in the so-called 'Whois database' managed by the registry. Without said change, there is no formal registration in the name of the new owner. In other words, the registry has not yet acknowledged a contract between the registry and the new holder. Traditionally, there are three fields to fill out in the Whois database: administrative contact, billing contact, and technical contact. Since the identity of these three contacts can be different, a question could arise as to who *really* is

---

33   Regulation No. 773/2002, On the Implementation of the .eu Top Level Domain, art. 4, § 2, 2002 O.J. (L 113) 1 (EC), *available 14 September 2015 at* http://eur-lex.europa.eu/legal-content/EN/TXT/PDF/?uri=CELEX:32002R0733&from=EN. It's also the case of the '.fr' since 2011. *See also* the French Code of Posts and Electronic Communications, art. L. 45-3 (26 July 2013), *available 14 September 2015 at* http://www.arcep.fr/fileadmin/reprise/textes/lois/cpce-legis.pdf.

34   UNINETT Norid AS, *Requirements for the Applicant – Who Can Apply?, Domain Name Policy for .no, available 14 September 2015 at* http://www.norid.no/navnepolitikk.en.html#link5.

35   Case C-376/11, Pie Optiek v. Bureau Gevers, 2012 E.C.R., *available 14 September 2015 at* http://curia.europa.eu/juris/liste.jsf?num=C-376/11.

36   For the circumvention of French registration rules, then contractual – they became regulation in 2011, requiring a domicile on the territory. *See* EuroDNS and Laurent Nunenthal v. AFNIC (Versailles Court of First Instance, 2004); France Printemps, Somewhere, Redcats, Free v. KLTE Ltd, AFNIC (Versailles Court of First Instance, 2006) (explaining a provision under which a Luxembourg registrar offered customers wishing to be registered and operate Internet services under the 'fr.' TLD but who do not fulfil the conditions required by AFNIC for Registration under the '.fr' TLD, to handle such registrations on behalf of such customers under the trusteeship of a French-registered company with headquarters in France).

the owner of the domain name. Responding to this confusion, registries have clarified this question by adding the category 'registrant' or by specifying that the administrative contact is at the same time the registrant. Used in practice by third parties who want to know who is the holder of a domain name, this information still lacks authority. For example, the information may not be immediately updated; thus, the information may have changed, but has not yet been reflected. Furthermore, the information could have been fraudulently modified. A U.S. District Court ruled in such a case that

> Defendants' arguments rest on changes to the WHOIS records and the registration contact information for the domain name. Such records, however, are not the equivalent of statutorily-created title systems. They are privately-maintained systems for providing contact information and keeping records for domain names.[37]

(c) Joint registration

A domain name can be registered in two names when there is no contrary requirement. One can take the example of a partnership between individuals that does not have the effect of creating a separate legal entity.[38]   **4.25**

2. The case of agreements on use

(a) General principles

When the registry has stated that the names it allocates must be used in a particular fashion, the holder who decides to let it be used by someone else should incorporate the registration rules in the license agreement in order to protect the object of the transaction. Moreover, the scope and meaning of the registration rules may need to be clarified in the agreement.   **4.26**

For example, the '.biz' TLD contains vague wording that would need explanation: **4.27**

> The registered domain name will be used primarily for bona fide business or commercial purposes and not (i) exclusively for personal use; or (ii) solely for the

---

37 Express Media Group, LLC, et al. & DVD.com v. Express Corp. & Gregory Ricks, 2007 WL 1394163 (N.D. Cal., 2007).
38 CAC, Kraftwerk GbR Ralf Hütter/Florian Schneider v. EURid (11 November 2006), *available 14 September 2015 at* https://eu.adr.eu/adr/decisions/decision.php?dispute_id=2661 (providing an example of the joint ownership allowed in Germany, where contracts can define the relationship between owners. 'In the absence of any agreement to the contrary, the effect of Joint Ownership is to create a legal entity sharing undivided interests in the intellectual property right – i.e. each party holds a nominal equal share, divided simply per head (Bruchteilsgemeinschaft, §§ 741 ff BGB) ... Joint Ownership can lead to a specific form of business entity (Gemeinschaft bürgerlichen Rechts, §§ 705 ff. BGB)').

purposes of (1) selling, trading or leasing the domain name for compensation, or (2) the unsolicited offering to sell, trade or lease the domain name for compensation.[39]

In the absence of a global understanding on the definition of what a '*bona fide business*' is, and given that a business that can be legal in State A and illegal in State B, it is advised that there should be a reference to a given State law or to the strictest of all laws in this field in the agreement.

4.28 Protecting the domain name does not just mean making sure the licensee will not use it in a manner that may infringe third parties' rights or violate the registration rules. It also means taking into account the elements that could affect the value of the domain name in the ecosystem in which it is used. For example, there are search engines which can penalize a name if it is used in conjunction with webpages that do not respect their guidelines and are conceived to trump these search engines.[40] Because the penalty is generally a de-ranking of the domain name, it affects the economic value of the domain name, and, thus, can deprive the owner of current or future revenues. Conversely, for a better understanding of what drives traffic to the domain name and what makes it valuable, the licensor may want to secure access to the traffic logs and data generated by the visitors.

4.29 When a domain name is registered by someone for the benefit of an organization that has no existence at the time the name is registered, like the case of a future partner of a company to be incorporated, the legal entity must make sure this electronic asset was registered with its identity. Similarly when an employee registers a domain name for her company, the firm must require and/or verify that the name was registered on its behalf and that the employee's identity does not appear in the Whois database: cases of employees 'leaving' with domain names are not rare. In both cases, the legal person must have access to and be able to change the account information that allows the domain name to be managed. Without them the name can be lost or cannot be the subject of a transaction.

(b) Situations of joint use

4.30 There are transactions where two parties (or in some instances more than two parties) decide to use a domain name in common. In this situation, the homepage will offer visitors the option to access two, or more, different

---

39 ICANN, EXHIBIT D: REGISTRY OPERATOR'S OPERATIONAL STANDARDS, POLICIES, PROCEDURES AND PRACTICES, art. I, § 2(a), .BIZ AGREEMENT APPENDIX 8 REGISTRY-REGISTRAR AGREEMENT (8 December 2006), *available 14 September 2015 at* www.icann.org/tlds/agreements/biz/appendix-08-08dec06.htm.
40 *See, e.g.*, Blogoscoped, *German BMW Banned From Google* (4 February 2006), *available 14 September 2015 at* http://blogoscoped.com/archive/2006-02-04-n60.html.

websites, usually accessible through a different domain name.[41] This was done, for example, for the names 'scrabble.com,' 'kaefer.de,' and 'winterthur.ch.' (the last name giving access to four different entities whose name includes this sign). The parties can decide to create a joint venture for this purpose, or decide to enter into a contract that sets the usage rules. In the latter case, this 'co-using' agreement is mechanically posterior to the registration or transfer. The holder remains unique in the eyes of the registry and of third parties. It also happened that a court ruled that the parties should 'share' the domain name in dispute.[42]

E. 'WHAT' IS THE NATURE OF THE TRANSACTION?

1. 'Sale' of a domain name

In practice, when a domain name changes hands after the former owner has received money from the new one, the transaction is referred to as a *sale*. Legally, for a sale to exist, there must be a transfer of *property*. Is a domain name property? Where registration rules or the law states that the registration only grants a right of use by the registrant, a domain name cannot be regarded as a property. For example, the domain names '.au,' '.uk,' '.be,' '.ch,' '.es,' and '.it' under the registration rules and the Regulation over the '.eu' domain[43] under the law sets out such restrictions. In Japan a court found the holder is just granted the right to use a domain name,[44] whereas in the famous <sex.com> ruling,[45] a U.S. court clearly ruled that the disputed name was a property right. Later, the European Court of Human Rights went in the same direction but referred to the concept of possession rather than the concept of property. The

4.31

---

41 Jacqueline Lipton, *A Winning Solution for YouTube and UTube? Corresponding Trademarks and Domain Name Sharing*, 21 HARVARD J. OF LAW AND TECH. 2 (2008), *available* 14 September 2015 at http://jolt.law.harvard.edu/articles/pdf/v21/21HarvJLTech509.pdf. For an example of ruling following when two companies decide to 'share' a name, *see* Microcaz v. Oceanet (Le Mans Court of First Instance, 29 June 1999).
42 Bundesgerichtshof Im Namen Des Volkes Urteil, I ZR 317/99 (April 2002), *available* 14 September 2015 at http://www.netlaw.de/urteile/bgh_15.htm (determining how the 'vossius.de' domain name should be shared).
43 Regulation No. 874/2004, Laying Down Public Policy Rules Concerning the Implementation and Functions of the .eu Top Level Domain and the Principles Governing Registration, art. 2, 2004 O.J. (L 162) 40 (EU), *available* 14 September 2015 at http://eur-lex.europa.eu/legal-content/EN/TXT/PDF/?uri=CELEX:32004R0874&from=EN (stating that 'a specific domain name shall be allocated for use').
44 Sonybank, [Tokyo Dist. Ct.] 2001, 2001(wa) no. 5603:

   A domain name registration is granted through a private contract that consists of the Rules of the Registration between an Internet user and JPNIC, the registry in Japan. The domain name registrant's right to use the domain name is a right arisen from such contract. Therefore, a domain name registrant's right to a domain name only exists in relation to JPNIC, and it is apparent that the domain name in this case is not something to which someone can claim his ownership.

45 Kremen v. Cohen, 337 F.3d 1024, 1030 (9th Cir. 2003).

doctrine in Europe tends to see a domain name not as a property.[46] This is not an academic debate: the question of the legal nature of a domain name has an impact on the nature of the transfer and also has fiscal incidences. If a domain name is a property that is being sold, there are countries where the Value Added Tax can be different depending on whether it is considered that the real object of the transaction is not the name itself, but the contractual claim the registrant has against the registry.

2. License of a domain name

4.32 The question of the legal nature of a domain name matters less when the name is not transferred, but licensed. There are numerous examples of licenses of domain names without payment. E-mail providers implicitly let their subscribers use their domain name not only for the technical exchange of messages, but also for display on a commercial, a website or a business card. Blogging platforms where users can post messages under the third level domain of their choice, for example 'xxxx.wordpress.com' or 'yyyyy.livejournal.com,' also give their consent to the use by their client of both the third and second levels domain name. The licenses that this chapter has dealt with are those which have a business purpose and are agreed for a fee, which can be substantial.[47]

F. CONCLUSION

4.33 Although they take place on the secondary market, domain names transactions are most entirely subject to domain name registration rules that apply on the primary market. The registration and/or renewal agreements form at the same time as the background and the foundation of the subsequent transactions that deal with domain names, as they contain rules that may affect those transactions. They may for example require that the domain name have a nexus with specific territories, others are reserved for specific entities, and other domain names are blocked in certain areas. These rules may place limits on

---

[46] Arguing that they should be subject to a property right: KONSTANTINOS KOMAITIS, THE CURRENT STATE OF DOMAIN NAME REGULATION: DOMAIN NAMES AS SECOND CLASS CITIZENS IN A MARK-DOMINATED WORLD (Routledge 2010). *But see* CÉDRIC MANARA, LE DROIT DES NOMS DE DOMAINE (2012). *See also* Xuan-Thao Nguyen, *Cyberproperty and Judicial Dissonance: The Trouble with Domain Name Classification*, 10 GEO. MASON L. REV. 183 (2001).

[47] In the case a domain name is being registered by a subsidiary in a country A and used by the mother company incorporated in a country B, the absence of a payment by the second can lead to a tax adjustment against the first. *See, e.g.,* Tribunal Administratif de Montreuil, 1ère Chambre, Jugement du 9 février 2012 (9 February 2012), *available 14 September 2015 at* www.legalis.net/spip.php?page=jurisprudence-decision&id_article=3492 (examining 'ebay.fr').

F. CONCLUSION

how and where the domain can be used, and thus can affect the value of the name which is the object of the transaction. An owner who licenses a domain name must conversely take into account the conditions in which the name will be used by the other party or third parties, as these conditions may affect the value of the domain name in subsequent transactions.

5

HOW TO MAKE TWO OUT OF ONE: THE INS AND OUTS OF TRADEMARK PORTFOLIO SPLITTING TRANSACTIONS

Gregor Bühler[*] and Luca Dal Molin[**]

A.	INTRODUCTION	5.01	restrictions on partial assignments	5.36
B.	PRELIMINARY NOTE ON APPLICABLE LAW	5.05	(e) License to register new trademarks	5.37
C.	BUILDING BLOCKS OF TRADEMARK PORTFOLIO SPLITTING	5.09	D. TRADEMARK PORTFOLIO SPLITTING AGREEMENTS	5.39
	1. Overview	5.09	1. Overview	5.39
	2. Free assignability as international standard	5.10	2. Typical provisions in trademark portfolio splitting agreements	5.42
	3. Partial assignment	5.12	(a) Trademark delimitation and allocation	5.42
	(a) Overview	5.12		
	(b) Effect of the partial assignment	5.14	(b) Implementation of the allocation	5.46
	(c) Limitations	5.16		
	(d) Technicalities under a Swiss law focus	5.19	(c) Coexistence, non-compete and mutual support	5.51
	4. Trademark license	5.23	(d) Scope	5.52
	(a) Overview	5.23	(e) Trademark maintenance	5.53
	(b) Limitations	5.26	(f) Duration and termination	5.55
	(c) Technicalities under Swiss law focus	5.28	(g) Conflict resolution, governing law, jurisdiction	5.56
	5. Partial assignment and license grant compared in practice	5.31	E. OTHER POSSIBLE OPTIONS AND CONSIDERATIONS	5.57
	(a) In general: ownership v. contractual rights	5.31	1. Shared ownership	5.57
			2. Joint ventures	5.60
	(b) Affected goods and services	5.33	3. Rebranding	5.61
	(c) Duration of the post-transactional arrangement	5.35	F. CONCLUSION	5.62
	(d) Flexibility of license grants v.			

A. INTRODUCTION

5.01 Trademarks are key assets for many businesses. Most companies own trademarks and use protected trade names, logos, and designations to distinguish

---

[*] Dr. iur. Gregor Bühler is a Partner in the IP/IT Practice Group of Homburger AG, Zurich, Switzerland.
[**] Lic. iur. Luca Dal Molin is an Associate in the IP/IT Practice Group of Homburger AG.

A. INTRODUCTION

their products and services in the marketplace. As such, trademarks can be a significant driver for mergers and acquisitions, and the trademark portfolios of the companies involved often play an important role in these transactions. One of the key issues in these transactions is how to separate the trademark portfolio affected by the transaction. This can be especially tricky if trademarks will have to be used not only by one of the parties following the completion of the transaction, but by both of them.

5.02 For instance, take a large public company that wants to divest its consumer electronic division. The consumer brand is very popular and a key asset in the deal. The buyer made it a condition that it can use this brand following the acquisition. The seller, however, has used the same brand in other divisions that will not be divested. Although the seller is willing to eventually transition to a new brand, it needs a certain time to do so. Hence, the seller and the buyer will have to use the same brand for some time following the transaction.

5.03 In such a situation, the parties need to agree on a way of coexisting, both of them with the same trademarks, following their transaction. This is usually done by means of a trademark portfolio splitting or trademark co-existence agreement. These arrangements can take a variety of forms, as required to mirror the parties' specific deal. Nevertheless, most of these arrangements are similar in that they are designed on the basis of two typical 'building blocks' of trademark portfolio splits, which are the following: a partial assignment of a trademark and a trademark license. Most often, these building blocks are integrated in agreements governing the split of the parties' trademark portfolio and their coexistence following the transaction.

5.04 The purpose of this chapter is to describe the practice of trademark portfolio splitting transactions. In doing so, we deliberately focus on practical aspects rather than trademark law theory. After briefly alluding to applicable law in Section B, we introduce the two building blocks of trademark portfolio splitting transactions that we have just mentioned, and compare their practical application in Section C. We then discuss how these building blocks are integrated in a typical trademark portfolio splitting agreement in Section D. Further, we briefly refer to other options that are sometimes considered in the context of a trademark portfolio split, such as shared ownership, joint venture companies as trademark owners, and rebranding, in Section E. The chapter is concluded by a summary and our recommendations in Section F.

B. PRELIMINARY NOTE ON APPLICABLE LAW

5.05 Transactions where the need for a trademark portfolio split arises are very often cross-border transactions and the split will affect trademarks registered in several jurisdictions. This brings up the question of applicable law: which law applies to cross-border trademark portfolio splits?

5.06 Broadly speaking, the answer to this question is twofold: While the law of the parties' choice usually governs the trademark portfolio splitting agreement, local law applies to required changes in local or regional trademark registrations and applications. The latter is based on the widely accepted notion that existence, scope, and duration of a trademark are subject to the law of the jurisdiction where protection is sought, the so-called principle of the *lex loci protectionis*.[1] In contrast, the contractual arrangements between the parties are not affected by this principle and the parties typically have the right to choose the governing law.[2] As it would go vastly beyond the scope of this chapter, we do not address the details of this issue. Nonetheless, it is crucial to bear in mind that local laws have a significant impact on cross-border trademark portfolio splits. For instance, irrespective of the parties' choice of the governing law in the trademark portfolio splitting agreement, local law will determine whether a partial assignment is permitted and what formalities have to be accomplished, or how a trademark license grant is qualified and what kind of requirements exists in order to grant such license under a locally registered trademark.

5.07 Hence, cross-border trademark portfolio splits usually require a country-by-country analysis to ensure that the agreement on the split can be implemented and enforced locally. This often requires parties without their own local expertise to retain local counsel, at least for key jurisdictions. Nevertheless, in order to keep drafting, negotiation, and implementation workable in practice, the parties to a global trademark portfolio split will typically attempt to adopt a 'one-size-fits-all' approach for their overall agreement governing the split, leaving room for required localization on a case-by-case basis. This way, they can decide on one globally applicable agreement, and deal with localization by

---

1 This is, for instance, codified in Article 110(1) of the Swiss Federal Act on International Private Law [hereinafter IPLA] of 18 December 1987, SR 291 and, at least regarding infringement, in Article 8(1) of the Rome II Regulation, Regulation (EC) No. 864/2007 of the European Parliament and of the Council of 11 July 2007 on the law applicable to non-contractual obligations, O.J. 2007 L 199/40 (EC) [hereinafter Rome II]; With respect to private international law aspects of trademark transactions, see chapter 12 in this book, Dai Yokomizo, *Choice-of-court and Choice-of-law Clauses in International Trademark Transactions*.

2 *E.g.*, Article 122(2), IPLA, *supra* note 1; Article 3(1) of the Rome I Regulation, Regulation (EC) No. 593/2008 of the European Parliament and of the Council of 17 June 2008 on the law applicable to contractual obligations, O.J. 2008 L 177/6 [hereinafter Rome I].

means of localized annexes, addressing local specifics, and 'catch-all'-language that requires the parties to agree in good faith on how to overcome unanticipated difficulties with local implementation.

This is the approach we mirror in this chapter: we focus broadly on the concepts that we see agreed upon in global trademark portfolio splits, leaving aside local particularities in the first place. When outlining this approach, to the extent relevant, we take into account the standards established by the Agreement on Trade-Related Aspects of Intellectual Property Rights of 15 April 1994 (TRIPS),[3] the Trademark Law Treaty of 27 October 1994 (TLT),[4] the Singapore Treaty on the Law of Trademarks of 27 March 2006 (STLT),[5] the Madrid Agreement Concerning the International Registration of Marks of 14 April 1891 (as amended 28 September 1979) (MMA),[6] the Protocol Relating to the Madrid Agreement Concerning the International Registration of Marks (as amended in 2006 and in 2007) (MMP),[7] the European Community Trademark Regulation (CTR),[8] and the European Trademarks Directive (TD).[9] As a result, the global approach addressed herein will not necessarily work in every single jurisdiction around the world, and may often require localization. To illustrate this, we exemplify localization and its technicalities at certain points from the perspective of our home jurisdiction, Switzerland, taking into account in particular the Swiss Federal Trademark Protection Act (TPA).[10]

5.08

---

[3] Agreement on Trade-Related Aspects of Intellectual Property Rights [hereinafter TRIPS], 1869 U.N.T.S. 299.
[4] Trademark Law Treaty, 27 October 1994, 2037 U.N.T.S. 298 [hereinafter TLT].
[5] Singapore Treaty on the Law of Trademarks, 27 March 2006, S. Treaty Doc. No. 110–2 [hereinafter STLT].
[6] Agreement Concerning International Registration of Trade Marks, Signed at Madrid, 14 April 1891, Revised at Brussels, 14 December 1900, and at Washington, 2 June 1911.
[7] Protocol Relating to the Madrid Agreement Concerning the International Registration of Marks, 15 U.S.C. § 1141a(b) (2004).
[8] European Council Regulation (EC) No. 207/2009, O.J. 2009 L 78/1 [hereinafter CTR].
[9] Directive 2008/95/EC of the European Parliament and of the Council of October 22, 2008 to approximate the laws of the Member States relating to trade marks, O.J. 2008 L 299.
[10] Swiss Federal Act on the Protection of Trade Marks and Indications of Source, Trade Mark Protection Act, of 28 August 1992, SR 232.11, *available 15 September 2015 at* http://www.admin.ch/opc/en/classified-compilation/19920213/index.html [hereinafter TPA].

C. BUILDING BLOCKS OF TRADEMARK PORTFOLIO SPLITTING

1. Overview

5.09 The following focuses on what may be referred to as the two 'building blocks' of trademark portfolio splitting. When two companies have to split a trademark portfolio between them, often as a result of an M&A transaction, their agreement on how to do so is typically built upon these building blocks. The building blocks are the following: first, a trademark can be *partially assigned* by one party to the other; and second, one party may retain (or acquire) exclusive ownership, but *license* certain rights to use the trademark to the other party. Before diving into these topics, we shall touch briefly on free assignability of trademarks, which is a prerequisite for many of the options we outline below.

2. Free assignability as international standard

5.10 The free assignability of trademarks, irrespective of whether or not the assignment takes place in connection with the transfer of a business, is a key requirement for many trademark portfolio splits. Over the past decades, this principle has become an international standard. Free assignability of trademarks has widely replaced the former idea that trademarks are inextricably linked to a certain business, and may therefore not be assigned unless by way of a transfer of that business. Today, as a matter of principle, trademarks are no longer tied to a certain business, as was the case under older trademark laws. Most importantly, this principle is reflected in TRIPS.[11] Free assignability is also the underlying assumption of the TLT[12] and the STLT.[13] Likewise, the Swiss TPA[14] and the European Community Trademark (CTM)[15] are built upon this principle.

5.11 Nevertheless, a few jurisdictions still tie a trademark to the *goodwill* associated with it, and do not permit the assignment of a trademark without the associated goodwill. The most important example of this is the United States

---

11   TRIPS, *supra* note 3, Article 21 states:

> Members may determine conditions on the licensing and assignment of trademarks, it being understood that the compulsory licensing of trademarks shall not be permitted and that the owner of a registered trademark shall have the right to assign the trademark with or without the transfer of the business to which the trademark belongs.

Id.

12   *See* TLT, *supra* note 4, Article 11.
13   *See* STLT, *supra* note 5, Article 11.
14   TPA, *supra* note 10, Article 17(1). *See also* BÜHLER, GREGOR, NOTH/BÜHLER/THOUVENIN (ED.), MARKENSCHUTZGESETZ (MSCHG), Art. 17 N 2, Bern 2009.
15   CTR, Article 17(1) CTR *supra* note 8.

C. BUILDING BLOCKS OF TRADEMARK PORTFOLIO SPLITTING

of America, where trademark assignments without associated goodwill are considered invalid.[16] It is, however, worth highlighting that goodwill and business are not the same; they typically have to be distinguished. At least in jurisdictions that adhere to TRIPS, trademark assignments without the associated business are permitted, even if the assignment of the associated goodwill is a prerequisite for a trademark assignment in that jurisdiction.[17]

3. Partial assignment

(a) Overview

5.12 The first building block of trademark portfolio splitting is the partial assignment of a trademark. In a partial assignment, a pre-existing trademark is split into two (or more)[18] surviving parts, each of which cover certain goods and services claimed by the original trademark, and one of the surviving trademarks is assigned to a third party. This enables the parties to the transaction to divide a trademark so that each of them can continue using the same brand for its respective business after carving one out of the other.

5.13 Take the example of the company divesting its consumer electronics business mentioned in the introduction. To achieve their goal, the parties can agree on a partial assignment of the relevant trademarks. They can split each of these trademarks into two surviving parts, one claiming consumer electronic goods and the other claiming the remaining parts of the seller's business. This way, the seller can retain ownership in the trademarks, claiming its remaining divisions to continue using the brand for the relevant products, while the buyer can use the same brand as owner of trademarks, claiming the acquired consumer electronics business. In short, a partial assignment allows the parties to split a trademark into two on the basis of the claimed goods and services.

(b) Effect of the partial assignment

5.14 Most importantly, the owners of the surviving trademarks each become owners of individual, independently registered trademarks, with all rights

---

[16] Section 10 of the Trademark Act of 1946 (Lanham Act), 15 U.S.C. § 1060(a)(1) states:

> A registered mark or a mark for which an application to register has been filed shall be assignable with the good will of the business in which the mark is used, or with that part of the good will of the business connected with the use of and symbolized by the mark.

Id. See further Irene Calboli, *Trademark Assignment 'With Goodwill': A Concept Whose Time Has Gone*, 57 FLA. L. REV., 771, 780 (2005).

[17] Article 21 of TRIPS requires the assignability of a trademark without the associated business, but it does not address goodwill. *See* TRIPS, *supra* note 3, Article 21; *see also* Calboli, *supra* note 16, at 819 et seq.

[18] To make this chapter easier to read, in the following Sections we address only splits of one trademark into two trademarks, but the explanations apply, mutatis mutandis, to splits into more than two trademarks.

vested in them. The surviving trademarks can claim the priority of the original trademark.[19] Also, the remaining duration of the surviving trademarks corresponds to the one of the original trademark.[20]

5.15 The owners have the right to assert the trademarks against third parties, and also against each other. In the latter case, conflicts may not be easily resolved. The surviving trademarks are identical (that is, they relate to the same registered signs), and will often claim similar goods or services. At the same time, none of them can claim priority over the other, as they share the same priority of the original trademark. In such a case, surviving trademarks that result from a partial assignment may have to coexist without any of the respective owners being able to claim and enforce priority rights against the other. In practice, this situation typically is – and should be – addressed in the parties' agreement on the trademark portfolio split, by containing language preventing the parties, unless in specified exceptional circumstances, from asserting their surviving trademarks against each other and governing dispute resolution.

(c) Limitations

5.16 Partial assignments are subject to certain limitations. Most importantly, the partial assignment cannot extend the scope of protection of the surviving trademarks as opposed to the original trademark.[21] It is not possible to add goods or services to any of the surviving trademarks that have not been claimed in the original trademark. In addition, it is not possible to claim the same goods or services of the original trademark in both of the surviving trademarks.

5.17 Further, the partial assignment may only divide the list of claimed goods and services, but not other elements of the trademark. Hence, other forms of a partial assignment, such as a split of the registered sign (for example, divide 'COCA COLA' in 'COCA' and 'COLA'),[22] or a territorial subdivision of the jurisdiction where the trademark is registered (for example, to split a Swiss trademark into parts each covering different regions based on local language), are not permitted.[23] The parties may choose though to distinguish themselves by virtue of the trademark and company name only. Recently, the Swiss

---

19 *See* TPA, *supra* note 10, Article 17a(3); TLT, *supra* note 4, Article 7(1)(a); STLT, *supra* note 5, Article 7(1)(a); CTR, *supra* note 8, Articles 44(7) and 49(7).
20 *See* Article 28(2) of the Swiss Ordinance on Trademark Protection of December 23, 1992 [hereinafter, TPO], *available 15 September 2015 at* http://www.admin.ch/opc/de/classified-compilation/19920365/index.html.
21 TPA, *supra* note 10, Article 17a(2); CTR, *supra* note 8, Articles 44(1) and 49(1).
22 BÜHLER, *supra* note 14, Art. 17a N 7.
23 *Id.*, Art. 17 N 16f; *see* Article 1(2) CTR, *supra* note 8.

Federal Supreme Court had to render a decision in a situation where the spun-off party was entitled to use the pre-existing name 'VON ROLL' with suffixes such as 'INFRATEC,' 'HYDROTEC' and 'HYDRO,' and a dispute arose when the selling party started using potentially similar suffixes, along with the 'VON ROLL' brand.[24]

Finally, limitations may result from the widely established ban on misleading trademarks: the use of a trademark by a party other than the one that has established the trademark's reputation may mislead consumers about the origin of the goods labeled with the trademark, and may be denied protection under trademark law, or even be considered a violation of unfair competition laws. In particular, this is relevant if the surviving parts of the original trademark both claim similar goods or services and the continued use by both parties for similar goods or services could lead to consumer confusion and even, along with this confusion, to a loss of distinctiveness of the surviving trademarks.[25] **5.18**

(d) Technicalities under a Swiss law focus

Under Swiss law, two different techniques can be used to give effect to a partial assignment, both of which can achieve a similar or even the same result. On one hand, the TPA provides for what we refer to as an *actual partial assignment* that directly causes the registration of a new trademark owned by the acquirer.[26] On the other hand, an owner of a trademark can request any of its trademarks be divided into two surviving parts without an immediate change in ownership.[27] This enables the owner to subsequently assign one of those surviving trademarks to a third party. **5.19**

The main difference between these two techniques is the following: in an *actual partial assignment*, the trademark has to be divided along the exact lines of the existing list of goods and services claimed in the original trademark, which may not be extended.[28] Hence, it would not be possible to split a trademark, which only claims the class heading 'furniture', into two surviving trademarks, of which one claims a sub-class 'beds' and the other a sub-class 'tables', if these sub-classes were not already expressly part of the list of goods **5.20**

---

24 Swiss Supreme Court Decision 4A_553/2014 of 17 February 2015 – VON ROLL. The Supreme Court remanded the case to lower court for further assessment of the contractual undertakings by the parties
25 Article 9ter(1) of the MMA even allows the member states to refuse a partial assignment 'if the goods or services included in the part so assigned are similar to those in respect of which the mark remains registered for the benefit of the assignor'. See MMA, *supra* note 6, Article 9*ter*(1).
26 TPA, *supra* note 10, Article 17(1).
27 *Id.*
28 BÜHLER, *supra* note 14, Art. 17 N 15.; DAVID, LUCAS, KOMMENTAR ZUM SCHWEIZERISCHEN PRIVATRECHT, MARKENSCHUTZGESETZ, MUSTER- UND MODELLGESETZ, Basel 1999, Art. 17 N 9.

and services in the original trademark. This is true even if 'beds' and 'tables' are, as a matter of fact, both covered by the class heading 'furniture', and the partial assignment would not cause the scope of protection to be extended.

5.21 To be able to amend and fine-tune the list of claimed goods and services, it is necessary to go for the second option, that is, a *division of the trademark* without immediate change in ownership combined with a *subsequent assignment* of one of the surviving trademarks to a third party. This allows the owner of the trademark, within certain limits, to modify the list of goods and services and to divide the claimed classes into sub-classes.[29] This way, the owner of the trademark claiming the class heading 'furniture' can in a first step divide its trademark into two surviving parts, each claiming sub-classes of 'furniture', such as 'beds' and 'tables'. Likewise, it is possible to further specify the goods and services claimed to reflect the delimitation as precisely as possible. For instance, a trademark claiming 'musical instruments' can be split into one claiming 'musical instruments, excluding string instruments' and another claiming 'string instruments'.[30] Following the actual separation of the trademark, in a second step, the owner of the surviving trademarks can assign one of them to a third party.[31]

5.22 To give effect to a partial assignment, a written request to the Swiss Institute of Intellectual Property ('IIP') is required, specifying the details of the split and, in case of the actual partial assignment, the assignee.[32] Swiss law allows the filing of a request for a division of a trademark at any time,[33] and, by doing so, goes beyond the minimum requirements of the TLT and the STLT.[34]

4. Trademark license

(a) Overview

5.23 The second building block of trademark portfolio splitting is the trademark license. By granting a license, the licensor agrees not to enforce the licensed trademark against the licensee and to tolerate the agreed use of the trademark by the licensee. In trademark portfolio splits, license grants enable the parties to split the affected trademark portfolio without requiring a change of ownership. Instead of an assignment of the trademark by the seller to the

---

29 BORTOLANI, SERGIO, § 22 no. 0.4, WEINMANN/MÜNCH/HERREN (EDS.), SCHWEIZER IP-HANDBUCH, Basel 2013.
30 BÜHLER, *supra* note 14, Art. 17a N 5; DAVID, *supra* note 28, Art. 17a N 7.
31 *Id.*, Art. 17a N 5.
32 *See* TPO, *supra* note 20, Article 28(1)(c).
33 TPA, *supra* note 10, Article 17a(1).
34 *See* TLT, *supra* note 4, Article 7; STLT, *supra* note 5, Article 7.

C. BUILDING BLOCKS OF TRADEMARK PORTFOLIO SPLITTING

buyer, the seller remains the owner of the relevant trademark, but contractually agrees not to exercise the rights conferred by the trademark against the buyer. Likewise, a trademark license can also be used in transactions in which the buyer of a business acquires ownership of the relevant trademark, but the seller shall be entitled to continue using the trademark during a transitional period, or even for an extended period of time.

Typically, exclusive, sole, and non-exclusive licenses are used to distinguish the scope of the rights granted to the licensee: an exclusive license entitles the licensee to exclusivity, even as opposed to the trademark owner who agrees not to use the licensed rights at all. Depending on local law, an exclusive licensee often has standing and the right to sue third parties for infringement.[35] The term sole license is typically used for a license grant in which the licensor retains the right to use the licensed trademark rights itself, but agrees to license it only to the sole licensee and not to any third party. Thus, if granted a sole license, the licensee obtains exclusivity vis-à-vis third parties, but not vis-à-vis the trademark owner. In case of a non-exclusive license, the licensor remains free to use the trademark itself or to license it to other third parties. Licenses granted in connection with a trademark portfolio split are typically sole or exclusive, at least in regards to the goods and services of the business sold to the acquirer. 5.24

In the example of the company divesting its consumer electronics business mentioned in the introduction, the parties could agree on a license grant to achieve their goal of enabling the seller to use certain trademarks during a transitional period: the buyer of the consumer electronics business could grant to the seller an exclusive license to use the relevant trademarks for the seller's remaining businesses during the agreed time period. 5.25

(b) Limitations

In the context of trademark portfolio splits, limitations may most importantly result from control requirements established in some, and from use requirements established in most, countries. Some jurisdictions, including the U.S., require the licensor to maintain reasonable control over its licensee in order to 5.26

---

[35] This is the default rule in Switzerland, TPA, *supra* note 10, Article 55(4). The CTR requires prior notice to the trademark owner and the owner's failure to bring an infringement suit within appropriate time, CTR, *supra* note 8, Article 22(3).

prevent the trademark from being considered abandoned.[36] Thus, each cross-border license grant, including in connection with trademark portfolio splits, should ensure that the appropriate safeguards are taken, if needed.

5.27 Even where such control is not required, a similar issue is presented by the fact that most jurisdictions require actual use of a trademark in commerce, in order to avoid abandonment of the trademark.[37] Where exclusive licenses are granted, the trademark owner can no longer use the trademark in the licensed scope and, as a result, has no means to prevent the abandonment of the trademark in that scope. Hence, most agreements providing for exclusive trademark license grants contain an obligation of the exclusive licensee to take necessary steps to prevent the abandonment of the trademark as a result of the lack of use, or at least disclaim the licensor's liability in case the licensed trademark is no longer enforceable due to the licensee's omission to use the trademark in the manner required for its maintenance.

(c) Technicalities under Swiss law focus

5.28 The TPA is based on the understanding that licenses can be freely granted without requiring control or oversight to be retained by the licensor, and without requiring a specific business relationship between the licensor and its licensee.[38] This mirrors the principle of the free assignability of trademarks referred to above (Section 2). As a result, license grants are an extremely flexible and powerful tool often used in trademark portfolio splits.

5.29 Although not required to be valid and enforceable, license grants should be fixed in a written instrument signed by both parties. This is not only a matter of diligence in general, but more specifically a prerequisite for the registration of the license grant in the trademark register.[39] While not mandatory, registering the license grant is advisable in order to protect the licensee against a third party acquiring the trademark in good faith without knowledge about prior license grants.[40]

---

36 Restatement (Third) of Unfair Competition § 33 cmt. b (1995); Kentucky Fried Chicken Corp. v. Diversified Packaging Corp., 549 F.2d 368, 387 (5th Cir. 1977).
37 *E.g.*, TPA, *supra* note 10, Article 11f.; TD, *supra* note 9, Article 10; CTR, *supra* note 8, Article 15. *See* further Article 19(1) of TRIPS, which permits the requirement of use to maintain a registration, provided that the minimum requirements set forth in Article 19(1) of TRIPS are met. *See* TRIPS, *supra* note 3, Art. 19(1).
38 BÜHLER, *supra* note 14, Art. 18 N 20; BORTOLANI, *supra* note 29, § 21 no. 0.2.
39 It is to be noted, however, that only a written document (and not necessarily the entire license agreement), must be filed with the trademark register; *see* TPA, *supra* note 10, Article 18(2); TPO, *supra* note 20, Article 29(1)(a).
40 *See* TPA, *supra* note 10, Article 18(2); BÜHLER, *supra* note 14, Art. 18 N 63ff; DAVID, *supra* note 28, Art. 18 N 13.

C. BUILDING BLOCKS OF TRADEMARK PORTFOLIO SPLITTING

5.30 The exclusive licensee has standing to enforce the licensed trademark against third parties, unless provided for otherwise in the license agreement.[41]

5. Partial assignment and license grant compared in practice

(a) In general: ownership v. contractual rights

5.31 In the context of trademark portfolio splits, partial assignments and license grants play an equally important role and the parties are often able to implement the same or a similar commercial agreement by either a partial assignment or a license grant. But from a legal perspective, the results are quite different: a partial assignment creates two independent trademark registrations, each having an independent owner with all right and title, including the right to assert the trademark against any third party, and to assign it to third parties. As opposed to this, a licensor retains sole ownership of the trademark, while its licensee has only contractual rights vis-à-vis the owner and often lacks standing to enforce the trademark against third party infringers. Hence, the assignee of a partially assigned trademark is more independent than a licensee, at least in theory.[42] As a result, the buyer of a business will initially prefer a partial assignment, while the seller will prefer to retain as much control as possible and will consequently focus on a license grant instead.

5.32 Leaving aside the parties' initial preferences, practical considerations direct towards either a partial assignment or a license grant: most importantly, the affected goods and services and the duration of the post-transactional arrangement have to be considered.

(b) Affected goods and services

5.33 In regards to the affected goods and services, partial assignments are often used where the carved-out businesses differ substantially enough so that the list of goods and services claimed in the original trademarks can be divided on the basis of reasonably clear criteria of distinction. In certain cases, however, it may be difficult to delimit two businesses on the basis of the goods and services claimed in trademark registrations, or the goods and services offered by each party following the transaction may be too similar to enable an adequate split of the list of goods and services. Opposing interests may further make the delimitation even more difficult: the desire to claim goods and services rather broadly in trademark registrations in order to create a safety

---

41 TPA, *supra* note 10, Article 55(4); BORTOLANI, *supra* note 29, § 21 no. 9.4.
42 In practice, the owners of the surviving trademarks and the newly carved-out businesses are, of course, still very much intertwined. Often, this continues long after the transaction, as the surviving trademarks are the same and only differ by the goods and services respectively claimed.

margin and room for future development may conflict with the parties' commercial deal on how to carve out their businesses. Even if one transaction party might not technically be using a certain trademark for specific goods or services following the transaction, that party may be reluctant to forfeit the trademark for these goods or services to the other party in a partial assignment because it fears losing its safety margin. In all these cases, and in others where the parties cannot agree on the division of the list of the claimed goods and services, they might instead agree on a license grant as feasible compromise,[43] either alone or in combination with a partial assignment of non-controversial goods and services.

5.34 In this context, further consideration has to be given to the risk of consumer confusion and of a loss of the trademarks' distinctiveness, especially if the goods or services claimed in each of the surviving trademarks are very similar. To minimize this risk, it is often advisable to limit partial assignments to cases where the surviving trademarks each claim sufficiently distinctive goods and services, and where the parties will use their respective trademarks to target different trade channels. This may be the case, for instance, if one of the surviving trademarks will be used for consumer goods, while the other will be used for goods and services offered to business customers. If not, where the surviving trademarks would claim very similar goods or services offered to the same market, a license grant might make more sense.

(c) Duration of the post-transactional arrangement

5.35 Partial assignments are often preferred if both parties continue using the carved-out trademarks for an unlimited time following the transaction. By contrast, if the agreement shall remain in force for a limited period in order to enable one or the other party to transition to a new brand, the parties will likely focus on license grants. Here, one of the risks associated with the contractual nature of the license grant also comes into play: license agreements and license grants may be subject to certain mandatory termination rights applying to contracts of unlimited duration.[44] Hence, the longer the parties' arrangement in the context of a trademark portfolio split is designed to last, the less comfortable a party typically is with its position as licensee. As a result, license grants tend to be used for short-term arrangements during transitional

---

43 In addition, local laws may not allow partial assignments if the goods and services in the surviving trademarks are too similar. *See* Article 9*ter*(1) of MMA, which allows member states to refuse a partial assignment 'if the goods or services included in the part so assigned are similar to those in respect of which the mark remains registered for the benefit of the assignor'. MMA, *supra* note 6, Article 9*ter*(1).
44 *See, e.g.*, BÜHLER, *supra* note 14, Art. 18 N 50; STIEGER, WERNER, ZUR BEENDIGUNG DES LIZENZVERTRAGES NACH SCHWEIZERISCHEM RECHT, 3, 11 (1999); decision of the Swiss Federal Supreme Court BGE 133 III 360.

C. BUILDING BLOCKS OF TRADEMARK PORTFOLIO SPLITTING

periods rather than for those designed to last for an unlimited duration or for an extensive period of time.

(d) Flexibility of license grants v. restrictions on partial assignments

License grants are often agreed upon where the commercial deal cannot be aligned with limitations imposed on partial assignments: as outlined above, partial assignments are limited to dividing the list of claimed goods and services, and the parties' ability to subdivide claimed class headings or sub-classes may be restricted. In contrast, a license grant is not restricted in this regard. The parties are free to agree on the scope of the license. They can decide to limit the license to a part of the sign that is registered as trademark (cf. below, Section E.3), they can agree on limitations in respect to the portion of goods and services for which the licensee may use the trademark (for example, to limit the license grant to very specific products that are not expressly distinguished in the list of claimed goods and services), or in respect of the specificities of the use (for example, use only for finished consumer goods and not parts and components to be integrated in another product).[45] In addition, a license grant enables the parties to subdivide the territory of a certain jurisdiction, which is not permitted for partial assignments.[46] Thus, when it comes to implementing the parties' commercial deal, licensing is often much more flexible.

5.36

(e) License to register new trademarks

Finally, license grants are sometimes used to enable one of the parties to the transaction to register new trademarks claiming the same sign that would, without the licensor's approval, infringe upon the licensor's registered trademarks or other intellectual property, in particular, copyright. There are two main hypotheses in which this can be considered: first, the parties may decide that they do not want to transfer any or certain trademarks as part of their trademark portfolio split, but rather enable one of them to register certain new trademarks claiming the same or slight variations of the pre-existing sign. In this case, the current owner of the trademark may grant to the other a license to enable the licensee to register an identical or similar sign as trademark for the goods and services relevant to the business continued by the licensee. Second, such a license grant may be part of an overall agreement splitting not only a trademark, but rather an entire brand, combining trademarks, copyrighted logos or designs, trade names, domain names, and so on. In this case,

5.37

---

45 See, e.g., Article 18(1) TPA, *supra* note 10: 'The proprietor of a trade mark may permit others to use the trade mark for the goods or services for which it is claimed, in whole or in part, and for the whole territory or a part of Switzerland only.' See also TD, *supra* note 9, Article 8(1); CTR, *supra* note 8, Article 22(1).
46 *Id.*

the licensor may license certain intellectual property rights to the acquirer of the business in the scope needed for the acquirer to take the steps necessary to protect those elements of the brand that are transferred to it as part of the transaction. This typically includes the acquirer's right to register the relevant trademarks. To be on the safe side, a license grant by the brand owner is often advisable even if the latter has no trademark registered in a relevant jurisdiction, but could, unless a license is granted, oppose to the buyer's trademark registration on the basis of copyright or unfair competition law. In some ways, a license grant to enable the licensee to register its own trademarks is the most straightforward option to implement a trademark portfolio split: one simple license grant specifying the scope of the business for which the license can be used would cover the entire trademark portfolio split. On this basis, the seller can avoid having to deal with partial assignments, and the buyer can control all registration filings.

5.38 But there is a significant downside attached to this option: by registering its own new trademarks, the buyer loses the priority rights of the original trademarks. This is often a key issue in transactions, in view of the risk of conflicts with trademarks that are younger than the original trademark, but predate the new registrations. Such rights could be asserted by the owner of the respective trademarks or even be cited by the trademark registries (in the course of an ex officio examination of trademark applications).

D. TRADEMARK PORTFOLIO SPLITTING AGREEMENTS

1. Overview

5.39 We have introduced the building blocks of trademark portfolio splits above, that is, partial assignments and license grants, which are not normally used on a stand-alone basis. As we have already seen, they are typically integrated in an agreement that addresses the trademark portfolio split and the parties' relationship regarding their trademarks after the transaction in a more general way. One of the main goals of these agreements is to govern the parties' coexistence in respect of their shared trademark history, taking into account the fact that the parties will use the same or similar signs after the transaction, be it for a transitional time period or for an unlimited duration.

5.40 This characterization has two implications. First, trademark portfolio splitting agreements often cover more than just trademarks; rather, these agreements tend to address the splitting of the pre-existing brands between the surviving businesses in general, and they often include not only provisions governing

D. TRADEMARK PORTFOLIO SPLITTING AGREEMENTS

trademarks, but also company names, unregistered trade names, and domain names. Accordingly, they are sometimes not referred to merely as trademark portfolio splitting agreements, but more broadly as coexistence or delimitation agreements. Second, trademark portfolio splitting agreements often do not only govern the actual split (that is, a one-time transaction that is completed together with the related M&A transaction), but they govern all trademark or brand-related forward-looking aspects of the parties' transactions. They are therefore agreements with ongoing rights and obligations that address the future relationship of the parties in respect of their shared trademark or brand history.

5.41 As a result, trademark portfolio splitting agreements are almost always a combination of provisions addressing several topics, which include the following issues: the actual trademark and brand delimitation and allocation, the legal implementation of this allocation, mutual support, scope, trademark maintenance, duration and termination, and conflict resolution. In the following, we briefly address each of these various issues.

2. Typical provisions in trademark portfolio splitting agreements

(a) Trademark delimitation and allocation

5.42 The first set of substantive rules in trademark portfolio splitting agreements is typically dedicated to the delimitation and allocation of the pre-existing trademarks. There are two steps involved in this: first, the identification of the trademarks relevant for the split by allocating the seller's signs to the surviving businesses; and second, the delimitation of the goods and services claimed in the identified trademarks by allocating them to the surviving businesses.

5.43 In the first step, the parties have to agree on the delimitation and allocation of the pre-existing signs. This is driven by the parties' commercial interests. While specific product names are often rather easy to allocate to the surviving businesses, signs that are used for a product range or even for all products, in particular if they include the selling company's name or other signs which are not attributable to a specific division, are more difficult to carve-out. Once the parties have agreed on this allocation, the trademark portfolio to be split can be identified by looking for all trademarks that protect the relevant signs. Trademarks that protect signs that are not used for the products of the sold business can typically be disregarded.

5.44 Then, in the second step, the parties have to allocate the products and, on this basis, the goods and services claimed in the identified pre-existing trademarks to the surviving businesses. For instance, in the example of the company divesting its consumer electronics business, all consumer electronics products are allocated to the acquirer's business, while the other products remain with the seller. On the basis of this product allocation, the goods and services claimed in the seller's trademarks are reviewed and allocated to one or the other party: those exclusively covering the consumer electronics business purchased by the buyer are allocated to that business, and those exclusively covering the remaining business to the seller. The remaining goods and services are those that cannot be allocated to one or the other exclusively and will or may be used by both surviving businesses following the transaction.

5.45 In this first set of substantive rules, often not only is trademark delimitation addressed, but the agreement further addresses whether certain entities have to be renamed following the transaction and the allocation and future use of domains. Given our focus on trademarks in this chapter, we do not further address this part of the parties' transaction.

(b) Implementation of the allocation

5.46 Once the parties have delimited and allocated the relevant signs and goods and services to the surviving businesses, the key of the trademark portfolio splitting agreement is to implement this allocation. Here, the building blocks discussed above come into play. As outlined in Sections C.3 to 5, the parties have several options to implement the allocation of the goods and services, which we only list briefly to avoid redundancy:

5.47 The parties may consider a partial assignment to carve-out those goods and services that can be exclusively allocated to the business sold to the buyer, while the remaining goods and services stay with the seller. Or they might agree that all trademarks stay with the seller, who agrees not to use them for any products allocated to the sold business and grant an exclusive license to the buyer for all uses in connection with that business. A vice-versa option may, of course, be considered as well.

5.48 Typically, the parties also have to agree on how to deal with those goods and services claimed in the seller's trademarks that will or may be used in connection with both surviving businesses. For these, a sole or an exclusive license grant by the party who is going to own the relevant trademarks to the other party is the most obvious choice, with or without the licensee's right to register its own trademarks for the relevant goods and services. As a result, the buyer may continue using the seller's trademarks for those goods and services that are allocated to the business sold to him, while the seller may continue using its trademarks for the remaining goods and services.

D. TRADEMARK PORTFOLIO SPLITTING AGREEMENTS

A license grant by the seller to enable the purchaser to register its own trademarks within the scope agreed for the continued operation of the sold business could also be considered as a general approach, that is, not just for the goods and services that cannot be clearly allocated to one of the surviving businesses, but also for those that can be allocated to the sold business. In this case, the seller would remain the owner of all of its trademarks, while the buyer simply registers new trademarks within the scope agreed for the continuation of the sold business. **5.49**

Apart from the actual implementation of the allocation, typically trademark portfolio splitting agreements also contain substantive provisions regarding the parties' future use of their respective trademark rights, and the parties expressly agree not to use any of their trademarks (particularly those with a distinctive logo) in a way conflicting with their agreement, or in a way that could create a misleading impression or confusion about the origin of the goods and services labeled with one of the party's trademarks. **5.50**

(c) Coexistence, non-compete and mutual support

Key provisions in trademark portfolio splitting agreements typically address the parties' agreement on their respective tolerance of certain acts by the other party and on the support that they owe to each other in respect of trademark registrations. In line with their agreement on the implementation of the trademark delimitation and allocation, the parties typically agree to tolerate, and not to oppose, certain acts by the other party, in particular the use of the relevant signs and trademark registrations in line with the agreement. In addition, the parties often agree not to assert their respective, deal-related trademarks against each other, provided that the other party complies with the delimitation foreseen in the agreement. This delimitation is often strengthened by non-compete undertakings by each party for the other party's field. Beyond that, the parties set forth their agreement on the provision of mutual assistance in case of registrations or other filings and, very importantly, on how to deal with infringements committed or alleged by third parties. This often includes rules on the provision of support in case of litigation. Finally, trademark portfolio splitting agreements typically provide for the parties' mutual obligation to consult with each other before taking any action that could impact the respective other party's business. **5.51**

(d) Scope

A trademark portfolio splitting agreement typically further specifies its territorial scope of application. In theory, the territorial scope of trademark portfolio splitting agreements could be limited to the jurisdictions in which **5.52** the seller of the business has registered trademarks. However, as already mentioned, the parties' agreement often extends not only to trademarks, but it is rather an agreement on how to split an entire brand. That brand might be present even in markets where trademarks have not yet been registered and proprietary rights may exist without any registration (for example, in case of copyright). What is more, as just mentioned, trademark portfolio splitting agreements also often contain obligations of each party to tolerate certain acts by the other party, such as the filing of a new registration in a jurisdiction without previous presence. Finally, there may be situations in which a trademark has not been registered (and not even used) in a certain jurisdiction. Absent specific reasons indicating otherwise, it is most often advisable to enter into a trademark portfolio splitting agreement on a geographically broad basis, irrespective of whether or not a trademark has been registered in each of the covered jurisdictions. The risk associated with such situations (no benefit of registrations or of at least prior use) will have to be addressed by parties in their agreement, typically in the section on representations and warranties.

(e) Trademark maintenance

5.53 The more technical parts of trademark portfolio splitting agreements are typically dedicated to trademark maintenance. Broadly speaking, the parties have to agree on how to maintain their trademark registrations that affect not only one of them, but also the other party. This applies mainly to trademarks that are licensed by one party to the other. It can even be relevant if the licensee, based on the license, has registered its own trademarks: given that new trademarks cannot claim the priority of the licensor's trademarks, the licensee may have an interest that the licensor maintains its trademarks in order to be able to support the licensee in case of a conflict with a trademark that predates the licensee's trademark, but over which the licensor's trademark can claim priority.

5.54 More specifically, the parties typically map out their agreement on which trademarks have to be maintained and by whom, who bears which costs, which party is responsible for interactions with trademark offices, procedures to be adhered to in case one or the other party intends to abandon a trademark, consultation obligations regarding trademark maintenance in general, how to deal with intra-group assignments, and so on.

(f) Duration and termination

5.55 As mentioned above, trademark portfolio splitting agreements are often more than just one-time transactions that are completed once the related M&A transaction is over. Rather, they are long-term, forward-looking agreements with ongoing rights and obligations of the parties. As a result, in most cases the parties have to set out the agreed duration and whether, and under what circumstances, the agreement may be terminated.

(g) Conflict resolution, governing law, jurisdiction

Last but not least, trademark portfolio splitting agreements typically contain provisions regarding conflict resolution, governing law, and jurisdiction. In this context, dispute resolution provisions are important; especially if the agreement is designed to last not just for a short period, future conflicts may not be excluded and the parties will want to agree on a reasonable and practicable process on how to attempt to amicably resolve these disputes. Further, as mentioned above, the parties are normally free to choose the law applicable to their overall agreement governing the portfolio split, but this does not impact the law that applies on the local trademark registrations that are affected by the split. 5.56

E. OTHER POSSIBLE OPTIONS AND CONSIDERATIONS

1. Shared ownership

At least in theory, certain goals of trademark portfolio splitting can be achieved by establishing shared ownership.[47] Instead of dividing an existing trademark into two independent parts that can each have different owners, the owner of a trademark can also create shared ownership together with a third party, typically by assigning an ownership interest to that third party. Depending upon the specifics of local law, the co-owners thereafter either jointly own an interest in the undivided trademark, or each of them is considered co-owner of an intangible fraction of the trademark. As a result, the co-owners can both use the trademark for the goods and services claimed therein, subject to the limitations set forth by applicable law and the parties' agreement. 5.57

Shared ownership is not very common. One reason for this is that it is rather counterintuitive, given that the main function of a trademark is to serve as indicator of origin: if owned by shared owners, to which one shall the product be attributed? This is, however, not the only reason for its infrequent use, especially taking into account that other forms of trademark portfolio splits 5.58

---

[47] With the wording 'shared ownership' we refer to any form of ownership shared between two or more owners and put aside the many forms of shared ownership that can take in various jurisdictions, such as joint ownership, co-ownership, or common ownership. The term 'shared ownership' is used to include all these different forms.

Chapter 5 HOW TO MAKE TWO OUT OF ONE

discussed in this chapter may give rise to similar uncertainties concerning the products' origin. Another reason, which is likely even more important, is that many jurisdictions lack explicit rules governing shared ownership. For instance, the TPA does not expressly address joint ownership, although its existence is acknowledged in practice.[48] Absent specific rules governing shared ownership, if needed, parties and courts try to use rules established for shared ownership in personal or real property analogously to trademarks. This is a difficult undertaking, mostly because of the quite different nature of a trademark as opposed to personal property or real estate. Uncertainties come up in particular with regards to the question of whether or not the parties have to account to each other for profits they each make of their independent use of the trademark, whether licensing transactions by one party need the approval of the other party, or whether one party may independently assign its share to a third party without the other party's approval. While these questions can in principle all be reasonably dealt with on a contractual basis, it may be unclear whether and, if so, to what extent mandatory local laws governing shared personal or real property ownership will apply to shared trademark ownership. All these issues combined often make shared ownership the least attractive option.

5.59   Hence, although there are a few well-known examples of trademarks owned by shared owners,[49] the usual approach is to avoid shared ownership if possible. Instead, parties look for options to structure their trademark portfolio split around shared ownership, choosing partial assignments and licensing transactions instead. Another option that may be considered to achieve a similar result from a business perspective is to establish a joint venture that becomes the sole owner of the trademark and grants the required licenses to the parties involved in the transaction.

2. **Joint ventures**

5.60   Rather than actually splitting the relevant trademark portfolio between them or establishing shared ownership, the parties can consider transferring the trademark portfolio to a joint venture company co-owned by them, which shall subsequently license the necessary rights to the businesses involved. Obviously, establishing a joint venture requires considerable resources (a

---

48   The TPO implicitly acknowledges shared ownership by making reference to registrations held by more than one person, *see* TPO, *supra* note 20, Article 4(1).
49   For instance, the U.S. trademarks 'SUPER HERO' and 'SUPER HEROES', which are co-owned by Marvel Characters, Inc. and DC Comics, U.S. serial no. 72243225 and 78356610. Another example is the U.S. trademark 'SWISS ARMY' that was originally jointly registered by Victorinox AG and Wenger SA, U.S. serial no. 74600279 (now owned solely by Victorinox AG after it acquired Wenger SA).

contract setting out the structure and the allocation of rights and obligations is to be agreed upon in a first place) and ongoing administration thereafter. As a result, this option is rarely used in connection with trademark portfolio splits, and if so, only if this is requested for other reasons, and specifically because other intellectual property rights will have to be shared by the parties beyond their transaction.

3. Rebranding

5.61 None of the building blocks discussed above allow amending the registered sign as such. The partial assignment, in particular, does not permit splitting an existing sign, for example, by splitting 'COCA COLA' in 'COCA' on the one side and 'COLA' on the other. However, there may be situations where the business deal to be implemented is to entitle one of the transaction parties to only use certain parts of the sign registered in the original trademarks. Doing so requires the registration of new trademarks that cannot claim the original trademark's priority. For this purpose, a license grant (and in certain countries a consent letter vis-à-vis the registers) is required, enabling the licensee to register the required new trademarks. At the same time, the owner of the original trademarks will likely be required to take the steps necessary to maintain these, at least for a limited duration, in order to ensure that the parties can still enjoy the protection resulting from the original trademarks.

F. CONCLUSION

5.62 The practice of trademark portfolio splitting focuses on two key issues. The first is the difficulty resulting from the fact that trademark law is largely dominated by local law, while trademark portfolio splits often have to be agreed upon and implemented globally. The second is the actual implementation of the parties' commercial deal into an efficient and workable agreement.

5.63 In regards to the first issue, the key is to take a global approach when it comes to drafting and negotiating a global trademark portfolio splitting agreement, at least to the extent reasonable. This is possible thanks to international agreements that have resulted in a much more uniform landscape of local trademark laws compared to a few decades ago. However, it is crucial to bear in mind that trademark law is still local law, and that the agreement has to be implemented locally. Hence, local expertise and the required room for localization are needed so that the global trademark portfolio splitting agreement can be implemented in the relevant countries.

5.64 In regards to the second issue, the key is to have a deep understanding of the building blocks of trademark portfolio splits and to be able to combine them most appropriately to implement the parties' deal. Trademark portfolio splitting agreements can take as many different forms as the commercial deal that they have to reflect. Here, thinking of the partial assignment and the license grant as building blocks of trademark portfolio splits and bearing in mind how each of them compares to the other and what other options might be considered can help the practitioner to reduce the complexity of drafting and negotiating trademark portfolio splitting agreements. This chapter has provided guidelines for implementing the commercials of the parties' transaction into an agreement tailored to their needs.

6

COMPETITION, MARKETS, AND TRADEMARK TRANSACTIONS

Shubha Ghosh[*]

A. INTRODUCTION	6.01	D. TRADEMARK TRANSACTIONS: TYING, TRANSFERS IN GROSS AND COVENANTS NOT TO SUE	6.71
B. COMPETITION, INTELLECTUAL PROPERTY, AND TRADEMARKS	6.15		
C. CONCEPTS, MODELS, AND TRADEMARK LAW	6.38	E. CONCLUSION	6.77

A. INTRODUCTION

6.01 With respect to the subject of business transactions, trademark law has a cryptic role in the scheme of intellectual property. While trademark's domain does not include original creations or new inventions, trademark serves a role in the commercialization of copyright's and patent's bounty by creating a brand that can be affixed to creative works or inventive products. This chapter explores the role of trademarks, and in turn the role of trademark transactions, in defining the competitive environment, which provides the soil in which innovation occurs.

6.02 One way to understand trademark's role in intellectual property is to note its parallels with trade secret. While the two fields are clearly distinct with the obvious distinction being trade secret's emphasis on private information internal to a firm, and trademark's focus on publicizing a firm's wares, they both share a common role in promoting the creation of information. Trade secret's fruit is valuable information that gives a firm an advantage over competitors. Trademark creates signals, in the forms of words and symbols, which generate information for consumers in typing and identifying products and services in the marketplace. Information under trade secret law defines the productive processes within a firm. The signals protected by trademark create a

---

[*] Vilas Research Fellow & George Young Bascom Professor of Business Law, University of Wisconsin Law School.

connection between a firm and consumers. Both trade secret and trademark together shape the supply side and the demand side of a competitive market. Within this market, copyright and patent serve to direct the pace and trajectory of innovation.

6.03 The connection between trade secret and trademark will be critical in Section C, which develops a conceptual and practical vocabulary for understanding competition. As background, it is worth noting how the delineation of trademark's role presented so far contrasts with the conventional wisdom. As Glynn Lunney has elegantly demonstrated,[1] scholars and practitioners have been split between trademark's ontological status as property and its status as monopoly. Trademark as monopoly proponents, with a pedigree going back to English common law, emphasize trademark law's creation of exclusive rights that allow the owner to prevent others from applying a word or symbol to a product. Critics of this view emphasize how trademark law promotes market entry by allowing firms to create a market identity that can attract consumers and displace existing firms. Trademarks, according to this view of critics, facilitate market entry by giving a firm a property right in a brand that allows it to publicize its products, and thereby create a presence in an existing market.

6.04 The view presented in this chapter goes beyond either conception of trademark to highlight how trademarks define competitive conditions in a marketplace, serving at times as a basis for market dominance and in other instances as a legal mechanism for facilitating market entry.

6.05 As Professor Lunney argues, those advocating for trademark as property would support interpretations of the law that strongly police free riding in order to protect an individual firm's brand. But these strong exclusionary rights reinforce the position of those conceptualizing trademark as monopoly.[2] In fact, Professor Lunney concludes his article by stating that trademark is better understood as a monopoly than as a property right, particularly in light of developments in jurisprudence that emphasize trademark's status as property.[3]

6.06 I approach the problem of trademark from the perspective that competitive markets foster innovation. This perspective is the subject of other strands of my research that explore the intersection of intellectual property law and competition policy. Taking this viewpoint as given, I make the case in this chapter that if trademark law is part of intellectual property (a point, again,

---

1 Glynn Lunney, *Trademark Monopolies*, 48 EMORY L.J. 367 (1999).
2 *Id.* at 371.
3 *Id.* at 417.

that is controversial), then its role serves largely to foster competitive markets. How it does so, and what competition means, are two pivotal questions that inform the analysis which follows.

6.07 Trademark's relationship with competition may be skewed by the relationship between trademark and products. Competitive markets serve to allocate products, not trademarks. In a few instances, such as fashion or other industries driven by the pursuit of status, trademarks may precisely be the product purchased. Blue jeans or jackets are desirable to consumers because of the labels they bear rather than any inherent difference in quality of the clothing, as compared to those sold by a competitor. At the same time, trademarks do serve as a way to differentiate products, which are the actual desiderata of consumers.[4] Trademark law does not make a distinction between these two roles of brands; nor should it. The law need not make judgments about what consumers buy or suppliers sell, absent clear social harm. Trademark can serve its ostensible information providing function whether consumers use a logo to find a product, or seek out a product for the logo.

6.08 The argument that the previous paragraph supports is a strong norm of consumer sovereignty. Trademark law and policy do not rest on judgments of what consumers should want. Instead they seek to mediate the communicative role between players in the marketplace, consumers and firms, and firms and competitors. Furthermore, the influence of trademark law can spill over into other constituencies as commercial brands are used in political, social, or cultural spaces. The competitive system has a wide reach, and the concerns of trademark law with market competition are writ large.

6.09 This last point underscores why limiting trademark to the ontological dichotomy of monopoly and property is impoverished as a doctrinal and policy matter. To say trademark is monopoly is to emphasize price competition – the ability to translate legal exclusion into higher prices in the marketplace. But market competition also has a non-price dimension with firms and consumers in rivalry over communicative aspects of brands and qualitative aspects of products. A richer context for trademarks in market competition requires seeing beyond monopoly.

6.10 As scholars and practitioners, we also need to see beyond property. Intellectual property as property is a tired trope, fueling a debate that has shed little light on how intellectual property can be practiced or reformed. As Professor Lunney points out, to use the label property is to say that there is a right to

---

4   Herbert Hovenkamp, The Opening of American Law, 198–99 (2015).

Chapter 6 COMPETITION, MARKETS, AND TRADEMARK TRANSACTIONS

exclude recognized by the state.[5] But the label provides no information on the scope or breadth of that right. There is agreement that intellectual property is distinct from real property, and therefore the legal entitlement of a fee simple is inapposite for intellectual property. Furthermore, there is recognition that the scope of the exclusive right depends on the goals of promoting innovation and progress. The analytical move of this chapter, to frame trademark law in terms of competition, provides a foundation for how to define the exclusive rights provided by trademarks, seeing beyond the label of property to the substance of exclusivity.

6.11 How then do you understand trademark law in terms of competition? A natural inclination is to turn to competition law, whether the antitrust doctrines of the United States or the precepts of competition law in the European Union. But it would be simplistic and conceptually wrong to reduce trademark law to competition law. The domain of competition law and policy includes markets for generic commodities for which trademark law may be irrelevant.[6] More to the point, the scope of competition law goes beyond aspects of an industry that intellectual property governs. Contracts with distributors, price regulation, and criminal price fixing are all examples of problems for competition law that have little relation to intellectual property. Competition policy in trademark law, put simply, will necessarily have a different emphasis than what we see in antitrust law.

6.12 But perhaps competition law can provide examples and models for how we address trademark law. That point seems more promising, and as I explore in Section B, there are many useful lessons from competition law that can instruct us in understanding trademark law. One of these issues is market definition. Another is the use of formal economic models as guideposts in gauging deviations from competition. Both market definition and economic models teach us conceptual problems in framing competition as a standard for designing law and policy. In Section C, I suggest an approach for trademark law (and by way of comparison other areas of intellectual property) that addresses the existing conceptual gap in defining competition.

6.13 In short, trademark is neither in opposition to intellectual property nor an estranged sibling. Instead, trademark law is integral to defining the competitive environment within which the intellectual property ecosystem of innovation flourishes. What I develop in this chapter instructs not only about trademark, but also about the relationship between intellectual property and

---

5 Lunney, *supra* note 1 at 368.
6 Hovenkamp, *supra* note 4 at 214–15.

competition. I leave this latter, broader question for future research. But the examination of trademark is a revealing first step towards the broader project.

6.14 Four sections follow this introduction. Section B examines the meaning of competition and its relationship to intellectual property. Section C offers an analytical approach drawing on the work of Albert Hirschman that informs the relationship between trademark and competition. I develop this analytical model not only to illustrate my arguments about trademark, but I also show how it applies to trade secret law. This parallel with trade secret law provides a comparison to trademark's role and broaches the bigger question of how the fields of intellectual property connect under the big tent of competition policy. Section D applies the analysis of competition and markets to trademark transactions. Finally, Section E offers concluding thoughts and implications for future research.

B. COMPETITION, INTELLECTUAL PROPERTY, AND TRADEMARKS

6.15 Transactions occur in a competitive environment. The word competition conjures up many images. Rivalry between opponents, agonistic contest among the talented, gamesmanship, and sportsmanship – all designed to provide entertainment for the passive voyeurs and generate the best value, whether measured in terms of the joy of the viewer and participants, or in pecuniary terms.[7] When applied to the marketplace, competition has associations with low price products and services delivered efficiently, and with high standards of care, customer relations, and professionalism. There is good competition and bad competition; the latter associated with oppressiveness, self-centeredness, greed, and lack of respect for the rules of the particular game or of social etiquette. Against the background of economic, business and sociological notions of competition exists a body of normative ideals of good and bad behaviour that are deemed appropriate.

6.16 Policy decisions about rules for the marketplace rest typically on the type of good to be provided to consumers. For the purposes of this chapter, it would be useful to divide goods, by which I mean products and services, as either private or public.[8] Private goods are ones whose value is enjoyed solely by the consumer of goods of that type. Examples include food, clothing, cell phones,

---

[7] See CLAUDIO COLAGUORI, AGON CULTURE: COMPETITION, CONFLICT AND THE PROBLEM OF DOMINATION (2012).
[8] See RICHARD CORNES & TODD SANDLER, THE THEORY OF EXTERNALITIES, PUBLIC GOODS, AND CLUB GOODS (1996); Shubha Ghosh, *Deprivatizing Copyright*, 54 CASE WES. L. REV. 368 (2003).

or computers. Public goods are ones where there is some degree of sharing in consumption. That sharing can take many forms. For example, a movie can be viewed by many people at once. The knowledge embodied in an automobile or a cell phone can be used in similar products. The word sharing in this context covers a wide range of situations. The sharing can be positive where a good is being enjoyed communally. It can also be negative where one person's consumption may produce a harmful effect on someone else, such as exhaust from a car or noise from playing music too loudly. In this way, the notion of a public good is connected closely to the concept of externalities, or third party effects from individual enjoyment of a good.

6.17 The presence of these third party effects explains why market provision of a public good may not be desirable. While a private good can be allocated through contracts between individual sellers and buyers that mediate through price and quantity terms, a public good cannot be readily allocated through competitive markets. The problem is that a public good cannot be readily divided up among consumers in a market. Private goods can be allocated to individuals through methods of exclusion and rivalry. A particular bite of a pizza can be enjoyed by only one person, and therefore price is based on the willingness to pay for that bite. In contrast, a range of people can enjoy a movie or a book. A price can be placed on it, but sharing may result in the supplier being undercompensated. Some form of state intervention is needed for public goods to be provided.

6.18 Most textbooks resolve the public goods problem by stating that the government must provide these goods.[9] Of course, there are many public goods that the government does provide, with national defense and roads being the canonical examples. But there are limitations to how much the government can do in providing public goods given the limited tax base and other sources of revenue.[10] The government faces information problems in determining the types of public goods to provide and their quality. As a result, shared goods are often priced in the marketplace, as the example of movies and books indicates. These markets are created through the legal definition of property rights, usually in the form of intellectual property laws. These laws impose a forced scarcity on shared goods, essentially privatizing them and minimizing the possibility of sharing.

6.19 Markets for public goods rest on a delicate trade-off between the consumption value that arises from sharing and the need to obtain private price information

---

9   *See* Cornes & Sandler, *supra* note 8.
10 Hovenkamp, *supra* note 4 at 102–3.

to effectively allocate the good. Market prices reflect the negotiated value based on the willingness to pay of consumers and the willingness to accept on the part of suppliers. Willingness to pay reflects consumption value while willing to accept reflects costs faced by the supplier. However, willingness to pay should include how much consumers value sharing the good in question. Even if I enjoy the story in a movie, others may enjoy it as well. There is value to each viewer from being part of a network of viewers that share in the experience. But this value may differ from consumer to consumer. The result is that for public goods, the quantity of the shared good is identical for all consumers in the marketplace while the willingness to pay will differ. So each consumer of a public good should be required to pay a different price for consuming the good. Compare this situation with the market for private goods in which consumers each pay the same price for a particular good but consume different quantities.

One way for suppliers of public goods to approximate the value of sharing is to charge consumers different prices reflecting the value they obtain from sharing. This phenomenon is referred to as price discrimination, and economists predict that we should see it frequently in markets for public goods.[11] Even if the government provides public goods, we would expect differential pricing with taxes across citizens who benefit from the provision of the public good. In markets for public goods, we see differential pricing as movies, books, songs, technologies, and know-how might be sold at different prices depending on the type of consumer (business or personal), the type of good (paperback or hardback, theatre exhibition or DVD), and the type of use (one time or repeated, pure consumption or research). **6.20**

My point is to describe what markets for private and public goods might look like. I make no claim as to their effectiveness, and most of the scholarly literature in economics, business, and law attempts to reach conclusions about ideal institutional arrangements to obtain a particular goal, usually allocative efficiency. This chapter, on the other hand, presents a discussion of different ways in which competition is conceptualized, and the difficulties of finding a unique set of institutional arrangements for designing competitive markets. The goal is one of pragmatism and identifying heuristics useful for legal policymaking. With this goal in mind, I bring the discussion of competition to the topic of trademarks. **6.21**

The key insight I am offering is that trademarked goods are typically a mix of public and private goods. A branded product consists of two attributes. The **6.22**

---

11   *See* Carl Shapiro & Hal Varian, *Information Rules* (1999).

first is the product, which is a private good, and the second is the brand, which is a public good. The brand is a public good because it can be enjoyed by all consumers either as a signal providing information about the underlying product, or as a symbol that every consumer is aware of whether they enjoy the underlying product or not. As a result, the market for a branded product is complex, entailing price competition over the sale of the underlying product and non-price competition over the sale of the brand. As I discuss at the beginning of Section C, these complexities can be translated into specific formal models of the market. One example of a pertinent formal model is that of monopolistic competition. My concern here, however, is not with the possible formal models, but with the concepts underlying competition for trademarks and goods.

6.23 If one agrees with the dual nature of competition over branded goods, the next question is: what are the implications for law and policy? One implication is that traditional market analysis, familiar in antitrust law, may not be particularly helpful in assessing competition. To illustrate this point, I turn to a scholarly analysis by Professors Mark Lemley and Mark McKenna on trademarks and markets.[12]

6.24 Lemley and McKenna's collaboration focuses on a provocative anomaly. Antitrust law offers special treatment to markets based on products and services protected by intellectual property. But, as Lemley and McKenna point out, if you apply antitrust market definition principles to such markets, there are doubts as to their competitiveness. There is no price at which some loyalists will switch from Pepsi to Coke, the Beatles to the Rolling Stones, Dan Brown novels to Stephen King ones, or Apples to PC's. Because of this lack of consumer response to a price change, the authors conclude, antitrust law should scrutinize intellectual property defined markets more closely.

6.25 Their solution to this apparent anomaly is to rethink market definition in intellectual property and antitrust. Courts engage in quasi-market definition analysis in several doctrinal areas of intellectual property, such as fair use, non-obviousness, and the first sale doctrine. The two authors conclude that these approaches are misguided. Instead, they revisit many of these doctrinal areas with a focus on the policies underlying these doctrines. Although they do not state so directly, presumably such rigorous policy scrutiny would also inform the issue of how intellectual property should be treated under antitrust

---

12 Mark A. Lemley & Mark P. McKenna, *Is Pepsi Really a Substitute for Coke? Market Definition in Antitrust and IP*, 100 GEO. L. J. 2055, 2059 (2013).

law. But that may be another paper. Lemley and McKenna's article develops implications for intellectual property alone, rather than its interaction with antitrust.

6.26 Lemley and McKenna take their cue from Professor Louis Kaplow's examination of market definition in antitrust law.[13] Professor Kaplow makes the convincing point that market definition in antitrust law is misguided. His argument is that the mechanics of market definition distract from the more pertinent questions of whether the alleged antitrust defendant has engaged in an exercise of market power. Market definition analysis requires the court to determine a market share, which is a measure of market power. This determination is quantitative, heavily expert dependent, and contentious, often generating more heat than light. Evidence of market power without market definition can bring clarity to antitrust scrutiny.

6.27 Lemley and McKenna draw a cautionary lesson about market definition from Kaplow. In antitrust, the requirement of market definition has arguably served as a way to claim assessment. Contentions about market definition can serve as a threshold basis for dismissing antitrust claims, or for challenging claims of antitrust violation. Market definition and the correlative market share serve as a rule-like way to determine the validity of an antitrust claim of monopolization. Analogously, Lemley and McKenna chronicle intellectual property cases where courts use a proto-market definition analysis to assess claims of genericide, functionality, patent damages, and un-copyrighted ideas.[14] Following from Kaplow's argument, however, this appeal to market definition is a distraction from the policies underlying these claims. The concern is that a rule-like concept, such as market definition, can serve to dismiss valid claims.

6.28 Market definition analysis is irrelevant for intellectual property cases. The chapter presents alternative approaches to address intellectual property cases that make reference to market effects without the use of market definition. I think this is correct. At the same time, there is another lesson to be gleaned from antitrust law, which I think can be developed. Antitrust law is a branch of competition policy. The normative foundations of desirable competition inform antitrust law. My point is that intellectual property law is also a branch of competition policy. Similarly, intellectual property doctrines should be based on a deeper appreciation of the norms of competition.

---

13   *See* Louis Kalpow, *Why (Ever) Define Markets?*, 124 HARV. L. REV. 437 (2010).
14   Lemley & McKenna, *supra* note 12, at 2080.

6.29 Lemley and McKenna state in their article: 'Competition doesn't occur in a vacuum; a company must compete with others in some market.'[15] Of course, competition has to occur in some space, physical or conceptual, but competition occurs in arenas outside a market. Lobbyists compete for legislative attention. Bloggers, advertisers, and commentators compete for the attention of consumers. Artists and inventors compete with each other for reputation and professional achievement. Competition occurs in many different social contexts, and social norms about how competition can and should occur inform decisions about the design of institutions. Design might entail limiting competition and deriving cooperative solutions.[16] Design might also entail channeling competitive energies towards socially valuable activities.[17]

6.30 What can we say about competition norms? Some guidance can be found in trade secret law, an area that is surprisingly absent from the Lemley and McKenna article, perhaps because of its focus on federal intellectual property policy. But trade secret law provides a model for my ideas with its focus on rules of disclosure and improper means as instruments for regulating the competitive process in information creation and dissemination.[18] Competition norms figure into when alternative mechanisms and informal rules for creating and disseminating creative works are developed, such as in areas like gourmet cooking, stand-up comedy, fashion, and databases.[19] Lemley and McKenna's article sets the stage for more discussion of competition norms in intellectual property (and in antitrust law).

6.31 As Lemley and McKenna indicate, there is a connection between competition and markets, but I see our understanding of the first as preceding our choices of institutional design for the latter. Markets could be structured as an unregulated free-for-all. Alternatively, markets could be highly structured and regulated through firm rules. One thing at stake in the stark choice between these two alternatives is a normative view of competition. In legal policy analysis, an implicit normative vision is embedded in the use of the term 'rent seeking'. As a dirty word, rent seeking describes behaviour of manipulating the laws to create and capture monetary or other gains. As a desideratum, rent

---

15 *Id.* at 2077.
16 *See*, for example, the work of Alvin Roth and Lionel Shapley, the 2012 Nobel Laureates in Economics whose scholarship engaged the economics of cooperation. *See* http://www.nobelprize.org/nobel_prizes/economic-sciences/laureates/2012/press.html (*available 15 September 2015*).
17 *See, e.g.*, J. Willard Hurst, Law and the Conditions of Freedom in Nineteenth Century America (1956).
18 *See, e.g.*, Pamela Samuelson & Suzanne Scotchmer, *The Law and Economics of Reverse Engineering*, 111 Yale L. J. 1575 (2002).
19 *See* Kal Raustiala & Christopher Sprigman, The Knockoff Economy: How Imitation Sparks Innovation (2012).

seeking entails identifying and meeting consumer and producer need through the creation of new products and services. Competition is about pursuing rents, but sometimes that pursuit can become corrupt. Discerning where the line is crossed requires engagement with the normative underpinnings of competition.

6.32 Economist George J. Stigler presents an important, and from what I can tell not often cited, narrative about the development of the idea of perfect competition.[20] In the context of presenting the history of competition as an idea, Stigler states: 'The merging of the concepts of competition and the market was unfortunate as each deserved a full and separate treatment.'[21] What he means is that competition, fully developed, can serve as a gauge of the effectiveness of the market as an institution, and a normative criterion for legal policy. Although his 1957 article focuses on price competition, a companion piece examines the relationship between price and non-price competition.[22] In this article, Stigler shows that price competition is more effective in reducing price than non-price competition because the marginal costs of engaging in non-price competition (such as advertising) are higher than the marginal costs of production.[23] But this analysis does not consider trademarks, which might allow a firm to economize on advertising costs, and may also give a firm market advantage in product differentiation.

6.33 Complementing Stigler, Albert O. Hirschman offers a view of competition that looks beyond the venue of the market to understand competition as a basis for institutional and social change.[24] This book is well-known, but its applications to intellectual property policy have not really been explored. As the subtitle says, Hirschman's concern is decline. That is a gloomy characterization, however, which perhaps reflects the pessimism of the late 1960s. I read the book in positive terms. Hirschman identifies three ways in which institutions change. One is by exit as the disaffected leave and form new organizations, and social and economic arrangements. The second is by voice as individuals express their concerns to promote change. Finally, loyalty serves as a bond that enhances voice and makes the threat of exit more credible. The three individually, and in combination serve as mechanisms for change and progress, and thereby help in understanding intellectual property.

---

20 *See* George J. Stigler, *Perfect Competition, Historically Contemplated*, 65(1) J. POL. ECON., 1–17 (1957).
21 *Id.* at 6.
22 *See* George J. Stigler, *Price and Non-Price Competition*, 76(1) J. POL. ECON., 149–154 (1968).
23 Id. at 151–2.
24 *See* ALBERT O. HIRSCHMAN, EXIT, VOICE, AND LOYALTY: RESPONSES TO DECLINE IN FIRMS, ORGANIZATIONS, AND STATES (1970).

6.34 So, what does all this mean for intellectual property, broadly, and for trademark law, more specifically? I will answer for intellectual property generally and then turn to trademarks. Hirschman's tools of exit, voice, and loyalty allow us to understand the dynamics underlying intellectual property policy. Consider the judicially administered doctrine of copyright fair use. Sometimes courts use fair use to promote exit by recognizing the need for users to shift to new technologies and platforms. The 1984 *Sony* decision about the VCR represents this view of exit.[25] In other cases, courts use fair use to promote voice, as in the *Campbell* case about the alternative riff on the song 'Pretty Woman' by 2 Live Crew.[26] The often neglected category of loyalty also plays a role, as courts find against fair use and in favor of copyright liability to spur alternative mechanisms for delivery of works. The controversial decision in *Grokster* from 2005 illustrates this approach.[27] When courts use exit, voice, or loyalty as mechanisms for competition is the subject of my current thinking about intellectual property policy and provides a way to gauge how norms of competition inform intellectual property decisions.

6.35 Other examples of the dynamics of competition, as seen through the lens of Hirschman, arise in patent and trademark law. Licensing is a mechanism of loyalty in both areas, but the question is how exit or voice can enter the relationship with either the patent or trademark owner. An appeal to voice can help to understand the controversial decision in *MedImmune*,[28] and could, as a conceptual matter, play a role in the disposition of the *Nike* decision from the Supreme Court in 2013.[29] Both cases raised the issue of when someone can challenge the validity of intellectual property (patent and trademark, respectively).

6.36 The question that Lemley and McKenna ask in the title of their article can be answered by Hirschman's concept of loyalty. Competition arises not through price or even quality, but through appeal to the consumer's interest in being affiliated with some group. Loyalty to Pepsi is like loyalty to the home team; it takes something other than a price change to force a switch. But loyalty serves as a mechanism for competition to obtain and maintain fan affinity. How either intellectual property or antitrust law should respond depends on the value we identify in such competition.

---

25 Sony Corp. of America v. Universal City Studios, Inc., 464 U.S. 417 (1984).
26 Campbell v. Acuff-Rose Music, 510 U.S. 569 (1994).
27 MGM Studios, Inc. v. Grokster, Ltd., 545 U.S. 913 (2005).
28 MedImmune, Inc. v. Genentech, Inc., 549 U.S. 118 (2007).
29 Already, LLC v. Nike, Inc., 133 S. Ct. 721, 184 L. Ed. 2d 553 (2013).

6.37 I could provide further examples, which I hope will be illustrative and provocative of my points here. But much of what I say here is made possible by Lemley and McKenna's article, as it helped to gel my various thoughts on markets, intellectual property, and competition. One bigger lesson from Lemley and McKenna's article, as well as from the Kaplow piece, is the relationship between formalism and realism in law. Market definition was intended to provide structure to the inquiry of market power by basing it in empirical measures of markets and elasticity. The good intention of realism, however, eventually lead to a stale formalism unmoored from the goals of addressing antitrust policies. Articles like Lemley and McKenna's guide us back to the policies and goals of intellectual property, to the ideas of competition presented in this chapter, as well as to many other salient ones.

C. CONCEPTS, MODELS, AND TRADEMARK LAW

6.38 Stigler correctly asks us to reconsider the concept of competition separate from a formal model of markets.[30] Upon returning to the first principles about the allocation of goods through competition, the key insight is the distinction between private goods and public, or shared goods. Price competition works for the first category, but not as well for the second. The challenge provided by trademark is the analysis of markets involving mixed public and private goods. The discussion in Section B shows that formally assessing these mixed markets is a complex task. Progress lies in rethinking the basic problems posed by competition, understanding its parameters, and determining ways to implement the concepts. Those tasks drive the discussion of this Section.

6.39 In gauging the relationship between intellectual property and competition law and policy, the main contribution is conceptualizing intellectual property as defining a regime of non-price competition. The quest for a formal model, however, may be elusive and, even if found, difficult to implement for legal policy. In this Section, I propose an analytical approach for understanding intellectual property in terms of non-price competition, which is derived from Albert Hirschman's famous model of exit, voice, and loyalty. The attractiveness of this approach is its conceptual rigor and focus on ideas that can be readily recognized and implemented by courts and debated by policymakers.

6.40 The motivation for this chapter is the longstanding legal and policy question of reconciling intellectual property and competition policy. The Supreme

---

30 *See* Hovenkamp, *supra* note 4, at 207 (describing degrees of competition within traditional models of monopoly and perfect competition).

Court's 2013 decision in *FTC v. Actavis*[31] brought this question to the forefront, offering an answer that has been interpreted as either quite narrow or game changing. Such contrasting views represent the language of the majority and dissenting opinions, and the unusual factual context for the decision. Whatever the scope of the opinion, the concept of 'freedom from competition'[32] arises in several antitrust cases involving intellectual property. Virtues of intellectual property as providing a refuge from competition contrast with claims that intellectual property is a monopoly, often a misuse of that term, perhaps a shorthand for 'strong exclusionary rights'. This chapter presents a conceptualization of these issues that provides normative balance and operability within legal policy debates.

6.41 While ostensibly offering freedom from competition, intellectual property actually entails different forms of competition. Scholars and policymakers characterize intellectual property rights as allowing the owner to set prices above marginal cost, and thereby obtaining a rent, or a monetary reward, for the legal exclusivity. This characterization of an intellectual property owner as price setter is often the basis for describing intellectual property as a monopoly. We can see such reference in recent Supreme Court cases. Kaplow's 1984 article on the patent-antitrust interface is an example of how price setting behaviour is assumed in the scholarly literature.[33]

6.42 But even if an intellectual property owner can set the price, and even if an intellectual property owner is free from price competition, non-price competition plays a critical role in the dynamics of innovation and intellectual property rights. Design around, transformative fair use, reverse engineering, trademark nominative and fair uses, and other practices and doctrines illustrate how an intellectual property owner faces competition along dimensions other than price. The scholarly literature on product differentiation and monopolistic competition represent formal economic approaches to recognizing non-price competition in intellectual property defined markets. The scholarly work tends to focus narrowly on copyright's access/incentive trade-off through specific models of markets. This chapter is conceptually broader and is not limited to particular 'market structures'. Therefore, the methodology presented in this chapter has broader appeal and implications.

---

31 FTC v. Actavis, Inc., 133 S.Ct. 2223 (2013).
32 *See* United States v. Line Materials Company, 333 U.S. 287 (1947).
33 Louis Kaplow, *The Patent-Antitrust Intersection: A Reappraisal*, 97 HARV. L. REV. 1813 (1984).

C. CONCEPTS, MODELS, AND TRADEMARK LAW

Albert Hirschman's idea of exit, voice, and loyalty provides an attractive framework for conceptualizing non-price competition. Hirschman's eponymous 1970 book presents the dynamic of exit, voice, and loyalty as tools in competitive struggles, especially in declining industries. The inspiration for the book came from Hirschman's study of government sponsored industries in Nigeria, and the failure of price competition to lead to improvements in such governmentally sanctioned monopolies, such as the railroads. His examples, however, also included then ongoing debates over public schools, and the forces for change in government and corporate governance in the United States. To the extent intellectual properties are instances of government-sanctioned monopolies, Hirschman's ideas about competitive dynamics have relevance. Even if the equation of intellectual property with forms of monopolies is incorrect, the forces of exit and voice have resonance in intellectual property debates, especially as counterweights to systems of loyalty that are often associated with intellectual property. 6.43

Competition law interacts with intellectual property law both internal to intellectual property doctrines (exhaustion, fair use, and so on) and external to intellectual property law (antitrust). My focus is on the first set of interactions. Non-price competition can inform an antitrust analysis of intellectual property practice, but I leave that in part for a later discussion. Here, the role of non-price competition in applying intellectual property doctrines is the focus. Leaving the broader normative discussion of competition versus 'freedom from competition' for another scholarly discussion, this chapter tries to unpack the different forces at work in competition using Hirschman's 1970 framework. 6.44

Exit, voice, and loyalty are different forces of competition that promote change in social institutions, such as the market. They are relevant to intellectual property as competition, of the non-price sort; they shape the dynamic of innovation and the implicit scope of intellectual property rights. 6.45

Exit refers to the movement of consumers and other participants within a particular organization in response to unfavorable decisions made by owners or managers within that organization. In the case of governmental organizations or voluntary associations, the exit can take the form of movement from the jurisdiction (moving to another state, disassociation with a homeowner's group). In the case of for-profit entities, exit takes the form of refusing to buy from a particular company or switching to a competitor. Competition analysis often focuses on entry of new firms. The strategy of exit is a corollary to the entry of new firms. Exit will sometimes be limited if new firms do not enter, and the viability of new firms will result in attracting customers that often would arise from exit of incumbents. 6.46

6.47 Exit occurs within the exclusive rights provided by intellectual property through brand switching, designing around a patent, reverse engineering a trade secret, developing expressive works that build upon without copying existing works of authorship, or through accessing different channels of distribution. The availability of exit depends upon the scope of intellectual property rights. The exit strategy also depends on the availability of alternatives for reasons other than the scope of intellectual property rights, such as institutional limitations and scope of the marketplace. In many instances, exit may not be an option, for example, in the case of pharmaceuticals or software products. At a broader level, one may not be able to exit the institutions of scientific investigation and research, or of expressive fields, such as book publishing or art exhibition.

6.48 Voice often can serve as an alternative to exit when the latter is not feasible. Voice is often described as change from within an organization. It can involve changing leadership or expressing dissenting viewpoints with the goal of fomenting change. Hirschman describes voice as 'political', while exit is 'economic'. However, voice can also have an economic dimension, such as through advertising or production of mainstream or alternative media. Exit, too, can have a political dimension, such as an economic boycott by consumers for disagreement with corporate investment policies. The particular label does not matter when it comes to understanding the competitive force, or the institutional and organizational context within which the force operates. Exit entails a refusal to deal with an entity. Voice, by contrast, assumes an ongoing communicative relationship with an entity.

6.49 Voice within intellectual property systems includes the use of trademarked or copyrighted works in the form of protest. Recognizing voice as a strategy may explain why fair use in copyright is more permissive when it is critical of the copied work, rather than a third work or a broader social issue. But restrictions on voice, even when aimed at issues broader than the work at hand, can be undesirable within an intellectual property system. The difficulty is in drawing boundaries on voice through intellectual property rights. Nonetheless, voice can have well-defined domains. For example, contracting can be a form of voice, and restrictions licensees, such as licensee estoppel, may be suspect from the perspective of voice. Furthermore, litigation is one channel for voice, and access to litigation can be important in supporting voice as a competitive force on intellectual property.

6.50 The dynamic between exit and voice is complicated. Exit is effective if the high-value customers leave a particular organization. But that may often leave behind less well-positioned individuals to exercise voice. Therefore, exit may undercut voice. At the same time, voice may facilitate access as individuals who may have low value for the organization put pressure through voice on high-value members to exit, which might put additional pressure on the organization to change. Policymakers and scholars need to consider the interplay between exit and voice in assessing particular policies.

Loyalty is another competitive force, but one that works counter to exit and voice.[34] Loyalty is the strategy often used by an existing entity to cement relationships with members in order to forestall change. At the same time, loyalty may be the key competition lever as organizations compete for members. Loyalty can work through emotional, cultural, and pecuniary appeals. However, the lever can be subject to cognitive biases and inertia, as existing members may downplay the need for change in order to obtain short term gains. Furthermore, loyalty may be won through superficial, short-run changes that do not address the underlying source of the discontent leading to exit and voice. **6.51**

Intellectual property systems are systems of loyalty. We can see this in the notion of trademark and branding. Copyright also illustrates a large element of loyalty through author-affinities and fandom. Patent licensing is a form of loyalty, especially through the use of most favored nation clauses and exclusivity provisions. Trade secrets operate to create within firm loyalty by making it difficult for existing employees to leave for other alternatives. The heart of my argument is that intellectual property serves to prevent exit and voice through mechanisms of loyalty. The goal of intellectual property policy is to allow room for exit and voice as competitive forces that can lead to change and innovation. **6.52**

Exit and voice provide the primary impetus for non-price competition. Loyalty acts to limit exit and voice by bonding individuals who might provide alternatives to the status quo from either leaving to pursue these alternatives, or engaging in advocacy to pursue these alternatives from within. These concepts map onto different types of intellectual property. **6.53**

In this chapter, I assume that non-price competition is a key driver of individual invention, market innovation, and technological change. Intellectual property operates within a world of non-price competition, and shapes its contours. Intellectual property rules shape the mechanisms of non-price competition as a facilitator of invention and innovation. Two implications **6.54**

---

34   *See* ALBERT HIRSCHMAN, ESSAYS IN TRESPASSING, 236–40 (1981) (presenting a discussion of the meaning of loyalty).

follow from this claim. First, even if intellectual property precludes competition (by establishing a price setting monopoly), non-price competition still exists. Second, intellectual property policy is designed to facilitate non-price competition.

6.55 The connection between non-price competition and intellectual property is apparent in different areas of intellectual property. Before proceeding to the examples, it is valuable to set forth the general structure of my argument. Intellectual property rights are exclusive rights that facilitate different types of loyalty. However, loyalty impedes non-price competition. Therefore, the design of intellectual property rights should facilitate exit and voice. This section shows how this view of intellectual property informs actual intellectual property doctrine and can guide policy reform.

6.56 Trade secret law best illustrates the dynamic of exit, voice, and loyalty in promoting non-price competition. From the 19th century to the 1930s, trade secret law in the United States evolved into a form of property owned by a firm.[35] Such developments reflected the evolvement of the corporate form, and the increased proprietary nature of tacit knowledge within a firm. Employee inventorship gave way to assignments through contracts and rules that facilitated firm management of valuable business knowledge.

6.57 After World War II, trade secret law shifted towards recognition of employee ownership, and the values of competition and employee mobility within trade secret regimes. The 1960 Pennsylvania Supreme Court decision, *Wexler v. Greenberg*,[36] illustrates the germ of start-up culture that is paramount today. At the same time, over half a century since the *Wexler* decision, we have witnessed some reversals from the role of exit in trade secret law. Inevitable disclosure, the use of contractual restrictions, such as grant back clauses, and the ongoing debates over invention assignment agreements illustrate pushback from the values of exit towards ones of loyalty, and preserving ownership and management within the firm of tacit knowledge.

6.58 Developments in trade secret law over a century illustrate a movement from loyalty to exit, and a return to loyalty. Non-price competition, as a normative basis for court decisions, advanced and then retreated in some areas. The benefits of non-price competition for trade secret regimes are apparent, however, and the role of trade secret as a means of imposing loyalty has

---

35 *See* CATHERINE FISK, WORKING KNOWLEDGE: EMPLOYEE INNOVATION AND THE RISE OF CORPORATE INTELLECTUAL PROPERTY 1870–1930, 211–13 (2009).
36 160 A.2d 430 (1960).

become less salient and perhaps undesirable. The challenge to firms, and to social policy, is recognizing some need for cohesion within a firm. As managers and employees view firms as mere platforms for individual mobility, the benefits that arise from the firms are potentially lost. An important legal basis for firm loyalty, however, need not be trade secret law. Instead, corporate law doctrines, such as the rule against usurpation of corporate opportunities, may facilitate firm loyalty without interfering with the benefits of non-price competition for invention and innovation. A combination of a fairly open trade secret regime, one that facilitates competition, with a strict fiduciary duty regime may provide the appropriate balance between loyalty and exit.

Trademark law also illustrates the dynamic of exit, voice, and loyalty. By contrast with trade secret law, trademark law provides a specific mechanism for loyalty. Within the trade secret law, the bond of loyalty is between the employer and the employee. Within trademark law, the bond is between the firm and the customer. Such a conception of trademark law is consistent with the traditional search cost rationale for the law. But the conception of trademarks as loyalty mechanisms goes beyond the traditional rationale. As a promoter of loyalty, trademarks aid not only in the location of goods, but also in developing connections among consumers and between the consumer and the trademark owner. **6.59**

Non-price competition through exit and voice can place limits on the exclusionary rights of the trademark owner, and facilitate innovation. Inter-brand competition is a canonical form of non-price competition as consumers can switch brand loyalties based on the bundle of amenities that a competing brand can provide. Brand switching is an example of exit. A competitor is free to attract consumers through many means, falling short of copying the trademark owner's mark. Exit to counterfeit brands poses an interesting challenge for the loyalty theory of trademarks. Under traditional search cost theory, counterfeits undermine the value of the trademark by attracting consumers to poor-quality products or services. Under the loyalty theory, consumers are demonstrating an element of loyalty to the brand by buying cheaper substitutes for products that may not otherwise be affordable. Counterfeits expand the brand, admittedly at the cost of quality in some instances. Counterfeit marks are not, therefore, an unalloyed negative under a loyalty theory of trademarks. This possibility may explain why trademark owners sometimes countenance counterfeit products in some markets, especially in the developing world. **6.60**

Voice, in addition to exit, facilitates non-price competition in the trademark regime. Those who are dissatisfied with a brand can express concerns through **6.61** the use of the trademark itself. Such use is protected as nominative fair use. Use of a protected mark to criticize the mark can also be a form of classical trademark fair use. Exclusions from trademark infringement, such as fair use, build on the communicative aspect of marks, especially as tools for exercising voice.[37]

6.62 One unexplored implication of voice in trademark law is the treatment of comparative advertising. While a consumer can make use of a mark to exercise her voice, the use of a mark by a competitor is controversial. However, comparative advertising may be an exercise of non-price competition through voice. Because of the important role of comparative advertising, courts and legislatures should be more facilitating towards this form of advertising against claims of unfair competition or trademark infringement. Effectively, comparative advertising may complement voice by consumers, and may serve as a conduit for communication between competitors and consumers.

6.63 Trademark's role in transactions and competition contrasts with those of copyright and patent, which also serve as mechanisms for promoting loyalty. Limitations on exclusionary rights under copyright and patent laws, as those under trademark law, can facilitate exit and voice. Copyright, like trademark, governs expressive activities, but ones that go beyond promoting brand loyalty. However, fandom under copyright regimes parallels branding under trademark. Copyright doctrines, such as fair use and first sale, facilitate non-price competition through exit and voice. The challenge is finding ways to promote exit and voice within digital copyright regimes. The broad recommendation is to have digital copyright mirror traditional copyright rules as much as possible.

6.64 Patent, perhaps less obviously, serves as a mechanism for promoting loyalty. Paralleling trade secret, patent is a mechanism for cementing loyalty within the firm by making it more difficult for employees holding within firm knowledge to exit. Licensing also acts as a mechanism for loyalty by, in some instances, aligning the interests of the licensee with those of the patent owner. The role of exit in licensing regimes comes into play through the treatment of patent remedies, of FRAND (Fair, Reasonable, and Non-Discriminatory), and of standard setting organizations.

---

[37] *See* Deven R. Desai, *From Trademarks to Brands*, 64 FLA L. REV. 981, 1036 (2012) (discussing co-branding and connection between trademarks and consumer communities). *See also* Deven R. Desai, *Speech, Citizenry, and the Market: A Corporate Public Figure Doctrine*, 98 MINN. L. REV. 455, 466–8 (2013) (connecting products markets to communication and speech).

6.65 Voice is also a pertinent mechanism for non-price competition in patent law. Challenges to patent validity rely on the mechanism of voice. Debates over licensee estoppel rest on the appropriate timing for the exercise of voice: during the licensing negotiation phase or afterwards. Administrative procedures for patent review also facilitate voice. Legal doctrines, such as standing, shape how and when voice can be exercised in the courts. Finally, the theory of voice can inform the understanding of experimental use as a limitation on patent rights. When experimental use facilitates voice as a challenge to a specific patent, the law should countenance such a limitation. However, since experimental use simply facilitates private gain, patent law should not allow an experimental use defense.

6.66 The theory of non-price competition presented here has three broad implications for intellectual property law: (i) understanding the boundary between intellectual property and competition policy; (ii) shedding light on intellectual property in development policy; and (iii) developing a broader understanding of the political economy of intellectual property.

6.67 Framing intellectual property within the terms of non-price competition opens up our understanding of the relationship between intellectual property and competition law doctrines. For those who see intellectual property as problematic because of the possibility of monopoly-like price setting, non-price competition suggests that the threat of intellectual property as monopoly may be limited. But this argument should not be the basis for complacency on the scope of intellectual property rights. The stronger counterargument is that intellectual property needs to be policed from the perspective of both price competition and non-price competition. The arguments in this chapter provide a more workable balance between intellectual property and competition law, suggesting an overlap and harmony in shared goals of promoting invention, innovation, and access. Such a view may aid in going beyond the narrow debate between the majority and dissent in the *Actavis* decision.[38]

6.68 Criticisms of the exit and voice framework may parallel that made of the raising rival's cost approach to antitrust enforcement. Both approaches focus on a potential mix of qualitative and quantitative analysis on the ease of entry into a particular market. The problem, however, is that in many instances, entry barriers may be desirable because they are a consequence of a firm providing a more innovative product than a competitor. I would argue that the exit/voice approach goes beyond the raising rival's cost approach by identifying specific mechanisms within a coherent theoretical framework for promoting

---

[38] *See* Shubha Ghosh, *Convergence?*, MINN. J.L. SCI. & TECH. (2014).

non-price competition. This framework does not rely on market definition, a target of criticism within antitrust analysis, and rests on both qualitative and quantitative information about competitive dynamics within which an entity operates. Therefore, the exit/voice approach serves to prove a theoretical bridge between intellectual property and competition law that can be applied to a complex factual context.

6.69 Hirschman's theory of exit and voice arose through his study of development and the failures of market-driven policies in developing countries.[39] The dynamics of non-price competition often undermined attempts at liberalization through price competition. The approach presented here, as applied to intellectual property, can be a basis for understanding the relationship between intellectual property and development. While often debated in terms of attracting foreign direct investment for large capitalized firms (that often will have some price setting capabilities in a market economy),[40] the role of intellectual property in promoting development also encompassed the promotion of indigenous innovation, and of start-up businesses that compete in distribution and manufacturing.[41] The exit/voice framework is instructive in how to design national intellectual property regimes that foster development through non-price competition.

6.70 Looking beyond developing countries, the exit/voice framework illuminates the political economy of intellectual property in developed countries, especially the interplay between incumbent firms, business models, and new entrants with alternative technologies and practices. Hirschman's framework can serve as a predictive model to explain industry responses and the influence on the law. Furthermore, the framework can be valuable in examining non-price competition as a normative virtue in the design of intellectual property regimes.[42] This chapter lays the foundation for how non-price competition

---

39 See Jeremy Adelman, Worldly Philosopher: The Odyssey of Albert O. Hirschman, 440–2 (2013) (background to writing of Exit, Voice, and Loyalty).
40 See Intellectual Property and Development: Lessons from Recent Economic Research, 35–6 (Carsten Fink & Keith Maskus eds., 2005); Robert M. Sherwood, Intellectual Property and Economic Development (2003 reprint).
41 See, e.g., J.M. Finger, Poor People's Knowledge: Helping People to Earn From Their Knowledge (2003).
42 Joseph Schumpeter is cited as extolling the virtues of monopoly in promoting innovation, especially through creating profits that can be used for research and development. Although monopoly precludes price discrimination in his analysis, innovation pressures still exist in Schumpeter's analysis through non-price pressures such as the entry of new firms. Kenneth Arrow, on the other hand, demonstrated that competition provided more innovative pressures than monopoly although his analysis focused on a model of technology change based on reduction of production costs. See discussion in Ghosh, supra note 38, and Hovenkamp, supra note 4, at 203–4.

operates in intellectual property systems and makes the case for addressing intellectual property policy through the lens of exit, voice, and loyalty.

D. TRADEMARK TRANSACTIONS: TYING, TRANSFERS IN GROSS AND COVENANTS NOT TO SUE

The analysis of competition and markets has application to specific examples of trademark transactions. The focus of this section is on three cases: tying arrangements involving trademarks, transfer in gross and merchandising, and the use of covenants not to sue to quell claims of trademark invalidity. 6.71

A tying arrangement is a requirement imposed on a purchaser to buy an item or service as a condition for the contract of sale or license of a product. For example, a patent owner sometimes requires a licensee to obtain a service contract as a condition for licensing the patented technology. Tying arrangements are subject to antitrust scrutiny for being anti-competitive. By forcing the purchase of a good or service, the seller may be leveraging monopoly power in the sale of one product (the tying product) into the sale of another, possibly unrelated, product (the tied product). Under antitrust law, tying arrangements are per se illegal if there is market power in the tying product, and anti-competitive effects in the market for the tied product.[43] The Supreme Court had held that ownership of a patent (and presumably other forms of intellectual property) does not create the presumption of market power for the purpose of tying analysis.[44] Instead, the challenger must show that ownership of a patent creates market power under the circumstances of the products involved in the tying arrangement. 6.72

Trademark licensees, often franchisees, have unsuccessfully challenged requirements by a trademark licensor to buy subsidiary goods, such as branded napkins or containers, as an illegal tying arrangement.[45] Typically, the ownership of a trademark does not, by itself, create market power, and there is little likelihood of monopolizing the market for napkins or other accessories. Furthermore, courts find a business interest in promoting a brand and developing recognition among consumers of the source of a product, such as a pizza or food at a restaurant.[46] Within the framework of Section C, the court's 6.73

---

43   Jefferson Parish Hospital District No. 2 v. Hyde, 466 U.S. 2 (1984).
44   Illinois Tool Works Inc. v. Independent Ink, Inc., 547 U.S. 28 (2006).
45   *See, e.g.*, Keener v. Sizzler Family Steak Houses, 597 F.2d 453, 456 (5th Cir.1979); Queen City Pizza, Inc. v. Domino's Pizza, Inc., 124 F.3d 430 (3d Cir. 1997).
46   *See* Queen City, 124 F.3d 430.

conclusions are found reasonable in identifying the role of loyalty. Furthermore, these contractual arrangements do not limit exit or voice. The licensees in these cases are aware of the conditions and can agree not to enter into the franchising arrangement. The trademark tying cases illustrate how loyalty is created in the competitive marketplace.

6.74 The second example of trademarks in gross illustrates the role of loyalty, and the possible need for limitations. Trademarks cannot be transferred to a licensee without a transfer of goodwill created by the licensor.[47] Trademark transfers cannot be personal or in gross, without invalidating the trademark. However, trademarks are often transferred for use on merchandising items, such as hats or t-shirts, which serve to advertise the branded product.[48] These transfers are not considered in gross because the trademark typically obtains trademark registration in the merchandising items. On the one hand, this business transaction serves to promote loyalty. On the other hand, the practice may limit the use of marks as parody or commentary on t-shirts or other merchandising items.[49] As a result, trademark law might serve to limit voice. Courts need to police this possibility.

6.75 The case of *Already v. Nike*[50] is troubling for the role of exit and voice in trademark law. As a counterclaim to Nike's claim against Already for trade dress infringement, Already argued that Nike's trade dress for the competing shoe was invalid. Nike settled its claim by granting Already a covenant not to sue. Already, however, proceeded with its counterclaim, which Nike argued was moot after the grant of the covenant not to sue. The Supreme Court ruled in favor of Nike, concluding that Already had no basis to challenge the validity of the trademark since there was no fear of being sued for trademark infringement in light of the covenant.

6.76 The Court's ruling in *Already v. Nike* creates a dangerous risk of foreclosing voice in trademark law. While the covenant not to sue provides Already freedom to operate, it also forecloses judicial review of the validity of the trademark. Perhaps future litigation can provide a basis for a challenge, but the covenant not to sue would be an effective means to silence claims of invalidity. The Court's ruling in *Already* is one that ignores considerations of voice

---

[47] *See, e.g.*, Hokto Kinoko Co. v. Concord Farms, Inc., 738 F.3d 1085, 1098 (9th Cir. 2013); In re XMH Corp., 647 F.3d 690, 696 (7th Cir. 2011); United Drug Co. v. Theodore Rectanus Co., 248 U.S. 90, 96–97, 39 S.Ct. 48, 63 L.Ed. 141 (1918); Green River Bottling Co. v. Green River Corp., 997 F.2d 359, 361–62 (7th Cir. 1993).
[48] See Kentucky Fried Chicken Corp. v. Diversified Packaging Corp., 549 F.2d 368 (5th Cir. 1977); Int'l Order of Job's Daughters v. Lindeburg & Co., 633 F.2d 912, 919 (9th Cir. 1980).
[49] *See, e.g.*, Hormel Foods Corp. v. Jim Henson Prods., Inc., 73 F.3d 497 (2d Cir. 1996).
[50] *See supra* note 29.

without any balancing need for developing loyalty. By quelling voice, the Court has upset the balance of exit, voice, and loyalty.

E. CONCLUSION

This chapter has made the case for fitting trademark law into competition policy. While, on the surface, that connection sounds straightforward given the parallel roots of trademark law and unfair competition, trademark as competition policy offers its own challenges. Traditional models of competition, with homogenous products and small firms competing over price, are not apposite to the realities of trademark. As this chapter has shown, the problem is that branded goods are distributed through two forms of competition: one for the product the consumer seeks, and one for the trademark. The former, typically, can be understood as a private good; the latter, as a public good. Price competition is adequate for distributing private goods, but markets for public goods rests more often on non-price competition. The challenge is to develop a conception of markets that takes into consideration both price and non-price competition.

6.77

Scholars and policymakers have struggled with these issues for nearly a century, searching for a formal mathematical model that can synthesize these complications. I have proposed a heuristic approach based on a theory of non-price competition, developed by economist Albert Hirschman. Exit, voice, and loyalty are ideas that are intuitive to policymakers and judges. These ideas also capture the underlying dynamics of non-price competition. The innovative contribution of this chapter is to make these concepts useful for analyzing trademark and other areas of intellectual property. For those wedded to formal mathematical models alone, the approach presented in this chapter is of little use. But for those who seek broader heuristics and frameworks, including, but not limited to, mathematical ones, the chapter moves forward the longstanding challenge of reconciling property and monopoly, and synthesizing the reality of competition and the exclusive rights of trademark.

6.78

Section C

VALUATION, TAXATION, SECURITY INTERESTS AND BANKRUPTCY

7

BRAND DIFFERENTIATION AND INDUSTRY SEGMENTATION: DRIVERS FOR TRADEMARK VALUATION IN CORPORATE TRANSACTIONS

Roy P. D'Souza[*]

A. INTRODUCTION	7.01	(c) Going concern business enterprise	7.31
B. BRAND MANAGEMENT PRINCIPLES	7.06	(d) Going concern business enterprise key transactions	7.32
C. COMMON APPROACHES TO VALUE BRANDS	7.09	2. Valuation of the brands transacted	7.37
1. Income approach	7.10	(a) Strategic vs. Financial Target	7.37
(a) Relief from royalty	7.13	(b) Summary	7.38
(b) Excess earnings	7.18	3. Asset purchase agreements containing trademarks	7.39
2. Market approach	7.20	E. PURCHASE PRICE ALLOCATION	7.40
D. HISTORICAL TRANSACTIONS INVOLVING BRANDS	7.22	F. WHY INDUSTRY MATTERS	7.41
1. Distressed vs. going concern (brand-only vs. business enterprise with brand)	7.23	G. ADDITIONAL BRAND VALUATION METHODS	7.45
(a) Distressed business enterprise (liquidation/brand only scenario)	7.24	H. THE WORLD'S MOST VALUABLE BRANDS	7.46
(b) Distressed enterprise key transactions	7.25	I. CONCLUSION	7.47

A. INTRODUCTION

Over the past decade, the fair value of intangible assets and intellectual property has been much more prominent on the balance sheets of private and public companies on a global level. While this transition has largely been driven by changes in financial reporting standards, as applicable to business **7.01**

---

[*] Member of the Valuation Practice of Ocean Tomo LLC. The Valuation Practice specializes in appraising patents, trademarks, brands, copyrights, and a variety of other intangible and intellectual property assets for transaction and monetization planning, capital raise, and restructuring/bankruptcy. The views expressed herein are solely those of the author and may not represent the views of Ocean Tomo. I would like to thank Elizabeth Quinlivan, Daniel McEldowney, Tyler Remick and Monica Linders for their contribution to this chapter.

combinations of all forms, a combined increase in licensing and asset (non-enterprise level) transactions has led to a renewed focus on the value creation opportunities afforded by this asset class.

7.02 Specifically, trademarks, trade names, and brands are a class of marketing-related intangible assets where it is not uncommon for corporations to have dedicated, and highly experienced professionals, whose sole focus is value creation and maximization through a combination of organic development, acquisitions, and licensing activities.

7.03 In this chapter our goal is to provide a foundation for how corporations and investors recognize and measure trademark value, particularly in the context of transaction considerations. We will first review the concept of trademark/brand life cycles, highlighting how managing brands and attempting to consistently measure value creation provides actionable information for corporate managers. As this knowledge base is commonly rooted in income- and market-based facts and assumptions, we will discuss how this data provides a valuation framework from which to expand on.

7.04 One of the most significant challenges in intellectual property valuation is finding independently verified comparable transactions of these assets, only where certain benchmarks can be established for commonly traded price ranges, depending upon key considerations such as industry, profitability, stage of life cycle, and so on. We will review available third party sources of information that also include data from financial reporting filings, and discuss the pros and cons of utilizing such information in practice.

7.05 We then conclude with an outline on additional brand valuation methods, and a comparison on the world's most valuable brands.

B. BRAND MANAGEMENT PRINCIPLES

7.06 Brand managers in the corporate environment must diligently analyze their brand's positioning in an effort to control its value. One common framework used to accomplish this is an analysis of a brand's strengths, weaknesses, opportunities, and threats (SWOT). An assessment of brand strength includes a review of the brand, its positioning, the market within which the brand operates, competition, past financial performance, future trajectory, and risks to the brand.[1] In the model developed by Interbrand PLC, brand strength is a composite of seven weighted factors, each of which is scored relative to the brand's competitors:[2]

Table 7.1   Interbrand PLC brand strength analysis

Factor	Weight	Analysis
Market leadership	25%	Strong brands have the ability to influence the market. Brands that have a better position in the market can better cope with pressure from competition.
Brand stability	15%	Brands with a long history that have shown high consumer loyalty over the years are strong, and therefore highly valuated.
Market	10%	The ideal market for a brand is stability, continually grows and possesses a lot of barriers of entry.
International degree	25%	Strong brands can cross barriers. Brands with further geographical and cultural expansion possess a high potential and are well protected from the market differentiations.
Brand trend	10%	The long tendency and ability of a brand to gain market share and to remain timely and consumer-oriented shows the brand's competitiveness.
Marketing support	10%	Brands with a targeted strategy, a continuous lead, and an important financial support can gain a stronger consumer loyalty than brands that are not steadily supported.
Legal protection of brand	5%	The legal protection of the brand rights is essential and decisive for its maintenance and differentiation.

Weaknesses of this model include the components of a built-in preference for older brands. A 'brand strength score' (BSS) is calculated by summing the weighted scores for each of the factors considered in Table 7.1. The relationship between brand strength, as measured by the BSS, and the brand risk (that is, discount rate) to be applied is displayed on the S-Curve in Figure 7.1. The stronger a brand the lower its risk, and the more certain future brand earnings. The industry weighted average cost of capital, (WACC) which is ideally composed of the same competitors assessed in the brand strength analysis, is used as the benchmark for the company's overall risk.[3]

7.07

As a legally, indefinitely lived asset, if a brand is used in a commercial context, it is an asset that requires consistent monitoring to ensure that the brand's legal

7.08

---

1   TATIANA SOTO J., METHODS FOR ASSESSING BRAND VALUE, A COMPARISON BETWEEN THE INTERBRAND MODEL AND THE BBDO'S BRAND EQUITY EVALUATOR MODEL 48 (2008).
2   Id.
3   SOTO J., *supra* note 1, at 49.

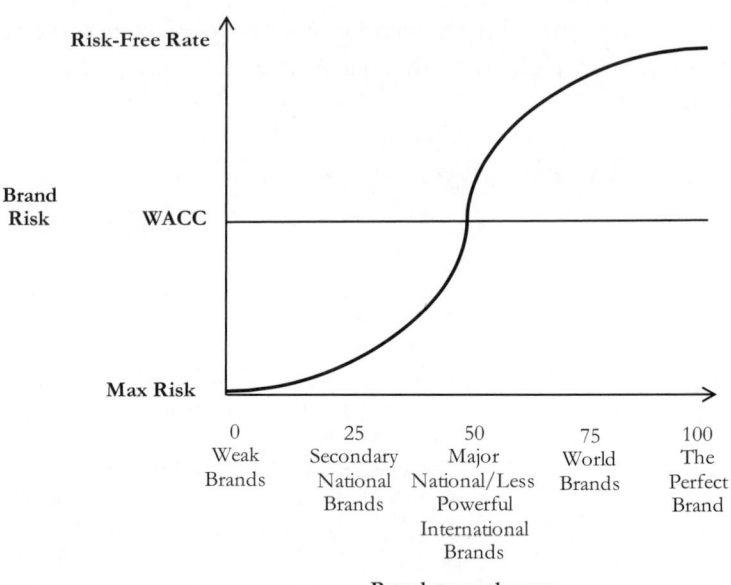

Figure 7.1 Interbrand PLC (S Curve)

value remains over time in preferable correlation with operational profits. Brand management is a job that is constantly in progress.

C. COMMON APPROACHES TO VALUE BRANDS

7.09 There are many approaches to valuing intellectual property. The two most common approaches are the Income Approach and the Market Approach. Additionally, there are many methods within each of these approaches. Determining which approach, and ultimately which method to use, depends on the circumstances and objective of the valuation, as well as the information that is available. The following section discusses each of these approaches, as well as some of the more common methods that are employed in trademark valuation.

1. Income approach

7.10 The Income Approach is often viewed as the superior approach to valuing an asset because future benefits of a business enterprise are measured in income. The Income Approach attempts to measure such future benefits by calculating the present value of the future income streams expected from the asset under consideration. There are a number of primary parameters that must be quantified in order to use this approach, including the amount and timing of

C. COMMON APPROACHES TO VALUE BRANDS

the expected cash flows attributable to the Subject Assets, and the risk associated with the realization of those cash flows.

7.11 The duration and timing of the cash flow stream are determined by forecasting the useful life of the property, which can be determined in any one of several ways, such as: (1) the physical or service life of the asset; (2) the statutory or legal life of the asset; (3) the economic life of the asset; or (4) the functional or technological life of the asset. The business risk associated with the realization of the stream of expected cash flows may be captured through the use of an appropriate discount rate, or the inputs used to forecast the cash flows, or through a combination of these factors.

7.12 The expected future cash flow stream derived from the assets, usually a series of periodic amounts, may be quantified using a variety of methods, depending on the specific circumstances of each case. In the context of valuing intellectual property, including brands and trademarks, the Relief from Royalty and Excess Earnings methods are frequently used.

(a) Relief from royalty

7.13 The Relief from Royalty methodology is based on the premise that a property's value can be measured by what the owner of the property would pay in royalties if it did not own the property and had to license it from a third party. Alternatively, this method may also quantify the amount of income the owner would generate by licensing the intellectual property to others. This method requires the determination of projected royalty payments, which are derived by applying a royalty rate to an appropriate royalty base.

7.14 The royalty base is the starting point in developing the Relief from Royalty method. The royalty base can be defined as the sales that are attributable to, and are covered by, the scope of the legal protection of the subject intellectual property assets. The royalty base is determined by projecting the expected revenues to be generated throughout the useful life of the intellectual property in question.

7.15 The royalty rate is the contractual percentage of the royalty base that is assigned to the underlying intellectual property. Arriving at the correct royalty rate is one of the most arduous tasks in trademark valuation. The most common practice is to find historical royalty rates from comparable agreements to use as a proxy. Comparable royalty rates can be found in publicly available agreements from database resources such as Royalty Stat, Royalty Source, ktMINE, or Intangible Spring. Additional royalty rate disclosures may also be available in U.S. Security and Exchange Commission (SEC) filings

Chapter 7 BRAND DIFFERENTIATION AND INDUSTRY SEGMENTATION

and through independent Internet research. Royalty rates are also often based on the amount of profits, cost savings, or other income associated with the asset being valued. Once an appropriate royalty rate and base have been determined, the lump sum fair value of the intellectual property is calculated as the net present value of the (avoided) royalty payments.

7.16 In order to provide a range of royalty rates associated with license agreements of brands/trademarks, independent research is necessary. For purposes of an example, a search was performed within ktMINE, a database service containing publicly available license agreement data, in order to investigate a typical range of rates garnered by these intangible assets. Table 7.2 summarizes these search parameters and associated search result 'hits.'

Table 7.2 ktMINE license agreement search criteria

	Step #	Search filter	Filter criteria	Step results	Search results
	1	Agreement type	Marketing intangible	5176	5176
AND NOT	2	Agreement type	Asset purchase, cross license, distribution, franchise, joint development, manufacturing/process intangible, other, service, software	13,975	1317

'Marketing Intangibles' is defined as when a 'License is likely to grant the right to use any of the following: Trademarks, Trade names, Trade dress, Copyrights, Service marks, Logos'. The performed search yields 1,317 search results, and the royalty rates associated with these agreements are presented in Table 7.3.

7.17 The royalty rates in Table 7.3 provide visibility into publicly available license agreement terms, which include the licensing of trademark assets. It is important to note that a valuation engagement would require the further parsing of data sources like ktMINE in order to eliminate licensing terms that are not deemed comparable to the asset(s) at issue in the valuation. Elements of comparability for royalty rates in a trademark valuation may include industry, price-point within the industry, geographic location, and breadth of sales/branding coverage. The royalty rate utilized in any trademark or brand valuation can have a major influence on the ultimate value conclusion, so this research is of particular importance within any relief from royalty analysis.

Table 7.3   ktMINE license agreement royalty rate summary

Common base	Observations	Min.	1st Quartile	Avg.	Median	3rd Quartile	Max.
Gross sales	308	0.05%	0.50%	5.82%	3.00%	7.00%	200.00%
Net sales	906	0.00%	3.00%	7.91%	5.00%	9.46%	200.00%
Costs	47	0.93%	71.25%	84.84%	110.00%	111.75%	125.00%
Gross profit	22	3.00%	10.00%	27.29%	18.50%	50.00%	50.00%
Operating profit	28	1.00%	12.00%	26.96%	25.00%	50.00%	50.00%
Net profit	3	50.00%	50.00%	50.00%	50.00%	50.00%	50.00%
Assets	3	0.01%	0.01%	0.67%	0.01%	1.01%	2.00%

(b)   Excess earnings

7.18   The Excess Earnings methodology is based on the premise that a property's value can be measured by the incremental earnings achieved by a proprietary product, relative to an essentially identical, but non-proprietary, product (for example, a generic version of the same product). The excess earnings may result from the proprietary product commanding a price premium, delivering manufacturing cost savings, or achieving larger sales quantities.

7.19   Usually, the most significant challenge in attempting to use the Excess Earnings method is finding a generic version of the proprietary product such that the only difference between the two is the presence or absence of the property being valued. For the earnings comparison to be appropriate, it is important that no other significant factors, aside from the property in question, contribute to the excess earnings achieved by the proprietary product. When such differences are present, the comparison may still be made as long as the impact of these differences is considered. Once the incremental earnings or cost savings have been identified, the future income is discounted to a lump sum net present value.

2.   Market approach

7.20   The Market Approach is also very common in brand valuation. This approach appraises assets based on the selling price of similar assets in the market. In the context of trademark valuation, the Comparable Transaction method is often used.

Chapter 7 BRAND DIFFERENTIATION AND INDUSTRY SEGMENTATION

7.21 The Comparable Transaction method appraises assets by observing historical transactions between unrelated willing buyers (or licensees), and willing sellers (or licensors) of similar assets. The degree of reliance on comparable transactions depends on an assessment of whether the transactions are sufficiently similar to provide an indication of the value of the assets in question. Factors to consider include the nature of the assets transferred, the industry and products involved, the agreement terms, the date of the transaction (that gives consideration to the economic environment in which the transaction occurred), the circumstances of the parties to the agreements, and other factors that may affect the agreed upon compensation.

D. HISTORICAL TRANSACTIONS INVOLVING BRANDS

7.22 When evaluating business transactions, it is difficult to accurately isolate the value attributable to trademarks. However, when brands themselves are one of the key drivers, it is reasonable to approximate relative value of trademarks based on the overall transaction size. In the following sections, a series of recent acquisitions and mergers involving the transfer of trademarks will be evaluated in an effort to emphasize the unique nature of determining a fair value for brands.

1. **Distressed vs. going concern (brand-only vs. business enterprise with brand)**

7.23 A key variable that drives the value of a trademark is the business with which it is associated. Brands gain recognition and acceptance for being associated with a particular product line or service, with varying degrees of sensitivity based on industry and relationship with end consumers. A brand is more valuable when associated with a successful, operating entity. However, brands may still retain value based on recognition even in the absence of a profitable enterprise. The following illustrates the effects of brand value depending on distressed versus non-distressed scenarios.

(a) Distressed business enterprise (liquidation/brand only scenario)

7.24 History has shown that brand value can drive transactions even in the absence of a profitable, or even existent, business. Purchasers are drawn to brand awareness and seek to capitalize on opportunities from reviving or rebranding. A series of recent distressed acquisitions, resulting from bankruptcy filings during the Great Recession, provide colour around these types of brand transactions.

D. HISTORICAL TRANSACTIONS INVOLVING BRANDS

(b) Distressed enterprise key transactions

(i) Old Hostess Brands

7.25 Hostess Brands filed for bankruptcy on 10 January 2012, as a result of excessive labour costs and mounting debt that management claimed inhibited the company's ability to compete and meet its financial obligations. At the time of insolvency, the company reported $981.6 million in assets against $1.4 billion in liabilities, and elected to sell off 37 of its brands.[4] Table 7.4 presents some of these brands.

Table 7.4 Hostess brand transaction activity

Acquirer	Business	Purchase price	Hostess brands acquired
Apollo & Metropoulos	Snacks	$410.0 million	Dolly Madison, Hostess
Bimbo Bakeries	Bread	$31.9 million	Beefsteak, Colombo, Cotton's, Emperor Norton, Fisherman's Wharf, J.J. Nissen, Parisian, Toscana
Flowers Foods	Bread	$360.0 million	Butternut Bread, Home Pride, Merita, Nature's Pride, Wonder Bread
Lewis Brothers	Bread	N/A	Blue Ribbon, Braun's, Bread du Jour, Continental, Countess, County Fair, D'Agostino's, Daffodil Farm, Di Carlo, Millbrook, Nancy Martin, Old World, Ozark Mill, Pantry Pride, Sap's, Weber's
McKee	Snacks	$27.5 million	Drake's
US Bakery	Bread	$30.9 million	Eddy's, Grandma Emile's, Standish Farms, Sweetheart Bakery

While some of the purchase price was associated with fixed assets, such as machinery and equipment, these operations alone were not profitable; meaning the majority of the value in the transactions could be attributed to the brands themselves. The transactions themselves support this notion, given that more recognizable brand names, such as Hostess and Wonder Bread, fetched a far greater premium than some lesser-known, regional brands.

(ii) Polaroid

7.26 In 2008, the 75 year-old company filed for bankruptcy after an alleged fraud by its owners, Petters Group Worldwide LLC. This was the second time in

---

4   Matthew Rocco, *Court OKs $800M Sale of Hostess Cake and Bread Brands*, FOX BUSINESS (19 March 2013), available 15 September 2015 at http://www.foxbusiness.com/industries/2013/03/19/hostess-gets-approval-for-800m-in-cake-and-bread-sales/.

Chapter 7 BRAND DIFFERENTIATION AND INDUSTRY SEGMENTATION

seven years the company had filed for Chapter 11 protection. The first, in 2001, was a result of a seismic shift in instant photo technology, as digital photography rapidly replaced the company's disposable and film camera offerings. The Polaroid brand was acquired by Petters Group, who licensed the brand until eventually purchasing the company outright for $426 million in 2005. The company was able to leverage its brand recognition and launch a series of DVD players, TVs, printers, and other electronics. The rebranding of Polaroid proved to be financially successful, as the resulting company was able to generate roughly $1 billion in sales and $400 million in profits.[5]

(iii) The Sharper Image

7.27 The Sharper Image filed for bankruptcy in February of 2008, citing declining sales, several consecutive years of losses, and litigation involving the efficacy of a major product.[6] The brands were sold to Gordon Brothers Group and its partners, who recognized the ongoing customer demand for The Sharper Image's products during the surplus inventory liquidation. The Gordon Brothers Group was able to transform the company's business model from a 'build/sell' to 'license/royalty' and secured over 30 license agreements. This new approach allowed The Sharper Image to continue capitalizing on strong name recognition among a broad base of consumers without requiring the intensive working capital needed in traditional retail or wholesale operations. Gordon Brothers Group sold The Sharper Image brand to Iconix in October 2011 for $65.6M, resulting in significant returns.[7]

(iv) Borders

7.28 After a series of missteps and rapidly declining brick and mortar book retail sales, Borders Group Inc. declared bankruptcy in February 2011, listing $1.29 billion in debt and $1.27 billion in assets.[8] Alongside being one of the main beneficiaries of the chain's demise, Barnes & Noble capitalized by purchasing the Borders' trade names and other intellectual property for $13.9 million.[9] By

---

5   Eric Larson & Michael Bathon, *Polaroid in Bankruptcy Again, Cites Petters Charges*, BLOOMBERG (19 December 2008), *available 15 September 2015 at* http://www.bloomberg.com/apps/news?sid=afOdWSvgMXtM&pid=newsarchive.
6   Jonathan Stempei & Justin Grant, *Sharper Image filed for Chapter 11 bankruptcy*, REUTERS, 20 February 2008.
7   Gordon Brothers Group, *The Sharper Image Case Study*, 13GBGCS009.
8   Julie Bosman & Michael J. de la Merced, *Borders Filed for Bankruptcy*, NEW YORK TIMES (16 February 2011), *available 15 September 2015 at* http://www.nytimes.com/2011/02/17/business/media/17borders.html?pagewanted=all&_r=0.
9   Tiffany Kary, *Borders to Sell Intellectual Property to Barnes & Noble*, BLOOMBERG BUSINESSWEEK (26 September 2011), *available 15 September 2015 at* http://www.businessweek.com/news/2011-09-26/borders-to-sell-intellectual-property-to-barnes-noble.html.

D. HISTORICAL TRANSACTIONS INVOLVING BRANDS

acquiring the Borders' brand, the company effectively eliminated the possibility of a rebranding effort and secured a dominant market share in the book retail space.

(v) Circuit City

In November 2011, Circuit City Stores Inc. filed for Chapter 11 bankruptcy protection. At the time the second largest U.S. consumer electronics retailer, the company listed $3.4 billion in assets and $2.32 billion in debt.[10] As the company was ultimately forced to liquidate its assets, the Circuit City brand, trademarks, and e-commerce business were sold to Systemax for $14 million and future revenue considerations in an auction that included other value consumer electronics online retailers, such as PC Connection and PC Mall.[11] After combining the Circuit City website with its primary brand, TigerDirect, Systemax decided to sell the Circuit City property in hopes that an investor would attempt to resurrect the iconic brand.[12]

7.29

(vi) Linens 'n Things

Linens 'n Things fell into bankruptcy in 2008, after a private equity firm aggressively levered the company before the Great Recession. The business was ultimately liquidated, selling off all assets. The brand name was acquired in February 2009 by a consortium of Hilco Global, Gordon Brothers Group, and Infinity Lifestyle Brands for a total of $1 million. After resurrecting Linens 'n Things as an e-commerce website, and striking deals with various home product suppliers, the brand was sold again to Galaxy Brand Holdings, a subsidiary of the Carlyle Group, for slightly more than $10 million in December 2013. Galaxy plans on leveraging the brand recognition by maintaining the website operations and potentially launching a 'store within a store' concept with major retailers.[13] This turnaround indicates how sensitive brand value can be to quantifiable economic factors as well as subjective factors such as public perception.

7.30

---

10   Karen Jacobs, *Circuit City files for bankruptcy protection*, REUTERS (10 November 2008), *available 15 September 2015 at* http://www.reuters.com/article/2008/11/10/us-circuitcity-idUSTRE4A936V20081110.
11   DealBook, *Circuit City Brand and Web Site Sold for $14 Million*, NEW YORK TIMES (14 May 2009), *available 15 September 2015 at* http://dealbook.nytimes.com/2009/05/14/circuit-city-brand-and-web-site-sold-for-14-million/.
12   Randy Hallman, *Circuit City name is for sale, again*, RICHMOND TIMES-DISPATCH (13 July 2013), *available 15 September 2015 at* http://www.newsadvance.com/work_it_lynchburg/news/circuit-city-name-is-for-sale-again/article_8fd9e71c-ebf9-11e2-b2d2-001a4bcf6878.html?mode=jqm http://www.newsadvance.com/work_it_lynchburg/news/circuit-city-name-is-for-sale-again/article_8fd9e71c-ebf9-11e2-b2d2-001a4bcf6878.html?mode=jqm.
13   Mike Spector, *Carlyle-Owned Company Buys Linens 'N Things Brand*, WALL STREET JOURNAL (9 December 2013), *available 15 September 2015 at* http://www.wsj.com/news/articles/SB10001424052702303330204579246284042383054?mod=rss_Business&mg=reno64-wsj&url=http%3A%2F%2Fonline.wsj.com%2Farticle%2FSB10001424052702303330204579246284042383054.html%3Fmod%3Drss_Business.

Chapter 7 BRAND DIFFERENTIATION AND INDUSTRY SEGMENTATION

(c)   Going concern business enterprise

7.31   In almost all merger and acquisition transactions, a major consideration of the acquiring or merging companies is the brand strategy of the resulting entity. The success of a brand strategy is predicated on the impact it makes on the entity's financial performance going forward. The value of this impact is highly case-specific, and it is measured by changes in such metrics as customer base, revenues, or margins.

(d)   Going concern business enterprise key transactions

(i)   Jarden Corporation acquires Yankee Candle Company

7.32   In September of 2013, Jarden Corporation (NYSE: JAH), a leading global consumer products company, announced the acquisition of Yankee Candle Company from Madison Dearborn Partners for approximately $1.75 billion in cash. The transaction was expected to extend Jarden's portfolio of market-leading, consumer brands in niche, and seasonal staple categories, while creating opportunities in cross-selling and broadening the global distribution platform. The acquisition was driven by Yankee Candle Company's leading market position and loyal customer base, driven heavily by brand recognition.[14] The acquisition's purchase price allocation listed the indefinite lived intangible assets at $1.0 billion (57.1 per cent of purchase price), which represent value attributable to Yankee Candle Company brand names, trade names, and trademarks.[15]

(ii)   American Airlines merges with US Airways

7.33   In an effort to create a stronger airline with greater scheduling and destination option, American Airlines (NASDAQ: AAL) merged with US Airways in a $17 billion transaction. While this transaction created the largest and, potentially, most recognizable airline in the world, the value attributable to trademarks was insignificant relative to not only the overall transaction, but also to intangible assets themselves. Details of this transaction are presented in Table 7.5.

---

[14]   Jarden Corporation, *Jarden Announces Agreement to Acquire Yankee Candle for $1.75 Billion*, COMPANY PRESS RELEASE (3 September 2013), *available* 15 September 2015 at http://www.jarden.com/latest-news-media/press-releases/jarden-announces-agreement-acquire-yankee-candle-175-billion.

[15]   Jarden Corporation 2013 10-K.

D. HISTORICAL TRANSACTIONS INVOLVING BRANDS

Table 7.5 Selected details of American Airlines merger with US Airways

US Airways identifiable intangible asset[1]	Fair value (millions USD)	Share
Slots[2]	$973	70.9%
Customer relationships	$290	21.1%
Marketing agreements	$80	5.8%
Trademarks	$30	2.2%
Total	$1,373	100%

Notes:
1. American Airlines Group Inc. DEFM14A, 10 June 2013.
2. The term 'slots' refers to landing and takeoff authorizations.

This observation is consistent with the notion that, due to relatively low brand loyalty, brand names and trademarks in the airline industry are less significant than those in other industries, such as consumer products.

(iii) Liberty Global acquires Virgin Media

7.34 Liberty Global (NASDAQ: LBTYA) acquired Virgin Media for $16 billion in cash and stock, representing $47.87 per Virgin Media share at the time of the transaction, a 24 per cent premium. The move was made to increase Liberty's competitive position internationally with companies like Comcast and News Corp, the latter of which owns British Sky Broadcasting, a direct competitor to Virgin in the U.K. and Ireland.[16] While the value of the deal was driven primarily by operational considerations, including existing infrastructure and customer relationships, other assets, including copyrights, represented roughly 12% of the assets transferred.[17]

(iv) T-Mobile (Deutsche Telekom) acquires MetroPCS

7.35 T-Mobile (NYSE: TMUS) acquired MetroPCS in an effort to compete with larger cellphone providers. The move effectively increased the resulting company's subscriber base to 42.6 million, closing the gap on the third ranked spring (56.4 million).[18] The transaction, which involved a reverse merger with the smaller MetroPCS acquiring T-Mobile with stock considerations, included a $233 million value for MetroPCS brands, representing less than

---

16 Amy Thomson & Kristen Schweizer, *Malone's Liberty to Acquire Virgin Media for $16 Billion*, BLOOMBERG (6 February 2013), *available 15 September 2015 at* http://www.bloomberg.com/news/2013-02-06/liberty-global-to-acquire-virgin-media-for-23-3-billion.html.
17 Virgin Media 10-Q for period ended 30 June 2013.
18 Deutsche Telecom Press Release, *T-Mobile USA and MetroPCS to combine, creating value leader in U.S. wireless marketplace* (3 October 2012), *available 15 September 2015 at* http://www.telekom.com/media/company/156296.

1 per cent of the $29 billion purchase price. The deal also included a 0.25 per cent trademark license to be paid on all products and services sold by the combined company.[19] While the majority of value was attributable to infrastructure and customer relationships, the value attributed to the brand was certainly not negligible.

(v) Swatch Group acquires HW Holdings Inc

7.36 In March 2013, Swatch Group (SWX: UHR) acquired HW Holdings, which owns high-end watchmaker, Harry Winston. The cash outflow for the acquisition totaled 684 million Swiss francs ($738 million), with value attributable to the Harry Winston brand totaling 83 per cent of the transaction price.[20] This transaction clearly indicates the premium that can be placed on high-end consumer products.

2. **Valuation of the brands transacted**

(a) Strategic vs. Financial Target

7.37 The motivation of a buyer is generally the driver of how one approaches valuation analysis. We see that historically, strategic buyers are generally willing to pay a premium relative to the market because of perceived synergies that management believes can be realized by incorporating the operations of the target with their own, or by eliminating potential competition from the market. On the converse, financial buyers approach trademarks like any other investable asset class by finding value in what is believed to be a mispricing in the market. We have also seen that brand value can be highly dependent on the industry, with brand recognition inconsistently driving value across the exemplary transactions.

(b) Summary

7.38 Utilizing historical transactions in evaluating trademark value is an exercise that should be undertaken with great awareness to the underlying circumstances involved in each transaction. As indicated in the transactions highlighted, pricing is highly sensitive to industry and motivation of the acquiring company, and no two transactions are the same. It is also difficult to quantify inherent subjectivity of certain intangible features such as brand loyalty.

---

19 T Mobile 2013 10-K for period ended 31 December 2013.
20 Swatch Group 2013 Annual Report.

3. Asset purchase agreements containing trademarks

7.39 An examination of ktMINE, a database service that isolates publicly available license agreements and asset purchase agreements, can shed light on historical royalty rates associated with trademarks as part of licensing or asset deals. By filtering within this database first for 'Asset Purchase' agreements only, we are able to generate a data set of royalty rates associated with asset purchase agreements, with marketing intangibles as the underlying assets. To attempt to isolate a 'typical' trademark royalty rate in these agreements, we have performed a three-level filtration analysis within the database; these search parameters and resulting 'hits' are summarized in Table 7.6.

Table 7.6 ktMINE asset agreement search criteria

	Step #	Search filter	Filter criteria	Step results	Search results
	1	Agreement type	Asset purchase	1113	1113
AND	2	Agreement T type	Marketing intangible	5175	794
AND NOT	3	Agreement type	Cross license, distribution, franchise, joint development, manufacturing/process intangible, other, service, software	13,833	84

ktMINE defines 'Asset Purchase' as a document involving the purchase of certain assets of one company by another company. The agreement will cover specific assets or the entire assets of the seller. 'Marketing Intangibles' is defined as when a 'License is likely to grant the right to use any of the following: Trademarks, Trade names, Trade dress, Copyrights, Service marks, Logos'. Because our search first isolates by asset purchase documents, we believe the royalty rates are another way of examining the value placed on brands/trademarks in transactional settings. As summarized in Table 7.6, this search yields 84 results, and a presentation of the underlying royalty rate data within these agreements is presented in Table 7.7.

Examining trademark asset purchase agreements and their underlying financial terms can provide one indication of value. These agreements describe transactions that deserve the same consideration and review as merger and acquisition activity surrounding a business enterprise incorporating brand or trademark assets. Similar to the license agreement review during the course of

Chapter 7 BRAND DIFFERENTIATION AND INDUSTRY SEGMENTATION

Table 7.7   ktMINE asset agreement royalty rate summary

Common base	Observations	Min.	1st Quartile	Avg.	Median	3rd Quartile	Max.
Gross sales	9	1.00%	10.00%	22.00%	10.00%	40.00%	50.00%
Net sales	49	0.80%	3.75%	26.92%	7.90%	25.00%	400.00%
Costs	5	17.50%	25.00%	25.50%	25.00%	30.00%	30.00%
Gross profit	1	33.30%	33.30%	33.30%	33.30%	33.30%	33.30%
Operating profit	11	9.00%	20.00%	32.93%	30.00%	46.90%	56.00%
Net profit	4	1.00%	5.50%	110.25%	20.00%	30.00%	400.00%

a relief from royalty analysis, it is important to consider elements of comparability and elements of non-comparability in order to isolate only asset purchase agreements that contain intellectual property attributes similar to the brand or trademark an appraiser is analyzing.

E. PURCHASE PRICE ALLOCATION

7.40   Most, if not all, business transactions involve the purchase and sale of various assets and liabilities. US GAAP (Generally Accepted Accounting Principles) and International Financial Reporting Standards require companies to disaggregate the value of these transactions into identifiable tangible and intangible assets for financial statement reporting purposes. The process of allocating the aggregated deal price is called a Purchase Price Allocation (PPA) and is based upon the *Business Combination* accounting rules in the U.S. and abroad. The acquiring company typically performs it after the sale has taken place. The process involves several steps, but generally starts by identifying the acquired assets net of their corresponding liabilities, writing up (or down) the value of these assets to their fair value, and allocating any residual value to goodwill and intellectual property or, in rare circumstances, dealing with a bargain purchase. While this approach is logical because it accounts for all assets in the purchase simultaneously, there are several shortcomings. For instance, unless the intellectual property in question is identifiable and licensable, the PPA does not consider the economic value of the intellectual property as it assumes the intellectual property value is the residual portion of the purchase price. Additionally, there are many assumptions surrounding the other assets and liabilities in the transaction that indirectly affect the residual purchase price. Some of these assumptions include the useful life of assets or liabilities, as well as their individual fair values. Furthermore, a PPA is performed for compliance or regulatory purposes, which may not have the same motivations as a valuation being completed to evaluate the true commercial licensing potential of the intellectual property. Therefore, a valuation completed for PPA purposes should not be solely relied upon, but should be considered a supplement, or a resource that can be used in conjunction with a current analysis based upon the facts and circumstances of the situation being addressed.

F. WHY INDUSTRY MATTERS

7.41 As a continuation to the Purchase Price Allocation discussion in the previous section, we have outlined major points from a study published by Houlihan Lokey. The 2012 Purchase Price Allocation Study is released annually and the 2012 edition, released in September 2013, marks the 12th year of its release. This study reviews U.S. public filings for 1,173 completed transactions throughout 2012 and provides summary statistics surrounding the transaction data.

7.42 The source material for the study consisted of 511 transactions (44 per cent of the original sample) that were narrowed down from the original sample by removing transactions that lacked sufficient information in the categories of purchase consideration (PC), goodwill, and identifiable intangible asset fair values. In this context, intangible assets include developed technology (including patents), in-process research and development (IPR&D), customer-related assets (including backlog, customer contracts, and customer relationships), trademarks and trade names (including domain names), and other assets (including non-compete agreements, licenses, contracts, and core deposits, among others).

7.43 The study divided the 511 transactions into 13 separate categories: aerospace, defense and government (ADG); business services; consumer, food, and retail (CFR); energy; financial institutions; healthcare; industrials; infrastructure services and materials (ISM); media, sports, and entertainment (MSE); real estate, lodging, and leisure; technology; telecom; and transportation and logistics. There was insufficient data to present in regards to the business services; MSE; and real estate, lodging, and leisure industries; this was due to the small number of transactions recorded for each of these industries.

7.44 This study demonstrates the quantifiable differences in Purchase Price Allocation and intangible asset allocation norms between various industries and types of intangible assets. For example, when broken down by industry, the study shows that the healthcare industry has the highest percentage mean of purchase consideration allocated to intangible assets (40 per cent). Please see Table 7.8, Summary Allocation Percentages, for individual industry statistics.

*Table 7.8 Summary allocation percentages**

		Purchase consideration		Intangible assets, % of PC			
	Count	Median ($)	Mean ($)	Low	High	Median	Mean
All industries	511	66	1007	0%	100%	30%	31%
Aerospace, defense, & government	9	46	421	12%	48%	17%	24%
Consumer, food, & retail	67	106	437	1%	99%	30%	33%
Energy	28	190	2206	0%	66%	19%	25%
Financial institutions	56	374	2828	0%	89%	1%	13%
Healthcare	75	80	1590	1%	100%	40%	40%
Industrials	99	46	421	1%	100%	27%	28%
Infrastructure services, & materials	12	83	871	3%	64%	22%	27%
Media, sports, & entertainment	4	5	15	2%	49%	34%	30%
Technology	153	39	397	1%	89%	35%	34%
Telecom	8	55	157	0%	69%	30%	31%

Note:
* Houlihan Lokey, *2012 Purchase Price Allocation Study*, 2013.

Developed technology, IPR&D, customer-related assets, and trademarks and trade names were the most common assets classified as identified intangible. Of these, trademarks and trade names contributed 45 per cent to the sample. Only 207 transactions (41 per cent) of the sample allocated PC to trademarks and trade names. The total mean allocation of these assets was 8 per cent. The consumer, food and retail industry reported the highest mean percentage allocation of PC with 21 per cent, while aerospace, defense, and government; energy; and financial institutions tied as the lowest mean percentage allocation of PC with 2 per cent. The technology industry reported the highest number of transactions allocating to trademarks and trade names with 65 transactions; however, it only reported an average of 3 per cent of purchase consideration being allocated. The 2012 study reported that 207 transactions (41 per cent of total sample) allocated purchase consideration to trademarks and trade names. Of those, only 127 transactions (61 per cent) allocated 5 per cent or less of purchase consideration to trademarks and trade names.[21] It is important to note that these value allocations should be considered as only a supplement to a licensing based valuation analysis. Regardless, the trends surrounding brand value and industry are an important observation to be made.

G. ADDITIONAL BRAND VALUATION METHODS

This chapter focuses special attention on the Relief from Royalty Income Approach to valuing brands; however, it is helpful to note that there are many alternative approaches[22] to brand valuation that may be utilized, depending on the practitioner's judgment and the context of the valuation. One alternative focuses on the equity value of the business enterprise underlying the brand or trademark. An analysis of the market value of a company's shares can provide one premise of value for a trademark owned by that company. Another alternative involves considering the brand's replacement value. Advertising and promotional expenses reflect specific trademark investments made, including concept development and consumer testing, among others. A method based on the formula of free cash flow minus assets employed, multiplied by required return, can be used as well. Finally, a method measuring company growth and optimization opportunities including new distribution channels, new international markets, new product lines, and higher/premium prices and/or volumes under the specific brand. As always, clearly defining the standard of value, and the premise of value, is an important and impactful component of any valuation.

7.45

H. THE WORLD'S MOST VALUABLE BRANDS

Each year, studies are published that attempt to attribute value to the top worldwide brands. The methodologies for each of the studies are unique in that different factors are accounted for, such as company revenue, advertising spend, and customer surveys. Table 7.9 presents the top 15 brands as rated by various institutions in 2013 and 2014.

7.46

---

21 Houlihan Lokey, *2012 Purchase Price Allocation Study*, September 2013, *available 15 September 2015 at* http://www.hlhz.com/us/press/insightsandideas/3938.aspx.
22 Pablo Fernández López, *Brand Equity and Brand Valuation*, Effective Executive, Vol. 8, No. 8, 35–39, August 2006.

Chapter 7 BRAND DIFFERENTIATION AND INDUSTRY SEGMENTATION

Table 7.9 The world's most valuable brands

Forbes rank	Brand	Forbes[1] 2013	Interbrand[2] 2013	Brand Z[3] 2014
1	Apple	$104,300	$98,316	$147,880
2	Microsoft	$ 56,700	$59,546	$ 90,185
3	Coca-Cola	$ 54,900	$79,213	$ 80,683
4	IBM	$ 50,700	$78,808	$107,541
5	Google	$ 47,300	$93,291	$158,843
6	McDonalds	$ 39,400	$41,922	$ 85,706
7	General Electric	$ 34,200	$46,947	$ 56,685
8	Intel	$ 30,900	$37,257	N/A
9	Samsung	$ 29,500	$39,610	$ 25,892
10	Louis Vuitton	$ 28,400	$24,893	$ 25,873
11	BMW	$ 27,900	$31,839	$ 25,730
12	Cisco	$ 27,000	$29,053	$ 13,710
13	Oracle	$ 26,900	$24,088	$ 20,913
14	Toyota	$ 25,600	$35,346	$ 29,598
15	AT&T	$ 24,200	N/A	$ 77,883

Notes:
1. Forbes, *The World's Most Valuable Brands*, 2013.
2. Interbrand, *Best Global Brands 2013*, 2013.
3. Millward Brown, *BrandZ Top 100 Most Valuable Global Brands 2014*, 2014.

When looking at these relative values in Table 7.9, it is apparent that, based on the purpose and methodology used to attribute value to brands, the results are highly sensitive to the inputs used. The inconsistency across the studies is indicative of the nuances in brand valuation analysis, and the varied perspectives of any given brands value. If one is to evaluate the effect of changing brand value over time, it is imperative that the results be generated in a manner that is methodologically consistent. Figure 7.2 shows the historical values for the top ten brands dating back to 2000 according to Interbrand.[23]

The trends represented in Figure 7.2 are unlikely to surprise observers of this data. Powerhouse tech brands like Apple and Google have seen brand value rise with an increasing revenue and user base, while the world's most recognized brand, Coca-Cola, has maintained its value as a consumer staple. It may also be noted that brand value is affected differently based on economic environment. As expected, GE and Toyota were negatively impacted during

---

23 Interbrand Interactive Charts 2013, *available 15 September 2015 at* http://www.bestglobalbrands.com/previous-years/2013.

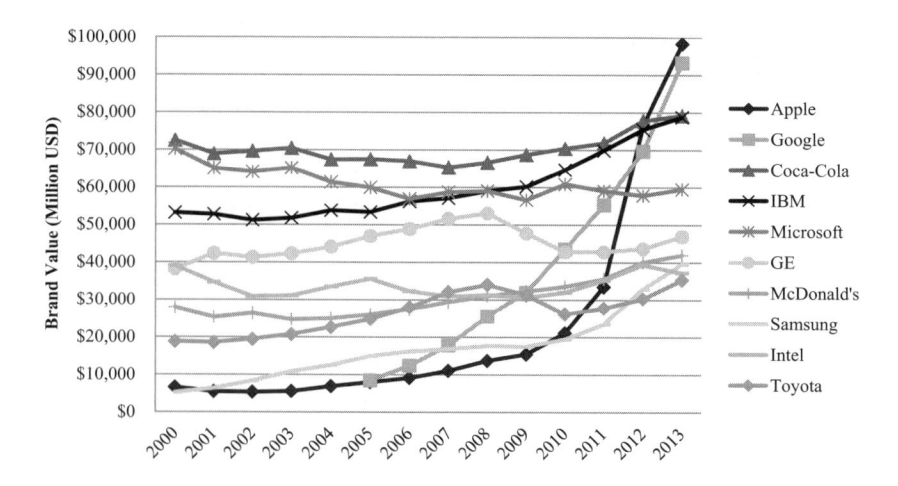

Figure 7.2 Brand value over time

the Global Financial Crisis, with value falling significantly from 2008 through 2010, while other top brands proved immune to the downturn.

I. CONCLUSION

As explored within this chapter, a brand is sometimes a supporting character that promotes the sales of a superior product or service – a superior technology, innovative idea, preferred taste, or reliability and shelf life of a product. The significance of branding shines brightest, perhaps, when correlated with a commodity product, such as vodka. Vodka is defined by Pace, the Beverage Tasting Institute, as being odourless and tasteless. The brand Grey Goose was intentionally produced as a luxury item, and differentiated itself from every other vodka brand on the market, successfully commanding a high-end price. The Grey Goose brand, created by Sidney Frank, is central to the product's reputation and success because there is absolutely no difference in taste between any two given vodka products. 'People are always looking for something new', says Frank. 'It's all about brand differentiation. If you're going to charge twice as much for vodka, you need to give people a reason.'[24] One reason Frank gave customers was the allure of French products. Unlike all other vodkas at the time of the brand's inception, Grey Goose was distilled and bottled in France, where many of the world's best luxury products originate. Frank also insisted on a distinctive bottle, and shipment to customers in wooden crates. These seemingly small touches augmented the power

7.47

---

24 Seth Stevenson, *The Cocktail Creationist*, NEW YORK MAGAZINE, *available* 15 September 2015 *at* http://nymag.com/nymetro/news/bizfinance/biz/features/10816/.

of the branding scheme. The tasteless and odourless obstacle was overcome, and only eight years after Sidney Frank created Grey Goose vodka, it was sold to Bacardi for more than $2 billion.[25] This story proves the potentially extreme heft of brand value when applied to an industry of otherwise indistinguishable products. Brand value, from commodity-driven companies to extremely specialized industries, cannot be overlooked and it is an important asset in the world of intellectual property valuation.

---

25   Id.

8

TRADEMARK TRANSACTIONS AND INTERNATIONAL TAX STRATEGIES

Jean-Frédéric Maraia[*]

A.	INTRODUCTION	8.01	D.	TRADEMARK TRANSACTIONS BETWEEN RELATED PARTIES 8.41
B.	OECD – BEPS: GENERAL PRESENTATION	8.05		1. Arm's length principle 8.43
				2. Arm's length price 8.47
C.	TRADEMARK TRANSACTIONS BETWEEN THIRD PARTIES	8.10		3. Domestic restructuring 8.54
	1. Licensing	8.12	E.	INTERNATIONAL TAX STRATEGIES 8.57
	(a) Tax treatment of royalties	8.14		1. Residence of companies 8.59
	(b) Impact of double tax treaties in an international context	8.18		2. Ownership 8.64
				3. Tax status 8.69
	2. Assignment	8.27		(a) Auxiliary status (intellectual property companies) 8.70
	(a) Royalties or capital gains?	8.27		
	(b) Tax treatment of capital gains	8.33		(b) Licence box 8.76
	(c) Impact of double tax treaties in an international context	8.36	F.	CONCLUSION 8.87
	3. Tax treatment of expenses	8.38		

A. INTRODUCTION

Trademarks are very often an important source of revenue for their holders. So it is not surprising to find that tax authorities, in Switzerland and abroad, are anxious to know whether profits generated by the use of trademarks (as in the case of other intangible assets) have been duly declared and taxed and, in an international context, duly allocated between the States concerned. **8.01**

In 2013, the Organization for Economic Co-Operation and Development (OECD) published an *Action Plan on Base Erosion and Profit Shifting*, a report now known as the BEPS[1] report (BEPS report). This document marks the start of fundamental changes in the area of international taxation. It seeks to establish consistency in the taxation of company profits at an international **8.02**

---

[*] Attorney-at-law, Partner, Schellenberg Wittmer SA; Lecturer, University of Geneva.
[1] ORGANIZATION FOR ECONOMIC CO-OPERATION AND DEVELOPMENT [hereinafter OECD], ACTION PLAN ON BASE EROSION AND PROFIT SHIFTING (2013), http://www.oecd.org/ctp/BEPSActionPlan.pdf (*available 15 September 2015*) [hereinafter OECD, ACTION PLAN ON BEPS].

level, through a rigorous application of tax rules based on economic substance and greater transparency. The OECD's action plan will be presented initially in part B of this chapter, showing the future importance, if this is not already the case, of its impact on the tax treatment of transactions involving trademarks and international fiscal strategies. In this part, the review of the plan, however, will be primarily a general overview, as the details of the specific actions related to certain transactions or fiscal strategies will be examined in detail in the other parts of this chapter.

8.03 It will then be necessary to address and elaborate on the fiscal consequences of trademark transactions, making a distinction between those transactions that take place between true third parties, as discussed in part C of this chapter, and those that take place between related parties, which are discussed in part D of this chapter. Finally, the last part of this chapter, part E, will be devoted to international fiscal strategies.

8.04 It should also be noted that this contribution is based essentially on Swiss tax law[2] and the international conventions of which Switzerland is part, which are based essentially on the OECD Model Tax Convention (OECD Model). In several cases, however, reference will still be made to other national law to illustrate certain particular features with respect to the topic of this chapter that exist in countries other than Switzerland.

B. OECD – BEPS: GENERAL PRESENTATION

8.05 As requested in the BEPS report dated February 2013, entitled *Addressing Base Erosion and Profit Shifting*, the OECD announced in a separate report published in September 2013 an action plan (hereinafter 'Action Plan on BEPS') aimed at preventing double non-taxation, as well as cases of no or low taxation 'associated with practices that artificially segregate taxable income from the activities that generate it'.[3] Fifteen actions have been proposed in this context.

8.06 In examining the taxable status of trademarks, the following actions in particular must be taken into account: Action 5 entitled *Counter Harmful Tax*

---

2 For cantonal and municipality taxes on profit, income, wealth and capital, we will refer to the Bundesgesetz über die Harmonisierung der direkten Steuern der Kantone und Gemeinden [StHG], [Federal Tax Harmonization Law] 14 December 1990, SR 642.14 (Switz.), *available 15 September 2015 at* https://www.admin.ch/opc/de/classified-compilation/19900333/201401010000/642.14.pdf [hereinafter Harmonization Law].

3 OECD, ACTION PLAN ON BEPS, *supra* note 1, at 15.

Practices More Effectively, Taking into Account Transparency and Substance; Action 6 entitled *Prevent Treaty Abuse*; and Actions 8–10 entitled *Assuring that Transfer Pricing Outcomes are in Line with Value Creation*.

In September 2014, seven initial elements of the Action Plan on BEPS were made public in connection with actions 1, 2, 5, 6, 8, 13, and 15.[4] Two highly detailed reports can be mentioned here: (i) Action 5, entitled *Countering Harmful Tax Practices More Effectively, Taking into Account Transparency and Substance* (BEPS Action 5),[5] and (ii) Action 8, entitled *Guidance on Transfer Pricing Aspects of Intangibles* (BEPS Action 8).[6] The first report finalizes the review of member country preferential schemes. The main goal is to realign taxation of profits with substantial activities, especially in the context of intangible regimes. In addition, the OECD aims to improve transparency through compulsory spontaneous exchange on rulings related to preferential schemes. The second report contains final revisions to chapters of the OECD Transfer Pricing Guidelines for Multinational Enterprises and Tax Administrations (2010) in order to clarify the definition of intangibles, to better identify transactions involving intangibles, and to provide additional guidance for determining arm's length conditions for transactions involving intangibles.[7] The report also contains numerous examples illustrating the application of the new rules. The chapter regarding ownership of intangible assets has to be viewed at this stage as 'interim drafts of guidance, not yet fully agreed by delegates'.[8]

8.07

These reports may themselves be the subject of an ad hoc scholarly publication reviewing them in detail. This chapter, instead, will not examine these reports in detail, but will limit its analysis to the main principles addressed in the reports. In particular, this chapter examines these reports when they relate to trasactions between related, parties, ownership, and tax status.

8.08

Finally, it is necessary to highlight the obligations of increased transparency resulting from the new rules governing the exchange of information. Specifically, Action 12, entitled *Require Taxpayers to Disclose their Aggressive Tax Planning Arrangements*, and Action 13, entitled *Re-examine Transfer Pricing*

8.09

---

4   OECD, *Centre for Tax Policy and Administration, BEPS 2014 Deliverables (September 2014)*, available 15 September 2015 at http://www.oecd.org/ctp/beps-2014-deliverables.htm.
5   OECD, ACTION 5, COUNTERING HARMFUL TAX PRACTICES MORE EFFECTIVELY, TAKING INTO ACCOUNT TRANSPARENCY AND SUBSTANCE (2014), *available 15 September 2015 at* http://dx.doi.org/10.1787/9789264218970-en [hereinafter OECD, ACTION 5].
6   OECD, ACTION 8, GUIDANCE ON TRANSFER PRICING ASPECTS OF INTANGIBLES (2014), *available 15 September 2015 at* http://dx.doi.org/10.1787/9789264219212-en [hereinafter OECD, ACTION 8].
7   *See generally id.*
8   *Id.* at 10.

Documentation. Here again, however, these aspects, which affect taxation in a more general sense and not trademarks specifically, will not be addressed in detail in this chapter, but only mentioned when necessary for the general analysis of the topic at issue.

C. TRADEMARK TRANSACTIONS BETWEEN THIRD PARTIES

8.10 This part deals with the fiscal treatment of trademark transactions between third parties, meaning parties that are legally and economically independent. The purpose of this definition, and distinction, is to make it possible to identify those tax-related questions that are raised in a general sense with respect to all trademark transactions and to deal separately with those questions that specifically concern transactions between related parties (see part D below).

8.11 With regard to trademark transactions, it is necessary to make a distinction between two categories of transactions, namely licensing contracts, referred to as licensing agreements, and transfer contracts, called assignments agreements. This distinction is necessary in light of the different tax treatments resulting from the definition of the revenues that are generated by the licensor and those that are generated by the transferor or assignor. In a third section we will look at the deductible expenses relating to trademarks.

1. Licensing

8.12 A licensing agreement is generally defined as an agreement in which one party grants the use of an intellectual property right to another party through an exclusive licence or through a simple licence to several parties.[9] In general terms, the granting of a licence will entitle the licensor to a consideration known as royalties.

8.13 As a rule, royalties are determined either contractually, in a fixed sum, or as a proportion of turnover on the business conducted. In the first case this may amount to a single or a periodic sum.

---

9 *See* Loi fédérale du 28 août 1992 sur la protection des marques et des indications de provenance [LPM], [Federal Act on the Protection of Trademarks and Indications of Source] [TmPA], 28 August 1992, ch. 232.11, art. 18 (Switz.), *available 15 September 2015 at* http://www.wipo.int/wipolex/en/text.jsp?file_id=332704 [hereinafter TMPA] (regarding trademarks in Switzerland).

(a) Tax treatment of royalties

(i) From the beneficiary's point of view

As a rule, royalties from the licensor's point of view are taxable. In Switzerland, they constitute revenue or profits, depending on whether an individual or a legal entity is involved in the transaction.[10]

8.14

In Switzerland, legal entities are subject to tax on profits based on the results shown in the profit and loss account. Furthermore, royalties received must be indicated and shown in the profit and loss part of the account of an (business or individual) entity, and are, therefore, taxed.[11] For individuals, royalties constitute income when the intellectual property asset (the trademark as the subject matter of this chapter) forms part of the taxpayer's private wealth,[12] and as income from self-employed activities when the asset belongs to the business.[13] This distinction in terms of the legal definitions does not, however, have any impact on the taxable base. On the other hand, this distinction becomes of fundamental importance when determining deductible expenses, and, above all, in the area of sales as capital gains. Therefore, this chapter will examine this distinction in detail below.[14]

8.15

(ii) From the debtor's point of view

From the licensee's point of view, the payment of royalties will, as a rule, be deductible if the debtor is a legal entity,[15] a partnership, or an individual who uses the trademark in the context of an independent lucrative activity.[16] In Switzerland, such deduction is permitted when it is commercially justified. It will always be the case, in principle, when the transaction is conducted between two completely independent parties. On the other hand, when the parties are associated with one another, for example within groups, tax deductibility is examined on a case-by-case basis, applying the arm's length

8.16

---

10 Licence box agreements will be discussed *infra* in Section E.
11 Bundesgesetz über die direkten Bundessteuern [DBG], [Federal Direct Tax Law] 14 December 1990, SR 642.11, art. 58, para. 1(a) (Switz.), *available* 15 September 2015 at http://www.admin.ch/opc/de/classified-compilation/19900329/index.html [hereinafter DTL]; Harmonization Law, *supra* note 2, at art. 24, para. 1(a).
12 DTL, *supra* note 11, art. 20, para. 1(f); Harmonization Law, *supra* note 2, art. 7, para. 1. *See also* MARKUS REICH, KOMMENTAR ZUM SCHWEIZERISCHEN STEUERRECHT I/2a, N 2, 124 at art. 20 (Martin Zweifel & Peter Athanas eds., 2008) [hereafter KOMMENTAR].
13 DTL, *supra* note 11, at art. 18, para. 1; Harmonization Law, *supra* note 2, at art. 8, para. 1.
14 *See infra* Section C.2 & 3.
15 DTL, *supra* note 11, at art. 58, para. 1; Harmonization Law, *supra* note 2, at art. 24, para. 1.
16 DTL, *supra* note 11, at art. 27, para. 1; Harmonization Law, *supra* note 2, at art. 10, para. 1. In other words, an individual who uses the trademark in a private context cannot deduct the royalties paid. This is a hypothetical case, however, because in most cases the use of a trademark by an individual is linked to the exercise of an independent activity.

principle.[17] The burden of proof rests with the taxpayer.[18] Therefore, the taxpayer must be able to demonstrate, for example, that the other party is independent, both legally and financially.[19]

8.17 It should be noted that Swiss tax law does not provide for the taxing of royalties at source, meaning there is no Swiss withholding tax.[20] Thus, the Swiss debtor is not required to make any withholding on the royalties due.

(b) Impact of double tax treaties in an international context

(i) Double taxation – treaties

8.18 From an international perspective, when royalties are paid by a taxpayer located in a given State to another taxpayer located in another State, the questions of the right to tax and how to prevent double taxation arise. In principle, royalties are subject to tax in the beneficiary's State of residence, and, very often, they are also subject to tax at source in the State in which the royalties arise.[21] This problem of potential double taxation may be resolved by applying double tax treaties. According to the OECD Model, which is the basis for most of the conventions signed by the OECD Member States, including Switzerland, royalties are taxable only in the beneficiary's State of residence.[22] This rule confers the right to tax income in the beneficiary's State of residence and forces the States of source to waive the levying of tax. However, in order to apply this rule and exclude the levying of tax in the State of source, the beneficiary has to be the beneficial owner of the royalties.[23] According to the majority of authors, the concept of beneficial owner is defined as the person who controls the use of the income.[24]

---

17 *See infra* Section D.1 & 2.
18 Xavier Oberson & Howard R. Hull, Switzerland in International Tax Law 172 (4th ed., 2012).
19 According to the case law of the Federal Court, the tax authority may presume the existence of a link with a shareholder or close contracting partner when this conclusion is obvious and no other explanation can be given for the unusual operation. Tribunal Fédéral (TF) [Federal Supreme Court] 119 Arrêts du Tribunal Fédéral Suisse [ATF] I 436 (Switz.).
20 Bundesgesetz über die Verrechnungssteuer [VStG], [Swiss Federal Withholding Tax Act] 13 October 1965, SR 642.21, art. 4, para. 1.
21 As indicated *supra* Switzerland is not one of the States where a tax at source is levied on royalties.
22 OECD, Model Tax Convention on Income and on Capital, art. 12 §1 (2014), *available* 15 September 2015 *at* http://www.oecd.org/ctp/treaties/2014-model-tax-convention-articles.pdf [hereafter the OECD Model].
23 *See* Cécile Brokelind, *Article 10*, *in* Commentaire Modèle de Convention fiscale OCDE concernant le revenu et la fortune 356 (Robert Danon et al. eds., 2013); Robert Danon, *Clarification of the Meaning of 'Beneficial Owner' in the OECD Model Tax Convention: Comment on the April 2011 Discussion Draft*, 65 Bull. Int'l. Taxn. 8 (2011); Robert Danon, *Le concept de bénéficiaire effectif dans le cadre du MC OCDE. Réflexions et analyse de la jurisprudence récente*, IFF Forum für Steuerrecht 38 (2007); Xavier Oberson, Précis de droit fiscal international 163 (4th ed. 2014).
24 *See* Oberson, *supra* note 23, at 169.

C. TRADEMARK TRANSACTIONS BETWEEN THIRD PARTIES

However, the allocation rule of article 12 § 1 of the OECD Model has not been incorporated into all double tax treaties. Indeed, many States wanted to authorize the State of source to withhold tax, but on a limited amount, generally 5 or 10 per cent,[25] while still maintaining the right to tax in the beneficiary's State of residence. Nevertheless, to prevent residual double taxation, the latter State would be required to offset the tax deducted at source from the additional tax charged through a credit mechanism. From a Swiss standpoint, the conventions that grant the State of source the right to withhold a limited amount of tax are, in this respect, in favour of the foreign State only because Switzerland, as a State of source, does not withhold tax at source on royalties in accordance with its domestic law. Thus, the treaty cannot, as a rule, constitute a legal basis for withholding tax in Switzerland, the so-called negative effect of conventions.[26]   8.19

In addition to the double taxation conventions, the problem with taxing royalties that flow between two States may also be resolved by applying the Savings Agreement with the European Union (EU) on the taxation of savings (Savings Agreement).[27] Indeed, according to Article 15, paragraph 1, of the Savings Agreement, the royalties paid out between associated companies or their permanent establishments are not taxed in the State of source when: 8.20

- such companies are affiliated by a direct minimum holding of 25 per cent for at least two years or are both held with a third company which has directly a minimum of holding of 25 per cent in the capital of the first company and in the capital of the second company for at least two years;
- one company has its fiscal residence, or a permanent establishment is located, in a Member State, and the other company has its fiscal residence, or a permanent establishment, located in Switzerland;
- none of the companies has its fiscal residence, and none of the permanent establishments is situated in any third party State (under the terms of the convention with any third State);
- both companies are subject to corporation tax without being exempted, and both are limited companies.[28]

---

25 *See* Jean-Frédéric Maraia et al., *Article 12*, in COMMENTAIRE MODELE DE CONVENTION FISCALE OCDE CONCERNANT LE REVENUE ET LA FORTUNE 471, 477 (Robert Danon et al. eds., 2013).
26 OBERSON, *supra* note 23, at 49.
27 Council Directive 2003/48, On Taxation of Savings Income in the Form of Interest Paments, 2003 O.J. (L 157) 38 (EC) [hereinafter Savings Agreement]. Agreement between the European Community and the Swiss Confederation providing for measures equivalent to those laid down in the Savings Agreement.
28 *Id.* at art. 15, para. 1.

8.21 Therefore, according to the Savings Agreement, an EU Member State may not levy any withholding tax on royalties paid by an EU limited liability company to a Swiss associated company or permanent establishment.[29] Therefore, only the State of residence has the right to tax royalties. Thus, the Savings Agreement is useful in cases where, contrary to the OECD Model Tax Convention, the applicable double tax treaty envisages a limited right to tax in the State of source, like France, Italy, Portugal, Spain, and so on. Application of the Savings Agreement and of the double taxation convention between the States concerned thus comes down to the taxpayer's choice and the latter may opt for the solution that is more favourable.

(ii) Anti-abuse rules

8.22 A double taxation convention, like the Savings Agreement, does not apply when the taxpayer makes improper use of the convention. In as much as Switzerland does not deduct tax at source on royalties, the risks of unlawful action will be found in the area of exemption, or refund, requests in connection with foreign taxes levied on royalties arising abroad and owed to a person or entity in Switzerland.

8.23 In this context mention must be made, first of all, to the 1962 Abuse Decree that introduced measures against the improper use of tax treaties concluded by the Swiss Confederation.[30] The purpose of the 1962 Abuse Decree is to prevent an exemption from foreign tax at source on income arising abroad, and requested by a Swiss resident when the latter's claim is improper.[31] The applicable conditions of the 1962 Abuse Decree were developed in the two Federal Tax Administration's circulars of 1962 and 1999. The 1962 Abuse Decree does not apply when the applicable convention contains special anti-abuse provisions, particularly in the double tax treaties with the United States, France, Great Britain, Italy, India, Japan and the Netherlands.[32] According to the 1962 Abuse Decree, as a general rule, tax relief is claimed abusively when a substantial part of it would benefit, directly or indirectly, persons not entitled to benefit from the tax treaty.[33] The purpose is to fight so-called conduit companies that simply transfer profits abroad, particularly in

---

29 This is also applicable when royalties arise in Switzerland and are paid to a EU associated company, but the application of the Savings Agreement is not necessary since there is no Swiss withholding tax levied on royalties.
30 Bundesratsbeschluss betreffend Massnahmen gegen die ungerechtfertigte Inanspruchnahme von Doppelbesteuerungsabkommen des Bundes [Federal Council Decree on Measures against the Improper Use of Tax Treaties concluded by the Swiss Confederation] 14 December 1962, SR 62.202 [hereinafter 1962 Abuse Decree].
31 *Id.* at art. 1, para. 2 (a)–(b).
32 OBERSON, *supra* note 23, at 234.
33 1962 Abuse Decree, *supra* note 30, art. 2, para. 1(a).

the form of interests or royalties. Thus, in order to avoid an abusive transfer, the Swiss company must show that (i) the received royalties are recorded in the accounting documents; (ii) a maximum of 50 per cent of the royalties are used to satisfy contractual rights or claims of persons not entitled to benefit from the treaty; and (iii) the rest can cover the corresponding expenses. However, these conditions do not apply to *active* companies, which include pure holding companies, the definition of which does not depend on the existence of the cantonal holding status but on a profit exclusively made up of returns on share holdings, with a tolerance in practice of 5 per cent,[34] or to companies listed on the stock market.

8.24 In practice, this anti-abuse rule plays a role when Swiss companies benefit from receiving royalties from licences and sub-licences.

8.25 Apart from the 1962 Abuse Decree, it is necessary to remember the beneficial owner condition that, in principle, should be applicable even in the absence of an express reference in a convention.[35] Thus, the relief of a foreign tax at source on the payment of royalties to a Swiss taxpayer would be denied in cases where the latter was not the beneficial owner.

8.26 Finally, the application of a double taxation convention may be excluded on the basis of an implicit anti-abuse clause. This approach is based on the good faith of the contracting States, as in the Vienna Convention on the Law of Treaties.[36] This implicit anti-abuse clause was confirmed by the Swiss Supreme Court in a decision regarding the application of the double taxation convention between Switzerland and Denmark. The case involved a dividend paid out by a Swiss company to a Danish company without adequate substance and held by shareholders domiciled in Guernsey and Bermuda; these States have no double taxation convention with Switzerland.[37] Consequently, the application of a convention to a payment of royalties arising abroad could also be excluded on the basis of the implicit anti-abuse clause in the context of an entity in Switzerland that would have no substance.[38]

---

[34] OBERSON, *supra* note 23, at 240.
[35] See *supra* Section C.2(c). See OBERSON, *supra* note 23, at 242 (concerning the implicit nature of this condition).
[36] Vienna Convention on the Law of Treaties, 23 May 1969, SR 0.111; Oberson, *supra* note 23, at 245.
[37] Tribunal Fédéral [TF] [Federal Supreme Court] 28 November 2005, 2006 RDAF II 239.
[38] Such an approach would also be in accordance with the principles resulting from the BEPS report and ACTION 5.

2. Assignment

(a) Royalties or capital gains?

8.27 In the case of an assignment, ownership rights are transferred between the parties. This operation is legally distinct from a licence agreement by which the licence merely grants a right to use the intangible asset.

8.28 A distinction between revenue in the form of royalties and capital gains must be made in light of the theory of the effect on substance of the asset.[39] Indeed, when the purpose of a transaction is the transfer of ownership of an asset, its substance is affected and the resulting profit must be regarded as a capital gain. On the other hand, when there is no effect on substance, the income will be considered as income from movable property, that is, royalties in the case of an intangible asset.

8.29 This distinction between revenue in the form of royalties and capital gains may also be made in light of Article 12 of the OECD Model. This international allocation rule, which serves to define the State with the right to tax royalties, contains a definition of royalties based on the distinction made between the granting of a right to use the asset and the transfer of the right to dispose of the asset.[40]

8.30 However, the two distinctions presented above converge and are based on the same criteria.

8.31 In light of the foregoing, where an assignment consists of the transfer of an ownership right to the intangible asset, like a trademark, and not of simply conferring a right of use, the profit that may result for the assignor must be regarded as a capital gain and not as royalties. Indeed, an assignment affects the substance of the asset, in contrast to a licence agreement.

8.32 The distinction between a capital gain and royalties is important for a number of reasons:

- If the assignor is an individual who holds the assigned trademark as part of his private assets, the capital gain represents an exempt capital gain, while the royalties received would have been taxable as an income from movable property as taxable revenue (see Section D below);
- If the assignor is an individual who holds the assigned trademark as part

---

39   OBERSON & HULL, *supra* note 18, at 153.
40   Maraia, *supra* note 25, at 483.

of his commercial assets, or if the assignor is a legal entity, the capital gain is taxable in the same way as royalties, but the allocation rules are different at the international level (see Section E below).

(b) Tax treatment of capital gains

8.33 The capital gains realized by an individual who holds the trademark as part of his private assets are exempt from income tax in Switzerland.[41] On the other hand, if the individual holds the trademark as part of his commercial assets, the gain would be subject to income tax as revenue from independent activities.[42]

8.34 In principle, a trademark belongs to the commercial assets of an individual when it is recorded in the financial statements on the professional activities carried on by a partnership. When the trademark is not recorded in financial statements, the question is a more delicate one. Some authors take the view that the taxpayer who himself creates an intangible asset is for that reason engaged in an independent activity and, consequently, define the asset as a commercial asset.[43] This position, which applies to all the intangible assets, is probably too categorical,[44] but is nevertheless seen as justified in most cases involving trademarks. Indeed, trademarks are, as a rule, used in association with the sale of a product or the supply of services, which in practice presupposes a commercial activity.

8.35 Finally, for a legal entity that sells a trademark that it owns, the gain is always taxable and, as such, subject to tax on profits.[45]

(c) Impact of double tax treaties in an international context

8.36 Where there is a capital gain, it is always taxed in the State in which the assignor is located. This fiscal treatment is distinct from the case of taxable royalties, in accordance with the applicable conventions, either wholly in the State in which the licensor is located, or in part in the State in which the licensee is located, taxing in the State of source.

8.37 The other State must avoid any double taxation, either by an exemption mechanism or by a tax credit system.

---

41 DTL, *supra* note 11, art. 16, para. 3; Harmonization Law, *supra* note 2, art. 7, para. 4(b).
42 DTL, *supra* note 11, art. 18; Harmonization Law, *supra* note 2, art. 8.
43 *See* Peter Locher, *I. Teil, in* KOMMENTAR ZUM DBG – BUNDESGESETZ ÜBER DIE DIREKTE BUNDESSTEUER. II. TEIL. ART. 49–102, 20 (2004).
44 *See* Jean-Frédéric Maraia, *Fiscalité et propriété intellectuelle, in* ENTREPRISES ET PROPRIÉTÉ INTELLECTUELLE 49, 51 (2010).
45 DTL, *supra* note 11, at art. 58; Harmonization Law, *supra* note 2, at art. 24.

3. Tax treatment of expenses

8.38 We can distinguish three types of expenses with reference to trademarks: (1) registration costs; (2) protection costs against third parties; and (3) marketing costs.

8.39 If the trademark holder who incurs the expenses is a legal entity, a partnership, or an individual who holds the trademark among his business assets, protection and marketing costs are in principle fully deductible. Registration costs should also be deductible. Indeed, according to Swiss commercial law, there is no obligation to record an asset in the balance sheet unless it can be used, identified, and valued independently.[46] This should not be the case with a newly registered trademark which, at that stage, does not usually have any useful value to the company.

8.40 With regard to a taxpayer who holds the trademark as a private asset, only the costs necessary for, or arising out of, the generation of revenue could be deductible.[47] Thus only the protection related expenses fall within this category.[48] In fact marketing costs should result in the trademark being deemed a commercial asset. With regard to registration costs, these should be regarded as non-deductible purchase costs.

D. TRADEMARK TRANSACTIONS BETWEEN RELATED PARTIES

8.41 In transactions between related parties the conditions fixed may differ from those that would have applied in transactions between independent third parties. The term related parties is generally used to describe the relationship between a company and its shareholder. The shareholder can be an individual person or a legal entity. Furthermore, when the shareholder is an individual, family members and those with a close relationship to the shareholder are also included in the definition of related party. Similarly, when a legal entity is a shareholder, companies in the same commercial group as the legal entity are considered related parties. Ultimately, these conditions can then result in a transfer of profits from one party to another, which would not have happened if the parties were economically independent of one another. In an international context, this situation arises when the advantage benefits a party

---

46 Robert Danon, *Commentaire des articles 57 à 59, 60, 62 à 65, 67 à 68 de la loi fédérale sur l'impôt fédéral direct (LIFD), in* IMPÔT FÉDÉRAL DIRECT 709–797, N 11, arts. 57–58 (Danielle Yersin & Yves Noël eds, 2008).
47 Yves Noël, *in* IMPÔT FÉDÉRAL DIRECT, N 6, art. 32 (Danielle Yersin & Yves Noël eds, 2008).
48 Bernard Zwahlen, *in* KOMMENTAR, *supra* note 12, at N 3, at art. 32; Locher, *supra* note 43, at N 15, at art. 32.

D. TRADEMARK TRANSACTIONS BETWEEN RELATED PARTIES

located in a State with a lower tax rate than in a State where the other party is located. In the case of a licensing contract or an assignment, a transfer of profits may take place if the amount of the royalties or the sale price is higher than or lower than the price that would have been set between independent enterprises.

It should be noted that, in the 2014 OECD report entitled *Guidance on Transfer Pricing Aspects of Intangibles*, the OECD proposed a whole new chapter in the 2010 edition of the Transfer Pricing Guidelines for Multinational Enterprises and Tax Administrations. The following considerations take account of this in general terms, without going into the details of the new rules. **8.42**

1. Arm's length principle

In order to adjust these transfers of profits, the OECD has recommended the application of the arm's length principle as the criterion for fixing transfer prices within a group. This principle, which came into existence in the 1930s in the United States, is clearly mentioned in article 9 § 1 of the OECD Model. According to this provision, when two related companies are linked, in their commercial or financial relations, by made or imposed conditions that 'differ from those which would be made between independent enterprises', the profits 'which would, but for those conditions, have accrued to one of the enterprises, but, by reason of those conditions, have not so accrued, may be included in the profits of that enterprise and taxed accordingly'.[49] Thus, when the transfer price differs from the market price, the State in which the enterprise has its registered office can make an adjustment of accounts, called an initial adjustment. This adjustment can take place even when the parties did not intend to reduce or evade any taxes.[50] **8.43**

However, Article 9 of the OECD Model cannot be an independent legal basis for upward income adjustments.[51] In other words, adjustments must be based on the provisions of domestic law. **8.44**

---

49 OECD Model, *supra* note 22, at art. 9 § 1.
50 OECD, Transfer Pricing Guidelines for Multinational Enterprises and Tax Administrations § 1.2, at 31 (2010), *available 15 September 2015 at* http://www.ilsole24ore.com/pdf2010/Sole OnLine5/_Oggetti_Correlati/Documenti/Norme%20e%20Tributi/2011/02/istruzioni-uso-societa-perdite-fiscali/ocse-linee-guida-2010-prezzi-trasferimento.pdf?uuid=3d4ba2c4-3c0b-11e0-9341-61eb1896ac2b [hereinafter OECD Transfer Pricing Guidelines].
51 Oberson, *supra* note 23, at 260, N 865.

8.45 Under Swiss law, there are various legal bases that permit adjustments, but none of them expressly refers to the arm's length principle.[52] However, the latter is recognised by the Swiss Supreme Court which has already referred to it in a number of cases regarding hidden dividends paid by a company to its shareholder.[53] Thus, the competent Swiss tax authority can adjust the taxation of a company when it finds that directly or indirectly, for example, through a related person or enterprise, a shareholder or a related party has acquired an advantage that would not have been granted to a third party under the same circumstances.[54] The amount of the adjustment is subject to profit tax and withholding tax at the level of the company that granted the advantage.

8.46 Thus, the arm's length principle applies in the same way in a Swiss or international context.

2. Arm's length price

8.47 In the case of a trademark, when it is necessary to seek comparable assets in order to determine the market price, one must take into consideration its characteristics as an intangible asset by looking at the nature of the trademark, the rights associated with the trademark, and any limitations involving the trademark.[55] The OECD notes that it is also necessary to take into account any other intangible assets transferred in the same transaction[56] or other transferred elements, like tangible assets or services.[57] The analysis must then 'consider the options realistically available to each of the parties to the transaction'.[58]

8.48 In order to determine whether the price determined is the market price, various methods have been developed by the OECD. These methods are

---

52 Brülisauer/Kuhn, *in* KOMMENTAR, *supra* note 12, at ad. art. 58, no. 117.
53 Tribunal Fédéral [TF] [Federal Supreme Court], 2A.588/2006 (Switz.); Tribunal Fédéral [TF] [Federal Supreme Court] 119 Arrêts du Tribunal Fédéral Suisse [ATF] Ib 116 (Switz.); Tribunal Fédéral [TF] [Federal Supreme Court], 2A.346/1992 du 9 mai 1995 in Archives 65 p. 51/57, StE 1995 B 72.11 no 3 consid. 3b.
54 Tribunal Fédéral [TF] [Federal Supreme Court] 115 Arrêts du Tribunal Fédéral Suisse [ATF] Ia 157; RDAF 1993, 407.
55 OECD ACTION 8, *supra* note 6, at 57 (Guidelines, no. 6.86).
56 *Id.* at 59 (Guidelines, no. 6.89). The OECD states, for example, that 'the trademark without the patent and regulatory marketing approval may have limited value since the product could not be sold without the marketing approval and generic competitors could not be excluded from the market without the patent'. *See id.* at 59 (Guidelines, no. 6.91). Identification of the other intangible assets transfers is important. 'For example, the transfer of rights to use a trademark under a licence agreement will usually also imply the licensing of the reputational value, sometimes referred to as goodwill, associated with that trademark, where it is the licensor who has built up such goodwill.' *See id.* at 59 (Guidelines, no. 6.92).
57 *Id.* at 60 (Guidelines, no. 6.95).
58 *Id.* at 65 (Guidelines, no. 6.108).

D. TRADEMARK TRANSACTIONS BETWEEN RELATED PARTIES

recognised in Switzerland. On one side, there are the so-called traditional methods based on the transactions, namely: (1) the comparable uncontrolled price method; (2) the resale price method; and (3) the cost plus method.[59]

8.49 The first consists of comparing the transaction between related enterprises with a comparable transaction between independent enterprises. The other two methods consist of taking a known amount as a basis, that is, the resale price, or the cost to be incurred by the seller, and then deducting, or adding, an appropriate margin that is determined on the basis of the margin that would have been determined by independent enterprises under the same circumstances.

8.50 These methods may not be particularly reliable for trademark transactions involving large sums. Indeed, the first method presupposes identifying a sufficiently similar trademark which has been the object of a transaction between third parties in order to apply the corresponding price. The third method is not particularly reliable in practice, because very often the costs incurred, and marketing costs in particular, do not correspond to the value of the asset.[60] As for the second method, it may be applied, but only in few cases because it presupposes reselling the asset to a third party, in other words, for a trademark, the existence of a licence between the related companies and a sub-licence with a third party company is necessary.

8.51 Consequently two other methods recognized by the OECD are more frequently used to validate the transfer price of a trademark, namely:[61] (1) the profit split method; and (2) the transactional net margin method.

8.52 Without going into the details of these methods, the first consists of dividing the profit derived from a transaction between the parties, taking into account the functions and risks assumed by each of them, by means of a comparative examination with situations between third parties. As for the second method, this is aimed at establishing a net margin that a party would achieve in a given transaction, in comparison with the same transaction between third parties. However, it is not regarded as a reliable method for directly valuing an intangible asset.[62]

---

59 OECD TRANSFER PRICING GUIDELINES, *supra* note 50, at § 2.12.
60 The OECD expressly mentions this in its report of 2014. OECD, ACTION 8, *supra* note 6, at 74 (Guidelines no. 6.139).
61 OECD TRANSFER PRICING GUIDELINES, *supra* note 50, § 2.56.
62 OECD ACTION 8, *supra* note 6, at 74 (Guidelines no. 6.138).

8.53 Unfortunately, no one method stands out as the most appropriate for trademark operations. It is necessary to take into account the reliability of the outcome of each of these methods and, by implication, of the available comparisons on a case-by-case basis. In the OECD 2014 report, however, the OECD stated that the two methods that, as a general rule, should be the most appropriate are the profit split method and the comparable uncontrolled price method.[63] Finally, 'in situations where reliable comparable uncontrolled transactions for a transfer of one or more intangibles cannot be identified, it may also be possible to use valuation techniques to state the arm's length price for intangibles transferred between associated enterprises' by calculating the discounted value of projected future income streams or cash flows derived from the exploitation of the intangible asset being valued.[64] However, these techniques have to be applied 'in a manner that is consistent with the arm's length principle'.[65]

3. Domestic restructuring

8.54 As indicated above, a trademark transfer between related entities must be carried out in accordance with market conditions, and at the market price, in order to avoid fiscal adjustments to the taxable profits. It is possible, however, to carry out transfers of intangible assets, including trademarks, at book value, but only if the conditions of a neutral restructuring are fulfilled. Among these conditions there is always the requirement of maintaining the tax liability in Switzerland, so that the tax authority can still tax the hidden reserves in the future, which would be the difference between the real value and the book value of transferred assets. In other words, the transfer of a trademark at book value can be contemplated from the perspective of fiscal neutrality, but the latent reserves associated with the trademark must remain subject to tax in Switzerland.

8.55 In Switzerland many operations can take place from the perspective of fiscal neutrality, particularly transformations, mergers, demergers, and transfers of assets. Each of these operations is subject to general conditions, namely maintaining the tax liability in Switzerland and the book value following transfer, as well as to special conditions for some of these operations.[66]

---

63 *Id.* at 75 (Guidelines no. 6.142).
64 *Id.* at 78 (Guidelines no. 6.150).
65 *Id.* at 78 (Guidelines no. 6.151).
66 DTL, *supra* note 11, at arts. 19 and 61; Harmonization Law, *supra* note 2, at arts. 8 and 24; OBERSON & HULL, *supra* note 18, at 249, note 83.

8.56 These transactions can, of course, include trademark transfers. However, among the special conditions applying to certain restructuring operations, like the transfer of assets, and demergers to create two sister companies, is that of transferring an enterprise or part of an enterprise.[67] Now the transfer of a trademark does not normally fulfil this condition. However the latter is deemed to be fulfilled in accordance with the practice of the Federal Tax Administration when the operation takes the form of a transfer of an economically independent operational unit, which presupposes the existence of services on the market or in connection with group companies and the use of a full-time person, or on the basis of a mandate, to perform the services.[68]

E. INTERNATIONAL TAX STRATEGIES

8.57 Trademarks can be an important source of revenue. Their location from an international perspective is important for tax purposes, in light of the different tax rates that apply in different States.

8.58 In the context of the analysis of international tax strategies, it is necessary to consider the following questions: (i) of the place of residence of the company that owns the trademark; (ii) ownership of the trademark; and (iii) the different tax rules that make the location of a business in a given State more advantageous.

1. Residence of companies

8.59 When there is a single company involved, the location of the trademark will depend directly on the company's location. However, a company cannot choose a State of residence based solely on the tax rates of the State, which might be lower for the company. A company should determine its place of residence by considering the economic reasons associated with the location. First, the company needs to be located in a State that has the necessary infrastructure, customer base, and is in the appropriate geographic market. Second, the company's registered office in a chosen State is not the only guiding criterion in fiscal terms for determining its tax residence in an international context. Thus, under Swiss domestic law, a legal entity is a resident and subject to full taxation for profits and capital taxes in Switzerland

---

[67] DTL, *supra* note 11, at art. 61, paras. 1(b), 3, and 4; Harmonization Law, *supra* note 2, at art. 24, paras. 3(b), 3–4, and 3–5.
[68] SWISS FEDERAL TAX ADMINISTRATION, CIRCULAR NO. 5, RESTRUCTURINGS 61, NO. 4.3.2.7 (1 June 2004).

if it is incorporated in Switzerland or if its place of effective management is located in Switzerland.[69]

8.60 Consequently, if the company has its registered office abroad, but is effectively managed in Switzerland, it will be subject to full tax liability on worldwide profits and capital. The place of effective management corresponds to the place of the daily management of the company's affairs (day-to-day business aspects), that is, the place where conduct aimed at accomplishing the company's statutory purpose are made.[70] The day-to-day business must be distinguished from the simple administrative activities and also from the activity of the supreme bodies of the company. The administrative activity must be limited to either monitoring the day-to-day management of the legal entity or to making certain fundamental decisions, which are strategic in nature.[71] The place where the documents are kept, the place where activities related to the bookkeeping and correspondence are carried on, as well as the place where the administrative work is done, are secondary criteria.

8.61 In the event of any conflict of tax liability between the State where the registered office is located and the State where the company is effectively managed, the OECD Model refers to the place of effective management.[72] According to the OECD Commentary, the place of management is 'the place where the key management and commercial decisions that are necessary for the conduct of the entity's business as a whole are in substance made'.[73] The reference to the place where the most senior person or group of persons makes its decisions has been deleted in the 2008 version of the OECD Commentary. Therefore, the OECD and Switzerland definitions of effective management are in agreement. In practice, it is likely that the place of the day-to-day business will correspond in most cases to the place where the key management and commercial decisions are made.[74]

8.62 As a consequence, a company intending to establish its registered office in a State where tax is low, particularly for the purpose of reducing the tax it must pay on profits, including those derived from trademarks, must ensure that it has its effective management in that State, excluding any other third party's

---

69 DTL, *supra* note 11, at art. 50; Harmonization Law, *supra* note 2, at art. 20, para. 1.
70 Tribunal Fédéral [TF] [Federal Supreme Court] 4 December 2003, 2004 [StR] 524.
71 *Id.* at 526; *see also* OBERSON & HULL, *supra* note 18, at 214; Jean-Frédéric Maraia, *Residence of Companies in Switzerland*, *in* RESIDENCE OF COMPANIES UNDER TAX TREATIES AND EC LAW 795, 806 (Guglielmo Maisto ed., 2009) [hereafter Maraia, *Residence*].
72 OECD MODEL, *supra* note 22, at art. 4, § 2.
73 OECD, COMMENTARY ON THE ARTICLES OF THE MODEL TAX CONVENTION ON INCOME AND ON CAPITAL, 24 and art. 4 [hereinafter COMMENTARY ON THE OECD MODEL].
74 Maraia, *Residence*, *supra* note 71, at 795, 816.

country. Thus, a company located in a country where tax is low, whose sole asset is one or more trademarks and other intangible assets, could have its effective management in Switzerland if the day-to-day business takes place in Switzerland, for example through its shareholders in Switzerland or a company in the same group located in Switzerland.

Finally, for all companies, the concept of effective management includes the requirement of substance in the place where its registered office is located. **8.63**

2. Ownership

In the case of a group of companies, in addition to the above considerations concerning the criterion of effective management, there could be a tax issue when the group decides to designate one of its subsidiaries, existing or yet to be set up, as the owner of the group's trademark or trademarks. **8.64**

This question of trademark ownership has important tax consequences. Indeed the owner has complete control over the rights attached to the trademark. For instance, the owner of a trademark has the power to transfer or to assign use, which is in principle taxable on the part of the beneficiary and deductible on the part of the debtor. Moreover, the owner of the trademark must bear the costs and risks associated with development and maintenance of the value of the trademark. In fiscal terms, these costs are deductible. **8.65**

In principle, the creator of the trademark is its owner. The trademark may be registered by any individual or legal entity. **8.66**

From a tax perspective, two approaches can be envisaged for determining who the owner of an intangible asset is for tax purposes when a multinational enterprise is involved. The first approach consists of referring directly to private law to determine legal ownership. The second approach involves the relegation of legal ownership to a subordinate position by taking into account economic factors, that is, the functions and the portion of the costs and risks borne by the members in creation of the asset to determine economic ownership. The latter criterion is based on the principle that the entity bearing the costs and risks associated with an activity must also be the entity that receives the profits.[75] **8.67**

---

75 Jean-Frédéric Maraia, Prix de transfert des biens incorporels 49, no. 161 (Schulthess Verlag ed, 2008).

8.68 Although the problem of the ownership of intangible assets has for a long time been debated in the United States, the OECD has not developed this question to any significant extent until it published *Interim Guidances* in Action 8.[76] The OECD has summarised its position as follows:

> If the legal owner of an intangible in substance:
> - Performs and controls all of the functions ... related to the development, enhancement, maintenance, protection and exploitation of the intangible;
> - Provides all assets, including funding, necessary to the development, enhancement, maintenance, protection and exploitation of the intangibles; and
> - Bears and controls all of the risks related to the development, enhancement, maintenance, protection and exploitation of the intangible,
>
> then it will be entitled to all of the anticipated, ex ante, returns derived from the Multinational Enterprise (MNE) group's exploitation of the intangible. To the extent that one or more members of the MNE group other than the legal owner performs functions, uses assets, or assumes risks related to the development, enhancement, maintenance, protection, and exploitation of the intangible, such associated enterprises must share the anticipated returns derived from exploitation of the intangible by receiving arm's length compensation for their functions, assets, and risks. This compensation may, depending on the facts and circumstances, constitute all or substantial part of the return anticipated to be derived from the exploitation of the intangible.[77]

3. Tax status

8.69 Many States have special tax regimes, and some of these are directly related to revenue generated from intellectual property. The purpose of this section is to present the regimes that exist in Switzerland, alongside an international perspective.

(a) Auxiliary status (intellectual property companies)

8.70 Companies that have an administrative activity in Switzerland or companies whose commercial activity is essentially oriented abroad and who only have a subsidiary activity in Switzerland, can request an auxiliary status. This status has consequences only at the level of cantonal and communal income taxes, which does not provide relief for federal income tax.

8.71 The regime does not provide for a special tax rate, but a reduced tax basis at cantonal and communal levels. A distinction is made between income deriving

---

76 OECD Action 8, *supra* note 6, at 38 (Guidelines no. 6.32 et seq.).
77 *Id.*

from domestic sources, of which 100 per cent is taxable, and from foreign sources, of which only of 10–20 per cent is taxed. Foreign-source income notably includes income derived from the use of intangible property abroad from, for example, licence fees, royalties, and so on.[78] In Geneva, when this scheme applies, only 20 per cent of foreign-source royalties is taxed at ordinary rates. Depending on the ratio of profits arising out of Swiss-based business activities and foreign-based business activities and on the canton of incorporation, the total tax burden on profits of the auxiliary company ranges between 9 and 12 per cent. Usually, the applicable rate for determining the taxable basis is negotiated with the Swiss tax authorities prior to the implementation of the Swiss company and is defined in a binding tax ruling. In addition, most cantons offer a reduced capital tax rate for auxiliary companies.

8.72 As mentioned previously, the basic condition for this regime to apply is for the Swiss company to conduct its business primarily abroad. Only ancillary business activities should be conducted in Switzerland. As test for the fulfilment of the aforesaid criterion, most cantons require that, cumulatively, (i) 80 per cent of the Auxiliary Company's income must derive from outside of Switzerland, and (ii) 80 per cent of the Auxiliary Company's expenses must be paid to non-Swiss recipients. Generally, a company holding intellectual property rights, including trademarks, will easily fulfil these criteria if the trademarks held by the Swiss company are licensed to foreign companies.

8.73 However, this regime will end soon. This is the result of a debate conducted by the EU against this regime, as well as the cantonal holding company regime. The EU has argued since 2007 that the auxiliary status must be abolished on the grounds that it would constitute public aid, which is contrary to the Free Exchange Agreement of 22 July 1972 between the EU and Switzerland. Independent of the legal debate on the validity of this position,[79] Switzerland has agreed to engage in a dialogue with the EU concerning this regime, as well as the holding company regime. Furthermore, the OECD has examined the particular nature of this regime that might be described as a harmful tax practice with the consequence of placing Switzerland on a black list.

8.74 In light of this situation, Switzerland has included this problem in its drafting of the Corporate Tax Reform III. In this context Switzerland has simply decided to repeal the auxiliary company regime. However, in order to compensate for this, measures have been considered. In particular, a reduction in the ordinary tax rate on profits at the cantonal level and the introduction of a

---

78   OBERSON & HULL, *supra* note 18, at 73.
79   *See* OBERSON, *supra* note 23, at 92 et seq.

regime of the type more familiar in the EU, such as the licence box and the notional interest deduction system has been discussed. A draft law has recently been published and, unsurprisingly, the legal basis for the status of auxiliary companies has been repealed.[80] However, a licence box regime is envisaged at the cantonal level.[81]

8.75 It is expected that these provisions will come into effect by 2018 or 2020. It is possible, of course, that changes could occur between now and 2018, but not with regard to the principle of repealing the auxiliary status, which at the moment is unanimously recognised.

(b) Licence box

8.76 Many European States have a *licence box* regime, particularly in Belgium, Luxembourg, the Netherlands, Spain and the United Kingdom. In essence, this regime provides for the preferential taxation of a certain type of revenue, that is, royalties, irrespective of their source, domestic or international. It is, thus, a measure that takes the form of a different and reduced tax rate for royalties from licences by comparison to the rate applicable to other forms of revenue, hence the concept of a *box*. In the above named countries the actual tax rate varies between 5 per cent, as in the Netherlands, and 15 per cent, as in Spain.[82]

8.77 Not all royalties from licences are included in these regimes. By way of example,[83] among the protected intangible assets included in the regime, Luxembourg includes patents, trademarks, software, domain names, models, and designs. In the Netherlands, the assets concerned are patents and other intangible assets with a *Dutch R&D Certificate*. In Spain, the licence box covers only royalties received from patents, models, drawings, formulas, and processes.[84] Finally, in the United Kingdom, the regime applies to royalties from patents and various additional protection certificates.

---

80 LES AUTORITÉS FÉDÉRALES DE LA CONFÉDÉRATION SUISSE, DÉPARTEMENT FÉDÉRAL DES FINANCES (2015), *available 15 September 2015 at* http://www.admin.ch/ch/f/gg/pc/pendent.html#DFF [hereinafter Swiss Confederation] (providing the draft law and explanatory report on the consultation in connection with the Federal Law on corporate tax reform of 19 September 2014).
81 SWITZERLAND, CORPORATE TAX REFORM III, DRAFT art. 24b (2014).
82 Peter R. Merrill et al., *Is it Time for the United States to Consider the Patent Box*, TAX NOTES 1667 (March 26, 2012), *available 15 September 2015 at* http://www.pwc.com/en_US/us/washington-national-tax/assets/Merrill 0326.pdf.
83 Swiss Confederation, *supra* note 80.
84 In Spain, due to historical reasons, the Basque Country has its own tax regime, subject to certain limits, and in particular a Patent Box regime which includes trademarks. *See* Roberto Bernales Soriano, *The Spanish IP Box Scheme*, *in* NOVITÀ FISCALI 126, 129 (Samuele Vorpe ed., 2013).

E. INTERNATIONAL TAX STRATEGIES

Thus certain regimes cover royalties from trademarks, but not all. **8.78**

In Switzerland the Canton of Nidwald introduced a licence box regime in 2011. The reduced tax rate applies to all the royalties contemplated in article 12 § 2 of the OECD Model. Thus, royalties received from licences on trademarks are included. **8.79**

The regime contemplated in the draft *Corporate Tax Reform III* include in the *box* revenue from patents, additional protection certificates, exclusive patent licences,[85] and protection of the first applicant in accordance with Article 12 of the law on therapeutic products. The *box* is, thus, designed as a basket for inventions. Trademarks are not included on this list. The draft law also expressly envisages that revenue from a patent is determined, in particular, by deducting the royalties that shall be paid as consideration for the use of trademarks. The licence box regime applies to legal entities which are the owners or authorised users of one of the intangible assets mentioned, provided they have played a significant part in development of the corresponding invention.[86] Purchased patents are thus excluded from the regime. The cantons are free to determine the extent of the reduction of the taxable base, but this reduction cannot exceed 80 per cent. Finally, the draft law does not contain any provisions relating to the deduction, but the Federal Tax Administration's report states that the charges relating to licence revenue, such as R&D and amortisation, must be recognised as deductions in this *box* scheme. **8.80**

It is regrettable, of course, that the regime proposed in the draft law does not also apply to trademarks since, apart from the Canton of Nidwald that already had a licence box regime applying to trademarks, Luxembourg, a Member State of the EU, also applies a licence box regime that includes royalties from licences on trademarks.[87] Neither the Federal Tax Administration nor the Federal Council has explained this position in particularly clear terms in the **8.81**

---

[85] According to the explanatory report, the licence is exclusive when its holder alone has the right to exploit the patent at least in Swiss territory. Swiss Confederation, *supra* note 80.

[86] According to the draft law, the term significant contribution to the development of the invention or product refers, in particular, to the creation or ongoing development of the invention or product based on that invention. Furthermore, in the case of group companies the term significant contribution also applies to control of the development of the invention and, in the case of authorised use or an exclusive licence, the holding of that invention by the group making the significant contribution. Harmonization Law, *supra* note 2, art. 24(b), para. 3.

[87] Liechtenstein also has a licence box regime whose area of application extends to trademarks in particular, as in Luxembourg. *See* Wolfgang Maute, Philipp Senn, & Benedikt König, *The Licence Box Model in Liechtenstein and Switzerland*, 6 REVUE FISCALE 416, 418 (2013), *available 15 September 2015 at* http://www.batlinergasser.com/sites/default/files/416-423.pdf.

Chapter 8 TRADEMARK TRANSACTIONS AND INTERNATIONAL TAX STRATEGIES

documents accompanying the draft law. One can imagine three reasons for the authors of the draft law to exclude trademarks from the licence box scheme.

8.82 The first would be the need to limit fiscal losses in connection with the introduction of such a regime. Indeed, if it turned out that this were the reason for excluding trademarks from the licence box scheme, one would have to regret the absence of a detailed analysis in this regard in the context of the explanatory report for the purpose of better identifying the financial consequences and weighing up the interests involved against the absence of any justification of a differentiated tax treatment of intellectual property rights.[88]

8.83 The second reason arising out of the existing regimes abroad could be the aim of focusing exclusively on returns on intangible assets that are the result of long research and development activities and a high level research effort, thanks to the use of highly qualified personnel. If, from our perspective, it is wholly desirable to encourage the development of R&D work in Switzerland, one should not exclude from the scope of the licence box regime revenue obtained from trademark licences. Indeed these intangible assets should be viewed as a whole for a company. A protected trademark could not, in principle, benefit from revenue produced by licence royalties if the trademark is not used in association with the product of work performed by employees through innovative work protected by a patent or expertise acquired. The subtle overlapping of intangible assets cannot easily justify making a distinction between them in the context of a licence box regime.

8.84 The third, and most likely, reason that might explain the content of the draft law could be the anticipation that the licence box rules will be reduced after the OECD, through the BEPS report, concludes their examination of such regimes. Indeed the OECD is currently working on setting stricter substantive requirements with the aim of avoiding arbitrary transfers of revenue from a country with high tax rates to a country with low tax rates, which includes examining cases in which licence box regimes are applied.[89] In concrete terms, the exclusion of trademarks from intellectual property assets that could qualify

---

88 An examination of the 'windfall effect' of the licence box regime does not distinguish the options as regards the intangible assets that are or are not to be taken into account, apart from the simple fact that 'the more extensive the box is, the greater the windfall effects are' (Swiss Confederation, *supra* note 80, at 104).

89 Action 5 in the OECD action plan contains the obligation of requiring a substantial activity for introducing any preferential regime. *See* OECD, ACTION PLAN ON BEPS, *supra* note 1, at 19; *see also* OECD, ACTION 5, *supra* note 5, at 27 et seq.

for tax benefits under a licence box regime rests on the *nexus approach*.[90] Indeed, under the nexus approach, it is not possible to establish a nexus between expenditures, marketing-related intellectual property assets, and income.

In its explanatory report on the consultation in connection with the Corporate Tax Reform III, the Federal Tax Authority has also identified four actions among the fifteen that are of a determining nature for examination of the licence box regime.[91] The first relates to application of the Controlled Foreign Company rules (CFC rules), which consist of preventing a company from accounting for profits in a State that generally has *too* low tax through a *controlled foreign company*. This would enable the shareholder's State of residence to tax the profits generated by the controlled foreign company, even in the absence of a distribution. Switzerland does not have such rules as part of its internal legislation, but many other countries have adopted such rules. It is possible, therefore, that the licence box regime will be exposed to the CFC rules. The second relates to the requirement of economic substance that is necessary for attributing to a company in question the profits that it shows in its accounts and the need for the exchange of information on any rulings granted with regard to that status. In this context, the report shows that a restrictive approach should prevail for determining the intangible assets that would be included in the intellectual property box regime, mentioning by the way the nexus approach.[92] Finally, from the perspective of transfer pricing, the report finds that the draft law is currently in accordance with BEPS Action 8, meaning that the prices are in accordance with the creation of value, and Action 13 titled *Documentation*. **8.85**

The OECD has not however adopted a formal position on the existing licence box regimes that also include trademarks.[93] In our view, it is necessary to wait for confirmation of the nexus approach and for a restrictive application of the intellectual property box to patents. However, if an examination of the OECD requirements with regard to the Luxembourg licence box regime and, in particular, its area of application extended to trademarks, does not result in restriction of the box to patent revenue only, Switzerland would also have to **8.86**

---

[90] According to the OECD, 'this approach looks to whether an IP scheme makes its benefits conditional on the extent of R&D activities of taxpayers receiving benefits.' 'The purpose of the nexus approach is to grant benefits only to income that arises from IP where the actual R&D activity was undertaken by the taxpayer itself.' OECD ACTION 5, *supra* note 5, at 29.
[91] *See* Swiss Confederation, *supra* note 80, at 134.
[92] *Id.* at 130.
[93] *See* OECD, ACTION 5, *supra* note 5, at 59. IP schemes still under review with respect to the elaborated substantial activity factor.

adopt this approach, in our view, in order to guarantee greater consistency in the taxation of intellectual property revenue.

F. CONCLUSION

8.87 The taxation of intellectual property, more specifically of trademarks, is an extremely broad subject, because many general, albeit complex, fiscal problems affect this category of assets including the definition of private assets/commercial assets, the definition of capital gains/return on assets, tax at source, reimbursement, the beneficial owner, and the anti-abuse rules in double tax conventions, transfer prices, restructurings, and auxiliary status, in addition to more specific questions about legal/economic ownership, licence box, and valuation difficulties.

8.88 There can be no doubt that this subject will remain a key issue for companies in the future, because trademarks and their often considerable value play a decisive role in the economic development of their owners and at the same time will logically constitute a significant source of revenue for tax authorities.

9

REGISTERING SECURITY INTERESTS OVER TRADEMARKS IN AUSTRALIA: THEORY AND PRACTICE

Robert Burrell[*] and Michael Handler[**]

A.	INTRODUCTION	9.01	2. Ongoing role of recording claims in the Trade Marks Register	9.23
B.	THE PRE-PPSA POSITION	9.03	3. Problems caused when title in property passes to the secured party	9.25
C.	THE PPSA REFORMS	9.08	E. CONCLUSIONS AND OPTIONS FOR REFORM	9.32
D.	TENSIONS BETWEEN THE TRADEMARK AND PPSA SYSTEMS	9.14		
	1. Imperfect information and transition costs	9.16		

A. INTRODUCTION

There should be very little to say about the registration of security interests **9.01** over trademarks in Australia. More precisely, one would expect that everything that might be said about this topic would constitute little more than an account of a general set of legal arrangements that have a field of operation extending well beyond trademark law. This is because the introduction of the Personal Property Securities Act 2009 (Cth) (PPSA), the key provisions of which came into effect on 30 January 2012, was meant to produce a single national record of security interests over all forms of personal property, both tangible and intangible. The resulting national Personal Property Securities Register (PPS Register) goes a long way towards achieving this aim; for the most part it succeeds in providing a single, *reliable* source of information. Most importantly, if a secured party fails to register its interest on the PPS Register,

---

[*] Professor, School of Law, University of Sheffield; Winthrop Professor of Law, University of Western Australia.
[**] Associate Professor, Faculty of Law, University of New South Wales.
  This chapter builds on the authors' earlier article, Robert Burrell & Michael Handler, *The PPSA and Registered Trade Marks: When Bureaucratic Systems Collide*, 34 UNSW LAW JOURNAL 600 (2011). The Australian legislation and case law referred to in this chapter is available at www.austlii.edu.au (*available* 15 September 2015).

Chapter 9 REGISTERING SECURITY INTERESTS OVER TRADEMARKS IN AUSTRALIA

its interest is 'unperfected', and a buyer will take the property free of the unregistered security interest. Conversely, a registered, perfected interest will be enforceable against entirely innocent and unaware third party purchasers. However, with regards to trademarks, the PPSA does not succeed in its aim of creating a unitary register that is determinative of all questions relating to the enforceability of security interests. This is because registration of the relevant interest on the Trade Marks Register will continue to offer the holder of the security interest a range of advantages and, in some cases, will continue to be essential.

9.02 We therefore proceed in this chapter to discuss suggestions as to how information might productively be shared between the two registration systems, together with some brief concluding comments on why such a seemingly innocuous suggestion for reform may, in fact, prove difficult to implement.

B. THE PRE-PPSA POSITION

9.03 In order to understand how the PPSA is intended to operate in the trademark field and why dual registration will continue to be important, it is necessary to understand something of how security interests in registered trademarks were recorded and dealt with under the Trade Marks Act 1995 (Cth) (TMA) before the PPSA reforms took effect on 30 January 2012.

9.04 In Australia, as in many other countries, it has never been mandatory to record security interests on the Trade Marks Register. Thus, a financial institution that has taken a security over a registered trademark – for example, by way of an equitable mortgage, or a fixed or floating charge[1] – has not been obliged to inform the Registrar of Trade Marks of its interest, or have it publicly recorded in the Register. To the extent that any obligations, pre-PPSA, were imposed on parties to register their security interests over trademarks, this was done through a separate regime under the Corporations Act 2001 (Cth). Corporations were required to lodge with the Australian Securities and Investments Commission notices of charges over personal property, including registered trademarks, which were then entered on the Australian Register of Company Charges.[2]

---

1 *See* further Jacqueline P. Lipton, *Security Interests in Trade Marks and Associated Business Goodwill*, 10 AUSTRALIAN INTELLECTUAL PROPERTY JOURNAL 157, 162–8 (1991) (discussing the types of security that can be taken over trademarks).
2 Corporations Act 2001 (Cth), ch 2K (before its repeal by the Personal Property Securities (Corporations and Other Amendments) Act 2010 (Cth)).

9.05 The TMA always provided for the voluntary recording of claims to security interests, with important consequences flowing from whether or not such information was recorded. The way in which the voluntary scheme under the TMA functioned, before its amendment as a result of the PPSA reforms, was that an owner of a registered trademark and a person claiming an interest in that mark could apply jointly to the Registrar of Trade Marks to have that claim recorded on the Trade Marks Register. Without checking the veracity of the claim, the Registrar was required to enter the particulars of the claim in the Register.[3] Importantly, the TMA contained the qualification that the mere record of a person's claim to an interest in a registered mark was not to be taken to be evidence that the person in fact had that interest.[4] Rather, the record was intended to provide a form of public notice as to the potential existence of an interest in the property, with parties whose claims were recorded being afforded certain benefits under the TMA. The fact that the scheme was voluntary made it nearly impossible to determine the proportion of securities in respect to which claims were recorded,[5] although it was thought to be relatively rare for parties to take advantage of the scheme, with ignorance of its existence and misconceptions as to its importance being offered as partial explanations.[6]

9.06 One complicated issue in this area of the law, pre-PPSA, was working out when a registered trademark was subject to a security interest at all. Determining priorities between securities was also complex. In this regard it should be noted that although the Corporations Act contained detailed provisions setting out priority rules in relation to charges (whether registered in the Australian Register of Company Charges or not),[7] it was also stated that these

---

[3] Trade Marks Act 1995 (TMA), s 113 (before its repeal and re-enactment by the Personal Property Securities (Consequential Amendments) Act 2009 (Cth)) and s 114(1). For applications for the recording of a claim to an interest in a trademark whose registration was being sought, *see* TMA, s 117 (before its repeal and re-enactment by the Personal Property Securities (Consequential Amendments) Act 2009 (Cth)) and ss 118, 114(2).

[4] TMA, s 116. For criticism of the model adopted in the TMA, *see* Samuel Murumba, *Recordal of Other Interests on the Trade Marks Register*, 21 AUSTRALIAN BUSINESS LAW REVIEW 75 (1993) (advocating a system of *registration* for all interests other than trusts, and *noting only* for interests arising from express, implied or constructive trusts).

[5] The problem of quantifying the use of the voluntary system is exacerbated by the fact that there is no easy way of searching the Trade Marks Register for claims to interests in registered marks. However, prior to the Personal Property Securities Act 2009 (Cth) (PPSA) coming into force, the authors identified, through rough and ready means, around 4,300 recorded claims, with at least 2,500 of these claims being for security interests. When one bears in mind that there are over 500,000 trademarks on the Register, and how common it is for floating charges over all of the assets of a company to be taken, it is probably fair to assume that a significant number of security interests were not recorded.

[6] John V. Swinson, *Uncertainties and Insecurities – Personal Property Security Reform and its Impact on Intellectual Property*, 66 INTELLECTUAL PROPERTY FORUM 12, 15 (2006).

[7] Corporations Act 2001 (Cth), ss 280–282 (before their repeal by the Personal Property Securities (Corporations and Other Amendments) Act 2010 (Cth)).

rules did not affect the operation of the law of registered trademarks. Thus the key provision in determining the impact of securities on dealings with registered trademarks was section 22 of the TMA. Before its amendment as a result of the PPSA reforms, section 22 provided:

(1) The registered owner of a trade mark may, subject only to any rights appearing in the [Trade Marks] Register to be vested in another person, deal with the trade mark as its absolute owner and give in good faith discharges for any consideration for that dealing.
(2) This section does not protect a person who deals with the registered owner otherwise than:
 (a) as a purchaser in good faith for value; and
 (b) without notice of any fraud on the part of the owner.
(3) Equities in relation to a registered trade mark may be enforced against the registered owner, except to the prejudice of a purchaser in good faith for value.

9.07 The intended effect of section 22(1) was tolerably clear.[8] If a registered owner wished, for example, to assign its mark, and a party's claim to a security over the mark was recorded in the Trade Marks Register, the assignee would have taken the mark subject to that security, if it in fact existed. Conversely, if the secured party's claim was not so recorded, then, subject to sections 22(2)–(3), the assignee would not have taken the mark subject to that interest. To use another example, assume that the registered owner first granted a charge over its mark to A, who failed to record its claim in the Register, and later granted a charge to B. Subject to the remainder of section 22, B would have taken priority over A, given that the registered owner was entitled to deal with B as the 'absolute owner' of the mark.[9] Even if A had its claim recorded after the charge to B was granted, A's interest would not have prevailed over B's, and this was true irrespective of whether B had taken the trouble to record its interest.[10] The impact of section 22(2)–(3), however, was that it was not the case that an assignee would never have acquired property subject to an

---

8 There were, however, aspects of its drafting that were problematic. One concerned the role of constructive notice, which we consider below. Prior to 2006, there were other problems with the wording of this section: for discussion, *see* Michael Pattinson, *Using Intellectual Property as a Security*, 7 AUSTRALIAN INTELLECTUAL PROPERTY JOURNAL 135, 142 (1996); John V. Swinson, *Security Interests in Intellectual Property in Australia*, 14 BOND LAW REVIEW 86, 113–14 (2002).
9 This was recognised to be a reversal of the ordinary rules of priority: *see* Pattinson, *ibid*, 139 (considering the similarly worded provisions of the Patents Act 1990 (Cth)).
10 If, however, B had failed to record its interest in these circumstances, it would have been vulnerable if the registered owner had granted a later charge to C, or if the registered owner had subsequently assigned the mark (subject to s 22(2)–(3)). As a further example of how these rules applied, if the registered owner granted a charge to A and a later charge to B, after which time A and B in turn applied to have their claims to their interests recorded in the Register, following which the owner assigned the mark, the assignee would have taken the mark subject to both A and B's interests (since both claims were recorded in the Register at the time of the assignment), with B having priority over A (because at the time B acquired its interest A's was not recorded).

'unrecorded' interest, or that a later security interest would always have prevailed over an earlier 'unrecorded' interest in a priority dispute. If, for example, an assignee of a registered mark had actual knowledge of the fact that there was a charge over the property, the assignee would not have been a purchaser 'in good faith', and thus not entitled to the protection afforded by section 22(1), meaning that it would have taken the mark subject to the charge. Perhaps the most difficult question left open by the wording of section 22(2) was whether an assignee who had only *constructive* notice of a security holder's unrecorded interest was no longer a purchaser 'in good faith', and thus disentitled to the protection afforded by section 22. This question was particularly important given the existence of the parallel, mandatory regime for registering charges over trademarks under the Corporations Act – would an assignee that failed to check the Australian Register of Company Charges have taken the trademark subject to a registered charge? While the courts never resolved this issue, a strong case could be made that both the wording of section 22(2) and the insular policy underpinning the TMA notification scheme meant that constructive notice would not have been sufficient to disentitle an assignee from protection in these circumstances.[11]

C. THE PPSA REFORMS

9.08 The PPSA reforms are most commonly discussed in terms of their role in setting up a new, centralized system for registration of security interests over personal property and, as the inevitable corollary, abolishing a large number of existing registration schemes, such as that for charges under the Corporations Act.[12] However, the reforms have also had a significant impact upon the registered trademark system in regards to determining whether dealings with registered marks are subject to security interests. The intention is that everything will now turn on whether such interests have been entered on the

---

11 *See* Robert Burrell & Michael Handler, *Australian Trade Mark Law* (Oxford University Press, 2010), 488 (noting the express reference to 'fraud' in s 22(2)(b) and pointing out that Australian legislatures tend to use different language when seeking to preserve constructive notice: *see, e.g.*, Proceeds of Crime Act 2002 (Cth), s 142; Pesticides Act 1999 (NSW), s 31. *See also* Swinson, *supra* note 8, at 99–100 (considering the analogous situation under the Patents Act 1990 (Cth) and reaching broadly the same conclusion).

12 *See* Personal Property Securities (Corporations and Other Amendments) Act 2010 (Cth), sch 1 item 18. Data from the Australian Register of Company Charges was migrated to the new PPS Register before the commencement of the PPSA regime on 30 January 2012: *see* PPSA, *supra* note 5, pt 9.4 div 6. It must be emphasized that data from the Trade Marks Register was not migrated. While no formal reasons were provided, the normative justification that would no doubt be offered is that this was because such data does not disclose whether a party in fact has the security interest claimed. However, the fact that there is no easy way to distinguish security interests from other types of interest recorded on the Trade Marks Register may well have played a significant role in practice. For a critical discussion of the data migration process *see* Rebecca Hope, *Migrated Security Interests: Lost in Transition*, 34 UNSW LAW JOURNAL 646 (2011).

new PPS Register. However, as will be seen in the next Section, considerable importance will still attach to whether a secured party's claim to its security interest continues to be, or is subsequently, recorded on the Trade Marks Register.

9.09 The PPSA recognizes that a registered trademark and a transferable trademark licence are both 'personal property' to which the Act applies.[13] Various types of 'security interest' can attach to such collateral.[14] 'Security interest' is given a functional definition in the PPSA as being 'a transaction that, in substance, secures payment or performance of an obligation'.[15] Importantly, this functional definition is intended to move away from the question of who has title to the property; the same rules are to apply irrespective of whether the transaction transfers title to the secured party (as with a chattel mortgage), or merely serves to create some lesser interest (such as by way of a charge).[16] In the case of trademarks, the functional definition means that a legal (as opposed to merely equitable) mortgage of a trademark, whereby a mark is assigned subject to a right of reassignment on redemption of the debt, will unquestionably be regarded as giving rise to a 'security interest' under the PPSA, and indeed the PPSA makes express provision to this effect.[17]

9.10 The PPSA provides that, once attached, a security interest is enforceable against a third party, provided there is a written security agreement in place, signed by the grantor, that describes the registered mark/licence, or states that the security interest is taken in all of the grantor's present and after-acquired property.[18] However, further significant consequences flow from whether or not a 'financing statement' with respect to such an enforceable security interest has been registered in the new PPS Register.[19] Where the collateral is a registered trademark or a licence over such a mark, this is a relatively straightforward process: as well as setting out details of the grantor and

---

13 PPSA, s 10 (definitions of 'personal property', 'licence' and 'intellectual property licence'). Notably, 'intellectual property' is defined to mean the *rights* to do certain acts under various statutes, for example, 'the rights held by a person who is the registered owner of a trademark that is registered under the *Trade Marks Act 1995*': PPSA, s 10 (definition of 'intellectual property' para (c)).
14 *See* PPSA, s 19(2) on attachment.
15 PPSA, s 12(1).
16 *See* PPSA, s 12(1) (transaction to be treated as giving rise to a security interest 'without regard to … the identity of the person who has title to the property'). *See also* s 12(2)(a)–(c) (making it clear that charges and chattel mortgages are within the definition of 'security interest').
17 PPSA, s 12(2)(j), (k).
18 PPSA, s 20(1)–(2). This (and the other matters we describe in the remainder of this paragraph) is the case for security interests arising on or after the registration commencement time: s 310(b). *See* s 311 on the enforceability of 'transitional security interests' (defined in s 308(a) as those arising before the registration commencement time under a security agreement that continues in force after that time).
19 *See* PPSA, s 150 for the application process.

secured party, the financing statement must describe the mark by 'serial number'.[20] This has been defined in regulations to mean the trademark registration number provided by IP Australia,[21] a decision that will greatly facilitate searches of the PPS Register for such collateral. The financing statement must also provide an 'end time' for the PPS registration, which is to be 'no later than … the end of the day 7 years after the registration time' but which can be renewed for further seven year periods.[22] Once the PPS registration is effective with respect to the collateral,[23] the security interest becomes 'perfected'.[24]

Whether or not the security interest has been perfected is critical in determining the position of third parties who acquire the property, and for determining priorities between secured parties. The key provision in looking at this issue is section 43(1) of the PPSA, which states that a buyer of personal property for value will take the property free of an unperfected security interest. Crucially, this is not subject to an exception, even in cases where the buyer has actual knowledge of the existence of the security interest. This creates a very strong incentive to register that goes beyond, for example, that

9.11

---

20 It is, however, worth noting that s 105(2) of the PPSA provides that in some circumstances a registered description of goods alone is taken to include a description of 'associated' intellectual property rights. This raises the possibility that a perfected security interest over a registered form of associated intellectual property might be hidden from searches of the PPS Register, because the collateral description in the financing statement merely describes the goods in respect of which the associated intellectual property rights subsist. As to some of the problems this may create, *see generally* Steve Pemberton & Robyn Chatwood, *Using Your IP to Get Finance? Implications of the Personal Property Securities Act 2009 for IP Lawyers and Their Clients*, 22 AUSTRALIAN INTELLECTUAL PROPERTY LAW BULLETIN 190, 193 (2010). However, the concept of 'associated' intellectual property is unlikely to cause concern in the trademark context. This is because s 105(2) only applies where separate security interests attach to goods and to a trademark, in circumstances where the exercise of rights in relation to the goods *necessarily* involves an exercise of the intellectual property rights: s 105(1). This threshold will not be satisfied in the case of trademarks given that the mere sale of goods bearing a mark applied by or with the authority of the owner will not constitute a potentially infringing use. This conclusion follows, *inter alia*, from s 123(1) of the TMA, *supra* note 3: *see* Crossmark Asia v. Retail Adventures [2013] NSWSC 55, [64]. Section 123 is a defence that applies to use of a mark that has been applied to goods by, or with the consent of, the trademark owner (although it must be acknowledged that the relationship between a 'necessary exercise' of an intellectual property right in s 105(1) of the PPSA and circumstances where the user has a defence to an action for trademark infringement is entirely unclear). *See* further Burrell & Handler, *supra* note 11, at 373–9.
21 PPSA, s 153(1) item 4 and Personal Property Securities Regulations 2010 (Cth), sch 1 cls 2.2(1)(c)(iii)(E)–(2), (3)(h). Strictly speaking, providing the registration number is mandatory only where the trademark is designated in the financing statement as 'commercial property'. This should be true in almost all cases: see PPSA, s 10 (definitions of 'commercial property' and 'consumer property').
22 PPSA, s 153(1) item 5(b). For the 'registration time', *see* s 160.
23 PPSA, s 163. *But see* ss 164–165 on defects that make a registration ineffective.
24 PPSA, s 21(1)–(2). For further details on the mechanics of PPS registration, *see, e.g.*, Nicholas Mirzai, *A Year with the Personal Property Securities Act 2009 (Cth): The Personal Property Securities Register, Amendment Demands and Judicial Proceedings*, 31 COMPANY AND SECURITIES LAW JOURNAL 295 (2013).

which applies under the Torrens system for land.[25] Importantly, this regime, which contemplates depriving secured parties of title to their property in certain circumstances, has survived its first constitutional challenge.[26] Further, section 44(1) provides that where the property is required to be described by serial number, but a search of the PPS Register only by reference to serial number would not disclose the registration (for example, because the financing statement contained an error), then a buyer of such property also takes it free of the security interest.[27] It should, however, be noted that at the time of writing, consideration is being given to removing this provision as it applies to trademarks and other forms of registered intellectual property.[28] A further, related provision stipulates that if a security interest is granted over a trademark licence, the trademark is later transferred, but the licensee continues to hold the licence after the transfer, the security agreement binds every successor in title to the licensor to the same extent as the security agreement was binding on the licensor.[29] Complex rules govern priorities,[30] but the default position is that a perfected security interest has priority over an unperfected security interest, priority between perfected security interests is governed by the time of

---

25 *See, e.g.*, Real Property Act 1900 (NSW), s 43(1); Land Title Act 1994 (Qld), s 184(3)(b); Transfer of Land Act 1958 (Vic), s 43 (each containing exceptions for fraud, which will catch some, but not necessarily all, cases where the buyer has actual knowledge of the unregistered interest).

26 *See* White v. Spiers Earthworks Pty Ltd (2014) 99 ACSR 214, 221–3 [35]–[40]. This case concerned s 51(xxxi) of the Australian Constitution, which prohibits the Commonwealth Parliament from legislating to acquire property other than on just terms. It must, however, be emphasized that this case turned on the operation of s 267(2) of the PPSA (which deals with the vesting of unperfected security interests in the grantor upon the grantor's winding up or bankruptcy) and not s 43.

27 This is subject to limited exceptions in s 44(2). In the PPSA as originally enacted, s 44(2)(b) contained an exception to s 44(1) if the buyer had actual knowledge that the sale constituted a breach of the security agreement. This exception was repealed by the Personal Property Securities (Corporations and Other Amendments) Act 2010 (Cth), sch 2 item 43 on the basis that it set up a 'complicated and potentially uncertain' test (Explanatory Memorandum, Personal Property Securities (Corporations and Other Amendments) Bill 2010 (Cth), 30), a decision that is perhaps surprising in light of s 46 of the PPSA, where the 'actual knowledge' exception is maintained where the property is sold in the ordinary course of the seller's business of selling property of that kind.

28 Bruce Whittaker, *Review of the Personal Property Securities Act 2009 Consultation Paper No 2: Creation and perfection of security interests; taking free rules; priority rules; and other dealings in collateral*, Attorney General's Department, [5.4.2.1.3] (2014), available 15 September 2015 at http://www.ag.gov.au/Consultations/Documents/PPSReview/Paper2Creationandperfectionofsecurityinterests.pdf. It is, however, to be hoped that this proposed reform will not be actioned: Robert Burrell & Michael Handler, *Response to Review of the Personal Property Securities Act 2009 Consultation Paper No 2* (2014), available 15 September 2015 at http://www.ag.gov.au/Consultations/Documents/PPSReview/ResponsesToPaper2/PPSReviewConsultationPaper2Response01.pdf.

29 PPSA, s 106(1), and *see* s 313 for application. Section 106(1) is, however, likely to be of little practical importance, since 'it is hard to imagine how a holder of … intellectual property, who gives a licence to use the intellectual property to a party who then gives a security interest, is bound by the security interest': Allens Arthur Robinson et al, Submission No 30 to Senate Standing Committee on Legal and Constitutional Affairs, Parliament of Australia, *Inquiry into the Personal Property Securities Bill 2008 [Exposure Draft]*, 9 January 2009, 56 (commenting on the near-identical s 127(1) of the Exposure Draft of the Personal Property Securities Bill 2008 (Cth)).

30 *See generally* PPSA, pt 2.6.

C. THE PPSA REFORMS

perfection, and priority between unperfected security interests is determined by the order of attachment of the security interests.[31]

If the PPSA reforms had gone no further than what we have just described, there would have been considerable uncertainty as to how they would have intersected with section 22(1) of the TMA, which, as shown above, made the power of a registered owner to deal with its mark as its absolute owner subject only to rights appearing in the Trade Marks Register. One option might have been to abolish the recordal scheme under the TMA, although this would have been problematic given that the Trade Marks Register is also designed to provide a record of claims to non-security interests, such as trademark licences, and to ensure that registered owners cannot deal with their marks unencumbered by such interests. Instead, in an attempt to ensure that the centralizing impact of the PPS Register was not undermined by the maintenance of the notification scheme under the TMA, section 22 of the TMA has been amended to add new sub-sections (2A) and (4), such that the section now reads as follows: 9.12

(1) The registered owner of a trade mark may, subject only to any rights appearing in the [Trade Marks] Register to be vested in another person, deal with the trade mark as its absolute owner and give in good faith discharges for any consideration for that dealing.
(2) This section does not protect a person who deals with the registered owner otherwise than:
   (a) as a purchaser in good faith for value; and
   (b) without notice of any fraud on the part of the owner.
(2A) Despite subsection (1), the recording in the [Trade Marks] Register of a right that is a PPSA security interest does not affect a dealing with a trade mark.
(3) Equities in relation to a registered trade mark may be enforced against the registered owner, except to the prejudice of a purchaser in good faith for value.
(4) Subsection (3) does not apply in relation to an equity that is a PPSA security interest.

'PPSA security interest' is defined as a security interest to which the PPSA applies, but specifically excludes an interest provided for under a security agreement that was made before 30 January 2012.[32] Thus, for security interests arising before this time, the two new sub-sections of section 22 of the TMA have no effect, and the pre-PPSA law, discussed above, continues to apply. For security interests arising from this date, the effect of the new sub-sections is that even if a claim to a security interest is recorded in the Trade Marks Register, this will have no effect on the registered owner's ability to deal with 9.13

---

31 PPSA, s 55(2)–(6).
32 TMA, *supra* note 3, s 6(1) (definition of 'PPSA security interest').

the mark or a third party's ability to enforce the security interest against the registered owner. Thus, whether an assignee takes a mark subject to a party's security interest that arises on or after 30 January 2012 will now depend entirely on whether that interest has been perfected under the PPSA. Similarly, where the registered owner has granted multiple securities over its mark from that date, priorities as between the secured parties will turn wholly on the operation of the priority provisions in the PPSA.

D. TENSIONS BETWEEN THE TRADEMARK AND PPSA SYSTEMS

9.14 In the previous Section, we saw that, consistent with the centralizing logic that underpins the entirety of the PPSA regime, questions as to the enforceability of security interests over registered trademarks arising on or after 30 January 2012, and of priority between competing security interests over registered trademarks, are to be determined solely by reference to the PPSA. Yet, despite the advent of the PPSA, and despite the amendments to the TMA discussed above, the voluntary scheme for recording interests in the Trade Marks Register remains in place, largely unchanged.[33] In this Section, we suggest that the continuation of this voluntary scheme of recording security interests will, to some extent, undermine the aims of the PPSA. Moreover, if the PPSA had been intended to protect purchasers of property completely from claims by secured parties with unperfected security interests, other amendments to the TMA would have been needed, most notably in relation to the grounds of rectification of the Trade Marks Register.

9.15 Before descending further into matters of detail, it is worth emphasizing that the mere presence of the voluntary facility, together with the authority that is generally claimed for the Trade Marks Register, is likely to mislead some groups into wrongly believing that the Trade Marks Register provides a reliable source of information about security interests. When coupled with complex transitional provisions that may make it difficult to determine when it is safe to rely on the PPS Register, and registration procedures that seem set to run in parallel with one another, there will be significant scope for error and confusion. Over and above the problems that flow from informational gaps

---

[33] It is worth noting, however, that from 30 January 2012, only the person claiming the right or interest in the registered mark may apply to the Registrar of Trade Marks for the recording of the claim, and the application must also 'be accompanied by proof to the reasonable satisfaction of the Registrar of the applicant's entitlement to the claimed interest or right': TMA, s 113 (as re-enacted by the Personal Property Securities (Consequential Amendments) Act 2009 (Cth), sch 2 item 21). *See also* TMA, s 117 (as re-enacted by the Personal Property Securities (Consequential Amendments) Act 2009 (Cth), sch 2 item 22) for applications in respect of trademarks whose registration is being sought.

and misconceptions, we draw attention to the ongoing advantages that recording of a claim to a security interest on the Trade Marks Register will confer on a secured party. Finally, we suggest that where title to a registered mark has been transferred to a secured party, it is difficult to see that the PPSA will operate as intended. Consequently, in the trademarks context, it seems that the aim of moving to a functional approach to security interests, where rights are divorced from the question of who has title to the property, will be partially frustrated.

1. Imperfect information and transition costs

9.16 The advent of the PPSA was the subject of extensive coverage. Government agencies expended considerable resources in an effort to generate public understanding of how the new regime would operate. There was also a long lead-time between passage of the core legislation in 2009, and the new regime coming into operation in early 2012.

9.17 Despite these efforts, and despite the fact that the PPSA regime has now been operational for a fair period of time, there is anecdotal evidence to suggest that some groups dealing with the registered trademark system are still not fully aware of the impact of the new regime set up by the PPSA. For such groups, there is considerable scope for confusion as to the role and effect of voluntary registration of a claim to a security interest in the Trade Marks Register. It is possible that some actors will mistakenly assume that recording a claim to a security interest in the Trade Marks Register will provide sufficient protection. In practice, however, this danger will almost certainly be mitigated by the fact that the party taking the security interest will, in most cases, be a large, well-advised financial institution with systems in place to ensure prompt registration on the PPS Register. The more apparent risk is probably the converse situation, that is, where a purchaser of a trademark does not think to look beyond the Trade Marks Register to determine whether the property is encumbered. When weighing this risk, it is important to bear in mind that potential purchasers may be being advised by trademarks attorneys, and the authors can state with some confidence that relatively little has been done to bring the PPSA regime to the attention of this profession. It is also important to bear in mind that it has been claimed that the voluntary system for recording interests on the Trade Marks Register has long been under-utilized.[34] If this is correct, there is a real danger that examination of the Trade Marks Register will not disclose the existence of a security interest. With the

---

34 Swinson, *supra* note 6, at 15.

advent of the PPS Register, it is conceivable that use of the voluntary recording facility will decline still further.

9.18 Developing understanding that the PPS Register is to have primacy in matters relating to security interests over trademarks is unlikely to be assisted by the complex transitional arrangements contained in the PPSA, and the treatment of these in the TMA.[35] As we saw above, the new sections 22(2A) and (4) of the TMA, which limit the operation of sections 22(1) and (3), do not apply to security interests that were in existence before 30 January 2012, that is, to what is defined in the PPSA as 'transitional security interests'. This appears to mean that a record of a claim to a pre-PPSA security interest in the Trade Marks Register will be necessary to protect a secured party. If a claim to such a security interest is not recorded, section 22(1) of the TMA will mean that assignees without actual knowledge of the security interest will take the mark unencumbered. From a casual examination of the PPSA, it would be tempting to conclude that this requirement only lasted for the duration of the two-year transitional period set out in section 322(2).[36] However, this is not the case. There is nothing in the PPSA to suggest that a 'transitional security interest' ever changes into a non-transitional one.[37] This means that even if a secured party subsequently registers its transitional security interest in the PPS Register, the new sub-sections of section 22 of the TMA never bite. To be clear, this means that a person who registers a transitional security interest in the PPS Register, but who never has its interest recorded in the Trade Marks Register, will remain vulnerable to a third party protected by section 22(1) of the TMA.[38] If the foregoing were not complex enough, it seems that in order for a secured party to be properly protected in relation to its transitional security interest now that the two-year transitional period has expired, it will also be necessary to register on the PPS Register. As has just been seen, the record of the claim in the Trade Marks Register is necessary to protect against a party falling under section 22(1) of the TMA. Registration on the PPS Register is necessary to protect secured parties against persons claiming the benefit of section 43(1) of the PPSA.

---

35   The complexity of the transitional provisions of the PPSA is an issue that has caused concern since the first drafts of the legislation were released for public comment. *See, e.g.*, DLA Phillips Fox, Submission No 13 to Senate Standing Committee on Legal and Constitutional Affairs, Parliament of Australia, *Inquiry into the Personal Property Securities Bill 2009*, 31 July 2009, 6 (the transitional provisions are 'overly complex and difficult to understand').
36   To be strictly accurate the transition period ended on 31 January 2014: PPSA, s 322(2)(f).
37   Rather, the focus is on requiring transitional security interests to be 're-perfected' to gain protection under the PPSA beyond the transitional period: PPSA, s 322(2).
38   To elaborate further, this consequence flows from the fact that the PPSA is purely negative in this context. Section 43(1) states that a purchaser is not bound by an unperfected security interest. At no point does the PPSA say that a purchaser *is* bound by a perfected security interest.

D. TENSIONS BETWEEN THE TRADEMARK AND PPSA SYSTEMS

9.19 If the complex transitional provisions mean that it will be many years before the PPS Register provides a 'one-stop shop' for those seeking to protect their security interests from third party claimants, there are other issues that will also complicate the relationship between the two registration systems. For instance, it seems surprising and unnecessary that PPS registrations of security interests, over registered trademarks, can only be of limited duration. As has been seen, the PPS registration for security interests over personal property identified by serial number is for a maximum of seven years. This period is entirely divorced from any of the timeframes under the TMA, where registration lasts for a renewable period of ten years,[39] and where records of claims to security interests have no fixed duration.

9.20 The obvious response to the issues we have identified is that no new system is perfect. Some parties will always remain ignorant of the law's requirements, and any reform as fundamental as the PPSA is always going to be accompanied by both complicated transitional provisions and by transitional costs as actors become accustomed to the demands of the new legal regime. It is not difficult to identify other parties that are likely to be caught out by the new system. For example, it seems inevitable that there will be traders that are accustomed to supplying goods in reliance on retention of title clauses who will be unaware that they now need to register their interests in order for them to be perfected. However, it can be argued that there is something special about forms of intellectual property that are built around registration.

9.21 Intellectual property registers are generally held out as having, and are understood to have, a privileged informational function. That is, they create a particular mindset amongst users who can be forgiven for not appreciating that such registers are not the sole repositories of information about the property in question. In this regard, it is noteworthy that some reform bodies have been attracted to the idea that security interests over registered intellectual property rights should not be treated like security interests over other forms of personal property, and have taken the view that registration on the specialized intellectual property register, rather than on a general personal property securities register, is to be preferred.[40] This is also an approach that

---

39 TMA, *supra* note 3, ss 72(3), 75.
40 United Nations Commission on International Trade Law, *UNCITRAL Legislative Guide on Secured Transactions*, Annex I, Recommendation 38(a) (2007), *available 15 September 2015 at* www.uncitral.org/pdf/english/texts/security-lg/e/09-82670_Ebook-Guide_09-04-10English.pdf ('[t]he law should provide that a security right in a movable asset that is subject to registration in a specialized registry ... may be made effective against third parties by ... [r]egistration in the specialized registry'). *See also* Law Commission, *Company Security Interests: A Consultative Report*, Consultation Paper No 176, [2.20], [2.48], [3.293], [3.337]–[3.342] (2004), *available 15 September 2015 at* http://www.lawcom.gov.uk/wp-content/uploads/2015/03/cp176_Company_Security_Interests_Consultative_Report.pdf (recommending that security interests over registered intellectual

attracted support from some interested parties during the passage of the PPSA through Parliament.[41] The logic underpinning this option is straightforward: the specialized register is where some parties will inevitably look to see if the property is encumbered.

9.22 Recommendations to treat registered intellectual property apart have proven controversial,[42] and we are not suggesting that Australia should go down this path in relation to securities over registered trademarks. On the contrary, we would emphasize that such an approach would create informational gaps, and risks of its own: some parties that become accustomed to dealing with the PPSA would very likely be confused by a system that creates a carve-out for registered trademarks. Rather, the point we are trying to make is that tension between the registered trademark and PPS systems is inevitable, and this is heightened by the advantages that will continue to flow to secured parties from recording their interests in the Trade Marks Register.

2. Ongoing role of recording claims in the Trade Marks Register

9.23 Turning to our second broad theme, there are a number of reasons why newly secured parties (that is, those with a new rather than transitional security interest) would want to have their claims recorded in the Trade Marks Register. By so doing, such parties will receive valuable information from the Registrar of Trade Marks in certain circumstances. In particular, under the TMA, recording of a security interest entitles the secured party to receive notice from the Registrar before the Registrar takes further action in relation to the mark. Specifically, the Registrar must give such notice before:

- cancelling the registration of a mark on the request of the registered owner;[43]

---

property be excluded from the company charges registration scheme); Law Commission, *Company Security Interests*, Report No 296, [3.39]–[3.41], [3.233]–[3.235] (2005), available 15 September 2015 at http://www.lawcom.gov.uk/wp-content/uploads/2015/03/lc296_Company_Security_Interests.pdf (acknowledging public concerns about its earlier recommendations and instead suggesting that security interests over intellectual property should remain registrable in both the companies and intellectual property registers, but that the priority rules under the latter register should take precedence over those under the former).

41 *See* Independent Film & Television Alliance, Submission No 25 to Senate Standing Committee on Legal and Constitutional Affairs, Parliament of Australia, *Inquiry into the Personal Property Securities Bill 2009*, 10 August 2009, 10.

42 Iwan Davies, *Secured Financing of Intellectual Property Assets and the Reform of English Personal Property Security Law*, 26 OXFORD JOURNAL OF LEGAL STUDIES 559, 582 (2006) (considering that a carve-out of intellectual property would be 'antithetical to the purpose of a modern personal property security regime where the focus is to harmonise and streamline transactions involving security over personalty').

43 TMA, s 84(2).

D. TENSIONS BETWEEN THE TRADEMARK AND PPSA SYSTEMS

- entering the particulars of an assignment of a registered mark on the Register and registering the assignee as the new owner of the mark;[44] or
- revoking the registration of a mark.[45]

In the first two cases, the Registrar can only act two months after giving the notice.[46] During this time the secured party can object to the Registrar's proposed course of action, and would have an opportunity to seek injunctive relief.[47] In the third case, the secured party also has the opportunity of being heard before the Registrar,[48] and has the right to appeal a decision to revoke the registration to the Federal Court or the Federal Circuit Court.[49] Since revocation invariably occurs following a third-party complaint to the Registrar that a mark has been registered in error, this final provision in effect gives a secured party the right to intervene in trademark disputes. Something similar can be seen in relation to proceedings before the Registrar to remove a mark from the Register on the grounds of non-use. The Registrar is required to give a copy of the removal application to 'each person who, in the Registrar's opinion, should receive one'.[50] The Trade Marks Office has interpreted this to mean that secured parties with claims recorded in the Register are to be given such notice.[51] Again, this gives such parties an opportunity to be heard or intervene in trademark proceedings.

9.24 To emphasize, there has been no amendment to the TMA to entitle secured parties that have registered their security interests over registered trademarks in the PPS Register to the same benefits as those outlined above. The Registrar of Trade Marks will never be obliged to examine the PPS Register before taking action in relation to a registered mark, and it seems that there are no plans for the Trade Marks Office to take it upon itself to check the PPS Register.

3. Problems caused when title in property passes to the secured party

9.25 The final issue that needs to be explored in this Section relates to whether the PPSA will operate as intended where the title to a mark has been transferred

---

44 TMA, s 111.
45 TMA, s 84A(4).
46 Respectively, Trade Marks Regulations 1995 (Cth) (TMR), regs 8.1, 10.5.
47 TMR, regs 8.1(3)(b), 10.4(1)(b), 10.4(4), 10.5.
48 TMA, s 84A(5). *See, e.g.,* Re Summit (2010) 90 IPR 404.
49 TMA, s 84D.
50 TMA, s 95(1); TMR, reg 9.6.
51 IP Australia, *Trade Marks Office Manual of Practice and Procedure*, pt 44.2 (last updated 15 May 2015), available 15 September 2015 at www.ipaustralia.gov.au/pdfs/trademarkmanual/trade_marks_examiners_manual.htm.

to a secured party, who appears on the Trade Marks Register as the owner of the mark. To reiterate, the PPSA seeks to render the question of who has title to the property irrelevant to the determination of whether an interest is enforceable against a third party – the PPSA looks to the function of the transaction and not its form. As a consequence, it should, for example, make no difference whether a security interest over a trademark is secured by way of a legal or an equitable mortgage. In either case, the question of whether the third party is bound should depend solely on whether the interest has been perfected by registration on the PPS Register. However, in cases where the secured party has taken title to the mark, such as by way of a legal mortgage, it is unclear that the PPSA can, in fact, function as intended. More specifically, it can be doubted whether section 43(1) of the PPSA can operate so as to allow the purchaser of a registered trademark claiming through the mortgagor to take it free from the interests of a secured party that has taken title to the mark but has not registered its interest in the PPS Register.

9.26 We should acknowledge two points about our analysis of this issue. First, we accept that, in practical terms, it is likely to be rare for a legal mortgage to be granted over a registered trademark. This is because a financier is unlikely to want to undertake the responsibility, as owner of the mark, for ensuring that the mark remains used under its control to prevent the mark from being vulnerable to removal on the grounds of three years of non-use.[52] Nevertheless, such dealing with a registered mark remains a possibility (particularly where short-term financing is contemplated, such that the non-use issue would not arise). Secondly, it might seem far-fetched to explore a situation where a purchaser seeks to acquire the trademark from a party (the mortgagor), whose name would not be on the Trade Marks Register as the owner of the mark. However, given the confusion that abounds as to the various systems governing trade names, it is not too much of a stretch to imagine a business sale agreement that purports to transfer all of the assets of a business (both tangible and intangible) being concluded without the purchaser ever consulting the Trade Marks Register. Indeed far from being a purely hypothetical scenario, one of the authors has direct experience of a dispute (albeit not one involving a security interest) arising from precisely this scenario. Moreover, irrespective of the probability of this situation arising, it is in any event worth considering because of what it tells us about the limits of the PPSA regime.

9.27 In order for an assignment of a registered trademark to take effect, a record of the assignment must be entered in the Trade Marks Register.[53] It is this

---

52 *See also* Lipton, *supra* note 1, at 163–4.
53 TMA, s 109(1).

D. TENSIONS BETWEEN THE TRADEMARK AND PPSA SYSTEMS

requirement that has the capacity to disrupt the operation of the PPSA, since it is not clear how a purchaser seeking to claim the benefit of section 43(1) of the PPSA in the circumstances described above could cause a change in ownership to be recorded, and hence to take effect. Assignees are entitled to apply to the Registrar of Trade Marks for a record of the assignment to be entered in the Register – the current owner does not necessarily have to initiate such a request.[54] However, any application must be accompanied by 'a document that establishes the title to a trademark of the assignee'.[55] It is difficult to see how a purchaser of a trademark claiming through the mortgagor could meet this requirement in a case where the security interest takes the form of a legal mortgage. In such a case, title to the mark would vest in the mortgagee, who would not be party to the agreement to transfer ownership. Any documentation evidencing the agreement would thus fail to establish the assignee's title to the mark, and the Trade Marks Office would refuse to transfer ownership.[56] Consequently, in order to secure its claim, the assignee would need to seek the assistance of a court. Most obviously, the assignee might seek rectification of the Register by way of an order of a prescribed court.[57] However, it is doubtful that an application for rectification could succeed.

9.28 The most significant hurdle that the assignee would face in seeking an order for rectification would be in demonstrating that any of the grounds on which rectification can be ordered apply. More specifically, although rectification can be ordered on a considerable number of grounds, as set out in sections 85–88 of the TMA, most of these grounds would be of no assistance to our hypothetical assignee. Indeed, the only provision that is even arguably relevant is section 85, which allows a prescribed court to make an order for rectification with a view to 'correcting any error in an entry in the Register'.[58] Details of ownership unquestionably constitute an entry in the Register, and hence there can be no doubt that section 85 can be used in some circumstances to force a change in ownership. What is much less clear, however, is whether it can be said that a failure to transfer title to a purchaser of a mark claiming the benefit of section 43(1) of the PPSA constitutes an 'error' in an entry in the Register that section 85 of the TMA can be used to correct. In our view, this language is inapt to cover the situation with which we are concerned. It needs to be borne

---

54   TMA, s 109(1)(b).
55   TMR, *supra* note 46, reg 10.1(a).
56   *See* further IP Australia, *Trade Marks Manual*, pt 43.3.2 (last updated 15 May 2015). For discussion of the role of the Registrar in the context of ss 109–10 of the TMA, *see* Mediaquest Communications LLC v. Registrar of Trade Marks (2012) 205 FCR 205.
57   For prescribed courts, *see* TMA, s 190.
58   TMA, s 85(b).

in mind that an order for rectification would be being sought not because of some defect in how the details of ownership were entered in the Register, but rather because the assignee would be seeking the benefit of provisions found in an entirely different Act of Parliament. To characterize the continued ownership of the mortgagee as being a product of an 'error' would be a significant stretch. That the language of an 'error in an entry in the Register' is not to be construed so broadly is reinforced when one turns to look at section 88 of the TMA. This provision allows the court to make an order for rectification by, *inter alia*, 'amending an entry wrongly made … on the Register'.[59] The TMA is clear that an application to amend an entry wrongly made can only be based on a small number of highly circumscribed grounds, for example, where an entry was made as a result of fraud, false suggestion, or misrepresentation.[60] By drawing a distinction between rectification of 'entries wrongly made' (tightly regulated by section 88) and rectification of 'errors in an entry' (dealt with in general terms by section 85), Parliament must have intended that the latter be read narrowly.[61] Thus, when read in context, we do not believe that section 85 could be of assistance to our hypothetical assignee.[62]

9.29 Moreover, even if the above conclusion is incorrect, there are two further barriers to an assignee seeking to invoke section 85. First, it should be noted that an application for rectification can only be brought by a person who has the requisite standing – such an application can only be made by an 'aggrieved person'. In our view, it is perfectly possible that a prescribed court might decline to treat an assignee as falling within this category. Admittedly, the High Court of Australia has indicated that this standing requirement in the TMA should be interpreted liberally.[63] However, this view was expressed in the context of a dispute between rival traders. In our view, a lower court would still be entitled to take a circumspect view of when a would-be purchaser of a mark falls within the rubric of an 'aggrieved person'. In particular, it would have to be remembered that the assignee's case for being regarded as 'aggrieved' would be undermined either (depending on the facts) by its own failure to consult the Trade Marks Register before taking an assignment, or by its deliberate decision to ignore the interests of the mortgagee and to seek to

---

59 TMA, s 88(1)(b).
60 TMA, s 88(2).
61 See further Burrell & Handler, *supra* note 11, at 259–60, on the limited role that s 85(b) ought to play in the TMA as a whole in light of the Full Federal Court's decision in Woolworths Ltd v. BP Plc (2006) 150 FCR 134.
62 We maintain this view notwithstanding that in the context of the PPS Register the Federal Court has been prepared to adopt a broad reading of the Registrar of Personal Property Securities' power to correct 'errors': *see* SFS Projects Australia Pty Ltd v. Registrar of Personal Property Securities (2014) 226 FCR 188.
63 Health World Ltd v. Shin-Sun Australia Pty Ltd (2010) 240 CLR 590, 597–9 [22]–[30] (French CJ, Gummow, Heydon and Bell JJ), 607 [54] (Crennan J).

rely on section 43(1) of the PPSA. Such a scenario is far removed from the type of case that motivated the High Court to insist that the standing requirement should be interpreted liberally. Second, it might be noted that an order for rectification under section 85 of the TMA is always discretionary. Given that an assignee with actual or constructive knowledge of the mortgagee's interest is unlikely to cut a sympathetic figure, it is perfectly conceivable that a court might refuse to order rectification even if it were otherwise convinced that section 85 might apply.

9.30 For the reasons canvassed above, we do not believe that an assignee of a mark over which an unperfected legal mortgage had been granted could obtain an amendment to the Trade Marks Register by means of the statutory rectification procedure. As an alternative, our hypothetical assignee might look to general equitable principles for assistance. The scenario with which we are concerned is somewhat different from the traditional type of case in which transferees have looked to equity for assistance in circumstances where there has been a failure to comply with legal formalities. Nevertheless, it would be possible to develop an argument along the following lines: the effect of section 43(1) of the PPSA is that anyone who purchases from a mortgagor a trademark over which an unperfected security interest has been granted takes the mark free from the mortgagee's interest. As such, the purchaser must be understood to be the absolute beneficial owner of the trademark, who is entitled to perfect its interest by requiring the mortgagee to effect a transfer in favour of the purchaser.

9.31 There can be no question that in certain circumstances a purchaser of a mark would be entitled to look to equity for assistance. It would have to be the case, for example, that a purchaser of a mark from its legal owner would be entitled to insist that the legal owner complete the formalities necessary to transfer legal title. This could only be done by means of a mandatory injunction – the statutory rectification provisions would not offer the purchaser any assistance in this scenario either. Consequently, general equitable principles might appear to offer considerable promise for our hypothetical assignee. However, to a far greater degree than other potential purchasers, our hypothetical assignee might face significant obstacles in securing equitable relief. The principal problem is that our hypothetical assignee might well not come to equity with clean hands – it is likely that the assignee will be found to have at least constructive notice of the mortgagee's interest, not least because of the record of the mortgagee's title in the Trade Marks Register. Moreover, at the very least, it is safe to say that in every case there would be a challenge to the assignee's right to seek equitable relief, and this will entail an analysis of the

Chapter 9 REGISTERING SECURITY INTERESTS OVER TRADEMARKS IN AUSTRALIA

assignee's state of mind – precisely the type of inquiry that the PPSA was designed to avoid.

E. CONCLUSIONS AND OPTIONS FOR REFORM

9.32 In the previous Section, we identified a number of areas where the PPSA will not work as intended. Some of these problems do not lend themselves to an obvious solution. A degree of confusion as to how the systems interoperate is inevitable, and although more could be done, for example, to reach out to trademarks attorneys, there is no simple or immediate solution to the problems that flow from an absence of (or at least delay in) public understanding of how a new legal regime is to operate. Other problems could be addressed more directly, but only by means of legislative intervention. This is true, for example, of the failure of the new regime to cope as intended with legal mortgages. It is also true of the requirement for double registration in the case of 'transitional security interests'.

9.33 To our mind, what is most interesting, however, is that in some cases the problems we have identified could be addressed purely through administrative action. In particular, there would seem to be scope to confer the informational advantages that flow from recording a claim to an interest in the Trade Marks Register on secured parties who have relied on the PPSA regime alone. This is most obviously true in the case of proceedings for the removal of a mark from the Register on the grounds of non-use. It will be recalled that one of the advantages that flows from recording a claim to an interest in the Trade Marks Register is that in the event that removal proceedings for non-use are commenced the party with the recorded interest will be given notice of the application for removal. Significantly, this result flows from the interpretation that the Trade Marks Office has placed on the requirement to give a copy of the application 'to each person who, in the Registrar's opinion, should receive one'.[64] What is interesting is that this language sets up a broad permissive power, and there can be no question that the Trade Marks Office would be within its rights to conduct a search of the PPS Register and to provide notice to secured parties accordingly. Somewhat more controversially, we would also suggest that the other notice requirements in the TMA that we discussed in the same Section could be read to achieve much the same end. In particular, we do not see any reason why the requirement in the legislation to give notice to parties with a recorded interest (for example, before revoking a registration)

---

[64] TMA, *supra* note 3, s 95(1); TMR, *supra* note 46, reg 9.6.

should be read as excluding the possibility of providing notice to other parties on a voluntary basis.

More generally, there is no reason why other informational links could not be created between the two systems through purely administrative action. For example, anyone seeking to record a claim to an interest in a mark recorded in the Trade Marks Register could be warned that in the case of a 'PPSA security interest', such an interest also needs to be perfected through registration on the PPS Register. In May 2015, the *Trade Marks Office Manual of Practice and Procedure* was amended to contain the following short statement in part 44.1: **9.34**

> All claimed interests in a trade mark should be recorded on the national Personal Property Securities Register (PPS Register), as the right of the registered owner to deal with the trade mark is limited only by those claimed interests that have been recorded on the PPS Register. Registration is voluntary and legal advice may be required on whether a claimant should register their interest on the PPS Register.
>
> Existing security interests recorded on the Trade Marks Register will remain but are of no legal effect. Secured parties can still record their interests in or rights in respect of a trade mark on the Register if those claimants wish to receive certain notifications under the *Trade Marks Act 1995*.

While we welcome the addition of information about the intersection of the registered trademarks and PPS systems, there are some problems with the wording of this statement, most notably in that it does not adequately deal with the ongoing position of 'transitional security interests', discussed above. Further, the change to the Manual does not appear to have been accompanied by a change in Office practice, whereby the party claiming an interest in the mark is informed individually, at the time of making the claim, of the separate PPS regime. As a separate matter, we would argue that the PPS Registrar could send the secured party a statement to the effect that it should also consider recording its interest in the Trade Marks Register as this will secure additional benefits in certain circumstances. The two registries might also encourage secured parties to describe their security interests in the same terms, to ensure maximum consistency between the information on the two Registers. Further, the PPS Registrar might seek to ensure that in fulfilling its obligation under section 156 of the PPSA to provide a 'verification statement' to a secured party, it crosschecks the Trade Marks Register to determine the accuracy of the information provided to it in the financing statement.[65]

---

[65] Section 155(a) of the PPSA, *supra* note 5, provides that the 'verification statement' need only verify 'the registration of a financing statement', which would not prevent the PPS Registrar from taking further, straightforward administrative steps to verify the accuracy of information in the financing statement.

Chapter 9 REGISTERING SECURITY INTERESTS OVER TRADEMARKS IN AUSTRALIA

9.35 It might reasonably be assumed that administrative reforms that could make the PPSA regime work more effectively would be readily adopted. We have been arguing for the creation of such linkages for several years,[66] but except for the minor change to part 44.1 of the *Trade Marks Office Manual of Practice and Procedure*, they remain to be created. This is not, we would hasten to add, because of any articulated policy position; rather, the problems we have identified appear not to have been acknowledged.

9.36 In this respect it is also notable that the Trade Marks Office historically made no attempt to contact parties who had registered a change over a trademark on the Australian Register of Company Charges. In a similar vein, it should be noted that proposals to create linkages between the registered trademark system and business name registers have been left to gather dust.[67] This is despite the fact that there is good evidence to suggest that many small and medium sized enterprises erroneously assume that registration of a business name both gives them positive rights over the name in question, and insulates them from a claim for trademark infringement. We should also mention the resistance the Trade Marks Office has shown to judicial demands that it take a broad range of legal questions into account when determining whether use of a mark 'would be contrary to law' for the purposes of section 42(b) of the TMA. The Office has consistently construed the leading decision of the Federal Court[68] as narrowly as possible, seemingly out of a desire to minimize the need for Office staff to take cognisance of issues other than those arising through direct application of the TMA and TMR. The introduction in 2006 of new revocation powers to allow a registered trademark to be removed from the Register through purely administrative action appears to have been similarly motivated by a desire to manage and maintain an operationally closed system. Registration 'errors' can now be corrected through internal office action (so long as they are discovered within 12 months of the trademark having been entered on the Register),[69] thereby reducing considerably the Registrar's reliance on the possibility of bringing rectification proceedings in the Federal Court under part 8 division 2 of the TMA.

---

66   *See* Robert Burrell & Michael Handler, *The PPSA and Registered Trade Marks: When Bureaucratic Systems Collide*, 34 UNSW LAW JOURNAL 600 (2011).
67   *Cf.* Advisory Council on Intellectual Property, *A Review of the Relationship between Trade Marks and Business Names, Company Names and Domain Names* (2006).
68   Namely, Advantage Rent-A-Car Inc v. Advantage Car Rental Pty Ltd (2001) 52 IPR 24.
69   TMA, *supra* note 3, s 84A (as introduced by the Intellectual Property Laws Amendment Act 2006 (Cth), sch 1 item 7).

E. CONCLUSIONS AND OPTIONS FOR REFORM

Consequently, if history is any guide, the matters we have identified seem very unlikely to be addressed through administrative action. Although seemingly innocuous, the bureaucracy is unlikely to embrace the necessary changes, despite the clear benefits that would result. **9.37**

10

THE INTERSECTION OF TRADEMARKS, LICENSES AND BANKRUPTCY: ENDING UNCERTAINTIES IN THE LAW

Xuan-Thao Nguyen[*]

A.	INTRODUCTION	10.01	3. Adding uncertainties: In re *Interstate Bakeries* and In re *Lakewood* (Sunbeam Prods., Inc. v. Chicago Am. Mfg, LLC)	10.57
B.	TRADEMARK IN ORDINARY LICENSES	10.12		
C.	TRADEMARKS IN CORPORATE TRANSACTIONS	10.18	E. ENDING THE UNCERTAINTIES	10.68
	1. *Chain v. Tropodyne*: sale of assets and trademark use within the acquired division	10.21	1. Looking beyond form, facing the substance	10.68
			2. Sales, not licenses	10.75
	2. *Seattle Brewing & Malting Co. v. Commissioner*: sale of assets and trademark use restricted to field of use and geographical territory	10.24	3. Concurrent use – assignment of trademark rights in different fields of use	10.79
			(a) Concurrent use doctrine	10.80
			(b) Co-existence separately	10.91
D.	CORPORATE DIVISION SALE OF ASSETS AND TRADEMARK USE IN IN RE *EXIDE TECHNOLOGIES*	10.33	(c) Imperfect coexistence, but do not touch the license	10.94
	1. In re *Exide Technologies*	10.34		
	2. Causing uncertainties	10.44	F. CONCLUSION	10.95

A. INTRODUCTION

10.01 Apple Corps, the record label founded by the Beatles in London, brought an action against Apple Inc., the Silicon Valley-based company over the trademark agreement entered by the parties back in 1991. Apple Inc. paid $26 million to Apple Corps for the coexistence right to use the Apple trademark. The agreement provided that Apple Inc. had the exclusive right to use the Apple trademark in connection with electronic goods, computer software, data processing, and data transmission services, while Apple Corps had the exclusive right to use the Apple trademark 'on or in connection with any current or future creative work whose principle content was music and/or musical

---

[*] Gerald R. Bepko Chair in Law, Director of the Center for Intellectual Property and Innovation, Indiana University McKinney School of Law. This chapter is based on *Selling It First, Stealing It Later: The Trouble with Trademarks in Corporate Transactions in Bankruptcy*, 44 GONZ. L.REV. 1 (2009).

A. INTRODUCTION

performances, regardless of the means by which those works were recorded, or communicated, whether tangible or intangible'. Both companies coexisted in their distinct fields of use, and each built goodwill in the trademark within their markets.

As technologies changed in the digital music business, the two companies' fields of use grew close to each other's market, although they did not foresee such a possibility at the time they executed the coexistence agreement. Apple Inc. developed their new products, iPod and iTunes software and music, resulting in litigation brought by Apple Corps for breach of the coexistence agreement. In the litigation, Apple Inc. prevailed, as there was no consumer confusion and no evidence to support the breach argument. The parties settled the case by entering into a new agreement wherein Apple, Inc. became the new owner of all trademarks related to 'Apple', and agreed that it would license the trademark back to Apple Corps for certain fields of use.[1] The path taken by the two parties would be better for Apple, Inc., but not Apple Corps, in light of the law intersecting trademark licenses and bankruptcy. Apple Corps, and many other existing trademark licensees, may not have known that they had just entered into a situation filled with uncertainty. **10.02**

This chapter will identify and discuss the uncertainty. **10.03**

Lawyers for the trademark licensee may not be aware about the intersection of trademarks and bankruptcy. They probably do not foresee that the licensor may be in bankruptcy in the future and that the licensee's trademark right will be in peril. When that happens, it would be too late for the licensee of the trademark to have protected itself against the loss of its rights. **10.04**

Consider this hypothetical: Twenty years ago, Alibaba, wishing to concentrate on its software business, decided to sell off its struggling map-making division. The sale of the corporate division included physical and intangible assets, facility and personnel. Alibaba found a willing purchaser (Yahoo@NewCo) for the division at a negotiated price. Alibaba and NewCo entered into an asset sale and purchase agreement, together with a perpetual, exclusive, royalty-free trademark license agreement. The parties bargained for and agreed that Alibaba would continue to use the trademark 'Mapquest' in business outside the division, and NewCo has the right to use the trademark 'Mapquest' in connection with the map products and services offered by the division. NewCo began the operation of the division after the acquisition. Things had **10.05**

---

1 Laurie J. Flynn, *After Long Dispute, Two Apples Work It Out*, NYT, 6 February 2007.

Chapter 10 THE INTERSECTION OF TRADEMARKS, LICENSES AND BANKRUPTCY

been going very well for NewCo; it had expanded into the digital map world with many new 'Mapquest' products, apps, and services.

10.06 Fast-forward 20 years. Alibaba is now going through reorganization under bankruptcy law. Alibaba seeks to terminate the exclusive trademark right used by NewCo in the map sector. Alibaba will not compensate NewCo for the trademark right to use. The reversion of the exclusive right to use the trademark 'Mapquest' in the map sector was never anticipated by either Alibaba or NewCo at the time of the sale and purchase of the corporate division 20 years ago. NewCo's executives are furious as they are facing a business and legal nightmare. How can NewCo proceed with its business without the trademark right that it has been using to market and sell products for the last 20 years? How can it be that the 'perpetual and exclusive' right to use the trademark in connection with the marketing and sales of map products and services now has no meaning? NewCo's bargained-for right to use the trademark faces elimination, even though it was never in breach of the trademark agreement.

10.07 Should Alibaba be allowed to grant the right to use the trademark 'perpetual[ly] and exclusive[ly]' with the sale of the map division and seize it back for free, 20 years later?

10.08 This chapter is part of an ongoing and broader inquiry into the intersection of trademark, contract, and bankruptcy laws in the United States. This chapter proceeds as follows. Section B describes trademark license arrangements that are typically utilized by the trademark owner to distribute and sell their products in the marketplace and not to sell an entire business unit to a purchaser. This type of trademark license arrangement is different from the uncommon transactions involving, in essence, a sale of trademark rights that accompany the sale of a corporate division to an unrelated company, as discussed in Section C. In this more uncommon transaction, the seller wants to sever ties with a particular corporate division while retaining the other divisions of the business. The seller sells the division to a purchaser, together with the grant of a perpetual, exclusive, and royalty-free right to use the trademark in the operation of the corporate division.

10.09 Section D examines the bankruptcy court decision, In re *Exide Technologies*,[2] where the transaction involving trademark rights, properly understood, falls within the type identified in Section B: the corporate sale of a business

---

2   In re Exide Techs., 340 B.R. 222 (Bankr. D. Del. 2006). This decision was later vacated in In re Exide Techs, 607 F.3d 957 (3rd Cir. 2010).

division together with the grant of right to use the trademark perpetually, exclusively, and without further payment beyond the lump-sum purchase price of the corporate business division. That trademark transaction should have been held to be a sale, not as a typical license granting merely the right to use. The Exide Technologies decision causes much uncertainty as potential purchasers may not be aware at the time of the acquisition that it may lose the perpetual and exclusive right to use the trademark in connection with the purchase of the corporate division. Why should a purchaser pay a large sum for all the assets, tangible and intangible, including the trademark right that it will not have in the future? Why should a purchaser pay for a property right and add value through extensive advertising to create one of the best brands, if it will eventually be taken away without any compensation?

10.10 Section E argues that this uncertainty must end, calling on the courts to recognize the reality and the substance of the corporate sale transactions of assets. If a grant of a perpetual, exclusive, and royalty-free trademark right is an outright sale of the right to the trademark, the purchaser can continue to operate the corporate division after the acquisition. This chapter argues that, if courts continue to adopt the traditional view espoused by the bankruptcy court in In re *Exide Technologies*, the purchaser will have no other option to ensure certainty that its purchased business will not be destroyed other than to negotiate for a concurrent use of the same trademark with the seller by means of an assignment of the trademark right in specified fields of use. The trademark concurrent use doctrine allows two or more owners of the same trademark to operate in distinct territories. The doctrine has its drawbacks as two owners attempt to coexist, but allows the purchaser to keep the trademark out of the debtor seller's bankrupt estate and alleviate the deadly reversion of the trademark right.

10.11 This chapter concludes that the intersection of trademark and bankruptcy law has brought more uncertainty and unpredictability to the corporate sales of assets transactions. The potential damages suffered by the purchaser who is also a non-debtor licensee serve as a reminder of a costly result of the uncertainty and unpredictability.

B. TRADEMARK IN ORDINARY LICENSES

10.12 The owner of trademarks can exploit the commercial power of the trademarks by licensing the trademarks to others. A trademark license is generally a contractual agreement between the trademark holder and a third party to use the trademark in connection with certain goods or services, and within a certain territory. The licensee enjoys the right to use the trademark, while the owner continues to possess the title to and ownership of the trademark.

10.13 A trademark license agreement can be oral, but most are in writing. A typical trademark license agreement contains provisions relating to the scope of the grant, quality control, duration of the license, royalty provision, best efforts of the licensee, registration, and termination. Trademark license agreements specify the scope of the grant so the parties know what the licensor is granting and what the licensee will receive as to the trademarks – the exclusivity of the right to use them, plus fields of use and territory.

10.14 Trademark license agreements often include a quality control provision to maintain the quality of the products or services bearing the licensed trademark. If the licensor fails to exercise quality control, the license arrangement may be viewed as 'naked' licensing, and the licensor may face the risk of losing the trademark. The trend in trademark licensing today with respect to quality control has changed as courts have adopted a flexible approach that allows licensors to rely on the reputation and expertise of the licensees for the quality control of the trademarked products; the licensor is no longer directly involved in quality control.

10.15 Trademark licensors want to be compensated for the use of trademarks pursuant to the license arrangement. Trademark license agreements include royalty provisions detailing the methods of calculation and payment schedules. Running royalty payments are dependent on the volume of sales, net sales, distribution, or production. Licensees generally prefer the running royalty payments because they want to minimize the exposure of paying the licensor a large sum in advance. From the licensor's perspective, including a minimum royalty payment plan is a necessary protection. Essentially, the licensor forces the licensee to use its best efforts and diligently exploit the licensee's rights under the license agreement by requiring that the licensee pay a minimum fixed amount regardless of the volume of sales, production, or distribution of the trademarked products. Additionally, the licensor will monitor and audit royalty payments, and to that end, the agreement typically includes provisions relating to record keeping, reporting, and audits.

10.16 Obviously, if the licensee fails to pay the required royalties, it is in breach of the license agreement. Generally, a trademark license agreement will allow for a cure period. If a breach is not timely cured, the license agreement is subject to termination. The termination provision may include a list of events deemed terminable. When the licensee fails to perform its obligations, such as lack of adherence to the quality control provision or breach of certain material provisions, it triggers the termination provision.

10.17 In summary, the devices used by trademark owners in their efforts to exploit their trademarks is the license or permission to third parties to limited use of the trademarks for a specific duration. The license agreement contains many provisions to protect the licensors as the owners of the trademark with a stake in the continued viability of the mark.

C. TRADEMARKS IN CORPORATE TRANSACTIONS

10.18 When a company, owning many divisions of its growing, expansive business under common trademarks or house marks, decides to unload a division of its business, it must determine how to structure the transaction to include the intangible assets such as the trademarks. Generally, a potential purchaser of the division needs to acquire the perpetual and exclusive right to use the existing trademarks in the operation of the purchased division. This is so the purchaser can market, distribute, and sell products and services while the seller company maintains its ownership in the trademarks for the continuation of the remaining divisions of its business. The company has several options to structure the transaction, depending on the circumstances. For example, the company may want to provide the purchaser with the right to use the trademark only within the division. Accordingly, the company will insist on a license agreement with field of use restriction. In some cases, where the trademarked products are confined within a particular territory, the company may furnish the purchaser the right to use the trademark in the specified territory. That means, in addition to the Asset and Purchase Agreement, the company will grant a license with a territorial restriction to the purchaser. Moreover, the company may reserve the right to use the trademark within the restricted territory on products or services outside of the field of use restriction.

10.19 The potential purchaser, contemplating the acquisition, will plan to pay either a lump sum or a combination of a lump sum and contingent payments to acquire the assets of the corporate division from the company seller. Spending significant financial resources to acquire the division, the purchaser obviously believes that the acquisition is a good business decision and that it will turn the division into a profitable enterprise, yielding a nice return on its investment. To achieve those goals, the purchaser will negotiate for a price that will give it the right to the physical assets, manufacturing facility, key personnel, and intangible assets, including the perpetual, exclusive trademark right to continue the operation of the division.

10.20 Below are illustrative examples from reported cases of corporate sales of assets transactions, together with the right to use trademarks within a field of use and a geographical territory.

1. *Chain v. Tropodyne*: sale of assets and trademark use within the acquired division

10.21 In *Chain v. Tropodyne Corp.*, the Jeffrey Chain division of Dresser Industries was in the business of manufacturing engineering grade chains.[3] In 1985, Dresser Industries sold the Jeffrey Chain division to a purchaser. Under the Asset Purchase Agreement, the purchaser acquired the manufacturing plant and the right to use the name 'Jeffrey Chain' as its corporate name. Pursuant to the ancillary License Agreement, as part of the transaction, Dresser Industries granted the new Jeffrey Chain Company a perpetual, exclusive license to use the 'Jeffrey' and 'J' marks in the sale of non-plastic sewage chains. Dresser Industries reserved 'sole and exclusive ownership' in the trademarks 'Jeffrey' and 'J' in the remainder of its business while it agreed not to use the trademarks contrary to the license terms specified in the License Agreement. After the acquisition, Jeffrey Chain used the 'Jeffrey Chain' name on engineering class chains, which included all types of metallic and plastic chains.[4]

10.22 Seven years later, in 1992, Dresser Industries struggled with its remaining business, spun off its plastic sewage chain division and sold it to Indresco. The sale of the plastic sewage chain division included an assignment of Dresser Industries' ownership interest in the 'Jeffrey' and 'J' trademarks. Three years thereafter, in 1995, Tropodyne acquired Indresco Company. From 1996 to 2004, Jeffrey Chain and Tropodyne engaged in trademark infringement and unfair competition disputes. The Sixth Circuit held that the original transaction between Jeffrey Chain and Dresser Industries gave Jeffrey Chain the exclusive right to use the mark 'Jeffrey' together with the word 'Chain' in the non-plastic chain business. Additionally, the court held that Jeffrey Chain was granted the exclusive right to use 'Jeffrey Chain' as a corporate name, the right to expand its business in the plastic chain business, and the right to use the corporate name in conjunction with the sales of plastic chain.

---

3 Chain v. Tropodyne Corp., 93 Fed. Appx. 880, 881 (6th Cir. 2004).
4 *Id.* at 882

C. TRADEMARKS IN CORPORATE TRANSACTIONS

The *Chain* case demonstrates that, when an entire division of a business is sold, the purchaser acquires the physical assets and the perpetual and exclusive license to use the trademark so it can continue to operate and later expand the products and services as it desires. In fact, the purchaser, Jeffrey Chain, did expand its chain business after the acquisition, and also expanded the use of the trademark on new products. The license in *Chain* is exclusive, which means only the purchaser Jeffrey Chain can use the trademark within the field. Although the seller continued to possess legal ownership of the trademark in the remaining areas of its business, it could not use the trademark in the same field pursuant to the Asset Purchase and License Agreements. Regardless of whether the seller continued to operate its remaining business or sold and assigned all of its rights, including the trademark rights, Jeffrey Chain was the only entity that had the sole right to use the trademark within the acquired division. The seller and its successors had already received the monetary sum for the sale of the assets of the division and could not go back to the purchaser to reclaim the trademark license. Consequently, the seller or its successors were not allowed to compete against Jeffrey Chain in the same market using the same trademark. If it did so, the seller or its successor would face trademark actions brought by Jeffrey Chain.

10.23

2. *Seattle Brewing & Malting Co. v. Commissioner*: sale of assets and trademark use restricted to field of use and geographical territory

In *Seattle Brewing & Malting Co. v. Commissioner*, the Tax Court held that the taxpayer's acquisition of a brewing plant, together with the perpetual, exclusive license to use the trademark for alcoholic beverages within a limited geographical territory, was not a 'license', but a capital asset.[5] Therefore, the cost of the transaction was not deductible from income as a business expense.

10.24

In that case, the taxpayer Century Brewing Association ('taxpayer' or 'Century') was a manufacturer of beer in Seattle, Washington. The Seattle Brewing & Malting Company ('Rainier') was also in the same business in the Seattle area with its corporate headquarters in California. The taxpayer and Rainier entered into an agreement entitled 'Licensing Agreement', wherein Rainier sold its physical plant, property, and equipment located in Seattle, together with the right to use the trademark 'Rainier' in Washington and Alaska, in consideration for payments contingent on either a production basis or a minimum royalty.[6] Pursuant to the Agreement, Rainier agreed that it would not sell or distribute alcoholic beverages in Washington and Alaska. The

10.25

---

5 Seattle Brewing & Malting Co. v. Comm'r, 6 T.C. 856, 873 (1946).
6 *Id.* at 858.

Chapter 10 THE INTERSECTION OF TRADEMARKS, LICENSES AND BANKRUPTCY

parties acknowledged that Rainier was the owner and would continue to have the sole and exclusive right to manufacture and distribute non-alcoholic beverages in the same territory under the same trademark.

10.26 The Agreement contained a provision wherein Rainier agreed to maintain all federal registrations of the trademark. With respect to quality control, Century agreed that it would manufacture alcoholic beverages of the same quality as those manufactured and marketed by Rainier, and that the alcoholic beverages would be produced under the same formulae used and provided by Rainier.[7]

10.27 Although Century acquired the title to the physical plant and real property from Rainier for the brewing business, Rainier demanded, and Century agreed, to provide security for all of its ongoing obligations under the License Agreement. To that end, the Agreement included a provision wherein Century agreed that if it was in default of any of its obligations, the title to the real property would pass to Rainier as liquidated damages.[8]

10.28 Rainier and Century devised an elaborate royalty payment plan dependent on the alcoholic beverage production levels. The parties also included a minimum annual royalty payment fee to ensure that Rainier would continue to receive a minimum sum, even if Century failed to meet its own production and sales. Century agreed to use its best efforts to increase the sales of alcoholic beverages within the territory, and to expend advertising amounts to market the products. In anticipating potential local prohibition laws on the manufacturing of alcohol, the Agreement also contained provisions to address how the minimum royalty payments would be adjusted accordingly.[9]

10.29 In addition, the Agreement contained an option provision. Pursuant to that provision, Century had the right and option to terminate all royalties by paying a sum of $1 million to Rainier after the Agreement had been in force for five years from the original execution date.

10.30 After the acquisition, Century spent large sums on advertising the Rainier trademarked products in the territory. Consequently, Century witnessed an increase in the production and sale of Rainier beer during the five-year period after the acquisition. Century anticipated that the payments at the barrelage rate for the next five years would exceed $1 million, and its board of directors thus decided to exercise the option provided in the License Agreement with

---

7   *Id.* at 859.
8   *Id.* at 860.
9   *Id.* at 859–60.

C. TRADEMARKS IN CORPORATE TRANSACTIONS

Rainier. Century executed a promissory note to pay Rainier the $1 million option price, together with interest. The Tax Court treated the transaction as a sale, and the $1 million price as the cost of acquiring a capital asset. Therefore, the cost was held not deductible from income as a business expense.[10]

10.31 The case above represents another example of a corporate transaction wherein the seller is not operating a very profitable division, and decides to sell the entire division to an unrelated company. The seller wants to continue to use the trademark outside of the specified field of use – alcoholic beverages in this case – for its future business. The seller also wants to limit the use of the trademark to a defined territory. The acquirer desires to obtain the manufacturing plant, real property, and equipment, in addition to the right to use the trademark so it can continue production upon acquisition. The acquirer pays the agreed amount according to the payment plan, provides security for its obligations in the event of default, and uses its best efforts to produce and market the trademarked products. In fact, the acquirer aggressively operates and expands its advertising expenditures and sales of the products after the acquisition. The seller receives what it wants: a monetary sum for its struggling business division, as it keeps its end of the bargain to restrain its trademark use in the specified territory. It continues ownership of the trademark and has the right to use the trademark in other fields of use. It maintains the federal trademark registration, and receives $1 million when the acquirer exercises the option to purchase the business and ceases to pay royalties.

10.32 Both *Chain* and *Seattle Brewing* serve as examples of sophisticated transactions in which corporations are often involved. These transactions are nothing new. Upon acquisition, the purchasers of the assets often face issues related to tax treatment of the amounts paid, that is, whether the acquisition cost is deductible as an expense or is a capital asset not deductible from the income earned during the year the expense was incurred. Another issue purchasers may confront is a breach of contract action involving the right to use the trademark, originally obtained from the seller, against the seller, its successors, or licensees. These two types of events are foreseeable at the time the purchasers decide to spend a large sum to acquire the business division from the seller. What the purchasers cannot imagine is that the perpetual, exclusive and royalty-free right to use the trademark for the operation of the business division could be taken away at some unknown future time if the sellers, after

---

10   Seattle Brewing, 6 T.C. at 873.

Chapter 10 THE INTERSECTION OF TRADEMARKS, LICENSES AND BANKRUPTCY

the sale of the assets to the purchasers, continue to struggle financially and file for bankruptcy.[11]

D. CORPORATE DIVISION SALE OF ASSETS AND TRADEMARK USE IN IN RE *EXIDE TECHNOLOGIES*

10.33 The unpredictability of the corporate transaction in which a purchaser has so willingly invested its resources to acquire the assets of the corporate division from a seller is seen in the following case, In re *Exide Technologies*.[12] In a nutshell, the purchaser paid millions of dollars to the seller in exchange for the entire corporate division of its industrial battery business, together with a perpetual, exclusive and royalty-free license to use the necessary trademark in the continuing operation of that business. Over the course of a decade, the purchaser had turned the business into a profitable enterprise while the seller continued to face financial hardship with its remaining divisions. When the seller filed bankruptcy, the purchaser confronted an unimaginable situation: losing the right to use the trademark in its purchased business because the seller was in bankruptcy and was seeking to reject the trademark license and recapture the right to use the trademark in the industrial battery business.

1. In re *Exide Technologies*

10.34 The Bankruptcy Court in the District of Delaware held that the debtor-seller Exide Technologies could reject the license agreement with EnerSys, Inc., which had purchased the industrial battery business from Exide Technologies along with the perpetual and exclusive right to use the trademark 'EXIDE' for that business.[13]

10.35 Ten years before Exide Technologies filed for bankruptcy, it decided to divest itself from the industrial battery business by selling the division to Yuasa, EnerSys' predecessor, for $135 million. The transaction was a typical asset sale and purchase, wherein Exide Technologies sold to EnerSys the manufacturing plants, equipment and other assets, assigned key employees to EnerSys, signed

---

11 *See, e.g.*, In re Exide Techs., 340 B.R. 222, 228 n.5 (Bankr. D. Del. 2006) (quoting the testimony of the purchaser EnerSys' President and CEO, Mr. John Craig for the description of the unexpected course of events wherein the debtor-in-possession decided to reject the perpetual, exclusive and royalty-free license that was part of the corporate assets sale transaction from Exide to EnerSys: 'Exide … is trying to … steal back the Exide trademark and I don't think that is fair.').
12 *See id.*
13 *Id.* at 227.

D. CORPORATE DIVISION SALE OF ASSETS AND TRADEMARK USE

a non-compete agreement for ten years and granted a perpetual, exclusive, royalty-free license to use the EXIDE trademark in the industrial battery business.[14]

10.36 Upon the acquisition of the battery business, EnerSys devoted its expertise and significant resources to continue to build the industrial battery business for nine more years by making high-quality products. EnerSys became successful in establishing a strong presence for EXIDE industrial battery and claimed to be the 'leading manufacturer of motive power batteries in the world'.

10.37 Almost a decade after its divestment from the industrial battery business, Exide Technologies decided to re-enter the business by terminating the non-compete agreement with EnerSys one year early. As a result, Exide Technologies purchased GNB Industrial Battery Company and competed directly against EnerSys. Exide Technologies wanted to sell the industrial battery products again under the EXIDE trademark. Exide Technologies made several overtures to take the trademark EXIDE back from EnerSys without success because it had granted EnerSys the perpetual and exclusive right to use the EXIDE trademark in the industrial battery business.

10.38 In April 2002, Exide Technologies filed for reorganization under Chapter 11 of the Bankruptcy Code. Exide Technologies sought to reject the perpetual and exclusive trademark agreement granted to EnerSys.[15]

10.39 The bankruptcy court found that the trademark license was an executory contract because there were material and ongoing obligations remaining unperformed under the agreement.[16] The court then evaluated the agreement and held that Exide Technology's rejection of it was an exercise of sound business judgment for the debtor's reorganization effort. EnerSys' right to use the trademark in the industrial battery business was extinguished upon rejection of the trademark license.

10.40 To support its conclusion that the trademark agreement was an executory contract, the court's legal analysis proceeded with the familiar 'Countryman standard'. Under that standard, the bankruptcy court stated that 'a contract is executory when "the obligation of both the bankrupt and the other party to the contract are so far unperformed that the failure of either to complete

---

14   *Id.* at 227–8.
15   *Id.* at 227; 11 U.S.C. § 365 (2000 & Supp. V 2005).
16   In re Exide Techs., 340 B.R. at 239. The court stated that 'the Trademark License, the Asset Purchase Agreement, the Administrative Services Agreement, and the December 27, 1994, letter agreement all comprise one, integrated agreement.' *Id.* at 229.

performance would constitute a material breach excusing performance of the other".' The court noted that it looked at the 'four corners' of the agreement to determine whether 'both parties have unperformed material obligations' under the Agreement.[17]

10.41 The court relied on the use restriction and quality control provisions of the trademark agreement, which prohibited EnerSys from using the trademark outside of the industrial battery business, and imposed on it the requirement to use the trademark in accordance with a quality control standard. The court found that the provisions were material and any default of either provision by EnerSys would result in a 'material breach' and therefore allow Exide to terminate the agreement.[18]

10.42 Also, the court stated that the Use Grant provision is a 'material obligation' on Exide, wherein Exide agreed not to use the trademark in conjunction with the industrial battery business sold to EnerSys and not to license the trademark to any other third parties after EnerSys purchased the battery division. Additionally, under the Registration provision, Exide was obligated to maintain registration of the Exide trademark, and such 'affirmative duty' to maintain the trademark and to give notice to EnerSys upon any lapse of the trademark rendered the provision a 'material, ongoing obligation' of Exide. Under the same provision, EnerSys was also required to comply with the trademark user registration in other countries for the use of the trademark in the battery division. Again, the provision was deemed by the bankruptcy court as imposing 'ongoing, material obligations' on EnerSys.[19]

---

17 *Id* at 229; *see also* In re Bradlees Stores, Nos. 00–16033 (BRL), 00–16035(BRL), 00–16036(BRL), 01-CV-3934 (SAS), 2001 WL 1112308, at *8 (S.D.N.Y. 20 September 2001) ('the executoriness analysis examines an agreement on its face to determine whether there are material obligations that require substantial performance from the parties.').

18 In re Exide Techs., 340 B.R. at 232. The court relied on the Termination provision to support its conclusion. The provision states:

> Termination. Licensor shall have the right to terminate this Trademark License if (a) products covered hereunder and sold by Licensee in connection with the Licensed Marks fail to meet the Quality Standards, or (b) Licensee uses, assigns or sublicenses its rights under the Licensed Trade Name or the Licensed Marks outside the scope of the Licensed Business and, in either such case, reasonable measures are not initiated to cure such failure or improper use within ninety (90) days after written notice from Licensor. Upon termination of this Trademark License, Licensee and its sublicensees shall, within a reasonable period of time not to exceed two (2) years, discontinue all use of the Licensed Marks and Licensee shall discontinue all use of the Licensed Trade Name and shall cancel all filings or registrations made pursuant to Paragraph 10 hereof and change its corporate or trade name registrations, if any, to exclude the Licensed Trade Name; provided, however, that if any failure to meet Quality Standards or improper use of, or assignment or sublicense of rights under, the Licensed Trade Name or Licensed Marks occurs in any jurisdiction other than the United States and is not remedied as permitted hereunder, this Trademark License will terminate only with respect to the jurisdiction in which such failure or improper use occurred.

19 *Id.* at 237.

D. CORPORATE DIVISION SALE OF ASSETS AND TRADEMARK USE

10.43 In summary, with those material obligations identified by the court, the agreement is deemed an 'executory contract'. Therefore, Exide could reject the agreement and EnerSys had to stop using the trademark upon rejection.[20]

2. Causing uncertainties

10.44 At a first glance, the In re *Exide Technologies* decision seems unremarkable as one of those reported and unreported cases where license agreements involving various forms of intellectual property, such as patents, copyrights, and trademarks, are either assumed or rejected by the debtor in bankruptcy. It is unremarkable since it addresses whether a license agreement is an executory contract, and thus whether the debtor has the right to assume or reject the contract under the relevant statute. Court after court has routinely held, either with a cursory analysis or none at all, that patent, copyright, and trademark license agreements are executory contracts because both parties to the agreements have some unperformed obligations to fulfill.[21]

10.45 However, a careful examination of In re *Exide Technologies* reveals a different picture. The agreement in Exide was not the typical, stand-alone license agreement between a debtor and non-debtor party. The perpetual, exclusive and royalty-free right to use the trademark in this case must be analyzed in connection with the outright sale and purchase of the industrial battery business division because the sale of the entire business included the right to use the trademark.[22] Unfortunately, the court ignored the reality underlying the inseparability of the sale of the battery division and the perpetual, exclusive and royalty-free right to use the trademark in the battery division. The transaction was an outright sale of that portion of the trademark related to industrial batteries, not a mere stand-alone license.

---

20 The Third Circuit later vacated the lower court's decision on executory contract based on New York's contract law. In re Exide Techs, 607 F.3d 957 (3rd Cir. 2010).
21 *See, e.g.*, In re Sunterra Corp., 361 F.3d 257, 264 (4th Cir. 2004) (the copyright license agreement for software was executory because 'each party owed at least one continuing material duty to the other under the Agreement'); In re CFLC, Inc., 89 F.3d 673, 677 (9th Cir. 1996) (concluding that the licensee must refrain from suing for infringement and the licensor must mark all products made under the license); Krebs Chrysler-Plymouth, Inc. v. Valley Motors, Inc., 141 F.3d 490, 498 (3d Cir. 1998) (concluding that trademark licenses are executory contracts subject to be assumed and assigned in bankruptcy); Institut Pasteur v. Cambridge Biotech Corp., 104 F.3d 489, 493 (1st Cir. 1997) (allowing debtor-in-possession to assume executory patent license agreement).
22 The goodwill of a business and a trademark are generally inseparable. *See* Coca-Cola Bottling Co. v. Coca-Cola Co., 269 F. 796, 806 (D. Del. 1920). The sale of the goodwill of business together with the right to use the trademark is characterized as a sale, not a license. *See* Griggs, Cooper & Co. v. Erie Pres. Co., 131 F. 359, 361–2 (W.D.N.Y. 1904).

10.46 By critically examining the transaction, it becomes apparent that the right to use the trademark in the In re *Exide Technologies* case was a property right sold to the acquirer as part of the entire industrial battery business. The plain language of the right granted (exclusive, perpetual and royalty-free) conveys the intention of an outright sale to the acquirer of a portion of the entire trademark.[23] Indeed, the reason that the right to use the trademark is perpetual is because the purchaser paid millions of dollars for the business, including the tangible and intangible property and rights, so it could continue to operate the business and generate profits from the acquisition. The purchaser did not just acquire the perpetual right to use the trademark as a stand-alone transaction, and the seller did not grant the right to use the trademark to the purchaser as a typical, stand-alone license in the ordinary course of business. By granting a perpetual right to use the trademark to the purchaser, the seller knew that it was severing itself from a particular business so it could concentrate on the remainder of its businesses. The purchaser acquired the right to use the trademark forever so it could achieve certainty for its ongoing activity in the acquired business.[24]

10.47 The right to use the trademark is exclusive, so the seller and its successors cannot compete directly against the purchaser within the defined market upon the acquisition of the business. The purchaser does not want to acquire the business from the seller for a very large sum, and then have to face direct competition from the seller and its other non-exclusive licensees in the same fields of use and in the same geographical territory. The purchaser's chance to succeed with the acquired business may be dissed if it was forced to operate among competitors with the right to use the trademark in the same field of use and geographic territory. That competition would render the acquisition meaningless. The purchaser's millions of dollars of investment in the acquisition would be wasted. The seller typically knows that payment for the transfer of the business represents the premium for the assets, as well as the goodwill of that business with the exclusivity of the right to use the trademark in connection with the operation of the specific business. The purchaser negotiates and pays a price for the business and the exclusivity of the trademark in

---

23 The grant to use the trademark EXIDE was perpetual, exclusive and royalty-free. In re Exide Techs., 340 B.R. at 228 (Bankr. D. Del. 2006). Such grant, as found in Seattle Brewing & Malting Co., was deemed a sale. Seattle Brewing & Malting Co., 6 T.C. at 869 (1946) ('If such grant is exclusive and perpetual, its characteristics more resemble a sale than a license, and this is particularly true where all the consideration has been paid.').

24 Seattle Brewing, 6 T.C. at 873 (holding the $1 million option purchase price the cost of the sale of the trademark because the right to use was perpetual and exclusive); *See* Ste. Pierre Smirnoff, Fls, Inc. v. Hirsch, 109 F. Supp. 10, 12 (S.D. Ca. 1952) ('It has been repeatedly held over a long period of time that the grant of an exclusive and irrevocable right to use a mark in a designated territory is an assignment and not a mere license.').

that operation in exchange for the certainty that no other entity beside it has the right to use the trademark. That certainty is important; the purchaser can prevent the seller and its successors from using the trademark in the field of use and in the territory.

10.48 The right to use the trademark is royalty-free because the purchase price for the business encompasses the price of the trademark right. Instead of a royalty payment plan, the purchaser paid a lump sum amount for all the property and rights, tangible and intangible, including the right to use the mark in the operation of the business. The trademark is not free; full consideration is paid as part of the purchase price of all of the assets of that business. The lump sum price in In re *Exide Technologies* reflected the seller's wishes to withdraw from the industrial battery business altogether. Also, the lump sum price established that Exide, at the time of the transaction, did not want to use the trademark again in connection with the industrial battery business. The right to use the trademark was granted royalty-free because the value of the trademark usage was included in the purchase price of the business; thus, the seller and the purchaser could each go their separate ways in order to implement their own future business plans with certainty.

10.49 In contrast, in a typical, stand-alone trademark license agreement, a lump sum payment is not the usual term because licensors generally want to maximize the royalties by having those royalties dependent on net sales (often with guaranteed minimum payments), and by imposing a best efforts standard on the licensees to ensure the royalties' generation. Paying for the total price, as EnerSys did in In re *Exide Technologies*, eliminated the periodic royalty payments dependent on production or minimum royalty payments, the maintenance of records for frequent audits conducted by the seller to verify the payments, or the enforcement of a best-efforts standard imposed on the licensee.

10.50 Most importantly, with the payment of the lump sum price, the purchaser attained a certainty, which it would not have had with a periodic royalty payment structure. In a royalty structure that demands a guaranteed minimum payment, the purchaser must make projections as to production, volume of sales and expenses in order to arrive at an accurate number for the guaranteed minimum. Also, in a royalty structure dependent on volume of sales or production, the purchaser must determine all the deductions so that it could arrive at a 'net sales' amount for each royalty payment period. The lump sum price establishes the purchaser's willingness to invest in the acquisition of the business, as well as the purchaser's strong desire to focus on the production and marketing of the products upon the acquisition. The purchaser has paid for the

Chapter 10 THE INTERSECTION OF TRADEMARKS, LICENSES AND BANKRUPTCY

new business and is thus motivated to use all of its efforts to make the business competitive and successful. The purchaser is not bound by any best-efforts provisions, and both the purchaser and the seller have no concerns as to whether the purchaser is using its best efforts in manufacturing, selling, and advertising the trademarked products.

10.51 In summary, the perpetual, exclusive and royalty-free right to use the trademark at stake in the *Exide Technologies* case was part of the acquisition of the industrial battery business division. That right is property acquired by the purchaser, EnerSys, for the continuing operation of the industrial battery division, just as if Exide had sold EnerSys a physical manufacturing facility or equipment as part of the sale of the division's assets. Those property rights should not be seized from the purchaser solely for the benefit of the seller-debtor. The seller-debtor already received its bargained-for-exchange in the form of the lump sum payment for all the assets of that division. The seller-debtor desired to rid itself of the industrial battery business and found a purchaser who was willing to pay a large sum for the business. The transaction as a whole was an outright sale, severing the seller's right to what it sold by transferring it to the purchaser. When the seller filed for bankruptcy, the perpetual, exclusive and royalty-free right to use the trademark in the battery division should not be considered to be part of the bankrupt estate, and the executory contract provision of the Bankruptcy Code should not be used to reacquire those transferred property rights.

10.52 An acquirer like EnerSys would never have thought, at the time of the acquisition that it would lose the perpetual and exclusive right to use the trademark in connection with the business purchased. The acquirer generally would believe it had negotiated and paid the purchase price for the entire property, tangible and intangible, including the perpetual and exclusive right to use the trademark necessary to operate the acquired business. EnerSys, like any acquirer in similar circumstances, naturally spent resources to manufacture, market, and sell the products in connection with the trademark. If the acquirer knew that the perpetual and exclusive right to use the trademark was subject to reversion to the seller without any compensation, the acquirer would have factored the reversion into the price. Why should the acquirer pay much more for a property right if it will not possess it in the future? Why should the acquirer pay for something that later increases in value, but is then taken away without any compensation?

10.53 Likewise, a seller, like Exide Technologies, would never have imagined that after pocketing the lump sum for the sale of the corporate division along with the grant of a perpetual, exclusive and royalty-free right to use the trademark

D. CORPORATE DIVISION SALE OF ASSETS AND TRADEMARK USE

in connection with the manufacturing, marketing, and sale of industrial batteries, it would have the right to take the trademark back. In fact, the seller Exide Technologies knew very well that after the sale of the corporate division to EnerSys, it had no right to use the trademark in the same fields of use ever again. Knowing the reality, ten years later Exide Technologies approached EnerSys several times with overtures to use the trademark, but EnerSys refused. At the time of the transaction, if the seller knew that it would obtain the windfall right to use the trademark again, and the purchaser knew that it would stand to lose the perpetual, exclusive and royalty free right to use the trademark in connection with the industrial battery business, it is unfathomable that the seller would have been able to fetch the high price that it received for the sale of the division. The purchaser would not be so naïve to pay for something for which it would invest substantial efforts, in addition to the original sum, just to lose it all.

10.54 In re *Exide Technologies* sends a chilling message to would-be acquirers that their investment in acquiring a business or corporate division might be wasted. At any given time in the future, the property negotiated and purchased for part of the acquisition might not be theirs to use in the operation of the business. Terms like 'perpetual', 'exclusive' and 'royalty-free' become meaningless as the acquirer faces the enormous risk of losing the right to use a trademark or brand name in the acquired business when the seller files for bankruptcy. The uncertainty of the transaction conveyed in In re *Exide Technologies* and similar cases is paramount.

10.55 Fortunately, the Third Circuit vacated the lower court's ruling.[25] The Third Circuit applied New York contract law's 'substantial performance' doctrine, which states that when a breaching party 'has substantially performed' before the breach, 'the other party's performance is not excused' to the present case.[26] Accordingly, the Third Circuit concluded that EnerSys had substantially performed its obligations under the 1991 trademark license agreement because it had paid the purchase price of $135 million for the transaction that included the industrial battery business and the right to use the 'Exide' trademark, and had assumed liabilities in connection with the acquisition. The Third Circuit also ruled that EnerSys's ongoing, unperformed obligations under the license agreement, such as the scope of the license grant, quality control, indemnity and assurances did not outweigh EnerSys's performance prior to Exide's

---

25 In re Exide Techs., 607 F.3d 957 (3rd Cir. 2010).
26 *Id.* at 963.

Chapter 10 THE INTERSECTION OF TRADEMARKS, LICENSES AND BANKRUPTCY

bankruptcy filing. In summary, the trademark license agreement was not executory and could not be rejected by Exide.[27]

10.56 The uncertainty, however, remains for trademark licensees when licensors are in bankruptcy because the Third Circuit did not address whether the rejection of a trademark license agreement by the debtor-licensor would automatically eliminate the licensee's rights in the licensed trademark. That means, under the traditional view in bankruptcy law on rejection of trademark license agreements, that the rejection allows the licensor to 'take back trademark rights it bargained away'.[28]

3. Adding uncertainties: In re *Interstate Bakeries* and In re *Lakewood* (Sunbeam Prods., Inc. v. Chicago Am. Mfg, LLC)

10.57 Still, layers of uncertainties pile on the life of trademark license agreements in bankruptcy, as seen in subsequent decisions rendered by the other circuit courts.

10.58 The Eighth Circuit in In re *Interstate Bakeries* decided to adopt a different approach from the Third Circuit, even though the facts are similar.[29] Indeed, IBC operated a bread baking business, among others. IBC then sold the bread-baking business to Lewis Brothers Bakeries (LBB) for $20 million. As in many typical corporate purchase and sale transactions, the parties allocated $11.88 million for the tangible assets and $8.82 for intangible assets, including the trademark license. The parties entered into an Assets Purchase Agreement and License Agreement for the transaction in 1996. Eight years later, on 22 September 2004, IBC and its subsidiaries addressed their financial trouble by filing for Chapter 11 bankruptcy. Subsequently, the debtor-in-possession asserted that the Trademark License Agreement with LBB was an executory contract subject to either assumption or rejection under bankruptcy law. LBB, relying on the Third Circuit's decision in *Exide*, argued that the Trademark License Agreement was part of the integrated agreement, the Assets Purchase Agreement, and was therefore substantially performed.[30]

10.59 In a split panel, 2–1, the majority stated that unlike the Trademark License Agreement in *Exide*, the Agreement in the present case included a provision for material breach if the licensee LBB violated quality control standards.[31]

---

27 *Id.* at 963–4.
28 *Id.* at 965–67 (Ambro J., concurring).
29 In re Interstate Bakeries Corp., 690 F.3d 1069 (8th Cir. 2012).
30 *Id.* at 1074–5.
31 *Id.* at 1075.

D. CORPORATE DIVISION SALE OF ASSETS AND TRADEMARK USE

The panel majority believed that because the inquiry of whether an agreement is an executory contract centers on 'whether any material obligations remain', the panel majority held that 'LBB's breach' of the quality control 'provision would be material ... that it constitutes a remaining material obligation'.[32] Accordingly, the agreement is an executory contract subject to the debtor's assumption or rejection under bankruptcy law.[33] Judge Colloton vigorously dissented and followed the reasoning articulated by the Third Circuit's decision in *Exide*.[34]

10.60 Two years later, the Eighth Circuit issued an *en banc* decision. Judge Colloton wrote the majority decision this time.[35] The Circuit viewed the Trademark License Agreement as an integrated agreement that included both the Asset Purchase Agreement and the License Agreement. By considering the Trademark License Agreement in the holistic approach, the Circuit held that the agreement was not an executory contract because LBB had substantially performed all of its obligations under the integrated agreement when it purchased IBC's assets, including the trademark license.[36]

10.61 In a different case, instead of a sale and purchase of corporate assets, involving a trademark license agreement that was part of an outsource deal, a product manufacturing agreement was entered into where the licensee incurred substantial cost to purchase equipment, hire employees and set up logistics for the sole purpose of fulfilling the manufacturing order from the licensor. The Seventh Circuit in In re *Lakewood or Sunbeam Products, Inc. v. Chicago Am. Mfg., LLC*, addressed the fate of the trademark license when the licensor was in bankruptcy and the bankruptcy trustee rejected the product manufacturing agreement.[37]

10.62 In that case, Lakewood was in financial trouble when it reached out to CAM for the manufacturing of box fans. CAM invested substantially in equipment, facilities, and human resources to meet the order pursuant to the Supply Agreement. Pursuant to the Supply Agreement, Lakewood licensed certain patents for CAM to use in the manufacturing of the box fans. Lakewood also licensed to CAM the trademark 'Lakewood' for use in connection with the box fans. Thereafter, when Lakewood was in further financial difficulty, it negotiated with CAM and allowed CAM to sell the box fans in the event that

---

32 *Id.*
33 *Id.* at 1076.
34 In re Interstate Bakeries Corp., 690 F.3d at 1076–9 (Colloton J. dissenting).
35 In re Interstate Bakeries Corp., 751 F.3d 955 (8th. Cir. 2014) (en banc).
36 *Id.* at 962.
37 Sunbeam Prods., Inc. v. Chicago Am. Mfg., LLC, 686 F.3d 372 (7th Cir. 2012).

Lakewood failed to purchase the fans from CAM in accordance with the orders detailed in the Supply Agreement.[38]

10.63 Lakewood then filed for bankruptcy. The trustee rejected the Supply Agreement and subsequently sold Lakewood's assets to a purchaser, Sunbeam. Sunbeam turned around and promptly filed patent and trade-mark infringement claims against CAM![39] The bankruptcy court carefully examined all the evidence surrounding the Supply Agreement. The bankruptcy court found that under the Supply Agreement: '(1) the license provided by the Supply Agreement extends to the fans that CAM manufactured before the agreement was executed; (2) the license extends to fans built after Lakewood had no further actual requirements; … and (4) CAM's remedy for breach was not limited to retention of Lakewood's equipment.'[40] Upon such findings, the bankruptcy court considered the impact of the rejection of the Supply Agreement on the trademark licensee.

10.64 Utilizing the court's equity power, the bankruptcy court gave the debtor a fresh start and prevented the licensor 'to take back trademark rights it bargained away'.[41] That meant the licensee CAM was permitted to use the trademark to survive the rejection of the Supply Agreement. CAM could continue to sell off the fans that it had invested substantially to manufacture pursuant to the debtor Lakewood's prior orders. These were the very fans that Lakewood did not have the funding to purchase, to the detriment of CAM.[42]

10.65 Subsequently, the case arrived at the Seventh Circuit. The Circuit upheld the bankruptcy court's decision, but on different grounds. Specifically, the Seventh Circuit declined to follow the 'equity grounds' reasoning that the bankruptcy court had adopted in ruling in favour of the licensee. The Seventh Circuit asserted that judges 'cannot over-ride' what the Bankruptcy Code provides 'by declaring that enforcement would be "inequitable".'[43]

10.66 The Seventh Circuit noted that the omission of 'trademark' from the definition of 'intellectual property' in the bankruptcy statute means that Section 365(n) 'does not affect trademarks one way or the other'.[44] Under bankruptcy

---

38 In re Lakewood Eng'g & Mfg. Co., Inc., 459 B.R. 306, 310 (Bankr. N.D. Ill. 2011) aff'd sub nom. Sunbeam Prods., Inc. v. Chi. Am. Mfg., LLC, 686 F.3d 372 (7th Cir. 2012).
39 In re Lakewood, 459 B.R. at 310, 325–6.
40 *Id.* at 338.
41 *Id.* at 344 (*quoting* In re Exide Techs., 607 F.3d at 967–8 (3rd Cir. 2010)).
42 *Id.* at 344–6.
43 *Sunbeam Prods*, 686 F.3d at 375.
44 *Id.*

law, the Circuit noted that 'rejection constitutes a breach of' the contract.[45] In both bankruptcy law and non-bankruptcy law, the Circuit observed, '[a]fter rejecting a contract, a debtor is not subject to an order of specific performance' and 'the other party's rights remain in place'.[46] Consequently, rejection of the contract 'frees the estate from the obligation to perform and has absolutely no effect upon the contract's continued existence'.[47] Moreover, rejection is not 'the functional equivalent of a rescission, rendering void the contract and requiring that the parties be put back in the positions they occupied before the contract was formed'.[48] Accordingly, the trustee's rejection of Lakewood's contract with CAM did not abrogate CAM's contractual rights. CAM could continue to use the trademark.[49]

10.67 In summary, the Third Circuit in *Exide* used equity power to allow trademark licensee to use the licensed trademark upon rejection. The Seventh Circuit in *Sunbeam* declined the use of court's equity power and provided an interpretation of the bankruptcy statutory provision itself to permit the licensee the right to use the licensed trademark. The Eighth Circuit in *Interstate Bakeries* relied on a holistic approach to conclude the trademark licensee's substantial performance and therefore removing the trademark license from being viewed as an executory contract.

E. ENDING THE UNCERTAINTIES

1. Looking beyond form, facing the substance

10.68 By examining a trademark agreement granted in connection with the corporate acquisition of a business division as a typical, stand-alone trademark license agreement in the ordinary business of the trademark owner, courts focus erroneously on the form, not the substance and the reality of the asset sale and purchase transaction. The proposed focus on substance requires the court to evaluate the operation of the provisions of the agreement to determine if they operate in a meaningful manner to place the attributes of ownership of the trademark rights transferred in the purchaser of the business.

10.69 For example, in a stand-alone license transaction, courts would know that a quality control provision is critical because without such a provision the

---

45　*Id.* at 377.
46　*Id.*
47　*Id.*
48　Sunbeam Prods, 686 F.3d at 377.
49　*Id.* at 378.

Chapter 10 THE INTERSECTION OF TRADEMARKS, LICENSES AND BANKRUPTCY

trademark holder risks abandonment of its trademark. In contrast, in the sale transaction of a business, which includes the perpetual, exclusive, and royalty-free right to use the trademark in connection with that business, the 'maintenance of quality' is 'for the mutual benefit of the parties' and does not possess the same importance.[50] The purchaser, not the seller, will be the one who will care about quality control.

10.70 Similarly, 'the agreement to protect the licensee against infringement', and other ongoing obligations of the agreement, such as the 'restriction of trademark use' provision, the registration provision, and the termination provision, 'no longer existed in a real sense' in the perpetual, exclusive, and royalty-free type of agreement in connection with the acquisition of the corporate division as once the price is paid, the triggers for termination of the right to use the trademark can no longer be realistically invoked.[51]

10.71 In a typical license arrangement, the 'use grant' provision generally sets forth the scope of the grant so each party knows exactly the parameters of the field of use and territory. The use grant in the context of a corporate sale of a business division means something more: it establishes what the seller sells and what the purchaser acquires with respect to trademark rights so the purchaser can continue to operate the business acquired and the seller may use the trademark in connection with its remaining business after the sale. This is akin to dividing one piece of property into two independent pieces of property, with the dividing line determined by the terms of the 'use grant' provision. That means the seller should not be able to come back, whether on the day after the transaction, or years later, to take back the acquired property of the purchaser by using the trademark contrary to the use grant provision. It has already sold that specified right of use to the purchaser. If a seller or its successor ignores the use grant, it might face a breach of contract action brought by the purchaser. Even in a trademark case where the facts are not as compelling as those in the In re *Exide Technologies* case, the court found in *Shoney's Inc. v. Schoenbaum* a breach of contract in favour of the exclusive licensee.[52]

---

50 Seattle Brewing & Malting Co. v. Comm'r, 6 T.C. 856, 868 (1946) (noting that the trademark license agreement with provisions 'such as the maintenance of quality, advertising, and the purchase of malt' were 'for the benefit of both parties, and the agreement to protect the licensee against infringement was no different than one to protect title … [p]rovisions for the mutual benefit of the parties became of relative minor importance' when the licensee paid the $1 million option price in lieu of the royalty payments). The Court held that the transaction was deemed a sale, not a license. *Id.* at 873.

51 *Id.* at 857–61 (identifying various ongoing obligations under the Trademark License Agreement between Rainier and Century); *Id.* at 868 ('agreement to protect licensee against infringement was no different than one to protect title'). The Court noted that as soon as the price was fully paid, all the obligations 'no longer existed in a real sense' and 'became of relative minor importance' because the 'most important provision in the contract was the payment of the price'. *Id.* at 868.

52 Shoney's, Inc. v. Schoenbaum, 894 F.2d 92, 97–98 (4th Cir. 1990).

10.72 In *Shoney's*, the licensor brought a declaratory judgment action against the licensee, seeking to determine whether the licensor could license the 'Shoney's' trademark for use in connection with motel services to a restaurant owner in the same geographic area. The licensor had originally entered into a license agreement for the exclusive right to use the 'Shoney's' trademark for restaurant services. The licensee countered with a breach of contract claim against the licensor because the licensor had licensed the same trademark to a different licensee for use in connection with different services in the same licensed territory. The licensee asserted that the license agreement failed to reserve the licensor's right to use and license the trademark for different purposes within the licensed territory. The license agreement contained the following provision:

> License and Licensed Territory. Licensor grants to licensee, for the terms and subject to the condition set forth herein, the exclusive right to use the Shoney's System, Trade Names and Marks within the licensed territory as hereinafter described.

The district court held that under the above provision, the licensor granted to the licensee the exclusive right to the name Shoney's in the territorial area and 'that in turn prohibits the licensor from granting the use of the Shoney's, or using the name themselves, in any other establishment in the [territorial] area. Thus, the licensee is assured that no other uses of the word will be made in the area'. The Fourth Circuit Court of Appeals agreed that such an interpretation 'is supported in logic and by the traditional canons of statutory construction' because the language of the above provision literally grants to the licensee, with no express limitations, the exclusive and absolute right to use the trademark within the territorial area. The Court of Appeals affirmed the breach of trademark license agreement claim asserted by the licensee against the licensor for licensing the same trademark to others for use in connection with other services, without reservations of such rights in the license agreement.[53]

10.73 In some instances, the seller or its successor may face a trademark infringement or unfair competition action brought by the purchaser. Indeed, in *Chain*, discussed above, the acquirer who purchased the engineering-grade chain corporate division from the seller, Dresser Industries, brought a trademark infringement and unfair competition claim against the seller's successor, Tropodyne. The use grant in the trademark license entered into in connection with the sale of assets in that case limited the purchaser to use the trademark only in the non-plastic sewage chains and the name 'Jeffrey Chain' as its

---

53 *Id.* at 97–8.

corporate name. Under the use grant, the purchaser had no right to use the trademark outside of the defined scope, and the seller could not use the trademark within the field of use, non-plastic sewage chains, and the corporate name 'Jeffrey Chain' for the engineering-grade chain division. The seller retained ownership and right to the trademark and could continue to use the trademark in other businesses outside the spin-off division. The seller, Dresser Industries, did use the trademark in its remainder business for some time after the sale of the assets, and then sold a different corporate division to Tropodyne, together with the exclusive right to use the trademark in that division. The seller's successor, Tropodyne, obtained what the seller had. The Sixth Circuit Court of Appeals held that Tropodyne could not prevent the purchaser from using the trademark in the field of use and that expanding its business was not in conflict with the license agreement between the original seller and Jeffrey Chain.

10.74 In summary, looking beyond form and focusing on the substance, the 'license' of a trademark in sale of a business is in substance a sale of the trademark right in connection with that sale.

2. Sales, not licenses

10.75 There are examples of cases where courts examined the substance of the transactions and held that the transactions were sales of trademarks or other intellectual property and not mere licenses. For example, in *Ste. Pierre Smirnoff, FLS., Inc. v. Hirsch*, the court found that there was enough evidence to establish that the plaintiff became the owner of the name 'Smirnoff' in the United States 'by virtue of a purchase for a lump sum of the entire exclusive and irrevocable right in the business, good will of the business, and the name ... '.[54] The court noted that other precedents supported its ruling 'the grant of an exclusive and irrevocable right to use a mark in a designated territory is an assignment and not a mere license'.[55] Similarly, in *A. Bourjois & Co., Inc. v. Katzel*, Justice Holmes observed that: '[a]fter the sale the French manufacturers could not have come to the United States and have used their old marks in competition with the plaintiff. That plainly follows from the statute authorizing assignments.'[56] Likewise, in *Reid v. Commissioner*, the Tax Court announced that 'an exclusive perpetual grant of the use of a trade name, even within narrower territorial limits than the entire United States, is a disposition

---

54 Ste. Pierre Smirnoff, FLS., Inc. v. Hirsch, 109 F. Supp. 10, 12 (S.D. Ca. 1952).
55 *Id.*
56 A. Bourjois & Co. v. Katzel, 260 U.S. 689, 691 (1923).

of such trade name falling within the "sale or exchange" requirements' rather than a license.[57]

10.76 The *Seattle Brewing* case discussed in Section D is also instructive. In that case, after the transaction with the Rainier Company, Century sought to deduct the $1 million option payments so it would not have to pay any royalties based on alcoholic production. Century claimed that the $1 million were royalties because it did not receive full title and right to the trademarks, and the payments were merely prepayments of future operating or production expenses. The Commissioner of the Internal Revenue rejected Century's characterization of the $1 million payments. It contended that the taxpayer Century's conversion of the Agreement from a royalty basis to a transaction under which it acquired exclusive and perpetual rights of a capital nature to manufacture and sell alcoholic beverages under the Rainier trademark; such cost may not be deducted as an expense.

10.77 The question for the Tax Court to decide was whether the $1 million should be regarded as an expense in the nature of prepaid royalties or a capital expenditure. If it is a royalty expense, the taxpayer can deduct the amount in the year incurred. The Tax Court held that the taxpayer acquired a capital asset when it exercised the option and paid the $1 million. The Court explained that Century's execution and delivery of the promissory note to Rainier eliminated the payment of royalties dependent on products sold, and that the $1 million was in the consideration for the exclusive and perpetual use of the rights in the territory. Since the transaction was a 'capital transaction', the amount paid by the taxpayer is not deductible from income. The Court proclaimed that '[w]e see no inhibition, where a corporation owns a trade name, to its assigning a right to use that name in a designated territory for a price, and if the right to use is perpetual and exclusive it is more consistent with the idea of a sale than a lease … '.

10.78 Under the logic of the above cases, the trademark transaction in In re *Exide Technologies* was a sale, not a typical, ordinary license that Exide regularly engaged in to sell its products and expand its market reach. The perpetual, exclusive and royalty-free rights wherein all consideration was paid as part of a lump sum purchase price of an entire business was a sale of a property right. The perpetual and exclusive rights granted rendered the subsequent conditions and obligations, which the court in *Exide Technologies* considered to be

---

57 Reid v. Comm'r, 26 T.C. 622, 632 (1956). 'Licenses' of other intellectual property, such as patents, trade secrets, and copyrights, are treated as 'sales' where the grant is perpetual and exclusive. *See, e.g.*, Merck & Co. v. Smith, 261 F.2d 162 (3d Cir. 1958); United States v. Carruthers, 219 F.2d 21 (9th Cir. 1955); Herwig v. United States, 105 F. Supp. 384 (Ct. Cl. 1952); Laurent's Est. v. Comm'r, 34 T.C. 385 (1960).

'material' obligations as 'no longer exist[ing] in a real sense'.[58] As Judge Learned Hand observed: 'It does not unduly strain the meaning of sale to make it include an exclusive license ...'.[59]

3. Concurrent use – assignment of trademark rights in different fields of use

10.79 If the bankruptcy court's decisions continue to result in uncertainties by following the In re *Exide Technologies* ruling and reasoning, a potential acquirer of a corporate division has no other option but insist on an assignment of trademark right concerning the division. Alternatively, the acquirer can attempt to rely on the concurrent use doctrine in its negotiation with the seller for an assignment of trademark right in the specific field of use for the corporate division.

(a) Concurrent use doctrine

10.80 Under the concurrent use doctrine, two different parties can own the same trademarks and agree to use the trademarks in two distinct, non-overlapping territories. The doctrine had its roots in two early important cases before it became part of the Lanham Act: the federal trademark and unfair competition statute. The cases are *Hanover Star Milling Co. v. Metcalf*[60] and *United Drug Co. v. Theodore Rectanus Co.*[61]

10.81 In *Hanover Star Milling Co. v. Metcalf*, the plaintiff used the trademark 'Tea Rose' in connection with its flour business in 1872 within the region encompassing Ohio and Pennsylvania. The defendant began to use the same

---

58 Seattle Brewing & Malting Co. v. Comm'r, 6 T.C. at 868 (1946). The Tax Court identified the ongoing obligations such as the quality control provision, the restriction of use provision, the registration provision, and the termination provisions in the Trademark License Agreement. *Id.* at 858–61. All of these provisions were no longer important. *Id.* at 868.
59 *See* Goldsmith v. Comm'r, 143 F.2d 466, 468 (Hand, J. concurring).
60 Hanover Star Milling Co. v. Metcalf, 240 U.S. 403 (1916). The plaintiff, Allen & Wheeler Company, brought its action against 'Hanover Star Milling Company on May 23, 1912 in the United States district court for the eastern district of Illinois'. *Id.* at 407. The Seventh Circuit Court of Appeals ruled in favor of the defendant, Hanover Star Milling Company,

> upon the ground that although the adoption of the Tea Rose mark by the latter antedated that of the Hanover Company, its only trade, so far as shown, was in territory north of the Ohio river, while the Hanover Company had adopted 'Tea Rose' as its mark in perfect good faith, with no knowledge that anybody else was using or had used those words in such a connection, and during many years it had built up and extended its trade in the southeastern territory, comprising Georgia, Florida, Alabama, and Mississippi, so that in the flour trade in that territory the mark 'Tea Rose' had come to mean the Hanover Company's flour, and nothing else.

Id. at 411–12.
61 United Drug Co. v. Theodore Rectanus Co., 248 U.S. 90 (1918).

trademark 'Tea Rose' on flour products in 1885 'in good faith without knowledge or notice' that the trademark had been adopted and used earlier by the plaintiff. The plaintiff and the defendant operated their business and sales within their respective geographical territories without any consumer confusion problem until 1904, when the defendant decided to mount 'a vigorous and expensive' campaign to advertise its products extensively outside its territory. The defendant advertised in Alabama, Mississippi, Georgia, and Florida. The defendant's advertising campaign, however, did not reach the plaintiff's market territory of Pennsylvania, Ohio, and Massachusetts. The parties were not aware of each other's products and trademarks since their products neither overlapped nor were sold within the same market.

The Court observed that through the extensive advertising campaign the defendant's Tea Rose Mill and Tea Rose flour products became known in the southern states. The plaintiff, on the other hand, confined their use of the 'Tea Rose' trademark to a limited geographical territory, 'leaving the southeastern states untouched'. The Court ruled that since 'Tea Rose' in the southern states meant the defendant's flour products, the plaintiff could not assert trademark infringement against the defendant in that territory. The Court reasoned that, to permit the plaintiff to use the trademark in the southern states, restricting the defendant's use of the trademark would cause 'the complete perversion of the proper theory of trademark rights'. **10.82**

Hanover Star Milling Co. v. Metcalf created the 'Tea Rose' standard for concurrent use, allowing two unrelated companies to own and use the same trademark in connection with different products in different geographical territories. The Court recognized that trademark rights are established in markets where the trademark is known, but those rights do not extend to markets which the trademark holder's products do not reach. **10.83**

Two years later, the Supreme Court addressed *United Drug*, which contained similar facts to the 'Tea Rose' trademark case. In that case, the plaintiff, Ellen M. Regis, used the trademark Rex, a derivation of her surname, to sell medicinal products for cases of dyspepsia and other ailments. The plaintiff registered her trademark in Massachusetts in 1898, and subsequently with the United States Patent and Trademark Office in 1900. The plaintiff also established its trademark priority against a retail drug company, 'Rexall,' and then purchased the retail store in 1911. At the time of the purchase, the retail drug company had its distribution and sales in the 'Rexall stores' in various states, including four stores in Louisville, Kentucky. **10.84**

10.85 In 1883, Theodore Rectanus of Louisville, familiarly known as 'Rex', began to use the word as a trademark for a blood purifier medicinal preparation. He advertised and sold his products without knowledge of the Regis' 'Rex' products. In 1906, Mr. Rectanus sold his business to a purchaser. The new owner continued to use the 'Rex' trademark to sell the blood purifier products in the Louisville area.

10.86 In 1912, the plaintiff Regis began to ship its 'Rex' dyspepsia products to its Rexall stores. Advertisements for the products were published by the stores in local newspapers. However, prior to the advertisements, no customer in Kentucky had heard of the plaintiff's Rex products. The customers in Kentucky only knew 'Rex' for the Rectanus Company and their blood purifier product.

10.87 The Supreme Court observed that the successors of Mrs. Regis' company and Mr. Rectanus' store conducted their respective businesses using the same trademark on medicinal products in two distinct geographical territories for 16 to 17 years until the plaintiff brought the trademark suit. Both parties had expended significant resources and efforts to build the goodwill of the trademark in their respective markets. There was no bad faith to use the goodwill of the other party. Consequently, the Court declined to grant an injunction against the defendant Rectanus Company's use of the trademark 'Rex'.

10.88 The Court noted that the present case was similar to *Hanover Star Milling Co. v. Metcalf*. The Court added to the 'Tea Rose' concurrent use standard a new rule that if a junior user has adopted a trademark in good faith, and built the goodwill in the trademark in a particular market, the senior user cannot enter that market with the same trademark used first in other geographical markets.

10.89 The Tea Rose-Rectanus doctrine was later superseded by the Lanham Act that explicitly permits concurrent registration of multiple, similar trademarks. Under the relevant statutory provision, registration for concurrent use trademarks is allowed if the parties can establish that they are entitled to use the trademarks based on 'their concurrent lawful use in commerce' prior to the filing dates of the pending applications and as long as there is no confusion, mistake, or deception. The Trademark Office may also issue concurrent use registrations when a court has determined that one or more persons are entitled to use the same or similar trademarks in commerce.

10.90 *Meijer, Inc. v. Purple Cow Pancake House* illustrates the application of the concurrent use statutory provision.[62] In that case, the applicant, Meijer, and the registrant, Purple Cow Pancake House, reached an agreement for concurrent use and registration for the trademark Purple Cow. Meijer would possess the trademark for its ice cream and confectionery stores east of the Mississippi River, while Purple Cow Pancake House would own the trademark for restaurant services west of the Mississippi River. The Board approved the agreement and allowed the concurrent use and registration to be granted to Meijer. The Board reasoned that the agreement contained provisions that impose restrictions on the advertisements and displays of the trademark in the specific territory. Any 'spill over' advertisements into the registrant's territory would carry a disclaimer of affiliation to the registrant, Purple Cow Pancake House.

(b) Co-existence separately

10.91 The concurrent use doctrine allows more than one owner for the same trademark. Extending the concurrent use doctrine, the seller of a corporate division and the purchaser can enter into an agreement wherein the seller assigns all of its rights in the trademark in the field of use for the continuation of the corporate division, while keeping the ownership of the same trademark in the other divisions of the business. With the agreement and assignment finalized, the purchaser can obtain federal registration of the trademark in the specific classes of goods and services in its own name.

10.92 The seller, however, may be reluctant to divide up its trademark into different fields of use. If the seller's remaining business and the purchaser's corporate division business approach closely to each other's fields of use, the seller may not want to assign the trademark in a particular field of use to the purchaser for fear that consumer confusion may occur in the future. To minimize consumer confusion, the parties must advance with care to keep their businesses distinct and apart. In other words, the parties must learn to co-exist together while selling or offering to sell distinct products in different markets but in the same nationwide geographical territory.

---

62 Meijer, Inc. v. Purple Cow Pancake House, 226 U.S.P.Q. 280, 280–81 (T.T.A.B. 1985). *See also* CDS, Inc. v. I.C.E.D. Mgmt., Inc., 80 U.S.P.Q. 2d 1572, 1585 (T.T.A.B. 2006) (holding that the applicant CDS is entitled to a concurrent use registration for the mark THE COPY CLUB in connection with document copying, publishing, and management services 'for the State of Kansas and that portion of the state of Missouri located within 50 miles of Lenexa, Kansas' while registrant I.C.E.D.'s has its trademark COPY CLUB for similar and overlapping services in the entire United States except for the territory of use identified for CDS's trademark registration).

10.93 Co-existence carries another risk that after the acquisition, either the purchaser or the seller may decide to manufacture and sell products of lower quality compared to those offered prior to the acquisition. Consequently, the other party has no right to intervene, as it is not the owner of the trademark in connection with products and services outside of its agreed field of use. Nevertheless, the co-existence option is still better than facing the complete loss of the trademark right if the seller is in bankruptcy and the bankruptcy court followed In re *Exide Technologies*. With the concurrent use doctrine, an outright assignment of the relevant trademark right to use in the acquired business, the buyer has a better chance of keeping its acquisition of the trademark right from becoming part of the seller's bankrupt estate.

(c) Imperfect coexistence, but do not touch the license

10.94 The Apple dispute demonstrates that even with the coexistence agreement, parties in such a dispute faced months of failed negotiation and costly litigation. With all the imperfection of concurrent use and coexistence of two owners of the same trademark, it may be tempting to go back to the one-ownership/licensing arrangement. That was the path Apple Inc. and Apple Corps took recently to move from concurrent ownership of the same trademark to a situation of a one-owner/license arrangement, a situation close to In re *Exide Technologies*. Lawyers for the licensee may not be aware of the intersection of trademarks and bankruptcy. They probably do not foresee that the licensor may be in bankruptcy in the future and that the licensee's trademark right will be in peril. When that happens, it would be too late for the licensee of the trademark to have protected itself against the loss of its rights.

F. CONCLUSION

10.95 The intersection of trademark and bankruptcy laws in the United States has brought to the attention of scholars and lawyers the uncertainty and unpredictability faced by non-debtor trademark licensees who have purchased the right to use trademarks as part of corporate transactions. The current legal landscape will not encourage potential purchasers to acquire a corporate division if in the future they might lose the perpetual, exclusive, and royalty free trademark right used in the operation of the business. In the event of the seller's future bankruptcy, in addition to retaining the original purchase price, the seller will reap the windfall of recapturing the trademark it effectively sold to another. The uncertainty must end, either by courts recognizing the transfer of the trademark as, in substance, the sale of a capital asset and not as a license of merely a limited right to use the trademark, or by the parties crafting assignments of divided trademark rights in different fields of use.

# Section D

DISPUTE PREVENTION AND SETTLEMENT MECHANISMS

11

OUT OF THE SHADOWS: THE UNIQUE WORLD OF TRADEMARK CONSENT AGREEMENTS

Neil Wilkof[*]

A. INTRODUCTION	11.01	PARTIES BY VIRTUE OF THE UNDERTAKINGS IN A CONSENT AGREEMENT	11.25
B. THE LEGAL FOUNDATION	11.02		
1. Assignment	11.03		
2. License	11.04	F. THE ROLE OF LIKELIHOOD OF CONFUSION	11.31
3. Consent agreement	11.06		
C. THE VARIOUS CIRCUMSTANCES IN WHICH A CONSENT AGREEMENT MAY ARISE	11.13	G. PUBLIC AND PRIVATE CONSIDERATIONS	11.35
		H. CONCLUSION	11.42
D. TYPES OF CONSENT AGREEMENT	11.20	APPENDIX	
E. IMPACT ON THE BEHAVIOUR OF THE			

A. INTRODUCTION

The focus of this chapter is on contractual arrangements that are popularly known as trademark consent agreements. The longtime use of consent agreements developed in trademark practice in response to the need by two (or more) parties to reach an agreement on the terms and conditions for the registration or use of their respective marks, presumably in such a way that does not cause a likelihood of confusion. Despite the temptation to treat these various kinds of arrangement as a single form of agreement, in practice there are multiple forms, reflecting the various contexts in which they arise. While a consent agreement is a contractual arrangement between private parties, its terms and conditions are fashioned in light of the requirements of the applicable domestic trademark laws and other public considerations. For all their prevalence in trademark practice, there is a paucity of professional **11.01**

---

[*] Member, Eyal Bressler and Company, Ramat-Gan, Israel. The author acknowledges the research assistance of Tanaya Sethi, a student at the Hidayatullah National Law University, Raipur, India.

literature on the subject.[1] This chapter proceeds as follows. First, this chapter distinguishes consent agreements from other types of trademark transactions. Building upon this Part, the remainder of the chapter considers the challenges posed in discussing consent agreements which are fourfold: (i) to identify the various contexts in which consent agreements have arisen; (ii) to consider the different forms of consent agreements that have developed in practice in response to these various contexts; (iii) to address the role of likelihood of confusion in consent agreements; and (iv) to elaborate on the various private and public considerations that can impact a consent agreement.

B. THE LEGAL FOUNDATION

11.02 At the outset, a useful way to view a consent agreement is to compare and contrast it with a trademark assignment and a trademark license, respectively. Each of these arrangements is a form of agreement between the owner of a trademark and a third party. However, the arrangements differ from each other with respect to the nature of the disposition of the trademark rights that are the subject of the agreement.

1. Assignment

11.03 An assignment is a transfer of ownership of the mark, sometimes together with the transfer of the goodwill attributed to the mark, whereby following the consummation of the assignment, the assignor no longer has any proprietary rights in the mark.[2] The rights that the assignor enjoyed as owner of the mark now belong to the assignee, which is now the owner of the mark. On occasion, following the assignment, the parties will enter into a so-called license back agreement in which the assignee, which is now the owner of the mark by virtue of the assignment, grants a license to the assignor for the right to use the mark

---

1   See, e.g., R. Storkebaum, *The Evolution of the Concept of 'Pre-Right Declarations,' into Coexistence Agreements*, 68 THE TRADEMARK REP. 47, 47 et seq. (1978); Michael Fawlk, *Trademark Delimitation Agreements under Article 85 of the Treaty of Rome*, 82 THE TRADEMARK REP. 223, 223 et seq. (1992); James van Santen & R. Dennis Claesens, *Consents to Register in Ex Parte Cases under Section 2(d) of the Lanham Act – a Forty Year Debate*, vol. 79, THE TRADEMARK REP. 89, at 89 et seq. (1989); Marianna Moss, *Trademark 'Coexistence' Agreements: Legitimate Contracts or Tools of Consumer Deception*, 18 LOY. CONSUMER L. REV. 197, 197 et seq. (2005); NEIL WILKOF & DANIEL BURKITT, TRADE MARK LICENSING, 2ND EDITION, 9–01 to 9–44 (2005); J. THOMAS MCCARTHY, 3 MCCARTHY ON TRADEMARKS AND UNFAIR COMPETITION, 4TH EDITION, 18:79–18:83 (2014).

2   Agreement on Trade-Related Aspects of Intellectual Property Rights, 1869 U.N.T.S. 299 [hereinafter TRIPS]. Article 22 of TRIPS in pertinent part provides that 'the owner of a registered trademark shall have the right to assign the trademark with or without the transfer of the business to which the trademark belongs'. Regarding the issue of goodwill, see Irene Calboli, *Trademark Assignment 'With Goodwill': A Concept Whose Time Has Gone*, 57 FLA. L. REV. 771 (2005).

as a licensee.[3] Whether or not an assignment is accompanied by a license back agreement, the basic structure of the agreement remains the same – the assignor has transferred its ownership right in the mark to the assignee.

2. License

A license does not result in transfer of the ownership; the owner merely grants to the licensee a right to use the mark.[4] Differences exist between jurisdictions regarding licenses, such as: the extent to which quality control of the licensee by the licensor is required; whether the jurisdiction provides for recordal of the license and, if so, the purpose of the recordal; and which party is properly viewed as the source of the licensed goods or services. Despite these distinctions, there are certain common legal features of a trademark license: the thread that brings the licensor and licensee together contractually is the licensor's ownership of the mark; the licensor maintains ownership of the mark; and both parties have continuing contractual obligations.[5]

11.04

Legal arrangements exist, other than a license agreement, whereby the trademark owner provides consent to a third party with respect to the owner's mark. Taking the distribution agreement as a prime example, the distributor receives the goods bearing the mark for further distribution and sale. As such, use of the trademark is not being made by the distributor, but by the trademark owner/manufacturer, which has caused the goods to be manufactured or selected and the mark to be applied to the goods.[6] The upshot is that while all trademark licenses require consent, not all forms of consent that involve use of a trademark constitute a license.

11.05

3. Consent agreement

A consent agreement is distinguishable from both an assignment and a license. Unlike an assignment, there is no transfer of rights inasmuch as the parties to a consent agreement remain the owners of their respective marks. Unlike a license, neither party to a consent agreement grants a right of use of its mark to the other party. Rather, a consent agreement addresses the terms of registration and/or aspects of the manner of use by each party with respect to such party's mark. In a license agreement, the licensee will have breached the

11.06

---

3 WILKOF & BURKITT, *supra* note 1, 6–41 to 6–43, regarding the assignment and license back of a trademark.
4 Article 21 of TRIPS provides in pertinent part that 'Members may determine conditions on the licensing … of trademarks, it being understood that the compulsory licensing of trademarks shall not be permitted.' TRIPS, *supra* note 2, at Article 21.
5 *See* WILKOF & BURKITT, *supra* note 1, especially chs. 4–6.
6 *See* WILKOF & BURKITT, *supra* note 1, ch. 7.

Chapter 11 THE UNIQUE WORLD OF TRADEMARK CONSENT AGREEMENTS

agreement if it uses the licensor's mark in a manner that is not permitted under the license. By contrast, in a consent agreement, a party will have breached if it registers or uses its own mark in a manner that it is not authorized under the agreement. As observed by Professor McCarthy, '[a] license integrates, while a consent differentiates.'[7]

11.07 There is a temptation to liken a consent agreement to a cross-license agreement, because in both agreements, each party continues to use its intellectual property right in accordance with the agreement. However, a cross-license agreement differs from a consent agreement because each party to the cross-license agreement is granting the other party the right to use its intellectual property right, rather than setting out the terms and conditions by which such party undertakes to use its own intellectual property right. A cross-license agreement regarding patent rights is well-recognized in practice within certain industries, such as in the telecommunications or semiconductor fields, where the plethora of patents may make a cross-license necessary as a commercial matter.[8] To the contrary (the most notable exception perhaps being the situation where two parties may co-brand a joint venture in which each of them is a partner), it is difficult to conceive of commercial circumstances in which two trademark owners would each need to obtain the right to use the trademark of the other party. Even if such circumstances do occur, a cross-license agreement is separate and distinct from the terms and conditions set out in a consent agreement.

11.08 While the notion of consent is found in various contexts within the trademark system, there is virtually no explicit provision for consent agreements per se. Article 16(1) of the Agreement on Trade-Related Aspects of Intellectual Property Rights (TRIPS) provides in part that '[t]he owner of a registered trademark shall have the exclusive right to prevent all third parties *not having the owner's consent* from using in the course of trade identical or similar signs for goods or services which are identical or similar to those in respect of which the trademark is registered where such use would result in a likelihood of confusion'.[9] The focus here is on the use of a mark by a party other than the trademark owner (no mention is made to registration) in the absence of consent. However, how this consent should be manifested is not set out.

---

7 3 McCarthy, *supra* note 1 at 18–79. The extent to which this observation is wholly applicable may depend on whether one feature of a consent agreement is that there is no likelihood of confusion regarding the respective marks. See, *infra*, section F, for further discussion on the role of confusion.

8 See, e.g., Alberto Galasso, *Broad Cross-License Agreements and Persuasive Patent Litigation: Theory and Evidence from the Semiconductor Industry*, The Toyota Centre, Suntory and Toyota International Centres for Economic and Related Disciplines, London School of Economics and Political Science (July 2007), *available 16 September 2015 at* http://eprints.lse.ac.uk/6718/.

9 TRIPS, *supra* note 2, at Article 16(1) (emphasis added).

Moreover, there are similar provisions regarding consent in the TRIPS Agreement with respect to patents, industrial designs and undisclosed information, for each of which there is no direct analog to the arrangements that characterize a trademark consent agreement. Accordingly, the better conclusion is that Article 16(1) does not specifically address a trademark consent agreement.[10]

11.09 Reference to consent can be found in various national trademark systems with respect to both registration and use. For example, considering trademark practice within the European Union, both the Community Trademark Regulation (CTMR) and the Community Trademark Directive provide that no third party may use a registered mark without consent from the proprietor of the mark.[11] Further, in appropriate circumstances, registration of a mark will not be declared invalid, or registration will not be denied, where the proprietor of the earlier trademark consents to the registration of the later trademark.[12] As a matter of implementation of the Community Trademark, if 'the Office is informed about a settlement between the parties … the opposition proceedings shall be closed'. However, the CTMR does not specify the nature or contents of the settlement.[13]

11.10 A notable example where a consent agreement between two applicants is contemplated is found in section 29 of the Israel Trademarks Ordinance.[14] Under this provision, the Commissioner, at his discretion, may declare that two or more applications are sufficiently similar, and order the parties to seek to negotiate an agreement between them, subject to the approval of the

---

10   It is noted that the TRIPS agreement contains similar provisions regarding consent for the use of industrial designs, patents and undisclosed confidential information in Articles 16, 28, and 39, respectively. TRIPS, *supra* note 2, at Articles 16, 28, 39.
11   Council Regulation (EC) No. 207/2009 of 26 February 2009 on the Community Trademark [hereinafter CTMR], [2009] O.J. L78, Article 9(1); Directive 2008/95/EC of the European Parliament and of the Council of 22 October 2008, [2008] O.J. L 299, to approximate the laws of the Member States relating to trademarks [hereinafter Directive], Art. 5. A similar provision is set out in the United States under the Lanham Act, 15 U.S.C. §1114 (1). *See infra* section H, for treatment of consent agreements pursuant to the United States Patent and Trademark Office Trademark Manual of Examining Procedure [hereinafter TMEP] in connection with registration practice, *available 16 September 2015 at* http://www.uspto.gov/trademarks/resources/TMEP_archives.jsp.
12   CTMR, *supra* note 11, at Article 52(2), and Directive, *supra* note 11, at Article 4(5).
13   Rule 18(2) of the Commission Regulation (EC) No. 2868/95 of 13 December 1995 implementing Council Regulation (EC) No. 40/94 on the Community Trademark, [1995] O.J. L 303/1 *also amended by* [2005] O.J. L 172/4. The current manual on Office practice provides that the parties need only state that settlement has been reached and the Office will close the proceedings. No details, except for costs, need be provided. See also reference to consent in connection with exhaustion (Article 13(1) of the CTMR and Article 7(1) of the Directive), genericness (Article 51(1)(c) of the CTMR and Article 12(20)(b) of the Directive); and invitation by the Office to settle a dispute, Trade Marks Act, 1996 (Community Trade Mark) Regulations, Art. 42(4), 2000.
14   Trade Marks Ordinance (New Version), 5732–1972 § 29.

Commissioner, which will enable the two applications to co-exist, provided that each satisfies the registration requirements. If no such agreement is reached, the Commissioner is authorized to decide which application has superior rights. By way of practice, the form of consent is subject to the approval of the examiner of a written agreement between the parties. However, there are no explicit guidelines regarding the contents of such an agreement.[15]

11.11 While there does not appear to be any statutory definition for 'consent agreement', extra-statutory attempts to do so have been made. Of particular note is the definition of 'coexistence agreement', proposed by the International Trademark Association (INTA) in 2005,[16] namely 'an [a]greement by two or more persons that similar marks can co-exist without any likelihood of confusion; allow[ing] the parties to set rules by which the marks can peacefully coexist'.[17] This definition is characterized by the following features: (i) the arrangement is an agreement between at least two parties; (ii) the agreement extends only to similar marks, it does not apply to dissimilar marks; (iii) consent is characterized in terms of co-existence, which itself is characterized by an absence of likelihood of confusion between the marks that are subject to the agreement;[18] (iv) the parties set the rules for the terms of co-existence;[19] and (v) no distinction is made between the various circumstances in which a co-existence agreement might arise, implying that the definition is circumstance-neutral.[20]

11.12 Despite the long-standing and widespread role that consent agreements have played in trademark practice, the upshot is that there is virtually no explicit

---

15   Guideline 012/2012, dated 23 February 2012, of the Israel Commissioner of Patents, Designs and Trademarks, as amended on 21 December 2014, provides some guidance regarding the conduct of an action under section 29 of the Israel Trade Marks Ordinance, but it does not address the contents of a settlement agreement pursuant to this section.
16   The International Trademark Association (INTA) is an international trade association focusing on trademark matters. For a detailed profile of the organization, see http://www.inta.org/Pages/Home.aspx, *available 16 September 2015.*
17   *See* Moss, *supra* note 1, at 209. *See also infra* Section D for discussion of multiple nomenclature that describe the arrangement. Interestingly, this definition has been somewhat altered in the currently available version of the INTA Glossary as follows: 'Agreement by two or more persons that similar marks can co-exist without any likelihood of confusion, allows the parties to set rules by which the marks can peacefully co-exist. To use the same mark in connection with the same or similar goods or services, usually limited by geographic boundaries.' http://inta.org/TrademarkBasics/Pages/glossary.aspx *available 16 September 2015*. The main difference between the two forms of the definition is the reference to geographic restrictions in the current version.
18   *See infra* Section F, for discussion of the role of confusion in a consent agreement.
19   *See infra* Section H, for discussion of the implications that follow from the fact that a co-existence agreement is a private agreement between the parties.
20   *See infra* Section C, for the various circumstances in which a consent agreement may arise and the implications therefrom.

legislative treatment of the subject, nor are there explicit guidelines regarding the requirements and contents of such an agreement. That said, no claim seems to ever have been raised that consent agreements are per se contrary to the trademark laws.[21] Rather, consent agreements have been, and should be viewed, as consistent with the trademark law and practice. What follows is a discussion of the various circumstances in which a consent agreement may arise.

C. THE VARIOUS CIRCUMSTANCES IN WHICH A CONSENT AGREEMENT MAY ARISE

The bedrock upon which a consent agreement rests is that, in various circumstances, two parties will enter into a contractual arrangement concerning the registration or use of their respective trademarks. The ultimate substance of the agreement will derive from these particular circumstances. Five principal circumstances can be identified:[22] **11.13**

1. A dispute between rival applicants for registration of their respective marks.
2. Citation of a third-party mark in an ex parte registration proceeding.
3. A trademark opposition or cancellation proceeding.
4. An action for trademark infringement.
5. A corporate transaction.

The circumstances described in (1)–(4) all derive from some type of administrative or legal action, while (5) is the result of a private action between the parties. Each of them will involve a different set of considerations by the two parties in fashioning the ultimate provisions of the agreement.[23]

In circumstance number (1), it is presumed that each of the parties has a roughly equal interest in securing registration of its respective mark. As such, there is a reasonable likelihood that an agreement can be reached, provided that the issue of likelihood of confusion between the respective marks is resolved to the satisfaction of the parties, and the trademark registry does not **11.14**

---

21 This does not mean that a consent agreement, even if it is consistent with the applicable trademark laws, cannot nevertheless still be at odds with other statutory provisions, such as competition law and contract law. *See, e.g., infra* Section H.
22 This list is not a closed one. However, it is presumed that any additional circumstances that give rise to a consent agreement will not fundamentally differ in substance from those discussed above.
23 These circumstances should be distinguished from those in which one of the parties seeks to rely on a pre-existing consent agreement.

otherwise reject the agreement.[24] An additional factor that could diminish the prospect that the agreement will be reached is whether the agreement that is being negotiated addresses only registration as opposed to both registration and use of the marks in question. If the latter, the relative bargaining power of the two parties is more likely to come into play. In any event, even if the bargaining power of the two parties is roughly equal, the parties will have to reach an agreement on two sets of parameters rather than one.[25]

11.15 Circumstance number (2) will typically occur either when the applicant (or prospective applicant) has identified the registered mark in a search, or the registered mark has been cited by the examiner as a possible bar to registration, in jurisdictions in which third-party rights are subject to examination or otherwise brought to the attention of the applicant. In either situation, both the balance of interests and the bargaining power between the two parties differ from that which is present in circumstance number (1), because the cited mark is usually registered. The major implication that follows from this is the degree to which the registrant will have an incentive to enter into a consent agreement regarding registration of the applicant's mark (much less entering into an agreement regarding use of the respective marks). Here, the issue of whether the registration or use of respective marks might implicate a likelihood of confusion is a central concern, because it is less likely that the registrant will consent to the registration (and use) of the applicant's mark in such a situation.[26] The principal way by which the applicant might be able to affect the registrant's considerations in this regard is to use the threat (or actual filing) of an action for cancellation of the registrant's mark.

11.16 Circumstance number (3) involves a situation where the moving party relies on its interest in its own trademark, usually, but not always, registered, as the basis for filing an action for the opposition to a pending application or the cancellation of a registered mark.[27] The motivation for filing either type of action will depend in part upon the law and practice of the jurisdiction involved. In a jurisdiction where the specification in the application is not limited to the goods or services of actual interest, it can be expected that the primary purpose in filing an opposition (or even a cancellation) proceeding is to cause the applicant (or registrant) to limit the specification of goods or

---

24 *See infra* Section F, regarding the issue of likelihood of confusion and Section H for the role of the registry in accepting the terms of a consent agreement.
25 *See infra* Section D, for discussion on the scope of a consent agreement with respect to registration and/or use.
26 *See infra* Section F, for discussion on the role of likelihood of confusion.
27 It is recognized that there exist bases, other than prior rights in a mark, which might give rise to the filing of an opposition or cancellation action.

C. THE VARIOUS CIRCUMSTANCES IN WHICH A CONSENT AGREEMENT MAY ARISE

services such that the likelihood of confusion is minimized, if not entirely eliminated.[28]

11.17 In jurisdictions in which the goods or services are limited to those in use or those with intent to use, the overlap between the respective goods or services may be less likely to be resolved by a consent agreement. The balance of bargaining power in either of these situations will usually be in favour of the moving party (subject to the financial ability of that party to maintain the opposition or cancellation action should no consent agreement be reached). The extent to which the issue of likelihood of confusion will affect the ability of the parties to reach a consent agreement will be more critical, as compared with those in numbers (1) and (2).

11.18 Circumstance numbers (1)–(3) each involve various aspects of the trademark registration process. By contrast, circumstance number (4) addresses the situation where a court action for trademark infringement is filed. Mutatis mutandis, the considerations discussed in connection with circumstance number (3), apply to circumstance number (4) as well. Perhaps the principal distinction rests on the fact that an infringement action deals directly with use, rather than registration of a mark by the defendant (although if the parties reach a consent agreement, the parties might also agree to changes to the terms of registration of the respective marks). As well, the cost of a civil court action is usually greater than an opposition or cancellation proceeding, which might place greater importance on the relative financial capabilities of the two parties.

11.19 As noted, circumstance number (5) does not involve any type of contentious action, but rather a private transaction that may give rise to the need for one of the parties to obtain consent from a third party regarding said third party's trademark. While not frequent, it sometimes occurs when an investor or purchaser of the shares or assets of the target entity will encounter a problematic trademark belonging to a third party, which is not a party to the transaction. In such a situation, the investor/purchaser may seek to require that a consent agreement be reached as a condition for the closing of the transaction. Unless the target successfully convinces the investor/purchaser to accept the risk posed by the third-party mark, the target may find itself confronted with a situation that is similar to circumstance number (2). The risk posed in such a situation, unless a consent agreement can be reached, is

---

28 *See infra* Section F, for discussion of circumstances where a consent agreement may not eliminate a likelihood of confusion.

that there may be a reduction in the valuation of the transaction or, in highly unusual circumstances, even a failure to consummate it.

D. TYPES OF CONSENT AGREEMENT

11.20 The previous section discussed the circumstances in which a consent agreement may arise. We now consider the types of consent agreements that can result. We first address the various provisions that will, depending upon the circumstances, typically be included in a consent agreement:[29]

- (i) identification of the trademark registrations (and applications) that are the subject of the consent agreement and any restrictions thereto (the form of the mark and the applicable goods and services);
- (ii) consent by one party to the registration (or use) of the trademark of the other party;
- (iii) recognition by one party of the rights of the other party's trademarks;
- (iv) undertaking by one party not to consent or challenge the registration (or use) of the trademark of the other party;
- (v) cooperation between the parties to enable each party to maintain its respective registration;
- (vi) withdrawal of any pending opposition or cancellation actions;
- (vii) attention to present confusion and steps to be taken to address any future likelihood of confusion; and
- (viii) territorial scope of the agreement.

11.21 The central provisions of a consent agreement are those that set out the goods and services and scope of use that each party undertakes for its respective mark(s), with the result that there will not be a current likelihood of confusion (see Appendix I for a visual representation of various possible outcomes based on the premise that the goal of the consent agreement is to prevent a current likelihood of confusion).[30] Since a consent agreement is an enforceable contract, additional provisions consistent with contract practice under the relevant national law may also be included. Nevertheless, the nature of the ongoing use by the parties of their respective marks may be more dynamic than can be fixed by the terms of the consent agreement, no matter how

---

29 *See also* WILKOF & BURKITT, *supra* note 1, Appendix B.
30 *See*, however, *infra*, Section F, for discussion of circumstances where the parties to a consent agreement may tolerate a current likelihood of confusion.

carefully crafted. Unavoidably, therefore, disputes may arise if future overlaps occur, despite the best present intentions of the parties.[31]

Based on the foregoing, while it can be said that virtually any consent agreement, whatever its form, will contain a core set of provisions, still there is no generic form of such agreement. An instructive approach to better highlight the various types of consent agreements is to consider the diversity of nomenclature that has been applied, and consider the substantive differences, if any, that are associated with such nomenclature. Heretofore, we have used the term 'consent agreement' to describe the arrangement between two parties regarding the registration and use of their respective marks, whatever the provisions of the specific agreement. However, other captions are also used in practice to describe the arrangement. In particular, the terms 'prior-rights agreement', 'delimitation agreement' and 'co-existence agreement' have also all been employed in lieu of 'consent agreement'. Are these terms synonyms or does each entail a separate form of agreement? **11.22**

Those in favour of treating these various captions as synonymous argue that the terms merely reflect a lack of harmonization in nomenclature rather than connoting any material difference in substance. The contrary position maintains that each of them embodies a different arrangement between the parties. Consistent with the second view, the following distinctions between the nature of the arrangement reached, based on the particular term that is used to describe the agreement, have been proposed:[32] **11.23**

(i) *Consent agreement* – consent merely to the registration of a third-party's mark without any other matters of substance being addressed (e.g., the submission of a 'letter of consent' to the relevant trademark office).
(ii) *Prior-rights agreement* – acknowledges the prior trademark rights of a third party together with an undertaking either not to become active in the field of such third party, or to restrict one's activities to a separate and distinct field, together with the toleration by the owner of the prior rights to these undertakings or restrictions.

---

31 Perhaps the most notable example was the lengthy dispute between the record company and the computer company regarding the permitted scope of use by both of the Apple trademarks. *See* 3 MCCARTHY, *supra* note 1, at 18.79. *See also* ROBIN FELDMAN, RETHINKING PATENT LAW, Introduction (2012) (discussing the analogous problem regarding the limitation of language in seeking to describe a patented invention).
32 The source for this information is based on a personal communication, and the party has asked to remain anonymous. Despite the distinctions set out in the text above, it is possible that in a given jurisdiction, the terms are used interchangeably without any fundamental difference in meaning.

(iii) *Delimitation agreement* – delimiting the business activities of the respective parties, such as by market or by the form of use of the marks, together with a mutual prior-rights declaration.

(iv) *Co-existence agreement* – mutual confirmation of existing business activities without any restrictions, typically without any prior-rights declarations.

11.24 There is no dispositive resolution of these pro and contra views. The term with the most widespread currency is 'consent agreement'. However, the term is often used with respect to an agreement that contains additional provisions. Further, in some jurisdictions, one or more of these other forms of caption is used without any systematic demarcation between them with respect to the contents of the specific agreement. This is particularly so with respect to the term 'co-existence agreement'. That said, the practice in some regions appears to have taken a more granular view, whereby each of these terms connotes an agreement with its own particular contents, as described above. As such, the significance of the caption given to a particular agreement may ultimately reflect the background of the parties and the jurisdiction in which the agreement has been reached. No aspect of the law and practice of consent agreements demonstrates more vividly that each such agreement derives from its own particular circumstances, set against the particular custom and practice that have developed.[33]

E. IMPACT ON THE BEHAVIOUR OF THE PARTIES BY VIRTUE OF THE UNDERTAKINGS IN A CONSENT AGREEMENT

11.25 Both a trademark assignment and a trademark license can be described as addressing the behaviour of both parties to the transaction, whether by virtue of the transfer of the ownership, or the setting of the terms and conditions for use of the mark in a license. For example, in an assignment, the former owner must refrain from exercising any proprietary rights in the mark, while in a license, the licensee is now permitted to use the mark subject to the terms and conditions of the agreement. By contrast, the extent to which the undertakings of the parties to a consent agreement transcend the realm of mere declaration and imply changed action by one or both of the parties depends upon the nature of the consent agreement that is reached.

---

[33] *See, e.g.*, Storkebaum, *supra* note 1, for the historical context in central Europe that gave rise to the use of a 'pre-rights declaration'.

E. IMPACT ON THE BEHAVIOUR OF THE PARTIES

11.26 Recall the definition for a consent agreement proposed by INTA, whereby the agreement 'allows the parties to set rules by which the marks can peacefully exist'.[34] To achieve peaceful coexistence, one or both parties can either continue to make use of its respective mark in the same manner as prior to the execution of the agreement, with no intention to alter the scope of its use (a form of 'more of the same'). Alternatively, one or both parties can undertake certain restrictions or other changes to the behaviour that such party might have taken, or contemplated taking, in the absence of the agreement.

11.27 Thus, as a matter of both negotiation and performance of a consent agreement, the undertakings made by a party may either be by maintenance of the status quo undergirded by a contractual declaration, or a material change in the party's behaviour regarding the registration and use of its mark.[35] At the one pole, take the situation where neither of the parties changes its behaviour as a result of entering into the consent agreement. In such a case, it can be asked why there is any need for two parties to agree that there is no likelihood of confusion between their respective marks. If, as a mixed matter of law and fact, the circumstances are such that there is no likelihood of confusion, then the agreement does not alter this situation ex ante. In fact, parties themselves have, and continue to enter into, such agreements on a consensual basis under such circumstances, which points to an ongoing felt-need to do so.

11.28 At a more analytical level, it can be argued that even if both parties merely agree to maintain the status quo in their behaviour regarding registration and use of their respective trademarks, such an arrangement can be viewed as akin to a mutual private declaration of non-infringement.[36] In a declaratory judgment action, there is no requirement that any action be taken by the parties. Rather, the court considers the allegations and gives judgment by means of a declaration of the rights of the parties in respect to the dispute.[37] In our situation, instead of the parties turning to a judge to declare the respective rights of each party, they do so themselves by private bargaining. Such an agreement is predicated on the assumption that there is, and will not be, any

---

34 *See supra*, text accompanying note 16.
35 *See infra*, Section C, for further discussion of the variety of circumstances in which forms of a consent agreement can arise.
36 This assumes that the outcome of the agreement is a non-infringing behaviour by the two parties. *But see infra* Section F, for discussion of circumstances where this assumption may not apply.
37 Consider the following definition of a declaratory judgment, namely '[a] binding judgment from a court defining the legal relationship between parties and their rights in the matter before the court. A declaratory judgment does not provide for any enforcement however. In other words, it states the court's authoritative opinion regarding the exact nature or the legal matter *without requiring the parties to do anything*' (emphasis added), http://www.law.cornell.edu/wex/declaratory_judgment, *available 16 September 2015.*

likelihood of confusion between the parties regarding the use of their respective marks, provided that the two parties continue to use their respective marks in the current manner, with no intention of altering their behaviour regarding the use of their respective trademarks.

11.29 At the other pole, if one or both of the parties undertake to alter its/their current or future behaviour, then the characterization of the consent agreement as a mutual private declaration of non-infringement, by analogy to a declaratory judgment, is inapt. Instead, modification of behaviour by the parties is necessary to prevent a situation where there is a current likelihood of confusion between the parties.[38] Nevertheless, here as well, private bargaining over the terms and conditions to ensure no current and future likelihood of confusion between the parties may well lead to a preferred result; each party undertakes to change its behaviour to prevent a likelihood of confusion. Such undertakings and their subsequent performance are presumed to obviate the need in the future to seek judicial relief against the other party.

11.30 The discussion above has focused on the two polar extremes. In practice, a given consent agreement may embody aspects of both the maintenance of ongoing behaviour as well as changes to a party's behaviour. Whatever the particular circumstances, the parties to the agreement need to pay close attention to the intended outcome based on the behaviour of the respective parties in fashioning the terms and conditions of the agreement.

F. THE ROLE OF LIKELIHOOD OF CONFUSION

11.31 Common wisdom holds that the very essence of a consent agreement is that it prevents confusion between registration and use of the respective marks. This was well-recognized more than a century ago in a leading U.S. case, which stated that a consent agreement 'is not an attempt to transfer or license the use of a trademark, or any rights therein, but fixes and defines the existing trademark of each, [in order] that confusion and infringement may be prevented'.[39] The centrality of coexistence and the absence of any likelihood of confusion also seem to be the position under Community Trademark and European Union General Court jurisprudence. Thus, the court recently confirmed that even where a party wishes to rely on co-existence between trademarks, it must demonstrate 'that such co-existence was based on any

---

38 *See infra* Section F, for discussion of the role of likelihood of confusion in a consent agreement.
39 Waukesha Hygiene Mineral Springs Co. v. Hygeia Sparkling Distilled Water Co., 63 F. 438 (7th Cir. 1894).

F. THE ROLE OF LIKELIHOOD OF CONFUSION

likelihood of confusion on the part of the relevant public between the earlier marks ...'.[40]

11.32 On its face, this seems like the correct position. After all, the fundamental basis for trademark protection is that it prevents confusion as to the source of the goods or services. As such, an agreement that has the effect of sanctioning confusion seems to be at odds with this fundamental tenet of the trademark system.[41] Moreover, because of this basic incompatibility between the goal of the trademarks system – to prevent confusion, and the outcome of such an agreement – which appears to sanction it, there is the suspicion that the parties have agreed to allow a likelihood of confusion for otherwise illegal purposes.[42] Accordingly, it can be argued that a consent agreement that provides for a likelihood of confusion should not be given effect.[43]

11.33 However, at least under United States law, the purity of this claimed principle has been challenged. In a leading case, the court upheld the validity of a consent agreement despite the fact that there was evidence of an existing likelihood of confusion between the parties. The court reasoned that there was no evidence that the agreement had been entered into with an intent to deceive the public, the goods of the respective parties were of similar quality and that, as a matter of public policy, contracts should be enforced.[44] This result puts in bas-relief the question of what interests are at issue in connection with a consent agreement, and the extent to which a court or registry is, and should be involved, in reviewing a private arrangement between the parties most directly affected by the arrangement.

---

40 The Cartoon Network, Inc. v. OHIM and Boomerang TV (Case T-285/12), EU General Court (Seventh Chamber), ¶ 55, October 2, 2013, *available 16 September 2015 at* http://curia.europa.eu/juris/document/document.jsf?text=&docid=142541&pageIndex=0&doclang=EN&mode=lst&dir=&occ=first&part=1&cid=199960.

41 *See also* Moss, *supra* note 1, at 209, who observed that:

> [regarding] coexistence agreements, if they create consumer confusion, then consumers would not be able to rely on the trademark as quality indicators. This would provide a disincentive for the manufacturer to maintain a certain level of quality, which, according to Judge Posner, would lead to the overall lower quality of the products affected by the coexistence agreement (footnote omitted). Thus, if coexistence agreements create consumer confusion, they will have adverse effects on the economics of trademark protection. Such agreements, in case of confusion, would increase consumer search costs and remove incentives to maintain the higher product quality.

42 *See infra* Section H.

43 *Cf.* KP Permanent Make-Up, Inc. v. Lasting Impression I, Inc., 543 U.S. 111 (2004), holding that a party raising the affirmative defence of fair use under the Lanham Act does not have the burden to negate all likelihood of confusion regarding the behaviour complained about. In that connection, Professor Dinwoodie observed '... that even where the harm that the prima facie cause of action seeks to prevent may be implicated, other concerns – for example, competition, or perhaps the protection of free speech – might warrant, on balance, that we live with some minor harm to the trademark owner in order to preserve those other values.' Graeme B. Dinwoodie, *Developing Defenses in Trademark Law*, 13 LEWIS & CLARK L. REV., 99, 134 (2009).

44 T & T Mfg. Co. v. A.T. Cross Co, 449 F.Supp. 819, aff'd in 587 F.2d 533, cert. denied, 441 U.S. 60 (1978).

Chapter 11 THE UNIQUE WORLD OF TRADEMARK CONSENT AGREEMENTS

11.34 It is well-recognized that a substantial number of jurisdictions have eliminated an examination of third-party rights ('relative grounds' of refusal) as part of the examination process, the rationale being that the private parties themselves are best placed to determine whether the likelihood of confusion is a matter of commercial importance that should give rise to a contentious action. If it is, then the aggrieved rights holder may seek to challenge the mark via an opposition or cancellation proceeding; if not, then the mark remains in effect without challenge. In either circumstance, the registrar or court is not involved at the examination stage. Even in jurisdictions such as the United States, where applications are still examined on relative grounds, there is a recognition, by at least some courts, that because a consent agreement is a private matter between the parties, a likelihood of confusion resulting from the agreement may not be sufficient to render the agreement ineffective.[45]

G. PUBLIC AND PRIVATE CONSIDERATIONS

11.35 The recognition that a consent agreement is not necessarily incompatible with a current likelihood of confusion reinforces the notion that the validity and scope of such an agreement is a function of the interaction between private and public considerations. At the one end, a consent agreement is a contract between private parties that is subject to the basic principle that private agreements should be enforced. As a result, its terms and conditions will bind the parties to the agreement. As such, disputes may arise over whether a party has exceeded the scope of the use of the mark with respect to the goods, territory, and even period of time.[46] Perhaps the most distinctive implication is that a consent agreement has long been held to operate as an estoppel on each of the parties.[47] This means that a party, which has agreed to the declaration that its mark is not confusingly similar with respect to the mark of the other party for specified goods, is estopped from later asserting infringement based on the same goods and the marks.

11.36 However, a consent agreement does not bind third parties. Moreover, if the terms of the agreement are incompatible with other laws, the fact that the parties have entered into a consent agreement does not exempt them from liability with respect to these laws. Indeed, the terms of the consent agreement may, in fact, give rise to such liability. This is most pronounced, at least in

---

45 *See infra* Section H, for discussion of examination of relative grounds for registration under United States practice in the context of consent agreements.
46 WILKOF & BURKITT, *supra* note 1, 9–33.
47 Waukesha Hygiene Mineral Springs Co. v. Hygeia Sparkling Distilled Water Co., 63 F. 438 (7th Cir. 1894).

principle, with respect to competition laws. If a consent agreement is found to have a deleterious impact on competition, then it may run afoul of the applicable competition law. In practice, there appears to be a significant difference in the treatment of the competition law aspects of a consent agreement under United States law and European Union law, respectively. Thus, a recent consideration of this topic under United States law raised several outcomes of a consent agreement that might be in violation of the United States antitrust laws, namely effect on marketing expenditure and resulting price effects, or on quality of products.[48] However, no actual cases were brought in support of the suggestion that such provisions in a trademark consent agreement, or the outcome of such provisions, have given rise to an antitrust violation under United States law.

11.37 To the contrary, so-called delimitation agreements have, on occasion, been found to be in violation of European Union competition law.[49] The basic principle was expressed by the European Court of Justice as follows:

> [a]greements known as 'delimitation agreements' are lawful and useful if they serve to delimit, in the mutual interest of the parties, the spheres within which their respective trademarks may be used, and are intended to avoid confusion or competition between them. This is not to say that such agreements are excluded from application of Article 85 of the Treaty if they also have the aim of dividing up the market or restricting competition in other ways.[50]

In an early case, the European Court of Justice (as it was then) upheld the decision of the Commission that a delimitation agreement that effectively kept one of the parties out of the German market, with respect to certain tobacco products, was unlawful.[51] Previously, the European Commission had ruled in a preliminary decision that there was an unlawful partitioning of markets when one party undertook not to sell the relevant goods in France, while the other party undertook not to sell the identical goods in the United Kingdom.[52] Courts, ruling under English law, took a similar position under the common law doctrine of restraint of trade, although the applicability of that doctrine in light of later English legislation can be questioned.[53] Against this backdrop, and at the national level, the German Federal Supreme Court has ruled that a prior rights agreement may have the effect of restricting competition if there is

---

48 Moss, *supra* note 1, at 219–21.
49 *See generally*, Fawlk, *supra* note 1; and WILKOF & BURKITT, *supra* note 1, 9–34 to 9–44.
50 BAT v. Commission, 35/83 [1985] 2 C.M.L.R. 470, 491.
51 *Id.*
52 Sirdar/Phildar [1975] 1 C.M.L.R. D 93.
53 *See* WILKOF & BURKITT, *supra* note 1, 9–42 and 9–43.

Chapter 11 THE UNIQUE WORLD OF TRADEMARK CONSENT AGREEMENTS

no basis to conclude that the undertakings and restrictions were directed at resolving a bona fide legal claim.[54]

11.38 Having regard to the position under European Union law and practice, it can be argued that the position may reflect a view of the relationship between trademarks and competition law different from that held in the United States. Until the 1970s, the general approach taken under United States antitrust law was that trademarks constituted a material anti-competitive risk, because a strong mark by virtue of extensive advertising could enjoy market power where demand, price, and output for the product could be manipulated ('monopolistic competition'). That view waned and was supplemented by the position that trademarks are pro-competitive, because they lower search costs for consumers seeking desired goods and services, and induce higher product quality.[55] Perhaps the continuing position under European Union law to view consent agreements as potentially anti-competitive reflects a fundamentally different view from that held in the United States regarding the market power of a trademark.[56]

11.39 The potential tension between the private and public aspects of a consent agreement is most pronounced in the context of the trademark registration process. The question raised is whether the registry is bound by virtue of the consent agreement to accept the declarations contained therein, especially with respect to the potential for likelihood of confusion between the marks covered by the agreement. The issue is most starkly presented when the particular national trademark registration system empowers examiners to evaluate the registrability of a mark based on third-party rights ('relative grounds' of examination). A notable example is the position in the United States, where examiners are charged with vetting an application inter alia on the basis of third-party rights. In such a situation, should a consent agreement have the effect of supplanting the professional discretion of the examiner by the private agreement of the parties?[57]

---

54 Jette Joop, Federal Supreme Court, Case KZR 71/08 (7 December 2010), 2011 GRUR 641–7.
55 *See* Jerre B. Swann, *The Evolution of Trademark Economics – From the Harvard School to the Chicago School to WIPO – as Sheparded by INTA and The Trademark Reporter*, 104 TMR 1132 (2014).
56 *See generally*, Carin Thomsen, *Trademark Coexistence Agreements in the Perspective of EU Competition Law*, MA Thesis, Department of Law, Gothenburg University, December 2012, *available 16 September 2015 at* https://gupea.ub.gu.se/bitstream/2077/32214/1/gupea_2077_32214_1.pdf.
57 A comprehensive summary of the position under U.S. practice was set, albeit nearly 30 years ago, by van Santen & Claessens, *supra* note 1.

272

11.40 While not addressed explicitly in the trademark statute itself, the issue of consent agreements in the context of registration is addressed in the Trademark Manual of Examining Procedure (TMEP).[58] The basic position taken, based on the jurisprudence of the Federal Circuit, is that 'consent agreements should be given great weight, and the USPTO should not substitute its judgment concerning likelihood of confusion for the judgment of the real parties without good reason'. This position applies, unless the consent submitted is a so-called naked consent, and 'on balance' the 'other relevant factors do not dictate a finding of a likelihood of confusion'. A 'naked consent' is a consent agreement that 'contain[s] little more than a prior registrant's consent to registration of an applied-for mark and possibly a mere statement that source confusion is believed to be unlikely'.

11.41 It should be carefully noted that the position taken under the TMEP is limited to United States examination practice. Other national trademark examination offices may reach different positions on how to reconcile the public and private aspects of giving effect to a consent agreement, reflecting the on-going tension between these two sets of interests. The upshot is that while the parties to a consent agreement are subject to the general principles of freedom of contract, there is no assurance that the understandings reached and the undertakings made will be given effect, especially with respect to registration.

H. CONCLUSION

11.42 Trademark consent agreements of various types and nomenclatures are a regular feature of, and cast a broad shadow over, contemporary trademark practice. However, as broad as the shadow is that they cast over trademark practice, so too is the degree to which consent agreements operate within their own shadow, removed from most statutory arrangements, sporadically addressed, if at all, by the guidelines and regulations that instruct trademark registry practice; only on rare occasion being the focus of commentator attention. This chapter has sought to bring consent agreements into the light of public discourse, and to highlight the issues that characterize them, both conceptually and as a matter of trademark law and practice. It is a first word, hopefully a worthy one, but it awaits those will follow with their further inquiries and discourse about this unique form of trademark agreement.

---

58 Trademark Manual of Examining Procedure (TMEP), at section 1207.01(d)(viii).

Chapter 11 THE UNIQUE WORLD OF TRADEMARK CONSENT AGREEMENTS

APPENDIX

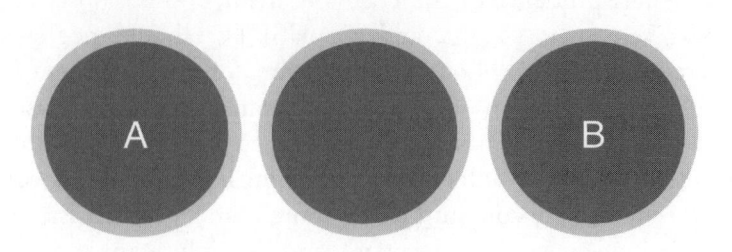

Figure 11.1   A, B, explicit 'no man's land'

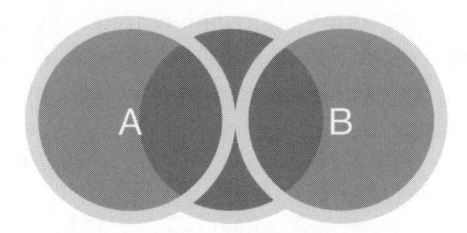

Figure 11.2   A, B, no explicit 'no man's land'

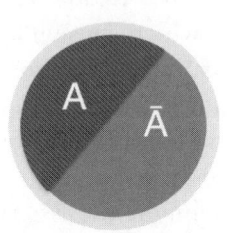

Figure 11.3   A, not Ā

Figure 11.4 A, not Ā, explicit no man's land

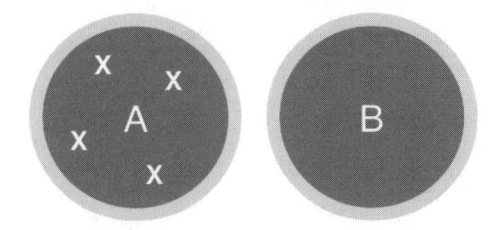

Figure 11.5 A, B, with explicit exclusions to A, or vice versa

12

CHOICE-OF-COURT AND CHOICE-OF-LAW CLAUSES IN INTERNATIONAL TRADEMARK TRANSACTIONS

Dai Yokomizo[*]

A. INTRODUCTION	12.01	(b) Limitation	12.20
		(c) Summary	12.25
B. CHOICE-OF-COURT CLAUSE	12.04	3. Summary	12.29
1. Practice	12.05		
(a) Which country's court is chosen?	12.05	C. CHOICE-OF-LAW CLAUSE	12.31
		1. Practice	12.32
(b) Is a choice-of-court clause exclusive or not?	12.06	2. Legal issues	12.34
		(a) Validity	12.35
(c) Choice-of-court clause or arbitration clause?	12.07	(b) Scope	12.39
		3. Summary	12.41
(d) Summary	12.08		
2. Legal issues	12.09	D. CONCLUSION	12.42
(a) Validity	12.13		

A. INTRODUCTION

12.01 This Chapter deals with choice-of-court and choice-of-law clauses in international trademark transactions. Typically, there are two kinds of international transactions with regard to trademark: licensing agreements and assignment of trademarks. The former relates to the authorization that is granted by a licensor to a licensee to use a trademark with respect to a variety of products, including collateral and promotional products. The latter concerns the transfer of the ownership of a trademark registered in one country or trademarks

---

[*] Professor of Law, Nagoya University, Graduate School of Law. This chapter is the outcome of the Grants-in-aid for Scientific Research (the Japanese Society for the Promotion of Science, for Scientists (A): 2012–2015) project: 'Establishment of a framework coordinating the international harmonization and diversification of IP law and competition law' (Principal Researcher: Prof. Masabumi Suzuki). I am grateful to Ms. Mitsuko Miyagawa (Attorney-at-Law, Partner of TMI Associates) for kindly accepting my interview about international trademark transactions.

A. INTRODUCTION

registered in several countries by its owner to another entity.[1] In this respect, a trademark assignment is similar to the transfer of other properties. Such transfer does not have specific relevance with regard to choice-of-court and choice-of-law, except that the assignment proceeding should generally be completed in accordance with the law of the country of registration, regardless of the law that the parties choose to apply to the assignment contract. For this reason, this Chapter focuses on the analysis of licensing agreements, which are more specifically relevant for the topic at issue.

12.02 In addition to a direct licensing agreement between a licensor in Country A and a licensee in Country B, there are cases where a licensor in Country A concludes a licensing agreement with a distributor in Country B, which in turn concludes a sub-licensing agreement with a sub-licensee in Country B.[2] There are also cases where a licensor in Country A establishes a subsidiary in Country B, and this subsidiary concludes a sub-licensing agreement with a sub-licensee in Country B. Although these kinds of transactions are popular in trademark practice, these sub-licensing agreements are not significant with regard to the choice-of-court and choice-of-law, since these agreements can be generally considered as domestic transactions in Country B. Accordingly, this Chapter focuses primarily on the analysis of direct licensing agreements between a licensor in Country A and a licensee in Country B, which again are more relevant for the topic at issue.

12.03 As a trademark licensing agreement constitutes a long-term relation between a licensor and a licensee, most often a dispute resolution clause such as a choice-of-court clause and a choice-of-law clause are inserted in the agreement.[3] With respect to these clauses, the following question could be asked: is there any special element in these clauses in a trademark licensing agreement as compared to similar clauses in other international contracts? If the answer is affirmative, and these clauses are in fact special with respect to trademark licensing agreements, then how should these clauses be regulated? In the following Sections, this Chapter analyzes the issues related to choice-of-court clauses and choice-of-law clauses in the context of trademark licensing agreements. In particular, this Chapter addresses issues related to the inequality of the bargaining power between the parties involved.

---

1   *See* Interview with Mitsuko Miyagawa, Attorney, TMI Associates (22 September 2014) [hereinafter *Interview with Ms. Miyagawa*] (highlighting that the typical case in this respect is that a foreign company under a financial difficulty assigns all trademarks registered in Japan to a Japanese company).
2   *See* IP High Court, Judgment, 29 September 2010, *available 16 September 2015 at* COURTS IN JAPAN, http://www.courts.go.jp/.
3   *Cf.* Tokyo District Court, Unpublished Judgment, 23 July 2009. The court denied the plaintiff's alleged existence of a contract by holding that it was unnatural that the parties had stipulated neither a choice-of-court clause nor a choice-of-law clause in concluding a long-term distributor agreement.

B. CHOICE-OF-COURT CLAUSE

12.04 In order to identify the choice-of-court clause in international licensing agreements with regard to trademarks, (1) the choice-of-court clause will be described[4] and (2) the two main legal issues of validity of a choice-of-court clause and limitation to the scope of the clause will be examined.

1. Practice

(a) Which country's court is chosen?

12.05 First, how is the country's court chosen in practice? In Japan, there are four cases about disputes on an international licensing agreement with regard to trademarks discussing the issue of choice-of-court clause. In these four instances, the parties agreed to the countries of litigation were France,[5] the State of California,[6] the United Kingdom[7] and the State of Hawaii.[8] These countries directly corresponded to the nationality or the place of incorporation of the licensors. The more advantageous position of the licensor in a licensing agreement could explain the fact that a country in which a licensor was incorporated was chosen as the place of litigation.[9]

(b) Is a choice-of-court clause exclusive or not?

12.06 Second, does a choice-of-court clause provide for the exclusive jurisdiction of the court of a country that the parties selected, or only for the additional jurisdiction of that court? Whereas it is generally considered that the majority of the clauses create an exclusive jurisdiction,[10] there is a case in which the choice-of-court clause referred to the non-exclusive jurisdiction of the designated court in addition to jurisdiction of the courts in other countries.[11] The court has also interpreted the following choice-of-court clause as the non-exclusive jurisdiction clause: 'Any dispute concerning or arising out of this

---

4 These developments are essentially based on information received from practitioners, since the experience of the author is limited because he is a scholar. Also, cases and practice referred to hereafter will be limited to Japan. Even so, it seems reasonable to think that the trend in Japan has a lot in common with other industrialized countries.
5 Tokyo District Court, Judgment, 26 March 2014, *available* 16 September 2015 at COURTS IN JAPAN, http://www.courts.go.jp/.
6 Tokyo District Court, Judgment, 31 March 2010, *available* 16 September 2015 at COURTS IN JAPAN, http://www.courts.go.jp/.
7 Tokyo District Court, Judgment, 28 January 1999, 995 HANREI TAIMUZU [Judicial Times] 242; 1670 HANREI JIHO [Judicial Reports] 75.
8 Tokyo District Court, Judgment, 26 September 2003, 1156 HANREI TAIMUZU 268. In this case, the parties did not arrive at the conclusion of a licensing agreement.
9 *Interview with Ms. Miyagawa, supra* note 1.
10 *Id.*
11 *See* Tokyo District Court Judgment, 28 January 1999, *supra* note 7.

Agreement shall be amicably settled between the parties hereto. Failing this, any dispute between the parties shall be submitted to the Commercial Court in Paris, France.'[12] In this case, a French individual living in Switzerland as the licensor initiated an action before a Japanese court against its Japanese licensee. It seems reasonable as a legal strategy for a licensor to conclude a non-exclusive jurisdiction clause designating the place of its incorporation, leaving the possibility that it would take an action before a court in the country in which the defendant resides. Thus, it depends upon the licensor's preference to assess whether the jurisdiction clause is exclusive or non-exclusive.

(c) Choice-of-court clause or arbitration clause?

12.07 Finally, which dispute resolution system is preferred in licensing agreements with regard to trademarks: litigation or arbitration? There is a case in Japan in which parties in a licensing agreement concluded an arbitration agreement and an arbitral award was rendered.[13] According to a leading lawyer in this field, the dispute resolution system chosen depends on the bargaining power of parties, but, generally speaking, an arbitration clause may be preferred in cases where the judicial system in the country of a licensor is not so trustworthy.[14]

(d) Summary

12.08 In practice, there seems to be no special element in choice-of-court clauses in licensing agreements with regard to trademarks, except to confirm the trend that a country in which a licensor is incorporated is chosen as the place of litigation. The question therefore arises whether it is necessary to intervene with parties' choice of court so that a licensee can choose other jurisdictions. Considering that licensing agreements are generally concluded between business entities and that parties tend to avoid going to court, which may harm their brand image, such intervention does not seem necessary.

2. Legal issues

12.09 In international transactions, a choice-of-court clause is often inserted in order to assure legal certainty and foreseeability. This is also the case in international licensing agreements regarding trademarks, and particularly in cases where a

---

12 *See* Tokyo District Court Judgment, 26 March 2014, *supra* note 5.
13 Tokyo District Court, Judgment, 26 January 2004, 1157 HANREI TAIMUZU 267; 1847 HANREI JIHO 123.
14 *Interview with Ms. Miyagawa, supra* note 1.

licensing agreement deals with corresponding trademarks in different jurisdictions, a choice-of-court clause is considered the most efficient way to avoid the fragmentation of litigation.[15]

12.10   Rules on choice-of-court agreements should be unified worldwide so that they could lead to legal certainty. However, rules on international adjudicative jurisdiction have not been unified and each country has had its own domestic law in this field, including rules on choice-of-court agreements. This situation appears to be changing. First, the Hague Choice-of-court Convention was signed on 30 June 2005 (hereafter referred to as 'Hague Convention').[16] Secondly, as for international IP disputes, soft-law-typed principles in matters of IP and conflict of laws have been drafted. For example, the American Law Institute published 'Intellectual Property: Principles Governing Jurisdiction, Choice-of-law, and Judgments in Transnational Disputes' (hereafter referred to as 'ALI Principles') in August 2008.[17] The European Max-Planck Group on Conflict of Laws in Intellectual Property (CLIP) published the 'Principles for Conflict of Laws in Intellectual Property' (hereafter referred to as 'CLIP Principles') in 2011.[18] The Group for Japanese Research Project 'The Transparency and Enrichment of Japanese Laws Concerning International Transactions in the 21st Century – Doing Cross-Border Business with/in Japan' ('Transparency of Japanese Law Project') drafted the 'Transparency Proposal on Jurisdiction, Choice-of-law, Recognition and Enforcement of Foreign Judgments in Intellectual Property' (hereafter referred to as 'Transparency Proposal').[19] Members of the Private International Law Association of Japan and Korea drafted a joint proposal 'Principles of Private International Law on Intellectual Property Rights' (hereafter referred to as 'Joint Proposal') in

---

15   Toshiyuki Kono & Paulus Jurčys, *General Report*, in INTELLECTUAL PROPERTY AND PRIVATE INTERNATIONAL LAW (Toshiyuki Kono ed., 2012).
16   Convention on Choice of Court Agreements, Hague Conference on Private International Law (30 June 2005), *available 16 September 2015 at* http://www.hcch.net/index_en.php?act=conventions.text&cid=98 [hereinafter Hague Convention]. The Hague Convention entered into force on 1 October 2015. *See* Marta Requejo, *The Hague Convention on the Choice of Court Agreements Enters into Force*, CONFLICT OF LAWS.NET (5 October 2015), *available 24 October 2015 at* http://conflictoflaws.net/2015/the-hague-convention-on-the-choice-of-court-agreements-enters-into-force/.
17   THE AMERICAN LAW INSTITUTE, INTELLECTUAL PROPERTY: PRINCIPLES GOVERNING JURISDICTION, CHOICE OF LAW, AND JUDGMENTS IN TRANSACTIONAL DISPUTES (2008) [hereinafter ALI PRINCIPLES].
18   EUROPEAN MAX-PLANCK GROUP ON CONFLICT OF LAWS IN INTELLECTUAL PROPERTY, CONFLICT OF LAWS IN INTELLECTUAL PROPERTY – THE CLIP PRINCIPLES AND COMMENTARY (2013) [hereinafter CLIP PRINCIPLES].
19   INTELLECTUAL PROPERTY IN THE GLOBAL ARENA – JURISDICTION, APPLICABLE LAW, AND THE RECOGNITION OF JUDGMENTS IN EUROPE, JAPAN AND THE US (Jürgen Basedow, Toshiyuki Kono & Axel Metzger eds., 2010) [hereinafter TRANSPARENCY PROPOSAL].

2010.[20] Finally, a special committee under the auspices of the International Law Association ('ILA') entitled 'Intellectual Property and Private International Law' was created in November 2010. It aims to draft guidelines that could be used by national and international lawmakers, as well as in international dispute resolution.[21]

These efforts to establish an international framework are influential and contribute to the unification of conflict-of-laws rules in matters of intellectual property (IP).[22] However, a question arises: how are these principles unified? As for choice-of-court agreements, the published materials are unanimously in favour of such agreements and tend to give the agreements a broad scope. Nevertheless, these principles and proposals are still different with respect to certain issues. 12.11

Among the many issues in choice-of-court agreements regarding trademark licensing agreements, two main issues will be focused on here: (1) validity, and (2) limitation to agreements. As for the validity of choice-of-court agreements, the formal and substantive validity and the capacity will be discussed. As for the limitation to agreements, issues with regard to exclusive jurisdiction, weak parties, and public policy will be discussed. 12.12

(a) Validity

(i) Formal validity

First, the conclusion of the choice-of-court agreement in writing is often questioned as a formal requirement of the agreement's validity. Even though the Hague Convention, the Transparency Proposal, and the Joint Proposal require the choice-of-court agreement to be in writing,[23] the CLIP principles allow parties to conclude a choice-of-court agreement in 'a form which accords with the practices which the parties have established between themselves', and, 'in cases of international trade or commerce, in a form which accords with a widely known usage'.[24] This liberal approach of the CLIP Principles is said to 12.13

---

20 CHITEKI ZAISAN NO KOKUSAI SHIHO GENSOKU KENKYU [RESEARCH ON PRINCIPLES OF PRIVATE INTERNATIONAL LAW IN INTELLECTUAL PROPERTY] 125 (Shoichi Kidana ed., Waseda University Comparative Law Study Series 2012) [hereinafter JOINT PROPOSAL].
21 INTERNATIONAL LAW ASSOCIATION, INTELLECTUAL PROPERTY AND PRIVATE INTERNATIONAL LAW COMMITTEE (2008), *available 16 September 2015 at* http://www.ila-hq.org/en/committees/index.cfm/cid/1037.
22 For example, the Supreme Court in the UK referred to the ALI principles and the CLIP Principles in Lucasfilm Ltd. v. Ainsworth [2011] UKSC 39, [2011] 3 W.L.R. 487 (appeal taken from Eng.).
23 Hague Convention, *supra* note 16, at art. 3(c); Joint Proposal, *supra* note 20, at art. 205(1); Transparency Proposal, *supra* note 19, at art. 107.
24 CLIP PRINCIPLES, *supra* note 18, at art. 2:301(3).

be in line with Article 23 of the Brussels I Regulation 44/2001.[25] Under the Brussels system, the form of international usage was added in 1978 in order to relax the writing requirement and to ease the use of standard contract.[26] Thus, proposed international norms reflect the current difference in respective jurisdictions.

12.14 As the above-mentioned principles and proposals provide the material requirements for the formal validity, the ALI Principles provide a choice-of-law rule relating to this issue: the formal validity of a choice-of-court agreement shall be governed by the law of the designated forum State, including its conflict of laws rules.[27] This approach seems based on the idea that the formal requirement for the validity differs from country to country and that it would be better to propose a choice-of-law rule on this issue than to define material requirements.

(ii) Substantive validity

12.15 Second, with respect to the substantive requirements for the validity of choice-of-court agreements, either the substantive law of the designated court or the law designated by a choice-of-law rule of the designated forum will determine which laws would be applicable to the requirement.

12.16 On one hand, the CLIP Principles and the Joint Proposal adopt the substantive law of the designated court, since 'it seems more favorable with regard to legal certainty'.[28] On the other hand, the Hague Convention and the ALI principles adopt the law designated by a choice-of-law rule,[29] since 'reference to the whole law permits the designated court to honor party autonomy'.[30] The newly revised Brussels I Regulation also adopts the latter approach,[31] inspired by the Hague Convention.[32]

---

25 Council Regulation 44/2001. On Jurisdiction and the Recognition and Enforcement of Judgments in Civil and Commercial Matters, 2000 O.J. (L 12) (EC).
26 EUROPEAN COMMENTARIES ON PRIVATE INTERNATIONAL LAW, BRUSSELS I REGULATION 415 (Ulrich Magnus & Peter Mankowski eds., 2nd edn. 2012).
27 ALI PRINCIPLES, *supra* note 17, at art. 202(3)(a).
28 CLIP PRINCIPLES, *supra* note 18, at art. 2:301(2); JOINT PROPOSAL, *supra* note 20, at art. 205(4).
29 Trevor Hartley & Masato Dogauchi, *Explanatory Report on the 2005 Hague Choice of Court Agreements Convention*, HAGUE CONFERENCE ON PRIVATE INTERNATIONAL LAW ¶ 125 (2007), *available 16 September 2015 at* http://www.hcch.net/upload/expl37e.pdf; ALI PRINCIPLES, *supra* note 17, at art. 202(3)(a). This provision is said to be consistent with the Hague Convention. *See* ALI PRINCIPLES. *supra* note 17, at Part III.
30 ALI PRINCIPLES, *supra* note 17, at Part III.
31 Council Regulation 1215/2012, art. 20, 2012 O.J. (L351) 1 (EU) [hereinafter Brussels I Regulation (Recast)].
32 Christoph Heinze, *Choice of Court Agreements, Coordination of Proceedings and Provisional Measures in the Reform of the Brussels I Regulation*, 75 RABELSZ 581, 584 (2011).

Other than those approaches, Japanese courts have held that the *lex fori* ought to govern the substantial validity.[33] However, this approach is criticized by the Joint Proposal since 'according to this idea, the existence and validity of the agreement on jurisdiction may not be decided until an action is filed'.[34]

(iii) Capacity

Third, the questions regarding the capacity of a party to conclude a choice-of-court agreement are twofold: First, is the law applicable to party capacity different from the law applicable to the substantive validity of the agreement? Second, if different, how is the applicable law decided?

Traditionally, the law applicable to capacity has been separately determined from the law applicable to the contract,[35] and it differs between countries whether nationality or domicile is chosen as the connecting factor. Among the international principles and proposals discussed here, the ALI principles follow the traditional approach and use a party's residence as a connecting factor.[36] In contrast, under the CLIP Principles, the law applicable to capacity is not distinguished from the law applicable to the substantive validity and shall be the law of the State of the designated court.[37] Finally, under the Hague Convention, since it was considered too ambitious to lay down a uniform choice-of-law rule, the Convention adopts a particular approach: capacity is determined both by the choice-of-law rules of the chosen court and by the choice-of-law rules of the court seized.[38]

(b) Limitation

(i) Exclusive jurisdiction

The question of exclusive jurisdiction should be mentioned first when discussing limitations on choice-of-court agreements. Some principles provide that a choice-of-court agreement shall be null and void if courts in a country (or countries) other than the country designated by parties have exclusive jurisdiction.[39] The same applies under other principles and proposals that refer the validity issue to the law (including or excluding the choice-of-law rules) of the country chosen by parties. Existing laws in different jurisdictions have the rule

---

33 [Supreme Court of Civil Reports], 28 November 1975, 29 Minshu 1554.
34 JOINT PROPOSAL, *supra* note 20, at 143.
35 *See* Ho no Tekiyo ni kansuru Tsusoku-ho [Tsusoku-Ho] [Act on General Rules for Application of Laws], Act No. 78 of 2006, art. 4(1) (Japan): 'A person's capacity to act is governed by his/her national law.'
36 ALI PRINCIPLES, *supra* note 17, at art. 202(3)(b).
37 CLIP PRINCIPLES, *supra* note 18 at 131. No explanation can be found about the reason why they adopt this approach.
38 Hague Convention, *supra* note 16, at art. 6(b); Trevor Hartley & Masato Dogauchi, *supra* note 29, at ¶ 150.
39 CLIP PRINCIPLES, *supra* note 18, at art. 2:301(4); JOINT PROPOSAL, *supra* note 20, at art. 205(5).

on exclusive jurisdiction, which would invalidate a relevant choice-of-court agreement.[40] Thus, the rule relating to exclusive jurisdiction as a limitation to choice-of-court agreements has been, at least generally, harmonized.

12.21 The next question is the scope of exclusive jurisdiction over IP disputes. The Transparency proposal rejects entirely the existence of exclusive jurisdiction over IP disputes.[41] However the controversy remains whether the country of registration of the IP right has exclusive jurisdiction over an infringement proceeding, if during such a proceeding the defendant raises an incidental question regarding the invalidity of the IP right or in the licensing dispute (for example, the trademark licensee claims that no royalties would be due because the trademark would not be valid). Although the Hague Convention, the CLIP Principles, and the Joint Proposal declare that when the validity issues arise as a mere incidental question, the choice-of-court agreement may not be invalidated,[42] the Brussels I Regulation was revised to the opposite direction,[43] following the ECJ's decision in the GAT/LuK case.[44] Thus, the scope of exclusive jurisdiction over IP disputes is still not unified.[45]

(ii) Weak party

12.22 Second, special considerations for the weak party limit the scope of choice-of-court agreements. The existing laws in the EU and Japan provide restrictions to a choice-of-court agreement with regard to contracts, such as consumer

---

40   Charalambos N. Fragistas, *La compétence internationale exclusive en droit privé*, in 2 STUDI IN ONORE DI ANTONIO SEGNI 197, 202–6 (1967).
41   TRANSPARENCY PROPOSAL, *supra* note 19, at 103.
42   Hague Convention, *supra* note 16, at art. 2(3); CLIP PRINCIPLES, *supra* note 18, at 132; JOINT PROPOSAL, *supra* note 20, at art. 205(5).
43   Brussels I Regulation (Recast), *supra* note 31, at art. 24(4) provides as follows:

The following courts of a Member State shall have exclusive jurisdiction, regardless of the domicile of the parties:

… (4) in proceedings concerned with the registration or validity of patents, trademarks, designs, or other similar rights required to be deposited or registered, irrespective of whether the issue is raised by way of an action or as a defense, the courts of the Member State in which the deposit or registration has been applied for, has taken place or is under the terms of an instrument of the Union or an international convention deemed to have taken place.

44   Case C-4/03, Gesellshaft fur Antriebstechnik mbH & Co.KG v. Lamellen und Kupplungsbau Beteligungs KG, [2006] E.C.R. I-06509.
45   In this respect, the Tokyo District Court in the Coral Sand Case explicitly denied the exclusive jurisdiction of courts of the state of registration for such cases, on the grounds that the decision on validity as a presupposed question would have effect only between the parties to the action and not *erga omnes* effect. Tokyo District Court, Judgment, 16 October 2003, 1874 HANREI JIHO 23. The position of this court seems more compatible with the ordinary framework of conflict of laws than the above-mentioned ECJ decision. Dai Yokomizo, *Intellectual Property and Conflict of Laws: Between State Policies and Private Interests*, 35 (3) AIPPI JOURNAL 119, 121 (2010).

contracts and employment contracts.⁴⁶ Based on the current situation of those two bodies, the Hague Convention excludes consumer contracts and employment contracts from its scope.⁴⁷ Also, the CLIP Principles do not include specific rules on consumer contracts, since 'the issue raised by such contracts are not specific to contracts related to intellectual property but are of a general nature'.⁴⁸ Thus, the drafted Principles and Proposals do not deal with contracts involving weak parties.

However, the existing rules relating to the above-mentioned contracts are different in their scope and their effects.⁴⁹ Thus, the harmonization of these rules will have an impact on IP disputes. Also, it should be noted that there is no provision for the protection of a licensee as the weaker party in these rules.   **12.23**

(iii) Public policy

Finally, limitation by the public policy should be mentioned. According to Article 6 of the Hague Convention, 'a court of a Contracting State other than that of the chosen court shall suspend or dismiss proceedings to which an exclusive choice-of-court agreement applies'. However, there are five exceptions to such obligation, one of which allows courts not chosen to reject an agreement when 'giving effect to the agreement would lead to a manifest injustice or would be manifestly contrary to the public policy of the State of the court seized'.⁵⁰ According to the Explanatory Report, 'manifest injustice' could cover the exceptional cases where one of the parties would not get a fair trial (that is, due to bias or corruption) and where the particular circumstances in which the agreement was concluded create injustice, such as fraud.⁵¹   **12.24**

---

46 For example, under Article 3–7(5) and (6) of the Japanese Code of Civil Procedure, a choice-of-court agreement with respect to a dispute arising in the future shall be effective only in cases where it is agreed that action can be filed to a court or courts of the state where the consumer had his/her domicile at the time of conclusion of the consumer contract, or in cases where a consumer files an action with a court of the state agreed in the agreement, or in cases where a business operator files an action in Japan or a foreign state and a consumer invokes the agreement in the proceedings in his/her favour. Also, a choice-of-court agreement with respect to a dispute arising in the future shall be effective only in cases where it is agreed at the time of termination of a labour contract and it is agreed that an action can be filed with a court or courts of the state where the place of performance of his/her labour at that time is located, or in cases where an employer files an action with a court of the state agreed in the agreement, or in cases where an employer files an action in Japan or a foreign state and an employee invokes the agreement in the proceedings in his/her favour. See Dai Yokomizo, *The New Act on International Jurisdiction in Japan: Significance and Remaining Problems*, 34 ZEITSCHRIFT FÜR JAPANISCHES RECHT [JOURNAL OF JAPANESE LAW] 95 (2012). As for the EU, *see* Toshiyuki Kono and Paulus Jurčys, *supra* note 15, at 128–9.
47 Hague Convention, *supra* note 16, at art. 2(1).
48 CLIP PRINCIPLES, *supra* note 18, at 134.
49 For example, there is no rule as to limitation of choice-of-court agreements with regards to insurance contracts in Japan whereas there is one in the Brussels I Regulation at Article 13. *See* Brussels I Regulation (Recast), *supra* note 31, at art. 13.
50 *Id.* at art. 6(c).
51 Trevor Hartley & Masato Dogauchi, *supra* note 29, at ¶ 151.

Although the same consideration can be seen in the current Japanese law[52] and the EU law,[53] the Principles and the Proposals do not follow this limitation provided by the Hague Convention. The ALI Principles explicitly rejected this idea, 'because it invites forum-shopping and therefore defeats the predictability that is the goal of the forum-selection clause'.[54] Thus, the necessity of such a limitation should be further discussed.

(c) Summary

12.25 This Part dealt with two main issues regarding choice-of-court agreements in international licensing agreements, namely validity and limitation to agreements. It was confirmed that despite a strong tendency to the harmonization of relevant rules among different jurisdictions and different international principles, significant differences still remain. Here two issues will be reflected: are there many specific issues on choice-of-court agreements within the context of international licensing agreements (or IP disputes)? Also, what issues would be easier or more difficult in the harmonization of the relevant rules?

(i) Special treatment of international trademark licensing agreements

12.26 The above-mentioned discussions about choice-of-court agreements in IP disputes (including licensing agreements) seem to apply not only to IP disputes but also to other international transactions, although the Principles and Proposals (other than the Hague Convention) cover specifically international IP disputes; the differences between the proposed rules with regard to the validity as well as limitation to choice-of-court agreements are principally not based on the particularity of IP law or IP rights. The only difference arising from that particularity is about exclusive jurisdiction: the question whether or not the scope of exclusive jurisdiction should cover the cases where a defendant raises the issue of validity (of the licensed trademark) as an incidental question in infringement proceedings or in a licensing dispute. The answer to this question would directly influence the scope of choice-of-court agreements in international IP contracts, such as trademark licensing agreements. However, this question in itself could be discussed within the rule on exclusive jurisdiction.

---

52 Article 3–7 (4) extends the cases where an agreement to the effect that an action can be exclusively filed with a court or courts of a foreign state may not be invoked by referring to the situation where such court or courts are unable to exercise their jurisdiction in fact. That situation would cover the cases of corruption.
53 In the EU, it is said that courts can declare null and void choice-of-court agreements which are considered unfair. Toshiyuki Kono and Paulus Jurčys, *supra* note 15, at 129.
54 ALI PRINCIPLES, *supra* note 17, at 40.

12.27 Thus, there seems no question with regard to choice-of-court agreements relating to which a special provision for IP contracts such as trademark licensing agreements would be necessary.[55] The harmonization of rules with regard to choice-of-court agreements should be discussed in a more general context, namely, within international contracts as a whole.

(ii) Issues difficult to harmonize and issues easy to harmonize

12.28 Which issues, then, are difficult and which issues are relatively easy to harmonize? Naturally the unification process with regard to conflict of laws (private international law) was frustrated a number of times, including during the Convention on Jurisdiction and Foreign Judgments in Civil and Commercial Matters. However, as the conclusion of the Hague Convention illustrates, issues with regard to choice-of-court agreements are relatively easy to find a consensus among states, probably because they do not directly concern the public interest of states. In contrast, issues concerning the limitation of choice-of-court agreements such as exclusive jurisdiction, weak party, and public policy directly concern the public interest and fundamental values of each state, thus they seem more difficult to lead to a consensus.

3. Summary

12.29 As has been mentioned above, the special committee 'Intellectual Property and Private International Law' in the ILA is working on the drafting of guidelines in matters of conflict of laws in IP issues. A rule on choice-of-court agreements is also on the agenda.[56] However, these issues should be discussed in a broader context and not be limited to the IP field. Thus, it is desirable not to touch on these issues in the agreement drafting process.

12.30 Also, within limitation to choice-of-court agreements, there are certainly greater differences between jurisdictions and it is unlikely that rules relating to the issues discussed in this Paper would be unified, due to the difference of state policies. However, harmonization is not unification, and if the direction

---

55 *Cf.* Alexander Peukert, *Contractual Jurisdiction Clauses and Intellectual Property*, in INTELLECTUAL PROPERTY AND PRIVATE INTERNATIONAL LAW 55, 69–71 (Joseph Drexl & Annette Kur eds., 2005). The author concluded (with the reservation about the question of exclusive jurisdiction) that the rationale and advantages of choice-of-court clauses and the compromise that may be found with regard to purely contractual aspects of forum selection can be applied without reservation to IP related transactions.

56 The ILA Guidelines on Intellectual Property and Private International Law (as modified and adopted in the Washington Conference (2014)) has a rule on choice-of-court agreements which provides as follows: 'The parties to a particular relationship should be allowed to designate in an agreement a court to have jurisdiction over their dispute. The chosen court shall have jurisdiction to decide all contractual and non-contractual obligations and all other claims arising from that legal relationship unless the parties express their intent to restrict the court's jurisdiction. Such jurisdiction shall be exclusive unless the parties have agreed otherwise.'

to which each state aims to proceed is common in the cases, (such as the protection of weak parties) differences of rules in different jurisdictions should be respected, as far as a certain degree of foreseeability of parties is assured.[57]

C. CHOICE-OF-LAW CLAUSE

12.31 As discussed above, the use of the choice-of-law clause in practice shall be (1) described and then (2) examined through legal issues.

1. Practice

12.32 Which country's law is chosen in practice? As mentioned *supra* Part B.1, the parties of the four Japanese cases discussing disputes of an international trademark licensing agreement, chose the laws of France,[58] the State of California,[59] the United Kingdom[60] and the State of Hawaii,[61] which were the countries in which the licensor had nationality or was incorporated. Similar to the choice-of-court clauses, this choice-of-law can be explained by the more advantageous position of the licensor in a licensing agreement making the decision.

12.33 Such a choice seems to have caused no great difficulties for licensees. The relevant rules in different jurisdictions have many commonalities and it is not difficult to obtain information about a foreign law because law firms have their networks worldwide.[62] Here again, it cannot be said from a practical point of view that there are special elements in these licensing agreements discussing the choice-of-law clause, which would require the intervention with the parties' choice of law.

2. Legal issues

12.34 In this Section, the (1) validity and (2) scope of the law applicable to licensing agreements will be discussed.

---

57 Other important topics with regard to choice-of-court agreements such as the relation with rules on parallel proceedings, consolidation and provisional measures cannot be touched upon in this chapter, since each topic would require more profound analysis.
58 *See* Tokyo District Court, 26 March 2014, *supra* note 5.
59 *See* Tokyo District Court, 31 March 2010, *supra* note 6.
60 *See* Tokyo District Court, 28 January 1999, *supra* note 7.
61 *See* Tokyo District Court, 26 September 2003, *supra* note 8.
62 *Interview with Ms. Miyagawa*, *supra* note 1.

C. CHOICE-OF-LAW CLAUSE

(a) Validity

12.35 The principle of party autonomy within international contracts has been established worldwide.[63] Based on this trend, the above-mentioned principles and proposals in matters of IP and conflict of laws also adopt the principle of party autonomy.[64] Three different issues about the validity will be mentioned: validity of a choice-of-law clause, formal validity, and substantive validity.

(i) Validity of choice-of-law clause

12.36 First, the CLIP Principles, the ALI Principles, and the Joint Proposal provide that the existence and validity of a choice-of-law clause has to be determined in accordance with the law that the parties purported to choose.[65] This solution is inspired by Article 3(4) of the Rome I Regulation (Reg. 593/2008),[66] and explained from the viewpoint of protection of the parties' expectations.[67] However, certain reservations are added. For example, the ALI Principles state that choice-of-law clauses in standard form agreements 'are valid only if the choice-of-law clause was reasonable and readily accessible to the nondrafting party at the time the agreement was concluded, and is available for subsequent reference by the court and the parties'.[68] Also, under the CLIP Principles, a party may rely on the law of the state in which he or she resides if it appears from the circumstances that it would not be reasonable to determine the effect of her or his conduct in accordance with the law that the parties purported to choose.[69] The purpose of this solution is to address the problem of silence by one party as to the formation of the contract, and to give a party which would otherwise be bound by the terms of the contract a veto right.[70]

(ii) Formal validity

12.37 As for the formal validity of a contract relating to the license of an IP right, it has been claimed in academic opinions that the *lex loci protectionis* should apply since specific formal requirements for licensing agreements are contained in

---

63 ALI PRINCIPLES, *supra* note 17, at 131.
64 *Id.* at art. 302(1); CLIP PRINCIPLES, *supra* note 18, at art. 3:501(1); TRANSPARENCY PROPOSAL, *supra* note 19, at art. 306(1); JOINT PROPOSAL, *supra* note 20, at art. 302(1).
65 ALI PRINCIPLES, *supra* note 17, at art. 302(4)(a); CLIP PRINCIPLES, *supra* note 18, at art. 3:501(4); JOINT PROPOSAL, *supra* note 20, at art. 302(3). There is no reference to this issue in the Transparency Proposal.
66 CLIP PRINCIPLES, *supra* note 18, at 270.
67 JOINT PROPOSAL, *supra* note 20, at 160.
68 ALI PRINCIPLES, *supra* note 17, at art. 302(5)(a).
69 CLIP PRINCIPLES, *supra* note 18, at art. 3:505(2).
70 *Id.* at 290.

different jurisdictions.[71] However, the Principles and Proposals referring to this issue utilize the *favor negotii* approach, following international contract practice.[72] Thus, the CLIP Principles that adopt this approach state that cases in which the contract would be invalid because the parties complied with *lex loci protectionis* (rather than any of the laws listed as the alternatives) are too rare to justify a tailor-made approach for IP contracts.[73] Under this principle, a contract (for example, relating to license) shall be formally valid if it satisfies the formal requirements of (a) the law which governs it in substance, (b) the law of the State in which either of the parties or its agent is present at the time of the conclusion of the contract, or (c) the law of the State in which either of the parties is habitually resident at that time.[74]

(iii) Substantive validity

12.38 As for the substantive validity of a contract relating to the license of an IP right, it is unanimously accepted in the above-mentioned Principles and Proposals that the law chosen by the parties governs,[75] although there is a slight difference about the determination of the parties' implied choice. In particular, the CLIP Principles admit that the choice shall be made by the clear demonstration of the terms of the contract or by the parties' conduct in the circumstances of the case. Also, it provides that a choice-of-court clause leads to a presumption that the parties have chosen the law of that State.[76] These rules are based on the Commission's Proposal for the Rome I Regulation of 2005.[77]

(b) Scope

12.39 The scope of a choice-of-law clause is limited to contractual issues such as interpretation, performance, the consequence of a breach of obligations, the nullity of the contract and so on,[78] and does not cover issues relating to infringement.[79] Thus, when a third party uses a trademark based on a sub-licensing contract with a licensee with whom a licensing agreement with a

---

71 EUGEN ULMER, DIE IMMATERIALGÜTERRECHTE IM INTERNATIONALEN PRIVATRECHT 100 (1975); DÁRIO MOURA VICENTE, LA PROPRIÉTÉ INTELLECTUELLE EN DROIT INTERNATIONAL PRIVÉ 312–316 (Martinus Nijhoff Publishers, 2009).
72 CLIP PRINCIPLES, *supra* note 18, at 289.
73 *Id.*
74 *Id.* at art. 3:504. *See also* TRANSPARENCY PROPOSAL, *supra* note 19, at art. 306(4).
75 ALI PRINCIPLES, *supra* note 17, at art. 315(1); CLIP PRINCIPLES, *supra* note 18, at art. 3:501(1); TRANSPARENCY PROPOSAL, *supra* note 19, at. 306; JOINT PROPOSAL, *supra* note 20, at art. 302(1).
76 CLIP PRINCIPLES, *supra* note 18, at art. 3:501.
77 *Proposal for a Regulation of the European Parliament and the Council on the law applicable to contractual obligation (Rome I)*, COM (2005) 650 final (15 December 2005). *See* CLIP PRINCIPLES, *supra* note 18, at 270–1.
78 *Cf.* CLIP PRINCIPLES, *supra* note 18, at art. 3:506(1).
79 However, in cases where parties conclude an arbitration agreement, infringement issues may also be determined by the law the parties choose if they so agree.

licensor has been terminated, and the licensor claims the infringement of his or her trademark against this third party, the law applicable to this claim should be the *lex loci protectionis*.

Although a licensing agreement does not concern the transfer of a trademark right, the context of an international trademark contract shall determine whether the transfer of a trademark right shall be governed by the *lex loci protectionis* or the *lex contractus*. In Japan, similar to cases of corporeal property transfer, courts have consistently confirmed a choice-of-law rule on the transfer of copyright: the law of the country for which the protection is sought shall govern the transfer.[80] This rule might also govern cases for the transfer of a trademark right; when a licensing agreement deals with several trademarks in different countries, each country's law shall determine the transfer of the trademark right granted by that country. However, the CLIP Principles adopt the *lex contractus* rule in order to keep away from any *dépeçage* between the contract provisions, including the obligation of the right holder to transfer the intellectual property right, and the contract language of the transfer itself.[81] Considering that the conditions with regard to transfer of the intellectual property right are closely related with state policy of each country, it seems preferable that its transfer shall be governed by *lex loci protectionis*. However, this issue should be examined in the future. **12.40**

3. Summary

The principle of party autonomy has been established worldwide and a choice-of-law clause is commonly used in a trademark licensing agreement, as well as in other international contracts. There is a perception that, in practice, the laws of the licensor's country of residence are chosen because of the difference of the bargaining power, but considering that a licensing agreement concerns a transaction between business entities, the necessity of protecting the weaker party by the choice-of-law does not seem as necessary as it would be in other contracts, namely consumer contracts or employment contracts. Also, the discussion of choice-of-law agreements in IP contracts is mainly developed on the assumption that international IP contracts are drafted as any **12.41**

---

80 For example, *see* Tokyo High Court Judgment, 30 May 2001, 1797 HANREI JIHO 111; Tokyo High Court, 28 May 2003, 1831 HANREI JIHO 135; Tokyo District Court Judgment, 26 October 2007 (unpublished); IP High Court, Judgment, 27 March 2008 (unpublished); Tokyo District Court, Judgment, 30 April 2009 (unpublished).
81 CLIP PRINCIPLES, *supra* note 18, at 271. The position of the ALI Principles is not clear. Whereas Article 315 (1) explicitly confirms the parties' freedom to choose the law applicable to a transfer of interest, the Reporter's Note states that the substantive conditions of a transfer are to be covered by the *lex loci protectionis*. ALI PRINCIPLES, *supra* note 17, at art. 315(1). The other Proposals do not refer to this issue.

international contract. The international contracts have no specific characteristics that would require special rules in IP contracts. Thus, the issues regarding choice-of-law in trademark licensing agreements should also be discussed in a broader context, namely, in the context of international contracts as a whole.

D. CONCLUSION

12.42 Choice-of-court and choice-of-law clauses work smoothly in international trademark licensing agreements and bring no significant problems in practice. Trademark licensing agreements concern brands. Disputes arising from those licensing contracts would harm the business reputation of the parties if the dispute resulted in litigation. The disadvantaged parties would have more difficulty finding the next licensor or licensee. Thus, parties rarely go to court to resolve the dispute.[82]

12.43 As for choice-of-court and choice-of-law clauses, there is a trend toward the court or the law of the licensor's country being selected, but, considering that a licensing agreement concerns a transaction between business entities, it is not necessary to jeopardize party autonomy by intervening.

12.44 As for legal issues with regard to choice-of-court or choice-of-law clauses in international trademark licensing agreements, there are no particular contract requirements that require a different treatment of these issues than in other contracts. Thus, these issues should be analyzed in a broader context, namely, in international contracts.

---

82 *Interview with Ms. Miyagawa, supra* note 1.

13

ALTERNATIVE DISPUTE RESOLUTION MECHANISMS FOR SOLVING TRADEMARK DISPUTES (MEDIATION, UDRP, ARBITRATION)

Jacques de Werra[*]

A. INTRODUCTION	13.01	1. Introduction	13.27
		2. Conditions and features	13.29
B. ADR METHODS FOR SOLVING TRADEMARK DISPUTES	13.02	(a) Objective arbitrability of intellectual property disputes	13.30
1. Mediation	13.03	(b) Consent of parties to submit to arbitration: the scope of the arbitration clause	
2. The UDRP	13.06		13.34
3. UDRP as a model for other ADR systems for trademark-related domain name disputes	13.12	3. Governing law	13.61
		4. Provisional measures	13.66
C. ARBITRATION OF (INTERNATIONAL) TRADEMARK DISPUTES	13.27	D. CONCLUSION	13.69

A. INTRODUCTION

The challenges and costs of litigating global trademark (and other intellectual property)[1] disputes before national courts are well-known. This explains and justifies the growing attention paid to alternative dispute resolution (ADR) mechanisms that are developed in order to solve trademark[2] (and other

13.01

---

[*] Professor of intellectual property law and of contract law and Vice-Rector, University of Geneva.
[1] This chapter will focus on trademark disputes, it being noted that the issue is essentially similar with respect to other categories of intellectual property rights; it is based on various papers by the author, including: Jacques de Werra, *Can Alternative Dispute Resolution Mechanisms Become the Default Method for Solving International Intellectual Property Disputes?*, 43 CALIFORNIA WESTERN INTERNATIONAL LAW JOURNAL 39 (2012); Jacques de Werra, *The Expanding Significance of Arbitration for Patent Licensing Disputes: from Post-Termination Disputes to Pre-Licensing FRAND Disputes*, 4 ASA Bulletin 2014 692 (2014), *available* 17 September 2015 at http://archive-ouverte.unige.ch/unige:46142.
[2] *See* James Morrison, *A Turning Tide, Arbitrating International Trademark Disputes and the Importance of the New WIPO Arbitration Rules*, 69 INTERNATIONAL TRADEMARK ASSOCIATION BULLETIN 10 (1 November 2014), *available* 17 September 2015 at http://www.inta.org/INTABulletin/Pages/ATurningTideArbitrating InternationalTrademarkDisputesandtheImportanceoftheNewWIPOArbitrationRules.aspx; for a more

intellectual property)[3] disputes, which are of particular importance in an international setting because of the interest that parties to an international trademark contract (potentially an international trademark license) may have in defining in advance to which alternative dispute settlement body they shall submit any potential dispute that may arise between them (instead of submitting their dispute to litigation).[4] This chapter will discuss certain alternative dispute resolution mechanisms (outside of arbitration) that may be used in order to solve trademark disputes (see below B), before turning to the use of arbitration (see below C). In light of the overall focus of this book on trademark transactions, this chapter will specifically address certain practical contractual issues that must be carefully assessed when considering the use of arbitration for solving (international) trademark disputes.

B. ADR METHODS FOR SOLVING TRADEMARK DISPUTES

13.02 Trademark disputes can be solved by the submission to various alternative dispute resolution mechanisms outside of the courtroom and outside of arbitration, and specifically to mediation (see below 1) and to the Uniform Domain Name Dispute Resolution Policy (UDRP) with respect to certain trademark-related Internet domain name disputes (see below 2), whereby the UDRP has served as a model for other intellectual property-related domain name disputes (see below 3).

1. Mediation

13.03 The trend of promoting the use of ADR mechanisms for solving certain trademark (and other intellectual property related) disputes is well underway.

---

restrictive view of the interest of arbitration for solving trademark disputes, *see* Frank J. Sullivan, *Is Arbitration Suitable for Trademark Problems?*, 58 TRADEMARK REP. 782 (1968).

3   *See* Joe Tirado/Alejandro I. Garcia, *Reasons to arbitrate IP Cases*, INTELLECTUAL PROPERTY MAGAZINE (8 December 2014), *available* 17 September 2015 *at* http://www.intellectualpropertymagazine.com/copyright/reasons-to-arbitrate-ip-cases-105157.htm.

4   An interesting recent example is the dispute between Pirelli and its former Spanish trademark licensee Licensing Projects SL, which led to an ICC arbitral award, and to litigation in Spain and in France, in which the arbitral award was annulled on procedural grounds (i.e. because of the principle of access to justice that may require to admit counterclaims that are raised by the defendant, here Licensing Projects SL, even if such party cannot pay the advance on costs as required under the relevant (ICC) arbitration rules). *See* Gómez-Acebo & Pombo Abogados, *Alicante Court Considers Trademark Infringement Stemming from Arbitration*, Lexology (14 November 2012), *available* 17 September 2015 *at* http://www.lexology.com/library/detail.aspx?g=9e7dc57d-6a08-4625-bf7a-f4e2ced6c3b5; Andrea Pinna, *La confirmation de la jurisprudence Pirelli par la Cour de cassation et les difficultés pratiques de garantir au plaideur impécunieux l'accès à la justice arbitrale*, 2013-2 THE PARIS JOURNAL OF INTERNATIONAL ARBITRATION 479 (2013), *available* 17 September 2015 *at* http://www.degaullefleurance.com/http://www.degaullefleurance.com/wp-content/uploads/2013/06/ParisJournalofInternationalArbitration_API_2013.pdf.

B. ADR METHODS FOR SOLVING TRADEMARK DISPUTES

At the European Union (EU) level, the Office for Harmonization in the Internal Market (Trademarks and Designs) (hereinafter OHIM) launched intellectual property mediation services in October 2011.[5] The intellectual property mediation services offered by OHIM initially resulted from a decision of the Presidium of the Board of Appeal of 14 April 2011, on the amicable settlement of disputes.[6] The basic idea was to promote mediation (without excluding other available alternative dispute resolution mechanisms).[7] The mediator must be chosen from a list provided by OHIM, whereby all the mediators are staff members of OHIM.[8] Mediation is only available during the course of appeal proceedings and on relative grounds relating to conflicts between the private rights of the litigants.[9] However, it is not available on grounds of public policy such as absolute grounds for refusal of European trademarks or designs.[10]

13.04 At the national level, national intellectual property offices also offer mediation services, such as is done by the United Kingdom Intellectual Property Office which promotes and institutes ADR mechanisms and specifically mediation for certain types of intellectual property disputes.[11]

13.05 The growing importance of these mediation services for trademark disputes has been widely recognized and it can be considered that the future of

---

5 OFFICE OF HARMONIZATION IN THE INTERNAL MARKET, MEDIATION, https://oami.europa.eu/ohimportal/en/mediation (*available 17 September 2015*).
6 Decision No. 2011–1, of the Presidium of the Boards of Appeal, 2011 O.J. 3.10, *available 17 September 2015 at* https://oami.europa.eu/tunnel-web/secure/webdav/guest/document_library/contentPdfs/law_and_practice/presidium_boards_appeal/in_force/2011–1_presidium_decision_on_mediation_en.pdf; this decision was replaced by Decision No 2013–3 of the Presidium of the Boards of Appeal of 5 July 2013 on the amicable settlement of disputes, *available 17 September 2015 at* https://oami.europa.eu/tunnel-web/secure/webdav/guest/document_library/contentPdfs/law_and_practice/presidium_boards_appeal/presidium_decision_2013–3_en.pdf [hereinafter Decision on Mediation].
7 *See id.* at recital 2 ('A friendly settlement should be easier to achieve with recourse to mediation, without prejudice to other alternative dispute resolution mechanism.').
8 'The Office shall maintain a list of qualified members of its staff, who are suitably prepared to intervene in mediation proceedings in the sense of the present decision' *Id.* at art. 7, para. 1. For the list of mediators, *see* OHIM, Mediators, https://oami.europa.eu/ohimportal/en/mediators (*available 17 September 2015*).
9 Decision on Mediation, *supra* note 6, at art. 1, para. 1. ('The request for mediation proceedings may be presented, by a joint declaration from the parties, at any time following the lodging of an appeal.').
10 *Id.* at art. 1, para. 2.
11 *See, e.g.*, INTELLECTUAL PROPERTY OFFICE, PATENTS HEARING MANUAL § 2.01 (July 2014), *available 17 September 2015 at* https://www.gov.uk/government/uploads/system/uploads/attachment_data/file/320984/Hearings_manual_web.pdf ('Alternative Dispute Resolution may provide the best opportunity for resolving the issues quickly, less expensively and with an increased chance of an amicable settlement.'); *see also* INTELLECTUAL PROPERTY OFFICE, INTELLECTUAL PROPERTY MEDIATION (14 May 2015), *available 17 September 2015 at* https://www.gov.uk/guidance/intellectual-property-mediation. However, the dispute may not always be appropriately submitted to an ADR system; this is also the case in Brazil based on a cooperation between the WIPO Arbitration and Mediation Center, see WIPO Mediation for Proceedings Instituted in the Brazilian National Institute of Industrial Property (INPI-BR), *available 17 September 2015 at* http://www.wipo.int/amc/en/center/specific-sectors/inpibr/.

trademark mediation and of intellectual property mediation is promising.[12] Beyond the regulatory framework that will enable and even promote the use of mediation for solving (international) trademark disputes, the offering of such services does not really raise major substantive legal issues from a trademark transaction perspective (by contrast to legal issues that may arise about the availability and interest of arbitration for solving trademark disputes). However, one aspect that must be taken into account by contracting parties who would include a multi-tier dispute resolution clause in their trademark agreement – that will include the preliminary obligation to submit to mediation before 'escalating' the dispute to court proceedings or arbitral proceedings – relates to the potential consequence that will apply in a case when one party would circumvent the obligation to submit to mediation before initiating the court or arbitral proceedings. While this issue is obviously not unique to trademark transactions as such, it should be emphasized that courts may consider that such circumvention is inadmissible so that the parties will be requested to first submit to mediation before initiating legal action. This point should, therefore, be duly considered in the drafting of the relevant dispute resolution clause of a trademark agreement, depending on the interests of the parties at issue and on the circumstances of the case.

2. The UDRP

13.06 One of the best examples of a successful ADR system in solving (international) trademark disputes is the Uniform Domain Name Dispute Resolution Policy (hereinafter UDRP), which was adopted by the Internet Corporation for Assigned Names and Numbers (hereinafter ICANN) on 26 August 1999.[13] ICANN is a 'California Nonprofit Public-Benefit Corporation.'[14] It is not a public state agency despite its contractual relationships with the United States (U.S.) government.[15] It is worth noting that the UDRP was based on policy recommendations, which were prepared under the aegis of the

---

12 For a discussion, *see* Nick Gardner, *Mediation and its Relevance to Intellectual Property Disputes*, 9 JOURNAL OF INTELLECTUAL PROPERTY LAW & PRACTICE 565 (2014).
13 *See* INTERNET CORP. FOR ASSIGNED NAMES AND NUMBERS, UNIFORM DOMAIN NAME DISPUTE RESOLUTION POLICY (24 October 1999), *available 17 September 2015 at* http://www.icann.org/dndr/udrp/policy.htm [hereafter UDRP].
14 ICANN, BYLAWS FOR INTERNET CORPORATION FOR ASSIGNED NAMES AND NUMBERS (30 July 2014), *available 17 September 2015 at* http://www.icann.org/en/general/bylaws.htm.
15 The independence of ICANN was reflected in 'the Affirmation of Commitments' between the U.S. Department of Commerce and ICANN dated 30 September 2009. *See* ICANN, THE AFFIRMATION OF COMMITMENTS – WHAT IT MEANS, (30 September 2009), *available 17 September 2015 at* http://www.icann.org/en/announcements/announcement-30sep09-en.htm#affirmation; it must be noted that ICANN is in a complex multistakeholder process of transition of certain functions (IANA Stewardship transition) that is still underway at the time of writing of this chapter, see https://www.icann.org/en/stewardship (*available 17 September 2015*).

World Intellectual Property Organization (hereinafter WIPO).[16] The UDRP has solved quite a phenomenal number of cybersquatting disputes (that is, several thousand) since its adoption.[17] In addition to the intrinsic quality of the UDRP's design features,[18] its success results particularly from the obligation imposed on all domain name registrars for *generic Top Level Domains* (gTLD) to be accredited with ICANN, whereby such accreditation obligates the registrars to contractually require clients who register domain names to submit to the UDRP.[19] The same obligation applies to cases in which the registrars enter into agreements with third-party resellers who ultimately contract with end-customers.[20] Consequently, the submission of disputes to the UDRP is imposed on all internet domain name holders of gTLD in a hierarchical way, starting from ICANN (top) to the holder of a given domain name (bottom). In other words, a chain of mutual contractual obligations ultimately imposes the UDRP to the relevant domain name holders.

Even if the merits of a complaint under the UDRP depend on the complainant's ability to show the ownership or control over a trademark[21] based on regulations of the country or region where the trademark is registered or protected,[22] the UDRP can generally be characterized by its delocalized nature, both in terms of geography and legal system. In other words, the UDRP applies regardless of the geographic localization of the parties in dispute, specifically the domicile of the owner of the disputed domain name. The UDRP is also legally delocalized and essentially independent from any

13.07

---

16 WORLD INTELLECTUAL PROP. ORG., WIPO INTERNET DOMAIN NAME PROCESS (1999), *available* 17 September 2015 *at* http://www.wipo.int/amc/en/processes/process1/report/finalreport.html [hereinafter WIPO].

17 17 *See* WIPO, *Total Number of Cases Per Year* (2015), *available* 17 September 2015 *at* http://www.wipo.int/amc/en/domains/statistics/cases.jsp.

18 *See* Nicholas Smith & Erik Wilbers, *The UDRP: Design Elements of an Effective ADR Mechanism*, 15 AM. REV. INT'L ARB. 215, 217–18 (2004).

19 *See* ICANN, Registrar Accreditation Agreement (2 August 2012), *available* 17 September 2015 *at* http://www.icann.org/en/registrars/ra-agreement-21may09-en.htm#3 [hereinafter Registrar Accreditation Agreement] ('During the Term of this Agreement, Registrar shall have in place a policy and procedures for resolution of disputes concerning Registered Names. Until different policies and procedures are established by ICANN ... under Section 4, Registrar shall comply with the Uniform Domain Name Dispute Resolution Policy identified on ICANN's ... website (www.icann.org/general/consensus-policies.htm).').

20 *See id.* at art. 3.12 ('If Registrar enters into an agreement with a reseller of Registrar Services to provide Registrar Services ("Reseller"), such agreement must include at least the following provisions ...'); *see also id.* at art. 3.12.2 ('Any registration agreement used by reseller shall include all registration agreement provisions and notices required by the ICANN ... Registrar Accreditation Agreement and any ICANN ... Consensus Policies, and shall identify the sponsoring registrar or provide a means for identifying the sponsoring registrar, such as a link to the InterNIC Whois lookup service.').

21 UDRP, *supra* note 13, at art. 4a(i) ('[Y]our domain name is identical or confusingly similar to a trademark or service mark in which the complainant has rights.').

22 Unregistered trademarks may suffice under certain exceptional circumstances. *See* WIPO, WIPO Overview of WIPO Panel Views on Selected UDRP Questions, *available* 17 September 2015 *at* http://www.wipo.int/amc/en/domains/search/overview2.0/index.html.

legal system because the substantive elements, on which the UDRP is based and decisions are rendered, are independent from any national or regional regulation,[23] except for the existence and control of a trademark by the complainant. The substantive criteria of a decision by the UDRP essentially relates to the good or bad faith registration and the use of the relevant domain name by its holder.[24] Consequently, the UDRP creates a corpus of autonomous rules for internet-related trademark disputes that can be compared to *lex electronic*.[25]

13.08 The adjudicatory power of experts appointed to decide a dispute under the UDRP is narrow in its scope; the decision can only grant the transfer or cancellation of the relevant domain name, or, alternatively, reject the UDRP complaint.[26] The UDRP also provides for the automatic enforcement of decisions that order a transfer or cancellation of the disputed domain name by notifying the registrar. This can only be avoided if the respondent, the holder of the relevant domain name, notifies the dispute resolution entity within ten business days of a lawsuit in the relevant jurisdiction.[27] The party may notify

---

23   It being noted that this independence may sometimes be problematic, particularly when the parties in dispute are located in the same country; decisions nevertheless refrain from importing national law into the UDRP. *See* Case No. D2004–0206, Covance, Inc. v. Covance Campaign, Administrative Panel Decision (WIPO 30 April 2004), *available 17 September 2015 at* http://www.wipo.int/amc/en/domains/decisions/html/2004/d2004-0206.html ('As a matter of principle, this Panel would not have thought that it was appropriate to import unique national legal principles into the interpretation of paragraph 4(c) of the Policy. This is so even if the effect of doing so is desirable in aligning decisions under the Policy with those emerging from the relevant courts and thus avoiding instances of forum shopping.'); *see also* Case No. D2007–1461, 1066 Housing Ass'n, Ltd. v. Mr. D. Morgan, Administrative Panel Decision (WIPO 18 January 2008), *available 17 September 2015 at* http://www.wipo.int/amc/en/domains/decisions/html/2007/d2007-1461.html ('This Panel would suggest that there is no real justification for such a local laws approach either in the Policy or the Rules and that such approach should be avoided wherever possible. It risks the UDRP fragmenting into a series of different systems, where the outcome to each case would depend upon where exactly the parties happened to reside. That way chaos lies.').
24   UDRP, *supra* note 13, at arts. 4b & c.
25   *See* Gralf-Peter Calliess, *Reflexive Transnational Law: The Privatisation of Civil Law and the Civilisation of Private Law*, 23 ZEITSCHRIFT FÜR RECHTSSOZIOLOGIE 185–216 (2002), *available 17 September 2015 at* http://ssrn.com/abstract=531063 (Ger.) (evidencing the structural and conceptual differences between the UDRP and lex mercatoria, which applies in the international business context).
26   UDRP, *supra* note 13, at art. 4(i) ('The remedies available to a complainant pursuant to any proceeding before an Administrative Panel shall be limited to requiring the cancellation of your domain name or the transfer of your domain name registration to the complainant.').
27   UDRP, *supra* note 13, at art. 4(k). The complaint must '[s]tate that Complainant will submit, with respect to any challenges to a decision in the administrative proceeding canceling or transferring the domain name, to the jurisdiction of the courts in at least one specified Mutual Jurisdiction.' ICANN, RULES FOR UNIFORM DOMAIN NAME DISPUTE RESOLUTION POLICY art. 3(b)(xiii), *available 17 September 2015 at* http://www.icann.org/en/help/dndr/udrp/rules. 'Mutual Jurisdiction means a court jurisdiction at the location of either (a) the principal office of the Registrar (provided the domain-name holder has submitted in its Registration Agreement to that jurisdiction for court adjudication of disputes concerning or arising from the use of the domain name) or (b) the domain-name holder's address as shown for the registration of the domain name in Registrar's Whois database at the time the complaint is submitted to the Provider.' *Id.* at art. 1.

B. ADR METHODS FOR SOLVING TRADEMARK DISPUTES

the dispute resolution entity by filing appropriate evidence such as a copy of a complaint file-stamped by the clerk of the court.[28]

13.09 The UDRP consequently institutes and provides an autonomous dispute resolution mechanism for victims of unauthorized domain name registrations that they consider as an infringement of their trademark. It is essential to note that the UDRP is not imposed on victims who have the option to resolve their disputes through domestic courts or other dispute resolution bodies. Such victims may have an interest in utilizing domestic courts or other dispute resolution systems rather than the UDRP if they wish to claim remedies that are not available under the UDRP,[29] such as damages resulting from online trademark infringement activities.

13.10 In contrast, even if the UDRP provides that parties can litigate their disputes in other fora,[30] the holders of disputed domain names – defendants in UDRP proceedings – are *contractually obligated* to submit to the UDRP if the UDRP is initiated against them by a third party trademark owner. The contractual obligation derives from the general terms and conditions of the domain name registrar. The registrar is, in turn, obligated to implement the UDRP based on its accreditation agreement with ICANN.[31] This is quite interesting from a trademark transaction perspective (which is the focus of this book) given that the UDRP ultimately derives from a contract: that is, the obligation of the domain name holders to submit to the UDRP results from the agreement that they had to accept in order to register their disputed domain name.

13.11 The UDRP interestingly institutes an *asymmetrical dispute resolution system* as it is mandatory for domain names holders to be subject to the UDRP, but it is only optional for complainants – who are victims of cybersquatting activities. The complainants instead can litigate their claims on other grounds such as a breach of contract, and/or an unfair competition claim in other fora. The UDRP is also *asymmetrical* because it can only be initiated by one category of stakeholders: the alleged victims of unauthorized registration of domain names. A domain name holder cannot initiate the UDRP proceedings to confirm the legitimacy of his or her entitlement to the relevant domain name.

---

28   UDRP, *supra* note 13, art. 4(k).
29   *Id.* at art. 4(i).
30   *See id.* at art. 4(k) ('The mandatory administrative proceeding requirements … shall not prevent either you or the complainant from submitting the dispute to a court of competent jurisdiction for independent resolution before such mandatory administrative proceeding is commenced or after such proceeding is concluded.').
31   *See* Registrar Accreditation Agreement, *supra* note 19, at art. 3.8.

3. UDRP as a model for other ADR systems for trademark-related domain name disputes

13.12 It is hardly disputed that the UDRP has been extremely successful and that it probably is, as of today, the most accomplished example of an affordable and efficient global alternative dispute resolution system for intellectual property disputes.[32] Therefore, it is not a surprise that the UDRP has been used as a model for designing dispute resolution mechanisms that involve domain names with national or regional extensions such as country code Top Level Domain Names (ccTLDs).

13.13 This is what was done for the policy relating to disputes about '.eu' domain names in the EU (the 'EU Policy').

13.14 The EU Policy, which applies to '.eu' domain names, is essentially based on a 2004 European Commission Regulation which established public policy rules concerning the implementation and functions of the '.eu' Top Level Domain and the principles governing registration.[33] The Regulation states that '[t]he Registry should provide for an ADR procedure which takes into account the international best practices in this area and in particular the relevant World Intellectual Property Organization (WIPO) recommendations, to ensure that speculative and abusive registrations are avoided as far as possible'.[34] Furthermore, it provides that 'ADR should respect a minimum of uniform procedural rules, similar to the ones set out in the Uniform Dispute Resolution Policy adopted by the Internet Corporation of Assigned Names and Numbers (ICANN)'.[35] These references show that the ADR process must follow 'the international best practices' and that the UDRP, as an element of these best practices, provided a valuable guidance in defining the procedural rules that have been adopted under the EU Policy.

---

32 It must, however, be noted that the UDRP has sometimes been criticized as being too protective of the interests of trademark owners. *See* Michael Geist, *Fair.com?: An Examination of the Allegations of Systemic Unfairness in the ICANN UDRP*, 27 BROOK. J. INT'L L. 903 (2002) (providing the solution to the forum shopping and bias issues); Michael Geist, *Fundamentally Fair.com? An Update on Bias Allegations and the ICANN UDRP*, available 17 September 2015 at http://aix1.uottawa.ca/%7Egeist/fairupdate.pdf (providing a statistical update and reinforcing the solution provided previously).

33 *See* Commission Regulation 874/2004 of 28 April 2004 Laying Down Public Policy Rules Concerning the Implementation and Functions of the .eu Top Level Domain and the Principles Governing Registration, 2004 O.J. (L 162) 40 (EC), *available 17 September 2015 at* http://eur-lex.europa.eu/LexUriServ/LexUriServ.do?uri=CONSLEG:2004R0874:20051011:EN:PDF; *see also* Regulation (EC) No 733/2002 of the European Parliament and of the Council of 22 April 2002 on the Implementation of the .eu Top Level Domain, art. 1, 2002 O.J. (L 113) 5 (implementing the '.eu' country code Top Level Domain within the community); *see also ADR Rules and Supplemental Rules*, ADR.eu, *available 17 September 2015 at* http://eu.adr.eu/adr/adr_rules/index.php, for '.eu' domain name dispute rules that implemented the ADR system.

34 Commission Regulation 874/2004, recital 16, 2004 O.J. (L 162) 44 (EC).

35 *Id*. at recital 17.

13.15 Even if the UDRP is nothing more than a private regulation imposed by contract, the explicit reference in the EU Policy to the UDRP as a model for dispute resolution services constitutes tangible evidence of the UDRP's influence on legislators and regulators. Thus, these regulations show the process of incorporation (*réception*) of *private best practice standards*, as reflected in the UDRP, into *public regulations*. The UDRP itself essentially reflects the recommendations from a report that was drafted under the aegis of WIPO, thereby evidencing the close interactions between private best practices and public regulations.

13.16 Although the substantive legal standards of decisions rendered under the UDRP are different from those under the EU Policy, the influence of the UDRP is important and covers both the procedural and the substantive aspects of the EU Policy, which targets 'speculative and abusive' domain name registrations.[36] It can thus be considered that the UDRP has shaped the EU Policy from both procedural and substantive perspectives.

13.17 These domain name dispute resolution systems also follow an asymmetric model similar to the UDRP as they are mandatory for the domain name holders, but optional on the victim-claimants.[37]

13.18 Similar to proceedings under the UDRP, these domain dispute proceedings should not be considered as arbitral proceedings.[38] The decisions rendered under the domain dispute proceedings are not enforceable in the same way as arbitral awards are, and these proceedings are not mandatory for the claimants.[39] In addition, contrary to the principle of confidentiality that generally applies to ordinary arbitration proceedings, the decisions rendered under these policies are published as a matter of principle.[40]

13.19 Despite the similarities the EU Policy share with the UDRP, an important element on which they noticeably differ is the nature of the rights that can be invoked by a complainant in such proceedings. While, as noted above, the UDRP only applies for the benefit of *trademark* owners, the EU Policy is significantly broader in its scope of protection. The regulation provides for a broad definition of protectable rights and includes 'registered national and

---

[36] Commission Regulation 874/2004, art. 21, 2004 O.J. (L 162) 44 (EC).
[37] *See id.*, art. 22 para. 2 ('Participation in the ADR procedure shall be compulsory for the holder of a domain name and the Registry.').
[38] *See* PHILIPPE GILLIÉRON, LA PROCÉDURE DE RÉSOLUTION EN LIGNE DES CONFLITS RELATIFS AUX NOMS DE DOMAINE 26, para. 46 (Lausanne 2002).
[39] *See supra* note 37 (and accompanying text).
[40] Commission Regulation 874/2004, art. 22 para. 11, 2004 O.J. (L 162) 44 (EC).

community trademarks, geographical indications or designations of origin, and, in as far as they are protected under national law in the Member-State where they are held: unregistered trademarks, trade names, business identifiers, company names, family names, and distinctive titles of protected literary and artistic works'.[41] Domain names infringing on these protectable rights are 'subject to revocation, using an appropriate extra-judicial or judicial procedure, where that name is identical or confusingly similar to a name in respect of which a right is recognized or established by national and/or Community law … and where it: (a) has been registered by its holder without rights or legitimate interest in the name; or (b) has been registered or is being used in bad faith'.[42]

13.20 In comparison to the UDRP, these ADR systems consequently have a broader scope of application as they also protect the owners or beneficiaries of other types of intellectual property rights and even those with rights such as family names, which do not formally belong to intellectual property rights.

13.21 The EU Policy illustrates a trend that can be of interest when considering potential shapes for ADR methods to be applied to other types of trademark disputes.

13.22 First, the EU Policy *integrates* the *acquis* ('best practices') that result from the rule and application of the UDRP and make them a part of local regulations. These policies consequently and expressly adopt as normative standard rules that were first conceived under the aegis of a non-state entity (that is, ICANN).

13.23 Second, the EU Policy provides an interesting example of how ADR mechanisms can potentially be imposed through a combined system of both *regulatory* and *contractual* measures. More precisely, the combined system is structured so that *regulations* addressed to one stakeholder (that is, the registrars of domain names) require such stakeholders to impose ADR clauses in their agreements with their own clients. Under the combined system, the *regulation*, therefore, dictates the *contract* by imposing the ADR system that will be included in the domain name registration agreements between the relevant registrars and their end-customers so that these customers have the *contractual obligation* to submit to the ADR system.

---

41 *Id.* at art. 10.
42 *Id.* at art. 21.

13.24 Third, in terms of the substantive criteria on which the decisions must be made, the EU Policy moves away from the UDRP's 'delocalized' factors and localizes disputes by reference to the substantive legal intellectual property principles resulting from the relevant national or regional laws. This indicates a process of *localization* of the substantive law on which the ADR proceedings are based by anchoring to the country or region associated with the registration of the relevant domain name. Therefore, these regulations show that these ADR systems do not necessarily apply transnational legal principles.

13.25 Fourth, the EU Policy extends the substantive scope of the relevant rules by allowing other prior rights to be invoked in addition to trademark rights. Thus, these regulations indicate that the set of legal rules and principles, which can be applied in these ADR systems, are not necessarily as limited as rules under the UDRP.

13.26 Fifth, ADR methods are imposed on all domain name registrants, some of which are private individuals who may potentially use the domain names for private or non-professional purposes, and thus, may qualify as consumers and be protected under certain consumer-protection regulations.[43] However, the adoption of these ADR methods has not raised any concerns about consumer protection, even though the claim has been made that such dispute resolution systems would be unfair, and therefore, are not binding on the clients,[44] because these ADR systems are imposed through standard and non-negotiable contracts.[45] This shows that if sufficient policy reasons justify their adoption, ADR systems can be imposed on weaker parties in the market such as consumers.

---

[43] *See* Council Directive 2011/83/EU of the European Parliament and of the Council of 25 October 2011 on Consumer Rights, Amending Council Directive 93/13/EEC and Directive 1999/44/EC of the European Parliament and of the Council and repealing Council Directive 85/577/EEC and Directive 97/7/EC of the European Parliament and of the Council, art. 3, 2011 O.J. (L 304) 64, 73 (EC), *available 17 September 2015 at* http://eur-lex.europa.eu/legal-content/EN/TXT/?qid=1444047065583&uri=CELEX:32011L0083 (applying consumer protections to any contract between a trader and a consumer with a limited number of exemptions).

[44] *See* Council Directive 93/13/EEC of 5 April 1993 on Unfair Terms in Consumer Contracts, art. 3, 1993 O.J. (L 095) 29 (EC), *available 17 September 2015 at* http://eur-lex.europa.eu/legal-content/EN/TXT/?qid=1444047203659&uri=CELEX:31993L0013; *see also id.* at annex (q) ('[E]xcluding or hindering the consumer's right to take legal action or exercise any other legal remedy, particularly by requiring the consumer to take disputes exclusively to arbitration not covered by legal provisions, unduly restricting the evidence available to him or imposing on him a burden of proof which, according to the applicable law, should lie with another party to the contract may be considered as unfair').

[45] The argument that the submission to an ADR system was mandatory under the standard contracts was also raised by certain respondents under the UDRP; however, it was not successful. *See* Case No. D2004-0749, Deutsche Telekom AG v. Oded Zucker, Administrative Panel Decision (WIPO 2004), *available 17 September 2015 at* http://www.wipo.int/amc/en/domains/decisions/html/2004/d2004-0749.html.

C. ARBITRATION OF (INTERNATIONAL) TRADEMARK DISPUTES

1. Introduction

13.27 In order to discuss the use of arbitration for (international) trademark disputes, it must first be emphasized that not all types of international trademark disputes can adequately be subject to arbitration (or other ADR mechanisms). This is particularly true for (large scale) counterfeiting activities for which ADR, which must generally be based on consent of all participants, will not necessarily offer the most adequate tools for redress because these activities may call for criminal sanctions and involve the official entities in charge of prosecuting criminal charges.

13.28 At the same time, it is important to note that ADR methods, which can take multiple forms ranging from an informal process to a formalized (though flexible and adaptable by the parties) dispute resolution system conducted with the assistance of a third party such as an arbitral tribunal,[46] are broadly viewed as useful alternatives for solving international intellectual property disputes.[47] This is particularly the case for disputes arising out of trademark transactions for which parties may decide to include an ADR/arbitration clause in their contracts by which they will thus agree to submit their potential future disputes to ADR/arbitration. The recourse to arbitration for solving trademark transaction disputes, as a proceeding which leads to an enforceable award, requires certain conditions to be satisfied.

2. Conditions and features

13.29 One preliminary question that arises is whether private arbitral tribunals have the power to decide on the issues that may fall under the exclusive jurisdictional power of domestic courts. This raises the issue of the objective arbitrability of the disputes, that is, the ability to submit these types of disputes

---

46 This chapter will not present all the different types of proceedings.
47 *See* Jacques de Werra, *Arbitrating International Intellectual Property Disputes: Time to Think Beyond the Issue of (non-)Arbitrability*, 3 INT'L BUS. L.J. 299, 311 (2012) [hereinafter de Werra] ('This trend ... [shows] a clear sign that arbitration is an adequate method for solving intellectual property disputes.'); *see also* Jacques de Werra, *Intellectual Property Arbitration: How to Use it Efficiently?*, SINGAPORE LAW GAZETTE, Jan. 2012, at 27–30, *available* 17 September 2015 *at* http://www.lawgazette.com.sg/2012-01/304.htm; Miriam R. Arfin, *The Benefits of Alternative Dispute Resolution in Intellectual Property Disputes*, 17 HASTINGS COMM. & ENT. L.J. 893, 896 (1995); Krešimir Sajko, *Intellectual Property Rights and Arbitration – Miscellaneous*, in 6 PATENTS AND TECHNOLOGICAL PROGRESS IN A GLOBALIZED WORLD 445 (Martin J. Adelmann et al. eds., 2009); Kamen Troller, *Intellectual Property Disputes in Arbitration*, 72 ARBITRATION: THE JOURNAL OF THE CHARTERED INSTITUTE OF ARBITRATORS 322 (2006), *available* 17 September 2015 *at* http://www.lalive.ch/data/publications/kt_IP_disputes_arbitration_2006.pdf (explaining arbitration as the ideal dispute resolution instrument involving intellectual property rights due to its complex and technical nature).

to arbitration (see below (a)). Even if arbitral tribunals are entitled to decide on these disputes as a matter of principle, the relevant arbitration clauses must be drafted in an appropriate way (see below (b)).[48] The issue of the choice of the governing law must also be carefully addressed (see below (c)), as well as the question of temporary injunctions (see below (d)).

(a) Objective arbitrability of intellectual property disputes

13.30 In order to adjudicate international intellectual property disputes through ADR mechanisms, particularly through arbitration,[49] it must be ensured that national or regional regulations do not subject these issues to resolution under their respective court systems.[50] This raises the issue of the conditions of objective arbitrability of intellectual property disputes, which has provoked a relatively intensive scholarly debate that cannot be analyzed in this chapter.[51]

13.31 As a matter of principle, it is adequate to consider that trademark disputes and, more generally, intellectual property disputes should be broadly arbitrable.[52] This liberal approach would indeed reflect the fact that intellectual property rights, and more generally intangible assets, have become standard assets of business entities that can be disposed of. In fact, many national arbitration regulations define the condition of objective arbitrability on the criterion of

---

48 For a discussion of certain issues which may arise in connection with the drafting of arbitration clauses, see below (b), (c) and (d) as well as de Werra, *supra* note 47, at 299–317.
49 It should be noted that the recourse to mediation or other informal ADR mechanisms is obviously less problematic to the extent that the third parties, which take part of the proceedings to solve disputes, do not have adjudicative power, and, thus, do not impinge on the power of domestic courts.
50 *See* Marc Blessing, *Objective Arbitrability, Antitrust Disputes, Intellectual Property Disputes*, in A COLLECTION OF REPORTS AND MATERIALS DELIVERED AT THE ASA CONFERENCE HELD IN ZURICH ON 19 NOVEMBER 1993, 13–15 (1994); Robert Briner, *The Arbitrability of Intellectual Property Disputes with Particular Emphasis on the Situation in Switzerland*, 5 AM. REV. INT'L ARB., at 28 (1994); *see* ANNE-CATHERINE CHIARINY-DAUDET, LE RÈGLEMENT JUDICIAIRE ET ARBITRAL DES CONTENTIEUX INTERNATIONAUX SUR BREVETS D'INVENTION (2006), for French law.
51 *See generally* NELSON HOLZNER, DIE OBJEKTIVE SCHIEDSFÄHIGKEIT VON IMMATERIALGÜTERRECHTS-STREITIGKEITEN (2001); Julian D.M. Lew, *Final Report on Intellectual Property Disputes and Arbitration*, 9 ICC INTERNATIONAL COURT OF ARBITRATION BULLETIN, 41–5 (1998); STEFAN LINIGER, IMMATERIALGÜTERRECHTLICHE STREITIGKEITEN VOR INTERNATIONALEN SCHIEDSGERICHTEN MIT SITZ IN DER SCHWEIZ (2002).
52 *See* Bernard Hanotiau, *L'arbitrabilité des litiges de propriété intellectuelle*, in LA RÉSOLUTION DES LITIGES DE PROPRIÉTÉ INTELLECTUELLE [RESOLUTION OF INTELLECTUAL PROPERTY DISPUTES] 156–74 (Jacques de Werra ed., 2010), for a detailed comparative overview of the issue; *see also* the dissenting opinion in the case Scherk v. Alberto-Culver Co., 417 U.S. 506, 527 (1974), which objected to the submission to arbitration of securities regulation claims and made the distinction between these non-arbitrable claims and trademark disputes that could be arbitrable ('There has been much support for arbitration of disputes; and it may be the superior way of settling some disagreements. If A and B were quarreling over a trade-mark and there was an arbitration clause in the contract, the policy of Congress in implementing the United Nations Convention on the Recognition and Enforcement of Foreign Arbitral Awards, as it did in 9 U.S.C. § 201 et seq., would prevail.').

whether the relevant matter can be freely disposed of by its owner.[53] Therefore, it seems appropriate to consider that intellectual property rights in general and trademarks in particular are disposable, and, therefore, should be fully arbitrable.[54]

13.32 However, the jurisdictional powers of private dispute resolution bodies may be problematic for disputes relating to the validity or nullity of trademarks and other industrial property rights (that is, registered intellectual property rights). The problem arises because the issue of whether an arbitral tribunal must have the power to decide on the validity or the nullity of registered intellectual property rights with *erga omnes* effect is an unsettled and delicate subject in certain jurisdictions.[55] Regardless, as national courts and authorities do not systematically examine the substantive conditions of protection of some intellectual property rights, it is doubtful that national courts can claim exclusive jurisdiction over these issues.[56] Thus, it has been argued that 'disputes concerning the validity of [intellectual property rights] for grounds which have not been pre-examined by the state authority ... should be considered as arbitrable'.[57] This view may particularly apply to the substantive conditions of validity of registered intellectual property rights (patents and designs), which are sometimes not examined at the time of filing.

13.33 Beyond this specific issue of the jurisdiction for decisions to be made *erga omnes* by arbitral tribunals on the validity of trademarks, it is generally admitted that other issues, such as the ownership, the transfer[58] and the infringement of trademarks, are arbitrable. Accordingly, trademark disputes should be considered as broadly arbitrable (depending on the relevant – national or regional – regulations).

---

53 The liberal Swiss arbitration regime, which is regulated under Chapter XII of the Swiss Act on Private International Law of 18 December 1987, is a good example. *See* François Dessemontet, *Arbitration of Intellectual Property Rights and Licensing Contracts, in* ENFORCEMENT OF ARBITRATION AGREEMENTS AND INTERNATIONAL ARBITRATION AWARDS: THE NEW YORK CONVENTION IN PRACTICE 556 (Emmanuel Gaillard & Domenico di Pietro eds., 2008).

54 *See* Anna P. Mantakou, *Arbitrability and Intellectual Property Disputes, in* ARBITRABILITY: INTERNATIONAL & COMPARATIVE PERSPECTIVES 263, 266–7 (Loukas A. Mistelis & Stavros L. Brekoulakis eds., 2009).

55 For a discussion, *see* Hanotiau, *supra* note 52.

56 *See, e.g.*, Mantakou, *supra* note 54, at 268; Francis Gurry, *Specific Aspects of Intellectual Property Disputes, in* OBJECTIVE ARBITRABILITY – ANTITRUST DISPUTES – INTELLECTUAL PROPERTY DISPUTES 110, 116 (1994).

57 *See* Mantakou, *supra* note 54, at 269 (applying the particular approach to patents).

58 *See* Andrea Mondini & Raphael Meier, *Patentübertragungsklagen vor internationalen Schiedsgerichten mit Sitz in der Schweiz und die Aussetzung des Patenterteilungsverfahrens*, 5 SIC! 289 (2015).

C. ARBITRATION OF (INTERNATIONAL) TRADEMARK DISPUTES

(b) Consent of parties to submit to arbitration: the scope of the arbitration clause

13.34 It is unanimously accepted that 'arbitration is a creature of contract',[59] whereby the consent of the parties to submit to arbitration is a basic tenet of (commercial) arbitration. This general principle is of particular importance for trademark (and other intellectual property) arbitration because the risk is that arbitration clauses are too narrowly drafted (see below (i)). The risk can also result from the (sometimes misguided) desire of the parties to exclude certain types of disputes from the scope of the arbitration clauses by way of carve-out clauses, which are also complex to handle (see below (ii)).

(i) Arbitration clauses covering contractual and non-contractual claims

13.35 It is critical to carefully draft the relevant arbitration clauses so that these clauses are effective and encompass not only purely contractual claims,[60] but also other trademark (or more generally intellectual property) related claims.[61]

13.36 While this principle sounds simple (or even simplistic), case law confirms that this point must be most carefully drafted in the relevant trademark transactions agreements. It is indeed (unfortunately) not infrequent that disputes arise about the scope of the jurisdictional power of an arbitral tribunal when the arbitration clause is drafted too narrowly. This can particularly happen if

---

59 Steelworkers v. American Mfg. Co., 363 U.S. 564, 569 (1960).
60 *See* Alexander Peukert, *Contractual Jurisdiction Clauses and Intellectual Property*, in 24 INTELLECTUAL PROPERTY AND PRIVATE INTERNATIONAL LAW 55, 57 (Josef Drexl & Annette Kur eds., 2005), for a similar issue with respect to the drafting of choice of jurisdiction clauses; for a case discussing the scope of a choice of court clause (in a dispute involving contractual claims and non-contractual – i.e. copyright infringement – claims), see Phillips v. Audio Active Ltd., 494 F.3d 378 (2nd Cir. 2007); it should also be noted that the trend supporting a growing freedom of parties to choose a court (beyond IP disputes) is confirmed by the recent case law of the ECJ, see Case C-352/13, Cartel Damages Claims (CDC) Hydrogen Peroxide SA v. Akzo Nobel NV et al, decision of 21 May 2015 (admitting the validity of choice of clause provisions under Article 23(1) of Regulation No 44/2001 for actions for damages for an infringement of Article 101 TFEU and Article 53 of the Agreement on the European Economic Area of 2 May 1992, in contracts for the supply of goods, even if the effect thereof is a derogation from the rules on international jurisdiction provided for in Article 5(3) and/or Article 6(1) of that regulation, provided that those clauses refer to disputes concerning liability incurred as a result of an infringement of competition law).
61 *See, e.g.,* Rhône-Poulenc Spécialités Chimiques v. SCM Corp., 769 F.2d 1569 (Fed. Cir. 1985) (interpreting the scope of an arbitration clause). In the case at hand, the arbitration clause provided that '[a]ny controversy or claim arising out of or relating to this Agreement or the breach thereof, shall, unless amicably adjusted otherwise, be settled by arbitration in Florida in accordance with the rules of the International Chamber of Commerce … .' *Id.* at 1571. The Federal Circuit determined that '[a]lthough the dispute involves claim interpretation, it arises out of the agreement … [and] hold that the determination of the scope and infringement of the 485 patent are the quintessence of the agreement and that the parties intended such central determinations to be included within the scope of its broad arbitration clause.' *Id.* at 1572; *see also* Simula, Inc. v. Autoliv, Inc., 175 F.3d 716, 720–21, 723 (9th Cir. 1999) (finding the nondisclosure of trade secrets to be a key part of the relevant agreements and therefore subjecting all claims 'arising in connection with' those agreements to arbitration).

the clause has a time limit (that is, the obligation to submit to arbitration is contractually limited in time).

13.37 This can be illustrated by a recent decision of the Swiss Supreme Court,[62] in which the Court held that certain claims raised by patent licensors against their ex-licensee after the termination of their patent license agreement were within the jurisdiction of the arbitral tribunal notwithstanding a contractual provision that seemed to provide for the submission to arbitration of only pre-termination disputes. While this decision essentially confirms the application of the well-established doctrine of separability[63] under which the validity of an arbitration clause does not depend on the validity of the underlying agreement (so that, in this case, the enforceability of the arbitration clause was not affected by the termination of the patent license agreement), this decision remains of high interest for several reasons (even if it was about a patent license agreement, it is also relevant from a trademark licensing perspective).

13.38 First of all, it confirms the risks of (apparently sophisticated) contractual clauses by which parties precisely define the obligations that are deemed to survive the expiration or the termination of the agreement. In this case, the parties had agreed that the dispute resolution mechanism (that is, good faith discussions between the parties followed by arbitration pursuant to Article 11 of their agreement) would survive the expiration or the termination of the agreement and would apply 'in respect of any matter arising prior to such expiration or termination'.[64]

13.39 The issue that arose was whether the arbitration clause should also cover disputes relating to matters arising *after* the expiration or termination of the agreement. The licensors (and claimants in the arbitration) had requested in the arbitration that their ex-licensee should stop manufacturing and selling contractual products that infringed on one of their patents (more specifically claim 21 of the U.S. patent 'qqq' – as identified in the decision) after the

---

62 Tribunal Fédéral [TF] [Swiss Federal Supreme Court] Feb. 27, 2014, ARRÊTS DU TRIBUNAL FÉDÉRAL SUISSE [ATF] 140 III 134.

63 '[P]rincipe adopté par la jurisprudence depuis des décennies ... et universellement admis en Europe occidentale et aux Etats-Unis sous la terminologie "severability" ou "separability".' Tribunal Fédéral [TF] [Swiss Federal Supreme Court] 2 September 1993, ARRÊTS DU TRIBUNAL FÉDÉRAL SUISSE [ATF] 119 II 380, para 4(a).

64 Tribunal Fédéral [TF] [Swiss Federal Supreme Court] 27 February 2014, ARRÊTS DU TRIBUNAL FÉDÉRAL SUISSE [ATF] 140 III 134, art. 8.3: 'Survival of Certain Rights Upon Expiration or Termination. All rights granted to and obligations undertaken by the Parties hereunder shall terminate immediately upon the expiration of the Term of this Agreement ... or the termination of this Agreement ... except for: ... (d) The procedures set forth in Article 11 herein in respect of any matter arising prior to such expiration or termination.'

termination of the license.[65] The licensee challenged the jurisdiction of the arbitral tribunal with respect to these claims made by the licensors on the ground of the narrow scope of the arbitration clause. By an interim award of 31 July 2013, the arbitral tribunal dismissed the jurisdictional challenge raised by the (ex-)licensee and held that it had jurisdiction to decide on the claims of the licensors. The licensee subsequently lodged an appeal against the award before the Swiss Federal Supreme Court by claiming that the arbitral tribunal had wrongly accepted its jurisdiction[66] and the Swiss Federal Supreme Court dismissed the appeal.

13.40 On the basis of a good faith interpretation of the relevant contractual provisions and in line with its established case law, the Swiss Federal Supreme Court held in this respect that the arbitration clause had to be construed extensively as to encompass post termination disputes so that the arbitral tribunal was correct in admitting its jurisdiction to decide the dispute. While this decision can be understood in view of the circumstances,[67] it should also serve as an important reminder of the risks resulting from the split of jurisdictional powers between courts and arbitral tribunals which may result from hastily drafted contractual clauses. Such a splitting scenario can arise in intellectual property-related contracts because parties are sometimes tempted to exclude intellectual disputes from the scope of arbitration clauses, which then materialize in 'intellectual property carve out' provisions (see below (ii)).

13.41 This decision of the Swiss Federal Supreme Court is also of relevance because it relates to a line of cases rendered in different countries (see for example, a previous decision of the Court in an unreported decision of 2003,[68] and a recent Australian case to which the Swiss Supreme Court referred).[69] In its previous decision of 2003, the Swiss Court had to decide whether the arbitration clause contained in a confidentiality agreement ('Secrecy Agreement')[70] that had expired several years before the dispute

---

65 Whereby the agreement provided (art. 8.2(e)) for a transition period during which the inventory of the licensee could be sold and the relevant royalties paid to the licensors.
66 Within the meaning of Loi fédérale du 18 décembre 1987 sur le droit international privé [LDIP] [Swiss Federal Act on Private International Law] 18 December 1987, art. 190, para. 2(b) [hereinafter Act on Private International Law].
67 Particularly because, as duly acknowledged by the Court (paragraph 3.3.4 of the decision), it would be unpredictable to hold that the jurisdiction of the arbitral tribunal would cease upon the termination of the agreement, because the parties are frequently in dispute about the validity of the termination, the time when it shall take effect and its consequences (as illustrated by this case).
68 Tribunal Fédéral [TF] [Swiss Federal Supreme Court] 19 May 2003, 4C.40/2003.
69 Services WA Pty. Ltd. Vs. ATCO Gas Australia Pty. Ltd. (2014) WA SC 10 (S) (cited in paragraph 3.3.4 of ATF 140 III 134).
70 The arbitration clause had the following wording:

arose[71] covered claims of assignment of various patent applications (which had been filed by one party supposedly on the basis of the confidential information obtained from the other party under the confidentiality agreement). Similarly to what it decided in ATF 140 III 134, the Swiss Federal Supreme Court held in that case that it would not be reasonable to hold that the jurisdictional power of the arbitral tribunal for a claim relating to the confidentiality agreement would be subject to a time limit.[72] The Swiss Federal Supreme Court consequently held that the expiration of the confidentiality agreement did not affect the validity and enforceability of the arbitration clause for deciding the dispute between the parties about their respective entitlement to the patent applications.

13.42 As demonstrated by these cases, this is ultimately a matter of contract interpretation. Parties should in any case be wary of the risk that arbitral tribunals might potentially be reluctant to admit their jurisdiction for post-contractual disputes relating to the infringement of the (previously licensed) intellectual property rights on the ground that the arbitration clause would be limited to contractual claims. This is what was decided in International Chamber of Commerce (ICC) case 4491[73] in which the sole arbitrator held that '… the Plaintiff's claims for damages and injunctive relief after the termination of the license agreement are not within the scope of the arbitration provisions of the licensing agreement …',[74] it being noted that the arbitration clause had a somewhat unusual wording.[75]

13.43 This decision of the Swiss Supreme Court further reminds us that certain regulatory instruments expressly state that contractual dispute resolution clauses survive the expiration or termination of the underlying contract.

> The parties shall try in good faith to settle amicably any difference or dispute resulting from or with regard to this agreement.
>
> Should they not succeed, the matter shall be settled under the Rules of Conciliation and Arbitration of the International Chamber of Commerce by one or more arbitrators appointed in accordance with the said rules …

71 The agreement was entered into in 1989 for a period of one year and the contractual obligation of confidentiality of the parties had a maximal term of 5 years (according to the information reflected in paragraph 5.4 of the decision) and legal proceedings were initiated before the court of Lucerne in 2001.
72 Tribunal Fédéral [TF] [Swiss Federal Supreme Court] 19 May 2003, 4C.40/2003, para. 5.4: 'Es widerspräche jeder Vernunft, die Zuständigkeit des Schiedsgerichts für einen mit dem Secrecy Agreement im Zusammenhang stehenden Anspruch lediglich mit einer zeitlichen Beschränkung vorzusehen'; the Court further held that the arbitration clause covered, from a substantive perspective, claims of patent assignments (that are claims resulting from patent law) and was consequently not limited to contractual claims.
73 As resulting from the excerpts of the award published in the JOURNAL OF INTERNATIONAL ARBITRATION 75 (1985).
74 Id., at 76.
75 Id., at 76 stating that 'the arbitrator found that the matters to be arbitrated under the licensing agreement are "possible disagreements between the (Plaintiff) and (the Defendant)" [sic]'.

C. ARBITRATION OF (INTERNATIONAL) TRADEMARK DISPUTES

Article 7.3.5 para. 3 of the Unidroit Principles of International Commercial Contracts provides that '[t]ermination [of the contract] does not affect any provision in the contract for the settlement of disputes or any other term of the contract which is to operate even after termination'.[76]

13.44 This decision confirms in any case the imperious need to take all the required measures in order to avoid or at least to minimize the risks of diverging interpretations of the scope of arbitration clauses, which frequently materialize in international intellectual property-related transactions. This is shown by the high profile dispute between a U.S. group (AMSC) and its former Chinese partner and client (Sinovel) which was recently submitted to the Chinese Supreme People's Court. This dispute raised contractual and intellectual property infringements issues (that is, infringement of copyright on computer source code for wind turbines) and led to various parallel judicial and arbitral proceedings in China. The Chinese Supreme Court recently held that the non-contractual claims for copyright infringement were not covered by the relevant arbitration clause and were thus to be submitted to Chinese courts (and not to the Beijing Arbitration Commission as claimed by Sinovel).[77]

13.45 This case and this issue also confirm the complexity of the interaction between court and arbitral tribunals, which is confirmed by case law. In a recent trademark licensing dispute about the Benihana restaurant brand,[78] one of the issues in dispute was whether a U.S. district could validly enjoin a licensee [Benihana of Tokyo] that was objecting to the termination of the agreement by its licensor [Benihana America] from making the argument before the arbitral tribunal that it should receive an extended cure period in lieu of termination. In that case, the licensee had initiated arbitration proceedings pursuant to the arbitration clause contained in the license agreement. This clause provided (in its relevant part) that: '13.1 If this Agreement shall be terminated by [Benihana America] and [Benihana of Tokyo] shall dispute [Benihana America's] right of termination, or the reasonableness thereof, the dispute shall be settled by arbitration at the main office of the American

---

76 See INTERNATIONAL INSTITUTE FOR THE UNIFICATION OF PRIVATE LAW, UNIDROIT PRINCIPLES, art. 7.3.5 (2010), *available 17 September 2015 at* http://www.unidroit.org/instruments/commercial-contracts/unidroit-principles-2010/405-chapter-7-non-performance-section-3-termination/1040-article-7–3–5-effects-of-termination-in-general.
77 For a comment of the dispute, *see* Arthur Dong & Meng Li, *Is an Infringement Claim within the Scope of Arbitration Clause under Laws of PRC?*, KLUWER ARBITRATION BLOG (29 May 2014), *available 17 September 2015 at* http://kluwerarbitrationblog.com/blog/2014/05/29/is-an-infringement-claim-within-the-scope-of-arbitration-clause-under-laws-of-prc/; for an update of the dispute, *see*, *AMSC Provides Update on Litigation With Sinovel Wind Group, Ltd*, American Superconductor Corporation (16 September 2014), *available 17 September 2015 at*, http://ir.amsc.com/releasedetail.cfm?ReleaseID=871066.
78 Benihana, Inc. v. Benihana of Tokyo, LLC, 784 F.3d 887 (2d Cir. 2015).

Arbitration Association in the City of New York in accordance with the rules of said association and judgment upon the award rendered by the arbitrators may be entered in any court having jurisdiction thereof.'[79] The Second Circuit held in this case that the District could not enjoin the licensee from making the argument before the arbitral tribunal that it should be granted an extended cure period: '[b]ecause the parties' dispute had been submitted to arbitration, the district court, rather than independently assessing the merits, should have confined itself to preserving the status quo pending arbitration'.[80]

13.46 This case confirms that the jurisdictional interactions and the risks of conflicts between courts and arbitral tribunals can be complex and that courts and arbitral tribunal should as a matter of principle work in a mutually supportive manner. This was precisely not the case here given that one party was trying to undermine and delegitimize the broad jurisdiction granted to the arbitral tribunal that the parties had agreed upon in the arbitration clause.

(ii) Intellectual property carve-out clauses

13.47 Parties to an intellectual property (and specifically a trademark) license agreement may be tempted to include sophisticated dispute resolution clauses in their agreement under which they would carve out certain types of disputes from the scope of the arbitration clause in so-called 'intellectual property carve out'[81] provisions. This can in turn lead to intricate difficulties when a dispute arises between the parties given that it is frequently complicated to distinguish intellectual property claims (excluded from the scope of the arbitration clause) from contractual claims (covered by the arbitration clause).[82] This is the lesson that we can learn from the interesting U.S. case *Oracle America Inc. v. Myriad Group*.[83]

13.48 In this case, the dispute resolution clause that had been agreed upon between the parties split the jurisdictional power between arbitration (for breach of contract claims) and state court litigation by carving out from the otherwise broad adjudication power of the arbitral tribunal certain types of disputes (essentially intellectual property infringement claims). While the decision only addressed the issue of who should get to decide on the interpretation of the

---

79 *Id.*
80 *Id.*
81 As formulated by the District Court, Oracle Am., Inc. v. Myriad Group AG, 2011 U.S. Dist. LEXIS 98830, 2011 WL 3862027, 20 (N.D. Cal. 1 September 2011).
82 For an example, *see* the US decision Oracle America, Inc. v. Myriad Group A.G., 724 F.3d 1069 (9th Cir. 2013).
83 *Id.*; this analysis is derived from Jacques de Werra, *Risks of IP carve-out in arbitration clauses*, 9 JOURNAL OF INTELLECTUAL PROPERTY LAW & PRACTICE 184 (2014), *available* 17 September 2015 *at*: http://jiplp.oxfordjournals.org/content/9/3/184.full.

C. ARBITRATION OF (INTERNATIONAL) TRADEMARK DISPUTES

scope and reach of the arbitration clause under U.S. law (that is, its arbitrability under the U.S. arbitration law terminology) between the California federal courts or the arbitral tribunal, its relevance is broader to the extent that this decision can (and should) serve as a useful warning/reminder of the risks of carve-out provisions contained in arbitration clauses, which are sometimes included by the parties in their intellectual property (and specifically trademark related) contracts for the purpose of reserving the power to enforce their intellectual property rights against the other contracting party before state courts.

13.49 In this case, Oracle America, Inc. licensed Java (its well-known computer programming language) so that its licensees were granted access to the Java programming language and use of Java trademarks in exchange for royalties. Myriad Group AG (a Swiss mobile software company) entered into a community source license with Oracle in 2002 ('the Source License'), whereby this license encompassed various license agreements and particularly the Technology Compatibility Kits License ('the TCK License'). The TCK License allowed a licensee to access Oracle's testing protocols and was intended to ensure compatibility of the licensee's products.

13.50 The arbitration clause contained in the Source License provided (in its relevant part) that: '[a]ny dispute arising out of or relating to this License shall be finally settled by arbitration as set out herein, except that either party may bring any action, in a court of competent jurisdiction (which jurisdiction shall be exclusive), with respect to any dispute relating to such party's Intellectual Property Rights or with respect to Your [that is, Myriad] compliance with the TCK license. Arbitration shall be administered: (i) by the American Arbitration Association (AAA), (ii) in accordance with the rules of the United Nations Commission on International Trade Law (UNCITRAL) ... and (iii) the arbitrator will apply the substantive laws of California and United States ...'.

13.51 Myriad stopped paying royalties (by relying on what it believed were its rights under one of the license agreements with Oracle, that is the Java Specification Participation Agreement), which Oracle considered as a breach of the Source License.

13.52 Oracle consequently filed suit against Myriad in the Federal District Court of the Northern District of California for breach of contract, violation of the Lanham Act, copyright infringement and unfair competition under California law. Myriad reacted by moving to compel arbitration on the basis of the arbitration clause in the Source License and submitted on 15 August 2011 a request for arbitration to the International Center for Dispute Resolution (ICDR), which is the international arm of the American Arbitration Association. On 1 September 2011, the District Court granted Myriad's motion to compel arbitration with respect to Oracle's breach of contract claim, but denied Myriad's motion with respect to the non-contractual claims.[84]

13.53 On 17 January 2012, the District Court granted an 'anti-suit injunction' against Myriad and thus enjoined Myriad from proceeding with arbitration of its non-contract claims. It consequently ordered Myriad to take all necessary measures to abate those proceedings insofar as they sought to adjudicate any claims or issues presented before the District Court, except as to Oracle's claim for breach of contract, pending further order of the Court.[85] The District Court held that because the arbitration clause stated that the court's jurisdiction is 'exclusive' with respect to a party's intellectual property claims or claims arising out of the TCK License, the parties intended for the court and not the arbitral tribunal to decide on the issue of arbitrability. Shortly after the decision, the parties agreed to stay all litigation before state courts (including a parallel litigation pending in the U.S. District Court of the District of Delaware), and the arbitration until such time as the Ninth Circuit Court of Appeals resolved Myriad's appeal against the injunction of the District Court, subject only to the completion of the process of appointing an arbitrator (in a parallel ICC arbitration proceeding which had been initiated).

13.54 By its decision of 26 July 2013, the Court of Appeal for the 9th Circuit reversed and held that the incorporation of the United Nations Commission on International Trade Law (UNCITRAL) Arbitration Rules in the arbitration clause constituted clear and unmistakable evidence that the parties intended to have the question of arbitrability decided by the arbitral tribunal, irrespective of which version (1976 or 2010) of the UNCITRAL Rules would apply.

13.55 This decision of the Court of Appeal for the 9th Circuit is to be welcomed given that it duly recognizes the power of arbitral tribunals to rule on their own jurisdiction, which is reflected in all major arbitration rules.[86] It further confirms the arbitration-friendly approach existing under U.S. law (as reflected in case law, particularly in the decision of the U.S. Supreme Court in

---

84 Oracle Am., Inc., 2011 U.S. Dist. LEXIS 98830.
85 Oracle Am., Inc. v. Myriad Group AG, 2012 U.S. Dist. LEXIS 5050.
86 *See, e.g.,* UNITED NATIONS COMMISSION ON INTERNATIONAL TRADE LAW, ARBITRATION RULES, art. 23, para. 1 (2010). The Court referred to the Arbitration Rules, which provide that '[t]he arbitral tribunal shall have the power to rule on its own jurisdiction, including any objections with respect to the existence or validity of the arbitration agreement'.

C. ARBITRATION OF (INTERNATIONAL) TRADEMARK DISPUTES

Scherk v. Alberto-Culver Co.,[87] – which related to an international trademark dispute), which is finding its way globally.

This case constitutes an important development in view of the fact that principles of international commercial arbitration and global arbitration institutions have sometimes not been fully appreciated by U.S. courts.[88]

13.56

The decision is of high practical relevance given that it clearly illustrates the risks of 'intellectual property carve-out' contained in arbitration clauses. In this dispute, the bifurcation of adjudication powers between the state courts and the arbitral tribunal led to a stay of all (state court and arbitral) proceedings for an extended period of time (some 18 months) and can, thus, hardly be considered as an efficient tool for solving international commercial intellectual property-related disputes. Parties should, therefore, duly assess the potential consequences and risks of inserting intellectual property carve-out provisions in their intellectual property agreements and, if they opt for such clauses, they should precisely draft them.[89] This concern is obviously not limited to intellectual property carve-out, but rather affects all contractual limits to the scope of arbitration clauses. This is clearly expressed in the International Bar Association Guidelines for Drafting International Arbitration Clauses (2010), which indicate that '[a]bsent special circumstances, the parties should not attempt to limit the scope of disputes subject to arbitration and should define this scope broadly'.[90] The Guidelines therefore wisely state that '[t]he parties should bear in mind that, even when drafted carefully, exclusions may not avoid preliminary arguments over whether a given dispute is subject to arbitration. A claim may raise some issues that fall within the scope of the arbitration clause and others that do not ... a dispute over the ownership or validity of intellectual property rights under a licensing agreement [which

13.57

---

87   Scherk v. Alberto-Culver Co., 417 U.S. 506 (1974).
88   *See*, by way of illustration, the decision of the United States Court of Appeal for the 5th Circuit in an international intellectual property contractual dispute, Bodum USA, Inc. v. La Cafetiere, Inc., 621 F.3d 624, 631 (7th Cir. Ill. 2010), evoking that the dispute 'would be submitted to an arbitral panel of business executives, the International Court of Commerce in Paris', while it seems that this refers to the ICC International Court of Arbitration which is the most established arbitration institution at the global level; *see also* the decision in Simula Inc. v. Autoliv Inc., 175 F.3d 716 (9th Cir. 1999), in which the Court stated that '[b]ecause the district court correctly concluded that all of Simula's claims were arbitrable and the ICC arbitral tribunal is authorized to grant the equivalent of an injunction pendente lite, it would have been inappropriate for the district court to grant preliminary injunctive relief', thereby ignoring that the arbitral tribunal had not yet been constituted at the time when the preliminary injunctive relief was requested.
89   As reflected by Patrick Rohn & Philipp Groz, *Drafting Arbitration Clauses for IP Agreements*, 7 JOURNAL OF INTELLECTUAL PROPERTY LAW & PRACTICE 652, 654 (2012), who suggest carefully defining the types of disputes to be carved out 'in order to avoid future jurisdictional disputes as to whether particular claims or defences are covered by the clause's scope'.
90   INTERNATIONAL BAR ASSOCIATION, IBA GUIDELINES FOR DRAFTING INTERNATIONAL ARBITRATION CLAUSES, guideline 3 (2010).

would have been carved out] may also involve issues of non-payment, breach and so forth, which could give rise to intractable jurisdictional problems in situations where certain disputes have been excluded from arbitration'.[91] This decision perfectly illustrates these problems and the negative consequences that they can provoke.

13.58 It should be emphasized that if an arbitral tribunal decides on an issue for which it had no jurisdictional power (based on the arbitration clause), this can constitute a ground for annulling the award and, in an international setting, for refusing the enforcement and recognition of a foreign award. In such a case, the enforcement of the foreign award could be refused on the ground that the award would supposedly exceed the scope of the disputes that the parties agreed to submit to arbitration. Article 5 para 1. of the New York Convention of 1958 provides that the '[r]ecognition and enforcement of the award may be refused, at the request of the party against whom it is invoked, only if that party furnishes to the competent authority where the recognition and enforcement is sought, proof that … (c) The award deals with a difference not contemplated by or not falling within the terms of the submission to arbitration, or it contains decisions on matters beyond the scope of the submission to arbitration, provided that, if the decisions on matters submitted to arbitration can be separated from those not so submitted, that part of the award which contains decisions on matters submitted to arbitration may be recognized and enforced'. This was precisely one of the arguments that was made in the dispute *Bad Ass Coffee Company of Hawaii Inc. v. Bad Ass Enterprises Inc.*,[92] which had a trademark component, about a franchise agreement in which the parties had agreed to carve out from the arbitration clauses certain disputes, that is, disputes concerning franchise fees, product purchase costs, advertising fees, and all other fees charged by the franchisor. The enforcement of an award rendered in Utah (in an arbitration governed by the rules of the American Arbitration Association)[93] was admitted by the Canadian (Alberta) court which rejected the argument that the dispute would allegedly fall within the scope of the carve-out clause (that is, that the dispute was not within the scope of the arbitration clause). The Court held that: '[27]

---

91 *Id.* at § 16.
92 Bad Ass Coffee Company of Hawaii Inc. v. Bad Ass Enterprises Inc., 2008 ABQB 404 (CanLII), *available* 17 September 2015 at www.canlii.org; *see also Summary of Decision*, 1958 New York Convention Guide (2015), *available* 17 September 2015 at http://www.newyorkconvention1958.org/index.php?lvl=notice_display&id=802.
93 The Utah award was confirmed as a judgment of the Utah District Court and the franchisor applied to a Master of the Alberta Court of Queen's Bench for a summary judgment to enforce the Utah judgment against the franchisees and P [a director of the franchisees and an Alberta resident], see Bad Ass Coffee Company of Hawaii Inc. v. Bad Ass Enterprises Inc., 2007 ABQB 581 (CanLII), *available* 17 September 2015 at www.canlii.org.

Clause 14 [of the relevant franchise agreements] specifically exempts disputes regarding franchise fees, product purchase costs, advertising fees and all other fees charged by the franchisor. The Defendants say that other fees includes royalties. The Defendants argue that the dispute between the parties is exactly what is exempted. Accordingly the Arbitrator did not have jurisdiction. [28] I do not accept the argument that the dispute is exempt. The dispute was not simply over royalties and fees. It dealt with a complete breakdown of the business relationship between the parties. It included the improper use of Hawaii's name and trademark. I reject that argument.'[94]

13.59 On this basis, the Court held that the award was enforceable and that it did not exceed the scope of the arbitration clause.

13.60 These cases show in any event that contracting parties (and their counsel) should be very careful in the drafting of the relevant arbitration clauses in order to avoid the risk of challenges to the jurisdiction or to the award on the ground that the dispute would go beyond the power granted by the parties to the arbitral tribunal.

3. Governing law

13.61 One advantage of arbitration consists in the broad choice left to the parties to decide the law that shall govern their dispute.[95] The interest in applying one single law in order to solve an international trademark dispute can be shown by reference to global trademark coexistence agreements. Some of these agreements give the right to one contracting party to register and use trademarks provided that they do not create any risk of confusion with the other party's trademarks.[96] In such a case, the issue of the risk of confusion,

---

94 *Id.*; for other examples of disputes about the scope of an arbitration clause containing carve-out provisions, see McKesson Corp., et al. v. Health Robotics, s.r.l,. 2011 WL 3157044 (N.D.Cal.) (in which the arbitration clause contained the following – carve-out – sentence: 'Notwithstanding the foregoing, either PARTY may elect to seek injunctive relief or other equitable remedies against the other PARTY from any court of competent jurisdiction, without waiving the PARTY's right to arbitrate disputes for money or damages'); see also Med. Creative Techs. v. Dexterity Surgical, Inc., 2004 U.S. Dist. LEXIS 11304, (E.D.Pa. 24 February 2005) (arbitration clause allowed court action for injunctive relief and permitted court to award money damages, leading court to construe arbitration clause as including exception for legal issues related to claims for equitable relief).
95 *See* Act on Private International Law, *supra* note 66, at art. 187, para. 1.
96 *See, e.g.* Tribunal Fédéral [TF] [Swiss Federal Supreme Court] 17 February 2015, 4A_553/2014, decided by the Swiss Supreme Court in a trademark / corporate name coexistence agreements in the framework of a corporate spin-off transaction in the Swiss industrial 'von Roll' group; on the issue of trademark coexistence agreements and on trademark splitting transactions, *see* the Chapters 11 and 5 respectively authored by NEIL WILKOF and by GREGOR BÜHLER & LUCA DAL MOLIN in this book; see also Apple Corps. Limited v. Apple Computer, Inc. [2006] EWHC 996 (Ch); *see also* Omega SA v. Omega Engineering Inc. [2011] EWCA Civ. 645.

which is a standard issue under trademark law, will be governed by the law of each country in which the alleged infringement takes place, thereby leading to the multiplication of governing laws. This would consequently imply, that even if the coexistence agreement were governed by a law chosen by the contracting parties, the existence of a risk of confusion could, depending on the interpretation of the contractual clause at issue, still be governed by multiple national trademark laws, in each of the countries in which the alleged infringement would have taken place. In order to avoid this consequence, parties involved in international commercial arbitration may prefer to submit all (contractual and non-contractual) issues to a single national (trademark) law. They could consequently select one (neutral) law in order to decide on the issues at stake, particularly on the issue of the risk of confusion, which could avoid the disadvantages of having to apply all different national laws[97] that may lead to conflicting results, in spite of the harmonization of international trademark protection standards (particularly thanks to the TRIPS agreement).

13.62 A choice of law clause could also cover issues relating to the validity or enforceability of the relevant trademarks (and other intellectual property rights), at least to the extent that the award to be rendered shall only have an effect between the parties (that is, *inter partes*). The parties to an international trademark agreement covering several countries should indeed have the power to decide in the agreement (in the arbitration clause) that the validity or enforceability of trademarks registered in different countries or regions shall not be governed by each and every national trademark law in the relevant countries or regions, but shall rather be analyzed on the basis of one single national trademark law.[98] This issue consequently leaves broad room for the freedom of parties in the drafting of the definition of the governing law (in the agreement itself or in the subsequent arbitration proceedings), whereby the choice of a unique law that shall apply to a global dispute, while facilitating the proceedings (in terms of time and costs), nevertheless creates the risk of the 'winner takes all' in the sense that if the parties choose by way of example to submit the issue of the validity or of the infringement of the relevant trademark to one single law, one answer will be given to this issue (which will turn out to be unfavourable to one party).

13.63 In any event, it is essential to realize that a choice of law clause, which would relate only to the law governing the contract and which would consequently

---

[97] For additional examples, *see* Trevor Cook & Alejandro Garcia, INTERNATIONAL INTELLECTUAL PROPERTY ARBITRATION, ARBITRATION IN CONTEXT SERIES 87 (2010).
[98] Cook & Garcia, *supra* note 97, at 93 sq.; Rohn & Groz, *supra* note 89, at 655.

not cover non-contractual issues, will not be sufficient.[99] The scope of the choice of law clause should therefore be formulated more broadly.[100] One approach could be to mirror the scope of the arbitration clause with the scope of the choice of law clause in the sense that the arbitral tribunal shall have the power to decide all relevant legal issues by application of one single governing law.[101]

13.64 This flexibility in the choice of the governing law can be an important advantage of arbitration over state court litigation in many areas of the world. This is particularly the case in the EU because of Article 8 of Regulation 864/2007 (Rome II), which provides that 'The law applicable to a non-contractual obligation arising from an infringement of an intellectual property right shall be the law of the country for which protection is claimed' (Article 8, para. 1), and that this rule is mandatory (that is, it cannot be overridden by contract pursuant to Article 8, para. 3[102]).[103]

13.65 It should in any case be kept in mind that the freedom of the parties to choose the law that shall govern their dispute does not (and cannot) affect the potential application of mandatory legal principles, and specifically of competition law. This is what was confirmed in the landmark Benetton – EcoSwiss case which was a trademark licensing dispute[104] and which was submitted to the Court of Justice of the European Union (at that time the Court of Justice of the European Communities).[105] In this case, the Court famously held that 'a national court to which application is made for annulment of an arbitration award must grant that application if it considers that the award in question is in fact contrary to article 81 EC (ex Article 85), where its domestic rules of procedure require it to grant an application for annulment founded on failure

---

99 See for instance the standard arbitration clause proposed by the London Court of International Arbitration (LCIA) which provides that '… the governing law of the contract shall be the substantive law of …'. See *Arbitration, Recommended Clauses*, LCIA (2015), available 17 September 2015 at http://www.lcia.org/Dispute_Resolution_Services/LCIA_Recommended_Clauses.aspx.
100 The standard arbitration clause of the WIPO arbitration and mediation center (*Arbitration and Mediation Center*, WIPO (2015), *available 17 September 2015 at* http://www.wipo.int/amc/en/clauses/#4) provides that: '… The dispute, controversy or claim shall be decided in accordance with the law of [specify jurisdiction]'.
101 Cook & Garcia, *supra* note 97, at 130.
102 'The law applicable under this Article may not be derogated from by an agreement pursuant to Article 14.
103 An arbitral tribunal having its seat in the European Union will not be bound to apply art. 8 (*see* Cook & Garcia, *supra* note 97, at 94), even if the application of Regulations Rome I and Rome II is debated in the legal literature: *see* BURGU YÜKSEL, *The Relevance of the Rome I Regulation to International Commercial Arbitration in The European Union*, 7 JOURNAL OF PRIVATE INTERNATIONAL LAW 149, 655 (April 2011), p. 149; Rohn & Groz, *supra* note 89, p. 655 who leave this issue open.
104 Benetton granted Eco Swiss the right to manufacture watches and clocks bearing the words 'Benetton by Bulova', which could be sold by Eco Swiss and Bulova.
105 Case C-126/97, Eco Swiss China Time Ltd v. Benetton International NV [1999] E.C.R. I-03055.

to observe national rules of public policy'.[106] On this basis, parties to an (international) trademark agreement should keep a close eye on the potential application of competition law which may affect or even jeopardize the enforceability of their contract (which may prove of strategic interest for the contracting party wishing to escape from its contractual liability, and can be of particular relevance for trademark licensees wishing to escape from the obligation to pay royalties under their license agreement). The critical impact of competition law on intellectual property licensing is confirmed by a case that is pending before the ECJ in which the issue (which was submitted by the Court of Appeal of Paris on 9 December 2014) is: 'Must the provisions of Article 81 of the Treaty (now Article 101 TFEU) be interpreted as precluding effect being given, where patents are revoked, to a licence agreement which requires the licencee to pay royalties for the sole use of the rights attached to the licensed patent?'[107]

4. Provisional measures

13.66 Given the necessity of quick action in the face of trademark infringement activities (also because of the risk of irreparable harm and of damage to the reputation),[108] provisional measures are of fundamental importance for trademark owners.[109] In such circumstances, it is very important to ensure that provisional measures can be obtained from state courts which can frequently be of critical assistance.[110] In licensing disputes, the victim who may claim protection by requesting provisional measures is not only the licensor,[111] but sometimes also the licensee.[112]

---

106   *Ibid*.
107   Case C-567/14, Genentech Inc. v. Hoechst GmbH, formerly Hoechst AG, Sanofi-Aventis Deutschland GmbH, 2015 O.J. (C 73) 12.
108   For an example, *see* the decision of the Tribunal Fédéral [TF] [Swiss Federal Supreme Court] 13 April 2010, ARRÊTS DU TRIBUNAL FÉDÉRAL SUISSE [ATF] 136 III 200, which was rendered against a procedural order issued by a sole arbitrator in a WIPO arbitration case which order the transfer of the stock of goods from the trademark licensee to the trademark licensor because the licensee was getting rid of the stock at depreciated prices which damaged the brand and the reputation of the licensor; for a comment of this case, *see* Jacques de Werra, *Liquidation d'un contrat de licence de marque et mesures provisionnelles: quelques observations à la lumière de l'ATF 136 III 200*, SIC! 662 (2010), *available 17 September 2015 at* https://www.sic-online.ch/fileadmin/user_upload/Sic-Online/2010/documents/662.pdf.
109   Cook & Garcia, *supra* note 97, at 221; Rohn & Groz, *supra* note 89, at 656.
110   One of the reasons is that a procedural order which would be rendered by an arbitral tribunal will not necessarily be enforceable, given that an arbitral tribunal does not have any coercive power to enforce by contrast to a state court, *see* Rohn & Groz, *supra* note 89, at 658.
111   *See* Performance Unlimited, Inc. v. Questar Publishers, Inc., 52 F.3d 1373 (6th Cir. 1995).
112   *See* Fairchild Semiconductors Corp. v. Third Dimension Semiconductor, 564 F.Supp.2d 63 (D. Maine, 12 December 2008).

13.67 The submission of a dispute to arbitration in a trademark contract shall not prevent one of the parties to request provisional measures from a state court, specifically at the place where the damage has occurred or may occur.[113] However, certain courts have adopted a restrictive approach about this,[114] which is not justified because there is no incompatibility and incoherence between requesting provisional measures before a state court and submitting the dispute on the merits to arbitration.[115]

13.68 A request for provisional measures can also be obtained from the arbitral tribunal. If the arbitral tribunal has not been constituted, some arbitration rules provide for the appointment of an 'emergency arbitrator'.[116] This need for quick action in international trademark disputes should also be taken into account by the parties negotiating a trademark agreement and an arbitration clause, who should consequently carefully select arbitration rules that will meet their needs and expectations (and specifically provide for emergency arbitration).[117]

D. CONCLUSION

13.69 ADR methods are growing in importance for solving global contractual business disputes. This is equally important for trademark-related agreements. Parties negotiating such agreements and considering the use of ADR are well advised to understand the specificities of such mechanisms in order to avoid

---

113 This is clarified in the WIPO arbitration rules (*see WIPO Arbitration Rules,* WIPO (2014), *available* 17 September 2015 *at* http://www.wipo.int/amc/en/arbitration/rules/newrules.html) as follows (Art. 48 d): 'A request addressed by a party to a judicial authority for interim measures or for security for the claim or counter-claim, or for the implementation of any such measures or orders granted by the Tribunal, shall not be deemed incompatible with the Arbitration Agreement, or deemed to be a waiver of that Agreement.'

114 Simula Inc. v. Autoliv Inc., 175 F.3d 716 (9th Cir. 1999): 'Because the district court correctly concluded that all of Simula's claims were arbitrable and the ICC arbitral tribunal is authorized to grant the equivalent of an injunction pendente lite, it would have been inappropriate for the district court to grant preliminary injunctive relief. Therefore, we affirm the district court's denial of preliminary injunctive relief'; *but see* In re Faiveley Transport Malmo AB, 522 F. Supp. 2d 639 (S.D.N.Y. 2007) (holding that the arbitration clause: '[a]ny dispute arising out of or in connection with this agreement shall be finally settled by arbitration without recourse to the courts' did not prevent the filing of temporary measures before courts in New York).

115 Sauer-Getriebe KG v. White Hydraulics, Inc., 715 F.2d 348 (7th Cir. 1983).

116 *See* WIPO Arbitration rules, *supra* note 113, at art. 49; ICC, ICC RULES OF ARBITRATION, art. 29 (2012), *available* 17 September 2015 *at* http://www.iccwbo.org/products-and-services/arbitration-and-adr/arbitration/icc-rules-of-arbitration/; on this issue, *see* Rohn & Groz, *supra* note 89, at 657.

117 *See* ICC, ICC INTELLECTUAL PROPERTY ROADMAP 64 (12th ed., 2014), *available* 17 September 2015 *at* http://www.iccwbo.org/products-and-services/trade-facilitation/ip-roadmap/ holding that '[t]o ensure that injunctive interim or conservatory relief is available even before arbitration commences. To that effect, parties should consider choosing arbitration rules that provide for interim measure to be granted by the arbitral tribunal but also for emergency relief even before the constitution of the tribunal (see for example the 2012 ICC Rules providing for emergency tribunals).'

traps and difficulties. As confirmed by this chapter, ADR mechanisms (and specifically mediation, UDRP and arbitration) can be of significant value for solving (international) trademark disputes and should consequently be duly considered by trademark owners, and by parties negotiating trademark-related agreements.

13.70 While the specificities of intellectual property (and specifically of trademark) arbitration should not be overestimated,[118] they must not be fully neglected. Contracting parties and their counsel should indeed take all required measures in order to benefit from the flexibilities that ADR mechanisms can offer and should consequently take into account their high potential, but also their limits, when drafting dispute resolution clauses in their trademark-related agreements.

---

118 *See* William W. Park, *Irony in Intellectual Property Arbitration*, 19 ARBITRATION INTERNATIONAL 451 (2003) (holding in the introduction that '[o]n scrutiny, the special nature of IP arbitration is not really all that special').

Part II

TRADEMARK TRANSACTIONS AT THE REGIONAL AND NATIONAL LEVEL

Section A
TRADEMARK TRANSACTIONS IN EUROPE

14

TRADEMARK TRANSACTIONS IN EU LAW: REFINING THE APPROACH TO SELECTIVE DISTRIBUTION NETWORKS AND NATIONAL UNFAIR COMPETITION LAW

Martin Senftleben[*]

A.	INTRODUCTION	14.01
B.	OVERVIEW OF HARMONIZED EU RULES	14.03
	1. Community Trade Mark Regulation	14.03
	2. Trade Mark Directive	14.10
	3. Reform plans	14.11
C.	SELECTIVE DISTRIBUTION NETWORKS	14.14
	1. The *Copad/Dior* case	14.14
	2. Expansion of the concept of product quality	14.17
	3. Impact on exhaustion of rights	14.19
	4. Open questions	14.23

	5. Rights against the licensee	14.29
	6. Rights against outside traders	14.37
	7. A more nuanced approach	14.40
D.	ROOM FOR NATIONAL UNFAIR COMPETITION LAW	14.43
	1. The *Martin Y Paz/Depuydt* case	14.43
	2. Mantra of complete harmonization	14.48
	3. Function theory unsatisfactory	14.52
	4. No pre-emption of national doctrines	14.57
E.	CONCLUSION	14.59

A. INTRODUCTION

Harmonized European Union (EU) trademark law contains rules on trademarks as objects of property, including transfers and licenses, in Articles 16 to 24 of the Community Trade Mark Regulation (CTMR)[1] and a provision on licensing in Article 8 of the Trade Mark Directive (TMD).[2] The rudimentary nature of this set of EU rules clearly comes to the fore in Article 16(1) of the CTMR: unless the CTMR provides harmonized norms, questions concerning Community Trade Marks (CTMs) as objects of property must be answered – for the whole EU territory – on the basis of the national law of a single EU   14.01

---

[*] Professor of Intellectual Property and Director, Kooijmans Institute for Law and Governance, Vrije Universiteit Amsterdam; Of Counsel, Bird & Bird, The Hague.
[1] Council Regulation No 207/2009 of 26 February 2009 on the Community trademark (codified version), 2009 O.J. (L 78) 1 (EC) [hereinafter CTMR].
[2] Directive 2008/95, of the European Parliament and of the Council of 22 October 2008 to approximate the laws of the Member States relating to trademarks (codified version), 2008 O.J. (L 299) 25 [hereinafter TMD].

Member State. The applicable national law is to be determined in accordance with the rules on points of attachment given in Article 16 of the CTMR. The seat or domicile of the trademark proprietor serves as the primary point of attachment.[3] An establishment can be used as an alternative.[4] As the EU trademark office – the Office for Harmonization in the Internal Market (OHIM) – has its seat in Alicante, Spain, the national law of Spain applies in default of a seat, domicile or establishment.[5]

14.02 The regulation of trademark transactions in the EU thus relies on a harmonious interplay of harmonized EU law and individual national legislation. This configuration of the system places a particular responsibility on the Court of Justice of the European Union (CJEU). When interpreting harmonized EU rules, the CJEU ought to consider the impact of its decision on the proper functioning of national law. An overambitious approach seeking to maximize the harmonizing effect of the rudimentary set of EU norms will almost inevitably lead to unsatisfactory results. After a short overview of EU 'objects of property' rules and present amendment proposals (following Section B of this Chapter), two decisions of the CJEU will be brought into focus to illustrate this point. The decision in *Copad/Dior* gives rise to concerns about harmonized rules in the TMD becoming a 'straitjacket' with insufficient breathing space for the reconciliation of licensor, licensee and third party interests (discussed in Section C of this Chapter). The case of *Martin Y Paz/Depuydt* sheds light on the potential corrosive effect of harmonized EU rules on national unfair competition law (discussed in Section D of this Chapter). The analysis shows the structural deficiencies of the current EU system and the need for additional fine-tuning based on both EU and national norms (concluding Section E of this Chapter).

B. OVERVIEW OF HARMONIZED EU RULES

1. Community Trade Mark Regulation

14.03 Article 16 of the CTMR sets forth the aforementioned rules on the interplay between harmonized EU norms and the application of the national law of a single Member State.[6] In line with Articles 20(2) and 23(3) of the CTMR, the points of attachment specified in this context (that is, seat/domicile/

---

3   CTMR, *supra* note 1, at art. 16.
4   *Id.*
5   *Id.* at arts. 16(1)(a), (b) and (2). *Cf.* TOBIAS COHEN JEHORAM, CONSTANT VAN NISPEN, TONY HUYDECOPER, EUROPEAN TRADEMARK LAW 534–5. (2010).
6   CTMR, *supra* note 1, at art. 16.

establishment) also serve as a basis for determining the national courts and authorities for levy of execution in respect of a CTM and the law governing effects vis-à-vis third parties.[7] Jurisdiction for involving a Community trade mark in insolvency proceedings depends on the question in which Member State the debtor has his main interests or – in case of an insurance undertaking or a credit institution – in which Member State that undertaking or institution has been authorized.[8]

14.04 Transfers are regulated in Articles 17 and 18 of the CTMR while Article 22 of the CTMR deals with licensing. The CTMR provides for whole or partial transfers independent of the underlying business or undertaking.[9] The underlying concept of 'transfer' includes assignment, legal succession (for example, in cases of heritage or merger), and changes of the legal structure resulting in the creation of a new legal person.[10] A sale of the whole of an undertaking entails the transfer of CTMs unless there is agreement to the contrary or the circumstances surrounding the transfer dictate otherwise.[11] In order to be valid, a transfer requires written form and the signature of the parties involved.[12]

14.05 For the successor in title to be able to invoke the rights in the CTM, the transfer must be registered.[13] OHIM will refuse to register a transfer if, as a result of the transaction, the CTM is likely to mislead the public with regard to the nature, quality or geographical origin of the goods or services for which it is registered.[14] For a transfer to be deemed misleading in cases of a trademark corresponding to the name of a natural person, it is not sufficient

---

7 *Id.*, at arts. 20(2) and 23(3).
8 *Id.*, at art. 21(1).
9 JEHORAM, VAN NISPEN & MUYDECOPER, *supra* note 5, at 536. For an overview of the different national traditions in the EU discussing the possibility and preconditions of independent transfers, *see* Annette Kur, *Die gemeinschaftliche Markenbenutzung – Markenlizenzen und verwandte Tatbestände*, GEWERBLICHER RECHTSSCHUTZ UND URHEBERRECHT INTERNATIONAL, 1, 2–4 (1990).
10 In case of the change of the legal structure, applicable national corporate law may provide for the predecessor and successor company to be considered the same legal entity. *See* Andreas Renck, *Community Trade Marks as Objects of Property*, *in* CONCISE EUROPEAN TRADEMARK AND DESIGN LAW, 90, 92–3 (Charles Gielen & Verena von Bomhard eds., 2011) (mentioning German law on the transformation of legal entities as an example).
11 CTMR, *supra* note 1, at art. 17(2).
12 *Id.* at art. 17(3). This requirement of a transfer in written form does not exist in all national laws of EU Member States. Some national systems, such as the German system, are more flexible and acknowledge contracts which are not concluded in writing as well. See the analysis conducted by ROLAND KNAAK, ANNETTE KUR, & ALEXANDER VON MÜHLENDAHL, MAX PLANCK INSTITUTE FOR INTELLECTUAL PROPERTY AND COMPETITION LAW, STUDY ON THE OVERALL FUNCTIONING OF THE EUROPEAN TRADE MARK SYSTEM 227, ¶ 2.19 (2011), *available 18 September 2015 at* http://ec.europa.eu/internal_market/indprop/docs/tm/20110308_allensbach-study_en.pdf.
13 *Id.* at art. 17(5). For the evidence of the transfer necessary for registration, *see* Renck, *supra* note 10, at 94–5.
14 CTMR, *supra* note 1, at art. 17(4).

that the successor continues to use the trademark even though the natural person has left the company.[15] As long as the characteristics and the quality of the goods or services remain guaranteed by the trademark owner, the link established by the trademark is considered correct unless the trademark owner has an intention to make consumers believe that the natural person is still involved.[16] The successor can also overcome the obstacle of a misleading transfer by limiting the registration to goods or services in respect of which the misleading effect does not arise.[17] In line with Article 6*septies* of the Paris Convention, Article 18 of the CTMR provides for the assignment of a CTM to the rightful proprietor in case an agent or representative registered the mark in his own name without proper authorization or justification.[18]

14.06 Given the unitary character of the CTM which, in line with Article 1 of the CTMR, leads to an equal effect throughout the EU, Article 17(1) of the CTMR only mentions the option of a partial transfer in respect of some of the goods or services.[19] A territorial restriction of the transfer of a CTM is invalid.[20] Licenses concerning a CTM, by contrast, can also be given for only part of the EU.[21] In general, the CJEU interprets the grant of a license to mean that:

> [T]he proprietor of a trade mark confers on the licensee, within the limits set by the clauses of the licensing contract, the right to use that mark for the purposes falling within the area of the exclusive rights conferred by that mark, that is to say, the commercial use of that mark in a manner consistent with its functions, in particular the essential function of guaranteeing to consumers the origin of the goods or services concerned.[22]

14.07 In case of doubt about the nature of a contract concerning a trademark, the authorization 'to use the trademark commercially in a manner consistent with its function' can play a decisive role.[23] In the absence of an entitlement to use

---

15 Case C-259/04, Elizabeth Florence Emanuel v. Continental Shelf *128* [2006] E.C.R. I-3110.
16 *Id.* at ¶¶ 49–50. *But see* Pier Luigi Roncaglia & Giulio Enrico Sironi, *Trademark Functions and Protected Interests in the Decisions of the European Court of Justice*, 101 TRADEMARK REP. 147, 172–3 (2011) (arguing that by focusing on material characteristics of the designer garments at issue, the CJEU neglected other features, such as style, which are central to the purchasing decision of consumers).
17 CTMR, *supra* note 1, at art. 17(4) and 17(5).
18 *Id.* at art. 18.
19 As to particular questions that can arise in the context of transfers with regard to seniority claims based on earlier national marks that have not been surrendered or allowed to lapse, *see* Renck, *supra* note 10, at 93.
20 JEHORAM, VAN NISPEN & HUYDECOPER, *supra* note 5, at 537.
21 CTMR, *supra* note 1, at art. 22(1).
22 Case C-376/11, Pie Optiek SPRL v. Bureau Gevers SA and European Registry for Internet Domains ASBL, ECLI:EU:C:2012:502 (2012).
23 *Id.* at ¶¶ 50, 51 and 53.

the trademark commercially to distinguish goods or services in the marketplace, a contract for the use of a trademark to obtain a registration of a corresponding domain name, for example, may be more akin to a contract for services than to a licensing agreement.[24]

Where a licensee contravenes a provision in the licensing agreement concerning the duration of the contract, the form of use, the scope of the goods or services, the territorial scope of the license or the quality of the goods or services, the trademark proprietor may invoke his trademark rights against the licensee.[25] For bringing infringement proceedings, the licensee, in principle, requires consent from the trademark proprietor. However, the holder of an exclusive license may bring infringement proceedings if the trademark proprietor does not take action himself within an appropriate period after formal notice.[26] The parties to a licensing agreement are free to depart from these default rules. In any case, however, the licensee is free to intervene in infringement proceedings brought by the CTM proprietor, to obtain compensation for damages which he suffered as a licensee.[27] If a counterclaim for revocation or a declaration of invalidity is brought in a legal action to which the trademark proprietor is not already a party, he must be informed of this development and may be joined as a party to the action in accordance with the conditions set forth in the applicable national law.[28]

14.08

Article 19(1) of the CTMR establishes the principle that a CTM may be given as security and be the subject of rights *in rem* independently of the undertaking.[29] Article 20(1) of the CTMR adds that a CTM, as already indicated, may be levied in execution. Unless a third party acquiring rights in a CTM had knowledge of a transfer, security interest, other right *in rem* or license, these legal acts will only have effect vis-à-vis third parties after they have been entered in the CTM register on request of one of the parties to the trademark transaction.[30] As Article 23(1) of the CTMR refers to positive 'knowledge' in this latter context, constructive or imputed knowledge are unlikely to suffice. A notice of the trademark transaction will thus normally be necessary to achieve third party effects in the absence of registration.[31] However, these rules on effects vis-à-vis third parties do not apply when the

14.09

---

24   *Id.* at ¶ 52.
25   CTMR, *supra* note 1, at art. 22(2).
26   *Id.* at art. 22(3).
27   *Id.* at art. 22(4).
28   *Id.* at art. 100(3).
29   For a discussion of different types of rights *in rem*, see JEHORAM, VAN NISPEN & HUYDECOPER, *supra* note 5, at 539–40.
30   CTMR, *supra* note 1, at arts. 17(5), 19(2), and 22(5).
31   Renck, *supra* note 10, at 101; JEHORAM, VAN NISPEN & HUYDECOPER, *supra* note 5, at 539.

trademark, or a right concerning the trademark, is acquired by way of transfer of the whole undertaking or by universal succession.[32] Levy of execution (by request of one of the parties in accordance with Article 20(3) of the CTMR) and involvement in insolvency proceedings (on request of the competent national authority in accordance with Article 21(3) of the CTMR) may be entered in the CTM Register as well.

2. Trade Mark Directive

14.10 In contrast to this set of legal norms in the CTMR, the rules in the TMD are limited to two aspects found in Article 8 of the TMD.[33] On the one hand, the first paragraph of the provision clarifies that a trademark – in this case a national trademark in a Member State – may be licensed for some or all of the goods or services for which it is registered and for the whole or part of the Member State concerned.[34] Article 8(2) of the TMD draws a parallel with Article 22(2) of the CTMR by making it clear that also in case of a national trademark, the trademark proprietor may invoke his trademark rights against a licensee breaching a provision in the licensing agreement regarding the duration of the contract, the form of use, the scope of the goods or services, the territorial scope of the license or the quality of the goods or services.[35]

3. Reform plans

14.11 The rules of harmonized EU trademark law are presently under review. The European Commission's package for amending the trademark legislation in the EU (the proposed new Regulation (Draft CTMR)[36] and Directive (Draft TMD)[37]) contains the proposal to supplement Article 8(1) and (2) of the TMD with further provisions taken from the CTMR.[38] This proposal is in line with recommendations made during the preparatory work for the new

---

32 CTMR, *supra* note 1, at art. 23(2).
33 TMD, *supra* note 2, at art. 8.
34 *Id.* at art. 8(1).
35 *Id.* at art 8(2).
36 Commission Proposal for a Regulation of the European Parliament and of the Council Amending Council Regulation (EC) No 207/2009 on the Community Trade Mark, COM (2013) 161 final, (27 March 2013) [hereinafter Draft CTMR].
37 Commission Proposal for a Directive of the European Parliament and of the Council to Approximate the laws of the Member States Relating to Trade marks, COM (2013) 162 final (27 March 2013) [hereinafter Draft TMD].
38 For general comments on the proposed new legislation, *see* Rolf Sack, *Kritische Anmerkungen zur Regelung der Markenverletzungen in den Kommissionsvorschlägen für eine Reform des europäischen Markenrechts*, 7/2013 GEWERBLICHER RECHTSSCHUTZ UND URHEBERRECHT 657, (2013); Tobias Cohen Jehoram, *Nieuw en verbeterd! Het Europees merkenrecht – Commissievoorstel doet 3 stappen vooruit, 1 achteruit*, 12–09–2013 BERICHTEN INDUSTRIËLE EIGENDOM 198–205 (2013).

trademark legislation. The *Study of the Max Planck Institute on the Overall Functioning of the European Trade Mark System* – the main preparatory work carried out for the new legislation – arrived at the following conclusion:

> The TMD should be complemented by a comprehensive body of rules addressing trade marks as objects of property. With the exception of rules regulating the third party effects of registration of legal transactions and the examination of transfer documents for risks of consumer deception, the rules to be introduced should follow those of the CTMR, so as to ensure coherence.[39]

14.12 Against this background, the Commission's reform package seeks to include the rules on transfers known from the CTMR in the TMD.[40] It supplements the existing licensing norms with the rules from the CTMR on possibilities for the licensee to bring infringement proceedings and intervene in proceedings initiated by the trademark proprietor.[41] Moreover, the Commission proposes to lay down rules ensuring that national trademarks can, independently of the undertaking, be given as security and be the subject of rights *in rem*,[42] and that they can be levied in execution.[43] With regard to transfers, licenses, security interests, other rights *in rem*, involvement in insolvency proceedings and licenses, the proposed amendment would include the option of registration in the national trademark register.

14.13 In the further legislative process, however, it became apparent that the Council of the European Union rejected several aspects of this broadening of the rules on trademark transactions in the TMD, such as the requirement of written form in the case of transfers, the possibility of recording insolvency proceedings in the register, and the rules on the initiation of, and intervention in, infringement proceedings in the case of licenses.[44] As the European Parliament also expressed doubts about provisions in the field of transfers,[45] it remains to be seen which elements of the Commission proposal will finally make their way into the new TMD.

---

39   *See* ROLAND KNAAK, ANNETTE KUR, & ALEXANDER VON MÜHLENDAHL, *supra* note 12, at ¶ 2.24 (2011). For a more detailed discussion of the individual rules that should be transposed into the TMD according to the Study, *see id.* ¶¶ 2.17–2.23.
40   Draft TMD, *supra* note 37, at art. 22.
41   *Id.* at art. 26(3) and (4).
42   *Id.* at art. 23.
43   *Id.* at art. 24.
44   Presidency Compromise Proposal, Council of the European Union, arts. 22–26 (18 July 2014), Interinstitutional File 2013/0089 (COD), no. 11827/14 PI 96 CODEC 1621.
45   Legislative Resolution on the Proposal for a Directive of the European Parliament and of the Council to Approximate the Laws of the Member States Relating to Trademarks (recast), EUR. PARL. DOC. (COM 0162) Amendments 37–39 (2014).

C. SELECTIVE DISTRIBUTION NETWORKS

1. The *Copad/Dior* case

14.14 On the basis of this overview of harmonized EU trademark transactions law and current amendment proposals, it becomes possible to explore specific problem areas in more detail. One of the controversial issues in the regulation of trademark transactions is the approach to selective distribution networks. To what extent should the trademark proprietor be able to invoke trademark rights to control the activities of licensees and further distribution of branded goods and services? In CJEU jurisprudence on trademark transactions, the issue of selective distribution networks featured prominently in *Copad/Dior*.[46] The case concerned a licensing agreement that Dior had concluded with Société industrielle lingerie (SIL) regarding the manufacture and distribution of luxury corsetry goods bearing the Dior trademark. Under this agreement, SIL was bound to refrain from sales to wholesalers and discount stores in order not to endanger the reputation and prestige of the luxury trademark. Nonetheless, SIL sold goods bearing the Dior trademark to Copad, a company operating a discount store business, even though Dior had explicitly refused SIL's request to grant permission for these sales outside its selective distribution network.[47]

14.15 In the light of Article 8(2) of the TMD, this case raised the question whether SIL's breach of contractual obligations amounted to trademark infringement or merely gave rise to contractual liability. As explained above, Article 8(2) of the TMD provides that the trademark proprietor can invoke trademark rights against a licensee who contravenes a provision of the licensing agreement dealing with duration, the form in which the trademark may be used, the scope of the goods or services falling under the license, the territory in which the trademark may be affixed, or the quality of the goods or services offered by the licensee. Given this enumeration of relevant contractual provisions, the CJEU was asked to give guidance on whether Article 8(2) of the TMD covered the contractual obligation to refrain from sales to discount stores.

14.16 Answering this question, the CJEU first addressed the issue of whether the list of categories of contractual stipulations in Article 8(2) of the TMD was exhaustive or merely illustrative. Tersely noting that Article 8(2) of the TMD contained 'no adverb, or an expression such as "especially" or "in particular",

---

[46] Case C-59/08, Copad SA v. Christian Dior Couture SA and Others [2008] E.C.R. I-03421.
[47] *Id.* at ¶¶ 7–10.

that would allow a finding that the list simply provides guidance',[48] the Court arrived at the conclusion that it followed from the 'very wording' that the list of contractual stipulations in Article 8(2) of the TMD was exhaustive.[49] To support this conclusion, the Court made a comparison with the text of Article 7(2) of the TMD regulating the right of the trademark proprietor to oppose the further commercialisation of goods after the exhaustion of trademark rights. As Article 7(2) of the TMD contains the adverb 'especially', the Court found that it had to be understood to offer an illustrative list of relevant circumstances, whereas Article 8(2) of the TMD set forth a closed list.[50] In other words, only a breach of contractual stipulations falling under one of the five categories listed in Article 8(2) of the TMD allows the invocation of trademark rights against a licensee.

2. Expansion of the concept of product quality

Taking this finding as a starting point, the question arose whether the contractual obligation to refrain from sales to discount stores could be brought within the scope of one of the categories listed in Article 8(2) of the TMD. The Court surmounted this hurdle by stating with regard to the category of 'the quality of the goods manufactured':

14.17

> [T]he quality of luxury goods such as the ones at issue in the main proceedings is not just the result of their material characteristics, but also of the allure and prestigious image which bestows on them an aura of luxury.[51]

According to the Court, the 'allure and prestigious image' thus forms part of the quality of luxury goods besides material characteristics. This holding offered the chance of including the ban on sales outside a selective distribution network in the concept of 'quality' in the sense of Article 8(2)(e) TMD. While this solution may reflect modern marketing strategies in the luxury goods industries,[52] it is doubtful whether this alignment of Article 8(2) of the TMD with luxury brand owners' interests rests on a proper policy basis. To this day, the justification for protecting brand goodwill is an unresolved question of trademark law.[53] Against this background, it becomes

---

48 *Id.* at ¶ 18.
49 *Id.* at ¶ 20.
50 *Id.* at ¶ 19.
51 *Id.* at ¶ 24.
52 *Cf.* Agnieszka Machnicka, *The Perfume Industry and Intellectual Property Law in the Jurisprudence of the Court of Justice of the European Union and of National Courts*, 43 INT'L REV. OF INTELL. PROP. & COMP. L. 123, 141–3 (2012) (describing the strategies applied by the luxury perfume industry).
53 For a detailed analysis of potential justifications, *see also* WOLFGANG SAKULIN, TRADEMARK PROTECTION AND FREEDOM OF EXPRESSION – AN INQUIRY INTO THE CONFLICT BETWEEN TRADEMARK RIGHTS

apparent that *Copad/Dior* took the protection of brand image to the extreme,[54] without giving a sufficiently strong explanation of the need to protect brand image and offering an unbiased analysis of effects on competitors, consumers, and society as a whole.[55] Instead, the CJEU simply focused on Dior's interest in the development of an aura of luxury and explained that:

> [S]etting up a selective distribution system such as that at issue in the main proceedings which, according to the terms of the licence agreement between Dior and SIL, seeks to ensure that the goods are displayed in sales outlets in a manner that enhances their value, 'especially as regards the positioning, advertising, packaging as well as business policy', contributes, as Copad acknowledges, to the reputation of the goods at issue and therefore to sustaining the aura of luxury surrounding them.[56]

14.18 This line of reasoning allowed the Court to conclude that the sale of Dior luxury goods to traders outside the selective distribution network might affect 'the quality itself of those goods'.[57] Dior's contractual provision prohibiting sales to discount stores could thus be deemed to fall within the scope of Article

---

AND FREEDOM OF EXPRESSION UNDER EUROPEAN LAW, 35–67 (2010) (casting doubt upon the justificatory basis of protection against dilution). Proponents of brand image protection in the framework of trademark law particularly point to the effort and financial expenses made by the brand owner. For instance, see Andrew Griffiths, *Quality in European Trademark Law*, 11 NW, J. TECH. & INTELL. PROP. 621, 635–7 (2013); Andreas Breitschaft, *Intel, Adidas & Co – Is the Jurisprudence of the European Court of Justice on Dilution Law in Compliance with the Underlying Rationales and Fit for the Future?* 30 EUR. INTELL. PROP. REV. 497, 499 (2009). Considering the costs for society involved in the grant of brand image protection – in particular restrictions of freedom of expression and freedom of competition – this fact alone, however, can hardly be deemed sufficient for the grant of broad exclusive rights. *See* Dominic Scott et al., *Trademarks as Property: a Philosophical Perspective*, in TRADEMARKS AND BRANDS – AN INTERDISCIPLINARY CRITIQUE 298, 296–7 (Lionel Bently, Jennifer Davis & Jane C. Ginsburg eds., 2011); Martin R.F. Senftleben, *The Trademark Tower of Babel – Dilution Concepts in International, US and EC Law*, 40 INT'L REV. OF INTELL. PROP. & COMP. L. 45, 59–61 (2009) (considering product differentiation, facilitation of consumer choice and incentives to purchasing and, nevertheless, reject utilitarian arguments). *Cf.* Mark A. Lemley, *The Modern Lanham Act and the Death of Common Sense* 108 YALE L.J. 1687, 1694–6 (1999); Ralph S. Brown, *Advertising and the Public Interest: Legal Protection of Trade Symbols*, 108 YALE L.J. 1619, 1622–34 (1999); Rochelle Dreyfuss, *We Are Symbols and Inhabit Symbols, so Should we be Paying Rent? Deconstructing the Lanham Act and Rights of Publicity*, 20 COLUMBIA-VLA J. L. & ARTS 123, 128 (1996). *See also* Mark A. Lemley & Mark P. McKenna, *Owning Mark(et)s*, 109 MICH. L. REV. 137 (2010) (commenting on intuitive protection against free-riding as a species of unjust enrichment law).

54   The CJEU made a similar statement already in Case C-337/95, Parfums Christian Dior SA and Parfums Christian Dior BV v. Evora BV [1997] E.C.R. I-6013.
55   In this context, *see* Glenn Mitchell, *Aura as Quality – A Sumptuary Law for Our Times?*, 103 TRADEMARK REP. 1273, 1277 (2013) (arguing that the expansion of the concept of quality in *Copad/Dior* 'does not serve the traditional source-identifying purposes of trademarks and the smooth and open functioning of markets. If anything, it serves to restrict markets, rendering otherwise legal transactions between a willing buyer and willing seller unlawful, as well as creating uncertainty in all transactions with licensees or other downstream sales. Moreover, *Copad*'s holding is socially regressive. The prevailing social and economic systems of the last several centuries eschew formal class structure. While private parties may, by contract (and within certain limits), restrict distribution of goods, preservation of the social *status quo* should not constitute a cognizable trademark function.').
56   Copad v. Dior [2008] E.C.R. I-03421, ¶ 29.
57   *Id.* ¶ 30.

8(2) of the TMD and allow the invocation of trademark rights against SIL. The factors to be considered in this context are the nature of the luxury goods bearing the trademark, the volumes sold, whether the licensee sold the goods to discount stores that were not part of the selective distribution network regularly or only occasionally, the nature of the goods normally marketed by the discount stores, and the marketing methods normally used in that sector of activity.[58]

3. Impact on exhaustion of rights

14.19 With regard to further sales in the distribution chain, the CJEU addressed the exhaustion of Dior's trademark rights in cases of a licensee contravening the contractual prohibition to sell to discount stores. This question had to be answered in the light of Article 7(1) of the TMD, which sets forth Community-wide exhaustion preventing the trademark proprietor from prohibiting use of its trademark on goods that have been put on the internal market 'by the proprietor or with his consent'. Therefore, the question was whether 'consent' in the sense of Article 7(1) of the TMD had to be determined based on the exhaustive list in Article 8(2) of the TMD.[59]

14.20 In this context, the Court first confirmed the general rule that, for the purposes of the exhaustion rule laid down in Article 7(1) of the TMD, a licensee putting trademarked goods on the market was considered to be acting with the consent of the trademark proprietor.[60] However, as Article 8(2) TMD expressly enabled the trademark proprietor to invoke trademark rights against a licensee contravening certain provisions in the license agreement, this general assumption of consent did not apply in cases falling under Article 8(2) of the TMD. The licensee's contravention of one of the clauses listed in Article 8(2) of the TMD thus precludes exhaustion of the rights conferred by the trademark for the purposes of Article 7(1) of the TMD.[61]

14.21 As the Court had already declared the list of relevant clauses in Article 8(2) of the TMD to be exhaustive and closed, the establishment of this link between Article 8(2) of the TMD and Article 7(1) of the TMD created a hierarchy of contractual stipulations: a breach of clauses falling under one of the five categories listed in Article 8(2) of the TMD leaves trademark rights intact, whereas exhaustion takes place when the contravention concerns clauses

---

58   *Id.* ¶ 32.
59   *Id.* ¶¶ 38–39.
60   *Id.* ¶ 46.
61   *Id.* ¶¶ 49–50.

falling outside the scope of Article 8(2) of the TMD. In this latter case, the trademark proprietor may still have the chance of opposing the further commercialization of goods marketed in contravention of the licensing agreement. According to Article 7(2) of the TMD, this is possible when the trademark proprietor has legitimate reasons to oppose the further commercialization, especially where the condition of the goods is changed or impaired after they have been put on the market. In *Copad/Dior*, the CJEU explained with regard to this 'last resort' that a balance had to be struck between the trademark proprietor's legitimate interest in safeguarding his luxury brand image and the discount store's legitimate interest in being able to resell the luxury goods using customary trade methods.[62] With regard to the balancing of these interests, the Court had already held in *Dior/Evora* that:

> [T]he fact that a reseller, who habitually markets articles of the same kind but not necessarily of the same quality, uses for trade-marked goods the modes of advertising which are customary in his trade sector, even if they are not the same as those used by the trade mark owner himself or by his approved retailers, does not constitute a legitimate reason, within the meaning of Article 7(2) of the Directive, allowing the owner to oppose that advertising, unless it is established that, given the specific circumstances of the case, the use of the trade mark in the reseller's advertising seriously damages the reputation of the trade mark.[63]

In this vein, the CJEU deemed it decisive in *Copad/Dior* whether further discount store commercialization of trademarked luxury goods, using methods which are customary in its sector of trade, damages the reputation of the prestigious Dior trademark.[64] If it does, the trademark proprietor had reason to oppose the further commercialization of goods in the sense of Article 7(2) of the TMD and the exhaustion rule of Article 7(1) of the TMD would not apply.

14.22 In sum, the decision thus offered Dior two options of neutralizing the exhaustion rule: it could argue first that the sale outside the selective distribution network affected the quality of the luxury goods itself in the sense of Article 8(2) of the TMD (no consent in the sense of Article 7(1) of the TMD); second, it could seek to show that the sale outside the selective distribution network damaged the reputation of the luxury trademark (consent

---

62 *Id.* ¶ 56.
63 Case C-337/95, Parfums Christian Dior SA and Parfums Christian Dior BV v. Evora BV [1997] E.C.R. I-6013, ¶ 46.
64 Copad v. Dior [2008] E.C.R. I-03421, ¶ 57.

in the sense of Article 7(1) of the TMD, but legitimate reason to oppose further commercialization by virtue of Article 7(2) of the TMD).

4. Open questions

While this solution may seem dogmatically sound as long as the analysis is restricted to Articles 7 and 8 of the TMD, it raises doubts when further provisions are taken into account. Article 5(1) of the TMD defines the exclusive right enjoyed by the trademark proprietor as the entitlement 'to prevent all third parties not having his consent from using [a conflicting sign] in the course of trade'. Article 5(2) of the TMD adds the option of providing protection against dilution. Article 5(3) of the TMD makes it clear that the right to prohibit use (and, thus, the freedom to give consent), *inter alia*, covers offering goods under a conflicting sign, putting them on the market, or stocking them for these purposes without indicating any confinement to the parameters listed in Article 8(2) of the TMD. Considering this broad description of the scope of exclusive trademark rights in the EU, the CJEU pointed out in *Copad/Dior* that:

14.23

> [c]onsent, which is tantamount to the proprietor's renunciation of his exclusive right within the meaning of Article 5, constitutes the decisive factor in the extinction of that right and must, therefore, be so expressed that an intention to renounce that right is unequivocally demonstrated. Such intention will normally be gathered from an express statement of consent.[65]

The Court went on to explain that, in the case of a licensee, consent could normally be assumed because of the economic link with the trademark proprietor. In this context, the Court attached particular importance to the licensing agreement offering the trademark proprietor the possibility of control over the activities of the licensee. Given this possibility of control, the Court was satisfied that in the case of use by a licensee, the trademark was still able to fulfil its essential function, namely 'to offer a guarantee that all the goods bearing it have been manufactured under the control of a single undertaking which is responsible for their quality'.[66]

14.24

In light of this description of the crucial role of the licensing agreement in safeguarding the appropriate functioning of the trademark, it is surprising that the CJEU finally arrives at the conclusion in *Copad/Dior* that consent in the sense of the exhaustion rule of Article 7(1) of the TMD is only absent in the

14.25

---

65 *Id.* ¶ 42.
66 *Id.* ¶ 45.

case of clauses falling under one of the categories listed in Article 8(2) of the TMD. If the licensing agreement is central to ensuring sufficient 'control of a single undertaking', it is conceivable to leave the definition of an appropriate standard of control to the trademark proprietor. In line with the broad rights found in Articles 5(1), (2) and (3) of the TMD, the trademark proprietor would then be free to make his consent dependent on those contractual obligations which he considers necessary to ensure 'control of a single undertaking', not only in the sense of contractual liability, but also for the purpose of reserving the possibility to invoke trademark rights against the licensee. As Advocate General Kokott mentioned in her opinion in *Copad/Dior*:

> One might assume that, where the licensee uses the trade mark in a manner that contravenes the licence agreement, the licensor is entitled to enforce his trade mark rights without restriction.[67]

14.26 Against this background, appropriate 'control of a single undertaking' (that is, control that renders the licensing agreement capable of securing the proper functioning of the trademark) could thus be understood to mean control in accordance with the standards set by the trademark proprietor himself and not by the closed list of Article 8(2) of the TMD. This seems plausible at least with regard to the relationship between the trademark proprietor and the licensee who has signed the licensing agreement and is fully aware of all conditions relating to the use of the trademark.

14.27 In sum, the assumption that the list in Article 8(2) of the TMD is exhaustive, thus, raises doubts in at least two respects. First, it implies the risk of an artificially broad interpretation of the listed categories, such as an interpretation of 'the quality of the goods manufactured' in the sense of Article 8(2)(e) of the TMD covering not only material characteristics, but also 'allure and prestigious image'.[68] Second, it seems counterintuitive to make inroads into the broad scope of Article 5 of the TMD by restricting this general concept to cases falling under one of the categories of Article 8(2) of the TMD when it comes to the question of using trademark rights to enforce contractual stipulations in a licensing agreement.[69]

14.28 Given these open questions, it makes sense to explore alternative approaches to the list in Article 8(2) of the TMD and its impact on the exhaustion of rights. For an alternative approach to be convincing, it would have to eliminate the doubts about the assumption of the list in Article 8(2) of the TMD being

---

67 Opinion of Advocate General Kokott, Copad v. Dior [2008] E.C.R. I-03421, ¶ 16.
68 Copad v. Dior [2008] E.C.R. I-03421, ¶ 24.
69 *Id.* ¶ 50.

closed and offer an appropriate balance between the interests of the trademark proprietor (Dior), the licensee (SIL), the third party trader outside the selective distribution network (Copad), and the public at large. Hence, a comprehensive reconciliation of interests is required.

5. Rights against the licensee

As to the relationship between the trademark proprietor (Dior) and the licensee (SIL), the licensing agreement must be seen as the core instrument for the trademark proprietor to exert control over the activities of the licensee and ensure a consistent use and presentation of the trademark.[70] Given this central role of the licensing agreement, it makes sense to let the broad description of exclusive rights in Articles 5(1), (2) and (3) of the TMD prevail over the closed list in Article 8(2) of the TMD. The trademark proprietor should be able to invoke trademark rights against the licensee not only with regard to contractual stipulations covered by Article 8(2) of the TMD, but also with regard to other conditions relevant to the use and presentation of the trademark in the broad sense of Articles 5(1), (2) and (3) of the TMD.

14.29

In this regard, the counterarguments on which the CJEU relied in *Copad/Dior* do not pose an insurmountable hurdle. As explained above, the CJEU arrived at the conclusion of a closed list in Article 8(2) of the TMD because, in contrast to Article 7(2) of the TMD, the enumeration of five categories of relevant contractual terms in Article 8(2) of the TMD contains no expression, such as 'especially' or 'in particular', which is normally used to indicate that the list has a merely illustrative character.[71] However, this argument based on the wording of Article 8(2) of the TMD disregards the broader context in which the provision is placed.

14.30

First, it is unclear why the CJEU viewed Article 8(2) of the TMD exclusively through the prism of Article 7(2) of the TMD. Given the direct link between the grant of a license and the scope of exclusive rights, it would have been more consistent to focus on Articles 5(1), (2) and (3) of the TMD instead. These provisions delineate the exclusivity enjoyed by the trademark proprietor and thus, the room for licensing. Obviously, the categories listed in Article 8(2) of the TMD are narrower than the scope of rights granted in Article 5 of the TMD. Besides duration, form of use, scope of goods and services, territory, and quality, the broad definition of exclusive rights in Articles 5(1), (2) and (3) of the TMD covers further parameters, such as the quantity of goods and the

14.31

---

70 *Id.* ¶ 45.
71 *Id.* ¶¶ 17–20.

reputation of the trademark.[72] A systematic interpretation including Articles 5(1), (2) and (3) of the TMD thus does not support the assumption that the list in Article 8(2) of the TMD is exhaustive.

14.32 Second, it must not be overlooked that Article 8 of the TMD is only a rudimentary regulation of trademark licensing. Obviously, this single provision does not constitute a complete legal system for the reconciliation of the interests of trademark licensors and licensees. Against this background, it is not advisable to understand Article 8(2) of the TMD as the 'final word' on situations in which the licensor may invoke trademark rights against the licensee. By contrast, the guarantee of freedom of contract must be factored into the equation. If the parties agree on further conditions defining the scope and reach of the license, this broader contractual framework should be accepted as a definition of the preconditions for safeguarding the functions of the trademark under the license in the sense of the jurisprudence of the CJEU.[73] Accordingly, additional contractual obligations supplementing the provisions falling under Article 8(2) of the TMD should justify the invocation of trademark rights as well.

14.33 If the contracting parties agree on a specific standard of control governing the use and presentation of the trademark, this standard should determine the scope of trademark rights against the licensee, not the list in Article 8(2) of the TMD. By definition, the list is incapable of covering all impact factors that the contracting parties may find relevant to the consistent use and presentation of the trademark. The broadening of the room for invoking trademark rights against the licensee is also in the interest of consumers. As long as products bearing the trademark are put on the market by the trademark proprietor or an undertaking belonging to the trademark proprietor's selective distribution network, consumers will have an expectation of consistent use of the trademark, not only with regard to product quality, but also with regard to product presentation and brand image.

14.34 Therefore, the list in Article 8(2) of the TMD should not be regarded as a closed list in the relationship between the trademark proprietor and the licensee. Instead of limiting the room for invoking trademark rights to cases

---

72 *See* Opinion of Advocate General Kokott, Copad v. Dior [2008] E.C.R. I-03421, ¶¶ 19–20 (discussing quantity as a relevant impact factor).
73 Copad v. Dior [2008] E.C.R. I-03421, ¶ 45 (noting that it is established case law of the Court that the possibility of control following a licensing agreement should suffice for the trademark to be able to fulfil its functions. Considering this expectation of a safeguarding role of the licensing agreement, however, it seems consistent to leave the development of a more refined standard of control – going beyond the parameters listed in Article 8(2) of the TMD – to the parties).

falling under the categories listed in Article 8(2) of the TMD, the trademark proprietor should be able to assert the rights granted and described in Articles 5(1), (2) and (3) of the TMD against the licensee with regard to all contraventions of the licensing agreement that have an impact on the proper functioning of the trademark in the marketplace.

14.35 Following this alternative approach, it is unnecessary to assume that 'allure and prestigious image' form part of the 'quality' of goods in the sense of Article 8(2)(e) of the TMD.[74] By contrast, it is sufficient to hold that 'allure and prestigious image' are relevant factors impacting the use and presentation of the trademark besides those factors listed in Article 8(2) of the TMD. They are relevant because the trademark proprietor has an interest in ensuring that the expectations of consumers dealing with a trader belonging to the selective distribution network are fulfilled.[75] Hence, the trademark proprietor should be entitled to invoke trademark rights against the licensee on the basis of Articles 5(1), (2) and (3) of the TMD without the need to artificially expand the concept of 'quality' in the sense of Article 8(2)(e) of the TMD.[76] Such an interpretation safeguards the exclusive rights granted and described in Articles 5(1), (2) and (3) of the TMD when it comes to licensing. Under this alternative approach, Article 8(2) of the TMD would not be understood to set forth an exhaustive, closed list of contractual terms justifying the invocation of trademark rights against the licensee in case of contravention. Instead, Article 8(2) of the TMD would be seen as a provision with a declaratory nature.[77] In any case, the trademark proprietor can assert trademark rights against a licensee who breaches a clause of the licensing agreement falling under one of the categories listed in Article 8(2) of the TMD. However, other contractual provisions concerning the proper functioning of the trademark can serve as a basis for a trademark claim as well. If the parties add further conditions of use to safeguard the proper functioning of the trademark under the licensing agreement, a breach of these additional conditions also justifies the invocation of trademark rights against the licensee. This approach underlines the central role of the licensing agreement in safeguarding the functions of the trademark, as described by the CJEU in *Copad/Dior*.[78]

---

74 *Id.* ¶ 24.
75 As to the guarantee of quality in cases of prestigious luxury trademarks, *see* Griffiths, *supra* note 53, at 635–7.
76 In this sense, *see also* Jochen Bühling, *Die Markenlizenz im Rechtsverkehr*, 1998 GEWERBLICHER RECHTSSCHUTZ UND URHEBERRECHT 196, 198 (1998) (arguing that, in case of contraventions of contractual provisions falling outside Article 8(2) of the TMD, it can be assumed that the trademark proprietor can invoke his trademark rights anyway because the use is no longer covered by the license and the licensee, in consequence, has no defense against an infringement claim).
77 *Cf. id.* at 198.
78 Copad v. Dior [2008] E.C.R. I-03421, ¶¶ 44–45.

14.36 Considering the safeguarding role of the licensing agreement, it is consistent to leave the development of a more refined standard of control – going beyond the parameters listed in Article 8(2) of the TMD – to the contracting parties and allow a trademark action in all cases where the proper functioning of the trademark is at stake. This alternative approach supports the assertion of trademark rights not only with regard to the control aspects listed in Article 8(2) of the TMD but also in other cases where the trademark proprietor legitimately seeks to secure the proper functioning of the trademark.[79] Indications for such additional cases can be derived from CJEU jurisprudence. In *L'Oréal/Bellure*, the CJEU broadened the range of trademark functions enjoying protection under EU law by holding that:

> [T]hese functions include not only the essential function of the trade mark, which is to guarantee to consumers the origin of the goods or services, but also its other functions, in particular that of guaranteeing the quality of the goods or services in question and those of communication, investment or advertising.[80]

Given this extension of the range of protected functions to communication, investment, and advertising,[81] the prohibition of sales to discount stores in the licensing agreement between Dior and SIL can be qualified as an additional legitimate aspect of control not mentioned in Article 8(2) of the TMD: to safeguard the proper functioning of the trademark under the licensing agreement, including the preservation of the prestigious brand image being the result of Dior's trademark-based communication, investment and advertising,

---

79 *But see* Mitchell, *supra* note 55, at 1276–7 (arguing that the intention to preserve an aura of luxury through the restriction of sales to approved retailers in a selective distribution network is socially regressive because it upholds formal class structures and, in consequence, cannot be qualified as a legitimate trademark function anyway). For an in-depth analysis of this aspect of intellectual property protection, *see* Barton Beebe, *Intellectual Property Law and the Sumptuary Code*, 123 HARV. L. REV. 809 (2010).
80 Case C-487/07, L'Oreal SA, et al v. Bellure et al [2009] E.C.R. I-05185, ¶ 58.
81 For a positive assessment of this development, *see* Haochen Sun, *Reforming Anti-Dilution Protection in the Globalization of Luxury Brands*, 45 GEO. J. INT'L L. 783, 794–5 (2014); Griffiths, *supra* note 55, at 635–7; Roncaglia & Sironi, *supra* note 16, at 183–4; Machnicka, *supra* note 52, at 138–9. For more critical comments, *see* Arpan Banerjee, *Non-Origin Infringement – Has Trade Mark Law Gone Too Far?*, 43 INT'L REV. INTELL. PROP. & COMP. L. 555 (2012); Martin R.F. Senftleben, *Trade Mark Protection – A Black Hole in the Intellectual Property Galaxy?*, 42 INT'L REV. INTELL. PROP. & COMP. L. 383 (2011); Annette Kur et al., *Sweet Smells and a Sour Taste – the ECJ's L'Oréal Decision* (Max Planck Institute for Intellectual Property, Competition and Tax Law Research Paper Series No. 09–12, 2009) *available* 18 September 2015 at http://ssrn.com/abstract=1492032. As to problems arising from the continuous expansion of the protection of branding efforts and goodwill functions in trademark law, *see* Martin R.F. Senftleben, *Adapting EU Trademark Law to New Technologies – Back to Basics?*, in CONSTRUCTING EUROPEAN INTELLECTUAL PROPERTY: ACHIEVEMENTS AND NEW PERSPECTIVES 137 (Christophe Geiger ed., 2011); TRADE MARKS AND BRANDS – AN INTERDISCIPLINARY CRITIQUE (Lionel Bently, Jennifer Davis & Jane C. Ginsburg eds., 2008); Graeme B. Dinwoodie & Mark D. Janis, *Dilution's (Still) Uncertain Future*, 105 MICH. L. REV. FIRST IMPRESSIONS 98 (2006); Barton Beebe, *Search and Persuasion in Trademark Law*, 103 MICH. L. REV. 2020 (2005); Mathias Strasser, *The Rational Basis of Trademark Protection Revisited: Putting the Dilution Doctrine into Context*, 10 FORDHAM INTELL. PROP. MEDIA & ENT. L. J. 375 (2000).

Dior legitimately[82] insisted on an enhanced standard of control in its relationship with SIL, including the prohibition of sales to discount stores.[83] As the clause supports the proper functioning of the trademark in the sense of *L'Oréal/Bellure*, it is consistent to allow the invocation of trademark rights against a licensee selling to discount stores even though a prohibition of sales outside a selective distribution network is not listed in Article 8(2) of the TMD. Following this alternative approach, an artificial extension of the concept of 'quality of the goods manufactured' in Article 8(2) of the TMD to 'allure and prestigious image' can thus be avoided without restricting trademark rights against a licensee.

6. Rights against outside traders

The balancing of interests is different with respect to the relationship between the trademark proprietor (Dior) and a trader outside the selective distribution network (Copad). For the trader outside the distribution network, the list in Article 8(2) of the TMD can be an important source of legal certainty. It limits the exposure to 'downstream' distribution restrictions that may be set in the licensing agreement. In line with the *Copad/Dior* decision, the assumption of the list in Article 8(2) of the TMD being closed implies that 'consent' in the sense of the exhaustion of rights under Article 7(1) of the TMD is only absent in the case of contraventions falling under Article 8(2) of the TMD. When the list in Article 8(2) of the TMD is seen as an exhaustive enumeration in the context of the exhaustion provisions, the outside trader can thus rely on consent and the exhaustion of rights in all cases that are not covered by Article 8(2) of the TMD. The trademark proprietor, then, can only use the remaining option to oppose the resale based on the argument that he has a legitimate reason in the sense of Article 7(2) of the TMD.[84] As the Court explained in *Dior/Evora*, this means freedom for the outside trader to use modes of

14.37

---

82 This conclusion seems in line with the interpretation of goodwill functions by the CJEU. In Joined Cases C-236, 237, & 238/08, Google France and Google et al. v. Louis Vuitton et al. [2010] E.C.R. I-02417, ¶ 91, the Court explained in respect of the advertising function that the trademark owner may have not only the objective of indicating the origin of its goods or services, 'but also that of using its mark for advertising purposes designed to inform and persuade consumers.' *Id*. In Case C-323/09, Interflora Inc. and Interflora British Unit v. Marks & Spencer plc and Flowers Direct Online Ltd. [2011] E.C.R. I-08625, ¶ 60, the Court elaborated with regard to the investment function that in addition to its origin and (potential) advertising function, a trademark may also be used 'to acquire or preserve a reputation capable of attracting consumers and retaining their loyalty'. *Id. See also* Machnicka, *supra* note 52, at 142–3, with regard to the legitimacy of preserving the fragile aura of luxury of certain goods.
83 This must not be misunderstood to mean that in the absence of a licensing agreement, the same standard of control should apply. By contrast, the legitimate interest of the discount store in being able to resell the goods in question by using advertising methods which are customary in his sector of trade, must be factored into the equation as well. *See* Case C-337/95, Dior v. Evora [1997] E.C.R. I-6013, ¶ 44.
84 Rolf Sack, *Die Erschöpfung von Markenrechten bei lizenzvertragswidrigem Vertrieb*, GEWERBLICHER RECHTSSCHUTZ UND URHEBERRECHT INTERNATIONAL 198, 201 (2010) (criticizing the line of reasoning

advertising which are customary in his trade sector, even if they are not the same as those used by the trademark owner himself or by his approved retailers.[85] In the context of trademark rights exhaustion, the assumption of the list in Article 8(2) of the TMD being closed could thus have the effect of preserving the freedom of customary advertising which the CJEU offered to resellers in *Dior/Evora*. To preserve this freedom, the contractual prohibition to sell to traders outside a selective distribution network would have to be kept outside the scope of the concept of 'quality of the goods manufactured' underlying Article 8(2) of the TMD.[86]

14.38 It does not place an unreasonably heavy burden on the trademark proprietor to assume that 'allure and prestigious image' does not form part of the 'quality' of goods. Article 8(2) of the TMD covers the duration of the contract, the form of use, the scope of the goods or services, the territorial scope of the license and the quality of the goods or services. Crucial contract parameters and, in particular, quality standards concerning the material characteristics of products are thus covered by Article 8(2) of the TMD anyway. The trademark proprietor would only lose the possibility of relying on Article 8(2) of the TMD and preventing the exhaustion of rights under Article 7(1) of the TMD with respect to contractual provisions prohibiting sales outside a selective distribution network. In line with the approach proposed above, this loss of trademark rights only applies to traders outside the selective distribution network. With regard to a licensee, the trademark proprietor keeps the option of bringing a trademark claim. In the internal relation with licensees, the trademark proprietor can draw on the full panoply of legal remedies and ensure compliance with contractual safeguards of a selective distribution system. This seems sufficient to ensure a functioning selective distribution network.[87] It also seems adequate to impose the obligation on the trademark proprietor to ensure compliance with selective distribution standards within the group of approved retailers. Outsiders, by contrast, should be able to rely on sufficient internal control. When entering into a business relationship with an approved retailer, an outside trader has a legitimate expectation of obtaining goods which he can further commercialize without having to fear that the

---

underlying the *Copad/Dior* decision, Sack arrives at a similar solution supporting the assumption of exhaustion on the basis of an analogous application of Articles 34 and 36 of the TFEU).

[85] Dior v. Evora [1997] E.C.R. I-6013, ¶ 46.
[86] In other words, the aim of the solution proposed here is to reinforce the beneficial role of the exhaustion doctrine vis-à-vis selective distribution networks. As to the importance of a proper ambit of operation of exhaustion in this context, *see* Irene Calboli, *Reviewing the (Shrinking) Principle of Trademark Exhaustion in the European Union (Ten Years Later)*, 16 MARQ. INTELL. PROP. L. REV. 257, 276–8 (2012).
[87] However, *see* Andrew Griffiths, *Trademarks and Responsible Capitalism*, 43 INT'L REV. OF INTELL. PROP. & COMP. L. 798, 819–820 (2012) (arguing in favour of broader control in line with the decision taken by the CJEU in *Copad/Dior* based on organisational behaviour).

trademark proprietor brings a trademark claim. In line with *Dior/Evora*, this legitimate expectation is only unjustified when the outside trader damages the trademark by using modes of advertising that fall short of customary advertising standards in his sector. In addition, the outside trader has no legitimate expectation of an entitlement to further commercialize trademarked goods when he acts in bad faith and seeks to profit from the breach of contractual provisions by an approved retailer. In this case, the trademark proprietor can invoke tort law against the outside trader.

Finally, the nuanced solution proposed here is likely to enhance consumer choice. When contractual terms concerning 'allure and prestigious image' fall outside of the scope of Article 8(2) of the TMD, the sale to discount stores in breach of the licensing agreement still allows the invocation of trademark rights against the licensee on the basis of the outlined alternative approach. However, this breach of the licensing agreement would not eliminate 'consent' and the exhaustion of rights in the sense of Article 7(1) of the TMD. A trader outside a selective distribution network can thus legitimately resell trademarked luxury goods as long as he uses customary modes of advertising and does not damage the trademark himself. As a result, consumers have a broader choice: they can opt for the full brand experience – including the allure, prestigious image and aura of luxury offered by approved retailers inside the selective distribution network – and pay extra for this enhanced brand experience. However, consumers are also free to pay less and purchase the goods from an outside trader without experiencing an aura of luxury.[88] In this latter case, the reference to quality standards in Article 8(2)(e) of the TMD still ensures that the material characteristics of the luxury goods comply with the standards inside the selective distribution network. In case of insufficient quality, no exhaustion takes place and the trademark proprietor can take action against the outside trader.[89] The difference, thus, lies in the enhanced brand experience of an aura of luxury and the freedom of consumers to pay for this experience.

14.39

7. A more nuanced approach

In sum, it is thus advisable to adopt a more nuanced approach. In the relationship between the trademark proprietor and a licensee, this list of

14.40

---

88 *Cf.* Mitchell, *supra* note 55, at 1276–7, who highlights the additional aspect of avoiding the artificial maintenance or establishment of formal class structures.
89 This is an important aspect of the nuanced approach recommended here. As to the importance of sufficient safeguards concerning product quality in case of trademark licenses, *see* Kur, *supra* note 9, at 5–6 and 8. As to the approach taken in the U.S., *see* Ann E. Doll, *Trademark Licensing: Quality Control*, 12 J. CONTEMP. LEGAL ISSUES 203 (2001).

contractual terms in Article 8(2) of the TMD should not be deemed exhaustive. By contrast, the trademark proprietor should be able to invoke trademark rights with regard to all contractual provisions concerning the proper functioning of the trademark, including communication, investment, and advertising functions. As a result, the trademark proprietor can enforce the prohibition of sales outside a selective distribution network without a need to artificially assume that 'allure and prestigious image' form part of the 'quality' of goods or services.

14.41 In the relationship between the trademark proprietor and an outside trader, however, the list in Article 8(2) of the TMD should be deemed closed and 'allure and prestigious image' should be assumed to fall outside the scope of Article 8(2) of the TMD. This enhances the legal certainty for outside traders. It leads to a clear boundary line between internal and external relations. Within the circle of approved retailers, the trademark proprietor can draw on the full panoply of legal remedies to ensure compliance with a selective distribution network. In the external relationship with outside traders, however, the trademark proprietor cannot prevent exhaustion as long as the material characteristics of products – the only relevant 'quality' in the sense of Article 8(2) of the TMD under this alternative approach – are in line with the contractual standard and the outside trader uses customary modes of advertising and does not damage the trademark himself.

14.42 As a result, consumers have a broader choice. They can purchase luxury goods from an approved retailer and pay extra for the enhanced brand experience including an aura of luxury. Alternatively, they are free to buy from a trader outside the selective distribution network at a discount price while renouncing the enhanced brand experience of allure, prestige and luxury.

D. ROOM FOR NATIONAL UNFAIR COMPETITION LAW

1. The *Martin Y Paz/Depuydt* case

14.43 The jurisprudence of the CJEU in the area of trademark transactions also sheds light on problems concerning the relationship between harmonized EU law and national unfair competition law. In *Martin Y Paz/Depuydt*, a leather goods manufacturer had sold the company name 'Nathan' to Martin Y Paz with regard to use for the production of a line of small leather goods, thereby guaranteeing the exclusive use of 'Nathan' in the manufacturing and distribution of the small leather goods. However, the leather goods manufacturer retained 'property in the name' with regard to the manufacture of handbags.

D. ROOM FOR NATIONAL UNFAIR COMPETITION LAW

The handbags business was later sold to David Depuydt together with the Benelux word mark NATHAN registered for leather items, clothing and shoes. To safeguard the guarantee of exclusivity given in the earlier contractual agreement with Martin Y Paz, the contract of the handbags business referred to the obligation not to manufacture or distribute small leather goods under the name 'Nathan'.[90]

During several years of collaboration, Martin Y Paz and David Depuydt both used additional signs on their respective goods: a horizontally stretched letter N and the word sign 'Nathan Baume'. Martin Y Paz acquired Benelux trademark registrations of these two signs on leather items, clothing, and shoes, and added a stylized version of the word 'Nathan'.[91] When relations between the two companies increasingly deteriorated, David Depuydt finally sought to have the Martin Y Paz trademark portfolio – consisting of the letter N, the stylized version of 'Nathan' and the mark NATHAN BAUME – declared invalid or, at least, limited to small leather goods. As this invalidation action was dismissed, Martin Y Paz invoked its trademark right to prevent David Depuydt from using signs that were identical or similar to the marks N and NATHAN BAUME for leather items, clothing, and shoes.[92]

14.44

At the national level, this trademark claim was rejected on the ground that Martin Y Paz had always recognized that David Depuydt could use signs identical to the marks for handbags and shoes. The Court of Appeals of Brussels was convinced of 'irrevocable consent' given by Martin Y Paz regarding David Depuydt's use of the marks N and NATHAN BAUME on handbags and shoes.[93] Appealing against this judgment, Martin Y Paz argued that it was free to withdraw its consent unilaterally at any time, and that a trademark claim brought after such withdrawal was not abusive, but a legitimate exercise of trademark rights. As the Court of Appeals of Brussels had also obligated Martin Y Paz to refrain from the manufacture and marketing of handbags and shoes under the marks N and NATHAN BAUME, Martin Y Paz added that the judgment amounted to an unjustified deprivation of its exclusive trademark right in those goods.[94]

14.45

---

90   Case C-661/11, Martin Y Paz Diffusion SA v. David Depuydt and Fabriek van Maroquinerie Gauquie NV, OFFICIAL WEBSITE OF THE COURT OF JUSTICE OF THE EUROPEAN UNION, *available 18 September 2015 at* http://eur-lex.europa.eu/legal-content/EN/TXT/?qid=1444064167090&uri=CELEX:62011CA0661, ¶¶ 10–15 (19 September 2013).
91   *Id.* ¶¶ 16–21.
92   *Id.* ¶¶ 22–25.
93   *Id.* ¶¶ 29–30.
94   *Id.* ¶¶ 32–33.

14.46 Against this background, the CJEU was asked three questions: whether a finding of irrevocable consent based on an indeterminate period of shared use could definitely prevent the proprietor of a registered mark from asserting its exclusive right against a third party, whether a national rule prohibiting wrongful and abusive use of a right could lead to a definitive ban on the exercise of exclusive trademark rights for part of the goods for which the trademark was registered, and whether the trademark proprietor could definitely be prohibited from recommencing the use of the mark for certain goods or services when this would amount to unfair competition because of free-riding on the publicity made by the third party and possible confusion of customers.[95]

14.47 Approaching these questions, the CJEU clarified first that Article 8 of the TMD – dealing with trademark licensing – was inapplicable because no contractual relationship could be found between the parties.[96] Therefore, the case had to be resolved on the basis of the exclusive rights conferred under Article 5 of the TMD. The central question, then, was whether national standards concerning the abuse of rights and unfair competition could deprive the trademark proprietor of the possibility to assert its trademark rights against a third party, and could also inhibit the trademark proprietor from using the trademark itself in respect of goods or services identical to those of the third party.

2. Mantra of complete harmonization

14.48 Insisting on complete harmonization of the rules relating to the rights conferred by a trademark in Articles 5 to 7 of the TMD, the CJEU answered this question by stating that:

> [S]ave for the specific cases governed by Article 8 et seq. of that directive, a national court may not, in a dispute relating to the exercise of the exclusive right conferred by a trademark, limit that exclusive right in a manner which exceeds the limitations arising from Articles 5 to 7 of the directive.[97]

The Court added that none of the limitations laid down in Article 6 of the TMD was relevant to the case. Exhaustion of trademark rights in the sense of Article 7 of the TMD could only play a role as long as Martin Y Paz had not withdrawn the consent given to David Depuydt.[98] Inherent limits of the

---
95   *Id.* ¶ 35.
96   *Id.* ¶¶ 48–49.
97   *Id.* ¶ 55.
98   *Id.* ¶¶ 56–57.

D. ROOM FOR NATIONAL UNFAIR COMPETITION LAW

exclusive rights granted in Article 5 of the TMD which can be derived from the Court's 'function theory', namely the limitation to use liable adversely to affect a protected trademark function,[99] could only support a decision in favour of continued use by David Depuydt if no encroachment upon protected trademark functions could be found. Otherwise, the decision to deprive Martin Y Paz of the possibility of exercising its exclusive right against David Depuydt would exceed the limitations arising from Articles 5 to 7 of the TMD.[100] A finding of unlawful conduct in the light of national rules on abuse of rights and unfair competition could not justify an obligation to prolong shared use of registered marks. However, the national court was free to impose a penalty on the trademark proprietor or award damages because of unlawful withdrawal of consent.[101]

14.49 Instead of leaving room for national doctrines reflecting general principles of fairness and equity, such as abuse of right and the prohibition of unfair competition, the CJEU thus postulated the precedence of harmonized EU trademark law and the pre-emption of flexible national standards. On the one hand, this approach may seem consistent when the rules of harmonized EU trademark law are qualified as *leges speciales* vis-à-vis more general national standards. On the other hand, it is evident that the specific rules in the TMD are hardly capable of offering a sufficiently rich and balanced set of norms for an appropriate assessment of the wide variety of trademark transactions taking place in practice. The error in the Court's line of reasoning clearly comes to the fore when considering the proviso 'save for the specific cases governed by Article 8 et seq. of that directive'[102] which precedes the mantra of complete harmonization through Articles 5 to 7 of the TMD in *Martin Y Paz/Depuydt*.

---

99 As pointed out above, the trademark functions enjoying protection in EU law range from the traditional origin function to the goodwill functions of communication, investment, and advertising. See Case C-487/07, L'Oréal v. Bellure [2009] E.C.R. I-05185, ¶ 58. For a discussion of the role of the function theory in EU trademark law, see Annette Kur, *Trademarks Function, Don't they?*, 45 INT'L REV. OF INTELL. PROP. & COMP. L. 434 (2014); Martin R.F. Senftleben, *Function Theory and International Exhaustion: Why it is Wise to Confine the Double Identity Rule in EU Trademark Law to Cases Affecting the Origin Function*, EUR. INTELL. PROP. REV.518 (2014); Tobias Cohen Jehoram, *The Function Theory in European Trade Mark Law and the Holistic Approach of the CJEU*, 102 TRADEMARK REP. 1243 (2012). As to the traditional focus of CJEU jurisprudence on the origin function, see Case C-206/01, Arsenal Football Club plc v. Matthew Reed [2002] E.C.R. I-10273, ¶ 51; Case C-245/02, Anheuser-Busch v. Budejovicky Budvar [2004] E.C.R. I-10989, ¶ 59; Case C-48/05, Adam Opel AG v. Autec AG [2007] E.C.R. I-1017, ¶ 21. For commentary, see P.J. Yap, *Essential Function of a Trademark: From BMW to O2*, 31 EUR. INTELL. PROP. REV. 81, 86–7 (2009); Ilanah Simon Fhima, *How Does 'Essential Function' Doctrine Drive European Trademark Law?*, 36 INT'L REV. OF INTELL. PROP. & COMP. L. 401 (2005); YANN BASIRE, LES FONCTIONS DE LA MARQUE, ESSAI SUR LA COHÉRENCE DU RÉGIME JURIDIQUE D'UN SIGNE DISTINCTIF (2014).
100 Case C-661/11, Martin Y Paz Diffusion SA v. David Depuydt and Fabriek van Maroquinerie Gauquie NV, ¶¶ 58–60 (19 September 2013).
101 *Id.* ¶ 61.
102 *Id.* ¶ 55.

14.50 The specific rules provided in Articles 8 and 9 of the TMD are of a rudimentary nature. Article 8 of the TMD only concerns licensing and is thus confined to a specific contractual relationship. Article 9 of the TMD concerns acquiescence of the proprietor of an earlier trademark in third party use of a conflicting subsequent trademark and is confined to the specific situation where both parties hold trademark rights. Against this background, the case *Martin Y Paz/Depuydt* shows the considerable gaps. As the case concerned consent instead of a license and the position of a defendant without trademark rights to the signs at issue, Articles 8 and 9 of the TMD offered no solution.[103] This finding should have led to the conclusion that there were no specific, harmonized rules of EU law that could pre-empt the application of national standards relating to abuse of rights and unfair competition.[104]

14.51 While the CJEU might have been correct in positing that the scope of rights conferred under EU trademark law is completely harmonized as a result of Articles 5 to 7 of the TMD, the Court was incorrect in assuming that this harmonization of the scope also implied complete harmonization of related legal norms and doctrines that may impact the exercise of EU trademark rights, such as trademark transaction rules, abuse of rights, and unfair competition law. Instead of holding that the effect of Articles 5 to 7 of the TMD was 'a complete harmonisation of the rules relating to the rights conferred by a trademark',[105] the Court should have limited its ruling to the finding that Articles 5 to 7 of the TMD had the effect of harmonizing the scope of trademark rights while leaving intact not only 'Article 8 et seq. of that directive'[106] but also national rules concerning the exercise of trademark rights.

3. Function theory unsatisfactory

14.52 The dilemma arising from the maximum harmonization approach taken by the CJEU clearly comes to the fore in the decision itself. Having precluded the application of flexible national doctrines, the Court was incapable of offering a satisfactory alternative source of equity and fairness in harmonized EU

---

103 As pointed out above, the CJEU itself, *id.* ¶48, found that Article 8 of the TMD was irrelevant to the case.
104 With regard to the state of law against unfair competition in the EU and the interplay between harmonized EU law and national regimes, *see* Frauke Henning-Bodewig, *Die Bekämpfung unlauteren Wettbewerbs in den EU-Mitgliedstaaten: eine Bestandsaufnahme*, GEWERBLICHER RECHTSSCHUTZ UND URHEBERRECHT INTERNATIONAL 2010, 273; Frauke Henning-Bodewig, *Nationale Eigenständigkeit und europäische Vorgaben im Lauterkeitsrecht*, GEWERBLICHER RECHTSSCHUTZ UND URHEBERRECHT INTERNATIONAL 2010, 549; LAUTERKEITSRECHT UND ACQUIS COMMUNAUTAIRE, (Reto M. Hilty & Frauke Henning-Bodewig eds., 2009); LAW AGAINST UNFAIR COMPETITION – TOWARDS A NEW PARADIGM IN EUROPE?, (Reto M. Hilty & Frauke Henning-Bodewig eds., 2007).
105 *Id.* ¶ 54.
106 *Id.* ¶ 55.

trademark law. In the absence of an open-ended 'due cause' provision covering cases of use of an identical sign for identical goods – the double identity situation that had arisen in *Martin Y Paz/Depuydt* left no room for invoking a general 'due cause' defence[107] – the closed catalogue of limitations in Article 6 of the TMD did not offer sufficient room to factor into the equation abuse of rights and unfair free-riding by the trademark proprietor.[108] Moreover, a solution based on the exhaustion of rights in accordance with Article 7 of the TMD was no longer available after the Court had abandoned the option of entitling the national court to declare the withdrawal of consent null and void because of an abuse of trademark rights and unfair competition. Once Martin Y Paz can lawfully withdraw its consent, the precondition of 'consent' in the sense of the exhaustion rule laid down in Article 7(1) of the TMD is no longer fulfilled.[109]

The CJEU could thus not do more than recall, as a last resort, its vague function theory as an inherent limitation of the rights granted in Article 5(1)(a) of the TMD.[110] According to this theory, use of a conflicting sign is not actionable in double identity situations as long as the use is not liable to adversely affect at least one of the trademark functions presently enjoying protection in EU trademark law. As explained above, the protected functions range from traditional origin and quality functions to the role of trademarks in

14.53

---

107 See the double identity rule set forth in TMD, *supra* note 2, at art. 5(1)(a) on the one hand, and the anti-dilution provision in TMD, *supra* note 2, at art. 5(2) on the other. While Article 5(2) of the TMD includes a flexible defense of 'due cause', a corresponding opening clause is sought in vain in Article 5(1)(a) of the TMD.

108 For the debate on this shortcoming of the present limitation infrastructure in EU trademark law, see ROLAND KNAAK, ANNETTE KUR, & ALEXANDER VON MÜHLENDAHL, *supra* note 12, at ¶ 2.266; Martin R.F. Senftleben, *Overprotection and Protection Overlaps in Intellectual Property Law: The Need for Horizontal Fair Use Defences*, in THE STRUCTURE OF INTELLECTUAL PROPERTY LAW: CAN ONE SIZE FIT ALL? 136 (Annette Kur & Vytautas Mizaras eds., 2011). As to the solutions found on the basis of the flexible 'due cause' defense available under TMD, *supra* note 2, at art. 5(2), see Case C-65/12, Red Bull v. Bulldog, OFFICIAL WEBSITE OF THE COURT OF JUSTICE OF THE EUROPEAN UNION, *available* 18 September 2015 at http://curia.europa.eu/juris/liste.jsf?num=C-65/12, ¶ 46; Case C-323/09, *Interflora et al. v. Marks & Spencer et al.* [2011] E.C.R. I-05185, ¶ 91; Bundesgerichtshof [BGH] [Federal Court of Justice], 11 March 2008, Neue Juristische Wochenschrift [NJW] 2110, 2008 (Ger.); Bundesgerichtshof [BGH] [Federal Court of Justice], 3 February 2005, Case I ZR 159/02, *Lila Postkarte*, GEWERBLICHER RECHTSSCHUTZ UND URHEBERRECHT 2005, 583; Cour de Cassation [Cass.] [French Supreme Court], 8 April 2008, Bull. 2008, Case 06–10961, Greenpeace v. Esso; Cour de Cassation [Cass.] [French Supreme Court], 8 April 2008, Bull. 2008, Case 07–11251, Greenpeace v. Areva; Court of Appeals of Amsterdam, Case LJN BS7825, 3 September 2011, Mercis and Bruna v. Punt, ¶ 4.1. *Cf.* Vincenzo Di Cataldo, *The Trademark with a Reputation in EU Law – Some Remarks on the Negative Condition 'Without Due Cause'*, 42 INT'L REV. OF INTELL. PROP. & COMP. L. 833 (2011).

109 Case C-661/11, Martin Y Paz Diffusion SA v. David Depuydt and Fabriek van Maroquinerie Gauquie NV, ¶ 57 (19 September 2013).

110 *Id.* ¶ 58. For a discussion of the function theory in EU trademark law, see the references *supra* note 99.

communication, investment, and advertising.[111] Attempts to define the protected functions, however, show that the CJEU has difficulty tracing their conceptual contours. In *Google/Louis Vuitton*, the Court explained in respect of the advertising function that the trademark owner may have not only the objective of indicating the origin of its goods or services, 'but also that of using its mark for advertising purposes designed to inform and persuade consumers'.[112] In *Interflora/Marks & Spencer*, the Court elaborated on the investment function, explaining that in addition to its origin and (potential) advertising function, a trademark may also be used 'to acquire or preserve a reputation capable of attracting consumers and retaining their loyalty'.[113] This investment function may overlap with the advertising function. Nonetheless, it had to be separated according to the Court because not only advertising was employed, but also 'various commercial techniques' when the trademark was used to acquire or preserve a reputation.[114]

14.54 These vague indications of potential objectives underlying the use of trademarks for advertising and investment strategies hardly qualify as reliable clarifications of the scope and reach of the protection which these functions should enjoy in double identity cases. The fact that the CJEU also recognized a trademark's communication function further enhances the legal uncertainty surrounding the function theory. As the Court did not comment on the communication function in any subsequent decision, this function still constitutes *terra incognita*. However, in *Martin Y Paz/Depuydt*, as a result of the pre-emption of national rules on abuse of rights and unfair competition, this openness of the function theory appears as an advantage rather than a shortcoming. In fact, the explicit reference to the function theory in the decision[115] can be understood as an indication that the CJEU is prepared to use the function theory as an alternative rule of equity and fairness to fill the gap resulting from the rejection of national law.

14.55 In fact, the Court has already used the function theory as a 'meta norm' of fairness and equity capable of forcing specific infringement criteria in EU trademark law onto the 'sidelines'.[116] In line with this use of the function theory, a trademark infringement action cannot succeed without a showing of

---

111 Case C-487/07, L'Oreal SA, et al v. Bellure et al [2009] E.C.R. I-05185, ¶ 58.
112 Joined Cases C-236, 237 & 238/08, Google France and Google et al. v. Louis Vuitton et al. [2010] E.C.R. I-02417, ¶ 91.
113 *Interflora v. Marks & Spencer* [2011] E.C.R. I-05185, ¶ 60.
114 *Id.* ¶ 61.
115 Case C-661/11, Martin Y Paz Diffusion SA v. David Depuydt and Fabriek van Maroquinerie Gauquie NV, ¶¶ 58–60 (19 September 2013).
116 *See also* Kur, *supra* note 99, at 443, (seeing the function theory as a basis for introducing a more flexible infringement analysis including considerations of fair and reasonable competition into EU trade mark law).

D. ROOM FOR NATIONAL UNFAIR COMPETITION LAW

adverse effect on at least one protected function. In this vein, the Court openly conceded in *Leidseplein Beheer/Red Bull* that the function theory was a means of putting absolute protection under Article 5(1)(a) of the TMD 'into perspective'.[117] In *Interflora/Marks & Spencer*, the Court saw the absence of a conflict with any protected trademark function as a relevant factor for determining if a trademark's unauthorized use for the purpose of informing consumers about alternative offers in the marketplace was made with 'due cause' according to Article 5(2) of the TMD.[118] Similarly, the Court pointed to the absence of a conflict with any protected trademark function as a reason for setting territorial limits to a prohibition against further infringement of a CTM in *Chronopost/DHL*.[119]

14.56 Advocate General Kokott gave an impressive demonstration of the use of the function theory as a 'meta norm' of fairness and equity in *Viking Gas/Kosan Gas*. Having concluded that the exhaustion doctrine could not be applied to the gas in the composite bottles at issue (an assumption which the Court did not adopt), Kokott embarked on an analysis of the refilling of gas bottles in light of the function theory.[120] Addressing communication, investment and advertising functions, Kokott postulated that:

> [N]ot every adverse affect on those functions justifies the application of [the double identity rule laid down in] Article 5(1) of Directive 89/104. The protection of those functions on the basis of that provision, first, must not undermine the requirements of specific protective rules and, second, must respect overriding other interests.[121]

The assessment of 'overriding other interests', then, led the Advocate General to conclude that even though the exhaustion doctrine did not apply, consumers' property rights in the composite bottles and the need to protect competition outweighed the affected functions of the trademark and justified the limitation of trademark rights. If consumers could only exchange empty gas bottles with Kosan as an exclusive supplier, they would not be free to exercise their property rights in the bottles by becoming customers of other

---

117   Case C-65/12, Leidseplein Beheer v. Red Bull, ¶ 32 (2014).
118   Interflora v. Marks & Spencer [2011] E.C.R. I-05185, ¶ 91, (clarifying that 'where the advertisement displayed on the internet on the basis of a keyword corresponding to a trade mark with a reputation puts forward – without offering a mere imitation of the goods or services of the proprietor of that trade mark, without causing dilution or tarnishment *and without, moreover, adversely affecting the functions of the trade mark concerned* – an alternative to the goods or services of the proprietor of the trade mark with a reputation, it must be concluded that such use falls, as a rule, within the ambit of fair competition in the sector for the goods or services concerned and is thus not without 'due cause' for the purposes of Article 5(2).' (emphasis added)).
119   Case C-235/09, DHL Express France SAS v. Chronopost SA [2011] E.C.R. I-02801, ¶¶ 46–48.
120   Case C-46/10, Viking Gas A/S v. Kosan Gas A/S [2011] E.C.R. I-06691, ¶¶ 36–37.
121   *Id.* ¶ 59.

suppliers. In this latter regard, the situation was comparable to the provision of repair services for a particular make of car, which also fell under a limitation of trademark rights.[122]

4. No pre-emption of national doctrines

14.57 Despite this remarkable potential to serve as a fairness and equity norm within EU trademark law, it remains unclear how the function theory could be a substitute for pre-empted national rules on abuse of right and unfair competition in Martin Y Paz/Depuydt. As Annette Kur pointed out, it is hard to see how the national court could avoid a finding of an adverse effect on the essential origin function in light of use of an identical sign in respect of identical goods.[123] As a way out, it would have to be assumed that David Depuydt does not cause confusion when using the marks N and NATHAN BAUME for handbags and shoes because the public is accustomed to Depuydt's products offered under these marks.

14.58 This twisted line of argument, however, can hardly be reconciled with the CJEU's further consideration that Martin Y Paz should be free to withdraw its consent for shared use of the marks. Hence, the lack of harmonized EU rules on abuse of right and unfair competition cannot be corrected by applying the open-ended function theory instead. As long as EU trademark law does not provide for a sufficiently robust body of fairness and equity norms, the CJEU should refrain from the overambitious pre-emption of national doctrines that provide indispensable room to manoeuvre. As Annette Kur concludes:

> [c]ases like Martin Y Paz therefore need a more comprehensive evaluation scheme which is equally based on overarching principles such as equity and fairness, but without being limited to the aspects on which the functions discussion is mainly focused. General principles informing such an evaluation (like 'unclean hands'; or 'Treu und Glauben') are found in practically every organically grown legal system. In contrast, European law, at least for now, does not represent a comprehensive, fully developed legal system providing for an overarching corpus of fundamental fairness principles ... This particular situation calls for a cautious approach; it would be wise not to interfere more than absolutely necessary with national correction mechanisms. Unfortunately, the CJEU does not always muster the kind of self-restraint one might wish for in such situations.[124]

---

122   Id. ¶ 65–67.
123   Kur, *supra* note 99, at 450–1.
124   Id. at 453.

E. CONCLUSION

14.59 Despite the rudimentary nature of trademark transaction rules in harmonized EU trademark law, the CJEU follows a maximalist approach. In *Copad/Dior*, the Court declared the list of contractual provisions justifying the invocation of trademark rights against a licensee to be exhaustive and closed in EU law. In *Martin Y Paz/Depuydt*, the Court assumed that the harmonized rules relating to the rights conferred by a trademark pre-empted flexible national standards in the area of unfair competition law and abuse of rights. The results of this jurisprudence are unsatisfactory.

14.60 Assuming that the list of contractual provisions justifying the invocation of trademark rights against a licensee is closed, the Court created a 'straitjacket' that requires an artificially broad interpretation of the relevant categories of contractual terms, such as the inclusion of 'allure and prestigious image' in the concept of 'quality'. Adopting a more nuanced approach based on the above analysis, the Court could arrive at a more convincing balancing of interests that ensures full control of the trademark proprietor over selective distribution rules within the circle of approved retailers, enhances legal certainty for traders outside the selective distribution network and offers consumers a broader choice.

14.61 Pre-empting flexible national standards in the area of unfair competition and abuse of rights, the CJEU created a considerable gap in the regulation of trademark transactions. The Court's use of the requirement of adverse effect on at least one protected trademark function as a precondition for the successful invocation of trademark rights cannot easily fill this gap. As a result, traders operating on the basis of consent from the trademark owner are exposed to the substantial risk of trademark protection becoming excessive in the sense that it minimizes the impact of limiting national doctrines without offering an adequate alternative at the level of harmonized EU law.

14.62 Given these shortcomings, the CJEU should seize future opportunities to recalibrate the interpretation of EU trademark transactions law and establish a system that leaves room for a more comprehensive consideration of all interests involved and a better interaction between harmonized EU rules and supplementary national fairness and equity norms.

15

UK PERSPECTIVES ON TRADEMARK TRANSACTIONS: A LIBERAL APPROACH

Laura Anderson[*]

A. INTRODUCTION	15.01	1. The nature of a trademark license	15.42
		2. Formalities	15.44
B. UK LAW AND TRADEMARK TRANSACTIONS	15.05	3. Key terms	15.47
		4. Grant and exclusivity	15.50
		5. Sublicensing	15.52
C. ASSIGNMENTS OF UK TRADEMARKS	15.11	6. Quality control	15.54
1. Assignment of part	15.16	7. Liabilities and indemnity	15.62
2. Unregistered trademarks	15.19	8. Rights of licensees to bring infringement proceedings	15.65
3. Requirements for valid assignment	15.20	9. Warranties	15.71
4. Language	15.21	10. Term and termination	15.72
5. Identification of the intellectual property rights being assigned	15.22	11. Assignment of licenses	15.77
6. Consideration	15.23	12. Contracts Rights of Third Parties Act	15.81
7. Assignment of the right to sue prior infringers	15.24	13. Registration	15.83
8. Implied covenants as to title	15.25	14. Licensing of unregistered trademarks	15.85
9. Registration	15.30		
10. Trusts and equitable assignments of trademarks	15.32	E. SECURITY INTERESTS	15.86
11. What is required for an equitable assignment?	15.35	F. UK COMPETITION LAW	15.91
12. Confirmatory assignments	15.37		
D. LICENSES OF UK TRADEMARKS	15.40	G. CONCLUSIONS	15.93

A. INTRODUCTION

15.01 Marks, signs and trade names have been an important part of commerce in the United Kingdom (UK) since the time of the Medieval guilds. The UK Trade Marks Register was established in 1876 and the first Registration on 1 January 1876 was The Bass Brewery's famous red triangle logo, which is said to be the world's first registered logo.[1] This mark is still registered and in use today.

---

[*] Partner, Bristows LLP. The author would like to thank Steven Willis and Ralph Giles for their help in the drafting of this chapter.
1   BASS & CO'S PALE ALE, Registration No. UK00000000001.

Trademarks are often hugely valuable assets. A key part of that value is the ability of a proprietor to deal with its trademark and to transact freely. The legal system in the UK supports this ability to transact and provides significant freedom for trademark owners. Transactions relating to trademarks can, of course, take many different forms; a merchandising arrangement, a sponsorship deal, a co-branding collaboration, the sale of a brand, or a brand finance deal are all transactions with trademarks at their core.

15.02

The role of the practitioner is to analyze the nature of any proposed transaction to establish whether it involves the transfer of a property right (an assignment); a permission to use (a license); the creation of a charge, mortgage, or other security (a security interest); or simply a contractual arrangement as to how a trademark proprietor will use its own mark (for example, under a trademark co-existence agreement). The practitioner will then seek to reflect relevant statutory provisions and, importantly, help to ensure appropriate clarity and control so as to preserve the value of the trademarks that are the subject of the transaction.

15.03

This chapter focuses on UK trademark assignments, licenses and security interests, as it is these transactions which form the legal basis of the vast majority of trademark-related deals in the UK.

15.04

B. UK LAW AND TRADEMARK TRANSACTIONS

The principal UK legislation governing the law of trademarks is the Trade Marks Act 1994 ('the 1994 Act').[2] The 1994 Act implemented the 1988 Council Directive to approximate the laws of the Member States relating to trademarks[3] and, as such, served to harmonize key issues of UK Trademark Law with the laws of other EU Member States. As far as trademark transactions are concerned, the 1994 Act goes into considerably more detail than the Directive, and includes specific provisions relating to assignments and other transmissions, licenses and the registration of transactions affecting registered trademarks.

15.05

The 1994 Act introduced significant changes to the law in respect of trademark transactions, establishing a much more permissive regime. The

15.06

---

2 Trade Marks Act 1994, 1994, c. 26 (U.K.), *available 21 September 2015 at* http://www.legislation.gov.uk/ukpga/1994/26/enacted [hereinafter Trade Marks Act 1994].
3 Council Directive 2008/95, 2008 O.J. (L 299) 25 (EU).

previous 1938 Trade Marks Act[4] reflected a long-held policy concern surrounding the separation of a trademark from the business producing the trademarked goods. Assignments were subject to control and any assignment of a trademark without the goodwill of the associated business was subject to Trade Marks Registry scrutiny.[5] In addition, any third-party use of a trademark had to be strictly controlled by a registered user agreement in accordance with legislative requirements.[6]

15.07 In contrast, the 1994 Act imposes no restrictions on assignments or licenses but instead gives trademark owners broad freedom and flexibility as to how they structure their trademark transactions. This reflects the concept of trademarks as property and the 1994 Act specifically identifies registered trademarks as 'personal property'.[7] The responsibility falls on the parties to a trademark transaction, and not the State, to ensure that their transaction is valid and effective and will not result in damage to the relevant marks.

15.08 In addition to registered trademarks, English Law protects unregistered trademarks or trade names through the tort of 'passing off'. While unregistered trademarks do not amount to personal property as such, they form part of the goodwill of a business and it is common to see transactions that deal in unregistered trademark rights as well as registered trademarks. The ability to bring an action in 'passing off' depends on ownership of goodwill and, as such, transactions concerning unregistered marks are generally structured and analyzed by reference to the transfer or exploitation of goodwill and associated enforcement rights.[8]

15.09 The vast majority of trademark transactions will require some form of contractual arrangement, with the exception perhaps of a simple gift of a registered trademark, and so in addition to the sources of UK trademark law, property law and 'passing off', it is, of course, important to consider relevant issues arising under contract law. Equity can also come into play in trademark transactions in the UK, as marks may be held on Trust and equitable interests may be created.[9] All of this adds to the rich legal basis of trademark transactions in the UK.

---

4 Trade Marks Act 1938, 1938, 1 & 2 Geo. 6, c. 22 (U.K.).
5 *Id.* at § 22(7).
6 *Id.* at § 28.
7 Trade Marks Act 1994, *supra* note 2, at § 24(1).
8 Reckitt & Colman Products Ltd. v. Borden Inc. [1990] 1 All E.R. 873 (Eng.).
9 Don King Productions Inc. v. Warren et al. [1998] 2 All E.R. 608 (D) 114 (Eng.).

15.10 When considering the contractual aspects of UK trademark transactions, there are a few key principles of English contract law that are worth bearing in mind. First, there is no general implied duty on the parties to act in good faith towards each other, although the courts will give meaning to any express obligation included in the contract.[10] Secondly, the English courts are generally very reluctant to imply terms into a written contract that are not there; for example, the right to assign a license cannot usually be implied into a contract 'unless there is more' to suggest otherwise.[11] As a result, when entering into a trademark transaction, the parties should turn to the statutes to see what might be implied and then must ensure that their transaction documents accurately reflect the terms of their deal.

C. ASSIGNMENTS OF UK TRADEMARKS

15.11 The assignment of a trademark is simply the transfer of ownership from one proprietor to another. Such transfers take place in many different circumstances, which may include intragroup reorganizations, the sale of a business, the setting up of a joint venture, the disposal of assets upon insolvency, the creation of certain types of security interests or a simple assignment. Irrespective of the type of transaction, the assignment of the trademark will need to be analyzed on the same basis.

15.12 Section 24(1) of the 1994 Act provides that:

> A registered trademark is transmissible by assignment, testamentary disposition or operation of law in the same way as other personal or moveable property.
>
> It is so transmissible either in connection with the goodwill of a business or independently.[12]

As such, it is clear that a UK trademark can be assigned separately from the business to which it relates and separately from any associated goodwill. A mark can also be assigned together with the goodwill associated with the mark itself, rather than goodwill associated with the business. Care is then needed to ensure that the parties have a clear understanding of what goodwill needs to

---

10 Compass Group UK and Ireland Ltd. (trading as Medirest) v. Mid Essex Hospital Services NHS Trust [2013] EWCA (Civ) 200, [2012] EWHC 781 (QB) (Eng.); *but see* Yam Seng Pte v. ITC Ltd. [2013] EWHC 111 (QB) (Eng.) (in which Justice Leggatt indicated that it may be possible to imply a general duty of good faith in certain long term 'relational' contracts, as followed in Bristol Groundschool Ltd. v. Intelligent Data Capture et al. [2014] EWHC 2145 (Ch) (Eng.)).
11 Lawson v. Donald Macpherson & Co. Ltd., [1897] 14 R.P.C. 696 (Eng.).
12 Trade Marks Act 1994, *supra* note 2, at § 24(1).

remain with the assignor and the extent to which the assigned goodwill can be separated from any retained business.

15.13 This freedom for trademark proprietors to exploit their trademarks as assets is balanced by section 46 of the 1994 Act which provides for the revocation of trademarks which have become deceptive by reason of the manner of their use.[13] There have been only a limited number of cases that have considered the relationship between section 24(1) and section 46 since the 1994 Act came into force. The first is *Scandecor Development v. Scandecor Marketing*[14] in which the Court of Appeal found that a trademark was invalid as a result of an arrangement under which it had been assigned without goodwill and was then the subject of a bare license back. However, the House of Lords disagreed with much of the Court of Appeal's reasoning[15] and put the stronger emphasis on the freedom to transact under section 24(1) of the 1994 Act, commenting that the fact that the mark was being used by two different entities on different goods did not, of itself, make the mark deceptive. The House of Lords put various questions to the Court of Justice, but the case was settled before the Court of Justice responded.

15.14 Another case that examined the relationship between assignments and deception was an action brought against Continental Shelf 128 Ltd (CSL) by the designer Elizabeth Emanuel[16] (who famously designed Princess Diana's wedding dress). Elizabeth Emanuel had set up a company and assigned to it her business, goodwill, and trademark. However, over a series of transactions, the trademark was assigned on to another company to which Elizabeth Emanuel had no connection. The question of deception was considered by the Court of Justice, which drew a distinction between a mistaken understanding on the part of consumers and actual deceit. The Court of Justice found that even though a consumer may assume that Elizabeth Emanuel was involved in the design of a product, the characteristics and qualities of the products bearing the mark were still guaranteed by the trademark proprietor. As such, the essential function of the trademark is maintained and the mark is not deceptive.

15.15 Overall, there is clearly a balance to be struck between the policy of freedom to exploit reflected in section 24(1) of the 1994 Act and the protections afforded by section 46 of the 1994 Act. Practitioners in the UK understand that

---

13 *Id.* at § 46.
14 Scandecor Development AB v. Scandecor Marketing AB and Another [1999] F.S.R. 26 (Eng.).
15 Scandecor Development AB v. Scandecor Marketing AB and Others and One Other Appeal [2001] UKHL 21, [34], [2001] All E.R. 29 (H.L.) [38] (appeal taken from Eng.).
16 Case C-259/04, Emanuel v. Continental Shelf 128 Ltd. [2006] E.C.R. I-3089.

instances of deception arising from otherwise lawful transactions will be very rare. However, the possibility of deception cannot, of course, simply be ignored and the role of the practitioner is to ensure that the parties do not overstate or overstretch their freedom with poorly structured arrangements that may result in misleading the public.

1. Assignment of part

15.16 Section 24(2) of the 1994 Act provides that assignments of registered trademarks may be partial[17] and so may be limited to apply:

(i) in relation to some but not all of the goods or services for which the trademark is registered; or
(ii) in relation to use of the trademark in a particular manner or a particular locality.

The Trade Marks Registry will, in effect, create a new trademark registration for the class of goods, use, or locality that has been assigned and issue that new registration to the assignee. The end result is two separate trademark registrations.

15.17 Practitioners in the UK are generally wary of partial assignments as there is a concern that a trademark may become deceptive where there are two owners using the same mark, particularly if they are using the mark on the same products. In most circumstances where a partial assignment may be contemplated, a license is likely to be a more appropriate arrangement, such that title can be preserved with one entity and appropriate controls exercised over use of the mark.

15.18 However, there are occasions when a partial assignment may be preferred, provided appropriate controls exist or coexistence arrangements can be put into place. For example, in an intragroup arrangement, ownership of a UK trademark may be divided on a geographical basis, with an English company owning a mark for England, Wales and Scotland and an Irish company owning the mark for the Republic of Ireland and Northern Ireland. Alternatively, following a business sale, both a licensor and a licensee may have been using a mark for different products over a long period of time and may have successfully distinguished their products from one another in the eyes of the consumer. In these circumstances, the licensor may wish to escape ongoing contractual obligations surrounding maintenance and enforcement associated

---

17   Trade Marks Act 1994, *supra* note 2, at § 24(2).

with a licensed mark and so may be prepared to split ownership of the registration. The key to such a transaction will be an arrangement akin to a coexistence agreement, which identifies how products will be branded, presented, and positioned so as to avoid consumer confusion.

2. Unregistered trademarks

15.19 An assignment of an unregistered trademark must be with goodwill as it is the goodwill that amounts to personal property (and not the unregistered mark) and gives the proprietor the ability to bring an action for 'passing off'. The 1994 Act specifically anticipates the assignment of unregistered marks in this way and section 24(6) states that:

> Nothing in this Act shall be construed as affecting the assignment or other transmission of an unregistered trade mark as part of the goodwill of a business.[18]

Where a business is sold together with all of its goodwill, any unregistered marks will automatically transfer to the assignee of the business unless those marks are expressly excluded.[19] If, for some reason, the parties wish to include unregistered marks in a transaction and yet do not wish to assign associated goodwill, the desired result can be achieved through contractual restrictions under which the proprietor agrees to cease all use of the mark and not to object to its use by the acquirer.[20] However, the acquirer will need to build up its own goodwill in the mark in order to be able to protect it.[21]

3. Requirements for valid assignment

15.20 An assignment of a registered trademark is not effective unless it is in writing signed by or on behalf of the assignor or, as the case may be, a personal representative.[22] There is no need for the assignee to sign for the assignment to be effective.[23] In practice, most practitioners do provide for assignments to be executed by both the assignor and the assignee in order to avoid any arguments as to the acceptance of the assignment by the assignee and account for the contractual provisions within the assignments, which the parties may wish to enforce against one another.

---

18   *Id.* at § 24(6).
19   *Id.*
20   *See generally id.* at § 24.
21   *Id.*
22   *Id.* at § 24(3).
23   *Id.*

C. ASSIGNMENTS OF UK TRADEMARKS

4. Language

15.21 It seems surprising but there are no UK statutory requirements as to how an assignment of trademarks (or, for that matter any intellectual property rights), should be worded. All that is required is that the language used must clearly demonstrate the intention that legal title to the intellectual property right will be transferred to a third party.[24] In practice, practitioners tend to use a seemingly random assortment of traditional words and phrases to try to achieve an effective assignment. Typical words and phrases used in trademark assignments include various combinations of the following: 'hereby assigns', 'assigns absolutely', 'assigns irrevocably', 'assigns unconditionally' and 'to hold the same unto the assignee absolutely'. Arguably, 'assigns' itself is sufficient provided there is nothing else in the document to indicate that the assignment is conditional, not absolute or revocable, or is not immediate.

5. Identification of the intellectual property rights being assigned

15.22 Also surprisingly, there appears to be very little case law as to how precisely one needs to identify the trademark rights that are being assigned. Presumably, if an assignment is too vague or ambiguous as to the identity of the intellectual property rights being assigned then there would be some risk that the assignment could be held void for uncertainty. In the case of a registered trademark, it is easy to identify the assigned right by referring to its registration or application number and its jurisdiction.

6. Consideration

15.23 An assignment can be by sale or it can be a gift. If the assignment is a gift, there is no need for an assignment to include consideration in order for it to be valid. However, most assignments include contractual rights and obligations in addition to the assignment itself. Consideration (even if only a nominal sum) is then needed to ensure these contractual terms are enforceable unless the parties execute the assignment as a deed, in which case no consideration need be included.[25]

---

[24] For general principles of English law contractual interpretation, see Investors Compensation Scheme Ltd. v. West Bromwich Building Society and Others [1998] 1 All E.R. 98 (Eng.).

[25] See CHITTY ON CONTRACTS, Part 1, ch. 1, § 6 (1–128) (Hugh Beale ed. 31st ed., Vol. 1, 2008); Plowd. 308; Morley v. Boothby (1825) 130 Eng. Rep. 455; 3 Bing. 107, 111–12.

7. Assignment of the right to sue prior infringers

15.24 If the assignee wishes to be able to take proceedings against infringers that engaged in infringing activities before the date of the assignment, then a specific provision must be included granting the assignee the right to do so.[26]

8. Implied covenants as to title

15.25 Trademark assignments in the UK commonly state that trademarks are assigned with 'full title guarantee' and this wording has a specific meaning. The Law of Property (Miscellaneous Provisions) Act 1994 (LP(MP)A 1994) implies certain covenants into dispositions of property where the phrases 'full title guarantee' or 'limited title guarantee' are used.[27] As registered trademarks are a form of personal property, these provisions apply to assignments of trademarks as well as other intellectual property, personal property, and real property in the UK. Both 'full title guarantee' and 'limited title guarantee' imply covenants that:

(i) the seller has the right to dispose of the property; and
(ii) the seller will, at the seller's own cost, do all the seller reasonably can to give the title the seller purports to assign.

However, the two title guarantees provide for different covenants concerning encumbrances and third-party rights. When giving a 'full title guarantee', the assignor covenants that the property is sold free from encumbrances and third-party rights, except those encumbrances disclosed to the assignee and those encumbrances the assignor did not know about and could not reasonably be expected to have known about.[28] There is some doubt as to how wide this covenant is; however, it is certainly not an absolute guarantee.

15.26 When giving a 'limited title guarantee', the assignor covenants that the assignor has not, since the last disposition for value, encumbered the trademark or subjected it to third-party rights.[29] The assignor therefore only makes a promise concerning the assignor's own dealings with the trademark. It is clear that neither the expression 'full title guarantee' nor the expression 'limited title guarantee' provide an absolute title guarantee.

---

26 *See generally* Trade Marks Act 1994, *supra* note 2, at § 17.
27 Law of Property (Miscellaneous Provisions) Act 1994, 1994, c. 36, § 1 (U.K.), *available 21 September 2015 at* http://www.legislation.gov.uk/ukpga/1994/36/enacted.
28 *Id.* at § 3(1).
29 *Id.* at § 3(3).

15.27 Many practitioners often use the phrase 'full title guarantee' or 'limited title guarantee' in assignments of trademarks but then go on to include express warranties as to the title which often duplicate or are inconsistent with the implied covenants as to title. This is clearly undesirable. Accordingly, it may be preferable to avoid using the phrase 'full title guarantee' or 'limited title guarantee' and include express warranties and representations concerning the title instead. The advantages of express warranties are:

- they will apply to all trademarks and any other intellectual property rights covered by assignment and not just the UK intellectual property rights;
- they can be drafted so as to provide an absolute warranty in relation to encumbrances; and
- they avoid the possibility of ambiguity if implied and express covenants are inconsistent.[30]

15.28 The parties will typically prefer to include an 'express further assurance' clause rather than rely on the covenants for title to ensure future cooperation. In doing so, they can include more specific details as to what acts an assignor will undertake at its own expense to ensure that title is effectively transferred and the assignment can be registered.

15.29 Breach of a covenant for title or warranty will give rise to a claim in damages but not a right to terminate.[31] Clearly, once a trademark has been assigned, the transaction has been completed and so cannot be terminated.

9. Registration

15.30 There is no requirement that an assignment of a UK registered trademark must be registered with the UK Intellectual Property Office. A proper assignment will be an effective transfer of legal title, even if it is not registered, and an assignee will be able to initiate proceedings for the infringement of the registered trademark, even if the assignment has not been recorded.[32]

15.31 However, registration protects the assignee from a person who acquires a subsequent conflicting interest[33] and also permits the assignee to recover damages for infringement of the mark.[34] Accordingly, assignees of registered

---

30 *See generally id.* at §§ 2–3.
31 *See* Hongkong Fir Shipping Co. Ltd. v. Kawasaki Kisen Kaisha Ltd. [1962] 2 Q.B. 26 (U.K.).
32 *See generally* Trade Marks Act 1994, *supra* note 2, at § 24.
33 *Id.* at § 25(3)(a).
34 *Id.* at § 25(4).

intellectual property rights have a strong incentive to ensure that the assignment to them is registered as soon as possible, as registration constitutes actual notice to the entire world of their interest. These days, registration of an assignment with the UK Intellectual Property Office is very straightforward and inexpensive. The process includes simply a form to complete and it is not necessary to provide a copy of the assignment itself.[35] The form may be signed by the parties or by an authorized representative of each party.

10. Trusts and equitable assignments of trademarks

15.32 As a matter of English law, it is possible for a UK trademark to be held on trust by one person for the benefit of another. Put simply, a trust occurs where legal and beneficial title to property are separated and the legal title is held for the benefit of another. Section 26(1) of the 1994 Act prohibits the entry of any trust on the UK Trade Marks Register and, as such, in a trust arrangement, the legal owner will be the registered proprietor.[36] However, the beneficial owner of a trademark can enjoy all the rights and benefits attributed to the applicable trademark, other than the legal title, such as the right to initiate infringement proceedings and the right to receive income in relation to the exploitation of the trademark.[37]

15.33 The splitting of legal and beneficial ownership can occur intentionally. For example, in the context of certain transactions (often intragroup arrangements) there may be tax advantages in splitting the legal title of trademarks from the beneficial or economic ownership of the marks. The split of legal and beneficial ownership can also occur unintentionally. For example, where a purported transfer of property is not effective because it does not comply with the formalities required to transfer legal title, it may still take effect as an equitable assignment with legal title effectively held on trust. The beneficiary of an equitable assignment has the ability to require that the legal title to the property concerned be transferred to it.[38]

15.34 In relation to trademarks, equitable assignments often arise when the language used in the relevant document indicates an agreement to assign (in the future) rather than an actual assignment with immediate effect. For example, the relevant document may state that the assignor 'shall assign' the trademarks to

---

35 INTELLECTUAL PROPERTY OFFICE, FORM TM16P, APPLICATION TO RECORD A PARTIAL ASSIGNMENT OF GOODS AND/OR SERVICES (2013), *available 21 September 2015 at* https://www.gov.uk/government/uploads/system/uploads/attachment_data/file/303731/tm16.pdf.
36 Trade Marks Act 1994, *supra* note 2, at § 26(1).
37 R. Griggs Group Ltd. & Ors v. Evans & Ors [2003] EWHC (Ch) 2914, [2003] 1 Ch. 153 (Eng.).
38 Saunders v. Vautier [1841] EWHC (Ch) J82, (1841) 41 E.R. 482 (Eng.).

the assignee rather than the assignor 'hereby assigns' the intellectual property rights to the assignee. In these circumstances, the registered proprietor will effectively hold the legal title on trust for the party to which it has agreed to assign the mark and can be called upon to perfect the transfer.

11. **What is required for an equitable assignment?**

No specific formalities or form of words are required to give rise to an equitable assignment but the key requirements appear to be:[39]

15.35

(i) a 'final and settled intention to transfer the property to the assignee there and then';[40]
(ii) a reasonable degree of clarity as to the property that is to be assigned; and
(iii) some 'act' by the assignor showing that the assignor is passing the property to the assignee.[41]

An 'act' for the purpose of the third requirement is construed broadly so there is no necessity for an actual deed to be carried out. Accordingly, in practice, this third requirement seems to add little to the requirement set out in the first limb above.

If equitable assignments have, to a large extent, the same practical effect as a legal assignment, why should practitioners ensure that assignees obtain a legal assignment? Legal assignments are preferable for the following reasons:

15.36

(i) Enforcement of an equitable assignment depends upon all the relevant circumstances of the case and the courts have considerable discretion over whether or not to give effect to an equitable assignment. For example, it is well known that equity will only come to the assistance of those with 'clean hands'.[42] Accordingly, an equitable assignee's conduct could affect whether or not a court would give effect to an equitable assignment.
(ii) As mentioned previously, it is advantageous for an assignee to register any assignment of registered intellectual property rights. However, section 26 of the 1994 Act states that no notice of any trust shall be entered

---

39 Phelps v. Spon-Smith and Co. (a firm) [1999] All E.R. (D) 1268 (Ch) (Eng.).
40 Re Williams [1917] 1 Ch. 1 at 8 (Eng.).
41 Kijowski v. New Capital Properties Ltd. [1987] 15 Con. L.R. 1 (Eng.).
42 This is a well-known doctrine that looks to see if there is any conduct by the claimant before applying to court that should preclude the claimant from applying for equitable relief. *See* Tinsley v. Milligan [1994] 1 A.C. 340 (H.L.) (appeal taken from Eng.).

on the Register.[43] Accordingly, there is a risk that a third party could subsequently acquire a conflicting interest, without having notice of the prior equitable assignment, and could take priority over the rights of an equitable assignee.

(iii) In addition, an equitable owner cannot bring enforcement proceedings in his or her own right and will require the legal owner to be joined as a party.[44]

12. Confirmatory assignments

15.37 Confirmatory assignments are not really a separate species of assignment or treated as a separate type of assignment in law. However, they are commonly used in relation to trademarks, particularly for registration purposes. A confirmatory assignment will often be used in the following circumstances:

- where there is some uncertainty regarding the validity of a previous assignment, perhaps because it was an agreement to assign rather than an actual assignment;
- where the assignee and/or assignor do not wish to disclose the document containing the original assignment to the Trade Marks Registry, perhaps because it includes confidential details about the transaction (such as the purchase price paid for the intellectual property right);
- where there was a transfer of a number of intellectual property rights, perhaps covering a number of territories and the national Registries are unable or unwilling to pick out the intellectual property rights relevant to their territory from the lengthy schedules; and/or
- to comply with the requirements of the national registry, for example that the assignment be in the local language or be in a particular prescribed format.

15.38 Arguably, the use of confirmatory assignments can be misleading, or perhaps even fraudulent in extreme circumstances, as they often purport to transfer title that has already been assigned. It is suggested that it is best to avoid confirmatory assignments wherever possible by not including actual assignments of trademarks in sale and purchase agreements but just agreements to assign. Then, on or after completion of a transaction, actual assignments can be entered into that conform to the requirements of local registries and do not disclose confidential information. Alternatively, as mentioned above, to register the assignment of a UK trademark, there is no need to submit the

---

43 Trade Marks Act 1994, *supra* note 2, at § 26.
44 *See generally id.* at § 23.

assignment itself to the Registry; a simple form is all that is required.[45] This can then remove the need to prepare confirmatory assignments for registration purposes in the UK.

Where use of a confirmatory assignment is unavoidable, it is suggested that a clear recital be added referring to the original assignment. The assignment provision should expressly confirm that title is only transferred to the extent it has not already been assigned by the original assignment.[46]

15.39

D. LICENSES OF UK TRADEMARKS

The license of a trademark is the grant of permission to do something that would otherwise amount to an infringement of a UK trademark. Section 10 of the 1994 Act sets out the acts of infringement;[47] essentially, these outline the use of another's mark in the course of trade. It follows then that a license is consent for another to undertake any of the 1994 Act section 10 acts of infringement and that, as a matter of English law, a license is not required to undertake any other acts, such as buying and selling goods as a distributor.

15.40

The provisions dealing with the licensing of UK trademarks are set out in sections 25 to 31 of the 1994 Act[48] and, unlike the provisions relating to assignments, the UK statutory regime relating to licenses closely follows the wording of the Trade Marks Directive.[49] The requirements are a 'light touch' and the parties to a trademark licensing arrangement are given considerable freedom to agree commercial terms. The 1994 Act section 28 sets out the core statutory licensing provisions as follows:

15.41

Licensing of registered trademark

(1) A licence to use a registered trademark may be general or limited. A limited licence may, in particular, apply:
   (a) in relation to some but not all of the goods or services for which the trademark is registered, or
   (b) in relation to use of the trademark in a particular manner or a particular locality.
(2) A licence is not effective unless it is in writing signed by or on behalf of the grantor.

---

45 *See* INTELLECTUAL PROPERTY OFFICE, *supra* note 35.
46 *See generally* Trade Marks Act 1994, *supra* note 2, at § 2.
47 *Id.* at § 10.
48 *Id.* at §§ 25–31.
49 Council Directive 2008/95, *supra* note 3, at art. 8(1).

Except in Scotland, this requirement may be satisfied in a case where the grantor is a body corporate by the affixing of its seal.

(3) Unless the licence provides otherwise, it is binding on a successor in title to the grantor's interest.

References in this Act to doing anything with, or without, the consent of the proprietor of a registered trademark shall be construed accordingly.

(4) Where the licence so provides, a sub-licence may be granted by the licensee; and references in this Act to a licence or licensee include a sub-licence or sublicensee.[50]

1. The nature of a trademark license

15.42 As a matter of English law, a registered trademark is a proprietary right. However, the same is not true of a license. As mentioned above, a trademark license amounts to consent to perform an act that would, in absence of the license, be an infringement of a UK trademark. In the case of *Northern & Shell v. Conde Nast*,[51] it was confirmed that a trademark license is not a property right but, is simply permission to do the licensed act.

15.43 In that case, the claimant had been granted an exclusive license and the court considered whether that exclusive licensee could bring an action for trademark infringement against a third party using the trademark with the consent of the proprietor. It was found that section 10 of the 1994 Act is clear; infringement requires acts to be undertaken without the proprietor's consent, and so no action in trademark infringement could be brought. The licensee's remedies would rest in a claim for breach of contract against its licensor if the proprietor had granted inconsistent rights in breach of the license agreement entered into with the licensee. This case was subsequently referred to and confirmed in *Leofelis SA v. Lonsdale Sports Ltd*.[52]

2. Formalities

15.44 As set out above in paragraph 15.41, Section 28(2) of the 1994 Act states that: 'A licence is not effective unless it is in writing signed by or on behalf of the grantor.'[53] This is consistent with the requirements for a valid assignment. However, it appears somewhat inconsistent with the position that a license is a permission to do something that would otherwise amount to an infringement, as clearly permission can be given formally in writing or informally orally.

---

50 Trade Marks Act 1994, *supra* note 2, at § 28.
51 *See generally* Northern & Shell plc v. Conde Nast and National Magazines Distributors Ltd. [1995] R.P.C. 117, at [117]–[127] (Eng.).
52 Leofelis SA & Anor v. Lonsdale Sports Ltd. [2012] EWHC (Ch) 485 (Eng.).
53 Trade Marks Act 1994, *supra* note 2, at § 28(2).

15.45 Many trademark licensing arrangements are not formally recorded in writing; for example, when they are between group companies and a transfer pricing structure has not been put into place or when the arrangements are non-exclusive and royalty-free and so a detailed commercial agreement is not a priority. Section 28(2) of the 1994 Act does not mean that a licensee under an informal, oral agreement is at risk of an infringement claim from the trademark proprietor. In these circumstances, the licensee has the consent of the proprietor and so is not committing an infringing act under section 10 of the 1994 Act. An informal, unwritten license will, therefore, be effective as against the licensor.

15.46 However, as a result of section 28(2) of the 1994 Act, an informal licensee is potentially at risk and does not have the benefit of the statutory protections of sections 28 to 31 of the 1994 Act, which are afforded to a licensee under a written license agreement. The informal licensee is at risk because its rights lie only against the licensor for so long as privity of contract remains. If the registered trademark were assigned to a third party, the new proprietor would not be bound by the unwritten permission granted to the licensee; an informal license is essentially a personal arrangement with the previous proprietor. In addition, the informal licensee is at risk if the proprietor grants a subsequent conflicting license to a third party, which may 'trump' the pre-existing oral arrangement. The informal licensee may have rights against the grantor but will have no security against any third party acquiring the trademark or any rights under the trademark. In addition, for an informal licensee to prove that it has rights against the grantor may well be problematic in light of the lack of a written agreement. There are, therefore, plenty of good reasons why licenses should be in writing and signed by both parties.

3. Key terms

15.47 The terms of a trademark license in the UK will, of course, vary depending on the circumstances, but key terms the parties will need to address will typically include the 'scope of grant and any exclusivity', 'controls over the licensee's use of the trademark', 'the rights and responsibilities of the parties for the maintenance and enforcement of the licensed trademarks', 'the ability of the licensee to sublicense or assign its rights', and 'term and termination and the parties' respective liabilities'.[54] In addition, any financial terms will, of course, need to be addressed where the licensee is paying royalties or other sums in consideration of the grant of the license.

---

54 *See generally id.* at §§ 28–31.

15.48 If a licensee uses a licensed trademark outside the scope of its licensed rights, the licensee risks an infringement action, as well as a possible claim for breach of contract. Any limitation on the field of use must be constructed with care so as to avoid any overlap and confusion between the different exploiting parties.[55]

15.49 The 1994 Act includes only limited regulation as to terms to be included in trademark licenses. With the exception of licensees' enforcement rights (as described infra at paragraph 15.65), the 1994 Act does not imply any terms into licenses of UK trademarks and it is for the parties to reach their own commercial deal and protect their own interests.

4. Grant and exclusivity

15.50 At the heart of any licensing arrangement will be the license grant. As set out in paragraph 15.41, section 28(1) of the 1994 Act states that any license may be general or may be limited, such that the grant may be restricted to some, but not all, of the goods or services for which the trademark is registered or may be for use in a particular manner or a particular geographical location.[56] For example, a license may be granted for a particular category of products for sale in Northern Ireland, but not the rest of the UK.

15.51 Licenses may either be exclusive, sole or non-exclusive and section 29(1) of the 1994 Act defines an exclusive license as a license authorizing the licensee to the exclusion of all other persons, including the person granting the license, to use a registered trademark in the manner authorized by the license.[57] Section 29(1) of the 1994 Act makes it clear that the exclusivity may be general or may be limited, for example, to certain goods or services or a particular area.[58]

5. Sublicensing

15.52 Under section 28(4) of the 1994 Act, it is clear that sublicensing is permissible, but that the right to sublicense will only apply 'where the license so provides'.[59] As a result, a right to sublicense will not be implied if a license agreement is silent on this issue. Where sublicensees are appointed, they will have the benefit of the same rights under the 1994 Act as any other licensee.

---

55 Doosan Power Systems Ltd. v. Babcock International Group plc and another company [2013] EWHC (Ch) 1364 (Eng.).
56 Trade Marks Act 1994, *supra* note 2, at § 28(1).
57 *Id.* at § 29(1).
58 *Id.*
59 *Id.* at § 28(4).

D. LICENSES OF UK TRADEMARKS

15.53 Where a licensor permits the grant of sublicenses, the licensor will typically want to ensure that the licensee imposes contractual controls on any sublicensees. The licensor will want to be able to bring a claim in damages against the licensee where the acts or omissions of any sublicensees cause harm to the licensor. The right to recover damages in these circumstances is not implied and needs to be expressly addressed in any license agreement.

6. Quality control

15.54 The 1994 Act does not impose any specific requirement on a trademark proprietor to exercise control over a licensee's use of a licensed trademark or notify the Trade Marks Registry of any such control. Again, licensors are given considerable freedom as to how they transact with their marks and it is the responsibility of a proprietor to look after its own interests. Under the previous 1938 Trade Marks Act, the accepted position was that a bare license without any licensor control would render the trademark deceptive[60] and licensors were subject to a statutory requirement to demonstrate the exercise of appropriate control.

15.55 However, the 1994 Act is less prescriptive and the requirement for formal quality control has been removed. That said, as noted supra at paragraph 15.13, the freedom for trademark proprietors to exploit their trademarks as assets is balanced by section 46 of the 1994 Act, which provides for the revocation of trademarks which have become deceptive by reason of the manner of their use.[61]

15.56 There have only been a very limited number of cases that have considered quality control requirements in trademark licenses under the 1994 Act. The leading case is *Scandecor*, as referred to above, in which the House of Lords ruled that use of a trademark under a bare license without any licensor control is not inherently likely to deceive the public; it will depend on the circumstances.[62] The House of Lords recognized that consumers understand the nature of trademark licensing with Lord Nicholls commenting that:

> Customers are well used to the practice of licensing trademarks. When they see goods or services to which a mark has been affixed, they understand that the goods have been produced either by the owner of the mark or someone else acting with his consent.[63]

---

60 Holly Hobbie Trade Mark [1984] R.P.C. 101 at (329–358).
61 Trade Marks Act 1994, *supra* note 2, at § 46.
62 Scandecor Development AB, *supra* note 14.
63 Scandecor Development AB and Another, *supra* note 15, at [34]; *id.* at [38].

Lord Nicholls also commented that consumers assume that a trademark proprietor will exercise control over a licensee's use of a licensed trademark as a result of the proprietor's own self-interest, as opposed to any formal legal requirement.

15.57 As a result, the absence of contractual controls in a license agreement does not make the licensed trademark inherently deceptive. However, in practice, the lack of actual control may increase the likelihood of the mark becoming deceptive. As such, the need for effective quality control remains. Without control, there remains the risk of a licensed trademark becoming generic or of its use misleading the public as to the nature, quality, or geographical origin of the goods or services in respect to which the trademark is used.

15.58 In any event, a licensor which sees any value in the licensed trademark will want to control the way in which that mark is used by a licensee. It will also want to ensure that the goods or services in respect to which the trademark is used meet certain standards of quality.

15.59 In any English Law trademark licensing arrangement, it is standard practice to include detailed provisions controlling both the use of the licensed trademark itself and the nature and quality of the applicable goods or services. A key feature of any licensing arrangement is, of course, the ability of the licensor to terminate in the event of breach. Detailed specific provisions will enhance the ability of a licensor to terminate where the licensee acts in a way that could damage the trademark.

15.60 While the formal legal requirement for licensor control may have been relaxed by the 1994 Act, the current tendency of UK trademark proprietors is to go for more, rather than less, in the way of contractual controls. This reflects licensors being ever more aware of their trademarks as valuable assets and being increasingly open to exploiting their trademark assets in different ways. As the number of third parties using a trademark under license increases, the need to ensure consistency of that use also increases. This move towards more rigorous and detailed contractual provisions also reflects the trend of trademark owners wanting to control strictly the messaging associated with their brands across all media and for all purposes.

15.61 As such, in any English law trademark licensing arrangement, it would be common to see the following control provisions:

- an obligation on the licensee to use the licensed trademark only in the form stipulated by the licensor, which will often include compliance with

the licensor's brand guidelines with specific requirements as to the size, colour, positioning and use of the trademark and relative size and prominence to any other marks which may appear;
- quality control requirements and specifications for all materials and products which bear the trademarks;
- a requirement for the licensee to submit samples of all materials and products which bear the trademarks to the licensor for approval, together with an approval process;
- a restriction preventing the licensee from seeking to register the licensed trademarks or any mark which is substantially similar;
- a statement that all goodwill associated with the use of the mark will accrue to the licensor, and not the licensee;
- a more general obligation on the licensee not to do anything which may damage the reputation of the licensor or the trademark or any associated goodwill; and
- an obligation to cease all use of the licensed trademark upon termination of the license agreement, subject to any appropriate 'sell off' period.

7. Liabilities and indemnity

In the event that a licensee supplies defective goods which bear a licensed trademark, liability can flow to the licensor under the Consumer Protection Act 1987 (the 'CPA').[64] The CPA implements European Product Liability Directive 85/374/EEC[65] and provides that a producer will be liable for damage caused by defective goods. This is a strict liability offence and the claimant need only show the presence of a defect and a causal link between the defect and the damage to bring a claim against the producer, as defined at section 1(2) of the CPA.

15.62

Section 2(2)(b) of the CPA also extends this strict liability to 'any person who, by putting his name on the product or using a trademark or other distinguishing mark in relation to the product, has held himself out to be the producer of the product'.[66] By licensing the use of a trademark, the proprietor will be considered to be 'holding itself' out as having a connection with the goods or services of the licensee which bear the trademark and may be liable for damages resulting from any defective goods, even if the proprietor is not directly involved in their manufacture and supply.

15.63

---

64 Consumer Protection Act 1987, 1987, c. 43 (U.K.), *available* 21 September 2015 at http://www.legislation.gov.uk/ukpga/1987/43/pdfs/ukpga_19870043_en.pdf.
65 Council Directive 85/374, 1985 O.J. (L 210) 29 (EC).
66 Consumer Protection Act 1987, *supra* note 64, at § 2(2)(b).

15.64 As a result, when licensing a trademark, the proprietor should consider both the reputation of the licensee and its ability to meet suitable standards of production and the proprietor should seek appropriate warranties and commitments from the licensee. It is also common practice for the licensor to obtain an indemnity from the licensee with respect to any claims brought against the licensor by third parties as a result of the acts or omissions of the licensee. The scope of such an indemnity will be the subject of negotiation but, ideally, the licensor will want a comprehensive indemnity without any financial cap covering any claims arising. In addition, the proprietor will typically require that the licensee clearly identify itself as the producer of the goods and give its contact details on all products to which the licensed trademark is applied so any complaints and claims are directed to the licensee.

8. Rights of licensees to bring infringement proceedings

15.65 The rights of a licensee of a registered UK trademark to bring proceedings in the event of an infringement of the licensed mark are set out in sections 30 and 31 of the 1994 Act.[67] These provisions are not mandatory and can be excluded by the parties in their trademark license agreement. However, if the agreement is silent, section 30 of the 1994 Act will apply and will confer rights on the licensee, provided the license has been registered at the Trade Marks Registry.

15.66 Section 30 of the 1994 Act sets out the rights of an exclusive or nonexclusive licensee while section 31 of the 1994 Act deals with rights of enforcement for an exclusive licensee which has been granted the rights of an assignee. Section 30 of the 1994 Act provides that in the event of an infringement that affects the interests of the licensee, the licensee may call on the proprietor of the trademark to take infringement proceedings. If the trademark proprietor either refuses to take action or fails to do so within two months of being called upon to do so, the licensee will be entitled to bring the proceedings in its own name.[68] Where the licensee brings proceedings, it must join the proprietor into the action unless the court gives permission for the licensee to bring the proceedings alone.[69]

15.67 In their license agreement, the parties may elect that an exclusive licensee will have the same rights and remedies as if the license were an assignment, in which case the provisions of section 31 of the 1994 Act will apply. These rights do not arise automatically and if they are not included in the license agreement

---

67 Trade Marks Act 1994, *supra* note 2, at §§ 30–31.
68 *Id.* at § 30.
69 *Id.*

section 30 of the 1994 Act will apply. Where section 31 of the 1994 Act applies, the licensee is entitled to bring infringement proceedings in its own name without having first to call on the proprietor, although such rights are concurrent with those of the proprietor.[70] A licensee who brings infringement proceedings is required to join in the proprietor unless the licensee obtains the court's permission to bring the action alone.[71]

15.68 A licensee cannot bring infringement proceedings against the proprietor or any third party who is acting with the proprietor's consent[72] although the licensee may have a claim against the proprietor for breach of contract if the proprietor has granted or exercised rights which conflict with those granted to the licensee.

15.69 Under both sections 30 and 31 of the 1994 Act, where a trademark proprietor brings proceedings for infringement, any loss suffered or likely to be suffered by licensees shall be taken into account and the court may direct that the proprietor hold any damages awarded on behalf of licensees. Where section 31 of the 1994 Act applies, the court may also take into account loss suffered by the trademark proprietor if the licensee brings the proceedings and will consider the terms of the license agreement when considering loss suffered, damages and any apportionment. These provisions are unusual as they permit the court to award damages for loss suffered by a person who is not a party to the proceedings. No such provisions apply in respect of patent infringement actions in the UK.

15.70 As mentioned above,[73] the parties are free to exclude these statutory enforcement rights and it is often the case that the parties will prefer to set out express contractual rights of enforcement in their license agreement. A trademark proprietor will often want to control enforcement proceedings itself and will be reluctant to give the licensee too much freedom, particularly where a trademark is licensed to a number of different licensees which will all have an interest in the action. The somewhat unusual damages position under sections 30 and 31 of the 1994 Act recognizes the fact that while it may be the licensee that is suffering direct financial loss as a result of an infringement, the licensor may still prefer to bring the proceedings itself and, in doing so, manage the defence of any counterclaim or attack on the validity of the licensed trademark.[74]

---

[70] *Id.* at § 31.
[71] *Id.*
[72] *See* Northern & Shell, *supra* note 51.
[73] *See id.*
[74] Trade Marks Act 1994, *supra* note 2, at §§ 30–31.

9. Warranties

15.71 As noted above, in the context of English Law assignments of trademarks, it is common to include the 'full title guarantee' or 'limited title guarantee' covenants for title implied by the Law of Property (Miscellaneous Provisions) Act 1994.[75] These covenants for title only apply to dispositions of property and so are not relevant in the context of trademark licensing. As a result, the parties will typically negotiate and agree to express warranties so as to provide financial redress for the licensee in the event that its investment is undermined. These might include warranties as to the status of the licensed trademarks, the licensor's title and the existence of any encumbrances and disputes.

10. Term and termination

15.72 In most trademark licensing arrangements, the ability of the licensor to terminate a trademark license and recover its rights is fundamental to the relationship between the parties. It is possible as a matter of English Law for a licensor to grant an irrevocable and perpetual license, however, such an arrangement would be unusual and may be more akin to a transfer of beneficial ownership.

15.73 Most English Law trademark licensing arrangements are entered into for a fixed period of time, often subject to renewal by the parties. In the event that an English law commercial arrangement does not include an express term or express termination rights, the courts will imply a right for either party to terminate on 'reasonable notice'.[76] What is 'reasonable notice' will depend on the facts and is left to the discretion of the courts, taking into account the actual arrangement, the nature of the parties, the degree of formality of the arrangement, and what is common practice in the industry in question. As a result, a trademark license arrangement that appears to be perpetual may, in fact, be subject to termination on, for example, six to twelve months' notice.

15.74 Most trademark licensing arrangements will also include an express right for the licensor to terminate in the event of the licensee's breach or insolvency. The threat of termination in the event of breach is, of course, a powerful tool to ensure the licensee complies with its commitments under its trademark license. If, following termination of a license agreement, a licensee continues to

---

75 *See* Law of Property, *supra* note 27.
76 Hamsard 3147 Ltd. (trading as Mini Mode Childrenswear) & Anor v. Boots UK Ltd. [2013] EWHC (Pat.) 3251 (Eng.).

apply the relevant trademark on an unlicensed basis, the proprietor may be able to bring a claim against the former licensee for breach of contract as well as an action for trademark infringement.[77] As a license is simply permission to do something that would otherwise amount to an infringement, it follows that once that permission has been revoked, the licensee loses its protection from an infringement claim.

A licensee may need to invest considerable sums to set up and run its business exploiting the licensed trademark. As a result, the licensee will want to ensure that its license is secure and that it has some certainty. It is common for a licensor's ability to terminate for breach to be limited to 'material breach' only. When determining what is a 'material breach', again the courts will look at the relevant facts and circumstances. In *National Power v. United Gas*, the court described a 'material breach' as a breach that 'has a serious effect on the benefit that the innocent party would have otherwise derived from the contract'.[78] The decision in *Crosstown Music v. Rive Droite* stated that materiality 'connotes the concept of significance, as opposed to triviality, and its materiality has to be measured in its total context'.[79] 15.75

To determine if the breach is, in fact, a material breach in its total context, all the circumstances of the contract and the breach should be considered, particularly: 15.76

- the nature of the contract;
- the nature and circumstances of the breach;
- the impact of the breach on the innocent party;
- any explanation for the breach or attempts to remedy the breach within an agreed timeframe; and
- the consequences of termination for the defaulting party.

As a result, the more a licensee has invested and the more the licensee's business is dependent on its trademark license, the more serious a breach would need to be to justify termination by the licensor.

11. Assignment of licenses

A trademark license can be a valuable asset and may amount to the cornerstone around which a business is founded. The ability of a licensee to assign its 15.77

---

77   *See generally* Trade Marks Act 1994, *supra* note 2, at § 30.
78   National Power plc v. United Gas Co. Ltd. and Another [1998] All E.R. (Q.B.) 321 (Eng.).
79   Crosstown Music Co. v. Rive Droite Music Ltd. & Ors [2010] EWCA (Civ) 1222 (Eng.).

license to a third party may make a significant difference to the licensee's ability to sell its business (as an asset sale, rather than a share sale) and realize value. In the event of a proposed business sale, the grant of a sublicense to the purchaser may be unattractive. The purchaser is likely to prefer a direct contractual relationship with the trademark proprietor and the existing licensee will want to be relieved of ongoing contractual commitments. As a result, an assignment of the relevant license agreement to the purchaser will be more desirable.

15.78 As a matter of English law, the parties to a contract can determine in advance whether or not the contract can be assigned to a third party. However, if the contract is silent and does not expressly permit or exclude assignment, general principles of English law will apply. As such, subject to the terms of the contract, the rights (or benefit) can be assigned without the consent of the party against whom the rights are held. However, a valid transfer of the obligations (or burden) of the contract to a third party requires the consent of the person entitled to benefit under the contract and is effected by novation.[80]

15.79 In the context of a trademark license, the right of the licensee to receive the benefit of the license is often subject to and dependent upon the licensee's compliance with the obligations set out in the agreement, for example, the obligation to pay royalties and the obligation to comply with quality control requirements. Often, the rights and the obligations cannot realistically be separated. As such, a transferring licensee will need to pass these obligations to any third-party purchaser. Thus, any common law right to transfer the benefit, but not the burden, is unlikely to be adequate.

15.80 As a result, a licensee may try to secure in its trademark license agreement the express ability to assign the agreement to a third party which may subsequently acquire the relevant business.[81] The ability to assign may be expressed to be dependent upon the assignee meeting certain standards that will satisfy the trademark proprietor as to its suitability. Alternatively, the proprietor may insist that the license agreement states that the agreement and any rights under it cannot be assigned except with the licensor's prior written consent. If a third party acquires a business that uses licensed trademarks and yet the license is not validly assigned, the new proprietor will be at risk of an infringement action from the trademark proprietor.

---

80 Trade Marks Act 1994, *supra* note 2, at § 24.
81 *See generally id.*

D. LICENSES OF UK TRADEMARKS

12. Contracts Rights of Third Parties Act

15.81 Nestled within the boilerplate language of English law contracts will be a 'third party rights clause' which can, at times, prove to be a useful provision when structuring trademark licensing arrangements. Contrary to the well established common law doctrine of privity (*Dunlop Pneumatic v. Selfridge*),[82] the Contract (Rights of Third Parties) Act 1999 ('CROTPA') allows a third party to enforce the terms of a contract if it specifically mentions the party as a person authorized to do so or if the contract purports to confer a benefit on the third party.[83]

15.82 Section 1(2) of CROTPA allows parties to exclude CROTPA from the contract, which is generally taken advantage of in licenses and commercial contracts as a standard boilerplate provision. However, there may be circumstances where the parties want expressly to ensure that a third party can enforce a benefit under a trademark licensing arrangement. For example, where the license granted is a sublicense, the trademark proprietor may seek direct enforcement rights in respect of certain provisions, including the benefit of any product liability indemnity given.

13. Registration

15.83 Registration of licenses is not a requirement under the 1994 Act but there are certain advantages in registering as set out in sections 28 to 31 of the 1994 Act.[84] These advantages include binding a successor in title or third party who subsequently acquires a conflicting interest. Under section 25(3) of the 1994 Act,[85] until an application has been made for registration of the license agreement, the license agreement will be ineffective against a third party who acquires a conflicting interest in or under the trademark in ignorance of the pre-existing license.

15.84 This provision appears to be inconsistent with section 28(3) of the 1994 Act[86] that states that a license will be binding on a successor in title to the grantor's interest. However, sections 25(3) and 28(3) of the 1994 Act need to be read together such that a successor in title will, in fact, only be bound if the license has been registered or if the successor was otherwise aware of its existence.

---

82 Dunlop Pneumatic Tyre Co. Ltd. v. Selfridge & Co. Ltd., [1915] A.C. 847 (H.L.) (Eng.).
83 Contract (Rights of Third Parties) Act 1999, 1999, c. 31, § 1(1) (U.K.), *available* 21 September 2015 at http://www.legislation.gov.uk/ukpga/1999/31/pdfs/ukpga_19990031_en.pdf.
84 Trade Marks Act 1994, *supra* note 2, at §§ 28–31.
85 *Id.* at § 25(3).
86 *Id.* at § 28(3).

14. Licensing of unregistered trademarks

15.85 It is possible for the owner of an unregistered trademark to grant a license to a third party permitting that third party to use the mark. However, the owner will need to have sufficient goodwill in the unregistered mark such that it can protect the mark in an action in 'passing off' and so will be able to attract a licensee. If the owner does not have sufficient goodwill, there will be no incentive for the prospective licensee to accept license terms, as the owner will not be able to prevent the prospective licensee from exploiting the mark independently.[87] Where the owner does have sufficient goodwill and the unregistered mark can be protected, any license will look very much like a license of a registered trademark and should include appropriate controls so as to preserve and enhance the value of the mark.

E. SECURITY INTERESTS

15.86 As well as transferring and licensing trademarks, it is clear under the 1994 Act that trademarks can be used as security. This is, of course, consistent with the principle of trademarks as property. Section 25(2) of the 1994 Act identifies registrable transactions as including 'the granting of any security interest (whether fixed or floating) over a registered trademark or any right in or under it'.[88]

15.87 The 1994 Act does not include a definition of security interest but from the wording of section 25(2) of the 1994 Act, fixed and floating charges are certainly covered.[89] In addition, section 24(4) of the 1994 Act provides that the provisions in section 24 of the 1994 Act relating to assignments 'apply to assignment by way of security as in relation to any other assignment'.[90] As such, a legal mortgage can also be created over registered UK trademarks.

15.88 A legal mortgage is a transaction where the title to the relevant asset (in this case a registered trademark) is transferred to the lender on the basis that it will be assigned back when the secured obligations are discharged. Where a legal mortgage is taken over a registered trademark, the proprietor will assign the trademark to the lender but will then typically need an exclusive license back in order to continue to exploit the trademark and maintain its value. The

---

[87] Harrods Ltd. v. Harrods (Buenos Aires) and Harrods (South America) Ltd. [1999] F.S.R. 187 (Eng.).
[88] Trade Marks Act 1994, *supra* note 2, at § 25(2).
[89] *Id.*
[90] *Id.* at § 24(4).

lender as assignee will clearly have an interest in ensuring that the trademark is maintained and enforced although, in practice, these activities are likely to be allocated to the assignor (or licensee) as the lender is unlikely to have the requisite skills or resources.

A legal mortgage gives the lender considerable control and power, but often the transfer of title is unattractive to the parties. In addition, setting up such an arrangement with a license back can be complicated. As a result, it is more common for practitioners in the UK to recommend the creation of a 'charge' over a registered trademark. Where a 'charge' is created, the borrower retains ownership of the trademark but the trademark is subject to an encumbrance. In the event the lender enforces the security, it will call for the assignment of the trademark into its name, and it may hold an assignment in escrow to facilitate such a transfer. Under such an arrangement, the lender will want to put terms in place with the borrower to ensure that it continues to renew the trademarks that are subject to the 'charge' and otherwise take steps to preserve their value. 15.89

'Charges' over trademarks may be registered at UK Companies House and also at the UK Intellectual Property Office. In accordance with section 25(3) of the 1994 Act, security interests are not enforceable against a third party acquiring a conflicting interest in ignorance of the prior security interest, unless the interest is registered.[91] 15.90

F. UK COMPETITION LAW

The main UK competition rules affecting trademark transactions and other types of commercial agreements are contained in Chapter I of the Competition Act 1998 (Competition Act 1998).[92] The so-called 'Chapter I prohibition' is concerned with anti-competitive agreements between independent undertakings, and is closely modelled on Article 101 of the Treaty on the Functioning of the European Union (TFEU).[93] When applying the 'Chapter I prohibition', the UK Competition and Markets Authority (CMA) and the UK Courts are obliged to ensure that any questions relating to competition within the UK are dealt with in a way that is consistent with the treatment of corresponding questions under EU law. The CMA and the UK 15.91

---

[91] *Id.* at § 25(3).
[92] Competition Act 1998, 1998, c. 41 (U.K.), *available 21 September 2015 at* http://www.legislation.gov.uk/ukpga/1998/41/introduction/enacted.
[93] CONSOLIDATED VERSION OF THE TREATY ON THE FUNCTIONING OF THE EUROPEAN UNION, art. 101, 26 October 2012, 2012 O.J. (C 326) 47.

Courts will take a particularly dim view of transactions which attempt to fix prices or which seek to share markets. If an agreement infringes the 'Chapter I prohibition', the anti-competitive provisions of the agreement may be unenforceable, and in serious cases the parties run the risk of heavy fines.

15.92 As a result, any trademark transactions that affect the UK need to be reviewed in line with EU competition law to ensure compliance. Exclusive licenses, territorial restrictions, and any controls on pricing will all require careful consideration. In particular, coexistence agreements can present challenges from a competition law perspective and the parties will want to ensure that the agreed-upon terms prevent consumer confusion without setting up anti-competitive market-sharing arrangements. Any analysis of UK trademark transactions under the Competition Act 1998 will reflect the analysis under EU competition law.

G. CONCLUSIONS

15.93 The UK does not have a particularly prescriptive legal regime governing trademark transactions. The principal UK legislation is derived from the 1988 Directive to approximate the laws of Member States relating to trade marks,[94] under which trademark proprietors are given considerable scope as to how they exploit their trademark assets. However, exploitation takes place within a legislative framework and an understanding of the regime is, of course, required. In addition, English law can present some surprises for foreign practitioners in the context of trademark transactions. English contract law places considerable emphasis on what the parties have written in their transaction documents and implying terms into an English Law assignment or agreement is not straightforward. That said, certain words and phrases really do matter and can give rise to commitments or consequences that may not be immediately apparent. The words 'full title guarantee' in a trademark assignment will imply covenants for title, a commitment that a trademark proprietor 'shall assign' rights in a trademark may create an equitable interest and references to a third party beneficiary in a trademark license may give a third party an enforcement right. When exploiting their trademarks, UK proprietors can enjoy the benefits of a flexible and accommodating system but should do so with the help of an experienced practitioner to ensure they preserve the value of their assets and establish a sound contractual basis.

---

94 Council Directive 2008/95, *supra* note 3.

16

TRADEMARK TRANSACTIONS IN GERMANY: A CONTINENTAL EUROPEAN SYSTEM MOVES TOWARDS COMMON UNDERSTANDING WITH THE US

Axel Nordemann[*] and Christian Czychowski[**]

A.	INTRODUCTION	16.01	(a) General	16.36
			(b) Restrictions imposed by antitrust law	16.40
B.	EXISTING LEGAL RULES ON TRADEMARK TRANSACTIONS IN GERMAN LAW	16.02	(c) License agreements and insolvency proceedings	16.46
	1. The legal framework – overview	16.02	(d) Trademark infringements	16.47
	2. Relations between European Union law and German trademark law	16.11	(e) Registration of a license	16.49
			3. Coexistence agreements	16.50
	3. Sections 27–31 MarkenG	16.19	(a) General	16.50
	4. The difference between transactions with regard to registered trademarks, company symbols, and titles of works	16.26	(b) Restrictions imposed by antitrust law	16.51
			(c) Applicable law	16.53
			4. Trademarks in mergers and acquisitions transactions	16.58
C.	TRADEMARK TRANSACTIONS IN PRACTICE	16.33	5. Trademarks as securities	16.61
	1. Purchase agreements	16.33		
	2. License agreements	16.36	D. CONCLUSION	16.64

A. INTRODUCTION

Trademark transactions are part of everyday practice in Germany, and are governed by different statutory provisions under European Union Law (EU law) and German law. Under German law, specific rules under German trademark law exist, but statutes from the General Civil Law also apply. The following outline gives an overview of these existing legal rules and furthermore takes a look into different typical agreements, such as purchase agreements, license agreements, and coexistence agreements, including a view from **16.01**

---

[*] Dr. jur., Honorary Professor, Faculty of Law, University of Konstanz; Partner, Boehmert & Boehmert, Berlin.
[**] Dr. jur., Honorary Professor, Faculty of Law, University of Potsdam; Partner, Boehmert & Boehmert, Berlin. The authors would like to thank their research fellow Inès Meri Duhanic for her great preparatory work in connection with this chapter.

387

antitrust law, as well as trademarks in mergers and acquisitions transactions and trademark securities.

B. EXISTING LEGAL RULES ON TRADEMARK TRANSACTIONS IN GERMAN LAW

1. The legal framework – overview

16.02 From a German law perspective, the word 'transaction' is a broader term than contract. A contract is a transaction, but a transaction is not necessarily a contract.[1] Since a commercial transaction is essentially an agreement between two or more parties to enter into a commercial relationship that involves any kind of exchange of items of value, the relevant laws and legal issues will therefore depend on a number of factors. The same applies when transferring one of the most valuable assets of a company: trademarks.

16.03 Notwithstanding the high complexity of trademark transactions, a uniform transactions codex does not exist in Germany. Representing a federation of 16 states (Länder), each with its own constitution, government, and independent court system, Germany is operating a national trademark system; unlike, for instance, the Benelux trademark system that also provides a regional basis for trademark applications. The provisions of German law involving trademark transactions derive from different laws, and are primarily supplemented and overlaid by provisions of the German Trade Mark Act (Markengesetz) (MarkenG).[2] For registered intellectual property rights, the transfer of rights should be filed with the relevant registers, even if it is not mandatory for the validity of a transfer, but necessary for later enforcement of rights against third party infringers. In Germany, trademark law is governed by the MarkenG and the European Community Trade Mark Regulation (CTMR).[3] Trademark applicants have the choice to apply for a national German trademark in accordance with the MarkenG, which will only be valid in Germany, or a Community trademark (CTM) in accordance with the CTMR, which will be valid in all 28 Member States of the European Union (EU), including Germany.

---

1 *See* in particular Sections 145 et seq. of the Bürgerliches Gesetzbuch addressing the legal requirements concerning the effective conclusion and validity of contracts. Bürgerliches Gesetzbuch [BGB] [Civil Code] 18 August 1896 [hereinafter BGB].
2 Markengesetz, BGBl. I, 3082 (1994) [hereinafter: MarkenG].
3 Council Regulation (EC) No. 207/2009 of 26 February 2009 on the Community Trade Mark, 2009 O.J. (L 78) 1 [hereinafter CTMR].

B. EXISTING LEGAL RULES ON TRADEMARK TRANSACTIONS IN GERMAN LAW

Yet, questions related to trademark due diligence in mergers and acquisitions, and other complex corporate transactions, in turn, affect the rules applicable to company and capital market law as laid down, for instance, in the Commercial Law Code (Handelsgesetzbuch) (HGB), or the Stock Corporation Act (Aktiengesetz) (AktienG).

16.04

In general, however, most of the trademark transactions may involve the application of the general civil law principles provided by the Civil Code (Bürgerliches Gesetzbuch) (BGB).[4] The late adoption of the BGB, which was extensively reformed and whose provisions on the transfer of intangibles were adapted to modern needs, specifically encompasses intellectual property rights as 'other rights', and makes the regime for the assignment of contract claims applicable to them under Section 413 BGB. The general civil law provisions are also of particular importance for the question of using trademarks as security. The book (sub-set of rules) of the BGB on property law addresses this issue by providing specific provisions for the use of intangibles as security. Other general principles of German civil law have to be considered, particularly when acquiring agreements that are not made in good faith, such as those intended to transfer the joint invention to one party with the goal of causing damage to a third party, are prohibited in Sections 226, 826 of the BGB. The interests of the other inventors/parties have to be considered according to the good faith (Treu und Glauben) rules in Sections 242, 241(2) of the BGB.

16.05

Other problems in the field of general civil law matters arise when, for example, negotiating agreements for research collaborations between two or more parties. If not otherwise agreed upon between the co-owners of a trademark right, the relationship between such co-owners is governed by Section 741 of the BGB, that is, the provisions on a 'community of part-owners'/'co-owners by defined shares' (Bruchteilsgemeinschaft). If the joint owners have entered into a partnership agreement, the relationship among them is governed by Sections 705 and 718 of the BGB, that is, the provisions on a 'community of joint owners' (Gesamthandsgemeinschaft), and rights to trademarks arising out of such activities may, depending on the particular facts, then be subject to these provisions.

16.06

A special aspect to be considered under German Law is whether a trademark may be exploited (for example, sold or out-licensed) in bad faith by someone other than the true owner or, respectively, may be acquired or in-licensed from someone other than the true owner by a third party in good faith. A registered owner who is not the real owner cannot validly sell the trademark. Thus,

16.07

---

4   BGB, *supra* note 1.

consistent with its general rules on transfer of claims and other rights under Sections 413 and 398 of the BGB, German law does not allow acquisition of trademark rights 'in good faith'.

16.08 With respect to [an exclusive] license, technology transfer, and research and development (R&D) agreements, no permit or registration is required, but there are certain anti-trust issues that merit attention as they could affect the validity of the agreement.

16.09 Additionally, the German Act Against Restraints of Competition (Gesetz gegen Wettbewerbsbeschränkungen) (GWB)[5] and European Antitrust Law (Articles 101 and 102 of the Treaty on the Functioning of the European Union (TFEU)[6]), and several guidelines and regulations, especially the Commission Regulation (EC) No 316/2014 of 21 March 2014 on the Application of Article 101(3) of the Treaty to Categories of Technology Transfer Agreements,[7] and the Commission Regulation (EC) No 1217/2010 of 14 December 2010 on the Application of Article 101(3) of the Treaty to Categories of Research and Development Agreements,[8] have to be obeyed when drafting an agreement containing terms and provisions covering intellectual property rights.

16.10 The relevant laws and legal issues will therefore depend on a number of factors when assessing the legal nature and structure of trademark transactions from the German perspective.

2. Relations between European Union law and German trademark law

16.11 German trademark law is, like all intellectual property rights, based on the principle of territoriality. The territorial nature of these rights means that each state or region determines, for its own territory and independently from any other state, what is to be protected as trademark, who should benefit from such protection, for how long they should be protected and how protection should be enforced.

---

[5] Gesetz gegen Wettbewerbsbeschränkungen [Act Against Restraints of Competition] of 26 June 2013 (BGB1.I No.32 S.1750) [hereinafter GWB].
[6] Consolidated Version of the Treaty on the Functioning of the European Union, 2008 O.J. (C 115) 47 [hereinafter TFEU].
[7] Commission Regulation (EC) No 772/2004 of 27 April 2004 on the application of Article 81(3) of the Treaty to Categories of Technology Transfer Agreements, 2004 O.J. (L 123) 11.
[8] Commission Regulation (EC) No 1217/2010 of 14 December 2010 on the Application of Article 101(3) of the Treaty to Categories of Research and Development Agreements, 2010 O.J. (L 335) 36.

B. EXISTING LEGAL RULES ON TRADEMARK TRANSACTIONS IN GERMAN LAW

16.12 However, as an EU Member State, Germany is required to comply with all European Community directives and regulations.

16.13 The European Union has, in turn, been obliged to settle the place of intellectual property, and thus also trademark law, in relation to a variety of its quintessential objectives, which include the elimination of: internal restrictions on the import and export of goods, a common commercial policy, and the creation of an internal market without obstacles on the free movement of goods, persons, services, and capital.[9]

16.14 Thus, for the purpose of pursuing these objectives, it was necessary to provide for EU-wide legislation on trademarks whereby undertakings can, by means of one procedural system, obtain EU-wide trademarks to which uniform protection is given, and which produce their effects throughout the entire area of the EU. According to Article 1(2) of the CTMR, CTM have a unitary character; they shall have equal effect throughout the EU, and be registered, revoked, or declared invalid only in respect of the entire EU.[10] In contrast hereto, national trademarks gained for the territory of Germany are geographically limited.

16.15 National trademark laws have been substantially harmonized in regards to substantive law since 1988 by the First Directive to Approximate the Laws of the Member States relating to Trade Marks (Trade Marks Directive) (TMD).[11] The MarkenG of 1994 has implemented the TMD, but is, in addition, a comprehensive law providing for protection of all distinctive signs including non-registered marks under Section 4, No. 2 of the MarkenG and commercial signs, such as company names or titles of works under Section 5 of the MarkenG. The requirements for obtaining trademark protection through registration in Europe are substantially the same in all Member States and in the Community trademark system because of the harmonization through the TMD so that the laws of the Member States are also congruent.[12] This does not mean, nevertheless, that the conditions for trademark protection and enforcement for national marks, and for CTMs are necessarily the same.

---

9 Consolidated Version of the Treaty Establishing the European Community, 2006 O.J. (C 321) E/37, at article 3.
10 CTMR, *supra* note 3, at Article 1(2).
11 Directive 2008/95/EC of the European Parliament and of the Council of 24 October 2008 to approximate the laws of the Member States relating to Trade Marks, codified version of the previous Council Directive 89/104/EEC of December 21, 1988 to approximate the laws of the Member States relating to Trade Marks, 2008 O.J. (L 299) 25 [hereinafter TMD].
12 *See*, in particular, CJEU, Judgment of 11 March 2003 in case C-40/01, Ansul BV v. Ajax Brandbeveiliging BV [Ansul] [2003] E.C.R. I-2439, 22, mn.44.

16.16 The relation between the German and EU trademark law is characterized by the principle of coexistence, which is one of the core elements of EU trademark law. Coexistence means that trademark law in the EU comprises both EU legislation as well as the national laws of the 28 Member States of the EU on the protection of marks; they exist alongside each other with an equal rights structure of trademarks at the EU level and the national level.[13] EU trademark law does not replace the law of the Member States on trademarks.[14] However, the Court of Justice of the European Union (CJEU) has further settled the issue by stating in its case law that EU law must be uniformly interpreted throughout the Member States.[15] The EU trademark system reflects the concept of the EU as a unitary territory with a single market.[16] Every single legal provision and legal concept has a reference at the end to the EU's goal to remove barriers to free movement of trade and competition by harmonization. The creation and maintenance of one internal market remains a guiding light. Another goal of the system, which is increasingly important, is to provide a harmonizing trademark model that is open and flexible for transnationally acting businesses. As the EU continues to expand,[17] the market is continuously opening itself more to competition by enabling businesses and citizens to benefit from a wide choice of goods and services.[18]

16.17 The EU is working towards simplifying the regulations to allow for this 'single marketplace' concept to come to full fruition. The CJEU reflects this goal in its opinions,[19] continuously allowing for, what the Max-Planck-Institute in its recently released *Study on the Overall Functioning of the European Trade Mark*

---

13 TMD, *supra* note 11, at Recital 2; CTMR, *supra* note 3, at Recital 5.
14 CTMR, *supra* note 3, at Recital 6.
15 *See*, e.g., CJEU, Judgment of 22 September 2011 in case C-482/09, Budějovický Budvar v. Anheuser-Busch [Budějovický Budvar], mn. 29 (2011).
16 TFEU, *supra* note 6, at Article. 26(2). Article 26(2) of the Treaty on the Functioning of the European Union (TFEU) states that 'the internal market shall comprise an area without internal frontiers in which the free movement of goods, persons, services and capital is ensured'. *Id.*
17 The last Member State joining the European Union [hereinafter EU] has been Croatia on 1 July 2013. Currently, the EU is negotiating memberships with the following countries: Iceland, Montenegro, Serbia, and Turkey. Macedonia has also applied for membership in 2004, but negotiations have not started. For further details, see http://europa.eu/about-eu/countries/member-countries/ (available 21 September 2015).
18 *See*, in particular, Communication of the European Commission COM, 2013 O.J. (L 348) 74.
19 *See*, in particular, CJEU, Judgment of 11 November 1997 in case C-349/95, Loendersloot Internationale Expeditie v. George Ballantine & Son Ltd and others [Loendersloot/Ballantine] [1997] E.C.R. I-6227, paras. 22 and 24; CJEU, Judgment of 29 September 1998 in case C-39/97, Canon Kabushiki Kaisha v. Metro-Goldwyn-Mayer Inc. [Canon/CANNON] [1998] E.C.R. I-5507, I-5531, mn. 28; CJEU, Judgment of 18 June 2002 in case C-299/99, Koninklijke Philips Electronics NV v. Remington Consumer Products Ltd. [Philips/Remington] [2002] E.C.R. I-5475, mn. 30.

B. EXISTING LEGAL RULES ON TRADEMARK TRANSACTIONS IN GERMAN LAW

System, has referred to as 'undistorted competition'.[20] This competition-centered approach keeps a balance between protecting trademark owners from unfair competition and simultaneously protecting the public interest by keeping the market free of deceptive signs. As the Max-Planck-Institute correctly identifies in its study:

> [T]he concept of undistorted competition as a guiding principle for interpretation of European trade mark law is not a one-way approach towards a protection scheme being faced with limiting effects only. Undistorted competition requires a basically strong and firm protection of trade marks that takes into account both the interests of the trade mark holders and the interests of competition.[21]

Even though trademark law grants owners a monopoly that may appear antithetical to this principle, the European understanding of free competition considers such monopolies in harmony with competition law's goal of promoting consumer welfare.

As in the case of the CTM system, the German trademark system relies solely on a registration based system, unlike the U.S., which operates under a common law system where a mark cannot be registered until it has been used as such in the sale of goods or services. This registration requirement fundamentally distinguishes EU and German trademark law.

16.18

3. Sections 27–31 of the MarkenG

The provisions governing the transfer of trademarks, as laid down in Sections 27–31 of the MarkenG, imply that all signs that are protected under this act within the meaning of Section 4, no. 1–3, of the MarkenG are part of the assets of the right holder.[22] The German legal philosophy underlying the entire trademark law is marked by the principle of non-accessoriness of trademarks and the connected legal relationship between the trademark and the undertaking (Konnexität).[23] Trademark transfer is possible by contract or by operation of law. The subject matter of Section 27(1) of the MarkenG concerns the transfer of trademark rights based on the registration, use, or notoriety. According to Section 27(1) of the MarkenG, the German concept of trademark transactions allows the proprietor to assign his rights in the

16.19

---

20 *See* Max-Planck Institute for Intellectual Property and Competition Law, *Study on the Overall Functioning of the European Trade Mark System*, 2011, 1, 51, *available 21 September 2015 at* http://www.ip.mpg.de/de/pub/aktuelles/trade_mark_study/synopses_tms.cfm.
21 *Id.*
22 MarkenG, *supra* note 2, Section 4, no. 1–3.
23 Karl-Heinz Fezer, *MarkenG*, § 3, mn. 202, in MARKENRECHT, KOMMENTAR, 4th ed. (2009).

trademark to third parties. Prior to the reform of German trademark law in 1995 – the year in which the new German Markengesetz replaced the former Warenzeichengesetz[24] – the former provision of Section 8 stated that trademarks were inseparable from the proprietor's place of manufacturing of the goods that bore the mark so that the mark could not be transferred independently of the production plant.[25]

16.20 In contrast, Germany nowadays permits separate transfers, although the provisions of the TMD have left it to the discretion of the Member States to determine whether they want to permit the separate transfer of trademarks. Regarding the trademark transfer policy at the international level, however, the Agreement on Trade-Related Aspects of Intellectual Property Rights (TRIPS) specifies in Article 21 that the owner of a registered trademark shall have the right to assign the trademark with or without the transfer of the business to which the trademark belongs. A trademark's proprietor is thus not restricted to transfer the mark, be it in whole or in part. In fact, the provision of Section 30(1) of the MarkenG allows him to grant licenses in the mark that reflect the general trademark policy on the Community level enshrined in Article 17 of the CTMR according to which the trademark should be capable of being transferred. This is remarkable considering the national implementing measures maxim in relation to the provisions of the TMD, which, in fact, does not contain any provisions concerning licensing. Notwithstanding the important role of Section 30 of the MarkenG for the legal examination of trademark licenses,[26] this rule remains incomplete. In addition to this provision, it is essential that an appropriate legal assessment of trademark transactions via license agreements be concluded through the general contract law, in particular Section 305 et seq. of the BGB. In this context, it is important to emphasize that according to German trademark law, the legal term 'license' only refers to genuine licenses, meaning that the licensor surrenders his trademark to the licensee for it to use as it has been registered.[27] It will not be seen as a license if the licensor has given consent to the licensee to use a sign that only appears to be identical or similar at random.[28]

---

24 Warenzeichengesetz of 5 May 1936, RGBl. II S. 134 (1936) [hereinafter WZG].
25 For examples of legislation, see the decisions of the Bundesgerichtshof (Federal Court of Germany, hereinafter BGH). *See* BGH, *Baader*, GRUR 363 (1973); BGH, *Peters*, GRUR 325 (1986).
26 *See* Axel Mittelstaedt, *Strategisches IP-Management*, GRUR-Prax 220 (2014) with further reference to the practical importance of using license agreements with regard to sustained corporate performance in Germany.
27 *See* the judgment to the former WZG. *See* BGH, *Micky-Maus-Orangen*, GRUR 485, 488 (1963).
28 *See* BGB, *supra* note 1, at Section 301.

16.21 On the other hand, Section 27(2) of the MarkenG states that the transfer of the whole of the undertaking does have effect on the trademark status. According to this provision, in case of doubt, it shall be presumed that the trademark passes to the transferee of the undertaking. Section 28 of the MarkenG provides the presumption of ownership as a consequence of the registration of the trademark in the register. Specifically, Section 28(1) of the MarkenG concerns the legal relationship in which registered trademarks are transferred, and the material ownership of rights does not concur with the formal registration in the Register. Section 28(1) of the MarkenG establishes the effect of legitimization of the trademark registration.

16.22 The assignment itself[29] is governed by the provision in the BGB on the transfer of claims, namely Section 389 of the BGB, which is applicable to 'other' rights by virtue of Section 413 BGB.[30] Unlike the rules concerning the transfer of CTMs,[31] in Germany, trademark rights are transferred by mere consensus of the parties – no act of publicity is required. For evidentiary reasons, however, it is advisable under German law to put the agreement in writing.[32] The fact that the German Trademark Register is afforded neither negative nor positive publicity fundamentally distinguishes the German approach to abandon the formal writing requirement in contract law. In turn, the Register tends to be rather generous in acknowledging validity of contracts which are not included in writing, which is in accordance with the civil law traditions in general. As a consequence, no third party may rely on the Register so that there is no room left for a bona fide acquisition of intellectual property and in particular trademark rights.

16.23 Unlike the copyright which cannot be transferred as such,[33] trademarks represent freely marketable assets under the German trademark transaction regime. Germany's Federal Constitutional Court (Bundesverfassungsgericht) (BVerfG) recognizes this important socioeconomic key position by highlighting the constitutional protection of the right of ownership in Article 14(1) of the GG and by distinguishing the protection of individual assets from the guarantee of protection under objective law provided under the competition

---

29 *See* BGB, *supra* note 1, at Section 389.
30 OLG Stuttgart 260, 261 NJWE-WettbR (1999).
31 CTMR, *supra* note 3, at Article 17(2) providing the writing requirement for Community trademark transfers. For further examination of the content of the register in the case of registered transactions, *see* KARL-HEINZ FEZER & REMBERT NIEBEL, HANDBUCH DER MARKENPRAXIS, Bd. II Markenvertragsrecht, mn. 779 (2011).
32 *See* AXEL NORDEMANN, JAN BERND NORDEMANN & ANKE NORDEMANN-SCHIFFEL, WETTBEWERBSRECHT-MARKENRECHT, mn. 1178 (11th ed. 2012).
33 *See* Urheberrechtsgesetz (German Copyright Act), Sec. 31(1) [hereinafter UrhG] (providing that the author may only grant exclusive or non-exclusive rights of use and exploitation).

rules.³⁴ Transferability and inheritability remain therefore important principles for trademark related transactions.³⁵

16.24 Furthermore, Section 29 of the MarkenG clarifies that the trademark may also be the subject of another right in rem, and that it may be subject to the enforcement of judgments and insolvency proceedings. The registration of in rem rights like usufruct (under Sections 1068(1), 1030, 1085 BGB) or pledges (under Section 1273 in conjunction with Sections 1228, 1235, 1247 BGB) is possible under Section 29(2) of the MarkenG and advisable, in order to prevent the trademark owner from partly or fully cancelling the trademark without the consent of the beneficiary of the in rem right, Section 48(2) of the MarkenG.

16.25 Section 31 of the MarkenG finally provides that the provisions of Sections 27–30 are also applicable to trademark applications. Additional provisions concerning the transfer in part of trademarks can be found in Sections 33–36 of the Trademark Regulation (MarkenV) and in Section 28 of the Ordinance Concerning the German Patent and Trade Mark Office (DPMAV).

4. The difference between transactions with regard to registered trademarks, company symbols, and titles of works

16.26 The MarkenG provides a unified national trademark protection system in Germany. In addition to trademarks under Section 1, No. 1, of the MarkenG, and geographical indications under Section 1, No. 3, of the MarkenG, the German trademark regime also covers protection in relation to commercial designations under Section 1, No. 2, of the MarkenG, which include company symbols and titles of works. Company symbols are pursuant to Section 5(2) of the MarkenG, which defines them as signs used in the course of trade as names, company names, or special designations of business establishments or enterprises. Section 5(3) instead defines titles of works as the names or special designations of printed publications, cinematographic works, musical works, dramatic works, software, or other comparable works. The legal requirements for these commercial designations were originally laid down in the area of unfair competition law, namely in Section 16 of the UWG (old version).³⁶ Any relevant case law and guiding principles adopted on this basis should be

---

34 BverfG, *Weinbergsrolle*, 51, BVerfGE 193; BverfG, *Esslinger Neckarhalde II*, 78, BVerfGE 58.
35 *See* Fezer, *supra* note 23, § 27, mn. 9, 39.
36 Gesetz gegen den unlauteren Wettbewerb of 7 June 1909 (Law on Unfair Competition), RGB 1. 499 (1909) [hereinafter UWG].

B. EXISTING LEGAL RULES ON TRADEMARK TRANSACTIONS IN GERMAN LAW

integrated in Sections 5 and 15 of the MarkenG, provided that this is not in conflict with the general principles of trademark law.[37]

Inherently distinctive commercial designations are generally protected throughout the whole federal territory of Germany.[38] This may be different, however, if the commercial activities of the company are geographically bound and are not aiming for expansion, as in the case of a single restaurant,[39] hotel,[40] or local retailers.[41] An entity that is transacting commercial designations in Germany must, therefore, ensure that the distribution system is not limited to specific geographical circles; the fact that the company in question is active on its presentation on the Internet does not necessarily mean that the relevant market is interregional.[42]

16.27

In accordance with their different nature, commercial designations identify different kinds of distinctive signs. Where trademarks identify the products and services of an undertaking from those of other undertakings, commercial designations constitute distinctive signs that identify the name of an undertaking as a whole, or function as its work titles.

16.28

This protection scheme has no equivalence in the CTMR. Here, the scope of protection is limited to registered trademarks. Accordingly, protection for the transferring of commercial designations originates directly in German law.[43] In regards to the establishment of the legal prerequisites and, in turn, the protection granted to these designations, the German Federal Supreme Court of Justice has clarified that EU law should always be duly taken into account in order to prevent diverging developments between those of registered trademarks and those of commercial designations.[44]

16.29

---

37 *See* the official justification for Sec. 5 MarkenG, BT-Drucks. 12/6581 from 14 January 1994, 64; for legislation on this issue *see* BGH, *Haus & Grund II*, GRUR 1104 (2008); BGH, *Buendgens*, GRUR 1164, 1165 (2001); BGH, *Altberliner*, GRUR 492, 493 (1999).
38 BGH, *Cambridge Institute*, GRUR 884 (2007); BGH, *soco.de*, GRUR 262, 263 (2005); BGH, *Altenburger Spielkarten*, GRUR 754, 757 (1995).
39 BGH, *Pic Nic*, GRUR 923, 924 (1993); BGH, *Rialto*, GRUR 155, 156 (1991).
40 BGH, *City Hotel*, GRUR 507, 508 (1995); BGH, *Hotel Krone*, GRUR 378, 379 (1984).
41 OLG Saarbrücken, *Bierstraße*, 62 NJWE-WettbR (1998).
42 BGH, *hufeland.de*, GRUR 159 (2006); BGH, *soco.de*, GRUR 263 (2005).
43 BGH, *Beta Layout*, 500, GRUR mn. 25 (2009); BGH, *Torres*, GRUR 825, 827 (1995), with further references.
44 BGH, *DB Immobilienfonds*, GRUR 344, 345 (2001). For trademark related examination of the jurisprudence of the CJEU *see* BGH, *Windsurfing Chiemsee*, BGH Bl. 210, 212 (2001).

16.30 This, in turn, has created a parallel approach between the scope of protection of company symbols and work titles and the scope of protection of registered trademarks. In particular, with respect to the claims of the right holder, one should refer to Sections 14, 15 and 18 et seq. of the MarkenG. Similarly, guidance for limits of protection can be found in Sections 20 et seq. of the MarkenG. This parallel approach does not apply, however, where the registered trademark has been legally considered as an asset that is independent from the company whose goods and services it labels. Still, when the mark is not considered as an independent asset, Section 27 of MarkenG applies the original principle of accessoriness between the business and its intellectual assets, according to which trademark protection could only be achieved in the case of the transfer of the whole business and which has been dropped for registered trademarks.[45] This principle remains essential in the context of distinctive signs under German trademark law.[46]

16.31 Certainly, under the German trademark law it could have been possible (likely via case law) to permit the transfer independently of the business, particularly in the light of the approximation of the different trademark rights. However, the overriding reason preventing the application of Section 27 et seq. of the MarkenG in these cases was the much closer bond of the company symbols with the businesses at issue.[47] Also, considering the fact that commercial designations only occur through concrete acts of use, and that these designations are specifically linked to the respective business, it appears appropriate to maintain the principle of dependent reciprocity.[48] Additionally, the close link and interaction between the rights holder and the company symbols is even more pronounced under the supplementary German rules of commercial law.[49] This difference of treatment between registered trademarks and company names has been declared admissible by the jurisprudence.[50] Separation of the company name from the undertaking may thus result in the invalidity of the sign.

---

45 *See* MarkenG, *supra* note 2, § 27.
46 BGH, *FROMMIA*, GRUR 972, 975 (2002); BGH, *Buendgens*, GRUR 1164, 1165 (2001).
47 REINHARD INGERL & CHRISTIAN ROHNKE, MARKENGESETZ KOMMENTAR, § 27 mn. 72 (3rd ed. 2010).
48 BGH, *FROMMIA*, GRUR 972, 975 (2002); BGH, *Buendgens*, GRUR 1164, 1165 (2001).
49 *See* Handelsgesetzbuch (HGB), §§ 30, 37 (2) (1897), with respect to the protection rules for the company name.
50 BGH, *Buendgens*, GRUR 1164, 1166 (2001); BGH, *FROMMIA*, GRUR 972, 974 (2002).

There is some disagreement in the case law and in the legal literature about the requirements for commercial transactions concerning work titles.[51] Although work titles are linked to a work, and not to a specific undertaking, German case law assumes that title rights will pass to the transferee only in connection with the rights of the respective work.[52] The voices to be found in the literature, however, prefer an isolated transaction system of title rights independent of the work itself. In particular, the literature stressed the significant practical need to allow the transfer of title rights of magazines to other publishers without the need to transfer the company or the work.[53] In this context, it became common to apply by analogy the same criteria as provided in Section 27(1) of the MarkenG.[54]

16.32

C. TRADEMARK TRANSACTIONS IN PRACTICE

1. Purchase agreements

Purchase agreements concerning trademarks follow the general rules of the purchase of other rights under German law. Since the introduction of the German Trade Mark Act (MarkenG), it has not been necessary to transfer the business operations with the transfer of the trademark. In other words: in Germany, trademarks are freely tradable assets.

16.33

German law differentiates, in respect to the transfer of a mark, between two legal transactions, first, a contract of obligation (Verpflichtungsgeschäft), with which the purchaser undertakes to transfer a mark, and second, a contract of disposal (Verfügungsgeschäft), with which the mark is then actually transferred. This disposal follows the rules of assignment (Section 398 of the BGB). Such a legal transaction is valid without any form requirement, meaning that the written form is not required and the transfer can occur by implication.

16.34

However, the subject matter of the transfer must be defined or definable; hence an obvious way would be to identify the number of the mark from the trademark register. In some cases, where large portfolios of marks are being

16.35

---

51 For a detailed examination of the dispute, *see* REINHARD INGERL & CHRISTIAN ROHNKE, KOMMENTAR, §§ 27–31 mn. 6 et seq.
52 BGH, *Verschenktexte I*, GRUR 218, 220 (1990).
53 Fezer, *supra* note 23, mn. 334, § 15; Eike Ullmann *in* FESTSCHRIFT FÜR MÜHLENDAHL, DER ERWERB DER RECHTE AN MARKE UND UNTERNEHMENSKENNZEICHEN 152 (Verena von Bomhard, Jochen Pagenberg, Detlef Schennen eds. 2005).
54 INGERL & ROHNKE, *supra* note 51, §§ 27–31, mn. 7.

transferred, specifying trademark numbers can be problematic. Where (non-registered) business names are subject to a purchase agreement the old rule still exists – they can only be sold together with the business itself. So it will be important to identify the assets of such business (for example, customer lists, price lists, know how) that will have to be transferred together with the business name in order to make it a binding purchase agreement.

2. License agreements

(a) General

16.36 In addition to the transfer of trademarks, the most common type of contractual arrangement involving marks is licensing. This type of contract is specially regulated in Section 30 of the MarkenG. With this contract, the trademark owner grants a third party the right to use his/her mark under particular conditions and in a particular scope. These types of agreements are also free of any form requirement under German law. In terms of their content, they follow common international standards.

16.37 Notably, these agreements contain provisions on the scope of the license (exclusive or non-exclusive), on the territorial extent of the license, the duration, but also, and in particular, on the content related restrictions of the license, meaning for what types of goods or services the marks may be used by the licensee. In addition, as in several other jurisdictions, licensing agreements contain provisions on the control of the quality of the goods or services produced or offered by the licensees, and also on the ability of licensors to effectively check this quality. Moreover, a license can be granted as an exclusive or a non-exclusive license. From a territorial standpoint, it can be granted for the whole territory of the Federal Republic of Germany, or only a part of it, according to Section 30(1) of the MarkenG.

16.38 In summary, the terms of these agreements tend to provide for a specific duration, form of use of the mark, the goods and/or services for which it shall be used, the territory of use, and the quality the goods or services shall have, as provided in Section 30(2), Nos. 1 to 5, of the MarkenG. If the licensee breaches the license agreement with respect to one of these aforementioned aspects, then the licensor can – next to a claim for breach of contract – also sue for trademark infringement, as per Section 30(2) of the MarkenG.

16.39 One of the primary obligations of the licensee is, of course, to pay the agreed license fee, which can be stipulated in the agreement as a flat rate amount, as volume-based or turnover-based royalties.

(b) Restrictions imposed by antitrust law

16.40 Even though German law adopts a liberal approach with respect to the terms of licensing agreements, these agreements are not fully exempted from the application of competition-related rules. In general, Germany offers attractive conditions for either forming or acquiring technology related companies, in particular Information Technology (IT) or IT-related companies. In this respect, it is indicative that four of the top ten European software developers and vendors, by revenue, are German, including SAP as one of the largest ones.[55] Still, this leading position for German undertakings in a technology-based environment also originates in a stable and predictable legal framework.

16.41 Notably, as of 1 May 2014, the Commission Regulation (EC) No 316/2014 of 21 March 2014 on the Application of Article 101(3) of the Treaty to Categories of Technology Transfer Agreements[56] (TTBER) came into effect.[57] It replaced the previous block exemption from 2004, and again set a 'safe harbour'[58] in which licensing agreements will not be challenged for antitrust reasons. This change may have been triggered, in part, by the fact that often licensors impose important restrictions as part of license agreements, for instance, as to the territory in which the licensee may use the trademark or other intellectual property rights.[59] Such restrictions may amount to restrictions of competition and have always been under antitrust scrutiny.

16.42 Notwithstanding the efforts to harmonize most of the intellectual property laws in the EU, the grant of intellectual property continues to be a matter for individual Member States. Even where the nature and scope of such rights are determined at the EU level, the rights themselves subsist and are enforced within national boundaries. Consequently, this is capable of conflicting with the EU's goal of market integration. On the other hand, certain licensing agreements are not simply anti-competitive, but, on the contrary, rather beneficial for consumers, as they spread information on technical innovation.[60]

---

55 Georg Licht & Eric A. Nerlinger, *New Technology-Based Firms in Germany – A Survey of the Recent Evidence*, ZEW DISCUSSION PAPERS, 2 et seq (1997).
56 Commission Regulation (EC) No 316/2014 of 21 March 2014 on the Application of Article 101(3) of the Treaty to Categories of Technology Transfer Agreements, 2014 O.J. (L 93) 17 [hereinafter TTBER].
57 The TTBER repealed Commission Regulation (EC) No 772/2004 of 27 April 2004 on the application of Article 81(3) of the Treaty to categories of technology transfer agreements, 2004 O.J. (L 123) 11.
58 *See* Gosta Schindler, *Wagging The Dog? Reconsidering Antitrust-Based Regulation of IP-Licensing*, 12 INTELLECTUAL PROPERTY L. REV. 49, 57 (2008).
59 Josef Drexl, *Die neue Gruppenfreistellungsverordnung für Technologietransfer-Vereinbarungen im Spannungsfeld von Ökonomisierung und Rechtssicherheit*, 716, 719 GRUR INT. (2004).
60 Commission Regulation (EC) No 316/2014 of 21 March 2014 on the Application of Article 101(3) of the Treaty to Categories of Technology Transfer Agreements, 2014 O.J. (L 93) 17, Recital 5.

Contracts promoting such static market efficiency are subject to the TTBER provisions.[61]

16.43 The TTBER renders Article 101(1) of the Treaty establishing the European Community[62] inapplicable on certain kinds of licensing agreements. Article 101(1) of the TFEU prohibits all agreements between undertakings that may affect trade between Member States, and which have as their object or effect the prevention, restriction, or distortion of competition within the common market. According to Article 101(3) of the TFEU, an agreement is exempt from the prohibition of Article 101(1) of the TFEU if it is beneficial to consumers. To benefit consumers, the agreement must ensure increased access to technology, and thus contribute to the improvement of production or distribution of goods.[63]

16.44 As can be seen from Article 1(1)(b) of the TTBER, the provisions of TTBER only cover license agreements concerning patents, know-how, mixed patent/know-how agreements, design rights, and software. In general, agreements relating to trademarks or copyright licensing are not covered by the TTBER.[64] In fact, pure trademark licenses are excluded; including those industrial franchise agreements that involve the supply of inputs produced know-how.[65] In any case, the trademark must not be the 'primary object' of the agreement, meaning products produced with the licensed technology.[66] The EU Commission established in the *Campari* case[67] that trademarks would be covered by the exemption where they are directly related to the exploitation of the licensed technology. On the other hand, trademark licenses can be covered by the regulation where they form part of a broader agreement involving the transfer of technology protected by patents, know-how, or license-agreement of software protected by copyright.

---

61 *See* Inger Berg Orstavik, *Technology Transfer Agreements: Grant-Backs and No-Challenge Clauses in the New EC Technology Transfer Regulation*, 36 INT'L. REV. INTELL. PROP. & COMP. L. 83 (2005) (with further references to Grant-Backs and No-Challenge Clauses in the TTBER). For a comparative perspective referencing to United States antitrust law, *see* Markus Feil, *The New Block Exemption Regulation on Technology Transfer Agreements in the Light of the U.S. Antitrust Regime on the Licensing of Intellectual Property*, 36 INT'L. REV. INTELL. PROP. & COMP. L 31 (2005).

62 Treaty Establishing the European Community, Official Journal C 325, P. 0033–0184 (2002) [hereinafter: ECT].

63 Fiona Carlin & Stephanie Pautke, *Last of Its Kind: The Review of the Technology Transfer Block Exemption Regulation*, The Symposium on European Competition Law, 24 NW. J. INT'L L. & BUS. 601, 603 (2003–2004).

64 Guidelines on the application of Article 81 of the EC Treaty to technology transfer agreements, 2005 O.J. (C 101) 2, 50.

65 *See* for further details NEIL J. WILKOF, TRADE MARK LICENSING 334 (2d ed. 2005).

66 TTBER, *supra* note 56, Art. 1(f).

67 Commission Decision 78/253/EEC, 1978 O.J. (L 70) 69.

16.45 However, the reliance on market share thresholds, and the fact that the party alleging legality of the agreement is – in contrast to national intellectual property laws, where the challenging party carries the burden of proof to establish invalidity or other improper conduct[68] – the one who is now in need of determining and evaluating all factors relevant for the analysis of Article 101(3) of the TFEU, has been widely criticized.[69] According to its Article 1(2), agreements that fall within the scope of Article 101(3) of the TFEU are now automatically legal, without prior evaluation by the Commission the undertakings bear a heavy burden of legal uncertainty. Some voices argue such a shift in the burden of proof might deter an intellectual property owner from licensing his rights.[70]

(c) License agreements and insolvency proceedings

16.46 A special problem can arise with respect to the protection of licensees in the case of insolvency of the licensor. In Germany, if a licensor becomes insolvent, the insolvency administrator has the right to choose, under Section 101 of the German Insolvency Act, whether he wishes to proceed with the continuing contractual obligation or not. It is predominantly accepted that licensing agreements constitute at least continuing obligations in this sense, if they are not exhausted in a one-time payment. This means, that the licensee is almost without any protection at all should the administrator refuse any further performance. In other words, in Germany, licensing agreements are generally not insolvency-proof. The issue has been recognized by the German legislator, which has twice attempted to regulate the situation under the law. Both legislative procedures failed. As a result, there is currently no absolutely secure solution in Germany for an insolvency proof licensing agreement. There is, however, currently a discussion on whether a general clause covering termination for cause and a limited transfer of licensing rights to the licensee in the case of termination could adequately safeguard the licensee.[71] However, the case law in question concerns software law, hence whether it can be transferred to general trademark licensing agreements remains to be seen.

---

68 *See* European Observatory on Counterfeiting and Piracy, Injunctions in Intellectual Property Rights, p. 7 (2009), *available 21 September 2015 at* http://ec.europa.eu/internal_market/iprenforcement/docs/injunctions_en.pdf.
69 Comments of the Max Planck Institute for Intellectual Property and Competition Law *Competition and Tax Law on the Draft Commission Block Exemption Regulation on Research and Development Agreements and the Draft Guidelines on Horizontal Cooperation Agreements* (2010), *available 21 September 2015 at* http://ec.europa.eu/competition/consultations/2010_horizontals/max_planck_institute_en.pdf.
70 *See* in particular Schindler, *supra* note 58, at 63.
71 BGH, *Softwarenutzungsrecht*, GRUR 435 (2006).

(d) Trademark infringements

16.47 Under German law, the licensee, even an exclusive one, is only entitled to file an action for infringement of the trademark right with the consent of the proprietor, Section 30(3) of the MarkenG. Under community trademark law, in contrast, Article 22(3) of the CTMR provides that the licensee is entitled to bring an action without consent if the trademark proprietor has not, upon request, itself brought an action within a reasonable time limit. This possibility does not exist under the MarkenG for national marks. Due to Section 30(3) of the MarkenG, which, unlike Article 22(3) of the CTMR, does not provide for action without consent, the consent can only be enforced, if the specific contractual provisions of the license agreement justify it. In this context, the trademark proprietor is also not entitled to impede the licensee in its commercial exploitation; an obligation to provide consent can therefore follow from this loyalty duty as resulting from Sections 241(2) and 242 of the BGB in conjunction with the license agreement.

16.48 The consent requirement already applies for a written notification stage (that is, cease and desist letter) and not only at the time of actual initiation of the court proceedings. The licensee can join the action of the trademark proprietor in order to assert claims based on its own damage suffered, Section 30(4) of the MarkenG. In the case of a trademark infringement action, which the licensee brings with the consent of the trademark proprietor, however, the licensee may only assert claims based on the damage suffered by the proprietor. The licensee is not entitled to any claims for damages of its own against the infringer. The BGH offsets the damage suffered by the licensee via the principle of set-off for damage suffered by third parties (Drittschadensliquidation) and a respective assignment under Section 398 of the BGB of the claim of the licensor to the licensee.

(e) Registration of a license

16.49 Under German trademark law, it is not possible to register any form of license with the German Patent and Trade Mark Office. Only the registration of in rem rights is possible under Section 29(2) of the MarkenG.[72] Contrary to that, under the Community trademark system, a license may be entered in the Register of the Community Trade Mark Office, and published upon request of one of the parties to the trademark license agreement, Article 22(5) of the CTMR. However, the registration of a license is not mandatory; if the license is not registered, this will have no effect on the license agreement.[73]

---

72 *See* Fezer, MarkenG, *supra* note 23, § 29, mn. 20–22.
73 *See* CTMR, *supra* note 3, Art. 22(5).

3. Coexistence agreements

(a) General

A coexistence agreement (Koexistenzvereinbarung) between holders of different trademark rights, which is just as commonplace in Germany as elsewhere, and is sometimes also called pre-right agreement (Vorrechtsvereinbarung) or differentiation agreement (Abgrenzungsvereinbarung), will be valid without any formal requirements, just like purchase and licensing agreements. However, such agreements only have the character of authorizations under the law of obligations; thus, they do not directly apply for and against a legal successor to whom the relevant mark is transferred. Therefore, such agreements usually contain clauses through which the parties undertake to impose respective requirements on their legal successors.

16.50

(b) Restrictions imposed by antitrust law

Coexistence agreements have to be viewed in relation to anti-trust law, too. German and also European antitrust law can be affected by a trademark coexistence agreement if the owners of the opposing trademarks agree to tolerate each other's trademarks, and to not attack the other's rights because the owner of the older mark, without such an obligation, could prevent the registration or the use of the younger mark. However, according to German case law and corresponding case law of the CJEU, such tolerance and no-challenge clauses are unobjectionable under antitrust law. Thus, such clauses are fully enforceable if the agreement has been concluded on the basis of serious and objective reasons that the conflicting trademarks may be confusingly similar, so that the parties taking into account their specific interests, and also the subject matter of the intellectual property rights in question, could adequately settle the dispute without running into a conflict with antitrust law.[74] Only if such clauses in trademark differentiation agreements also include any allocation of customers or of the market, do they become objectionable under antitrust law.[75]

16.51

Therefore, in order to avoid challenges of the validity of a coexistence agreement, it should quite clearly be shown that there had been serious and objective arguments that the trademarks involved were confusingly similar, and that a serious trademarks conflict had arisen. Furthermore, the parties

16.52

---

[74] See CJEU, *Toltecs/Dorcet II*, 399, GRUR Int. (1985); BGH, *Jette Joop*, 641, GRUR 642 mn. 19 (2011); BGH, *Heilquelle*, WUW/E 1385 (1975).
[75] See CJEU, *Toltecs/Dorcet II*, 399, GRUR Int. (1985); BGH, *Jette Joop*, GRUR 641, 642 mn. 19 (2011).

should always limit the scope of their mutual obligations to allow a solution of their trademarks conflict as such without any allocation of customers or markets.

(c) Applicable law

16.53 In practice, coexistence agreements often do not contain a provision on the applicable law. In such case, the applicable law is normally determined looking at the conflicts of law rules based upon the venue of the court. Presuming that the court would be in Germany, German conflict of law rules would apply.

16.54 As a general rule, German conflict of laws rules are universal. In other words, they apply whether they lead to the application of German or any other national law. Conflicts of law for contracts are currently determined by the European Union Regulation No. 593/2008 of 17 June 2008 on the law applicable to contractual obligations (Rome I Regulation).[76] However, according to Article 28 of the Rome I Regulation, these rules only apply to contracts concluded after 17 December 2009. For contracts concluded before this date, Articles 27 and 28 of the Introductory Law to the BGB (EGBGB) apply to contracts concluded on or after 1 September 1986.[77] However, both rules have the same effect, namely, they provide that the national law of the country with which the contract has the closest links will be applied.[78]

16.55 For contracts concluded and fulfilled before 1 September 1986, general (case law) conflict of law rules applicable to contracts will apply also to coexistence agreements. There is only very limited case law – and no Supreme Court decision – on the question as to whether a contract concluded before 1986, but stipulating continuing obligations, should be subject to the law determined by the conflict of law rules at the time of its signature, or whether the applicable law may be determined by conflict of law rules coming into effect at a later date (and without any specific intervention of the parties). The one published decision by the Court of Appeal of Koblenz opts in favour of the conflict of law rules applicable at the time of signature.[79]

16.56 Still, German conflict of law applicable to contracts concluded before the 1986 reform generally applied a multitude of elements to determine the (geographical) center of gravity of a contract. This method was very close – and led to

---

[76] Regulation (EC) No. 593/2008 of the European Parliament and of the Council of 17 June 2008 on the law applicable to contractual obligations (Rome I), 2008 O.J. (L 177) 6 [hereinafter Rome I].
[77] Introductory Act to the German Civil Code, Einführungsgesetz zum Bürgerlichen Gesetzbuch (EGBGB) BGBl I p. 2494 (1994).
[78] Compare Rome I, *supra* note 76, at Article 2 with German EGBGB, *supra* note 77, at Article 3 & 4.
[79] *See* OLG Koblenz 935, 936 Recht der Internationalen Wirtschaft [hereinafter RIW] (1993).

identical results in the large majority of cases – to the rules in Article 28, Paragraph 1 EGBGB and, currently, in Article 4, Paragraph 4 of the Rome I Regulation, that is applying the national law of the country with which the contract has the closest links.[80] If, for example, a German and a foreign entity, or even two foreign entities, conclude a coexistence agreement in order to settle a trademark conflict that has arisen in Germany because an earlier German trademark has been enforced in an opposition proceeding against a younger German trademark registration, the coexistence agreement should, in most cases, have the closest links to Germany, so that a German court would apply German law.

16.57 Independent of the specific applicable law to the agreement, German law may apply to specific issues of the agreement in case of overriding mandatory provisions by virtue of Article 9 of the Rome I Regulation. Such overriding mandatory provisions may be, for example, found in German antitrust law. These mandatory provisions will only override the law applicable to the agreement regarding the specific points that the mandatory provisions cover. Therefore, if, for example, Japanese law would apply to a coexistence agreement, Japanese law would be applicable to the agreement as such, whereas German antitrust law may apply to the specific provision having effect on the German market.

4. Trademarks in mergers and acquisitions transactions

16.58 Provisions covering trademark rights can often be found in separate sections of agreements governing larger merger and acquisitions transactions, whether they are asset deals or share deals.

16.59 As a rule, these are the so-called representations and warranties. In this context, there are no peculiarities to Germany compared to international standard practice. However, in respect to the certainly complex legal situation concerning earlier marks, one must be cautious before issuing comprehensive guarantees regardless of negligence or fault in respect of the transferred trademark rights. While it is true that trademark rights are somewhat easier to search than, for example, patents, absolute certainty can usually not be achieved as a result of such search, so that absolute guarantees, irrespective of

---

80 See PALANDT-THORN, BÜRGERLICHES GESETZBUCH, KOMMENTAR (74th ed. 2015), Einl v. EGBGB (IPR), mn. 21; Anke Nordemann-Schiffel *in* FRIEDRICH K FROMM, AXEL NORDEMANN, JAN BERND NORDEMANN, WILHELM NORDEMANN, URHEBERRECHT, KOMMENTAR §§ 120ff mn 82 (11th ed. 2014).

negligence or fault, certainly represent a risk. This applies, in particular, if the scope of such guarantees extends to include the owners of the business personally.

16.60 In the case of standard contractual agreements that are considered to be general terms and conditions of business in Germany, one must also take into account that restrictions of liability are only possible to a limited extent according to the law governing terms and conditions in Germany. Similarly, there are limits to guarantees in terms and conditions that are issued irrespective of negligence or fault.

5. Trademarks as securities

16.61 Trademark rights can also be used as securities for the purpose of obtaining financial credit. Section 29 of the MarkenG expressly reflects this possibility.[81] In practice, the relevant mechanisms to use trademarks are securities which are called 'pledges' or 'security assignments' (transfers by way of security) of entire trademark portfolios. While credit institutions primarily use a pledge or lien for securing a financial credit, security assignments are far more common in the area of private equity financing deals.

16.62 Both contractual agreements are possible without formal requirements. However, pledges can also be noted in the Trademark Register. Pledges differ from security assignments in that the former must be enforced through a somewhat more complicated procedure involving mandatory enforcement through a bailiff; ultimately meaning that the trademark rights are auctioned off. This is one of the reasons that security assignments, which are nothing more than a de facto transfer of ownership in trust of marks, are preferred.

16.63 Alongside pledges and security assignments, German law also provides for the possibility of establishing a right of usufruct (a right to use without owning the property under civil law). In this instance, the owner grants a third party the right to use the asset, that is, the trademark right, without transferring the actual ownership of it. The registration of in rem rights, like usufruct or pledges, is possible under Section 29(2) of the MarkenG and often it is advisable, in order to prevent the trademark owner from partly or fully cancelling the trademark without the consent of the beneficiary of the in rem right, Section 48(2) of the MarkenG.

---

81 *See also* Fezer, MarkenG, *supra* note 23, § 29, mn. 20–22.

D. CONCLUSION

Existing legal rules on trademark transactions under German law cover the wide variety of transactions that exist in practice. As explained in this Chapter, the legal framework of EU and German trademark law, as well as implications from German General Civil Code and antitrust law, provide for the necessary legal structure that shall govern trademark transactions in Germany. Moreover, a wide variety of legal questions may arise, in practice, with respect to coexistence agreements, restrictions imposed by antitrust law, and instances in which trademarks are used as securities. **16.64**

17

FRENCH PERSPECTIVES ON TRADEMARK TRANSACTIONS: FROM THE CIVIL CODE TO THE BUSINESS LAW?[*]

Nicolas Binctin[**]

A. INTRODUCTION	17.01	2. Transfer of trademark	17.42
B. CONTRACTUAL FREEDOM	17.06	D. TAX CONSIDERATIONS AND	
1. General principles of contract law	17.07	TRADEMARK TRANSACTIONS	17.46
(a) Trademark assignment	17.08	1. Trademark operations for free	17.49
(b) Trademark licensing	17.13	2. The tax qualification of a trademark	
2. Specific dispositions	17.23	license as an asset	17.52
		3. Tax influence on a merger and	
C. THE TRADEMARK AS AN ELEMENT OF THE *FONDS DE COMMERCE*	17.32	acquisition qualification	17.54
1. Trademark and securities	17.33	E. CONCLUSION	17.57

A. INTRODUCTION

17.01 This chapter focuses on the analysis of the French perspective regarding trademark transactions. It is important to note in the beginning that French trademark law currently follows the general principles set forward by European Union (EU) law. In addition, the interpretation of French trademark law is directly influenced by the decisions of the Court of Justice of the European Union (ECJ) in this area. Presenting a French perspective on trademark law and trademark transactions can, therefore, be difficult in a legal environment that is less and less national and is, instead, harmonized throughout the EU. In fact, while there is certainly a European perspective on the issue, the question may now be whether there is still one from a national perspective, in this case a French perspective.

17.02 Still, despite the process of EU harmonization, some elements of the trademark law remain clearly outside the realm of EU influence. This is true, in

---

[*] The text of this chapter has been adapted by the editors.
[**] Professor, Faculty of Law, Université de Poitiers.

particular, for the rules on trademark transactions. More specifically, EU trademark law establishes the principle that a trademark can be assigned or licensed.[1] But, the legal conditions under which trademarks are assigned or licensed are not directly established by EU law. Of course, any assignment or licensing agreement has to be in compliance with the EU competition law,[2] but the substantial conditions of these agreements continue to be regulated under French contract law. In this respect, in the EU, we are still waiting for the possible adoption of common principles of EU contract law, which could later impact transactions of intellectual property-related products in the EU.[3]

17.03 Because contract law is still regulated by national laws, we can, thus, refer to a French perspective on trademark transactions. Moreover, because French trademark law as harmonized includes few specific provisions relating to trademark transactions, the general principles of the French Civil Code apply to trademark transactions. In particular, the general principle of French contract law applies to the acts of selling, licensing, or using a trademark as an 'in kind' contribution or security for the incorporation of a company or to secure financial support by banks or venture capitalists.[4] Accordingly, presenting the French perspectives on trademark transactions ultimately results in presenting the interaction and relationship between the general principles of French contract law and those of trademark law.

17.04 The first part of this Chapter focuses on an analysis of contractual freedom as it relates to trademark transactions. Further, however, as a trademark is one of the main elements of a business. Notably, French commercial law has developed a specific concept for the legal analysis of the business: the *fonds de commerce*. In particular, the *fonds de commerce* is:

> A body of corporeal elements (equipment, machinery, commercial goods, merchandise) and incorporeals (right to lease, name, sign, patents and trademarks, goodwill), which belong to a merchant or to a manufacturer and gathered together to enable him to exercise his activity. This body constitutes a universality of assets and is treated as an incorporeal movable subject to specific rules (notably in case of sale or pledge).[5]

---

1   European Parliament and Council Directive 2008/95 to Approximate the Laws of the Member States Relating to Trade Marks, 2008 O.J. (L 299) 25 (EC) replacing Council Directive 89/104, 1989 O.J. (L 40) 1 (EEC).
2   CONSOLIDATED VERSION OF THE TREATY ON THE FUNCTIONING OF THE EUROPEAN UNION art. 81, 10 October 2012, 2012 O.J. (c 326) 47 [hereinafter TFEU]; *see also* TFEU art. 102.
3   Nicolas Binctin, *Le Droit Européen de la Vente et la Propriété Intellectuelle*, *in* LES CONTRATS DE LA PROPRIÉTÉ INTELLECTUELLE 101 (Jean-Michel Bruguière ed. 2013).
4   CODE CIVIL, Title III (Fr.) [hereinafter FCC] (official translation *available 22 September 2015 at* http://www.legifrance.gouv.fr/Traductions/en-English/Legifrance-translations).
5   GÉRARD CORNU, DICTIONARY OF THE CIVIL CODE, *Fonds de Commerce* (2014); *see also* DICTIONNAIRE DU DROIT PRIVÉ, *Définition de Fonds de Commerce*, (2015), *available 22 September 2015 at* http://

Accordingly, the French perspective on trademark transactions includes addressing the analysis of these transactions from the viewpoint that a trademark is an element of the *fonds de commerce* (which can be translated with the corresponding legal concept of 'business' in English). A typical question in this respect is whether a trademark can be sold without the *fonds de commerce*, in other words, without the business to which the mark refers. This question was discussed at length, especially before the adoption of the Agreement on Trade Related Aspects of Intellectual Property Rights (TRIPS).[6] Today, following the general principle of Article 21 of TRIPS,[7] Article L. 714–1 of the French Code of Intellectual Property or *Code de la Propriété Intellectuelle*, (CPI) provides that '[t]he rights under a mark may be transferred in whole or in part, independently of the company that exploits them or has them exploited'.[8] This clarifies that a trademark can be included in a transaction without the *fonds de commerce*. Still, in some cases, a trademark requires some connection with the *fonds de commerce* in order to be assigned or licensed. Therefore, the analysis of the *fonds de commerce* in this chapter will offer some specific and complementary approaches to the French perspectives on trademark transactions.

17.05 Furthermore, since a trademark is a specific intangible asset, which may represent an important part of the value of a company, trademark transactions may also be subjected to the application of tax law. Thus, tax-related considerations are of fundamental importance in structuring and practice of trademark transactions. These tax-related considerations will be addressed in the final section of this chapter with an emphasis on examining the influence of tax law on the choice, structure, and details of trademark transactions.

B. CONTRACTUAL FREEDOM

17.06 Under French trademark law, a trademark is a property,[9] an intangible asset, which can be the subject of any contract that deals with goods. Therefore, in a

---

www.dictionnaire-juridique.com/definition/fonds-de-commerce.php. The concept of *fonds du commerce* corresponds to the concept of 'tangible and intangible goodwill' in common law jurisdictions.

6 *See generally* AGREEMENT ON TRADE-RELATED ASPECTS OF INTELLECTUAL PROPERTY RIGHTS, 15 April 1994, Marrakesh Agreement Establishing the World Trade Organization, Annex 1C, LEGAL INSTRUMENTS – RESULT OF THE URUGUAY ROUNDS Vol. 31, 33 I.L.M. 83 (1994) [hereinafter TRIPS].

7 *Id.* at Article 21.

8 CODE DE LA PROPRIÉTÉ INTELLECTUELLE, Article L714-1 (Fr.) [hereinafter CPI] (official translation available 22 September 2015 at http://www.legifrance.gouv.fr/affichCodeArticle.do;jsessionid=F886C02 DDBAE48F100E0DB9C05583774.tpdjo11v_3?idArticle=LEGIARTI000006279716&cidTexte=LEGIT EXT000006069414; http://www.wipo.int/wipolex/en/text.jsp?file_id=179120).

9 NICOLAS BINCTIN, DROIT DE LA PROPRIÉTÉ INTELLECTUELLE 702 (3rd ed. 2014).

B. CONTRACTUAL FREEDOM

situation involving a trademark transaction, the contract simply needs to address the intangible nature of the trademark. In such a situation, the basic principle of contractual freedom in France is applied, as described in Part B.1 below. But, trademark law has specific requirements that have to be followed for trademark transactions to be valid, as explained in Part B.2 below.

1. General principles of contract law

17.07 The CPI states that the owner of a trademark can transfer or license the rights in the trademark either on an exclusive or non-exclusive basis, as well as in whole or in part.[10] To perform these transactions, the trademark owner has to refer to the general principle of French contract law. French contract law is built on the principle of freedom of contract. Even if the law provides some model agreements, the parties are not bound by them and can draft their own terms of contract, and thus develop different and alternative models. The major limits to contractual freedom are public order and competition law.[11] In other words, the assignment and the license of a trademark can be structured broadly, and generally under an open legal framework.[12] In particular, any of the three principal types of trademark transactions (that is, the assignment, the license, and the use of the intellectual property as collateral) can be designed to respond to the specific needs of the parties in the transaction, based on the circumstances of each individual case, ranging from a very simple assignment to a very complex operation such as using the mark as security or collateral for securing financing or venture capital.[13]

(a) Trademark assignment

17.08 With respect to a trademark assignment, an assignment is perfected and the ownership of a trademark is transferred when the parties agree on the property to be transferred and the price to be paid for the transfer.[14] This assignment occurs even if the property has not yet been delivered and the price has not yet been paid.[15] In regard to trademark transactions, the only specific French sale law requirement is that the agreement at issue must be in writing. Furthermore, the price has to be either determined and stated in the contract or

---

10   CPI, *supra* note 8, at art. L. 714–1. 'The rights under a mark may be transferred in whole or in part ... the rights under a mark may be wholly or partially licensed on an exclusive or non-exclusive basis or pledged.' *Id.*
11   Jacques Raynard, *Aspects civilistes des contrats de transfert de technique*, in LES CONTRATS DE LA PROPRIÉTÉ INTELLECTUELLE 9 (Jean-Michel Bruguière ed, 2013).
12   *See* WILLIAM DROSS, CLAUSIER – DICTIONNAIRE DES CLAUSES ORDINAIRES ET EXTRAORDINAIRES DES CONTRATS DE DROIT PRIVÉ INTERNE (2nd ed., 2011); GENEVIÈVE HELLERINGER, LES CLAUSES DU CONTRAT – ESSAI DE TYPOLOGIE 536 (2012).
13   FCC, *supra* note 4, at Title VI.
14   *Id.* at art. 1583.
15   *Id.*

determinable, meaning that the price has to be comparative to the value of the trademark and more than a symbolic gesture.[16] When a trademark is the subject of an assignment contract, the general provisions of contract law apply directly to the assignment. This means that the assignment of a trademark is treated like an ordinary sale of property. The parties to the agreement have to have legal capacity and be able to sell the property at issue.[17] If there is joint ownership of the property by more than one party, the capacity of all parties has to be established according to the general principles of French contract law or based on an undivided ownership agreement.[18]

17.09 In this respect, it is important to distinguish between the assignment of a trademark and the sale of a part of the undivided ownership. Only the assignment part of the transaction needs to follow the principles provided by trademark law. Furthermore, the priority right is not an accessory of the trademark, thus, the transfer of the priority right has to be included in the assignment agreement explicitly or it could be assigned on its own.[19] In case of the absence of a specific indication in this respect, the seller continues to own the priority right.[20] If there is a trademark co-existence agreement, the co-existence agreement has to be included in the conditions of the assignment to remain in force after the assignment is perfected. It is possible that the co-existence agreement can ultimately affect the validity of the assignment of a trademark. If the assigned trademark is later involved in an infringement proceeding, the assignment can include the transfer of the judicial action. Still, this has to be explicitly mentioned in the agreement.

17.10 The major developments involving trademark assignment laws in France comes from case law. The French Court of Cassation has abandoned the *numerus clausus* doctrine, which applies to real property rights.[21] It means that, based on the principle of contractual freedom, it is possible to sell any kind of quasi-property right on a trademark and to enter into any kind of division or sub-division of the right of ownership on a given trademark. Moreover, one can not only transfer the full ownership, but also some isolated elements of a trademark. For example, one can transfer the right in a mark only with respect

---

16 *Id.* at Title VI, art. 1591.
17 *Id.* at Title II, art. 1123.
18 FCC, *supra* note 4, art 1123.
19 *Id.* at Title VIII, art. 1692.
20 Cour de Cassation [Cass.] [Court of Cassation] com., 18 June 1996, Bull. civ. IV, No. 94–44654 (Fr.); Cours d'appel [CA] [Regional Court of Appeal] Paris, 11 May 1987, JCP E. 1988, No. 69, obs. Jean-Jacques Burst et Jean Marc Mousseron.
21 Anna di Robilant, *Property and Deliberation. The Numerus Clausus Principle, New Property Forms and New Propery Values*, AMERICAN J. COMP. L. 7 (2014); *see also* Cour de Cassation [Cass.] [Court of Cassation] req., Feb. 13, 1834 S. Jur. 1 (Fr.).

to some of the goods and services for which the trademark is registered.[22] In such cases, the subject-matter of the agreement is the conventional property right in the mark. The agreement, and the transfer, can be either temporary or permanent.[23] All in all, the conditions set by the parties in these agreements can be a great area for contractual creativity.[24]

For any assignment, the price stipulated between the parties can be an inclusive price, which can be paid in a lump sum or in several instalments, or the price can also be a fully proportional price.[25] It can also be both (that is, a part of the price is an inclusive price and the other part is proportional). In case of a proportional price, the assignment agreement has to define the basis and the rate for calculating this part of the price.[26]   **17.11**

For the warranties, the general provisions set forth in the French Civil Code apply.[27] Where the assignment agreement is stipulated amongst professionals, warranties can be excluded. A deal is done by professionals when it involves persons who are acting in their professional capacity.[28] If there are only business entities in the agreement, the agreement is always the result of a professional operation. To the contrary, if there is even a single individual as a party to the agreement, then the purpose of the agreement needs to be determined to ensure that the agreement is not a consumer agreement or a non-professional act.   **17.12**

(b) Trademark licensing

An approach similar to the one described for trademark assignments is also followed for trademark licensing. A trademark licensing agreement is similar   **17.13**

---

22 *See generally,* CPI, *supra* note 8.
23 R. Charles Henn Jr., et al., *Trademark Licensing Basics, Intellectual Property Desk Reference,* Kilpatrick Stockton LLP, 69, *available 22 September 2015 at* https://clients.kilpatricktownsend.com/IPDeskReference/Documents/Trademark%20Licensing%20Basics.pdf.
24 Louis d'Avout, *Démembrement de propriété, perpétuité et liberté,* 29 RECUEIL DALLOZ, 1934 (23 May 2012); Thierry Revet, *Propriété et droits réels,* 3 REVUE TRIMESTRIELLE DE DROIT CIVIL 2012, 549 (23 May 2012); William Dross, *La perpétuité des droits réels sui generis,* LA SEMAINE JURIDIQUE EDITION GÉNÉRALE 930 (3 September 2012); Frédéric Danos, *Perpétuité, droits réels sur la chose d'autrui et droit de superficie,* RÉPERTOIRE DEFRÉNOIS, 15 November 2012, at 1067; Louis d'Avout & Blandine Mallet-Bricout, *La liberté de création des droits réels aujourd'hui,* 1 RECUEIL DALLOZ 53 (31 October 2012).
25 Henn Jr. et al., *supra* note 23, at 71.
26 *Id.*
27 FCC, *supra* note 4, at art. 1641.
28 *See generally id.* at ch. IV, § 3, sub-section 3; *see also* Eloise Roca et al., *No-Warranty Clauses in Europe,* ASSOCIATION OF CORPORATE COUNSEL (25 March 2013), *available 22 September 2015 at* http://www.acc.com/legalresources/quickcounsel/nwce.cfm.

to a rental agreement, that is, a lease on an intangible property.[29] In the absence of specific provisions under French sale law, the general principles applied to leasing apply, which can be found in the French Civil Code.[30] The general principles of French lease law are similar to the general principles of French sales law. The main difference between the two principles is that there is no ownership transfer involved in a trademark licensing agreement. And, in terms of determining the capacity and the undivided ownership, the rules for licensing are the same as the sales rules. In the case of a sub-license, the licensor can be a tenant himself. French intellectual property law has no specific rules on sub-licensing. The common French contract law leaves the possibility of sub-license agreements to be determined by the parties during negotiations. The licensor can either agree or prohibit the licensee from granting sub-licenses. If the licensor allows the licensee to sub-license, the sub-license is limited to the terms and scope of the original license agreement.[31]

17.14 The license can either cover all or only some of the economical uses of a trademark, and, similarly, the license can cover one or several territories.[32] Furthermore, the license can be granted for either a limited or unlimited duration,[33] which is an important distinction because the duration of the license agreement influences the termination conditions. The license agreement can include or exclude any element and/or economical use depending on the licensee's interests and the licensor's strategy.

17.15 One of the main questions involved in a licensing agreement is exclusivity. French law allows the parties freedom to negotiate a license agreement with territorial and/or product exclusivity.[34] The legality of exclusivity is a question of competition law rather than contract law. The ECJ assesses the exclusivity of a license in the Treaty on the Functioning of the European Union.[35] There is no specific French provision on this issue.

---

29 Jacques Raynard, *De l'originialité de la licence de brevet en tant que louage de chose*, in LE DROIT DE LA PROPRIÉTÉ INTELLECTUELLE DANS UN MONDE GLOBALISÉ – MÉLANGES EN L'HONNEUR DU PROFESSEUR JOANNA SCHMIDT-SZALEWSKI 267 (Christophe Geiger ed. 2014).
30 FCC, *supra* note 4, art. 1708.
31 Henn Jr., et al., *supra* note 23, at 71, 73.
32 CPI, *supra* note 8; Henn Jr. et al., *supra* note 23, at 70–71.
33 Marie-Elodié Ancel, *La clause de durée dans les contrats de licence de marque*, COMMUNICATION COMMERCE ELECTRONIQUE 9 (2012).
34 CPI, *supra* note 8.
35 Case C-403/08 and C-429/08, Football Association Premier League and Others v. QC Leisure and Others [2011] ECR I-09083; *see also* Consolidated Version of the Treaty on the Functioning of the European Union, Article 101, 2012 O.J. (C 326) 47 (EN).

17.16 The license can be for free or can include royalty payments to the licensor. The royalties are defined broadly as either a fixed or proportional rate, meaning that the royalty is proportional to any element of the business as defined in the licensing agreement.[36] Moreover, the rate can be adjusted and the agreement can include a minimum amount guaranteed.[37] According to the ECJ case law, the basis of the rate has to be in accordance with the use of the trademark.[38] However, the royalties are based on the existence of the trademark, so, when the trademark enters into the public domain, the licensing agreement is no longer valid because the trademark is no longer owned by the licensor. But, the parties can include in the license agreement a provision relating to the payment of royalties after the trademark has entered the public domain. In the event that the trademark enters the public domain, because the royalty payments began prior to the trademark entering the public domain and were based on the use of the trademark, the royalty payments will continue until the date specified in the agreement. The agreement must specify the payment terms and conditions, the necessary amount of control exercised by the licensor over the licensee's use of the trademark, and all the technical dispositions of the license.[39]

17.17 The warranties included in the license agreement are similar to the ones included in the sale contract for the existence of the good, the existence of the ownership, and the qualities of the trademark.[40] Certain special warranties may be added in a license agreement. Many license agreements include a warranty covering the mismanagement of the trademark by the licensor.[41] For example, the licensor warrants to pay all the taxes necessary to maintain the trademark in the license area. If the licensor does not comply with this warranty, the licensor has to cover the licensee's damages.

17.18 The relationship between the transfer of a license and the licensed trademark is an important question under French Law. The licensor can assign the licensed trademark to a third party without being in conflict with the provisions of the French Civil Code.[42] The assignment of the trademark is possible as long as the parties have fulfilled and continue to fulfill their

---

36 Henn Jr. et al., *supra* note 23, at 71.
37 *Id.*
38 Case C-193/83, Windsurfing International Inc. v. Commission [1986] ECR 611. For observations on the case, *see* Gorges Bonet, *Propriétés intellectuelles*, REVUE TRIMESTRIELLE DE DROIT EUROPÉEN 313 (1987).
39 *See generally,* Henn Jr. et al., *supra* note 23.
40 Yan Basire, *Les clauses de non-garantie dans les contrats de licence de brevet*, PROPRIÉTÉ INDUSTRIELLE (Jan. 2012, No. 1).
41 CPI, *supra* note 8, at L714–6; *see also* FCC, *supra* note 4, at art. 1645.
42 FCC, *supra* note 4, at art. 1237. 'The obligation to do cannot be performed by a third party against the will of the obligee-creditor, when the latter has an interest in having it performed by the obligor-debtor himself.' *Id.*

obligations under the license agreement. The trademark buyer must respect the license agreement finalized before the transfer and perform all the obligations of the licensor under the agreement. The trademark buyer also has to respect the licensee's position under the agreement. But, if the license agreement provides for certain personal obligations (*intuitus personae*) of the licensor, the transfer of the licensed trademark can be limited. If those commitments are not *intuitus personae*, like, for example, to pay the taxes, the trademark buyer has to perform them. But, if there are some *intuitus personae* obligations in the license agreement, for example, to transfer special knowledge about the trademark to the buyer, the licensor cannot transfer the ownership of the trademark unless the licensor has received prior authorization from the licensee. In general, the transfer of the trademark license can be achieved in the French legal system, as a kind of sale; the buyer is taking the contractual place of the seller.[43] To secure such a transaction, it is best to explicitly include a provision in the license agreement regarding the possible sale of the trademark.

17.19 Under a trademark license, the licensor is liable for any defective good in the market bearing the trademark under the liability for defective goods provided for by the EU Product Liability Directive.[44] The licensor is identified as the producer of the goods associated with the trademark according to the Product Liability Directive because the trademark is used to identify the producer of the goods,[45] and, thus, the license makes the trademark owner liable on this basis.

17.20 The licensee also has to perform obligations under the agreement. Particularly, the licensee has to use the licensed trademark.[46] The use of the trademark is a condition for the continued ownership of the trademark. If the licensee does not use the trademark in the course of business, the licensor may lose the trademark as a result.[47] Under the French Civil Code, the obligation on the licensee to use the trademark in the course of business is not an obligation that the licensee's use of the trademark be successful, but simply that the licensee has to use the trademark (*obligation de faire*).[48] This requirement is included to

---

43 *See* LAURENT AYNES, LA CESSION DE CONTRATS ET LES OPÉRATIONS JURIDIQUES À TROIS PERSONNES (1984); NICOLAS BINCTIN, LE CAPITAL INTELLECTUEL 123 (2007).
44 Council Directive 85/374/EEC on the Approximation of the Laws, Regulations and Administrative Provisions of the Member States Concerning Liability for Defective Products, 1985 O.J. (L 210) (EC). The liability is applied in case of exploitation of a product; the license is a kind of exploitation.
45 *Id.*; *see also* FCC, *supra* note 4, at art. 1386–6.
46 DENISE BAUMANN, L'OBLIGATION D'EXPLOITER LES MARQUES EN DROIT FRANÇAIS ET ALLEMAND – ÉTUDE COMPARATIVE 14 (1978).
47 CPI, *supra* note 8, at art. L714–5.
48 FCC, *supra* note 4, at art. 1142.

protect the licensor from losing ownership over the trademark because of the licensee's failure to use the trademark. According to the ECJ case law, the licensee has to use the trademark in accordance with the business habits of the licensee.[49] The licensee's obligation to use the trademark is also in line with a proportional royalty scheme if the license is negotiated and agreed on such a business model.[50] When the royalty is proportional to the use of the trademark, the licensee has the obligation to use the trademark.

17.21 For the use of a trademark as an 'in kind' contribution for incorporating or for securing collateral for loans, there is no legal limit under French law.[51] The incorporation act can be structured as a sale or a license, for a long or short period, and with or without exclusivity. The incorporation act is able to adapt any kind of contractual operation, like a trademark assignment or licensing agreement. The incorporation act simply exchanges the money for a counterpart of stocks. If there is an ownership transfer through the incorporation, the company becomes the owner of the trademark. In the case of incorporation that is limited to a license, the licensor remains the owner of the trademark, not the company, and a standard license agreement, as discussed above, between the licensor and the company has to occur.[52] If the incorporation is for a short or limited period, for example, two years, the company no longer has the right to use the trademark after the term of the license agreement has expired, but the trademark owner partner remains a stockholder in the company.

17.22 Different types of trademark transactions can be involved in such agreements according to French contract law. Of course, a French trademark can be the object of a sale, assignment, or licensing agreement, but any EU trademark is also able to be the subject of a trademark transaction. In addition to French and EU trademarks, any trademark in the world can be the subject of a trademark transaction that is governed by French law.[53] The contractual freedom of the parties to negotiate and determine the governing law of the agreement is important to expressly include agreement, especially if elements of the agreement can create conflicts in different countries. For example, any trademark transaction can be governed by French law, but any French trademark can also be the subject of a foreign trademark transaction and

---

49 CPI, *supra* note 8, at art. L714–5.
50 Jacques Raynard, *Clause d'Obligation d'Exploitation Insérée dans une Cession de Brevet*, PROPRIÉTÉ INDUSTRIELLE 20–21 (1 January 2003, No. 1).
51 About the incorporation of intellectual goods in the French Law, for a global study, *see* Binctin, *supra* note 43, at 75.
52 Henn Jr. et al., *supra* note 23, at 69.
53 IP IN BUSINESS TRANSACTIONS: FRANCE OVERVIEW (1 March 2012), *available 22 September 2015 at* http://uk.practicallaw.com/6-501-8761?q=&qp=&qo=&qe=.

subject to foreign laws. It will be the same question for the issue of jurisdiction. Contracting parties may designate either French Courts or foreign ones for a French or EU trademark transaction. They can also consider an arbitral jurisdiction. The only limit to the jurisdiction of a foreign court or an arbitral jurisdiction for a trademark generally lies in the disputes concerning the validity of the trademark. For this type of disputes, the jurisdiction of a foreign court or of an arbitral jurisdiction can be excluded.[54]

2. Specific dispositions

17.23 The contractual freedom for trademark transactions is subject to some limits under French law. These limits are typically formal requirements, which the transaction has to satisfy to be valid. For example, the agreement has to be in writing, has to be available to the public, the agreement has to expressly state who has the right to initiate an infringement suit against third-parties (opposability of the trademark), and who has the right to use the trademark.[55]

17.24 Under French law, the agreement that relates to a trademark has to be in writing.[56] The written form helps prove the validity of the agreement, its publicity, and its opposability.[57] The type of agreement determines what kind of writing is necessary to be a valid agreement.[58] For example, if the transaction is a transfer of trademark ownership, a written agreement is required to prove the validity of the transfer. If the transaction grants exclusive rights to the trademark, again, a written agreement is necessary.[59] But, for a non-exclusive license, French law upholds the validity of the license with or without an accompanying written agreement.[60] This policy of not requiring a written agreement for non-exclusive licensing agreements is based on the opinion that the law does not require publicity when the agreement relates to a non-exclusive license. This policy is interesting in practice because generally any trademark license is executed by a written agreement. The exception, however, is used only in case a conflict arises to justify the use of a trademark without any written authorization. In any case, the written form can be an authentic act or a private agreement.

---

54 On trademark and arbitration in France, *see* Binctin, *supra* note 9, at 1357.
55 *See generally* CPI, *supra* note 8, Book VII, Title 1; *see also* Henn Jr. et al., *supra* note 23.
56 CPI, *supra* note 8, art. L714–1. 'Transfer of ownership or pledging shall be recorded in writing, under pain of invalidity.' *Id.*
57 *Id.*, art. L714–7. 'Any transfer or modification of rights under a registered mark shall only have effect against others if entered in the National Register of Marks.' *Id.*
58 *Id.*
59 CPI, *supra* note 8, art. L714–1.
60 *Id.* 'A non-exclusive license grant may result from an unwritten agreement concerning its use.'

B. CONTRACTUAL FREEDOM

The publicity of the agreement is required to ensure that third-parties and the public are aware of the transaction.[61] The agreement has to be known to everyone, which is a legal requirement of the agreement. The publicity of the agreement is required for the agreement itself to be valid, but it also has to be in writing to satisfy other elements relating to the trademark statute and the owner's situation. Registration of the transaction is required to maintain public notice of the agreement. If the transaction is not registered, the agreement is not known to the public, but is only known to the parties involved in the agreement. Some mandatory information, however, is accessible to third-parties, like the new owner's or licensee's name, the licensee's business nature, the licensor and the licensor's address. But even if such information is not mandatory, the lack of additional information can lead to some difficulties, such as missing a new address. Typically the interested party initiates the registration process and the registration can be recorded any time after the agreement has been executed.[62] As is the practice in any office, the National Industrial Property Institute (INPI) prefers to have one employee act as the registration chair throughout the registration process until the registration is finalized; this approach is certainly an oversight issue by the INPI.[63] This request can create some difficulties for a new owner to perform the registration of its trademark. The INPI does not have much, if any, power to control past registrations of the trademark at issue and, accordingly, should only focus on whether or not the register can show the status of the trademark as it relates to registration now. The registration does not ensure the existence or the quality of the trademark, but only provides the identity of the present owner and of the licensees. An uninterrupted chair of registration, however, is not necessary in order to achieve this goal. For a third-party, the possession and the appearance theory should allow third-parties to identify the owner of the trademark. If the register is not up to date, but someone knows that a trademark is owned by a company, this appearance may affect the capacity of the company owner to use its trademark. **17.25**

However, if the trademark is not registered, the owner or the licensee of a trademark can directly provide proof of trademark ownership to any third-party through a notification.[64] The owner or the licensee can show legal power **17.26**

---

61 *Id.*, Book VII, ch. II.
62 *Id.*, art. R714–6.
63 *Id.*, Book VII, ch. II. For more information regarding the trademark registration process of the National Industrial Property Institute, *see French Trademark Registration Costs and Registration Procedures, available 22 September 2015 at* http://www.bycpa.com/html/news/20076/721.html.
64 CPI, *supra* note 8, art. L714–7.

and rights associated with the trademark and warn third parties of potential infringement by showing this document.[65]

17.27 The effective date agreement published in the official intellectual property journal is the constructive date for public knowledge.[66] The registration has no retroactive effect regarding public knowledge and, therefore, the date of public knowledge is not the date of the agreement, but the date of the registration's publication.[67] A licensee or a new owner cannot claim damages in an infringement case during the administration procedure period, but the licensee or new owner can directly communicate proof of its power on the trademark and show standing to sue the infringer. Whatever the importance of the registration, this procedure remains optimal for the trademark owner, without affecting the validity of the agreement.[68] Lack of public knowledge is a sanction for a rule aimed at protecting third-parties. In 2008, the regulator limited the effect of the lack of public knowledge for trademark transactions. Even if the license, simple or with exclusivity, was not registered with the national register, the licensee can be a party to an infringement action initiated by the trademark owner. In this action, the licensee could claim damages for its own prejudice. The consequence of the non-opposability is, therefore, limited to the inability of the licensee to sue the infringer independently.

17.28 To initiate the registration, the parties must provide the INPI a document that explains the nature of the trademark transaction.[69] If the owner is a legal entity, it is not necessary to mention the legal form of the legal entity (that is, the corporate name is sufficient). If the legal entity is in the process of incorporation without legal personality nor its own assets, it cannot be the owner and cannot be registered as such. In that case, the registration has to be made in the name of another person and mentioned that this person is acting for the company that will be incorporated. After the incorporation, it will be possible to modify the registration. If the registration is done by an individual, the name of the person must be used.[70] This means that if the person is married, it is not necessary to use the marital name. The same is true when the registration is done by a couple: the registration must be done in the name of Mr. W. and Mrs. Y. If the registration mentions Mr. and Mrs. W., the office

---

65 *Id.*, art. L716–2.
66 Cour d'appel [CA] [Regional Court of Appeal] Lyon, com., 11 February 1999, Bull. Civ. IV, No. 96LY00297 (Fr.).
67 Cour de Cassation [Cass.] [Court of Cassation] com., June 24, 1986, Bull. civ. IV, No. 84–14379 (Fr.).
68 Heloise Deliquiet, *L'incidence de la publicité des contrats sur l'action en contrefaçon*, *in* LES CONTRATS DE LA PROPRIÉTÉ INTELLECTUELLE 19 (Jean-Michel Bruguière ed, 2013).
69 CPI, *supra* note 8, art. R712–2.
70 Cabinet Chaillot, *Requirements for filing a French Trademark Application*, available 22 September 2015 at http://www.chaillot.com/french-trademark-attorney/filing-requirements.html.

may assume that they are brother and sister, not a married couple. If the registration is done after a merger and acquisition transaction, the registration is made based on a summary of the merger and acquisition agreement. The INPI accepts a summary that describes the agreement.[71] The summary only includes the necessary elements that are needed in order to prove the legal nature, the legal effects of the trademark transaction, and the identity of the parties.[72] The agreement and summary also have to be signed by the parties. Providing a summary is the best way to respect the legal publicity of the agreement and preserves the business secrets of the transaction. A copy of the original act is always sufficient for the registration.[73] Any act written in a foreign language must be translated in French. Both the original and the translation have to be communicated to the office; no official translation is required though.[74]

17.29 To fulfil the registration requirements, the applicant has to pay taxes for the procedure. The registration is usually published within six to eight months after the registration process began, but it is possible to ask for a quicker procedure, but this requires additional taxes to be paid. In a single registration procedure, it is possible to ask for multiple registrations for the same category of IP rights, for example, trademarks, and for the same nature of operation, sale or license, or pledge.

17.30 The INPI can reject the request for registration procedure if it does not comply with the rules.[75] In that case, the INPI notifies the applicant of the rejection with instructions that the application be modified and corrected and then resubmitted to the INPI again. It is possible to challenge the INPI's decision before the Paris Court of Appeal.

17.31 If the request is accepted, the registration is recorded on the national register.[76] The INPI sends the party who initiated the procedure a document with the identification number and the date of the registration. The INPI then proceeds with the publication.[77] Any person interested in the procedure/

---

71 CPI, *supra* note 8, art. R714–4.
72 *Id.*; Casey Cogut, *Getting the Deal Through, Mergers & Acquisitions 2012*, 128 (Law Business Research Ltd., 2012), *available 22 September 2015 at* http://www.bersay-associes.com/fr/wp-content/uploads/2012/08/MA2012-France.pdf.
73 CPI, *supra* note 8, art. R714–5.
74 Law No. 94–665 of 4 August 1994, JOURNAL OFFICIEL DE LA REPUBLIQUE FRANCAISE [J.O.], 5 August 1994.
75 CPI, *supra* note 8, at art. R714–7.
76 *Id.*, art. L713–1.
77 *Id.*, art. R714–8.

transaction can send a request to the office to obtain an excerpt from the register with the registration.[78]

C. THE TRADEMARK AS AN ELEMENT OF THE *FONDS DE COMMERCE*

17.32 From an economic point of view, a trademark is one of the most beneficial assets of a business, acting as tool that drives consumer choice in the market. Because of this important role of a trademark for the business, the debate over the conditions for the assignment of a mark always involved long discussions about whether or not a trademark could be sold on its own, without the underlying business. Under the current French approach, the transfer of a trademark does not necessarily entail the transfer of the business or, similarly, the *fonds de commerce*. In fact, under the current law, 'the rights under a mark may be transferred in whole or in part, independently of the company that exploits them or has them exploited'.[79] But, a requalification of the transaction is always possible, especially when considering the tax law as we will see later. Moreover, should the mark be transferred as an element of the *fonds de commerce*, this may facilitate its use in new operations.

1. Trademark and securities

17.33 The major area of law supporting the transfer of the *fonds de commerce* along with the trademark is French securities law. By transferring the trademark with the *fonds de commerce*, the security interest of using the trademark as collateral or as a pledge protects the owners of the trademark and the other investors.[80] Still, according to French law, a trademark can be used alone as collateral. French intellectual property law is concerned with the publication of the agreement; the common French securities law, however, is concerned with the type of agreement entered into by the parties. A trademark, as an asset of a person, is an element of the general pledge of the creditors,[81] and a lien can be requested by any creditor on a trademark,[82] but more likely on the goods displaying the trademark.[83]

---

78 *Id.*, art. R714–8.
79 *Id.*, art. L714–1.
80 Brian W. Jacobs, *Using Intellectual Property to Secure Financing after the Worst Financial Crisis since the Great Depression*, 15 MARQ. INTELLEC. PROP. L. REV. 449, 457–8 (2011).
81 *See* NATHALIE MARTIAL, DROIT DES SÛRETÉS RÉELLES SUR PROPRIÉTÉS INTELLECTUELLES (2007). *See also* FCC, *supra* note 4, at art. 2284–2285.
82 Alexandra Le Corroncq & Prudence Cadio, *La Saisie Conservatoire de Marque: Pourquoi et Comment?*, LA SEMAINE JURIDIQUE ENTREPRISE ET AFFAIRE 1073 (31 January 2013).
83 The right of lien can be engaged in the condition of article 2286. *See* FCC, *supra* note 4, art. 2286.

C. THE TRADEMARK AS AN ELEMENT OF THE *FONDS DE COMMERCE*

17.34 A trademark can also be used as a security.[84] As an intangible good, the security of the trademark has to be distinguished between whether the security is on the trademark or whether the security is on the trademark receivables, or products.[85]

17.35 A security on a trademark is a security on an intangible property, either present or future, that is used to secure the loan and, also, ensures repayment of the loan.[86] The security on a trademark can be executed by agreement or by a court decision. The French Civil Code defines few principles for the security on intangible products and the principles applicable to intangible products are similar to those principles applicable to tangible products.[87] The only limiting provision relates to collective trademarks, which are specifically excluded from the security mechanism.[88] French intellectual property law only requests a publication of the security for notice purposes for third parties. This provision is compatible with the French Civil Code provision of disposition. For the perfection of the security, the agreement must be in writing, has to identify the debt, and has to describe the trademark given as a pledge.[89] The debtor, (that is, the trademark owner), must preserve the quality of the trademark.[90] In the event that the trademark owner breaches his provision to preserve the trademark, the creditor can ask for a close-out netting provision or for a complementary security.[91] For a trademark, this means that the owner has to pay the INPI taxes to maintain the trademark right, and that the trademark owner has to use the trademark in the business life. The trademark owner cannot abandon an application or a registration for all or part of the goods or services to which the mark applies without previous authorization from the creditor. If the owner does not pay the debt, the creditor can request from a court the sale of the trademark or the transfer of the trademark ownership to the creditor.[92] In the event that ownership is transferred, the valuation of the trademark must be done by an expert on the day of the transfer.[93]

---

84 Nicolas Borga, *Pour un renouveau des garanties conventionnelles sur droits de propriété intellectuelle*, LES CONTRATS DE LA PROPRIÉTÉ INTELLECTUELLE 117 (Jean-Michel Bruguière ed, 2013).
85 FCC, *supra* note 4, art. 2329.
86 *Id.*, art. 2355.
87 CPI, *supra* note 8, art. L714-1. This article opens the application of the legal solution to the trademark with any additional elements.
88 *Id.*, art. L715-2-4. 'A collective certification mark may not be subject to assignment, pledge or any measure of enforcement.' *Id.*
89 *See generally* FCC, *supra* note 4, at Title II, ch. II, § 1.
90 *Id.* at art. 2344.
91 *See generally* David Mengle, *ISDA Research Notes, The Importance of Close-Out Netting*, INTERNATIONAL SWAPS AND DERIVATIVES ASSOCIATION (2010), *available 22 September 2015 at* http://www.isda.org/researchnotes/pdf/Netting-ISDAResearchNotes-1-2010.pdf.
92 FCC, *supra* note 4, art. 2346.
93 *Id.*, art. 2348.

17.36 With respect to EU trademarks, the national security system could be the basis for a security. A community trademark (CTM) can be used as a security,[94] but if such use occurs, it must be published.[95] However, the EU does not provide what law governs the use of a CTM as a security, so, French law can be designated as the applicable law if the parties so determine.

17.37 A security can also be created on trademark receivables.[96] A security on receivables is typically used more often and is easier to organize. A security on trademark receivables is a type of security on the rights of a trademark structured as a security on an intangible produce.[97] The security on trademark receivables does not need to comply with the specific provision of trademark law because it is governed only by the French common security law.

17.38 A security can also be created based on the *fonds de commerce*. A security on a trademark is long and expensive to set up. On the one hand, the security can be based only on a French trademark, but this security is limited in scope. On the other, the security can include trademarks registered in various countries, but the publicity is complex, expensive, and the effect can be different country by country. Furthermore, the security is vastly complex and quite expensive to organize.

17.39 As indicated earlier, the *fonds de commerce* can be the subject of a security under French law. In this case, all the elements of the *fonds de commerce* could be covered by the security, especially when the security agreement explicitly states that all trademarks, either registered in France or in foreign countries, included in the *fonds de commerce* are covered by the security agreement.[98] In such an agreement, a broad security is formed, which includes fewer administrative procedures. In practice, when a trademark is used as a security, the creditor checks that there are no other securities on the trademark. Then, the creditor requests a security on the *fonds de commerce* explicitly including all the

---

[94] Council Regulation No 207/2009, On the Community Trade Mark, art. 19, 2009 O.J. (L 78) [hereinafter Community Trade Mark Regulation].

[95] *Id.*, art. 33.

[96] The European Legal Alliance, *Taking Effective Security in European Jurisdictions*, Field Fisher Waterhouse, 6 (November 2005), *available 22 September 2015 at* http://jweinsteinlaw.com/pdfs/3dc4e342-e283-45ab-9b06-c472b877f876.pdf.

[97] FCC, *supra* note 4, art. 2355.

[98] *See generally* Community Trade Mark Regulation, *supra* note 94; *see also* CODE DE COMMERCE, art. L142-2 (March 20, 2006), *available 22 September 2015 at* http://www.wipo.int/wipolex/en/text.jsp?file_id=180801 [hereinafter Commercial Code].

trademarks. The trademarks or the trademark receivables can also be transferred to a security trust.[99]

17.40 In more complex agreements, trademark receivables can be used in a securitization agreement. The securitization of intellectual property was introduced in France in 1998.[100] This legal framework changed in 2008[101] in order to harmonize French law with the EU Directive on Reinsurance.[102] According to the Monetary and Financial Code, the purpose of securitization structures is, first, to be aware of the risks associated with the securitization of intellectual property.[103] These risks include insurance risks from the acquisitions of receivables, from the finalization of agreements that secure future financing, and from insurance transfer risks. The second purpose is to fully finance or cover these risks by issuing shares, units, or debt securities through securitization funds or securitization companies.[104] The Monetary and Financial Code adds that the nature and characteristics of trademark receivables for securitization may be established by decree. The decree[105] has a major importance for intellectual property securitization in the French law system: only receivables can be included in securitization structures, irrespective of the receivable's origin.[106] By contrast, Luxembourg has another legal solution. In Luxembourg, securitization can be done with any asset, including trademarks, and not just debt. However, the legal limitation of the securitization under French law does not exclude intellectual property securitization. Any kind of receivables can be included in a securitization transaction, among them trademark receivables (for example, receivables of trademark licenses, especially long term trademark licenses). French intellectual property law and French securitization law may accept such a transaction. The main question that arose concerned the debt repayment for securities in the event that the trademark was cancelled. Two elements should be considered concerning this problem: (1) cancellation is specific to intellectual property rights and only a

---

99 Law No. 2008–776, 4 August 2008, on the Modernisation de l'Economie, art. 18, JOURNAL OFFICIEL DE LA RÉPUBLIQUE FRANÇAISE (4 August 2008) *available 22 September 2015 at* http://www.legifrance.gouv.fr/affichTexte.do;jsessionid=0BD623A9DF38C5646CCB41B7681335D8.tpdila20v_1?cidTexte=JORFTEXT000019283050&dateTexte=&oldAction=rechJO&categorieLien=id&idJO=JORFCONT000019283047. (Such a trust was created in France in 2008.)
100 ALEXANDRE QUIQUEREZ, LA TITRISATION DES ACTIFS INTELLECTUELS (2013).
101 European Parliament and Council Directive 2005/68/EC of 16 November 2005 on Reinsurance and Amending Council Directives 73/239/EEC, 92/49/EEC as well as Directives 98/78/EC and 2002/83/EC (Text with EEA relevance) 2005 O.J. (L 323) 1.
102 *Id.*
103 Commercial Code, *supra* note 98, art. L214–42–1.
104 *Id.*
105 Decree No. 2008–711, 17 July 2008 amending the provisions applicable to securitization funds (fonds communs de créances), JOURNAL OFFICIEL DE LA RÉPUBLIQUE FRANÇAISE 11554 (19 July 2008), *available 22 September 2015 at* http://www.legifrance.gouv.fr/eli/decret/2008/7/17/2008–711/jo/texte.
106 Commercial Code, *supra* note 98, art. L214–43.

minority of intellectual property rights are cancelled every year, so, if there are intellectual property rights in the securitization transaction, the risk is low that the trademark will be cancelled; (2) in any securitization transaction, the risks associated with the underlying asset or underlying contract must be assessed. This cancellation would not arise from the ownership, but from any underlying contract. For the securitization agreement, the result is the same. In drafting the securitization, a provision should be included to protect against the risks mentioned above. At this time, there have been no purely trademark securitization developments in France, so the legal solutions and protections for trademark securitizations are unclear. If the securitization is based on a trademark receivable model, the original company maintains ownership of the trademark, but it must continue to use the trademark. The success of the securitization is the result of the use of the trademark in the market. The securitization agreement must be precise concerning this use obligation, and it can include economic sanctions if there are not sufficient revenues.

17.41 Despite the limits of French law, French trademarks can be involved in a securitization deal entered into in another European country, for example, Luxembourg. For these reasons, it appears that securitization of trademarks seems available in France, beyond French securitization law.

2. Transfer of trademark

17.42 As indicated above, a trademark can be sold independently from the *fonds de commerce*, but typically the trademark is transferred with the *fonds de commerce*, or part of it. According to French law, the main issue is to determine whether a transfer of the company or a transfer of the *fonds de commerce* has occurred because the two are not the same. The transfer of a company is a stock transfer and includes the company debts (that is, a share deal). The transfer of a *fonds de commerce* includes only tangible and intangible assets and excludes the buildings and debts (that is, an asset deal).[107] It is possible to sell the *fonds de commerce* without some of its elements if it is explicitly mentioned in the sale agreement.

17.43 In this way, it is possible to have a trademark transfer that includes the value of the brand image and the accessories of the trademark. The *fonds de commerce* can be primarily composed of trademarks, such as the *Lacoste* trademark. In that case, it is important to understand the special function developed by the

---

[107] *Id.* at art. L141–5; *see also* Buying a Business, How to Take Over a Business in France (2015), *available* 22 September 2015 at https://www.justlanded.com/english/France/Articles/Business/Buying-a-Business.

fonds de commerce, in that it becomes a vehicle for trademark transactions. The *fonds de commerce* has special legal conditions for security and for leasing. For example, the *fonds de commerce* could be a way to create special licenses on trademark. Moreover, when a merger and acquisition agreement is executed, it is typical that, during the administrative management period for the merger and acquisition agreement, the *fonds de commerce* of the acquired entity is leased to the buyer to start the business venture.

The link between the sale of a trademark and the *fonds de commerce* transfer is important in France. Case law considers that if the sale of the trademark transfers the seller's customers to the buyer, such an operation is a *fonds de commerce* transfer, even if the sale object is only a trademark.[108] Such a qualification is important because the legal procedure to sell a *fonds de commerce* is different from the one relating to selling a trademark. The consequence regarding the definition of the transaction's legal nature is not only a tax effect question, but it is also a question of agreement qualification, formalities, and publicity. The Code de Commerce provides an extensive and special procedure for a *fonds de commerce* transfer to protect the creditors.[109] The legal nature of the trademark transfer has to be clarified before the execution of the transfer. A guide for defining the legal nature of the transaction determines that a non-used trademark can be sold directly (that is, out of the *fonds de commerce* procedure). If the trademark is used, it is necessary to check if the customers of the seller are willing to follow the trademark. While this is the case for a significant trademark, it may not be the case for a secondary trademark, which relates to certain elements of a product. The division of the *fonds de commerce* in order to sell different elements of it through two agreements does not seem to be efficient because the Court of Cassation can requalify the agreement.[110] The tax aspect of the qualification is important too. Any transfer of a trademark forces the parties to declare it to the tax administration and to pay a registration fee (*Droit d'enregistrement*). The *Droit d'enregistrement* can be fixed at €125, but it can also be proportional. The tax is fixed when the trademark is not qualified as a *fonds de commerce*. But, when the trademark is qualified as such, the *Droit d'enregistrement* must be proportional to the value of the trademark.[111] Since 2008, the rate has been 0

17.44

---

108 YVES REINHARD, SYLVIE THOMASSET-PIERRE, & CYRIL NOURISSAT, DROIT COMMERCIAL – ACTES DE COMMERCE, COMMERÇANTS, FONDS DE COMMERCE, CONCURRENCE, CONSOMMATION (8th ed. 2012).
109 Commercial Code, *supra* note 98, at art. L141–1. Although this aspect will not specifically be addressed here, it is important to note it for future reference.
110 Cour de Cassation [Cass.] [Court of Cassation] com., 23 October 2007, Bull. civ. IV, No. 06–18570 (Fr.).
111 CODE GÉNÉRAL DES IMPÔTS, art. 719 (Fr.), *available* 22 September 2015 at legifrance.gouv.fr/affichCodeArticle.do?cidTexte=LEGITEXT000006069577&idArticle=LEGIARTI000006310743&dateTexte=&categorieLien=cid.

to 1 per cent for amounts less than €23,000, 2 per cent for amounts between €23,000 and €107,000, between 0 and 60 per cent for amounts between €107,000 and €200,000, and between 2 and 60 per cent when the amount exceeds €200,000.[112] The qualification has, therefore, a direct effect on the cost of the agreement.

17.45 As a result, it appears that a presentation of French perspective on trademark operations is closely connected with the French regulation of the *fonds de commerce*.

D. TAX CONSIDERATIONS AND TRADEMARK TRANSACTIONS

17.46 It is not the goal of this chapter to extensively analyze the taxation of trademarks. However, trademark transactions are influenced by tax considerations. The idea of this last part of the chapter is not to expose the French tax system applied to trademarks, but rather to outline the influence of the tax system on trademark transactions.

17.47 Roughly speaking, in France, the tax rate for companies is 33.33 per cent, except for small companies which enjoy a reduced rate of 15 per cent if the benefit is under €38,120, the annual turnover is over €7.63 million, and 75 per cent of the stocks are owned directly or indirectly by individuals.[113] Trademark royalties have no specific treatment under tax law in France,[114] whereby trademark royalty tax is one-third of the royalty income.[115] From this standpoint, the French position is not the most attractive, especially for the transfer price strategy. France will not be the beneficiary country for transfer price purposes: the companies will rather try to put money out of France than to attract a part of their profits in France. But, the French tax administration also focuses on the practices of transfer price from France to a third country. The evolution of tax law is to develop control mechanisms and to limit the legality

---

112 *Id.*
113 Taj, Deloitte Touche Tohmatsu Ltd., *Corporation Tax System in France, Direct Taxes at a Glance* (2012), available 22 September 2015 at http://www.internationaltaxreview.com/pdfs/taxdata/france-corporation-tax-system_august-2010.pdf; *see also* Deloitte, *Taxation and Investment in France 2015, Reach, Relevance and Reliability (2015)*, available 22 September 2015 at http://www2.deloitte.com/content/dam/Deloitte/global/Documents/Tax/dttl-tax-franceguide-2015.pdf.
114 The patent royalties know a special taxation with a 15% rate tax.
115 Tax rules may vary when the trademark is owned by an individual. In that case, depending on the type of transaction, the royalties can be qualified as commercial or non-commercial revenues. The respective qualification has an influence on the tax rate in the specific cases at issue, and on the taxation of the valuation gains.

of the transfer price model, but only in accordance with the OECD recommendations. The *Conseil Constitutionnel* (Constitutional Council) decided to preserve the contractual freedom and the respect of the ownership in December 2013 by a cancellation of the main provisions of the 2014 Finances Law that had introduced control tools against transfer pricing strategies, whereby this development is not specific to France and, therefore, does not need to be further analysed here.[116]

17.48 In terms of contractual practice, the tax qualification is independent from the commercial or civil qualification: a license, under commercial law, can be a sale from the tax law point of view. It means that the drafting of the agreement can be adapted in order to reach a special tax law qualification of the operation.[117] Concerning the strict contractual practice, two hypotheses need to be addressed: (1) the trademark operation for free; and (2) the tax qualification of a license as an asset. Finally, a third hypothesis will be addressed: the influence of the tax qualification for a merger and acquisition agreement.

1. Trademark operations for free

17.49 Typically, trademark transfers are free or accompanied by a symbolic amount, like a single euro. The symbolic nature of transferring the trademark for a single euro has important social aspects, but it is also important for tax purposes. According to the tax point of view, the transfer of the trademark for a symbolic price reduces the value of the agreement. This kind of agreement, however, can be executed in order to reorganize the assets of a company or to transfer the trademark from the owner of the trademark to the founder company. The idea is not to abuse the tax system, but to adapt a company asset for better development. Nevertheless, regardless of the parties' intentions, the tax administration can qualify the agreement and the qualification will be different according to the nature of the parties: either as legal entity or as an individual.

17.50 For an individual, the reduced value can change the tax nature of the agreement. After finalizing the sale agreement and transferring the trademark for free as a donation, the tax administration will qualify the agreement as a gift, not a sale.[118] This qualification determination will impact the amount of

---

116 Conseil Constitutionnel [CC] [Constitutional Council] decision No. 2013–685DC, 29 December 2013, Rec. 1127 (Fr.).
117 Nicolas Binctin, *Les Prévisions Fiscales dans les Contrats de la Propriété Intellectuelle*, COMMUNICATION COMMERCE ELECTRONIQUE 17 (No. 5, 2007).
118 ORGANIZATION FOR ECONOMIC CO-OPERATION AND DEVELOPMENT, *Glossary of Tax Terms*, available 22 September 2015 at http://www.oecd.org/ctp/glossaryoftaxterms.htm.

tax paid. The general tax rate for donations, with the exception of family donations and non-profit organizations, is 60 per cent of the value of the goods. In the event of a gift, the tax administration first evaluates the trademark and then calculates the due tax on the value.[119] For example, a trademark is sold by an individual to the individual's company in order to concentrate the main assets in the company and to help find new partners. The transfer is executed for a symbolic euro. The tax administration may challenge not the transfer itself, but its tax qualification. To the tax administration, the value of the trademark is €50,000, and the taxes that have to be paid are €30,000, in addition to any potential penalties. In this situation, the transaction, executed in order to boost the attractiveness of the small company, can actually put the company into bankruptcy.

17.51 The tax qualification for a legal entity in the same situation will be quite different. A company has to realize benefits and save money. Any act of the company that is not done for that purpose can be qualified by the tax administration as an irregular management action.[120] This can occur because of a symbolic euro transaction, which limits the incomes without a direct commercial interest. Such a transaction can be executed in order to switch assets from a division to another one. For example, company A sells to company B a trademark for one euro that has a value of €50,000. This irregular management action creates a loss of €49,999 for A. This amount will be integrated in the taxable benefits of company A which will pay the 33,33 per cent tax on the value of the trademark and not on its effective income. The tax administration can also correct the value added tax for the transaction[121] and levy penalties.

2. The tax qualification of a trademark license as an asset

17.52 The qualification of a trademark license as an asset has many consequences on the tax management of license agreements. French case law analysed this question in 1984.[122] Since then, the *Conseil d'Etat* (Council of State) has maintained the same position. Three cumulative criteria must be met in a license agreement to qualify a trademark license as an asset. The criteria that

---

119 See e.g. *Vins&Spiritueux, Current Legal, Tax and Labor Issues, Valuing Wine Trademarks: Bombshell at the Bordeaux Administrative Court of Appeal*, PriceWaterhouseCoopers (February 2011), *available 22 September 2015 at* http://list2.pwc.fr/valuing-wine-trademarks-bombshell-at-the-bordeaux-administrative-court-of-appeal.html.
120 *Tax Audit, What is an Irregular Management Action?*, Cabinet Stephane Haddad (2006), *available 22 September 2015 at* http://www.cabinet-haddad.com/spip.php?article57.
121 Conseil d'Etat [CE] [Council of State] No. 328762, CE Sect., 26 September 2011, Rec. Lebon.
122 Conseil d'Etat [CE] [Council of State] No. 43573, CE, 5 November 1984, Rec. Lebon; *see also*, Conseil d'Etat [CE] [Council of State] No. 262219, CE Sect., 14 October 2005, Rec. Lebon.

D. TAX CONSIDERATIONS AND TRADEMARK TRANSACTIONS

must be satisfied are the territorial exclusivity, the duration, and the licence transferability.

(a) The territorial exclusivity means that the license must confer to the licensee an exclusive right to use the trademark in France. The exclusivity forbids any other license and any use of the trademark by the trademark owner in the French territory. It means that, if the license agreement defines the exclusivity differently, these criteria will not be met.

(b) The needed duration is a minimum: the license has to be long enough in order to become an asset according to tax law. It is not a fixed duration. Less than a year is too short, but over a year may be sufficient, depending on the development of the company's business.[123] It can be similar with the accounting approach.[124] Again, it is possible to adapt this criterion in a trademark license in order to satisfy the qualification or to exclude it.

(c) The transferability of the license is the last criterion. As previously mentioned, the transferability of a license is possible under French law and can be done under different circumstances. This criteria is discussed because it is a pure tax law criterion that is not shared by accounting law.[125] It means that a trademark license may be qualified as an asset according to accounting law and not according to tax law. The transferability of the license must be possible without any intervention or control of the licensor. The licence should be free to transfer from the licensee to a sub-licensee. From a tax law perspective, the idea is that the transferability of an asset is the proof of its value for the company. Consequently, an *intuitus personae* license cannot be qualified as an asset. Regarding other licenses, the parties can adapt the drafting of the agreement to fulfil the criteria or not, and the license can explicitly mention its free transferability.[126]

17.53 A recent case illustrated the sensitivity of how the license agreement is drafted in light of the tax qualification as an asset of a sub-license.[127] The dispute was about a patent, but the resolution is the same for a trademark. For the duration criterion, the Pfizer France sub-license, concluded with Pfizer NL, was subject

---

[123] Conseil d'Etat [CE] [Council of State] No. 64092, CE, 24 July 1987; Conseil d'Etat [EC] [Council of State] No. 189904, CE, 18 May 1998, Rec. Lebon.
[124] INTERNATIONAL ACCOUNTING STANDARDS 38, § 4 and 6.
[125] REPUBLIQUE FRANÇAISE, BULLETIN OFFICIEL DES IMPÔTS, DIRECTION GÉNÉRALE DES IMPÔTS, No. 213, No. 8 (30 December 2005) (analysing the importance of the criteria).
[126] Practical Law, Intellectual Property License Agreement Transferability, Thomson Reuters (20 May 2014), *available 22 September 2015 at* http://us.practicallaw.com/6-567-5046?q=&qp=&qo=&qe=.
[127] Conseil d'Etat [CE] [Council of State] No. 308494, CE Sect., 16 October 2009, Rec. Lebon. *See also* the review of the decision by Yann de Kergos & Julien Monsenego, *L'arret Pfizer Holding France: la Jurisprudence SA Sife Est Perenne!*, REVUE DE DROIT FISCAL 94 (No. 4, 28 January 2010).

to an unlimited duration with the possibility, for both the licensor and the licensee, of terminating the license within a 60-day period without indemnity. The *Conseil d'Etat* concluded that such a duration does not meet the duration criterion irrespective of the effective duration of the license and the capital links between the licensor and the licensee.[128] For the transferability criterion, the license authorized the transfer of the contract with the previous written approval of the licensor, except in the case of a global transfer. This restriction on transferability was too important to permit the qualification as an asset according to the tax law approach. The *Conseil d'Etat*, therefore, concluded that the license cannot be qualified as an asset, and followed the Pfizer argument. For Pfizer, the exclusion of the qualification was important because if the license is not an asset, all the license costs are qualified as charges and can therefore reduce the taxable benefit, and, thus, the tax paid. This solution is important for the organisation of a transfer price strategy.

3. Tax influence on merger and acquisition qualification

17.54 It is typical to organise the assets of a parent company and share them between different subsidiaries. Such an operation is allowed in France and creates a special tax qualification, which is the *apport partiel d'actifs*. Trademark law and tax law may have to be articulated to fulfil such an operation. A recent decision of the *Cour de Cassation* of 2013[129] shows the complexity of the articulation. The company operates as a business and produces decorative arts products. The company has four shops and many franchises. The company modifies its organization and realizes an *apport partiel d'actifs* (partial transfer of business assets) to a subsidiary of its franchise activity. The incorporation agreement puts the operation under the special tax rules of French tax law, which gives the company the opportunity to pay only a fixed tax rate of €375 for the transfer.[130] The tax administration challenges the benefit of the special rules. The first panel of judges rejected the tax administration reclamation. The Court of Appeal held that the franchise activity transferred to the subsidiary is different from the other activities of the original company, and, so, it can be the object of an *apport partiel d'actifs*. In the decision, the Court of Appeal stated that the trademark license without any restriction provides the subsidiary the necessary elements of a real, efficient, and independent activity. But, the Court of Cassation did not follow this approach. The Court determined that the Court of Appeal should have examined whether the trademark license,

---

128 Conseil d'Etat [CE] [Council of State] No. 308494, CE Sect., 16 October 2009, Rec. Lebon.
129 Cour de Cassation [Cass.] [Court of Cassation] com., 29 January 2013, Bull. civ. IV, No. 11–24713 (Fr.); *see also* Nicolas Binctin, *Droit Fiscal des Societes – Apport Partiel d'Actifs et Droit d'Usage d'une Marque*, REVUE DES SOCIÉTÉS 578 (29 January 2013).
130 CODE GÉNÉRAL DES IMPÔTS [CGI] art. 210 A, art. 210 B (Fr.).

included in the incorporation treaty, granted enough freedom to the subsidiary to develop a long term activity. In the decision, the Court decided that the qualification of *apport partiel d'actifs* depends on the nature and quality of the trademark license. If it is not necessary to transfer the full ownership of the trademark to meet the qualification, the transferred benefits of the trademark must still be sufficiently important in order to benefit from the qualification.[131] The Court also excluded the qualification of *apport partiel d'actifs* for an operation including a *fonds de commerce* without a trademark.[132] In its 2013 decision, the Court of Cassation followed its previous position. Still, it also included the tax analysis of the asset qualification, specifically the *Conseil d'Etat* approach to qualify a license as an asset. The Court thus adopted a restrictive position for the qualification of the *apport partiel d'actifs*.

17.55 This holding may have some effects on the opportunity to use such a qualification. The goal of the qualification changes depending on the operation. The drafting of a license agreement in order to exclude the asset qualification is made to reduce the taxable benefit and could be an element of tax optimization and transfer price policy. Such a strategy is quite clear to follow and the tax qualification influences the drafting of the license, but only for some marginal elements. In the 2013 case, the goal was the opposite. The reached tax qualification was to benefit the special rule of *apport partiel d'actif*. According to the elements of the decision, the license agreement may not be sufficiently sustainable, but the incorporation act may explicitly present the three criteria developed by the *Conseil d'Etat* case law to reach the qualification.

17.56 The mistrust of the French judges for the license should be discarded with a modification of the legal nature of the rights on the trademark given to the licensee. It is now possible, as mentioned previously, to create rights in rem, temporary or not. Such a right in rem may offer the same benefits as a classical trademark license, but the nature of the right is different. If the parties switch the qualification from a personal right to a right in rem, it may have an effect on the qualification, including the tax qualification. The right in rem on the trademark should be an asset. The contractual freedom, stepping up by the Court of Cassation in 2012, may be an answer to the difficult tax qualification question.

---

131 *France, Taxation of Cross-Border Mergers and Acquisitions*, KPMG (2010), *available 22 September 2015 at* http://www.kpmg.com/Global/en/IssuesAndInsights/ArticlesPublications/Lists/Expired/TAX-MA-2010/MA_Cross-Border_2010_France.pdf.
132 Cour de Cassation [Cass.] [Court of Cassation] com., 13 May 1980, Bull. civ. IV, No. 78–15666 (Fr.).

E. CONCLUSION

17.57 The French legal framework for trademark transaction accepts a broad contractual freedom approach. The owner, the licensor, the licensee, and any other contractual figures can decide the contractual conditions, for the most part, and include these conditions onto their agreement. The law related to any type of trademark transaction asks, however, for a formal obligation, a written form and a publication of the operation for an *erga omnes* opposability. As a result of this contract freedom, a considerable legal creativity has developed in this area in order to allow the parties to maximize their options and the value that can be granted to the mark to be transacted. As an element of the *fonds de commerce*, the trademark can also be involved in all transactions involving the *fonds de commerce*. This affords trademark owners additional options for trademark transactions, especially for securities. In any instance, however, trademark transactions are subject to tax law, and in turn to the principles of tax law that apply to these types of transactions.

Section B

TRADEMARK TRANSACTIONS IN NORTH AND SOUTH AMERICA

18

TRADEMARK TRANSACTIONS IN THE UNITED STATES: TOWARDS A DE FACTO ACCEPTANCE OF TRADING IN GROSS?

Irene Calboli[*]

A.	INTRODUCTION	18.01	1. The current rule on trademark licensing 'with control'	18.21
B.	A BRIEF PRIMER OF TRADEMARK LAW	18.03	(a) Rationale of the rule	18.27
			(b) Origin of the rule	18.29
C.	TRADEMARK ASSIGNMENT	18.06	2. Judicial developments	18.32
	1. The current rule on trademark assignment 'with goodwill'	18.06	(a) The evolution of the standard	18.33
			(b) Recent developments	18.36
	(a) Rationale of the rule	18.10		
	(b) Origin of the rule	18.12	E. STRATEGIC TRADEMARK TRANSACTIONS	18.38
	2. Judicial developments	18.16		
	(a) Early (conservative) decisions	18.17	1. Trademark assignment and license-back	18.39
	(b) Shifting towards trademark assignment 'in gross'?	18.19	2. Security interests in trademarks	18.42
D.	TRADEMARK LICENSING	18.21	F. CONCLUSION	18.45

A. INTRODUCTION

In this chapter, I elaborate on the current laws regarding trademark transactions in the United States (U.S.). In particular, I address the rules and requirements that apply to trademark assignments and trademark licensing agreements. Based on the principle that trademarks are not protected as property rights, U.S. trademark law has historically forbidden trading trademarks 'in gross'. As a result, trademarks must be assigned with the associated goodwill of the business to which the marks belong and, in licensing agreements, licensors must control the quality of the products that are produced by the licensees under the license agreement. Since their introduction, however, **18.01**

---

[*] Visiting Professor and Deputy Director, Applied Research Centre for Intellectual Assets and the Law in Asia (ARCIALA), Singapore Management University School of Law; Professor of Law, Texas A&M University School of Law. This chapter builds upon my research in this area. In particular, portions of this chapter update and adapt my previous articles *Trademark Assignment 'With Goodwill': A Concept Whose Time Has Gone*, 57 FLA. L. REV. 771 (2005), and *The Sunset of 'Quality Control' In Modern Trademark Licensing*, 57 AM. U. L. REV. 341 (2007).

these rules have proven ambiguous, primarily due to the lack of clear definitions as to what constitutes 'trademark goodwill' and 'quality control'. As a result, the courts have applied these rules inconsistently. Furthermore, because of the ambiguity surrounding these concepts, the courts have de facto moved away from a strict application of these rules and have instead assessed the validity of trademark transactions based primarily on whether the quality of the products at issue remains consistent and whether or not the public is confused as to this quality.

18.02 My analysis proceeds as follows. In Section B, I offer a brief primer of trademark theory. In Section C, I examine the rule on trademark assignment. In this Section, I describe how the courts have increasingly moved away from assessing whether goodwill has been transferred with a mark and, instead, have inferred such valid transfer by assessing the continuity of the quality of the products at issue. In Section D, I examine the rule on trademark licensing. In this Section, I again conclude that the current requirement has become increasingly formalistic and the courts tend to focus on the continuity of product quality in order to uphold the validity of trademark licensing agreements. In Section E, I address the strategic use of trademark transactions in litigation and other settings. In particular, I examine the practice of trademark assignment and license-back in settlement agreements and the use of trademarks as collaterals in secured transactions. In this Section, I highlight the increasing disconnect between theory and practice, as trademarks are de facto used as property rights in practice despite the language of the statute. I conclude this chapter by noting that, even though current trademark practices and judicial decisions seem to favour a liberal approach and freedom of transactions, this area remains filled with ambiguity and inconsistency and trademark lawyers need to be cautious when advising their clients on these matters.

B. A BRIEF PRIMER OF TRADEMARK LAW

18.03 Analyzing the rules on trademark transactions requires a brief overview of the general principles regarding the scope of trademark protection. Unsurprisingly, trademark owners have historically advocated for minimal restrictions on their ability to trade in their marks, arguing that a mark often represents the most valuable aspect of a business. Yet, the generally accepted justification for limited trademark protection in the U.S. rests on consumer protection.[1] In

---

1 'The central purpose of the rule regarding the assignment of trademarks is to protect consumers.' *See generally*, 3 J. THOMAS MCCARTHY, MCCARTHY ON TRADEMARKS AND UNFAIR COMPETITION § 18:1–10 (4th ed. 2015).

particular, in the U.S., it has long been supported that trademarks are not protected 'in gross' – as property rights per se – but as symbols of business goodwill and as conveyers of information to consumers.[2]

18.04 As a direct result of this position, trademark law has traditionally required that trademarks be assigned with their goodwill and that licensors control the quality of the products produced under license. Against this position, trademark owners have repeated that trademarks are valuable business assets per se, and, as such, deserve absolute protection and free alienability.[3] This position was also originally supported by the courts at common law. However, at the beginning of the 20th century, it was accepted that property rights in trademarks could hinder competition in the marketplace. Accordingly, the courts began protecting trademarks on the grounds of consumer protection. The adoption of the Lanham Act in 1946 confirmed this position, which remains the basis for trademark protection to date.[4] Nevertheless, the idea that trademarks should be protected per se as property was never abandoned by trademark owners who routinely continued to trade in trademarks as 'things' in and of themselves. Generally, this trade in trademarks has been conducted 'through a widespread ignorance'[5] of the law, or by 'making the most of [its] exceptions'.[6]

18.05 Besides advocating that trademarks should be traded with no requirements attached, trademark owners have also vocally supported additional protection for their marks beyond the limits of consumer protection. In the past half century, these calls have brought increased acceptance of protection for trademarks per se in several areas. Perhaps the most explicit example in this respect was the (highly contested) adoption of the Federal Trademark Dilution Act (FTDA) of 1995, which extended the protection of famous marks beyond confusingly similar products and simply based it on a likelihood of dilution of the distinctiveness of the mark.[7] Even before the adoption of the FTDA, the

---

2 *See* William M. Landes & Richard A. Posner, *Trademark Law: An Economic Perspective*, 30 J.L. & ECON. 265, 265–66 (1987) ('Trademark law ... can be best explained on the hypothesis that the law is trying to promote economic efficiency.'); *see also* Nicholas Economides, *The Economic Aspects of Trademarks*, 78 TRADEMARK REP. 523 (1988).
3 *See* Frank I. Schechter, *The Rational Basis of Trademark Protection*, 40 HARV. L. REV. 813, 819 (1927) ('The true functions are, then, to identify a produce as satisfactory and thereby to stimulate further purchases by the consuming public.'). *Cf.* Glynn S. Lunney, Jr., *Trademark Monopolies*, 48 EMORY L.J. 367 (1999).
4 The Trademark Act of 1946, 15 U.S.C. §§ 1051–1141 (2014) [hereinafter Lanham Act]; *See* S. Res. 1333, 79th Cong. (1946) (enacted).
5 Nathan Isaacs, *Traffic in Trade-Symbols*, 44 HARV. L. REV. 1210 (1930–1931).
6 *Id.*
7 Federal Trademark Dilution Act of 1995, Pub. L. No. 104–98, §§ 3(a) & 4, 109 Stat. 985 (effective 16 January 1996) (codified as amended at 15 U.S.C. §§ 1125, 1127); Trademark Dilution Revision Act (TDRA) of 2006, Pub. L. No. 109–312 §§ 2, 3(e), 120 Stat. 1730 (codified as amended at 15 U.S.C.

courts started to considerably loosen the traditional interpretation of the standard for trademark infringement – the 'likelihood of consumer confusion'. In particular, from its original interpretation of confusion as to the source of the products in terms of actual product manufacturing, the courts also started to include confusion as to the 'control', 'sponsorship', 'endorsement', or 'affiliation/association' with the products.[8] This expanded interpretation of 'consumer confusion' was introduced into the Lanham Act in 1988.[9] In recent years, the courts have gone even further.[10] In several instances, the courts have even protected trademarks by directly adopting a property-based approach.[11] As I elaborate in the next sections, this expansionist trend has considerably affected the area of trademark transactions.

C. TRADEMARK ASSIGNMENT

1. The current rule on trademark assignment 'with goodwill'

18.06 Section 10(a)(1) of the Lanham Act sets forth the conditions for the assignment of registered trademarks under U.S. law.[12] Specifically, the provision recites that:

> [a] registered mark or a mark for which an application ... has been filed shall be assignable *with the goodwill* of the business in which the mark is used, or with that part of the goodwill of the business connected with the use of and symbolized by the mark.[13]

---

§§ 1125, 1127) (effective 6 October 2006); *see also* Jesse A. Hofrichter, *Tool of the Trademark: Brand Criticism and Free Speech Problems with the Trademark Dilution Revision Act of 2006*, 28 CARDOZO L. REV., 1923, 1935 (2007).

8   For a detailed reconstruction and criticism of the expansion of the concept of 'confusion' in trademark law, see Mark P. McKenna, *Testing Modern Trademark Law's Theory of Harm*, 95 IOWA L. REV. 63 (2009).
9   Lanham Act § 43(a), 15 U.S.C. § 1125(a) (2012).
10 For example, the courts developed doctrines such as initial interest confusion and post-sale confusion. For a detailed recount and critique of these doctrines, see Jennifer E. Rothman, *Initial Interest Confusion: Standing at the Crossroads of Trademark Law*, 27 CARDOZO L. REV. 105 (2005); Jeremy N. Sheff, *Veblen Brands*, 96 MINN. L. REV. 769, 794 (2012).
11 *See, e.g.*, Frank H. Easterbrook, *Intellectual Property is Still Property*, 13 HARV. J.L. & PUB. POL. 108, 118 (1990) (arguing that 'we should treat intellectual and physical property identically in the law').
12 Lanham Act § 10, 15 U.S.C. § 1060(a)(1). Trademark assignment is defined as '[the] transfer by a party of its right, title and interest in a ... registered mark or a mark for which an application has been filed'. UNITED STATES PATENT AND TRADEMARK OFFICE, TRADEMARK MANUAL OF EXAMINATION PROCEDURE, § 501 (9th ed. 2015), *available 23 September 2015 at* http://tmep.uspto.gov/RDMS/detail/manual/TMEP/Jan2015/d1e2.xml [hereinafter T.M.E.P.].
13 Lanham Act § 10, 15 U.S.C. § 1060(a)(1) (2014).

C. TRADEMARK ASSIGNMENT

Under this rule, trademarks must be assigned with the associated goodwill of the business to which the mark belongs or the assignment can be deemed invalid and the mark may be cancelled according to Section 14 of the Lanham Act.[14] Assignments 'without goodwill' can also lead to the abandonment of the assigned mark as indicated in Section 45.[15]

18.07 Section 10(a)(1) also prohibits the assignment of intent-to-use (ITU) trademark applications.[16] Instead, for a trademark assignment to be valid, a mark should be used in commerce prior to the assignment. This includes marks that are already registered and trademark applications for marks that are already in use in commerce at the time of the application for registration.[17]

18.08 According to Section 10(a)(2), the requirement of the transfer of goodwill only applies, however, to the marks that are validly assigned and not to any additional mark that may also be used by the assignor as part of the same business.[18] Furthermore, under Section 501.06 of the Trademark Manual of Examination Procedure (TMEP) of the United States Patent and Trademark Office (USPTO), trademark owners are free to assign their marks only with respect to some of the products for which the mark is registered, while still retaining the right to use the mark to identify other products. The same provision states that joint owners may assign their interest in the mark independently.[19] Similarly, the sole owner of a mark can assign only 'a portion (*e.g.*, 50%) of his or her interest in the mark to another party', while retaining control of the remaining portion of the mark.

18.09 Finally, to constitute a valid transaction, the trademark assignment must be executed in writing, which serves as 'prima facie evidence of the execution of

---

14 Lanham Act § 14, 15 U.S.C. § 1064(3) (2014) ('[a] petition to cancel ... a mark ... may ... be filed ... [a]t any time ... if the registered mark is being used by, or with the permission of, the registrant so as to misrepresent the source of the goods or services on or in connection with which the mark is used').
15 Lanham Act § 45, 15 U.S.C. § 1127 (2014) ('[w]hen any course of conduct of the owner, including acts of omission as well as commission, causes the mark ... to lose its significance as a mark').
16 Lanham Act § 10, 15 U.S.C. § 1060(a)(1) (2014) ('no application to register a mark under Section 1051(b) ... shall be assignable prior to the filing of an amendment under Section 1051(c) ...').
17 Lanham Act §1, 15 U.S.C. § 1051(a)(1)-(2) (2014) (under the general trademark rules, the assigned trademark application should include and specify 'the date of the applicant's first use of the mark, the date of the applicant's first use of the mark in commerce, the goods in connection with which the mark is used, and a drawing of the mark').
18 Lanham Act § 10, 15 U.S.C. § 1060(a)(2) ('it shall not be necessary to include the goodwill of the business connected with the use of and symbolized by any other mark used in the business or by the name or style under which the business is conducted').
19 The Trademark Manual of Examining Procedure defines a partial assignment as a trademark: 'owned by two or more persons, and a co-owner may assign his or her interest in a mark. Also, a party who is the sole owner of a mark may transfer a portion of his or her interest in the mark to another.' *See* T.M.E.P., *supra* note 12, at § 501.

Chapter 18 TRADEMARK TRANSACTIONS IN THE UNITED STATES

an assignment'.[20] In addition, the assignment must be recorded with the USPTO. Assignments are recorded after filing a Recordation Form Cover Sheet and a copy of the trademark assignment contract with the Assignment Recordation Branch of the USPTO.[21] Once a mark is validly assigned, the assignee gains all of the rights and obligations of the assignor, including the right to sue third parties.[22]

(a) Rationale of the rule

18.10 As indicated in Section B, the rationale for the rule of trademark assignment 'with goodwill' rests on the principle that trademarks deserve protection only as symbols of goodwill and because of the information they convey to consumers.[23] As a corollary to this principle, a mark can be protected so long as it guarantees the *continuity* of the quality of marked products.[24] Considering that a trademark assignment in gross could jeopardize this continuity,[25] the traditional position is that trademarks should be transferred with the associated goodwill in order to reduce the likelihood of disrupting this product continuity.[26]

18.11 The rule of assignment 'with goodwill' has additionally been justified based on the position that assignments without goodwill may bring undeserved economic advantages for assignees to the detriment of consumers. In particular, consumers could be deceived when the quality of the assignees' products is of

---

20 Lanham Act § 10, 15 U.S.C. § 1060(a)(3); Lanham Act § 10, 15 U.S.C. §1060(a)(5); *see also* T.M.E.P., *supra* note 12, at § 500.

21 Lanham Act § 10, 15 U.S.C. § 1060; UNITED STATES PATENT AND TRADEMARK OFFICE, *Trademark Assignment: Change & Search Ownership* (2015), *available 23 September 2015 at* http://www.uspto.gov/trademarks/process/assign.jsp [hereinafter USPTO]; Assignments can be recorded online with the USPTO online for a fee of $ 40.00. For more information, *see* USPTO, *Electronic Trademark Assignment System (ETAS)* (2015), *available 23 September 2015 at* http://etas.uspto.gov.

22 For the assignee to assert his/her rights under the assignment, the assignee has to prove ownership of the mark. In this respect, ownership can be established by submitting a signed statement to the Office that identifies the assignee, in addition to a copy of the executed agreement and a copy of the assignment records from the Office. *See* ANNE GILSON LALONDE, 1–3 GILSON ON TRADEMARKS § 3.06 (Matthew Bender 2015) [hereinafter GILSON ON TRADEMARKS].

23 *See* 3 MCCARTHY, *supra* note 1, at § 23:1–124.

24 *See, e.g.*, Dawn Donut Co. v. Hart's Food Stores, Inc., 267 F.2d 358 (2d Cir. 1959); Land O'Lakes Creameries, Inc. v. Oconomowoc Canning Co., 221 F. Supp. 576 (D. Wis. 1963), aff'd, 330 F.2d 667 (7th Cir. 1964).

25 *See, e.g.*, PepsiCo, Inc. v. Graphette Co., 416 F.2d 285, 290 (8th Cir. 1969); Glow Indus., Inc. v. Lopez, 273 F. Supp. 2d 1095, 1107 (C.D. Cal. 2003).

26 3 MCCARTHY, *supra* note 1, § 18:10. Notably, to require that trademarks be transferred with goodwill could avoid 'a fraud on the purchasing public who reasonably assumes that the mark signifies *the same thing*, whether used by one person or another'. Marshak v. Green, 746 F.2d 927, 930 (2d Cir. 1984) (emphasis added).

lesser quality than those of the assignors.[27] Moreover, in instances where the quality changes in favour of higher product quality, consumers' reliance on the mark as an indicator of a 'certain type of quality' is also disrupted. Simply put, any discontinuity in product quality would thwart consumer expectations when consumers unintentionally purchase products qualitatively different from what they expect, regardless of the high, low, or average quality level of these products.[28] As a result, this would hamper the most important functions of a mark: to provide accurate information about product quality to consumers and thus promote economic efficiency by reducing consumer search costs.[29]

(b) Origin of the rule

18.12 The rule against assignment in gross was first developed as a judicial doctrine by the courts. In 1905, Congress incorporated this rule into Section 10 of the Trademark Act of 1905 (1905 Act). Section 10 of the 1905 Act stated '[e]very registered trade-mark ... shall be assigned with the goodwill in which the mark is used'.[30] The legislative history of the Lanham Act reveals that proponents of broader trademark protection[31] sought to change the wording of Section 10 in order to facilitate trademark assignment also without the associated goodwill.[32] Ultimately, the Lanham Act confirmed the text of the 1905 Act. However, Section 10(a)(2) departs from the previous interpretation that trademark assignment required the transfer of the whole business in which a mark was used. As I noted in Section C.1, the provision recognizes that trademark owners can assign their marks individually with the respective associated goodwill, and still retain the ownership of their businesses.[33]

18.13 In the decades that followed, the text of Section 10 was partially amended. In 1962, the language providing for the cancellation of a mark used to mislead the public as a result of an assignment was stricken from the provision[34] to be

---

27 *See, e.g.*, WILLIAM M. LANDES & RICHARD A. POSNER, THE ECONOMIC STRUCTURE OF INTELLECTUAL PROPERTY LAW 184 (2003).
28 *PepsiCo, Inc.*, 416 F.2d at 287.
29 LANDES & POSNER, *supra* note 27, at 186.
30 Trademark Act of 1905, ch 592, § 10, 33 Stat. 724, 727 (repealed 1946) [hereinafter 1905 Act].
31 *See* Trade-marks: Hearings Before the Comm. on Patents Subcomm. on Trade-marks *on H.R. 4744*, 76th Cong. 81 (1939) (testimony of Edward S. Rogers).
32 When the trademark bill was introduced in the Seventy-fifth Congress, it provided that '[a] registered trade-mark shall be assignable either with or without the goodwill of the business'. H.R. 9041, 75th Cong. § 10 (1938). The same language was retained when the bill was reintroduced in the Seventy-sixth Congress. H.R. 4744, 76th Cong. § 10 (1939); *see* DAPHNE ROBERT, THE NEW TRADE-MARK MANUAL 23–24 (1947); Walter J. Halliday, *Assignments Under the Lanham Act*, 38 TRADEMARK REP. 970, 970 (1948).
33 *See* Walter J. Halliday, *Assignment Under the Lanham Act*, 38 TRADEMARK REP. 970, 973 (1948). 'The purpose of this provision, as stated by the congressional committee, is to permit 'a registrant who own more than one mark to dispose of one mark if he wishes to do so.' *Id.*
34 The original 15 U.S.C. § 10 (1946) provided that: '*[p]rovided*, [t]hat any assigned registration may be cancelled at any time if the registered mark is being used by, or with the permission of, the assignee so as to

incorporated, as a general requirement applying to all registrants, into Section 14 of the Lanham Act.[35] In 1988, the Trademark Revision Act[36] amended the language of Section 10 with respect to the prohibition against the assignment of ITU trademark applications.[37] As a result of the Trademark Law Treaty Implementation Act,[38] which followed the ratification of the Trademark Law Treaty (TLT) by the U.S.,[39] ITU applications could be assigned after the filing of an amendment to allege use rather than a statement of actual use.

18.14 After over a century from the introduction of the rule at common law, neither the courts nor the trademark statute provide a clear or consistent definition of what constitutes goodwill. This remains the *Achilles heel* of the provision and the cause for the ambiguity surrounding its application. In past decades, the courts have tried to elaborate on this definition based on consumer attitudes and habits to describe goodwill by evaluating 'the consumers' favorable reactions to a mark', 'the lure of the place', 'the lure to return', 'buyer momentum', 'the legal and economic recognition of buying habits', and 'the expectancy of continuous patronage'.[40] However, the lack of a statutory definition of goodwill has led to inconsistent case law.[41]

18.15 Moreover, since the adoption of the Agreement on Trade-Related Aspects of Intellectual Property Rights (TRIPS) in 1994,[42] no member of the World Trade Organization (WTO), including the U.S., can request that trademarks be assigned with the associated business. Instead, Article 21 of TRIPS establishes that 'the owner of a registered trademark shall have the right to assign the trademark with or without the transfer of the business to which the trademark belongs'.[43] Literally interpreted, the provision prohibits requiring the transfer of any tangible business asset as part of a trademark assignment. As a result, the provision in Section 10 of the Lanham Act now has to be

---

misrepresent the source of the goods or services in connection with which the mark is used.' Trademark Act of 1946, Pub. L. No. 79–489, § 10, 60 stat. 427, 431–32.

35 S. Rep. No. 87–2107, at 5–6 (1962).
36 Trademark Revision Act of 1988, Pub. L. No. 100–667, Sec. 112, § 1060, 102 Stat. 3935.
37 *Id.* at sec. 112, § 1060.
38 Pub. L. No. 105–330, 112 Stat. 3064 (1998), *available 23 September 2015 at* http://www.uspto.gov/web/offices/com/sol/tmlwtrty/index.html.
39 Trademark Law Treaty, 28 October 1994, S. Treaty Doc. No. 105–35 (1998), 2037 U.N.T.S.
40 J. Thomas McCarthy, 1 McCarthy on Trademarks and Unfair Competition §§ 2:15–17 (4th ed. 2015) (summarizing existing case law and doctrines on goodwill). Goodwill is 'the best semantic term we have to describe the consumer recognition or drawing power of a trademark'. *Id.* § 2:15.
41 For a detailed analysis of the judicial decisions in this respect, see Irene Calboli, *Trademark Assignment 'With Goodwill': A Concept Whose Time Has Gone*, 57 Fla. L. Rev. 771, 788–95 (2005).
42 Agreement on Trade-Related Aspects of Intellectual Property Rights, 15 April 1994, Marrakesh Agreement Establishing the World Trade Organization, Annex 1C, Legal Instruments – Result of the Uruguay Rounds vol. 31, 33 I.L.M. 81 (1994).
43 *Id.* at art. 21.

interpreted as only requiring the transfer of intangible goodwill – lest requiring the transfer of tangible goodwill, that is, business assets, would be a violation of Article 21 of TRIPS.

2. Judicial developments

Even though the language of the rule of assignment 'with goodwill' continues to stand, its application has changed considerably since the rule was first adopted. 18.16

(a) Early (conservative) decisions

At common law, the critical inquiry for the validity of an assignment was whether a simultaneous transfer of tangible business assets had occurred.[44] Without such a concurrent transfer, the courts held that assignments were invalid and, in most instances, cancelled the mark at issue or declared it abandoned.[45] In addition, an assignment was not valid if the assignor continued to sell similar products under a different trade name after the transfer.[46] However, starting in the 1920s, the courts started to acknowledge a difference between goodwill and the business, and adopted the position that an assignment was still valid if the assignee had acquired only the part of the business that was necessary for producing the same goods as those manufactured by the assignor.[47] Under the 1946 Lanham Act rule, the courts increasingly acknowledged that transfer of tangible assets was not essential for a valid transfer of goodwill. Starting in the 1960s, the courts further relaxed this interpretation and gradually recognized that assignments were also valid if tangible assets had not been transferred and if the products identified by the mark were not identical nor substantially similar, but only 'similar in kind'.[48] 18.17

The 1962 decision in *Hy-Cross Hatchery, Inc. v. Osborne*[49] represented the first break from the traditional test. In this case, the Court of Custom and Patent Appeals upheld an assignment where the assignee had used the mark on a 18.18

---

44 *See* MacMahan Pharmacal Co. v. Denver Chem. Mfg. Co., 113 F.2d 468, 474–5 (8th Cir. 1901).
45 Bulte v. Iglehart Bros., 137 F. 492, 499 (7th Cir. 1905) ('To uphold such a transfer would be to ignore the fundamental office of a trademark, would be to disregard its purpose and object, would be to sanction a fraud upon the public purchasing article.').
46 *See, e.g.*, Bulte, 137 F. at 499; MacMahan, 113 F.2d at 474–5. This conservative approach initially continued under the rule of the 1905 Act. *See, e.g,* Sexton Mfg. Co. v. Chesterfield Shirt Co., 24 F.2d 288 (D.C. Cir. 1928); Carroll v. Duluth Superior Milling Co., 232 F. 675, 680 (8th Cir. 1916); Sauers Milling Co. v. Kehlor Flour Mills, *Co.*, 39 App. D.C. 535, 542 (D.C. Cir. 1913). The Supreme Court affirmed Section 10 of the 1905 Act in 1918 in United Drug Co. v. Rectanus Co., 248 U.S. 90, 97 (1918).
47 *See* Mulhens & Kropff, Inc. v. Ferd. Muelhens, Inc., 43 F.2d 937 (2d Cir. 1930).
48 *Cf.* Lunney, *supra* note 3, at 410–17.
49 Hy-Cross Hatchery, Inc. v. Osborne, 303 F.2d 947 (C.C.P.A. 1962).

product that was not of the exact same kind as that of the assignor.[50] By the beginning of the 1970s, most courts integrated the *Hy-Cross* principle into their rulings and started to declare assignments valid as long as 'sufficient continuity' or 'substantial similarity', rather than 'identity', existed between the marked goods.[51] Specifically, the courts generally affirmed that trademark assignments did not require the transfer of tangible assets,[52] and that transfer of goodwill could be interpreted as 'intangible goodwill'. This line of reasoning continued in most subsequent decisions on trademark assignment, regardless of the outcomes of the disputes. In a series of leading cases between 1999 and 2001,[53] the courts held the assignments under scrutiny invalid because the assignees used the mark on products that, according to the judges, were different from those of the assignors and this use could mislead consumers in their legitimate expectation of product continuity. Still, in all the decisions at issue, the courts focused primarily on the 'reality of the transaction',[54] rather than on the transfer of goodwill to declare the assignments void.[55]

(b) Shifting towards trademark assignment 'in gross'?

18.19 This trend away from the 'goodwill requirement' brought the majority of the judiciary to an unprecedented liberal approach toward trademark assignment until 2004. Particularly, from 2001 until 2004, the courts upheld all trademark assignments under scrutiny, finding that they included the goodwill of the assigned mark.[56] In 2004, a minority of the courts returned to a more conservative position. Specifically, the courts declared assignments void in two cases related to domain names,[57] arguing that the transfer of a registered domain name is not a sufficient element to satisfy the requirement of Section 10. Yet, these decisions primarily reflect the intention of the judiciary to prevent traffic in domain names.

---

50 *Hy-Cross*, 303 F.2d at 950. The ruling was heavily criticized, and the decisions that followed returned to a more conservative interpretation of the rule. *See* PepsiCo, Inc., 416 F.2d 285; Mister Donut of Am., Inc. v. Mr. Donut, Inc., 418 F.2d 838 (9th Cir. 1969).
51 PepsiCo, Inc., 416 F.2d at 288.
52 *See, e.g.*, Money Store v. Harriscorp Fin., Inc., 689 F.2d 666, 678 (7th Cir. 1982); Visa, U.S.A., Inc. v. Birmingham Trust Nat'l Bank, 696 F.2d 1371, 1375 (Fed. Cir. 1982).
53 *See, e.g.*, Sugar Busters LLC v. Brennan, 177 F.3d 258 (5th Cir. 1999); Pilates, Inc. v. Current Concepts, Inc. 120 F. Supp. 2d 286 (S.D.N.Y. 2002); McGraw-Hill Compensation Inc. v. Vanguard Index Trust, 139 F. Supp. 2d 544 (S.D.N.Y., 2001), aff'd 27 Fed. Appx. 23 (2d Cir. 2001).
54 *See* Archer Daniels Midland Co. v. Narula, 2001 WL 804025, at *7 (N.D. Ill. 12 July 2001).
55 *See generally* Pilates, 120 F. Supp. 2d 286, at *2–21 (quoting McCarthy, *supra* note 1, at § 18:24).
56 Vittoria North America L.L.C. v. Euro-Asia Imports Inc., 278 F.3d 1076 (10th Cir. 2011); International Cosmetics Exchanges, Inc. v. Gapardis Health & Beauty, Inc., 303 F.3d 1242 (11th Cir. 2002); Glow Indus., Inc., 273 F. Supp. 2d 1095 (C.D. Cal. 2003).
57 Pure Imagination v. Pure Imagination Studios, No. 03 C 6070. 2004 WL 2222269 (N.D. Ill. Sept. 30, 2004); InterState Netbank v. Netb@nk, 348 F. Supp. 2d 340 (D.N.J. 2004).

18.20 This trend in favour of trading in trademarks has continued to date with minor exceptions. In 2008, in *Burgess v. Gilman*,[58] in 2010, in *Fizpatrick v. Sony-BGM Music Corp*,[59] and in 2012, in *BLT Restaurant Group LLC v. Tourondel*, the courts upheld the assignments at issue finding that the goodwill had been transferred. In particular, in *BLT Restaurant Group*, the court held not only that the contractual provision, which specified that the requisite goodwill would be transferred along with the mark, was sufficient for the validity of the assignment, but it also held that no business assets had to be transferred with the goodwill.[60] However, in 2014, in *Brown Bar II, L.P. v Dixie Mills, LLC*, the court invalidated the assignment because the assignor went out of business and no longer possessed any goodwill to assign along with the mark.[61] The courts found that the mark was merely transferred as a piece of property, and was, thus, an assignment in gross. Still, the court noted that the assignment was invalid because the assigned mark was not used on substantially similar products of the same quality. Had the mark been used on substantially similar products, the court would have likely (but not certainly) found the assignment valid.

D. TRADEMARK LICENSING

1. The current rule on trademark licensing 'with control'

18.21 Sections 5 and 45 of the Lanham Act set forth the current conditions for the validity of trademark licensing. Specifically, Section 5 states that:

> [w]here a registered mark or a mark sought to be registered is or may be used legitimately by related companies, such use shall inure to the benefit of the registrant or applicant for registration, and such use shall not affect the validity of such mark or of its registration, provided such mark is not used in such manner as to deceive the public.[62]

The Lanham Act also permits licensing of ITU trademark applications in addition to marks that are already in use.[63]

---

58 Burgess v. Gilman, 316 Fed. Appx. 542 (9th Cir. 2008).
59 Fitzpatrick v. Sony-BMG Music Entm't Inc., 99 U.S.P.Q.2d 1052 (S.D.N.Y. 2010).
60 BLT Restaurant Group LLC v. Tourondel, 855 F. Supp. 2d 4, 21 (S.D. N.Y. 2012).
61 Brown Bar II, L.P. v. Dixie Mills, LLC, 732 F.Supp.2d 1353, 4 (N.D. Ga. 2010).
62 Lanham Act § 5, 15 U.S.C. § 1055 (2014). *See also* RESTATEMENT (THIRD) OF UNFAIR COMPETITION § 33 cmt. b (1995) ('If the trademark owner exercises reasonable control over the nature and quality of the licensee's goods or services, the benefits of the licensee's use accrue to the trademark owner.').
63 Lanham Act § 5, 15 U.S.C. § 1055 (2014). The second sentence of Section 5 was introduced with the Trademark Revision Act of 1988 and states, '[i]f first use of a mark ... is controlled by the registrant or

18.22 Section 45 defines a 'related company' as 'any person whose use of a mark is *controlled* by the owner of the mark with respect to the nature and quality of the goods or services on or in connection with which the mark is used'.[64] Similar to the rule on trademark assignment, lack of quality control can lead to the forfeiture of trademark rights if consumers are misled under Section 14 of the Lanham Act. In addition, invalid licenses can lead to abandonment of the licensed mark under Section 45.[65] Also under Section 45, failure to control a license can also render trademark owners liable for false advertising under the Federal Trade Commission Act[66] when the licensees use the marks as instruments to defraud the public.[67]

18.23 In general, trademark owners can license their marks to one or more parties on an exclusive or non-exclusive basis. A licensing agreement typically contains the following information: 'the licensee's right to use, whether exclusive or nonexclusive; royalty payment, if any; geographic area of use; nature of the licensed products or services; sublicensing rights, if any; and the terms of the agreement.'[68]

18.24 Exclusive licensing agreements grant to the licensee the sole right to use the mark in commerce.[69] Additionally, the licensor will often refrain from using the mark in commerce and the licensee is able to sublicense the mark to third parties.[70] An exclusive licensing agreement 'may be limited to a certain territory and/or product or service line, and may include the right to sublicense to third parties'.[71] In contrast, a non-exclusive licensing agreement allows the licensor to grant multiple license agreements to multiple parties in the same

---

applicant for registration of the mark with respect to the nature and quality of the goods or services, such first use shall inure to the benefit of the registrant or applicant, as the case may be'. *See* Pub. L. No. 100–667, 102 Stat. 3935, 3938 (1988).

64   Lanham Act § 45, 15 U.S.C. § 1127 (2014) (emphasis added). Originally, a 'related company' was defined as 'any person who legitimately controls or is controlled by the registrant or applicant for registration in respect to the nature and quality of the goods or services in connection with which the mark is used'. Lanham Act § 45, Pub. L. No. 79–489, 60 Stat. 427, 443 (1946). This definition was amended in 1988 with the adoption of the Trademark Law Revision Act. Pub. L. No. 100–667, 102 Stat. 3935, 3947 (1988).

65   Lanham Act § 45, 15 U.S.C. § 1127 (2014); 15 U.S.C. §§ 41–77 (2000 & Supp. V 2005).

66   *See, e.g.*, Barcamerica Int'l USA Trust v. Tyfield Imps., Inc., 289 F.3d 589, 597–98 (9th Cir. 2002) (holding that abandonment of trademarks occurring when an owner fails to exercise adequate quality control over a licensee is purely an involuntary forfeiture of trademark rights).

67   *See* McCarthy, *supra* note 1, at § 18:48 (citing Waltham Watch Co. v. FTC, 318 F.2d 28, 29 (7th Cir. 1963), cert. denied, 375 U.S. 944 (1963) (finding Federal Trade Commission Act violation)).

68   2–6 Gilson on Trademarks, *supra* note 22, at § 6.01. 'During the entire term of a trademark license, the trademark owner/licensor retains full ownership rights in the mark. Its overall relationship with its licensee, and the nature and scope of the license, are governed by the terms of the license agreement.'

69   *Id.* at § 6.03(1). ('With an exclusive license, the licensor promises to refrain from licensing others to use the mark.')

70   *Id.*

71   *Id.*

area and for the same products.[72] A non-exclusive licensing agreement gives the licensee simply the right to use the licensor's mark.[73] In general, non-exclusive licensees do not have the right to sublicense to another party the right to use the mark, while exclusive licensees commonly are entitled to sublicense the mark to third parties.

18.25 Exclusive licensees enjoy the same rights and protections that trademark owners have under the Lanham Act,[74] which includes standing to sue. Under a non-exclusive licensing agreement, however, the licensee is not granted the same rights as the licensor. The licensor, under the non-exclusive licensing agreement, retains all the rights to the trademark. 'Nonexclusive ... licensees may not sue to challenge trademark infringement under section 32(1) of the Lanham Act, but they may sue under Section 43(a), which allows "any person who believes that he or she is likely to be damaged" to sue.'[75]

18.26 Licensing agreements can either be written or oral even though agreements are typically in writing due to the fact that written agreements allow the courts to interpret the exact language of the contract.[76] A license agreement is not required to be recorded with the USPTO, but it can be, and it is advisable to record an agreement with the USPTO as best practice and in order to create a public record of the licensing agreement.[77]

(a) Rationale of the rule

18.27 Similar to the rule on assignment with goodwill, the rule on licensing with control is based on the principle that trademarks are not protected per se, but as symbols of goodwill and conveyers of information to consumers. Using trademarks as information conveyers also includes maintaining consistent quality of the marked products, regardless of the actual manufacturer. In particular, the requirement of licensing rests on the assumption that a lack of control by the trademark owners could create a breach in the continuity of product 'nature and quality'.[78] In turn, this could lead to consumer confusion or deception if the public continued to purchase the products while relying on

---

72 *Id.* at § 6.03(2).
73 *Id.*
74 *Id.* at § 6.03(1). ('Because courts analogize [the licensee's] rights to those of a trademark owner, exclusive licensees generally have standing to sue.'). Lanham Act § 45, 15 U.S.C. § 1127.
75 2–6 GILSON ON TRADEMARKS, *supra* note 22, at § 6.03(2); Lanham Act § 32, 15 U.S.C. § 1114(1); Lanham Act § 43, 15 U.S.C. § 1125(a).
76 2–6 GILSON ON TRADEMARKS, *supra* note 22, at § 6.01.
77 T.M.E.P., *supra* note 12, at § 503.02.
78 Lanham Act § 45, 15 U.S.C. § 1127 (2000). Originally, a 'related company' was defined as 'any person who legitimately controls or is controlled by the registrant or applicant for registration in respect to the nature and quality of the goods or services in connection with which the mark is used'.

the products' previous characteristics.[79] Hence, requiring trademark owners to control the nature and quality of the licensed products maintains consumer reliance based on the information conveyed by the licensed mark because the quality of the licensed products remains consistent with that of the licensor's products.[80]

18.28 Similar to the rule on assignment with goodwill, the rule on licensing with control is also justified based on the rationale that changes in product quality can increase consumer search costs. In particular, without the quality control requirement, unscrupulous licensors or licensees could change product quality and take advantage of unwary consumers.[81] Licensors could be tempted to maximize revenues by asking licensees to decrease product quality when facing difficulties in the market, bankruptcy, or awareness that their marks have no future.[82] Similarly, licensees could decide to change product quality when they face financial problems or because of other reasons. Although licensees should also be concerned with producing a consistent product quality (or they risk losing customers), their lack of direct ownership of the mark could make them less interested in the long-term success of the products.[83] Accordingly, they could be more inclined to increase short-term profits by decreasing product quality.

(b) Origin of the rule

18.29 Despite the fact that trademark licensing is a widespread practice today, it was not until the adoption of the Lanham Act in 1946 that the practice was officially accepted in the U.S. Both at common law and under the rule of the Trademark Act of 1905, trademark licensing was prohibited as a violation of the primary function of a mark, which at that time was accepted to be that of indicating the origin of the marked products in terms of physical 'source'.[84]

---

79 *See* F. Vern Lahart, *Control – The Sine Qua Non of a Valid Trademark License*, 50 TRADEMARK REP. 103, 107–09 (1960).

80 *See Dawn Donut Co.*, 267 F.2d at 367 (2d Cir. 1959). ('Clearly the only effective way to protect the public where a trademark is used by licensees is to place on the licensor the affirmative duty of policing in a reasonable manner the activities of his licensees.')

81 *Id.* 'The public is hardly in a position to uncover deceptive uses of a trademark before they occur and will be at best slow to detect them after they happen.'

82 *See* James M. Treece, *Trademark Licensing and Vertical Restraints in Franchising Arrangements*, 116 U. PA. L. REV. 435, 453–54 (1968). ('A licensee ... is somewhat more likely than a mark owner to vary product quality, giving rise to a requirement that a mark owner who chooses to license the use of his mark must eliminate this additional increment of risk to the consumer by supervising his licensee.')

83 LANDES & POSNER, *supra* note 27, at 184–5.

84 Irene Calboli, *The Sunset of 'Quality Control' in Modern Trademark Licensing*, 57 AM. U. L. REV. 341, 344 (2007); Irene Calboli, *What if, After All, Trademarks were 'Traded in Gross'?*, 2008 MICH. ST. L. REV. 345, 348 (2008).

D. TRADEMARK LICENSING

Based on this strict interpretation of trademark functions, the majority of the courts initially saw this practice as 'philosophically impossible',[85] and, thus, prohibited it[86] because licensing necessarily implied the outsourcing of product manufacturing to third parties – thus, running against the principle that marks guarantee the physical source of the products.

Still, despite this majoritarian position, a few courts started to indirectly allow licensing several decades prior to the adoption of the Lanham Act.[87] In 1879, the Supreme Court ruled in *Kidd v. Johnson*[88] that the owner of a trademark, who entered into a partnership and used a trademark for the benefit of the partnership did not need to transfer ownership of the mark to the partnership.[89] A few decades later, in the 1916 *Hanover Star Milling Co. v. Metcalf* decision,[90] the Supreme Court held that a trademark was not abandoned and could continue to serve its function as a mark even though it had been licensed.[91] Building upon these decisions, other courts permitted limited forms of licensing in different factual situations.[92] It was then that the 'quality assurance' theory was developed.[93] Courts in their decisions and scholars in their academic writings reconciled this theory with the traditional 'source theory' of trademarks by postulating that trademarks could indicate not only 'actual' product source, but also source 'at large', including the source 'controlling' the product manufacturing process.[94]

18.30

---

85 *See* 3 MCCARTHY, *supra* note 1, at § 18:39.
86 *E.g., MacMahan*, 113 F. at 471–72 (8th Cir. 1901). 'A trademark cannot be ... licensed, except as incidental to a transfer of the business or property in connection with which it has been used.' *Id.* at 474–5.
87 *See* Hicks v. Anchor Packing Co., 16 F.2d 723, 725 (3d Cir. 1926) (noting that in Section 7(c) of the 1918 Trading with the Enemy Act, Pub. L. No. 65–233, 40 Stat. 1020 (codified as amended at 50 U.S.C. app. § 7(c) (2000)), Congress authorized seizure of enemy trademarks and their license to U.S. companies; the grant of such a license did not create ownership of the mark in the licensee); Keebler Weyl Baking Co. v. J. S. Ivins' Son, Inc., 7 F. Supp. 211, 214 (E.D. Pa. 1934) (describing a subsidiary licensing other subsidiaries of United Biscuit Co.); Nelson v. J. H. Winchell & Co., 89 N.E. 180, 183–4 (Mass. 1909) (upholding the concept of a licensed right to use as distinct from the right to use flowing from ownership).
88 Kidd v. Johnson, 100 U.S. 617 (1879).
89 *Id.* at 619.
90 Hanover Star Milling Co. v. D.D. Metcalf, 240 U.S. 403 (1916), superseded by statute, Lanham Act § 22, Pub. L. No. 79–489, 60 Stat. 427, 435 (1946).
91 *See id.* at 418–19 (setting forth that 'trademark rights, like others that rest in user, may be lost by abandonment').
92 3 MCCARTHY, *supra* note 1, at § 18:39.
93 *Id.*, at § 3:10 (recognizing a new concept that 'a trademark did not necessarily have to indicate only manufacturer or merchant source, but could also serve to indicate a level of consistent quality'); *see also* Isaacs, *supra* note 5, at 1215–16; Treece, *supra* note 82, at 445.
94 In the early 1930s, trademarks were seen as fulfilling two different but interrelated functions – indicating the source of the products in terms of 'single controlling source' and guaranteeing to the public that all products bearing the same mark shared the same quality. MCCARTHY, *supra* note 1, § 18:40.

18.31 Yet, while they stressed the importance of control, courts never elaborated on how much control was adequate for licensing to be valid. Instead, individual judges decided how much control is necessary on a case-by-case basis.[95] Even after the enactment of the Lanham Act, courts did not elaborate on how to interpret 'control' or how much control had to be exercised by trademark owners. Instead, this task was left, again, with individual judges as a fact-intense issue. Not surprisingly, the result has been judicial inconsistency.

2. Judicial developments

18.32 With the exception of minor linguistic clarifications, Sections 5 and 45 of the Lanham Act have remained formally unchanged since the enactment of the statute. The interpretation of quality control, however, has changed considerably in the past century. The changes in interpreting the requirement have directly followed the variations in the judicial interpretation of the concepts of 'control of related companies' and 'product quality'.

(a) The evolution of the standard

18.33 Soon after the adoption of the Lanham Act in 1946, courts started drifting away from the position that, for a license to be valid, trademark owners had to enforce strict quality control.[96] Several courts adopted a broader interpretation and upheld licensing agreements as long as trademark owners could prove that the control they exercised was 'adequate' to guarantee consistent quality.[97] Courts never elaborated, however, a specific test to assess whether the control used by licensors was in fact 'adequate'. Rather, they adopted a case-by-case analysis and assessed control based on how licensors guaranteed product quality and whether the agreements included quality control provisions. Several courts affirmed that 'adequate' could be interpreted as 'reasonable'[98] and that findings of 'reasonable' control could dismiss claims of naked licensing.[99] Part of the judiciary lowered this threshold even further and interpreted 'adequate' to mean merely 'sufficient'.[100]

---

95 *E.g.*, Barcamerica, 289 F.3d at 596–97 (9th Cir. 2002).
96 Calboli, *The Sunset of 'Quality Control' in Modern Trademark Licensing*, supra note 84, at 368.
97 *E.g.*, Susser v. Carvel Corp., 206 F. Supp. 636, 641 (S.D.N.Y. 1962), *aff'd*, 332 F.2d 505 (2d Cir. 1964); Morse-Starrett Prods. Co. v. Steccone, 86 F. Supp. 796, 805 (N.D. Cal. 1949).
98 *See generally* Siegel v. Chicken Delight, Inc., 448 F.2d 43, 48–49 (9th Cir. 1971) (finding that as long as the licensor exercises reasonable control over the product's quality, as opposed to maintaining control over specific component articles used in operation and production, a license can be valid).
99 TMT N. Am., Inc. v. Magic Touch GmbH, 124 F.3d 876, 885–86 (7th Cir. 1997).
100 *E.g.*, Susser, 206 F. Supp. at 641.

D. TRADEMARK LICENSING

As part of this favourable trend, the judiciary also developed the position that 'actual' rather than contractual control could support valid licensing.[101] This tendency to look outside the contractual provisions to find indicia of control was first affirmed in the 1959 decision of *Dawn Donut Co. v. Hart's Food Stores, Inc.*,[102] where the court held that the language of the contract was not directly relevant to the validity of the license as long as the licensor exercised actual control.[103] Since then, this principle has commonly been affirmed by the judiciary and, building upon it, some courts have declared that, if actual control is present, an oral agreement can also constitute valid licensing.[104] Courts continued to lower the bar for what constituted 'adequate' control in the following decades. In particular, the judiciary stated that 'adequate' control was a very low standard and that even 'minimal' control was sufficient for a license to be valid.[105]

18.34

Over the past decades, courts have also started to increasingly focus their attention onto the element of product quality, rather than on control, to assess the validity of trademark licensing. In particular, courts started to assess the quality of the products produced under the licensing agreements and assumed that licensors had exercised 'sufficient' quality control provided that the quality of the products was consistent. This approach was first established in 1964 in *Land O'Lakes Creameries, Inc. v. Oconomowoc Canning Co.*[106] In this case, the court held that even if Oconomowoc Canning had not exercised affirmative control on its licensee, the agreement was still valid because the company had justifiably relied on its licensee to control quality since the licensee had maintained consistent product quality for more than 40 years of their licensing relationship. In subsequent years, several courts followed this decision.[107] Still,

18.35

---

101 *E.g.*, Embedded Moments, Inc. v. Int'l Silver Co., 648 F. Supp. 187, 194 (E.D.N.Y. 1986); Nat'l Lampoon, Inc. v. Am. Broad. Cos., 376 F. Supp. 733, 737 (S.D.N.Y. 1974), aff'd per curiam, 497 F.2d 1343 (2d Cir. 1974).
102 Dawn Donut Co., 267 F.2d at 368 (2d Cir. 1959).
103 *Id.* However, the court clarified that in the absence of actual control, abandonment could still be found even if the agreement contained quality control provisions. *Id.* at 368. *Cf.* Robinson Co. v. Plastics Research & Dev. Corp., 264 F. Supp. 852, 864 (W.D. Ark. 1967) ('it is the *right* to control rather than the actual exercise of control which determines whether or not a license is valid').
104 Transgo, Inc. v. Ajac Transmission Parts Corp., 768 F.2d 1001, 1017–18 (9th Cir. 1985).
105 This approach was first elaborated in 1972 in Kentucky Fried Chicken Corp. v. Diversified Packaging Corp. 549 F.2d 368, 387 (5th Cir. 1977) ('Retention of a trademark requires only minimal quality control, for in this context we do not sit to assess the quality of products sold on the open market.').
106 Land O'Lakes, 330 F.2d 667 (7th Cir. 1964).
107 *E.g.*, Haymaker Sports, Inc. v. Turian, 581 F.2d 257, 262 (C.C.P.A. 1978); Embedded Moments, Inc., 648 F. Supp. at 194 (E.D.N.Y. 1986); Eva's Bridal Ltd. v. Halanick Enterprises, Inc., 639 F.3d 788 (7th Cir. 2011); Original Rex v. Beautiful Brands International, 792 F. Supp. 2d 2442 (N.D. Okla 2011).

no court has openly rejected the requirement so far, and some courts have continued to assess agreements conservatively.[108]

(b) Recent developments

18.36 Current trademark practices have also contributed to the growing distance between the quality control requirement and its application in practice. This includes the rise of a new form of licensing agreement: promotional trademark licensing.[109] This practice – which is commonly referred to as trademark merchandising – usually involves the use of a licensed mark on unrelated products, which are not directly produced by trademark owners. The purpose of trademark merchandising is to build, enhance, and exploit brand image and consumer affiliation by affixing the licensed mark to various types of promotional products (for example, T-shirts, mugs, pens, etc.).[110] As commentators have pointed out, trademark merchandising deeply challenges the traditional notion of quality control, since trademark owners most often lack expertise in the promotional goods industry.[111] Hence, the judiciary has rarely questioned the validity of this type of licensing based on lack of quality control. Here again, the courts have commonly relied on the consistent quality of the marked products – that is, on the 'reality of the transaction' test – to assume that such control has been exercised.[112]

18.37 Finally, the courts have further undermined the possibility of strictly enforcing quality control by developing the so-called doctrine of licensee estoppel.[113] Under this doctrine, licensees are barred from bringing claims against licensors for lack of quality control throughout the whole duration of the licensing

---

108 Bach v. Forever Living Prods. U.S., Inc., 473 F. Supp. 2d 1110 (W.D. Wash. 2007). 'The general rule is that a trademark owner who "fails to exercise adequate quality control over [a] licensee" of a trademark creates a "naked license" and thereby abandons the trademark.' *Id.* at 1120 (citation omitted). *See* Dep't. of Parks & Recreation v. Bazaar Del Mundo, Inc., 448 F.3d 1118, 1131 (9th Cir. 2006) ('[W]ell-established trademark law imposes a duty upon the licensor to retain sufficient control over the mark to prevent public deception.'); Barcamerica, 289 F3d 589.

109 The recognition of this practice dates back to the decision in Boston Professional Hockey Ass'n v. Dallas Cap & Emblem Manufacturing, Inc., 360 F. Supp. 459 (N.D. Tex. 1973), *rev'd in part*, 510 F.2d 1004 (5th Cir. 1975). *But see* Stacey L. Dogan & Mark A. Lemley, *The Merchandising Right: Fragile Theory or Fait Accompli?*, 54 EMORY L.J. 461, 471–3 (2005) (criticizing the decision and the foundation of trademark merchandising per se).

110 *See* Calboli, *The Case for a Limited Protection of Trademark Merchandising*, 2011 UNIV. ILL. L. REV. 101 (2011); W. J. Keating, *Promotional Trademark Licensing: A Concept Whose Time Has Come*, 89 DICK. L. REV. 363 (1985).

111 *See generally* Lisa H. Johnston, *Drifting Toward Trademark Rights in Gross*, 85 TRADEMARK REP. 19, 35 (1995) (noting that '[t]he argument for abolishing the quality control requirement focuses on the fact that in promotional merchandising the consumer does not expect a preordained quality level').

112 *See* Calboli, *The Sunset of 'Quality Control' in Modern Trademark Licensing*, *supra* note 84, at 371.

113 *See* MCCARTHY, *supra* note 1, § 18:63; *see also* Treece, *Licensee Estoppel in Patent and Trademark Cases*, 53 IOWA L. REV. 525 (1967).

agreement.[114] The courts have generally justified this doctrine based on equitable principles stating that it aims primarily at safeguarding predictable contractual relations.[115]

E. STRATEGIC TRADEMARK TRANSACTIONS

Besides the rise of promotional licensing, additional trademark practices have contributed to reinforcing the position that the U.S. is de facto drifting toward the acceptance of trading in gross. **18.38**

1. Trademark assignment and license-back

In particular, the past two decades have witnessed the expansion of the practice of assignment and license-back agreements, where a trademark owner assigns his/her mark to an assignee, who in turn grants back to the assignor a license to continue using the mark. Most often, this type of agreement is used by trademark holders as a useful means to settle claims of trademark infringement[116] or to secure priority over a mark in order to assert claims of opposition or trademark infringement.[117] During the past decades, trademark holders have also increasingly adopted this type of agreement to use their marks as collateral for loans.[118] **18.39**

The rationale behind this practice, however, profoundly deviates from the traditional view of trademark law.[119] Specifically, the primary purpose for the **18.40**

---

114 See Prof'l Golfers Ass'n of Am. v. Bankers Life & Cas. Co., 514 F.2d 665 (5th Cir. 1975) (dismissing claim of abandonment based on uncontrolled licensing because estoppel barred the defence). But see RESTATEMENT (THIRD) OF UNFAIR COMPETITION § 33 cmt. d (1995) ('The case for estoppel is weaker when the licensee asserts a lack of control by the licensor over other users.').
115 Calboli, *The Sunset of 'Quality Control' in Modern Trademark Licensing*, supra note 84, at 386; Calboli, *What if, After All, Trademarks were 'Traded in Gross'?*, supra note 84, at 357–8.
116 See 3 MCCARTHY, supra note 1, at § 18:9 ('[I]n settlement of pending litigation, plaintiff may obtain an assignment of rights in the mark and license back [to] the defendant. If there was evidence of customer confusion, this arrangement would bring commercial reality into congruence with customer perception that plaintiff was controlling defendant's use.').
117 See Calboli, supra note 41, at 795 (2005) (citing Glow Indus., Inc., 273 F. Supp. 2d at 1097, 1104).
118 In this respect, the RESTATEMENT (THIRD) OF UNFAIR COMPETITION recites:
> An assignee may license the assignor to use the trademark after an assignment. If the assignment satisfies the requirements stated in this Section and the subsequent license back to the assignor satisfies the requirements stated in § 33, the priority arising from the assignor's original use of the trademark is maintained.

§ 34 cmt. c (1995).
119 This practice strongly resembles a coexistence agreement. A coexistence agreement creates 'concurrent use rights' in a particular mark. Marianna Moss, *Trademark 'Coexistence' Agreements: Legitimate Contracts or Tools of Consumer Deception?*, 18 LOY. CONSUMER L. REV. 197 (2005).

assignees/licensors is to acquire control of the assigned mark and avoid claims of trademark abandonment, or laches and acquiescence on the part of future infringers, rather than entering 'substantially similar' businesses.[120] On their part, assignors/licensees enter these transactions primarily to avoid a finding of trademark infringement and to continue using the mark at issue for the same products as prior to the signing of the agreement, rather than producing or distributing under a licensing program. Likewise, when a mark is used as collateral for a loan, the purpose of the agreement for the assignee/licensor/lender is just to acquire nominal control over the mark and, for the assignor/licensee/borrower to continue disposing of it as previously.[121]

18.41 The judiciary has confirmed the validity of this procedure[122] as a 'well-settled commercial practice'.[123] This further supports the contention that the judiciary is moving away from assignment with goodwill and licensing with quality control. Theoretically, courts have continued to affirm that these transactions are valid only as long as they do not disrupt the continuity of the marked products and provided that assignees/licensors maintain control over their quality.[124] Yet, these limits have proved sterile and formalistic,[125] and the courts have generally relied on the language of the agreement regardless of the effective control exercised by licensors.[126] In other words, by using assignments and license-back agreements, trademark owners and other market players bypass the legal requirement for trademark assignment and licensing

---

120   Calboli, *supra* note 41, at 795.
121   *E.g.*, Visa, U.S.A., Inc., 696 F.2d at 1374 (Fed. Cir. 1982).
122   *See* MCCARTHY, *supra* note 1, at § 18:9 n.4 (citing Brewski Beer Co. v. Brewski Bros., 47 U.S.P.Q.2d (BNA) 1281, 1288–9 (T.T.A.B. 1998)); Sands, Taylor & Wood v. Quaker Oats Co., 18 U.S.P.Q.2d (BNA) 1457, 1467–68 (N.D. Ill. 1990), *aff'd in part and rev'd in part*, 978 F.2d 947 (7th Cir. 1992); Raufast S.A. v. Kicker's Pizzazz, Ltd., 208 U.S.P.Q. (BNA) 699, 702 (E.D.N.Y. 1980); Syntex Labs, Inc. v. Norwich Pharmacal Co., 315 F. Supp. 45, 55–56 (S.D.N.Y. 1970), aff'd, 437 F.2d 566 (2d Cir. 1971).
123   *See* E. & J. Gallo Winery v. Gallo Cattle Co., 967 F.2d 1280, 1290 (9th Cir. 1992) (quoting *Visa*, 696 F.2d at 1377). This practice has 'the beneficial effect of bringing "commercial reality into congruence with customer perception".' *Id.* (citation omitted).
124   *See, e.g.*, Haymaker Sports, Inc., 581 F.2d at 261 (C.C.P.A. 1978) ('A licensor may license his mark if the licensing agreement provides for adequate control by the licensor over the quality of goods or services produced under the mark by a licensee.'); *see* Visa, 696 F.2d at 1377.
125   *See* Visa, 696 F.2d at 1377 ('Contrary to the view of the Board, it is not determinative that there was "no evidence showing to what extent Visa has actually exercised real and effective control over the nature and quality of the services performed by Alpha Beta under the licensed mark".').
126   Glow Indus., Inc., 273 F. Supp. 2d at 1114–15 (C.D. Cal. 2003).

> The language of the agreement demonstrates that [defendant] maintained control over the quality of the … products distributed by [the assignor] pursuant to the license-back, and the burden thus shifts to [plaintiff] to demonstrate that [defendant] did not exercise that control. [The assignor]'s lack of recollection [of such control] is not sufficient to meet that burden, and *it must be assumed* … that [defendant] maintained control over the quality of the products [the assignor] distributed under the mark.
>
> *Id.* at 1111 (emphasis added).

under the implicit consent of the courts and exchange marks as 'things' in the market place as they seem convenient.

2. Security interests in trademarks

As additional evidence of the growing trend toward a revival of a property approach to trademark protection, the judiciary has also shown increasing acceptance toward security interests in trademarks in recent years.[127] Theoretically, secured transactions involving trademarks[128] can be structured as collateral assignments, where title to the mark is immediately transferred to the lender; as conditional assignments, where title is not transferred to the lender until default; or as Uniform Commercial Code ('UCC') security interest liens.[129] In the latter case, Article 9 of the UCC governs consensual transactions of personal property as collateral for loans.[130] Pursuant to Article 9 of the UCC, 'the lender generally must file a UCC-1 financing statement with the Secretary of State of the state in which the borrower resides in order to perfect a security interest'.[131] The UCC-1 financing statement must include the name of the debtor, the name of the lender, and what the collateral is covering.[132] In addition, the lender can also file the security interest with the USPTO.[133] This registration is advisable so that the public is aware of the security interest on the mark.[134]

18.42

---

[127] For a discussion favouring the amending of federal law to allow the use of trademark as security, *see* Allison Sell McDade, *Trading in Trademarks – Why the Anti-Assignment in Gross Doctrine Should Be Abolished When Trademarks Are Used as Collateral*, 77 TEX. L. REV. 465, 482 (1998). *See also* 3 MCCARTHY, *supra* note 1, at § 18:7 (discussing the practice of trademark owners using their marks as security interest).

[128] *See, e.g.*, In re TR-3 Industries, 41 B.R. 128 (Bankr. C.D. Cal. 1984). 'Neither Section 10 of the Lanham Act nor any other section of the Lanham Act specifies a place of filing a claim of security interest in a trademark application for registration of a trademark.' *Id*. at 131.

[129] In this respect it is unclear whether a single filing of the security instrument with the United States Patent and Trademark Office (USPTO) is sufficient perfection for the security interest, or whether an additional recordation in state registries is required under the Uniform Commercial Code (U.C.C.). *See* U.C.C. § 9–109(c) (2000); *see also* Patterson Labs., Inc. v. Roman Cleanser Co. (In re Roman Cleanser Co.), 802 F.2d 207 (6th Cir. 1986). 'I conclude that [appellee]'s security interest in the debtor's trademarks, formulas and customer lists, perfected under the Article 9 filing, did not violate federal trademark law and was valid and enforceable.' *Id*. at 212. Currently, the practice has evolved in recording a financing statement under Article 9 at the state level, and a copy of the security agreement with the USPTO. Courts have generally upheld this practice, but the issue is still partially unclear. The original draft of Section 10(b) of the 1988 Revision Act introduced new provisions relating to the definition and federal registration of security interests in trademarks. These provisions were not enacted, however, in the final version of the Act. *See* MCCARTHY, *supra* note 1, at § 18:7.

[130] U.C.C. § 9–301 (2002).

[131] *Id.;* Baker Botts, *Perfecting Security Interests in IP*, (June 2007), *available 23 September 2015 at* http://www.law360.com/articles/29111/perfecting-security-interests-in-intellectual-property; Heather M. Barnes et al., *Perfection at the Intersection of the UCC and Federal IP Law*, 31-APR AM. BANKR. INST. J. 60 (2012).

[132] U.C.C., *supra* note 129, §9–502.

[133] T.M.E.P., *supra* note 12, at § 503.02.

[134] *Id.*

18.43 Because lenders rarely have an interest in using a mark, collateral assignments are typically structured as assignments and license-back agreements. To avoid the duty of monitoring the quality of the products,[135] secured transactions are generally structured as conditional assignments.[136] However, the Lanham Act does not distinguish between conditional and final assignments.[137] As a result, if parties want to record the transaction with the USPTO as future notice against third parties, conditional assignments should also include the transfer of goodwill.[138] Confirming the trend toward a flexible interpretation of Section 10, the majority of the judiciary has lowered the standards for the validity of both collateral and conditional assignments in secured transactions in the past years. *In re Roman Cleanser*[139] enunciated this shift. Roman Cleanser secured a loan from a competitor using only its mark as collateral. When the company defaulted, the Bankruptcy Court stated, against the position of the trustee, that the fact that no tangible assets were part of the secured transaction did not make the trademark security interest unenforceable or the assignment invalid.[140] The Sixth Circuit affirmed.

18.44 This decision, along with many similar rulings during the past decades, provides additional evidence showing the shift toward a generally more flexible interpretation of Section 10. Still, consumer protection is not a secondary consideration for the courts,[141] and the majority of the courts requires some degree of continuity of product type and quality.[142] Nevertheless, trademarks have become so property-like that they can serve as collateral for loans.[143]

---

135 Haymaker Sports, Inc., 581 F.2d at 261 (C.C.P.A. 1978) (noting that if the borrower-licensee's trademark activities are not sufficiently controlled by the lender-licensor, the license will be considered a 'naked license' resulting in the abandonment of the trademark).

136 Technically, conditional assignments do not vest legal title under the U.C.C. and become operative only if lenders enforce or foreclose the security upon borrowers' default. *See* U.C.C. § 9–108.

137 37 C.F.R. § 3.56

> Assignments which are made conditional on the performance of certain acts or events, such as the payment of money or other condition subsequent, if recorded in the Office, are regarded as absolute assignments for Office purposes until canceled with the written consent of all parties or by the decree of a court of competent jurisdiction.

Id..

138 *See* Clorox Co. v. Chem. Bank, 40 U.S.P.Q.2d (BNA) 1098, 1103–04 (T.T.A.B. 1996); Haymaker Sports, 581 F.2d at 261–2.

139 Patterson Laboratories, Inc., 802 F.2d at 212 (6th Cir. 1986).

140 *Id.* at 208. 'The issue here is whether a security interest in a trademark constitutes an impermissible 'assignment in gross' under the Act if the security interest fails to cover machinery and equipment needed to produce the trademarked goods. We hold that it does not.' *Id.*

141 *See, e.g.*, Glow Indus., Inc., 273 F. Supp. 2d at 1107.

142 *See, e.g.*, Vittoria N. Am., 278 F.3d at 1083; *see also*, RESTATEMENT (THIRD) OF UNFAIR COMPETITION § 34, cmt. b.

143 'Indeed, "[t]he notion of security interests in intellectual property presupposes the capacity of such property to attain significant values in and of themselves".' McDade, *supra* note 127, at 466 (quoting Ian Jay Kaufman et al., *Securities Interests in Intellectual Property*, N.Y.L.J., 28 June 1991, at 5).

F. CONCLUSION

Despite the important changes in the economy that have taken place in the past half century – the transformation of the manufacturing sectors, the rise of the service economy, and consumerism – the requirements for the validity of trademark assignment and licensing agreements in the U.S. remain essentially the same (with some amendments) as those that were first adopted with the enactment of the Lanham Act, or even prior to it. Still, the judicial interpretation of these requirements has profoundly changed in the past decades. In most instances, judicial decisions have drifted away from a strict interpretation of the requirements of assignment with goodwill and licensing with control. This said, some courts have continued to interpret the requirements conservatively. As a result, competitors, interested third parties, and trademark owners in general, are often left wondering what represents a valid agreement. Accordingly, trademark lawyers are advised to use caution when advising their clients as the notion of 'trademark goodwill' and 'quality control' remain ambiguous and the validity of a given transaction will likely be assessed by the courts based on the facts that apply to the case on a case-by-case basis.

18.45

19

NEW DRESS CODE FOR BUSINESS TRANSACTIONS IN BRAZIL: ESSENTIALS AND PECULIARITIES OF TRADEMARKS IN THE SPOTLIGHT

José Carlos Vaz e Dias*

A. INTRODUCTION	19.01	E. TRADEMARK AS COLLATERAL AND SECURITY INTEREST	19.35
B. THE LEGAL NATURE OF TRADEMARKS: OPPORTUNITIES AND LIMITS	19.06	F. ASSIGNMENT OF THE TRADEMARK APPLICATION AND/OR REGISTRATION	19.46
C. TRADEMARKS LICENSING	19.13	G. CONCLUSION	19.63
D. TRADEMARK AND FRANCHISING IN BRAZIL	19.22		

A. INTRODUCTION

19.01 The number of trademark filings at the Brazilian National Institute of Industrial Property (INPI) has been taken into consideration to measure the level of the Brazilian economic development and the perspective of business transactions.[1] The Brazilian Government has also referred to this index to assess the level of consciousness of local businessmen towards intellectual property rights and to tailor specific public policies to foster trademark

---

* Partner, Vaz e Dias Advogados; Professor, State University of Rio de Janeiro; LL.M and Ph.D in Intellectual Property Rights and Foreign Investment Laws, University of Kent at Canterbury, United Kingdom.

1 For an interesting study about the statistics indication of economic development by trademark filing, see PATRÍCIA MARIA DA SILVA BARBOSA, USO DE MARCAS COMO INDICADORES ESTATÍSTICOS DE CIÊNCIA E TECNOLOGIA. ESTUDO DE CASO DAS MARCAS COLETIVAS NO BRASIL (author's translation: 'Use of Trademarks as Statistic Indicator of Science and Technology: Case Study of Collective Marks in Brazil'), *available 23 September 2015 at* http://nbcgib.uesc.br/nit/ig/app/papers/0315093107138519.pdf. This study explores the origins of the use of trademark with statistic indicators, and points out the different impact of trademarks in diverse economic sectors. The study further developed discussions about trademarks in different regions of Brazil. For example, trademarks are regarded as important instruments to attract consumers in food and beverages and protect textile, chemical and electronic companies from piracy in the Brazilian market.

A. INTRODUCTION

protection and innovation for locals.[2] Such policies could encompass reduction of the official fees for registration, possible increase of tax benefits to trademark use, and the promotion of workshops, among others.

19.02 There seems to be a direct relationship between the trademark filing index and the variation and changes of the Brazilian economy.[3] According to the data published by the INPI in 2013,[4] the number of trademark filings has been on the rise since 2007. From 2007 onwards the filings have reached a yearly rate of over 100,000.[5]

19.03 It may be implied by the data that the greater the number of trademark filings,[6] the more promising and the better are the perspectives which arise for investments by local and foreign companies.

19.04 These figures are evidence that local businessmen believe in the economy's growth. Most importantly, there is a more consistent understanding that trademarks may aggregate value to products and services in a market, draw the awareness of consumers, and maintain the identity and reputation of a business. Further, the available data underlines the opportunities for trademark exploitation by means of direct and indirect business. Therefore, trademarks are crucial to business transactions.

19.05 The objective of this chapter is therefore to address possible commercial arrangements that applicants/titleholders may explore and their peculiarities in Brazil. For this purpose, four examples of business transactions are discussed. Franchising, trademark licensing, trademark assignment and security interest.

---

2   José Matias Pereira, *A gestão do Sistema de proteção à propriedade intelectual no Brasil é consistente?* (author's translation: 'Is the Management of the Intellectual Property Protection in Brazil Comprehensive?'), 45(3) REVISTA DE ADMINISTRAÇÃO PÚBLICA 567–90 (June 2011), available 23 September 2015 at http://www.scielo.br/pdf/rap/v45n3/02.pdf.
3   Manuel Mira Godinho, Sandro Mendonça & Tiago Santos Pereira, *Trademarks as an Indicator of Innovation and Industrial Change*, 33(9) RESEARCH POLICY 1385–404 (2004).
4   *See* Instituto National da Propriedade Industrial [hereinafter INPI], *Marcas Depositadas* (author's translation: 'Brands Filed'), available 23 September 2015 at http://www.inpi.gov.br/sobre/arquivos/dirma_estat_portal_ago_13_tabela_1.pdf/view.
5   According to the data published by the INPI, more than 75% of the trademark filings have been done by Brazilian companies, which expresses the awareness of locals of the importance of trademarks and possibly the discredit and criticism of foreign companies to the existing delays on trademark prosecution and registration grant. Further, it may be highlighted that Brazilian businessmen are aware of the delay in trademark prosecution at the INPI. Nonetheless, they continue filing in view of the recognized importance of trademarks to their business.
6   A greater number of registrations can foster economic development, as the titleholder may undertake investments based on the established rights granted by registration, including that the trademarks do not violate third parties' rights. However, the registration index only offers partial information to economic operators, due to the existing backlog of work on trademark prosecution proceedings in Brazil. Obtaining a registration before the INPI can take up to four years.

The first two refer to the exploitation of a mark by authorized third parties, while the latter two involve the direct use of the mark by its holder via the direct assignment of the mark to third parties. The legal framework related to trademark protection and exploitation will be discussed when addressing each of these types of transactions.

B. THE LEGAL NATURE OF TRADEMARKS: OPPORTUNITIES AND LIMITS

19.06 Before addressing the perspective on trademark transactions, it is important to determine the nature of trademark rights in which the commercial exploitation will be grounded.

19.07 A trademark is understood as any visually perceptive sign used in competition to distinguish and/or certify industrial products, commercial articles, and professional services from those that are manufactured or rendered in the market, especially by third parties.[7]

19.08 Since it is considered an important asset for companies' competitiveness, subsection XXIX of Article 5 of the Federal Constitution expressly provides fundamental rights in trademarks.[8] Trademarks are also recognized as subject matters of ownership and property, which secure exclusive rights to the owner, which is

---

7 DENIS BORGES BARBOSA, TRATADO DA PROPRIEDADE INTELECTUAL, Vol. I, 876–9 (2010). *See also* Articles 122 and 123 of Law 9,279 of 14 May 1996 [hereinafter Brazilian Industrial Property Law] *available 23 September 2015 at* http://www.wipo.int/wipolex/en/text.jsp?file_id=125397. In particular, Article 122 of the Brazilian Industrial Property Law states that 'Any distinctive visually perceivable signs that are not included in legal prohibitions shall be eligible for registration as a mark'. Article 123 of the Brazilian Industrial Property Law states:

   For the purposes of this Law, the following definitions apply:

   I.   product or service mark: one which is used to distinguish a product or service from another that is identical, similar, or alike, but of different origin
   II. certification mark: one that is used to attest to the conformity of a product or service with certain technical standards or specifications, particularly regarding its quality, nature, material used and methodology employed; and
   III. collective mark: one that is used to identify products or services provided by members of a certain entity

   Id (translation from the website).

8 *See* Constitution of the Federative Republic of Brazil, Article 5:

   All persons are equal before the law, without any distinction whatsoever, Brazilians and foreigners residing in the country being ensured of inviolability of the right to life, to liberty, to equality, to security and to property, on the following terms …

   XXIX – the law shall ensure the authors of industrial inventions of a temporary privilege for their use, as well as protection of industrial creations, property of trademarks, names of companies and other distinctive signs, viewing the social interest and the technological and economic development of the country …

   Id. (translation from the Digital Library of the Chamber of Deputies. Constitution of the Federative Republic

provided by Article 5 of the Industrial Property Law,[9] as it classifies trademarks as chattels or moveable property, and therefore makes the Theory of Property Rights under the Brazilian Civil Code[10] applicable to trademark exploitation.[11]

19.09 The Theory of Property Rights under the law of the land has the objective of expressly stipulating the rights granted to the proprietor over its objects or intangibles and setting the boundaries of property to prevent abusive practices by the proprietor and violation of third parties. Accordingly, the property rights are viewed under two different – but evolving – perspectives,[12] which provide the legal attributes and obligations to be complied with by the proprietor.[13] The first is the structural perspective, which expresses the proprietor's powers to extensively exercise the property and obtain profit from it by means of exploiting the involved object directly or granting rights to third parties.[14] It also opens the possibility for the proprietor to recover the protected object or intangible against unauthorized use by third parties (*rei vindication*) and obtain losses and damages. Therefore, the remedies are secured to infringement of property rights, as stipulated by the Civil

---

of Brazil Constitutional text of 5 October 1988, with the alterations introduced by Constitutional Amendments No. 1/1992 through 64/2010 and by Revision Constitutional Amendments No. 1/1994 through 6/1994. Documentation and Information Center Publishing Coordination Brasília, 3rd ed. 2010).

9 Brazilian Industrial Property Law, *supra* note 7, at art. 5: 'For legal effects, industrial property rights are deemed to be movable property.'

10 Article 1215, Law 10,406 (Jan. 10, 2002) [hereinafter Brazilian Civil Code] *available 23 September 2015 at* http://www.wipo.int/wipolex/en/details.jsp?id=9615. Article 1225 of the Brazilian Civil Code states: 'the following are real rights: Property.' *Id*. Article 126 states that 'Real rights over movable things, when constituted or transmitted by *inter vivos* acts, are acquired only on delivery of the thing.' *Id*.

11 The theory of property rights may be applicable also to industrial property rights (trademarks and patents) bearing in mind the peculiar nature of such rights, such as the intangible characteristic and its limited existence in time and territory. Moreover, the protection requires compliance with specific principles, such as the First-to-File, the Territory and Specialty and the patentability and trademark registration requirements.

12 GUSTAVO TEPEDINO, A NOVA PROPRIEDADE (O SEU CONTEÚDO MÍNIMO, ENTRE O CÓDIGO CIVIL, A LEGISLAÇÃO ORDINÁRIA E A CONSTITUIÇÃO) (author's translation 'The New Property (Its Minimum Content Between the Civil Code, the Ordinary Legislation and the Constitution')) 306 REVISTA FORENSE 73–75 (1989).

13 Under Brazilian law, legal attributes of property are those legal powers secured to proprietors directly and immediately related to the protected object and intangibles. This means that the titleholder or proprietor may use and dispose of the concerned objects and intangibles by any means insofar it does not violate third parties and complies with the Social Functionality. CAIO MÁRIO DA SILVA PEREIRA, 4 INSTITUIÇÕES DE DIREITO CIVIL 159–72 (8th ed. 2004) (author's translation: 'Institutions of Civil Law').

14 The legal powers are set out by Article 1,228 of the Brazilian Civil Code and encompass the direct exploitation of the right (*ius utendi*), the rights to receive the fruits from third parties' exploitation ('*ius fruendi*'), and the assignment or sale of the rights to someone else ('*ius abutendi*'). The provision states that 'The proprietor has the power to use, exploit and dispose of the thing, and the right to recover it from the power of anyone who wrongfully possesses or hold it.' Brazilian Civil Code, *supra* note 10, at art. 1,228.

Procedural Code and other specific laws, such as the Industrial Property Law.[15]

19.10 The second perspective involves its functional aspects, which requires the exercise of the property rights to the economic and social objectives related to the nature of the object or intangible and the characteristics of granted rights.[16] Therefore, a trademark is an adequate intangible for property rights and the titleholder may extensively exploit it in the market, including the use of it as a transaction.

19.11 It is important to note that Brazil requires trademark registration at the INPI to secure the exclusive rights to its titleholder or to third parties to exploit the registered trademark commercially and enforce its rights in court, as provided by Article 129 and 130 of the Industrial Property Law. Such requirement is justified by the fact that registration is seen under the law as a right recognized by a competent state agency and therefore granted and secured by it. On the other hand, trademarks under prosecution by the INPI are viewed as 'expectation of rights' where the registration requirements (distinctiveness, visual perception, originality and observance to the local laws) are yet to be examined.

19.12 Notwithstanding the aforementioned, the Industrial Property Law secures to the trademark applicant the possibility of exercising some legal attributes related to the property rights. According to Article 130 of the Industrial Property Law, the trademark applicant or the owner may use the mark directly by means of identifying products and services in the market, assigning the

---

15   The *rei vindication* comes under the industrial property rights at a great extent from the exclusive rights (right to exclude others) granted by the Industrial Property Law. In particular, stating:

> The property of a mark is acquired by means of registration, when validly granted pursuant to the provisions of this Law, *and its exclusive use throughout the national territory is assured to the titleholder*, with due regard, as to collective and certification marks, to the provision in Articles 147 and 148.

Brazilian Industrial Property Law, *supra* note 7, at art. 129 (emphasis added).

16   The social function of intellectual property rights is broadly outlined in the first paragraph of Article 1228 of the Brazilian Civil Code, which states:

> 1. The right of ownership must be exercised in a manner consistent with its economic and social ends that, in conformity with the provisions of special legislation, so as to preserve the flora, fauna, natural beauty, ecological equilibrium and artistic and historical patrimony, avoiding pollution of the air and water.

Brazilian Civil Code, *supra* note 10, at art. 1,228. The Brazilian Industrial Property Law sets out forfeiture as an event for the end of trademark rights and an effect for non-compliance with the social functionality principle. Forfeiture takes place due to the non-use of a registered trademark for a period of five years as from the grant or if the registered trademark has been used in a modified form that implies modification in its original characteristic as granted by the INPI. *See* Brazilian Industrial Property Law, *supra* note 7, at arts. 143–5.

property rights and licensing its use to third parties[17] and taking extrajudicial or court measures against infringers.[18]

C. TRADEMARKS LICENSING

One of the most common ways to exploit a trademark in the Brazilian territory is granting rights for third parties to use it by means of a trademark licensing agreement. Such rights may be extensive or limited, and include the possibility for the licensee to defend the license mark in court due to infringement. In view of the binding nature of trademark licensing, the contractual terms and conditions will be regarded as law between the parties. Therefore, the contracting parties should stipulate all involved rights, obligations and requirements in the agreement.   19.13

In addition, trademark licensing may be of different nature, as detailed below: 19.14

(a) *Exclusive*: the licensee will be the only party to exploit the trademark in the market, excluding the licensor/titleholder from the exploitation.

---

[17] The rights to exploit trademarks applied for at the INPI are limited by cogent laws, including public order laws (i.e. foreign exchange control laws, taxation, consumer laws and antitrust) and other mandatory laws that cannot be disposed of by third parties (i.e. prior recordation of trademark licensing at INPI for royalty remittances overseas and the formality requirements). Public order laws are those essentially aiming to protect the best interest of the community or to preserve directly the values of the Brazilian society. Such laws are usually public administration laws, taxation laws, consumer rights and antitrust laws. *See, e.g.*, Marcelo Figueiredo & Maria Alice Deucher Brollo, *Anotações a respeito dos planos econômicos – Alteração da política salarial – Reajuste de salários pela lei antiga – Direito adquirido, merca expectativa de direito e normas de ordem pública – Resenha doutrinária e jurisprudencial* 6 REVISTA TRIMESTRAL DE DIREITO PÚBLICO 234 (1992). An example of public order laws is the Consumer Code that applies to each and every business that affects in any sense the effectiveness of consumer rights. Contractual provisions excluding a licensee or licensor from repairing and indemnifying consumers are neither valid nor enforceable in Brazil, since Article 12 of the Consumer Code (Law 8,078 of 11 September 1990) [hereinafter Consumer Code] grants to consumers the possibility of seeking repair and indemnification from any party involved in the delivery of goods or rendering of services.
  Mandatory laws are cogent but do not aim to protect directly the community. Instead, it aims to balance business relationship or stipulate specific formalities for some acts and business. Article 4 Law 8,955 of 15 December 1994 [hereinafter Brazilian Franchise Law], *available 23 September 2015 at* http://www.wipo.int/wipolex/en/text.jsp?file_id=205219, determines the obligation of franchisor to deliver a disclosure document to the perspective franchisee so-called Franchise Offering Circular, at least 10 days before the executing of a franchise agreement or the receipt of any remuneration derived from the franchise relationship.

[18] The guarantee comes from the need to protect the existing reputation and integrity of the mark, despite the fact that a trademark is being prosecuted at the INPI. Currently, this guarantee is justified due to the backlog of work at the INPI, which has been delaying the examination proceedings substantially. According to Article 130 of the Brazilian Industrial Property Law 'It is also secured to a trademark titleholder or applicant the following rights: I. assign the registration or application; II. license its use; III. ensure its material integrity or reputation.' Brazilian Industrial Property Law, *supra* note 7, at art. 130.

Therefore, the licensee may prevent third parties from manufacturing and marketing products identified by the licensed trademarks.

(b) *Non-Exclusive*: the licensor will retain the rights to use the trademark and will be further entitled to grant concurrent licenses to third parties.

(c) *Sole License*: the licensee will be authorized to exploit the license agreement, but the licensor will retain the right to also use the trademark.

(d) *Master License*: the licensee is empowered by the licensor to concentrate the exploitation in a determined region or territory and grant to sub-licensees specific rights for trademark exploitation. This kind of license is very common in licensing where licensors identify the regions in which its licensed products and trademark will be commercialized.

19.15 Trademark licensing agreements in Brazil are subject to prior recordation of the agreement at the INPI for the following reasons:[19]

(a) to produce the effect of agreement before third parties, including the Brazilian Central Bank for remittances overseas and to entitle the licensee to proceed in court against the infringement of the trademark, when the agreement so provides;

(b) to entitle the licensee to proceed with royalty remittances to a foreign licensor; and

(c) to empower the licensee to fiscally deduct the remitted/paid royalties to the licensor.

This means that recordation is not needed for the validity of the agreement between the parties or for maintaining the validity of the trademarks in Brazil and to prevent forfeiture. The adequate use of a trademark in Brazil may be evidenced by the licensee's use insofar as the licensing agreement is signed between the parties and invoices evidencing the sale of the identified product are presented to the INPI during forfeiture proceedings.

19.16 In the absence of a legal compilation addressing the ruling of trademark licensing (only scattered rules address licensing in Brazil to date), the provisions in Articles 565 to 578 and 579 to 592 of the Civil Code with respect to leasing agreements should also be taken into account by the licensor/licensee when drafting the agreement.[20]

---

19 José Carlos Vaz e Dias et al., *Brazil*, in WORLD INTELLECTUAL PROPERTY RIGHTS AND REMEDIES 25–6 (Dennis Campbell ed., 2002).

20 The applicability of these ancillary rules of the Civil Code is possible in view of the fact that trademarks are chattels or moveable property under Article 5 of the Industrial Property Rights. A licensee in this regard is considered equal to a lessee of movable property.

19.17 Further, trademark licensing is subject to foreign exchange control laws and the unwritten rules of the INPI applied during the recordation proceedings of trademark licensing.[21] As a result, the parties need to comply with specific rules, as follows:

(a) licensing agreements are required to be in writing;
(b) the licensor needs to list the trademarks duly filed/registered in Brazil that will be subject to licensing by specifying the number of the application/registration;
(c) the licensor requires maintenance of the validity of the enlisted trademarks in Brazil, including the obligation to defend them in court, unless the licensee is entitled to do so;
(d) adequate designation of the parties;
(e) the term of the agreement should be matched to the duration of the validity of the enlisted trademarks in Brazil;
(f) stipulation of the remuneration for the license rights; contractual omission in this regard is understood as royalty free;
(g) indication of the responsible party for the collection/payment of withholding taxes applicable to royalty remittances; among others.

It is important to note that royalty remittances overseas suffer restraints from the foreign exchange control laws when the contracting parties are related. Accordingly, when a licensor directly or indirectly controls a licensee,[22] the applicable royalties may not surpass the amount of 1 per cent of the net sales revenue obtained by the licensee from the exploitation of the product identified by the licensed trademark. This amount is determined by the cap royalties used by Ministerial Ordinance 436/58 for fiscal deductibility.

---

21 The foreign exchange control laws applicable to trademark licensing include Law 4,131 of 3 September 1962, Law 4,506 of 30 November 1964, Law 8,383 of 31 December 1991, and the regulations of the Brazilian Central Bank (BACEN). Unwritten rules derived from revoked INPI's regulations are still applicable by the agency when recording technology transfer agreements and licensing agreements. This practice is considered illegal in view of the Principle of Legality that the INPI and other public agencies are subject to comply. José Carlos Vaz e Dias, *Os princípios da legalidade e da competência e os limites de atuação do INPI no direito de concorrência*, REVISTA DO IBRAC 13–21 (1998) (author's translation 'The principles of legality and competence and the limits of INPI's role in competition law').

22 The controlling party is the company that owns more than 50% of the voting shares and the power to elect the majority of the controlled parties' administrators. *See* Article 1,098 of the Brazilian Civil Code:

A company is controlled where:

I – another company holds, through the capital of the controlled company, a majority of votes on resolutions put to meetings or to the assembly of partners, members or shareholders, as the case may be, and the power to elect a majority of the administrators of the controlled company;

II – control over the company referred to in the preceding item is held by another company, through shares or quotas held through other controlled companies.

Brazilian Civil Code, *supra* note 10, at art. 1,098.

19.18 Royalty calculation and remittance can only take place from licensed trademarks that are already registered before the INPI. Therefore, trademark applications cannot generate royalties or remittances of any kind to a licensor.

19.19 When the contracting parties are unrelated, no royalty limits are imposed and therefore, the parties may freely stipulate the value of the remuneration. No other specific regulations are imposed in principle to limit the freedom to contract of a licensing trademark.[23] The parties may further renew the contractual period, and extend or modify the terms and conditions of the agreement. However, any modifications are valid and effective when proposed in writing and executed by the parties and two witnesses. The signature of a foreign licensor requires notarization by a Notary Public and further legalization at the Brazilian Consulate.[24]

19.20 Modifications, renewals, and extension of any kind require prior recordation at the INPI. Recordation will be applicable only to those trademarks filed or registered at the INPI, as they need to be valid and effective in Brazilian territory.

19.21 As to the formalities, the agreement needs to be signed by the parties and two witnesses. The signature of the foreign party's representative should be notarized and legalized before the Brazilian Consulate. The parties and witnesses should further place their initials on each page of the agreement.

D. TRADEMARK AND FRANCHISING IN BRAZIL

19.22 Franchising is one of the most effective businesses for the promotion of goods and services in Brazilian territory. It currently generates a total revenue of BR$111,582 billion (approximately $50 billion USD), as published by the Brazilian Franchise Association, as shown in Figure 19.1.

---

23 Nevertheless, the antitrust regulations and the Consumer Rights Code are laws of public order and the terms and conditions of a licensing agreement and the exercise of the rights by the parties cannot violate them. Article 12 of the Consumer Code states:

> The manufacture, producer, and builder, both Brazilian and foreign and the importers are liable, independently of fault for redress for damages caused to consumers by defects, resulting from the design, manufacture, construction, assembly, formulas, handling and making up, presentation or packing of their product, as well as for insufficient or inadequate information on the use or hazard thereof.

Brazilian Consumer Code, *supra* note 17, at art. 12.

24 Trademark licensing agreements executed by a French licensor are exempt from legalization in view of the existing treaty.

D. TRADEMARK AND FRANCHISING IN BRAZIL

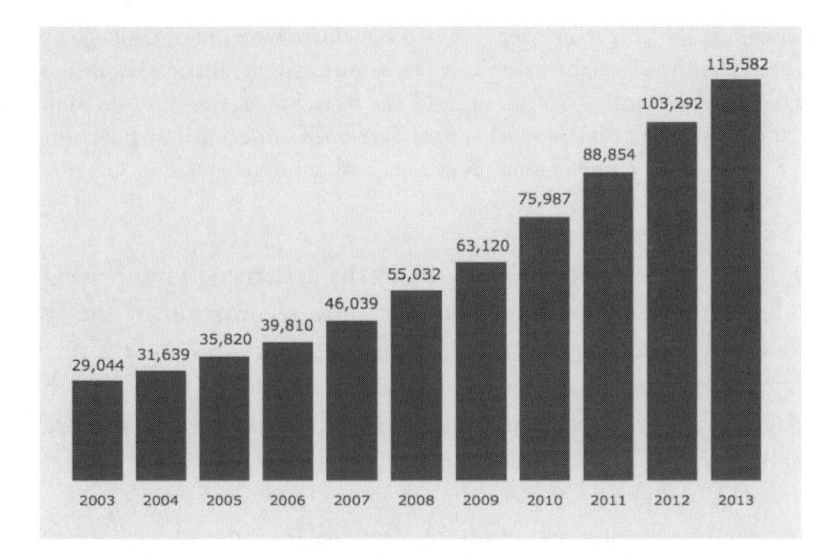

Source: Brazilian Association of Franchising (http://www.portaldofranchising.com.br).

Figure 19.1 Revenue from franchising (BR$)

Further to that, the sector consisted in 2013 of 114,400 franchising units operating locally, which generated more than 1,029,681 jobs in the same year.[25] Additionally, there are 2,703 established franchisors in various economic sectors,[26] among them being 168 international franchise networks. There are 112 Brazilian franchised trademarks exploring its products and services in 53 countries.[27]   **19.23**

The trademark role in the success of franchising comes from the prevailing Business Format Franchising in the country where prescribed operational, commercial and marketing methodologies are granted to franchisees[28] together with trademarks and trade dress peculiar to the business/service.[29]   **19.24**

According to the Brazilian Franchise Law, a franchise is defined as: **19.25**

---

25 Evolução do Setor 2003–2013 (author translation: 'Industry Evolution 2003–2013'), Associação Brasileira de Franchising (2013).
26 *Id.*
27 CANDIDA CAFFÉ ET AL., CHAPTER ON BRAZIL. This article was first published in THE FRANCHISE LAW REVIEW (Mark Abel ed., 1st ed. 2014).
28 BARBARA BESHEL, AN INTRODUCTION TO FRANCHISING, (IFA Educational Foundation, 2010), *available* 23 September 2015 *at* http://www.franchise.org/uploadedfiles/franchise_industry/resources/education_foundation/introtofranchising_final.pdf.
29 The prescribed business and operation method and the reputation of the trademark provide third parties with an opportunity to be adequately trained in how to operate an unknown business thus, it is believed, reducing the risk of business failure. The success of franchising in Brazil may be explained by different reasons, including the lower risk involved than in using traditional methods in a country with continental size and market diversity.

the system by which a franchisor grants to franchisee the right of trademark or patent use, associated to the right to exclusive or semi-exclusive distribution of products or services and, eventually, also the right of use of technology of business implantation and administration or operational system developed or detained by franchisor against direct or indirect remuneration, however, without characterizing an employment relationship.[30]

19.26 In view of that, trademarks are essential to the existence of franchising and to the validity of a franchise agreement. Because recordation of the franchise agreement is also needed for overseas remittance purposes and tax deductibility, the agreement requires prior recordation at the INPI. Therefore, the INPI demands that the franchised trademarks filed/registered in Brazil are adequately specified in the agreement.

19.27 Trademarks are also looked upon by franchisees, in practical terms, as a convincing business argument for investment or the heart of the business decision or franchise deal. In this matter, it should be highlighted that trade dress of a service and business is protected by Brazilian laws when it presents distinctive business element. Such protection takes place under the unfair competition rules set out by Articles 186 to 188,[31] and 884[32] of the Civil Code, and those specific rules to unfair competition in the Industrial Property Law.[33]

19.28 Because a trademark is the carrier of the reputation of a franchise in the market, it is understood that the goodwill of a single unit franchise belongs entirely to the franchisor who is the titleholder of the mark. Any poor performance by franchisees may affect the trademark concerned, the image of the franchisors thereby causing damages to the franchise network and other franchisees.

19.29 Franchising agreements hold stringent rules on trademark use in this regard. Among them, one can point out the franchisee's obligation to use the trademark and the trade dress concerned in a manner determined by the franchisor so that all single unit franchises in a network look the same and signal quality and product/service reliance to consumers. Moreover, quality

---

30 Brazilian Franchise Law, *supra* note 17.
31 These provisions deal with the identification, concept and limits of illicit acts committed by any person that may generate indemnification from losses and damages.
32 Article 884 of the Brazilian Civil Code addresses illicit enrichment, including the unauthorized use of trade dress or products and services by third parties. Brazilian Civil Code, *supra* note 10, at art. 884.
33 Article 195 of the Brazilian Industrial Property Law enlists those unfair competition practices regarded as crime, including the *use of fraudulent means* by a competitor to divert, for his own or a third party's benefit, another clientele. Brazilian Industrial Property Law, *supra* note 7, at art. 195.

control of the products sold in a single unit franchise belongs entirely to franchisor, which is empowered by the agreement to determine those products that will be sold in the store and their source.

19.30 In order for a franchise to be valid and effective in Brazil, the Brazilian Franchise Law requires compliance with the following obligations: (i) the franchise rights need to be granted in writing and the agreement requires signature by the contracting parties and two witnesses; (ii) specification of the trademarks involved for the use of franchisee, which are applied for/registered at INPI; (iii) specification of franchisor and franchisee's rights, including remuneration, among others.[34]

19.31 Further, the law determines the obligation of a franchisor to deliver to the prospective franchisee a document, the so-called Franchise Disclosure Document (FDD).[35] The FDD needs to specify the following items, as follows[36]:

I) resumé abstract, societary structure and full name or commercial style of franchisor and all enterprises to which it is directly linked, as well as respective trade names and addresses;
II) balance sheets and financial statements of the franchising enterprise relative to the last two fiscal years;
III) precise indication of all litigation in which the franchisor, the controlling enterprises and titleholders of trademarks, patents and copyrights relative to the operation and their subfranchisors may be involved, specifically challenging the franchising system or those which may directly make it impossible for the franchise to function;
IV) detailed franchising description, general description of the business and the activities that will be performed by the franchisee;
V) profile of 'ideal franchisee' concerning previous experience, education level and other characteristics;
VI) requirement concerning the direct involvement of franchisee in the operation and administration of the business;
VII) estimated total of the initial investment, royalty rates and other required investments for the franchising installation;

---

34 Brazilian Franchise Law, *supra* note 17, at art. 6 (stating '[t]he franchise agreement must always be signed in the presence of two (2) witnesses and shall be valid independently of being registered before a public notary's office or a public agency.'). *See also id.*, at art. 8 ('the provision of this law apply to the franchise established and operated within the national territory').
35 The FDD is a document that comprises commercial and operation information about the franchisor and the franchise network needed for a prospective franchisee to decide about investing in the proposed franchise network.
36 *See* Brazilian Franchise Law, *supra* note 17, at art. 3.

VIII) complete list of franchisees, subfranchisees and subfranchisors of the franchise network;
IX) information on the territory, including exclusivity and any possibility of rendering services or realizing sales outside the territory;
X) clear information about the franchisee's obligations to acquire any real estate, services or manufacturing components for implementation, operation and administration of its franchise from specific suppliers;
XI) indication of what is effectively offered to the franchisee by the franchisor concerning manuals, supervision, training and assistance;
XII) specification of the situation of the trademarks or patents the use of which is being authorized by the franchisor before the INPI;
XIII) situation of franchisee after expiry of the franchising agreement regarding know-how or industrial secrets to which the franchisee has had access and the possibility of the franchisee competing with the franchisor; and
XIV) delivery of a model of the standard franchise agreement.

The FDD needs to be delivered to the prospective franchisee at least ten days before the execution of the franchise agreement or pre-agreement or the payment of any kind of fees by the franchisee to the franchisor or to an enterprise or person linked to it.

19.32 This obligation also binds international franchises in Brazil since Article 8 of the aforementioned law stipulates, 'the obligations under this law apply to all franchise systems introduced and operated in the Brazilian territory'.[37] Furthermore, the INPI requires evidence of the delivery of the FDD to Brazilian franchisees in order to record the Franchise Agreement and permit remittances abroad. Therefore, international franchisors are required to deliver the FDD to the local potential franchisees and most importantly, international franchisors are bound by the penalties specified by the law.[38]

---

37 *Id.* at art. 8.
38 The penalty for not complying with the delivery of the FDD and/or providing false information in the FDD is the possibility for the franchisee to demand the annulment of the franchise agreement and the return of all amounts that have been paid to franchisor deriving from the operation of the franchising, including the initial franchise fee and the royalties. The franchisee may also request losses and damages in court caused by non-compliance with the legal obligation. Article 4 of the Brazilian Franchise Law states:

> The Franchise Disclosure Document will be prepared annually by franchisor and should be delivered to the applicant at least 10 (ten) days before the signature of the franchise agreement or pre-agreement or the payment of any fees by franchisee to franchisor or to a company or person linked to it.

Brazilian Franchise Law, *supra* note 17, at art. 4. In addition, the Brazilian Civil Code sets the statute of limitation for a person to initiate court proceedings. There are two different rules that may be related to late delivery of the FDD to the prospective franchisee. For the annulment of the franchise agreement, franchisees may proceed in court within two years from the date of execution of the franchise agreement. *See* Brazilian Civil Code, *supra* note 10, at art. 179. ('When the law provides that a given act is voidable, without

19.33   An important note is that trademark applications may generate royalties and remittances from a franchise agreement, in view of the broader rights granted to the franchisee, including the delivery of operational manuals, training and so on. This treatment differs from licensing.

19.34   The same formalities as in the trademark licensing agreement apply to franchising, as the parties and two witnesses should sign the agreement. The signature of the foreign party's representative should be notarized and legalized before the Brazilian Consulate. The parties and witnesses should further place their initials on each page of the agreement.

E. TRADEMARK AS COLLATERAL AND SECURITY INTEREST

19.35   Since trademarks have become valuable assets to a company's competitiveness, such intangibles are being increasingly used by business and in court decisions as collateral to secure obligations.

19.36   To perfect and enforce the security interest agreement bearing a trademark as collateral, the Industrial Property Law provides for the need to register any limitation or pledge on trademark applications and registrations.[39] The objective of registering the security interest is to place any interested party or businessmen on constructive notice that the pledge of the trademark prevents any assignment to or guarantee of other third parties.[40]

---

establishing the period of time within which annulment must be claimed, the time period shall be two years from the date in which the act was concluded.') To seek losses and damages due to the non-compliance of the FDD, the limitation period for the franchisee is ten years, as from the date of execution of the franchise agreement. *See id*, Article 205 (which states that '[p]rescription occurs in ten years, unless the law has fixed a lesser period') (translation from LESLIE ROSE, THE BRAZILIAN CODE IN ENGLISH, 2nd ed. (2012)).

39   The need of registration of the pledge before the public agencies and register of titles and deeds are set out by Article 1,432 of the Brazilian Civil Code, according to which '[t]he instrument of pledge must be registered by either of the contracting parties; an instrument of common pledge shall be registered in the Office of Titles and Documents', Brazilian Civil Code, *supra* note 10, at art. 1,432.

40   The debtor is further required to proceed at the INPI to remove the recordation of the lien when the corresponding debt is adequately paid, as it is of its interest to do so and free the trademark for further transactions. This statement is derived from the interpretation of Article 136 of the Brazilian Industrial Property Law that establishes the general ruling for recordation of the trademark lien and Article 1437 of the Brazilian Civil Code. In particular, Article 136 of the Brazilian Industrial Property Law states:

The INPI shall make the following entries: I. of the assignment, containing the full identification of the assignee; II. of any limitation or onus that applies to the application or registration; and III. of changes in the name, headquarter or address of the applicant or titleholder.

Brazilian Industrial Property Law, *supra* note 7, at art. 136. *See id*. at art. 137 ('[e]ntries shall become effective with regard to third parties beginning on the date of their publication') (translation from website). *See also* Brazilian Civil Code, *supra* note 10, at art. 1,437 ('The extinction of the pledge produces effect after cancellation of registration is recorded, upon production of proof of extinction') (translation from ROSE, *supra* note 38).

19.37 This means that recordation of the pledge by the INPI will make the agency refuse to record assignments, mortgages, or any additional collateral specified as a security for the satisfaction of a debt.

19.38 The Industrial Property Law provides a novelty in relation to the prior law, as it recognizes that recordation will be applicable to any kind of limitation, not only to those derived from case law and decisions of government authorities. Under the new wording of Article 136 of the Industrial Property Law, any limitation on trademark applications or registration will be taken into account for recordation, including those privately agreed by the titleholder in commercial agreements, such as any 'Trademark Mortgage Agreement', 'Security Interest Agreement', among others.

19.39 The indication of trademark applications or registrations as security for a debt does not exempt the applicant or registrant from complying with its obligation of maintaining the trademarks involved as valid and effective. In fact, the applicant or registrant of the lien is placed in the position of a trustee and therefore holds an obligation to maintain the security in good order.

19.40 In view of that, the applicant/titleholder is obliged to comply with its basic obligations, such as paying the official fees for registration and requesting registration renewals during the legal time frame, among others.

19.41 Articles 1,431 to 1,472 of the Brazilian Civil Code deal with security interests as collateral for guarantees, as they determine that moveable things and rights may be offered and disposed to secure payment or performance of a contractual obligation. The basic requirements of the lien are that: the moveable thing becomes subject to property in existence and by law; and the moveable thing is capable of conveyance to the creditor's possession following the peculiarities of the thing and the existence of a main agreement creating the credit.[41]

19.42 It is important to highlight that 'moveable thing' should also include immaterial rights, as the Civil Code has eliminated the requirement of effective conveyance and possession of the collateral by the debtor. Accordingly, the effective conveyance of the chattel is dispensable and the 'fictitious' transfer may take place by means of an agreement that secures the lien.

19.43 It is a common practice adopted by commercial banks and financing institutions to accept products/goods as security for a debt and empower the debtor

---

[41] José Carlos Vaz Diaz & Daniel Pitanga, *Brazil*, in TRADEMARKS IN 42 JURISDICTIONS WORLDWIDE (Callum Campbell ed., 2010).

as a trustee of the product thereby maintaining with the debtor the pledge products/goods. This may apply to trademarks.

Security interest in trademarks is usually affected in the form of a separate agreement or within the contents of a loan agreement, which should contain the following matters: 19.44

- the nature of the loan or the main obligation that created the amount;
- the precise amount of the credit, or its estimated value or total amount;
- the time frame for payment of the credit;
- the peculiarities of the secured trademark, including the specification of the registration or application of the mark before the INPI; and
- the estimated value of the secured mark.[42]

As to the formalities, the agreement needs to be signed by the parties and two witnesses. The signature of the foreign party's representative should be notarized and legalized before the Brazilian Consulate. The other party's signature should be notarized locally. The parties and witnesses should further place their initials on each page of the agreement. 19.45

F. ASSIGNMENT OF THE TRADEMARK APPLICATION AND/OR REGISTRATION

Trademark registrations and applications may be subject to commercial sale by means of assignment to third parties, as they comply with the general requirements set out by Article 481 of the Civil Code, which are (a) the effective transfer of property rights to the buyer and (b) payment of the agreed price to the seller. 19.46

The Industrial Property Law complements this by making the recordation of the assignment at the Brazilian INPI indispensable. This is due to the peculiar nature of trademarks – intangible and immaterial – which does not permit the 19.47

---

42 The requirements for the validity of a security interest are set by the combination of provision 1,424 of the Brazilian Civil Code and the existing information in the Trademark Manual issued by the INPI by means of Resolution n. 142 of 27 November 2014 (*available 23 September 2015 at* http://manualdemarcas.inpi.gov.br/). In particular, Article 1,424 of the Brazilian Civil Code states,

> Contracts of pledge, antichresis and hypothec shall state, on pain of inefficacy: I – the amount of the debt, its estimated amount, or its maximum amount; II – the term fixed for payment; III – the interest rate, if any; IV – the property given as security, with its specifications.

Brazilian Civil Code, *supra* note 10, at art. 1,424.

'physical transfer of the trademark to the seller'.[43] Therefore, the recordation of the assignment is viewed as evidence to third parties of the transfer of the trademark rights to the buyer.

19.48 It is understood that a trademark assignment needs to fulfill three independent stages that produce effects to the parties. The first is the actual execution of the agreement. The second is the filing of the assignment at the INPI for recordation purposes and the third and final the publication of recordation, when the assignment will effectively produce effects between third parties.

19.49 In practical terms, this means that the validity of the trademark assignment agreement will commence with its execution by the contracting parties, not against third parties. Without the publication of the assignment at the Industrial Property Gazette, the assignee will not be able to defend its ownership on the assigned trademarks or initiate court proceedings against infringers that violate the trademark rights. Further to that, BACEN will require the prior recordation of the assignment in order to authorize remittances of payment arising from the acquisition of trademark applications/registrations.

19.50 Notwithstanding the information provided on the effects of an assignment agreement, the Brazilian courts have accepted the legitimacy of the assignee in taking court action against third parties that infringe its rights derived from the assignment (secure the property rights and exclusivity to exploit goods and services and defend the assigned mark) with the filing of the assignment agreement at the INPI. This acceptance comes from the fact that recordation is a formal requirement where the INPI examines if the assignee holds the same activity of the class of goods/services of the mark, if the registration/application is valid and if the agreement complies with the formalities. Moreover, the courts wish to prevent the existing backlog of work of the INPI[44] from jeopardizing the assignee's rights, including the damage that the assigned trademark may suffer from infringers.

---

43 *See* Articles 134, 135 and 137 of the Brazilian Intellectual Property Law, *supra* note 7. According to Art. 134, 'The trademark application and the registration may be assigned, provided the assignee satisfies the legal requirements for applying to register it.' *Id*. Article 135 states '[t]he assignment must comprehend all the registrations or applications, in the name of the assignor, for the same or similar marks, related to an identical, similar, or alike product or service; under penalty of having the registrations cancelled or the unassigned applications dismissed.' *Id*. For the text of Article 137, *see supra* note 40.
44 According to common practice on trademark prosecution, the recording of an assignment agreement may take up to two years to be concluded. The recording of a licensing agreement with the INPI of an assigned trademark (not yet published by the Industrial Property Gazette) is also possible insofar as the licensor evidences to the Technology Transfer Department that the assignment has been filed at the INPI.

F. ASSIGNMENT OF THE TRADEMARK APPLICATION AND/OR REGISTRATION

19.51 During the recordation procedure, the assignor will be the responsible party for maintaining the validity of the assigned trademark and responding to all debts related to the sold product.[45] Therefore, if an assigned trademark is declared forfeit due to non-user or it suffers revocation proceedings, the assignor will take all requested steps to preserve its validity. The parties may stipulate that the assignee will lead all court proceedings in the maintenance of the validity.

19.52 According to Article 135 of the Industrial Property Law, the assignment must include all applications or registrations in the name of the assignee involving identical or similar marks relating to a product or a service under the penalty of the cancellation of the registrations or the shelving of the unassigned applications. The rationale behind this rule comes from the need to prevent the assignor from continuing the use of a similar trademark to the assigned one for the same activity. This would interfere with the objective of the trademark assignment, which is the transfer of the property rights to the buyer, encompassing exclusivity in the market.

19.53 Therefore, it can be stated that the assignment of a trademark may not be partial or limited (for example, the authorization for one party to exploit a trademark linked to a product of one class and for another party another product of the same class).

19.54 In this matter, the assignment of a mark for the identification of specific products of a class is further prevented by Article 144 of the Industrial Property Law. This provision states that the use of a mark encompasses the products and services specified in the Registration Certificate. The use of the mark in part of the products may lead to the partial forfeiture of the registration with respect to those products or services not similar or akin to those for which use of the mark has been approved.[46]

19.55 It is also understood that assignment cannot be granted to different parties for different regions of Brazil, since the transfer of rights relates to applications/registrations filed/granted at the INPI, which has effect for the whole Brazilian territory.

---

45 *See* Article 502 of the Brazilian Civil Code: 'Unless it is otherwise agreed, the seller is liable for all the debts that encumber the thing up to the moment of delivery' Brazilian Civil Code, *supra* note 10, at art. 502.
46 Brazilian Industrial Property Law, *supra* note 7, at art. 144:
> Use of the trademark must be made in respect of the products or services indicated on the certificate, under penalty of the registration being partially cancelled regarding the products or services that are neither similar nor related to those in respect of which use of the mark was proven.

Id.

19.56 It should be stated that the transfer of the rights over a registration/application does not in principle involve the assignment of the goodwill of the assignor's business derived from reputation of the mark. The assignment will involve the property rights under the trademark registrations/applications, which encompass solely the exclusivity and the possibility of obtaining profits from its use.

19.57 Nevertheless, the Industrial Property Law determines that a trademark not registered, but protected under the concept of prior use,[47] may only be assigned if the assignor's business or part of the assignor's business that has links to the trademark is also transferred.[48]

19.58 Articles 1143 to 1149 of the Civil Code provide the possibility of a trademark assignment together with the goodwill when the assignor also transfers its commercial and industrial business to the assignee by means of a so-called 'Trespasse' agreement ('Transfer of a commercial establishment').[49] In the 'Trespasse', the business is assigned as a whole, including intangibles, list of clients, the lease of where the business is located, credits, and debts, among others.

19.59 In view of that, the assignee will be prohibited from competing with the assignor for a period of five years as from the execution of the 'Trespasse'. The violation of this obligation set out in Article 1,147 of the Civil Code is classified as unfair competition practice thereby applying losses and damages for such violation.

---

47 Although the Brazilian trademark system adopts the First-to-File Principle, Paragraph 2 of Article 129 of the Industrial Property Law protects those trademarks that have been in use in good faith and for more than six months. Such protection comes under the title 'right or precedence' to request the registration of the mark in use at the INPI. Brazilian Industrial Property Law, *supra* note 7, at art. 129(2).

48 *See id*. The stipulation of this rule comes from the concept that the use in the market of a mark not registered relates to a small business where the trademark is embedded in the business run by the holder. In view of this understanding, the transfer of a mark not registered to a third party without the goodwill generated by the mark would be bizarre.

49 The Brazilian Civil Code has created specific rules for the assignment of a business, including those applicable to the assignee's and the assignor's responsibility to pay the existing debts from the business and assure the payment of debtors. According to Article 1,145 '[i]f Alienor does not have sufficient assets to meet his liabilities, the efficacy of the alienation of the establishment depends on payment of all creditors or on the consent of such creditors, either express or tacit, within 30 days from their notification' Brazilian Civil Code, *supra* note 10, at art. 1,1145. Under Article 1,146:

> The acquirer of the establishment is liable for the payment of all debts prior to the transfer, provided that such debts have been duly entered in the accounts. The original debtor remains solitarily liable for a period of one year from the date of publication, with respect to debts that have fallen due, and from the due date, with respect to all other debts.

Id. at art. 1,146.

19.60 A strong evidence of unfair competition practice, in this matter, would be the assignor's attempt to use, file and attempt to register the assigned trademark or similar under the 'Trespasse'.

19.61 In order for a trademark assignment to be valid against third parties, the assignment agreement requires the prior recordation at the INPI. In practical terms, such recordation will be required for the assignee to proceed in court in defense of the assigned trademarks and maintain the registration at the INPI as valid and effective. Assignment to third parties will be effected as from the date the recordation is published in the Industrial Property Gazette.

19.62 Recordation is not required for the validity of the assignment between the parties, which takes place as from the execution of the agreement. Therefore, there are no penalties for not recording the assignment agreement at the INPI.

G. CONCLUSION

19.63 The use of trademarks as an instrument to promote transactions and investments is a reality in Brazil, as businessmen have been aware of the commercial possibilities in exploiting a trademark besides identifying products and services in the market.

19.64 The awareness is combined with the economic strength of the Brazilian economy, which has resulted in a higher interest for locals and foreigners to expand their businesses, and with the existing legal framework that recognizes a trademark as an adequate subject matter of property rights.

19.65 Among the various possibilities for using a trademark as a business transaction, this chapter has highlighted the assignment and use of the trademark as a collateral as a means of direct use by the titleholder. Licensing rights and franchising were chosen to evidence the indirect exploitation and the possibilities for the titleholder to acquire royalties and other kinds of remuneration from third parties' use.

19.66 Despite the existing framework for trademark use, one has to realize the applicability of ancillary regulations and laws to transactions, as Brazil is a country that still imposes foreign exchange control laws and government approval for remittances overseas. Furthermore, taxation and public order legislation (such as antitrust and quality control linked to consumer laws and taxation) is also applicable to the transactions, and needs to be adequately examined by the titleholder and possible third parties.

19.67 For all business transactions, compliance with the basic rule is indispensable, which is the filing and the registration of a trademark in Brazilian territory and the maintenance of its validity. The lack of a valid trademark in Brazil jeopardizes any attempt at exploitation by its titleholder.

Section C
TRADEMARK TRANSACTIONS IN ASIA

20

CHINESE TRADEMARK LAW AND TRADEMARK TRANSACTIONS: A LAW IN TRANSITION IN THE GLOBAL ECONOMY

He Guo[*]

A.	INTRODUCTION	20.01		(a) Supervision of the quality of the marked goods	20.43
B.	EVOLUTION OF THE CHINESE TRADEMARK LAW	20.03		(b) Maintenance of trademark rights	20.48
C.	ESTABLISHING TRADEMARK RIGHTS	20.12	3.	Ownership of the goodwill and legal responsibilities after a trademark license contract is terminated	20.50
	1. Registered trademarks	20.13			
	(a) Application for trademark registration	20.13		(a) Ownership of the goodwill	20.50
	(b) Examination of the application for trademark registration	20.16		(b) Legal responsibilities after a trademark license contract is terminated	20.51
	2. Unregistered trademarks	20.20			
D.	ASSIGNMENT OF TRADEMARKS	20.26	F.	PLEDGE OF TRADEMARKS	20.53
	1. Concept and formalities for trademark assignment	20.26		1. Definition and legal basis of trademark pledge	20.53
	2. Procedures and regulations on trademark assignment	20.34		2. Procedural requirements for the pledge of the trademark rights	20.60
E.	TRADEMARK LICENSING	20.37		3. Effects of the pledge contract of trademark rights	20.65
	1. Type of trademark licenses	20.40			
	2. Obligations of the trademark owners and licensees	20.42	G.	CONCLUSION	20.67

A. INTRODUCTION

Trademark law in the People's Republic of China (PRC) has undergone a significant evolution in the past century to respond to the economic needs of consumers and manufacturers in a globalized economy. The PRC's change in its trademark system signified not only this drastic change, but also the desire of the national government to have significant regulation over what trademarks are registered, the registration process itself, and the rights associated with the mark once registered. **20.01**

---

[*] Dr. and Professor of Law, Renmin University of China.

Chapter 20 CHINESE TRADEMARK LAW AND TRADEMARK TRANSACTIONS

20.02 This chapter proceeds as follows. First, it will discuss the developments of China's trademark system from the mid-1900s. Second, it will discuss the conferral of trademark rights on different types of marks, including registered marks and unregistered marks. Third, it will address current issues in assigning trademark rights between parties. Fourth, it will discuss procedures for licensing trademark rights to third parties to the benefit of the original trademark owner. Finally, it will address the process for pleading a trademark.

B. EVOLUTION OF THE CHINESE TRADEMARK LAW

20.03 The adoption of national trademark law and the institution of a national trademark registration system is generally the result of the economic development from a national economy towards a market economy. For over a century, we have witnessed the relentless evolution and improvement of the Chinese trademark legislation. The emergence of the Chinese trademark system is to a large extent the result of the political, economic, and cultural transition that has characterized modern China, also as a consequence of the West's legal and economic cultural influence. It is also a consequence of the harmonization in international trademark laws, with the interest of China in playing an active role in international trade.

20.04 In 1904, under the pressure from foreign powers, the Qing government promulgated the first regulation on trademarks in Chinese history through the Experimental Regulations on Chinese and Foreign Trademark Registration.[1] Although not ultimately implemented, it laid the foundation for future trademark legislation. In 1923, the Republic of China promulgated the Trademark Law and Regulations for the Implementation of the Trademark Law, which were later reformulated and revised several times.[2]

20.05 When the PRC was founded in 1949, the trademark law system of the Republic of China was abolished, and in 1950, Provisional Regulations for Trademark Registration were promulgated.[3] Though concise, this emphasized

---

1 ZUO XUCHU, HISTORY ON CHINESE TRADEMARK LAW 83 (Intellectual Property Press (Beijing), 2005); Zhao Yukun, *The Legislation and Protection of Trademark In The Republic of China*, 3 JOURNAL OF HISTORICAL ARCHIVES 119 (2003).
2 ZUO, *supra* note 1, at 168, 239–45; Zhao, *supra* note 1, at 120.
3 SU WANJUE ET AL., TUTORIAL TRADEMARK LAW 30 (Law Press (Beijing), 1986); Zhang Naigen, *On The Transformation of China Intellectual Property System Under The WTO*, 5 JOURNAL OF WORLD TRADE ORGANIZATION FOCUS 19 (2011).

the protection of trademarks,[4] in 1963, the Regulations on the Management of Trademark stipulated the compulsory registration of trademarks.[5] The legislative aim of these Regulations was to strengthen the country's administration of the market,[6] and more importantly, to define and accordingly protect trademarks as the symbol of quality for the goods that they identify.[7] Additionally, the Regulations were to institute a system of compulsory registration for trademarks,[8] which was necessary in – and also heavily influenced by – the Chinese system of 'planned economy,' that is, an economy based on organized and centralized planning, in which production, prices, investment and incomes are decided and fixed by the central government.

Ultimately, the National People's Congress' Standing Committee of the People's Republic of China promulgated the Trademark Law of the People's Republic of China ('Trademark Law of PRC') in 1982. The newly implemented 'reform and opening up' policy pushed the economic model of the whole country to transform from a centralized planned economy to a diversified market economy. As a result, every aspect of Chinese society was transforming from closure to opening up, including the national approach to trademark law and policy. Nonetheless, as the first promulgated law within the PRC's intellectual property system, the 1982 trademark law was still influenced by and characterized by a system of planned economy.

20.06

In 1993, the Trademark Law of PRC was revised for the first time. This revision was prompted by the establishment of a socialized market economy.[9] With respect to trademarks, the main revision was the addition of the provisions on the protection of service marks and the cancellation of trademarks whose registration was acquired by unfair means, which reinforced to some extent the penalties for trademark infringement.[10]

20.07

---

4   Provisional Regulations for the Trademark Registration, (promulgated by the Gov't Admin. Council, 28 July 1950) GOV'T ADMIN. COUNCIL, 28 August 1950, at art. 1 (China). The regulations are enacted for the purposes of protecting the exclusive right to use trademarks in general industry and commerce.

5   SHEN GUANSHENG, THE THEORY AND PRACTICE ON CHINESE TRADEMARK LEGAL SYSTEM 39 (People's Court Press, 1993); Deng Hongguang, *The Improvement of The Trademark Law From The Perspective of The Legislative Purpose of Trademark Law*, 5 JOURNAL OF INTELLECTUAL PROPERTY 53 (2005).

6   Regulations on the Management of Trademark (promulgated by the Gov't Admin. Council, 1963) 8 ST. COUNCIL GAZ. 1963, art. 1 (China). The regulations are enacted for the purposes of strengthening the administration of trademark, and urging the enterprises to guarantee and improve the quality of their products.

7   *Id.* at art. 3 ('Trademark is a symbol of certain quality of goods.').

8   *Id.* at art. 2 ('Enterprises shall apply to Central Administration for Industry and Commerce for trademark registration.').

9   Jin Wuwei, *The Review and Summary of The Third Revision of The Trademark Law*, 10 JOURNAL OF INTELLECTUAL PROPERTY 3 (2013).

10 *Id.* at 3.

20.08 In 2001, the second revision of the Trademark Law of PRC was launched as a result of the need for the Trademark Law of PRC to comply with the Agreement on Trade-Related Aspects of Intellectual Property Rights (TRIPS) as part of the accession process of China to the World Trade Organization (WTO).[11] In October 2001, the Trademark Law of PRC was thus amended. Through this revision, significant changes were made in the following respects: first, the scope of trademark ownership was extended to include natural persons, where the previous laws and regulations had only included enterprises and public institutions, or privately or individually-owned businesses; second, categories of trademarks under protection were widened to include three-dimensional trademarks (3D trademarks); third, there were explicit stipulations on the conditions and requirements of the recognition and protection of well-known marks; fourth, it was explicitly stipulated that collective marks and certification marks can be used to protect geographical indications; fifth, there were explicit stipulations on the pre-emptive registration of a trademark another person had used and the corresponding handling of such registration.[12]

20.09 The third revision of the Trademark Law of PRC was made in 2013. This revision was different from the previous two revisions in that it was necessary to meet the requirements of the development of the domestic market economy and the implementation of an intellectual property (IP) strategy. The revision process lasted for more than seven years until 2013. Through this revision, the categories of registerable trademarks were broadened to include sound marks. And at the same time, the penalties for trademark infringement were raised from 500,000 to 3 million yuan.

20.10 The general standards of the Trademark Law of PRC were brought to a higher level in accordance with international standards through newly included provisions on the term of examination of the application for trademark registration, limitation on the qualification for the opposing party in trademark opposition, and the aim of the protection of well-known marks, and so on.[13]

---

11 *Id.*
12 He Ping, *The Third Revision of The Trademark Law*, 10 JOURNAL OF CHINA TRADEMARK 11 (2013).
13 Liu Shaojun, *The Trademark Law of PRC In Progress*, 12 JOURNAL OF INTELLECTUAL PROPERTY 30 (2013).

In summary, through several revisions in the past 30 years, the specific **20.11**
provisions of the Trademark Law of the PRC have been aligned to the
requirements of the related international treaties.[14]

C. ESTABLISHING TRADEMARK RIGHTS

In theory, trademark rights are established either by trademark registration or **20.12**
trademark use.[15] Under the Trademark Law of the PRC, trademark rights are
established based on trademark registration, with use not being necessary for
registering a trademark. Upon the granting of registration, trademark registrants enjoy the exclusive right to use the trademark.[16] With that being said,
trademarks that are used in commerce without registration also enjoy some
protection under Chinese law.[17] The protection of unregistered trademarks is
primarily limited to acts of unfair competition, such as imitation of the
trademarks by another person, instead of the exclusive right to use such
trademarks. To a certain extent, use based on unregistered trademarks may
foreclose the possibility of registering the marks by third parties in the
future.[18]

---

14 The People's Republic of China (PRC) is a member, inter alia, of the following international agreements: Paris Convention for the Protection of Industrial Property, 19 December 1984, 828 U.N.T.S. 305 [hereinafter Paris Convention]; Agreement on Trade-Related Aspects of Intellectual Property Rights, 28 November 2007, 1869 U.N.T.S. 299 [hereinafter TRIPS]; Madrid Agreement, 4 July 1989, 828 U.N.T.S. 389 [hereinafter Madrid Union]; Protocol Relating to the Madrid Agreement Concerning the International Registration of Marks, 1 September 1995, 28 INDUS. PROP. L. & TREATIES, 3–007 [hereinafter Madrid Protocol]; Singapore Treaty on the Law of Trademarks, World Intellectual Property Organization, 29 January 2007; Trademark Law Treaty, 28 October 1994, 2037 U.N.T.S. 298.
15 IGNACIO S. SAPALO, translated by Zhang Yinhu, BACKGROUND READING MATERIAL ON INTELLECTUAL PROPERTY 164–6 (Zhang Yinhu trans., World Affairs Press, 2010).
16 *See* Trademark Law of the People's Republic of China (promulgated by the Standing Comm. Nat'l People's Cong., 23 August 1982, effective 30 August 2013) 5 STANDING COMM. NAT'L PEOPLE'S CONG. GAZ. ART. 3, § 1 (China) [hereinafter Trademark Law of PRC]. 'The trademark registrants shall enjoy the exclusive right to use the trademarks, and be protected by law.'
17 *Id.* at art. 15, § 2. 'Where an applicant for registration of a trademark identical with or similar to an unregistered trademark in prior use by another party on identical or similar goods has any contractual, business or other relationship except the relationship described in the preceding paragraph with the other party and knows the existence of the unregistered trademark, the trademark shall not be registered upon opposition from the other party.'
18 Wang Ze & Xu Lin, *On The Protection of Unregistered Trademarks In Prior Use Under The Trademark Registration System*, 12 JOURNAL OF CHINA TRADEMARK 46 (2010).

1. Registered trademarks

(a) Application for trademark registration

20.13 In China, any civil entity can apply for trademark registration to the Trademark Office of the State Administration for Industry and Commerce. Anyone applying for trademark registration must submit to the Trademark Office one copy of the application for trademark registration and reproductions of the trademark.[19] The applicant must also submit a duplicated copy of the valid credentials that can certify identity.[20] Applicants claiming the right of priority must submit the certification of the priority,[21] and applicants entrusting a trademark agency must submit a Power of Attorney and other relevant documents.[22]

20.14 Applicants must pay attention to the following aspects for different kinds of trademark registration:

- First, if applying for the registration of a three-dimensional sign as a trademark, the applicant must make a statement in the application, and submit a reproduction thereof by which the three-dimensional shape can be determined, with the reproduction including at least a three-view drawing, and state the use of such trademark.
- Second, if applying for the registration of the combination of colours as a trademark, the applicant must make a statement in the application, and state the use of such trademark.
- Third, if applying for the registration of a sound sign as a trademark, the applicant must make a statement in the application, and submit a sample of the sound as required, describe such sound trademark, and state the use of such trademark. To describe a sound trademark, a stave or musical notation shall be used together with the written description; if the sound cannot be described by a stave or musical notation, the written description shall be used; and the description shall be in accordance with the sound sample.
- Fourth, if applying for the registration of a collective mark or a certification mark, the applicant must make a statement in the application, and

---

19 *See* Regulations of the Implementation of Trademark Law of PRC (promulgated by the State Council of People's Republic of China, 3 August 2002, effective 15 September 2002) ST. COUNCIL GAZ., art. 13, § 1 (China) [hereinafter Regulation of PRC Trademark Law].
20 *See id.* at art. 14, § 1.
21 *See id.* at art. 20, § 1.
22 *See id.* at art. 5, § 1.

submit the documents certifying the qualifications of the subjects and the rules on the administration of the use of the mark.[23]

Where a trademark is, or consists of, foreign words, their Chinese meanings shall be indicated.[24]

In the application for trademark registration, categories of goods or services on which a trademark is used and the names of goods or services must be listed as specified in the Classification of Goods and Services. In the current effective International Classification of Goods and Services for the Purpose of the Registration of Marks – Nice Classification (10th edition), there are in all 45 categories: 34 for goods and 11 for services.[25] Under the Trademark Law of PRC (2013 version), an applicant for trademark registration may, in a single application, apply for registration of the same trademark on goods or services in different classes.[26] Through 'cross-class' application, it is more convenient for the applicants to get trademark registration in different classes, which was not allowed before the Trademark Law of PRC 2013 version came into effect.[27]

20.15

(b) Examination of the application for trademark registration

The starting point of the examination process of the Trademark Office is to judge whether the application meets the requirements for acceptance. Where the application formalities are complete, the application documents are completed as required, and the fees are paid, the Trademark Office shall accept the application, determine the serial number of the application, and send the acceptance notice.[28] The date of filing the application (hereafter referred to as the application date) is one of the most important parts in the acceptance notice. Generally, the application date shall be the date on which the application documents are received by the Trademark Office; where an application enjoys the right of priority, the priority date shall be deemed as the application date. If other parties have already applied for registration prior to that date, it is difficult for the latter application to be approved because under the Chinese trademark system, where two or more applicants apply for the registration of identical or similar trademarks for the same or similar goods, the first application filed shall be accepted. The standard for determining the

20.16

---

23 See id. at art. 13, §§ 3–7.
24 Id.
25 Nice Agreement Concerning the International Classification of Goods and Services for the Purposes of the Registration of Marks, 5 May 1994, 1154 U.N.T.S. 89.
26 See Regulation of PRC Trademark Law, supra note 19, at art. 22, § 2.
27 See Trademark Law of PRC, supra note 16, at art. 20 (updated 2001).
28 See Regulation of PRC Trademark Law, supra note 19, at art. 18, § 2.

sequence of application is the application date. Where applications are filed on the same date, the application for the trademark which was the first used shall be accepted.[29] If they start using the trademark on the same date, or fail to submit the evidence of prior use of such trademarks, the Trademark Office shall determine one of them by drawing lots.[30] In the examination process, if the application is found to be in conflict with any prior right acquired by another person, the Trademark Office will not approve the application for trademark registration.[31]

20.17 Distinctiveness is the key point in the examination process of the application for trademark registration. Distinctiveness means that the trademark can distinguish the origin of goods or services. This is the common practice in the trademark law of all countries. Under the Trademark Law of PRC, 'any trademark in respect of which an application for registration is filed shall be so distinctive as to be distinguishable'.[32] Based on this principle, the Trademark Law of PRC stipulates several examples of lack of distinctiveness, such as signs comprising the generic names of the goods, having direct reference to the quality, main raw materials or other features of the goods, and geographical names known to the public and so on.[33]

20.18 Signs cannot be approved for trademark registration if they are detrimental to public order, social morals or customs. Under the Trademark Law of PRC, the stipulations as to these features mainly include the following aspects: first – like trademark law in many countries – signs identical with or similar to State names, national flags, national emblems or military flags of countries, and the names, flags or emblems of international organizations cannot be used as trademarks. Thus, any official sign cannot be registered as a trademark in China. Second, signs bearing racial discrimination cannot be used as trademarks. Third, trademarks cannot be detrimental to social morals or customs, or have other unhealthy influences. Fourth, trademarks cannot be deceptive in composition or meanings.[34] In summary, distinctiveness is necessary for a sign

---

29 *See* Trademark Law of PRC, *supra* note 16, at art. 31.
30 *See* Regulation of PRC Trademark Law, *supra* note 19, at art. 19.
31 *See* Trademark Law of PRC, *supra* note 16, at art. 9, § 1.
32 *See id.* at art. 9, § 1.
33 *See id.* at art. 10.
34 Trademark law of PRC, *supra* note 16, at art. 10, § 1.

> The following words or devices shall not be used as trademarks: (1) those identical with or similar to the State name, national flag, national emblem, military flag, or decorations, of the People's Republic of China, with names of the places where the Central and State organs are located, or with the names and designs of landmark buildings; (2) those identical with or similar to the State names, national flags, national emblems or military flags of foreign countries, except that the foreign state government agrees otherwise on the use; (3) those identical with or similar to the names, flags or emblems or names, of international intergovernmental organizations, except that the organizations agree otherwise on the use or

to be approved as a trademark. And signs detrimental to social morals or customs, or having other unhealthy influences, cannot be used as trademarks and thus can also not be approved for registration.

After the substantial examination – where a trademark the registration of which has been applied for is in conformity with the relevant provisions of the Trademark Law of PRC – the Trademark Office shall, after examination, preliminarily approve the trademark and publish it. After publication, approving the application still depends on the opposition process. Where no opposition has been filed, or the opposition cannot be established after the expiration of the time limit from the publication, the registration shall be formally approved by the Trademark Office.[35] **20.19**

2. Unregistered trademarks

Even though the Trademark Law of PRC was enacted when the Chinese planned economy was about to be substituted by a more diversified and market-oriented economy, the original version of trademark law was inevitably influenced by the past. For example, this influence included favouring a system of registered trademarks as a means for the government to intervene in – and supervise the functioning of – the economy via the trademark registration process. This change also explains why registered trademarks were given, and are still given, stronger rights under the trademark system in force in China. Moreover, in the 1980s, unregistered trademarks were not offered any legal protection. Instead, under the original 1982 version of the Trademark Law of PRC, the exclusive right to use a trademark was granted only to registered trademarks. **20.20**

After China joined the Paris Convention for the Protection of Industrial Property (Paris Convention), unregistered trademarks were offered protection as specified in the Paris Convention (that is, under the general principle of unfair competition).[36] For several years, this protection was nominal rather than practical. In fact, it was difficult to invoke such protection, which entailed a heavy burden of proof for owners of unregistered trademarks, including **20.21**

---

that it is not easy for the use to mislead the public; (4) those identical with or similar to official signs and hallmarks, showing official control or warranty by them, except that the use thereof is otherwise authorized; (5) those identical with or similar to the symbols, or names, of the Red Cross or the Red Crescent; (6) those having the nature of discrimination against any nationality; (7) those having the nature of fraud by which the consumers may easily be confused and misled on the features of the goods such as quality or origin; (8) those detrimental to socialist morals or customs, or having other unhealthy influences.

35 *See* Trademark Law of PRC, *supra* note 16, at art. 33.
36 Paris Convention, *supra* note 14, at art. 10*bis*.

well-known marks. The issue of protecting unregistered trademarks was raised many times in the revisions of the Trademark Law of PRC in 2001 and 2013. As a result, in the 2001 revision, unregistered well-known marks were granted additional legal protection, following the language of Article 6-*bis* of the Paris Convention.[37] 2001 version also offered legal protection to unregistered well-known marks in other classes based on the language of Article 16.3 of TRIPS.[38] The 2011 version of the Trademark Law of PRC adopted the principle that 'any trademark in respect of which an application for registration is filed shall be so distinctive as to be distinguishable, and shall not conflict with any prior right acquired by another person'.[39]

20.22 Most recently, the 2013 version of the Trademark Law of PRC added the principle according to which

> [W]here an applicant for registration of a trademark identical with or similar to an unregistered trademark in prior use by another party on identical or similar goods has any contractual, business or other relationship except the relationship described in the preceding paragraph with the other party and knows the existence of the unregistered trademark, the trademark shall not be registered upon opposition from the other party.[40]

Furthermore, the 2013 revision of the Trademark Law of PRC included additional provisions against unfair competition, such as the provision that the principle of good faith shall be followed with respect to the application for registration or use of a trademark.[41] Besides this principle, the 2013 revision also adopted the rule that the holder of a trademark registration cannot foreclose the use of a similar or identical mark to those third parties who have been using the mark prior to the registration.[42] All in all, these provisions have greatly reinforced the legal status of unregistered trademarks in China.

20.23 Still, as for all trademarks, unregistered trademarks must also meet certain requirements to be protected. In the current Chinese trademark system, only unregistered well-known marks and unregistered trademarks with a certain reputation are offered legal protection. In particular, 'the holder of a trademark well known to the relevant public may file a request for protection of the said

---

37 *Id.* at art. 6*bis*.
38 *See generally* Madrid Union, *supra* note 14; TRIPS, *supra* note 14, at art. 16.3.
39 *See* Trademark Law of PRC, *supra* note 16, at art. 9, § 1 (remaining unchanged in the 2013 revision).
40 *See* Trademark Law of PRC, *supra* note 16, art. 15, § 2.
41 *Id.* at art. 7, § 1.
42 *See id.* at art. 59, § 3.

mark as a well-known mark under this law if believing that there is any infringement upon its rights'.[43]

In addition, under the Trademark Law of PRC, 'an application for the registration of a trademark shall not create any prejudice to the prior right of another person, nor unfair means shall be used to pre-emptively register the trademark of some reputation another person has used'.[44] Whether a trademark is of some reputation firstly depends on whether it has already been 'used'. There are also special regulations on the use of a trademark in the 2013 version of the Trademark Law of PRC. For example, the 'use of a trademark' means using a trademark on goods, on the packages or containers of goods, in the trade documents of goods, or for advertisements, exhibitions, and other commercial activities for the purpose of identifying the origin of goods.[45]

20.24

Ultimately, the scope of protection for unregistered trademarks is relatively broad. Any distinctive commercial sign that is used on goods can be deemed as a trademark, for example, including specific name, packaging, and decoration of goods. In turn, under Section 2, Article 5, of the Anti-Unfair Competition Law of PRC, to use the specific name, package, decoration of the famous or noted commodities, or use a similar name, package, decoration of the famous or noted commodities, which may cause confusion, and mislead consumers into regarding the commodities as famous or noted commodities, can constitute unfair competition.[46]

20.25

D. ASSIGNMENT OF TRADEMARKS

1. Concept and formalities for trademark assignment

Trademark rights grant private property rights to their owners. Accordingly, trademarks can be assigned as other types of private property. Naturally, the assignment of trademarks shall follow the principle of autonomy of contracts. Trademark assignment constitutes an important way to acquire trademark rights in China.

20.26

---

43 *See id.* at art. 13, § 1.
44 *See id.* at art. 32.
45 *See id.* at art. 48.
46 *See id.* at art. 58; Law Against Unfair Competition (promulgated by Standing Comm. Nat'l People's Cong., 2 September 1993, effective 1 December 1993) 21 STANDING COMM. NAT'L PEOPLE'S CONG. GAZ. 938, art. 5, § 2 (China).

20.27   As in other countries, the analysis of trademark assignment in China also focuses on the concept of 'trademark goodwill'. Notably, after having been in use for a certain period, a trademark acquires a certain goodwill in the mind of consumers. Consumers buy the goods identified by that mark because they are satisfied with certain qualities of the goods, and expect these qualities to continue to be part of these goods, even if the mark is assigned to a third party.

20.28   Precisely in order to guarantee the continuation of the same business activity even when trademarks were assigned to third parties, the trademark provisions of many countries originally established that assignors must transfer the business to which the trademark belongs together with the trademark. The transfer of tangible business assets along with the mark was then considered to be the only way to guarantee the continuation of the same business activity and, in turn, the consistency in quality of trademarked goods in order to protect consumers.

20.29   This principle was nonetheless abandoned in recent decades. Now, national trademark laws of most countries provide that the assignment of business is no longer a compulsory requirement as part of the validity of a trademark assignment. Some countries, however, still require transfer of goodwill, at least intended as intangible assets and control of the quality of the trademark goods identified by the assigned trademarks. China is indeed one of the countries that still requires that trademark assignees control the quality of the products identified by the assigned marks.

20.30   In particular, Section 1, Article 42, of the Trademark Law of PRC states:

> [W]here a registered trademark is assigned, the assignor and assignee shall conclude a contract for the assignment, and jointly file an application with the trademark Office. The assignee shall guarantee the quality of the goods in respect of which the registered trademark is used.[47]

Under this provision, even though the transfer of business together with the trademark is not a compulsory requirement for the validity of a trademark assignment, the assignee remains responsible for controlling the quality of goods once the mark has been assigned. Simply put, consumers expect a consistent quality for these goods, and the national legislators emphasize the connection between the goodwill and the goods; if the assignee fails to comply

---

47   *See* Trademark Law of PRC, *supra* note 16, at art. 42, § 1.

with this obligation, the industrial and commercial administration shall impose a fine upon it.[48]

20.31 In this context, it should be noted that the Paris Convention does not impose this requirement,[49] under Article 21 of TRIPS, the owner of a registered trademark shall have the right to assign the trademark with or without the transfer of the business to which the trademark belongs.[50] Article 21 does not refer to 'trademark goodwill', which leaves TRIPS Members free to introduce the obligation that marks be transferred with the goodwill, as long as this does not require contextual transfer of business assets. Accordingly, the current provision in Section 1, Article 42, of the Trademark Law of PRC is fully in line with the provision provided in Article 21 of TRIPS.

20.32 Under the Trademark Law of PRC, the owner of a registered trademark intending to assign a registered trademark shall also concurrently assign any additional similar or same trademark registrations for similar or identical goods to the same assignee, so as to prevent confusion amongst consumers caused by separate assignments to different assignees.[51] For example, a Hong Kong company registered the trademark 'Satch' in international classifications No. 18 and No. 25 respectively, then assigned the trademark in two classes to a company in Guangzhou and a company in Beijing respectively, which caused confusion in the Chinese domestic market about the two different assignees. To prevent this confusion, the rule was included in the 2013 revision of the Trademark Law of the PRC.[52] In particular, if the owner of a registered trademark intending to assign the registered trademark does not concurrently assign all its similar registered trademarks on identical goods or all its identical or similar registered trademarks on similar goods, the Trademark Office shall, according to the circumstances, order rectification of the situation within a specified period; if the situation fails to be rectified at the expiry of the said time limit, the application for assignment of the registered trademark shall be considered abandoned.[53]

20.33 Generally, where the assignment of a registered trademark is likely to cause confusion, or have other inappropriate consequences, it shall also be prohibited by law. For example, due to historic reasons, some geographical names were

---

48   *See id.* at art. 7, § 2.
49   *See* Paris Convention, *supra* note 14, at art. 6 *quarter*.
50   *See* Madrid Union, *supra* note 14, at art. 21.
51   *See* Trademark Law of PRC, *supra* note 16, at art. 42, § 2.
52   *See id.*
53   *See* Regulation of PRC Trademark Law, *supra* note 19, at art. 31, § 2.

registered as trademarks in several countries. The assignment of these trademarks to parties in unrelated geographical regions is likely to cause confusion, so it will be rejected by the Trademark Office.[54] In principle, trademark assignments can thus be limited for consideration of public interest.[55]

2. Procedures and regulations on trademark assignment

20.34 Under the Trademark Law of the PRC, both registered and unregistered trademarks can be assigned. The assignment of unregistered trademarks should be in conformity with the public order, social morals or customs or compulsory requirements set in laws such as the Anti-Unfair Competition Law of PRC and the Trademark Law of PRC and so on, and the principle of equality, voluntariness, fairness, making compensation for equal value, and autonomy of will in the civil law. The following discussion is focused, however, on the necessary formalities for the assignment of registered trademarks. As the registration system is dominant in the Chinese trademark system, assignments of registered trademarks represent the largest share of trademark assignments in China.

20.35 Besides the requirement mentioned in the previous Section, the assignment of a registered trademark in China will undergo related formalities. In particular, 'the assignment of a registered trademark shall be published after it has been approved, and the assignee enjoys the exclusive right to use the trademark from the date of publication'.[56] Still, the principle that the assignee enjoys the exclusive right to use the assigned trademark from the date of publication is not detrimental to the legal effect of the trademark assignment contract prior to the publication date. Thus, the trademark assignment contract shall enjoy legal effect after the contracting parties reach an agreement. However, before the publication date, the assignee cannot claim trademark rights against a third party according to the assignment contract, in that the assignment of trademarks must be published before taking legal effect toward third parties.

20.36 Moreover, where trademark rights are transferred between different parties due to reasons except assignment such as heritage, the owner of the trademark intending to transfer the trademark shall concurrently transfer all its similar

---

54 *See* Trademark Law of PRC, *supra* note 16, at art. 42, § 3.
55 *See id.* at art. 42, §§ 2–3. 'The owner of a registered trademark intending to assign the registered trademark shall concurrently assign all its similar registered trademarks on identical goods or all its identical or similar registered trademarks on similar goods; and where an assignment is likely to cause confusion, or have other unhealthy influences, it shall be rejected for registration by the Trademark Office, the applicant shall be notified in writing and the reasons thereof shall be given.'
56 *See* Trademark Law of PRC, *supra* note 16, at art. 42, § 4.

registered trademarks on identical goods or all its identical or similar registered trademarks on similar goods.[57]

E. TRADEMARK LICENSING

In addition to being entitled to transfer the ownership of the mark by assignment, any trademark owner may, by signing a trademark license contract, authorize other parties to use the trademark under certain conditions. This contract is called trademark licensing, and the trademark owner shall be the licensor, and the user of the trademark shall be the licensee. After the trademark licensing contract is concluded between the licensor and the licensee, the trademark owner still owns the exclusive rights related to the trademark, and the licensee only acquires the right to use the trademark. **20.37**

Trademark licensing is a common business model used by trademark owners in modern society. For example, the licensing of trademarks is an important part of franchising agreements. **20.38**

Since, unlike the assignment of a trademark, trademark licensing only relates to the transfer of the right to use the trademark, trademark licensing contracts are generally subject to recordation without further need of approval by the Trademark Office. A system of thorough recordation permits third-party stakeholders to search whether trademarks are used under licensing agreements and other related issues. Likewise, such system facilitates the government's supervision of the quality of the licensed goods, so as to guarantee the consistency and predictability of the quality of these goods for consumers.[58] Specifically, under the Trademark Law of PRC, 'the licensor shall submit the licensing of the trademark to the Trademark Office for recordation, and the Trademark Office shall publish it. An unrecorded license cannot be used as a defense against a third party in good faith'.[59] **20.39**

1. Type of trademark licenses

Under the Interpretation of Several Questions on the Application of Law in Trial of Trademark Civil Dispute Cases issued by the Supreme Court, the **20.40**

---

57 *See id.* at art. 42.
58 Liu Chuntian, Intellectual Property Law 314 (Higher Education Press, 4th ed. 2010).
59 *See* Trademark Law of PRC, *supra* note 16, at art. 43, § 3.

licensing of a trademark includes the following three types based on the scope of the licensee's right to use the trademark and the standing of the licensee in litigation:[60]

1. *Exclusive license*: the trademark owner gives an exclusive license to a licensee with respect to the use of the registered trademark for an agreed period, within a specified territory and in an agreed manner; moreover, the trademark owner, in accordance with the agreement, may not use the registered trademark.
2. *Sole license*: the trademark owner licenses a single and exclusive license to a licensee to use the registered trademark for an agreed period, within a specified territory and in an agreed manner; however, the trademark owner, in accordance with the agreement, may continue to use the registered trademark but may not license other parties to use the registered trademark.
3. *Non-exclusive license*: the trademark owner licenses to a third party the right to use the registered trademark for an agreed period, within a specified territory and in an agreed manner; but the trademark owner can still use the registered trademark as well as license it to other parties.

In China, the above-mentioned types of trademark license are all recognized by law in legal practice.[61]

20.41 In addition, based on the different types of licensing agreements, licensees enjoy different litigation rights in instances of the infringement of the licensed trademark. Notably, a licensee under an exclusive licensing agreement can file a legal action for infringement in front of the people's courts in lieu of the licensor. A licensee under a sole license contract can also file a legal action for infringement in front of the people's courts together with the trademark owner or independently if the trademark owner does not file an action. However, a licensee under a non-exclusive license contract can only file a legal action for infringement provided that she has been given clear authorization to do so by the trademark owner.[62] This difference is based on the different roles of the licensee in these agreements, and in turn, the interests in the licensed mark. Obviously, after an exclusive license has been issued by the trademark owner, all market interests of the trademark within the duration of the contract are

---

60 *See* Interpretation by the Supreme People's Court of Several Issues Relating to Application of Law to Trial of Cases of Civil Dispute Over Trademarks (promulgated by Adjudication Comm. of the Supreme People's Court, 12 October 2002, effective 16 October 2002) 32 SUP. PEOPLE'S CT. GAZ., art. 3 (China) [hereinafter Interpretation of Trademark Disputes].
61 *See id.*
62 *See id.* at art. 4.

transferred to the licensee. Similarly, within the duration of a sole license, the interests of the trademark are shared by the trademark owner and the licensee. In contrast, for a non-exclusive license, the licensee shares these interests with other licensees in the market, thus he cannot enjoy the same rights as an exclusive or sole licensor.

2. Obligations of the trademark owners and licensees

In a trademark licensing agreement, the relationship between the trademark owner and the licensee cannot be described simply as the trademark owner receiving the royalty, and the licensee acquiring the right to use the trademark. In theory, the party receiving the profit shall be liable for the damage that might be caused by the activities that can bring the profit. That is to say, obligations follow the profits that are part of a licensing agreement. In particular, should problems arise with respect to the quality of the goods produced under license, or damages be caused by such problems, both the trademark owner and the licensee shall be liable for such problems or damages.[63] More specifically, the obligations of trademark owners and licensees are reflected in the following aspects. 20.42

(a) Supervision of the quality of the marked goods

Under the Trademark Law of PRC, 'any user of a trademark shall be responsible for the quality of the goods in respect of which the trademark is used'.[64] In other words, both the trademark owner and the licensee shall be obliged to guarantee the quality of goods as long as the trademark is used with respect to those goods. 20.43

Besides this provision, the lack of consistency in goods quality could also create liability under product quality laws.[65] In particular, under the Product Quality Law of PRC, 'producers shall be responsible for the quality of products they produce', and 20.44

> [T]he quality of products shall meet the following requirements: first, products shall be free from any irrational dangers threatening the safety of people and property, and if there are State standards or trade standards for ensuring the health of the human body and safety of lives and property, the products shall conform to such standards; second,

---

63 Ma Haixia, *On the Product Liability Undertaken by Trademark Licensors*, 3 JOURNAL OF NORTH CHINA UNIVERSITY OF WATER RESOURCES AND ELECTRIC POWER, SOCIAL SCIENCES EDITION (2014).
64 *See* Trademark Law of PRC, *supra* note 16, at art. 7, § 2.
65 *See* Product Quality Law of the People's Republic of China (promulgated by the Standing Comm. Nat'l People's Cong., 22 February 1993, effective 8 July 2000) 4 STANDING COMM. NAT'L PEOPLE'S CONG. GAZ. art. 41, § 4.

products shall have the property they are due to have, except cases in which there are explanations about the defects of the property of the products, and third, products shall tally with the standards prescribed or specified on the packages and with the quality specified in the instructions for use or shown in the providing samples.[66]

Under this law, the products shall be in conformity with the stipulations, no matter whether a trademark is used on the products or not. With regard to product quality, trademark law only plays a minor role, rather than a leading role.[67]

20.45   Moreover, under the Trademark Law of the PRC,

> Any trademark registrant may, by signing a trademark license contract, authorize other persons to use its or his registered trademark. The licensor shall supervise the quality of the goods in respect of which the licensee uses the registered trademark, and the licensee shall guarantee the quality of the goods in respect of which the registered trademark is used.[68]

Here again, trademark law provides a statutory obligation that the trademark licensor guarantee the quality of goods as a general rule to balance freedom of contract in trademark law and the public interest of consumers to receive products of consistent quality. Accordingly, improperly using or misusing the trademark by the licensee may infringe the interests of the consumers, and may render the licensing agreement void. To protect the interests of consumers, the Trademark Law of PRC also provides that, 'where any party is authorized to use a registered trademark of another person, the name of the licensee and the origin of the goods must be indicated on the goods that bear the registered trademark'.[69]

20.46   The supervision or control of the product quality of the licensee by the licensor is not only an obligation of the licensor to consumers, but also a right that it or he can claim against the licensee. If the products of the licensee are of low quality, it will do harm to the goodwill of the trademark and then the interests of consumers. In this sense, the trademark licensor is entitled to supervise the product quality of the licensee.[70]

20.47   In this respect, the recordation of the licensing agreement with the Trademark Office becomes crucial for trademark owners and their licensees. In particular,

---

66 *See id.* at art. 26.
67 *Id.*
68 *See* Trademark Law of PRC, *supra* note 16, at art. 43, § 1.
69 *See id.* at art. 43, § 2.
70 *See id.* at art. 43, § 1.

an unrecorded license may not be used as a defense against a third party using an identical or similar mark in good faith. More specifically, unless it is put on record at the Trademark Office, a license is only binding between the parties concerned in the contract.[71] As mentioned above in the Interpretation of Several Issues on the Application of Law in Trial of Trademark Civil Dispute Cases, a licensee under an exclusive or sole licensing agreement can file a claim for trademark infringement independently in front of the people's court.[72] These actions, however, can only be filed subject to the record of the licensing agreement by the Trademark Office.[73]

(b) Maintenance of trademark rights

20.48 Since a licensing agreement is a contract, it will also be bound by the Contract Law of PRC. Trademark owners have an implied obligation to maintain the validity of trademark rights, and facilitate that licensees enjoy full trademark rights ('purity of the contract') within the duration of the licensing agreement. To the contrary, any deviation from these general principles may constitute a breach of contract.[74]

20.49 The validity of the trademark rights in this context refers to the fact that the trademark owners are obliged to guarantee that the trademarks are valid within the duration of the licensing agreement, and the validity of trademark rights should not be jeopardized due to the trademark owner's fault. And the expression 'purity of the contract' refers to the assurance that the right to use the licensed registered trademark shall not be foreclosed by existing elements that may jeopardize the licensee fully enjoying her rights under the contract. For example, the licensor shall not sign exclusive licenses with two or more parties in the same region; nor infringe third parties' rights when using the trademark; or decide not to file legal action in time in the event of trademark infringement occurring.[75]

---

71   *See id.* at art. 43, § 3.
72   *See* Interpretation of Trademark Disputes, *supra* note 60, at art. 4, § 2.
73   *See* Trademark Law of PRC, *supra* note 16, at art. 43, § 3.
74   *See* Contract Law of the People's Republic of China (promulgated by Standing Comm. Nat'l People's Cong., 15 March 1999, effective 1 October 1999) 15 ORDER OF THE PRESIDENT OF THE PRC, art. 60, § 2 [hereinafter Contract Law of PRC].
75   Zhu Iianjun & Wang Hong, *Analysis of The Types of Trademark Licensing Disputes*, 8 JOURNAL OF CHINA TRADEMARK 53 (2007).

3. Ownership of the goodwill and legal responsibilities after a trademark license contract is terminated

(a) Ownership of the goodwill

20.50 After the termination of a trademark licensing agreement disputes may arise about the ownership of interests, such as the goodwill attached to the trademark, and to the packages and decoration of goods. In general, after a licensing agreement is terminated, the goodwill of a trademark naturally belongs to the trademark owner together with the transfer of the full right to use the trademark. Accordingly, licensees should cease to use the licensed trademark, and the goodwill accumulated on the trademark shall belong to the trademark owner.[76]

(b) Legal responsibilities after a trademark license contract is terminated

20.51 Under Article 115 of General Principles of the Civil Law of PRC[77] and Article 97 of the Contract Law of PRC,[78] the parties concerned can claim compensation for any losses that may be caused by the breach or the termination of a contract. The same principles apply to a trademark licensing agreement.

20.52 In practice, a licensing agreement may be terminated due to declaration of invalidation of the registered trademark. This is directly provided in the Trademark Law of PRC:

> [a] decision or ruling to declare invalidation of a registered trademark is not retrospective to a judgment, ruling, or consent judgment made and enforced by a people's court, a trademark infringement case decision made and enforced by an administrative department for industry and commerce, or a trademark assignment contract or license contract executed before the trademark is declared to be invalid. However, the trademark registrant shall compensate others for losses caused by its bad faith.[79]

Moreover, the provisions state that the damages due to trademark infringement, trademark assignment fees, and trademark royalties that are not returned 'shall be all or partially returned if the principle of fairness is evidently

---

[76] Cui Guobin, *The Allocation of The Goodwill Attached To the Trademark After The Termination of The Trademark License Contract*, 12 JOURNAL OF INTELLECTUAL PROPERTY 10 (2012).
[77] General Principles of the Civil Law of the People's Republic of China (promulgated by Standing Comm. Nat'l People's Cong., 12 April 1986, effective 12 April 1986) 4 STANDING COMM. NAT'L CONG. GAZ., art. 115.
[78] *See* Contract Law of PRC, *supra* note 74, at art. 97.
[79] *See* Trademark Law of PRC, *supra* note 16, at art. 47, § 2.

violated otherwise'.[80] In this context, one could infer that a trademark owner in good faith would be exempted from the above-described liability after the declaration of invalidity of the registered trademark.[81]

F. PLEDGE OF TRADEMARKS

1. Definition and legal basis of trademark pledge

A pledge is a type of guarantee, and the pledge of a trademark means the trademark's owner uses the trademarks as a transferrable guarantee according to law related to creditor's rights. If the debtor defaults on his debt, the creditor shall be entitled to the priority of having the debt paid with the money converted from the sale or auction of the pledged property (in this case the trademark) according to the provisions of law.[82] **20.53**

Under the Property Law of the People's Republic of China (Property Law of PRC), the exclusive right to use a registered trademark can be transferred as a pledge.[83] Similarly, under the Guaranty Law of the People's Republic of China (Guaranty Law of PRC), rights that may be pledged include the exclusive right to use 'trademarks, the property rights among patent rights and copyrights transferable according to law'.[84] **20.54**

Compared with the pledge of other movable properties, in the pledge of trademarks, the value of the pledged property is less stable. Accordingly, even though trademarks that can be pledged are not limited to registered marks under the Guaranty Law of PRC from 1995,[85] under the more recent Property Law of PRC from 2004, only the exclusive right to use registered trademarks can be pledged.[86] This reflects the prudence of the legislature on this issue. **20.55**

As the pledged property (the object of the pledge) is used to guarantee the performance of the obligation between the creditor and the debtor, the **20.56**

---

80 See id. at art. 47, § 3.
81 See id. at art. 47.
82 See Guaranty Law of the People's Republic of China (promulgated by Standing Comm. Nat'l People's Cong., 30 June 1995, effective 1 October 1995) 5 STANDING COMM. NAT'L PEOPLE'S CONG. GAZ., art. 63 [hereinafter Guaranty Law].
83 See Property Law of the People's Republic of China (promulgated by Standing Comm. Nat'l People's Cong., 16 March 2007, effective 1 October 2007) 3 STANDING COMM. NAT'L PEOPLE'S CONG. GAZ., art. 223, § 5 [hereinafter Property Law].
84 See Guaranty Law, supra note 82, at art. 75, § 3.
85 See id.
86 See Property Law, supra note 83, at art. 223, § 5.

pledged property must meet a series of requirements under the law. For example, based on the nature of the pledge, the pledged property must be the carrier of a certain kind of property benefit. Undoubtedly trademark rights are a type of property interests, and thus meet this requirement. In addition, the pledged property must be transferable according to the law, and interests that are not transferable cannot be used as guarantees. As trademark rights can be classified as property rights, they meet the requirements to be used as a guarantee.

20.57 In China, trademark owners should meet two requirements in order to validly use a trademark to establish a guarantee. First, the pledged trademark should be a valid trademark. Registered trademarks can meet this requirement more easily than unregistered trademarks. If parties wish to establish a guarantee on an unregistered trademark, they must consider that the unregistered mark is not detrimental to public order, social morals or customs, and is thus a valid right. The principle of freedom of contract applies, but the creditor or pledgee should carefully judge the validity of the unregistered mark when concluding a guarantee contract. For example, the parties should consider whether the unregistered trademark is recognized as a well-known mark by a court or the national office; or whether the publicity or influence of the trademark is confirmed in a related judgment made by a court or administrative decision; or whether the publicity or influence of the trademark has been confirmed in related court decisions or administrative resolutions; or whether the publicity can be demonstrated by evidence in the form of commercial advertising and marketing. At the same time, the pledge of an unregistered trademark may encounter difficulties in the registration procedure of the pledge itself, as to date Chinese law does not elaborate on this issue.[87]

20.58 Second, the pledged mark should not carry any previous burden that may influence or limit its transferability. For example, a mark could in theory be under multiple pledges, but additional pledges may limit the ability of the mark to be an effective guarantee. Additionally, any existing trademark license prior to the pledge – especially an exclusive license with a long duration – may influence the real value of the trademark as a guarantee for the creditor. These (and similar) factors should be clarified between the parties when concluding a pledge contract.

20.59 Following the general rules on trademark assignment, in the transfer of a trademark that is necessary to establish a pledge, the owner of the registered

---

87   *See* Guaranty Law, *supra* note 82, at art. 79.

trademark should concurrently assign any additional similar registered trademarks on identical goods or any additional identical or similar registered trademarks on similar goods.[88] The owner of a registered trademark intending to pledge the mark should also concurrently register the pledge of any additional similar registered trademarks on identical goods and services or any additional identical or similar registered trademarks on similar goods and services. To the contrary, obstacles may arise with respect to the performance of the guarantee contract, and the exercise of trademark rights by the creditor. Only by following these steps, can the pledged trademark guarantee the loan granted by the creditor, in case of default of the pledgee/former trademark owner.[89]

2. Procedural requirements for the pledge of the trademark rights

20.60 Unlike the pledge of other types of movable property, where the possession of the actual property can be transferred, in the pledge of trademark rights, only the trademark registration certificate can be delivered to the pledgee for safekeeping. In the specific stipulations of the Property Law of PRC and the Guaranty Law of PRC, it is stressed that where the trademark rights are pledged, the parties concerned shall conclude a contract in written form.[90]

20.61 Another issue is the right of pledge as a type of *jus in re aliena*, which is a security interest set on the property of others and requires an ad hoc registration procedure. In China, a pledge contract shall take effect from the date of its registration, and the right of pledge shall take effect from the time the registration authorities register the pledge contract. This leads to the conclusion that the pledge of trademark must be registered, or otherwise the pledge contract and the right of pledge shall have no legal effect, and will not achieve the goal of protecting the interests of creditors.[91]

20.62 In particular, the Trademark Office of the State Administration for Industry and Commerce is responsible for trademark registration and administration throughout the country, including the registration of the pledge of trademarks. The State Administration for Industry and Commerce has already enacted the Procedures for the Registration of the Pledge of the Exclusive Rights to use

---

88 *See* Trademark Law of PRC, *supra* note 16, at art. 42, § 2.
89 *See* Regulations of the State Administration for Industry and Commerce on the Procedures for the Registration of Pledges of the Exclusive Right to Use Registered Trademarks (promulgated by St. Admin. For Industry and Commerce, 10 September 2009, effective 1 November 2009) 13 ST. COUNCIL GAZ., 2010, art. 3 [hereinafter Exclusive Rights Registration Procedures].
90 *See* Property Law, *supra* note 83, at art. 227, § 1; *see also* Guaranty Law, *supra* note 82, at art. 79.
91 *See* Property Law, *supra* note 83, at art. 227, § 1; *see also* Guaranty Law, *supra* note 82, at art. 79.

Registered Trademarks.[92] Under this Regulation, a pledge shall not be registered under any of the following circumstances: first, the pledger is not the rightful owner of the exclusive right to use the trademark; second, the attribution of the exclusive right to use the trademark is unclear; third, there are other circumstances detrimental to the related laws and regulations.[93]

20.63 The regulation also stipulates the main required content in a pledge contract on the exclusive right to use a trademark:

- name and address of the pledger and the pledgee;
- reason and aim of the pledge;
- the trademark under pledge and the time limit for the pledge;
- the value of the exclusive right to use the trademark under pledge and the evaluation report issued by the trademark evaluation institution designated by the State Administration for Industry and Commerce;
- other issues related to a trademark under pledge that the parties deem necessary to include in the contract.[94]

20.64 In the application for the registration of the pledge for the exclusive right to use a trademark, the parties should submit the following documents: Certificate for the Registration of the Pledge of the Exclusive Rights to Use a Trademark, a copy of the business licenses of the pledger and the pledgee, a duplicate copy of the pledge contract (for contracts in foreign languages, the Chinese translation shall be attached and taken as final), a copy of the certificate of trademark registration for the pledged trademark, and so on.[95]

3. Effects of the pledge contract of trademark rights

20.65 Under the Property Law of PRC and the Guaranty Law of PRC,[96] if trademark rights are pledged, the pledger may not assign such rights, or license to another person the right to use the mark unless agreed upon by the pledger and the pledgee through consultation.[97] Moreover, the proceeds obtained by the pledger through the assignment of such rights or through licensing another person to use such rights shall be used to pay the debts owed to the pledgee in advance or be deposited with a third party.[98]

---

92 *See* Exclusive Rights Registration Procedure, *supra* note 89.
93 *See id.* at art. 8.
94 *See id.* at art. 5.
95 *See id.* at art. 4.
96 *See* Property Law, *supra* note 83, at art. 227, § 2; *see also* Guaranty Law, *supra* note 82, at art. 80.
97 *See* Property Law, *supra* note 83, at art. 227, § 2; *see also* Guaranty Law, *supra* note 82, at art. 80.
98 *See* Property Law, *supra* note 83, at art. 227, § 2; *see also* Guaranty Law, *supra* note 82, at art. 80.

20.66 Additional special provisions on the pledge of trademarks can be found in the Interpretation of Several Questions on the Application of the Guaranty Law of PRC.[99] In particular, these guidelines state, with respect to the scope of rights that can be exercised by the trademark owner after the said trademark is pledged, that:

> [I]f the exclusive right to use trademarks, the property rights among patent rights and copyrights transferable according to law are pledged, and the pledgor assigns or licenses the pledged rights to others without the pledgee's prior consent, such assignment and license shall be deemed as null and void. And the pledgor shall compensate for the losses caused to the pledgee or a third party.[100]

From the provisions indicated above, and this interpretation, it seems clear that a pledged trademark should not be assigned or licensed by the pledger under the Chinese trademark system, or else such assignment and license shall be deemed as null and void.

G. CONCLUSION

20.67 The current trademark system in China dates back to the 1980s. The past 30 years have witnessed great progress in this interesting area of the law. Especially after three revisions, in 2001, 2011 and 2013, the current laws and regulations related to trademark rights have met the general international standard. After China joined the WTO in 2001, many foreign companies have applied for trademark registration and routinely engage in trademark transactions in China.

20.68 But after all, China is still in a transitional period. The market economy has just been established, and its overall framework needs improvement, including the current trademark system. Compared to the legal principles that have been generally well implemented in China, following international agreements there are still several practical problems. These include coordinating the Administration for Industry and Commerce, stepping up enforcement in the court, addressing different decisions made by different courts of final resort in the same case, increasing compensation for the losses in trademark infringement cases, which is still relatively low, coordinating the relationship between trademarks and other commercial signs, such as trade names, domain names,

---

99 *See* The Judicial Interpretation of the Supreme People's Court on Some Issues Regarding the Application of the Guarantee Law of the People's Republic of China (promulgated by Judicial Comm. Sup. People's Ct., 29 September 2000, effective 13 December 2000) 44 SUP. PEOPLE'S CT. GAZ., art. 105.
100 *Id.*

geographical indications, trade dress, and the conflicts between trademarks and other intellectual property rights, such as works and industrial designs.

20.69 As China is moving towards a prominent role in the global economy, new requirements will emerge due to economic development, and this in turn will influence changes in the trademark legal system. In this respect, the Chinese trademark system will continue to improve together with the development of the global economy.

21

JAPANESE PERSPECTIVES ON TRADEMARK TRANSACTIONS: IS EXPANSIVE TRADEMARK PRACTICE PREVAILING OVER THE CONSERVATIVE STOICISM?

Shinto Teramoto[*]

A.	INTRODUCTION	21.01	6. Governing laws of licensing agreements	21.38
B.	WHAT IS A 'TRADEMARK'?	21.03	7. Japanese taxes imposed on royalties	21.39
	1. Scope of 'trademarks' in the context of trademark transactions	21.03	8. Termination of licensing agreements	21.48
	2. 'Trademarks' under the Trademark Act	21.05	9. Application of the Anti-Monopoly Act	21.51
	3. What has changed and what has not in the legal definition of trademarks	21.07	D. TRADEMARK ASSIGNMENTS AND SECURITY INTERESTS	21.53
	4. Laws to be considered when negotiating trademark transactions	21.11	1. General principles	21.53
			2. Trademarks that simultaneously represent the goodwill of diversified suppliers	21.56
C.	LICENSES	21.12	3. Marks that represent the collective goodwill of multiple suppliers	21.58
	1. Definition of 'license'	21.12	4. Non-assignability of regional collective trademark rights	21.61
	2. 'Right to use' trademarks provided under the Trademark Act	21.13	5. Security interests in trademarks	21.63
	3. Non-exclusive right to use	21.17		
	4. Proprietary right to use	21.24		
	5. Licensing agreements for marks not registered under the Trademark Act	21.29	E. CONCLUSION	21.67

A. INTRODUCTION

This Chapter introduces the various facets of trademark transactions under Japanese law. It connects the rules and regulations of trademarks in Japan with the applicable principles of Japanese contract law. This overview includes the most recent legal changes and should aid the understanding of those interested

21.01

---

[*] Professor, Faculty of Law, Kyushu University, Fukuoka, Japan.

in this area as well as help highlight what the standards of practice are and what issues to avoid.

21.02 The first Section delves into the various definitions for registered and unregistered trademark rights within Japanese law and the conventions surrounding the legal rights of ownership and enforcement. Against this background, the next Section explores the various aspects of licensing terms and provisions in trademark transactions. This Section identifies the different types of ownership and the implications of the transfers of particular rights. Additionally, this Section offers guidance as to the considerations to be aware of when structuring a licensing agreement including limitations under Japanese law and the resulting tax classifications. Finally, the last Section examines the assignability of various types of trademark rights in Japan, including the rules surrounding collective marks and the customs applicable within the context of bankruptcy or secured transactions.

B. WHAT IS A 'TRADEMARK'?

1. Scope of 'trademarks' in the context of trademark transactions

21.03 As with almost all legal concepts, the concept of a 'trademark' under Japanese law is established by carving out a certain part of a broader concept of a 'trademark' in the practice of trademark transactions (Figure 21.1). If attorneys were to confine the scope of a trademark to the scope defined under one or more specific laws when they are negotiating trademark transactions or drafting contracts, they would not be meeting the needs of their clients. Moreover, we should note that industries and attorneys, domestic as well as abroad, are constantly lobbying law makers and governments to expand the legal scope of trademarks protected by the Trademark Act or other existing or new laws. Also, attorneys often try to extend legal protection to every kind of mark, symbol, appearance, and so on by means of unfair competition[1] and tort claims.[2]

21.04 In consideration of these conditions, and because the purpose of this chapter is to outline the Japanese perspective on 'Trademark Transactions,' the scope of a 'trademark' discussed herein must be broader than that of a 'trademark' under the Trademark Act of Japan.[3] For the convenience of readers, the discussion

---

1 *Fusei Kyōsō* in Japanese.
2 *Fuhō Kōi* in Japanese.
3 Shōhyō-hō [Trademark Act], Law No. 127 of 1959, as amended.

B. WHAT IS A 'TRADEMARK'?

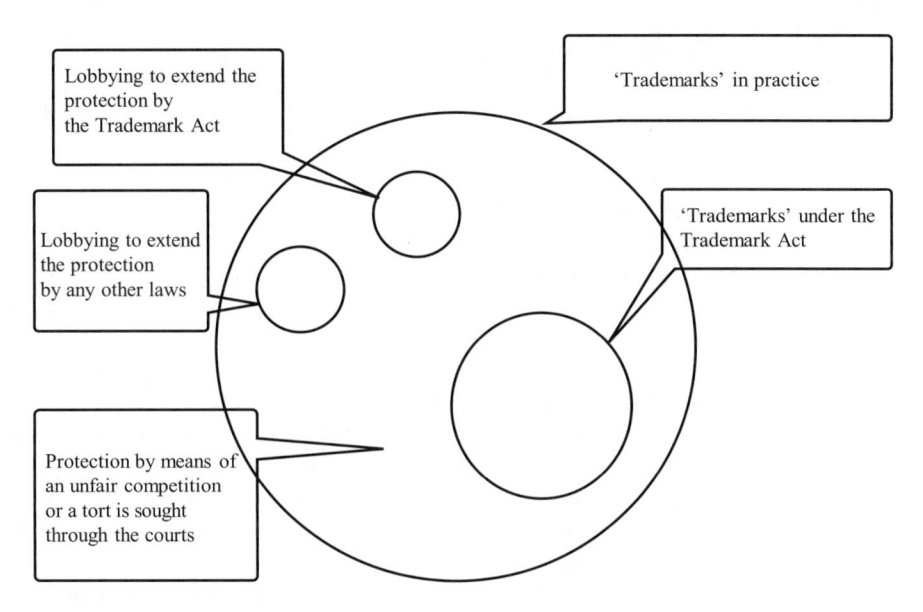

Figure 21.1 The concept of a 'trademark'

herein includes not only transactions concerning trademarks under the Trademark Act, but also marks and symbols that play roles similar to trademarks in the course of business dealings.

2. 'Trademarks' under the Trademark Act

The Trademark Act in effect until 31 March 2015[4] defined a 'trademark' in paragraphs 1 to 4 of Article 2 as follows: **21.05**

(1) 'Trademark' in this Act means any letter(s), figure(s), sign(s) or three-dimensional shape(s),[5] or any combination thereof, or any combination thereof with colors (hereinafter referred to as a 'mark') which is:

    (i) used in connection with the goods of a person who produces, certifies or assigns the goods as a business; or

    (ii) used in connection with the services of a person who provides or certifies the services as a business (except those provided for in the preceding item).

(2) 'Services' set forth in item (ii) of the preceding paragraph shall include retail services and wholesale services, namely, the provision of benefits for customers conducted in the course of retail and wholesale business.

(3) 'Use' with respect to a mark as used in this Act means any of the following acts:

---

4 On 1 April 2015, the amendment of Trademark Act by the Law No. 26 of 2014, as explained below, has become effective (Cabinet Order No. 27 of 28 January 2015).

5 The amendment of the Trademark Act, enacted on 1 April 1997, expanded the scope of trademarks to include three-dimensional shapes. *See* Shōhyō-hō no Ichibu o Kaisei Suru Hōritsu [Act for Partial Revision of the Trademark Act], Law No. 68 of 1996.

513

(i)   to affix a mark to goods or packages of goods;
(ii) to assign, deliver, display for the purpose of assignment or delivery, export, import or provide through an electric telecommunication line, goods or packages of goods to which a mark is affixed;
(iii) in the course of the provision of services, to affix a mark to articles to be used by a person who receives the said services (including articles to be assigned or loaned; the same shall apply hereinafter);
(iv) in the course of the provision of services, to provide the said services by using articles to which a mark is affixed and which are to be used by a person who receives the said services;
(v)   for the purpose of providing services, to display articles to be used for the provision of the services (including articles to be used by a person who receives the services in the course of the provision of services; the same shall apply hereinafter) to which a mark is affixed;
(vi) in the course of the provision of services, to affix a mark to articles pertaining to the provision of the said services belonging to a person who receives the services;
(vii) in the course of the provision of services through an image viewer, by using an electromagnetic device (an electromagnetic device shall refer to any electronic, magnetic or other method that is not recognizable by human perception; the same shall apply in the following item), to provide the said services by displaying a mark on the image viewer;[6] or
(viii) to display or distribute advertisement materials, price lists or transaction documents relating to goods or services to which a mark is affixed, or to provide information on such content, to which a mark is affixed by an electromagnetic device.

(4) To affix a mark to goods or other articles provided for in the preceding paragraph shall include to form in the shape of the mark goods, packages of goods, articles to be used for the provision of services, or advertisement materials relating to goods or services.[7]

---

6 For example, when you open a web page to use Google search engine, 'Google's' logo is displayed. *See* Figure 21.2. This is an example of the use of a trademark that falls within Article 2, Paragraph 3, item vii.

   A business entity often provides information on its products or services, or provides services through its web pages. A potential consumer is likely to reach such a website by using a search engine. Such business entities often embed certain information as a 'meta tag' into the HTML or XHTML documents for their web pages, so that such information (a 'snippet') is displayed in the results generated by the search engine. Embedding a trademark in such a meta tag to show such mark as a snippet is also considered to fit under the trademark use described in Article 2, Paragraph 3, item vii. *See* Figure 21.3. *See also* Ōsaka Chihō Saibansho [Osaka Dist. Ct.] 8 December 2005, Heisei 16 (wa) no. 12032, CHITEKI ZAISAN KŌTŌ SAIBANSHO HANKETSU SHŌKAI HANREI KENSAKU SHISUTEMU [CHIZAI KŌSAI WEB], *available 24 September 2015 at* http://www.ip.courts.go.jp/app/files/hanrei_en/268/000268.pdf.

7 Figure 21.4 shows a trademark gazette for the registered trademark of Yakult Honsha Co., Ltd. having a three-dimensional shape, Registration No. 5,384,525. For more on the company, see YAKULT HONSHA, http://www.yakult.co.jp/english/index.html (*available 24 September 2015*). Figure 21.5 shows a small plastic bottle containing lactobacillus beverage, which is sold by Yakult Honsha. This is a typical example 'to form in the shape of the mark packages of goods'.

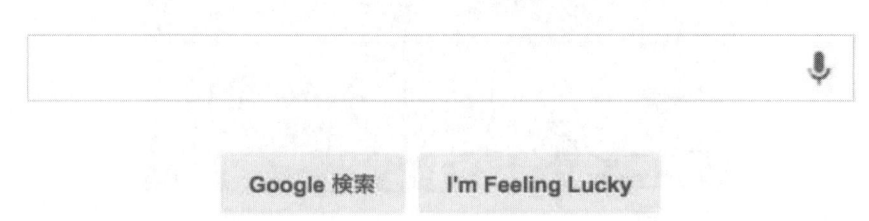

Figure 21.2 The 'Google' logo displayed on the web page of Google Inc. that provides a search engine service

Figure 21.3 Example of a snippet containing a trademark displayed by a search engine

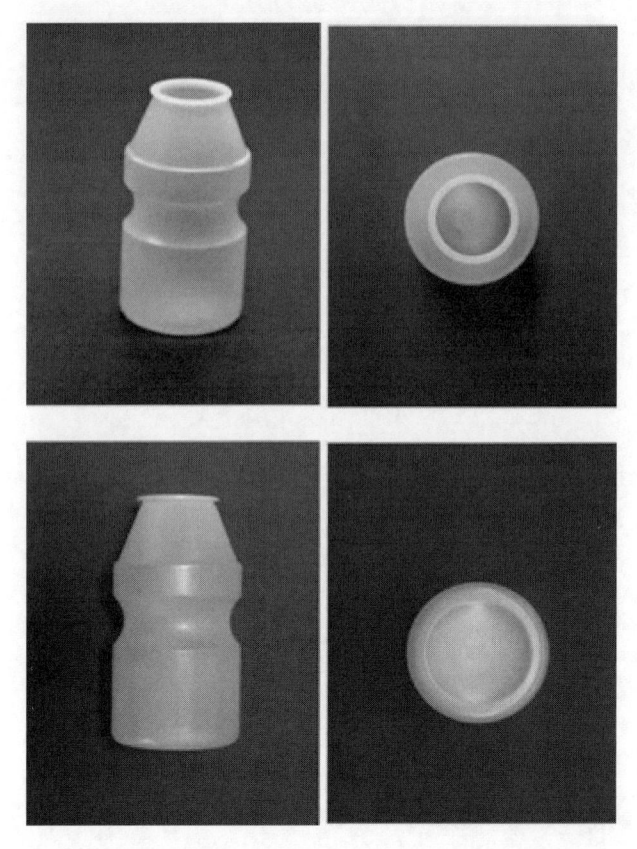

Figure 21.4 Example of a registered trademark in a three-dimensional shape

Figure 21.5 Example of a registered trademark in a three-dimensional shape used as a product container

The basic definition of the trademark as provided in Article 2, Paragraph 1 of the Trademark Act was extended to the following scope by the Law No. 26 of 2014:   **21.06**

> 'Trademark' in this Act means any letter(s), figure(s), sign(s), three-dimensional shape(s), or *color(s)* or any combination thereof, or *sounds or any others as provided by Cabinet order, as recognized by a person's perception which is* ...[8]

This new extended definition of a trademark is effective on and from 1 April 2015. According to Article 5, Paragraph 2 of the Trademark Act, as amended by the said Law No. 26 of 2014, and other official publications,[9] the newly introduced types of trademarks include motion marks, hologram marks, color *per se* marks, sound marks, and position marks. However, taste, scent, and touch marks are not yet covered.

3. What has changed and what has not in the legal definition of trademarks

The scope of a 'trademark' registrable under the Trademark Act has been repeatedly extended by amendments to the Act. However, the role and the basic nature of what is assumed to be a trademark by the Act remains unchanged.   **21.07**

That is, a trademark is not a product or service itself, although a trademark is often incorporated in the appearance or another product or service aspect that is recognizable by human perception. The role of a trademark is to convey certain information concerning a product or service, for example, its origin, quality, prestige, suitable or targeted class of consumers, and so on.[10] In summary, a trademark is a vehicle that is expected to convey certain information about a product or service.   **21.08**

The scope of a trademark transaction between private parties is not regulated or restricted by the legal definition of a trademark, even though it is often affected by such a definition. Notably, the scope of the object of a trademark   **21.09**

---

8 *See* Trademark Act, at art. 2 Paragraph 1, as amended by Law No. 26 of 2014, *supra* note 4 (emphasis added).
9 *See The Trademark Examination Guidelines*, JPO (March. 2015), *available 24 September 2015 at* https://www.jpo.go.jp/shiryou/kijun/kijun2/syouhyou_kijun/htm; Order for Enforcement of the Trademark Act (Cabinet Order No. 19 of 1960, as amended) amended by Cabinet Order No. 26 of 2015.
10 For example, a Supreme Court judgment pointed out that a trademark has the role of indicating the product's origin and guaranteeing its quality. *See* Saikō Saibansho [Sup. Ct.] 27 February 2003, Heisei 14 (ju) no. 1100, 57 Saikō Saibansho minji hanreishū [Minshū] 125, *available 24 September 2015 at* http://www.courts.go.jp/app/hanrei_en/detail?id=625.

transaction often extends to any vehicle having the said role and characteristics. Such scope often includes marks; the names of human beings, living things, or goods; the appearance of products; a catch line used in connection with the provision of a service, and so on, some of which are protected under laws other than the Trademark Act – for example, the Unfair Competition Prevention Act,[11] the Copyright Act,[12] and protection by a tort claim under the Civil Code[13] – and some of which are subject to ongoing debates as to whether or not they should be given legal protection. Naturally, the scope of the discussion in this chapter should cover not only trademarks registrable under the current Trademark Act, but also those marks or vehicles that play roles similar to trademarks as defined under the Trademark Act.

21.10 This understanding of trademarks, focused on the intrinsic characteristic of a trademark in its role to convey certain information concerning a product or service, is also consistent with the concept of Article 15, Paragraph 1 of the Agreement on Trade Related Aspects of Intellectual Property Rights (TRIPS), which provides as follows:

> Any sign, or any combination of signs, capable of distinguishing the goods or services of one undertaking from those of other undertakings, shall be capable of constituting a trademark. Such signs, in particular words including personal names, letters, numerals, figurative elements and combinations of colours as well as any combination of such signs, shall be eligible for registration as trademarks. Where signs are not inherently capable of distinguishing the relevant goods or services, Members may make registrability depend on distinctiveness acquired through use. Members may require, as a condition of registration, that signs be visually perceptible.[14]

4. Laws to be considered when negotiating trademark transactions

21.11 The discussion above suggests that the Trademark Act is not the only law that defines the scope of the objects of trademark transactions. Lawyers who design, negotiate and draft trademark transactions often take into consideration and refer to the following laws:[15]

---

11 Fusei Kyōsō Bōshi-hō [Unfair Competition Prevention Act], Law No. 47 of 1993, as amended.
12 Chosakukenhō [Copyright Act], Law No. 48 of 1970, as amended.
13 Minpō [Civil Code], Law No. 89 of 1896, as amended.
14 Article 15(1), Agreement on Trade-Related Aspects of Intellectual Property Rights, 15 April 1994, Marrakesh Agreement Establishing the World Trade Organization, Annex 1C, 1869 U.N.T.S. 299, 33 I.L.M. 1197 (1994) [hereinafter TRIPS Agreement].
15 This is not an exhaustive list, and it will not be possible to explain in details the application of each law in this chapter.

- The Trademark Act.
- The provisions concerning a trade name[16] under the Commercial Code,[17] the Companies Act,[18] and other laws that regulate the establishment, operation, liquidation, and so on of corporations and other entities. Obviously, the trade name of a business entity often conveys certain information concerning its products or services, while the trade name itself comprises of neither products nor services.
- The Unfair Competition Prevention Act, which protects an indication of goods or business (meaning a name, trade name, trademark, mark, container or packaging for goods that is connected with a person's operations, or any other indication of a person's goods or business; the same shall apply hereinafter) and its appearance.
- The Copyright Act.[19] Literary, visual or audio works are often employed by business entities as vehicles to convey certain information about their products or services.
- The Act Concerning the Protection of the Indications of Specific Products of Agriculture, Forestry and Fisheries,[20] which provides protection of the geographic indication of these products.

C. LICENSES

1. Definition of 'license'

Needless to say, grants of license are one of the most typical and most frequently used types of trademark transaction. However, it is not so easy to define what a 'license' is. The on-going efforts for a Civil Code Reform confirm such difficulty.[21] The *Interim Draft 2013 for Reforming the Civil Code (Law Of Obligations)* published by the Ministry of Justice of Japan on March 11, 2014, presents three alternatives regarding how to deal with licenses in the Civil Code, which are not provided for under the current Civil Code:

21.12

---

16 *Shōgō* in Japanese.
17 Shōhō [Commercial Code], Law No. 48 of 1899, as amended.
18 Kaisha-hō [the Companies Act], Law No. 86 of 2005, as amended.
19 Copyright Act, *supra* note 12.
20 Tokutei Nōrin Suisan Butsu tō no Meishō no Hogo ni Kansuru Hōritsu [Act Concerning the Protection of the Indications of Specific Products of Agriculture, Forestry and Fisheries], Law No. 84 of 2014 (effective from 1 June 2015).
21 *See Civil Code Reform*, MINISTRY OF JUSTICE, *available 24 September 2025 at* http://www.moj.go.jp/ENGLISH/ccr/CCR_00002.html.

(1) To place new provisions concerning licenses under the provisions concerning leases. This proposal reflects the understanding that a license is deemed as a specific variation of a lease, or, at least, a contract that resembles a lease. This proposal defines a grant of license as a contract between parties, under which the licensor agrees not to object to the licensee's use of intellectual property protected by the licensor's rights, while the licensee agrees, in exchange, to pay royalties to the licensor. This proposal intends that, in general, the provisions concerning leases will apply to licenses.

(2) To categorize a grant of license as a type of contract independent of a lease. This proposal reflects the understanding that a grant of license is not a variation of a lease nor a relative thereof.

(3) To not draft specific provisions concerning licenses. This proposal reflects the understanding that regulating licenses under the law is useless or ineffective because there is an extremely wide variety of licenses.[22]

2. 'Right to use' trademarks provided under the Trademark Act

21.13 In contrast to the heated discussions over whether or not the Civil Code should be amended to include provisions concerning licenses, the Trademark Act has provisions concerning the 'right to use a trademark'[23] from the beginning, and no one questions the need for these provisions in the Act.

21.14 The Trademark Act gives a trademark rightholder the power to exclude others from using the trademark registered with the Japan Patent Office (JPO) in his name in connection with the goods or services designated in the relevant registration. However, other users of registered trademarks are able to defend themselves against the exercise of exclusive power by the trademark rightholder, if they can prove their use fulfils certain conditions. The Trademark Act calls such conditions the 'right to use a trademark'.

21.15 The fact that a person has the right to use a certain trademark does not necessarily mean that he or she is granted a license to use that trademark by the trademark rightholder. For example, a person, using a certain trademark in a fair manner, prior to the JPO trademark registration application date of the relevant rightholder of the same trademark, has a right to use that trademark

---

22 For example, the public commentary presented by the Japan Business Federation (*Keidanren* in Japanese) as of 11 June 2013, *available* 24 September 2015 at https://www.keidanren.or.jp/policy/2013/058.html, supports this proposal. The author also agrees with this proposal.
23 *Shiyō-ken* in Japanese.

subject to certain conditions.[24] This right to use a trademark is called the 'right to use a trademark arising from prior use'.[25]

However, without a doubt, the most frequently recognized cause for a right to use a trademark is a contract between the relevant trademark rightholder and the person who wants to use the trademark. According to the experiences of the author, such a contract constitutes the core of most trademark licensing agreements. **21.16**

3. Non-exclusive right to use

The first prong of a right to use a trademark granted by a contract is a 'non-exclusive right to use a trademark'.[26] The grant of a non-exclusive right to use a trademark is given by the trademark rightholder or by a proprietary licensee of the registered trademark at issue. The explanation below assumes a more common situation where the trademark rightholder grants this non-exclusive right to a licensee. **21.17**

The Trademark Act assumes that a grant of a non-exclusive right to use is accompanied by the following conditions: **21.18**

(a) the designation of the relevant trademark. This can be identified by indicating the trademark registration number with the JPO;
(b) the designation of the goods and/or services in connection with which the licensee is granted to use the relevant trademark. This can be chosen from among the designated goods and/or services in the relevant trademark registration at the JPO;
(c) the demarcation of any other scope within which the licensee can use the relevant trademark. For example, the scope can be a geographical range that corresponds to all or a part of the domain of Japan.

Those who use the relevant trademark within the scope of the granted non-exclusive right to use such trademark are able to claim that the trademark rightholder is not entitled to exclude such use.[27] However, the holder of a

---

24 *See* Trademark Act, *supra* note 3, at art. 32.
25 *Senshiyō-ken* in Japanese.
26 *Tsujō-shiyō-ken* in Japanese. 'The holder of a trademark right may grant to another person a non-exclusive right to use the trademark to which he/she holds the right'. Trademark Act, *supra* note 3, at art. 31, para. 1.
27 'The holder of a non-exclusive right to use shall have the right to use the registered trademark for the designated goods or designated services to the extent provided by the agreement under which such right is granted.' *Id.* at art. 31, para. 2.

non-exclusive right to use a trademark has no power to exclude others from using the same trademark.

21.19 The trademark rightholder, as a licensor, may authorize a licensee as the sole licensee with permission to use the relevant trademark within a certain scope (for example, within Japan). Such a right granted to the licensee, often called an exclusive license, will also fall within the category of a *non-exclusive* right to use, unless a *proprietary* right[28] to use the trademark is registered with the JPO. An 'exclusive' licensee in this context has no power to exclude others from using the licensed trademark.

21.20 The registration of a non-exclusive right to use a trademark with the JPO is not compulsory. However, without such a registration, the relevant licensee cannot make a claim of his or her rights against any subsequent assignees or proprietary licensees of the relevant trademark.[29]

21.21 Additionally, the bankruptcy trustee of the licensor, subject to certain conditions, may terminate the contract that gives the licensee a non-exclusive right to use the relevant trademark,[30] unless such a non-exclusive right is registered with the JPO.[31]

---

28 *See infra* Part C.4 (explaining the meaning of proprietary right).
29 *See* Trademark Act, *supra* note 3, at art. 31, para. 4.
30 Hasan-hō [Bankruptcy Act], Law No. 75 of 2004, art. 53, paras. 1–2:
> If both the bankrupt and his/her counter party under a bilateral contract have not yet completely performed their obligations by the time bankruptcy proceedings have commenced, a bankruptcy trustee may cancel the contract or may perform the bankrupt's obligations and request the counter party to perform his/her obligations.
>
> In the case referred to in the preceding paragraph, the counter party may specify a reasonable period and demand the bankruptcy trustee to give a definite answer within that period with regard to whether he/she will cancel the contract or request the performance of the obligation. In this case, if the bankruptcy trustee fails to give a definite answer within that period, it shall be deemed that he/she has canceled the contract.

Id. See also id. at art. 56.
> The provisions of Article 53(1) and (2) shall not apply where the counter party of the bankrupt under a contract for the establishment of a leasehold or any other right of use or to make a profit has registered such right or meets another requirement for duly asserting such right against any third party.

Id.
31 It should be noted that the non-exclusive right to work a patented invention (*Tsujo-jisshi-ken* in Japanese) can be claimed against subsequent assignees of the patent and the holders of the exclusive right to work the relevant invention without registration. *See* Tokkyo-hō [Patent Act], Law No. 121 of 1959, art. 99. Moreover, the receiver in bankruptcy of the patentee cannot arbitrarily terminate a licensing agreement that grants the non-exclusive right to work the invention. *See* Bankruptcy Act, *supra* note 30, at art. 56. Practitioners engaged in licensing or bankruptcy procedures should be careful about this difference between the non-exclusive right to use a trademark and the non-exclusive right to work a patented invention. A patent license (especially, in the case of a cross-license or patent pool arrangement) often covers a considerable number of patented inventions. Moreover, such patented inventions are often replaced or newly patented inventions are added. Therefore, it is not practical for patent licensees and licensors to register such non-exclusive rights to practice

21.22 A licensee that is granted a non-exclusive right to use a trademark is not entitled to assign the right to any other party, unless it is approved by the relevant trademark rightholder. However, a non-exclusive right belonging to the licensee who is a natural person may be succeeded by his or her heirs without the approval of the trademark rightholder. Also, without the approval of the relevant trademark rightholder, the non-exclusive right belonging to a licensee that is a corporation may be transferred to another corporation due to a merger of the licensee with such other corporation.

21.23 Such transfers of the non-exclusive rights without the approval of the trademark rightholder cause concern because the proposed, new non-exclusive licensee might be in competition with the trademark rightholder. Even if the proposed, new non-exclusive licensee is not in competition with the trademark rightholder, trademark rightholders are usually careful about whether their licensees have control over the quality of the products and services with which the licensed trademarks are connected. In light of this consideration, trademark licensing agreements often authorize the trademark rightholder, as the licensor, to cancel and to terminate the license at the commencement of an inheritance or merger proceeding, or upon a change of control over the licensee.

4. Proprietary right to use

21.24 The second prong of the right to use a trademark as granted through contract is the 'proprietary right to use the trademark',[32] which becomes effective only after its registration with the JPO.[33] The holder of a proprietary right to use a trademark is entitled to exclude others from using the same trademark within the scope designated in its registration with the JPO.

21.25 '*Senyō-shiyō-ken*' is often translated as the 'exclusive right to use a trademark'. However, when drafting licensing agreements for trademarks registered with the JPO in English, an 'exclusive right to use a trademark' or an 'exclusive license to use a trademark' usually refers to a *non-exclusive* right to use a

---

patented inventions. In contrast, such a difficult situation is not found with respect to trademark licenses. This difference of conditions regarding patent licenses and trademark licenses is reflected in the differences in the regulations on the registration of non-exclusive rights. For an example of an explanation prepared by the JPO, see http://www.jpo.go.jp/shiryou/hourei/kakokai/pdf/tokkyo_kaisei23_63/01syou.pdf (*available 15 September 2015*).

32 *Senyō-shiyō-ken* in Japanese. 'The holder of trademark right may establish a proprietary right to use the trademark to which he/she holds the right.' Trademark Act, *supra* note 3, at art. 30, para. 1.
33 Article 98, Paragraph 1 of the Patent Act which is applied *mutatis mutandis* by Article 30, Paragraph 4 of the Trademark Act.

Chapter 21 JAPANESE PERSPECTIVES ON TRADEMARK TRANSACTIONS

trademark that is granted solely to the licensee.[34] Those who draft and negotiate the said trademark licensing agreement should refer to the relevant provisions of the Trademark Act and also expressly define the scope of the rights to be granted to the licensee. This includes whether the licensor is obligated to register such rights with the JPO; whether the licensing agreement grants exclusive rights against third parties; and whether the licensee's rights to use the relevant trademark are also exclusive against the licensor, to avoid confusion or misunderstanding in case of future disputes.[35]

21.26 Even if the trademark rightholder agrees to grant the licensee a proprietary right to use a trademark, the licensee does not have such right until it is registered with the JPO. The registration of a proprietary right to use a trademark must be jointly applied for by the registered trademark rightholder (as the licensor) and the licensee.[36] A licensing agreement that is intended to grant a proprietary right to use a trademark may contain a provision that obligates the licensor (the relevant trademark rightholder) to cooperate with the licensee in the registration of such a right. In order to ensure such licensor's cooperation in the registration of the right, licensees often require licensors to provide a power of attorney, giving a patent attorney who is designated by or acceptable to the licensee the right to file the application for registration with the JPO, upon or prior to the execution of the licensing agreement.

21.27 The scope of the right to use the trademark granted to the licensee through the proprietary right may exclude the licensor's use of the same trademark within such a scope depending on the conditions designated in the registration of the right with the JPO.

21.28 Trademark rights holders usually maintain their interest by controlling the use of the relevant trademark by others since the use of a trademark may affect its brand value or even the sales of the products or services provided by the licensee, which also may affect the royalties payable by the licensee to the trademark rightholder. Accordingly, trademark rightholders do not necessarily lose their right to exclude others from the use of the trademark.[37]

---

34 *See infra* Part C.3.
35 In Sunstar, Inc. v. Alberto-Culver Co., 2009 U.S. Lexis 23759 (7th Cir. 28 October 2009) (addressing the meaning of *Senyo-shiyo-ken* in a licensing agreement based on Illinois law as the main issue of disputes between the licensor and the licensee).
36 Article 18 of the Patent Registration Order (Cabinet Order No. 39 of 1960, as amended) applied *mutatis mutandis* by Article 10 of the Trademark Registration Order (Cabinet Order No. 42 of 1960, as amended).
37 The Supreme Court of Japan held that patentees do not necessarily lose their right to demand that others do not exercise their patented invention when they grant licenses for the proprietary right to exercise the patented invention. *See* Saikō Saibansho [Sup. Ct.] 17 June 2005, Heisei 16 (ju) no. 997, 59 Saikō Saibansho Minji Hanreishū [Minshū], *available 24 September 2015 at* http://www.courts.go.jp/app/hanrei_en/detail?id=753.

5. Licensing agreements for marks not registered under the Trademark Act

Licensing agreements are often made for marks that are not registered **21.29** trademarks under the Trademark Act. Some of these marks are within the scope of trademarks registrable under the Trademark Act, but are not registered. Others are out of the scope of registrable trademarks. For example, photographs of celebrities, performers, and athletes are often used in advertisements to entice consumers to purchase goods or services. These are typical examples of marks that are out of the scope of registrable trademarks.[38] The terms and conditions provided by a contract that grants a licensee the use of such marks are almost the same as those provided by a licensing agreement concerning registered trademarks.

Figure 21.6 Example of a registered trademark using an illustrated portrait of a person (Japan Trademark Registration No. 4582803)

---

38 If the face or appearance of a person is fixed as an illustration or otherwise, it is registrable as a trademark under the Trademark Act. Figure 21.6 shows an example of such registered trademark. A *Sushi* restaurant uses an illustration of its founder as its trademark.

Chapter 21 JAPANESE PERSPECTIVES ON TRADEMARK TRANSACTIONS

21.30 Japanese laws do not provide for any specific ownership status for marks that are not registered under the Trademark Act.[39] However, during the term of a licensing arrangement, the parties assume that the licensor has substantial ownership of the mark licensed to the licensee. Under these agreements, the licensor may assign ownership of the relevant mark to a third party. However, licensees of marks not registered under the Trademark Act have no means of registering their rights to use the marks. Accordingly, licensees cannot make a claim for their right to use the mark against the assignees. Additionally, subject to certain conditions, a bankruptcy trustee for the licensor may terminate a contract that gives the licensee a right to use the relevant mark.

21.31 Under specific conditions, several laws entitle the owner of a mark[40] that is not registered under the Trademark Act to exclude others from using the same mark. The Unfair Competition Prevention Act is an example of such a law and is most often employed by owners of marks to achieve their purpose.

21.32 For example, the characteristic pleats used on a line of women's clothing are considered 'an indication of goods or business that is well-known among consumers'[41] which enables the owners of such an indication to exclude others from using the same indication as a mark for the others' products and services.[42] As an additional example, the Supreme Court has suggested, although in dicta, that the unauthorized use of images of celebrities or entertainers for the purpose of utilizing their power to attract customers can be characterized as a tort under the Civil Code.[43] These court opinions outline the qualifying requirements for injunctive relief for marks not registered under the Trademark Act.

21.33 However, because these marks are not trademarks registered under the Trademark Act, it is debatable whether the owners of these marks can legally exclude others from using the same marks until the owners prove that the marks satisfy the relevant requirements for injunctive relief in the particular court.

---

39 The Trademark Act provides for the ownership of the exclusive right to use a registered trademark, but it does not provide for the ownership of the trademark itself.
40 Here, the word 'owner' is used in a practical context.
41 *See* Unfair Competition Prevention Act, *supra* note 11, at art. 2, para. 1, item 1.
42 *See* Tōkyō Chihō Saibansho [Tokyo Dist. Ct.] 29 June 1999, Heisei 7 (wa) no. 13557, *available* 24 September 2015 *at* http://www.courts.go.jp.
43 *See* Saikō Saibansho [Sup. Ct.] 2 February 2012, Heisei 21 (ju) no. 2056, 66 SAIKŌ SAIBANSHO MINJI HANREISHŪ [MINSHŪ], *available* 24 September 2015 *at* http://www.courts.go.jp/app/hanrei_en/detail?id=1137.

21.34 If it is debatable whether a mark satisfies the requirements for injunctive relief, those who may want to use the same mark might naturally consider whether they should try to obtain a license from the mark owner by paying a royalty or whether they can just use the mark without a license.

21.35 The user of a mark not registered under the Trademark Act may weigh various considerations in deciding whether to obtain a license from the mark owner. For example, the user may compare the cost of paying royalties to the cost of defending against a possible lawsuit from the mark owner. Some users may obtain their own licenses, others may develop a business practice of obtaining licenses in order to use such unregistered marks, and still others may refuse to pay even small royalties amounts.

21.36 Such a gap, between the attitudes of the mark owners and unlicensed users of unregistered marks, can cause mark owners to seek injunctions and compensatory damages against the mark users. For example, the owner of a racehorse demanded that a software company stop using the name of his horse and that they compensate him for damages because they used his horse's name as the name of a virtual racehorse in a video game they produced and sold.[44]

21.37 The 2014 Amendment to the Trademark Act[45] has extended the scope of registrable trademarks. Therefore, quite a few marks that have not previously qualified as registrable trademarks will become registrable under the Trademark Act. We can reasonably expect that those who have refused to obtain a license to use any such trademarks will likely come to accept the license conditions offered by the mark owners.

6. Governing laws of licensing agreements

21.38 The governing laws of licensing agreements are not restricted by the Trademark Act or otherwise, irrespective of whether the agreement grants the licensee the right to use a trademark registered under the Trademark Act or an unregistered mark. A licensing agreement governed by foreign law can grant the licensee a non-exclusive right or proprietary right to use a registered trademark under the Trademark Act, keeping in mind that a proprietary right to use a registered trademark is not effective until registered with the JPO.[46]

---

44 *See* Saikō Saibansho [Sup. Ct.] 13 February 2004, Heisei 13 (ju) nos. 866, 867, 58 SAIKŌ SAIBANSHO MINJI HANREISHŪ [MINSHŪ] 311 (rejecting the demand of the owner of the racehorse).
45 *See supra* Part B. 2.
46 *See* Sunstar, Inc. v. Alberto-Culver Co., 2009 U.S. Lexis 23759 (7th Cir. 28 October 2009). *See also, e.g.*, the discussion *supra* Part C.

Chapter 21 JAPANESE PERSPECTIVES ON TRADEMARK TRANSACTIONS

7. Japanese taxes imposed on royalties

21.39 A license to use marks is often granted to corporations doing business in Japan by foreign corporations that have no branch offices or other permanent establishments (PEs) in Japan.[47] Naturally, the possibility of Japanese taxes being imposed on the royalties payable by the licensee to the licensor is a matter of concern for both the licensor and the licensee.

21.40 The classes of income for foreign corporations that have no PE in Japan on which Japanese Corporation Tax is imposed are, in general, limited to 'Domestic Source Income' as itemized in Article 141 of the Corporation Tax Act of Japan.[48] The list of 'Domestic Source Income' does not include 'royalties for an industrial property right or any other right concerning technology, a production method involving special technology or any other equivalent thereto, or consideration for the transfer thereof', as specified in Article 138, item 7(a) of the Corporation Tax Act.[49] Accordingly, in principle, Japanese corporation tax is not imposed on the royalties payable by a licensee using relevant marks in Japan to a licensor that has no PE in Japan.

21.41 In contrast, royalties are subject to Japanese income tax, which must be withheld by the licensee and payable to the Japanese tax authorities.[50] In principle, the withholding tax rate is 20 per cent[51] of the royalty amount payable by the licensee to the licensor.[52]

21.42 However, this withholding income tax rate – the sum of the income tax rate and the special income tax rate – is reduced by bilateral double tax treaties (that is, treaties for the avoidance of double taxation). For example, the rate is reduced to 10 per cent by the tax treaties between Japan and Korea, China, Singapore, Indonesia, and so on. Moreover, such withholding income tax is

---

47   *See* Hōjinzeihō [Corporate Taxation Act], Law No. 34 of 1965, art. 141, items 1–3, as amended.
48   *See id.*
49   According to the National Tax Agency Commissioner's Directive on the Interpretation of the Corporate Taxation Act 20-1-21, it is reasonably understood that marks not registered under the Trademark Act also can fall within 'an industrial property right or any other right concerning technology, a production method involving special technology or any other equivalent thereto'.
50   Shotokuzei-hō [Income Tax Act], Law No. 33 of 1965, art. 161, item 7(b), as amended.
51   From 1 January 2013, the withholding tax rate was increased to 20.42% to cover reconstruction after the 3.11 scale earthquake. This rate will continue for a 25 year period through 31 December 2037. *See* Higashinihon Daishinsai Kara no Fukkō no Tame no Shisaku o Jisshi Suru Tame ni Shūeki no Hitsuyōna Sōsu no Kakuho ni Kansuru Tokubetsu Sochi-hō [Act on Special Measures Concerning the Securing of the Necessary Sources of Revenue to Implement Measures for Reconstruction from the Great East Japan Earthquake], Law No. 117 of 2011.
52   *See* Income Tax Act, *supra* note 50, at art. 212, para. 1, art. 213, para. 1, item 1.

rescinded by the tax treaties between Japan and Holland, Switzerland, France, the U.S., and so on.

Cross-border licensing agreements typically contain a so-called 'gross-up' clause. Suppose that the royalty amount payable by the Japanese licensee to the foreign licensor is 100 and the withholding tax rate is 10 per cent. The gross-up clause requires the licensee to pay 100 directly to the licensor, in exchange for 90.[53] According to the National Tax Agency Commissioner's Directive on Interpretation of the Income Tax Act 221–1(1), the royalty amount should have been 100 × 100/90 = 111. Accordingly, the licensee is required to pay withholding income tax in the amount of 100 × 100/90 × 10% = 11. **21.43**

Suppose that a Japanese corporation (or person) has the trademark rights to a trademark registered with the JPO under the Trademark Act. Also, suppose that this domestic trademark rights owner, as a licensor, grants another domestic corporation (or person) the right to use this trademark. This transaction is termed a 'lease' of assets carried out by a business entity within Japan.[54] Accordingly, the royalty paid by the licensee to the licensor is subject to consumption tax, which is currently at 6.3 per cent of the said royalty,[55] and local consumption tax, which is 17/63 of the said consumption tax amount.[56] The total of the consumption tax and local consumption tax is 8 per cent[57] of the relevant royalty amount.[58] Hereinafter, the wording 'consumption tax' is used to refer to both the consumption tax and local consumption tax, as is often used in the course of business practice. **21.44**

Suppose that the same mark is registered under both the Japanese and foreign trademark acts and that the trademark rights owner grants a Japanese domestic licensee with the right to use the mark both in Japan and the relevant foreign state. This transaction is deemed as a 'lease' of assets carried out in the state of the principal office of the licensor (or the location of the licensor's residence, if the licensor is a natural person).[59] For example, if the licensor is a **21.45**

---

53 The result can be described with the following mathematical formula: 100 − 100 × 10/100 = 100 × 90/100 = 90.
54 *See* Shōhizei-hō [Consumption Tax Act], Law No. 108 of 1985, art. 4, para. 1, as amended; Shōhizei-hō Shikōrei [Consumption Tax Act Enforcement Ordinance], Law No. 360 of 1988, art. 6, para. 1, item 5, as amended.
55 *See* Consumption Tax Act, *supra* note 54, at art. 29.
56 *See* Chihō Zeihō [Local Tax Act], Law No. 226 of 1950, art. 72–83, as amended.
57 6.3% + 6.3% × 17/63 = 8%.
58 This total rate will be increased to 10%, although the government's decision about when this increase will be made is still pending.
59 *See* Consumption Tax Act Enforcement Ordinance, *supra* note 54, at art. 6, para. 1, item 5.

corporation with its principal office in Japan, the transaction is considered as having been carried out in Japan for the purposes of consumption tax, and consumption tax is imposed on the royalty payable by the licensee to the licensor. However, if the licensor is a corporation with its principal office outside of Japan, the transaction is considered an exporting transaction for the purpose of calculating the consumption tax, and is exempted from the consumption tax.[60]

21.46 The method for deciding whether licensing agreements for copyrighted works or unpatented technologies (often called 'know-how') are conducted in Japan and whether it is an exporting transaction is the same as the method for determining those issues for licenses of registered marks.[61] And, in practice, the same method is also applicable to licenses of unregistered marks. Accordingly, the conclusions concerning licensing agreements of registered marks are just as applicable to the licenses of unregistered marks.

21.47 As explained above, whether Japanese consumption tax is imposed on the royalty calculations for trademark licensing transactions is decided according to the locations of the trademark's registration, the licensor and the licensee.

8. Termination of licensing agreements

21.48 According to general Japanese legal practice, a party to a continuing transaction contract that does not specify a period for the continuation of the transaction may terminate the contract; however, the terminating party must give the other party reasonable advance notice or must compensate the other party for damages incurred due to the immediate termination of the contract.[62]

21.49 In order to avoid the legal uncertainty concerning the reasonableness of notice periods, as well as the justifiability for terminations of the contracts themselves, licensing agreements are usually made for fixed periods, such as one to three years. In order to facilitate the continuation of licensing agreements for longer periods, licensors and licensees often include within the contract provisions the capability of an automatic renewal of the terms as long as both parties present no objections. However, it should be noted that repeated

---

60 *Id.,* at art. 7, para. 1, item 5, art. 8, para. 1; Consumption Tax Act Enforcement Ordinance, *supra* note 54, at art. 6, para. 1, item 5, art. 17, para. 2, item 6.

61 *See* Consumption Tax Act Enforcement Ordinance, *supra* note 54, at art. 6, para. 1, item 7, art. 17, para. 2, item 6.

62 *See, e.g.,* Tōkyō Chihō Saibansho [Tokyo Dist. Ct.] 30 July 2010, Heisei 17 (wa) no. 25703, *available* 24 September 2015 *at* http://www.courts.go.jp.

automatic renewals of contracts may give one party the justification to claim that the relevant contract is a continuing transaction contract with no fixed period and that the other party should be required to give reasonable notice before terminating the contract.

21.50 For example, suppose the trademark rightholder of a mark grants a licensee the right to sublicense the right to use the mark to another party and that the licensee, in turn, grants a sublicensee the right to use that same mark. In such cases, the sublicensees may claim their due rights to use the mark against the trademark rightholder. However, once the primary licensing agreement between the original trademark rightholder and the licensee terminates, any such authorization to a sublicensee is deemed automatically terminated as well.[63]

9. Application of the Anti-Monopoly Act

21.51 Trademark rightholders may leverage their rights to secure their own advantages in a particular market. Such advantages may be beyond the scope of the legal effects of the trademark rights themselves. For example, a trademark rightholder that manufactures consumer products might grant retailers the right to use their trademark in order to market such products on the condition that the retailers do not market any competing products. In this way, the rightholder effectively prevents the retailers from selling competing products and maintains their market advantage.

21.52 Article 21 of the Act on Prohibition of Private Monopolization and Maintenance of Fair Trade of Japan[64] (Anti-Monopoly Act) states that '[t]he provisions of this Act do not apply to acts found to constitute an exercise of rights under the Copyright Act, Patent Act, Utility Model Act, Design Act or Trademark Act'. However, it should be noted that this provision does not exempt or permit any such leveraging of the trademark rights on the part of the rights holder.[65]

---

[63] *See, e.g.*, Ōsaka Chihō Saibansho [Osaka Dist. Ct.] Dec. 9, 1987, Showa 59 (wa) no. 6274, Showa 62 (wa) no. 3283, *available 24 September 2015 at* http://www.courts.go.jp.

[64] Shiteki Dokusen no Kinshi Oyobi Kōsei Torihiki no Kakuho ni Kansuru Hōritsu [Act on Prohibition of Private Monopolization and Maintenance of Fair Trade], Law No. 54 of 1947, as amended.

[65] *See, e.g.*, *Guidelines for the Use of Intellectual Property Under the Anti-Monopoly Act*, JAPAN FAIR TRADE COMMISSION (28 September 2007); *Recommendation Decision*, JAPAN FAIR TRADE COMMISSION (13 September 1965).

D. TRADEMARK ASSIGNMENTS AND SECURITY INTERESTS

1. General principles

21.53 The owners of trademarks use the marks as representations and symbols of consumers' loyalty to their products and services. Consumers that are satisfied with the products or services are likely to become loyal to such marks and seek them out. Naturally, some merchants are interested in utilizing this consumer loyalty to others' marks in order to encourage the purchase of their own products or services. Thus, trademark owners are able to generate revenue through having others utilize their consumers' loyalty to their marks. One way in which mark owners can make this happen is to grant others a license to use their mark. Another way is to assign the mark or the rights to the mark to others.

21.54 The Trademark Act explicitly provides that trademark rights are assignable.[66] Still, an assignment of a trademark right is not effective until the registration of such assignment with the JPO.[67]

21.55 Contrastingly, assignments of marks that are not registered under the Trademark Act may be made at the discretion of the relevant parties. However, a third party may not necessarily recognize any such assignments as legally effective beyond the assignor and assignee.

2. Trademarks that simultaneously represent the goodwill of diversified suppliers

21.56 It is quite common for multiple products and services to be designated with just one registered trademark. In such cases, the trademark right to the mark is divisible into multiple trademark rights, each of which may have different designated products or services. Additionally, each of these trademark rights is assignable to different assignees.[68]

21.57 If such assignments of the trademark rights occur, one trademark may simultaneously represent consumer loyalty to one supplier – for example, the assignee or trademark rightholder for particular designated products or services – as well as loyalty from a different group of consumers to another

---

[66] *See* Trademark Act, *supra* note 3, at art. 24–2, para. 1.
[67] Article 98, Paragraph 1 of the Patent Act, applied *mutatis mutandis* by Article 34, Paragraph 4 of the Trademark Act.
[68] *See* Trademark Act, *supra* note 3, at art. 24–2, para. 1.

supplier – for example, the assignee or trademark rightholder for other designated products or services. This situation of simultaneous representations by one trademark may cause confusion among consumers. In order to prevent such confusion, one trademark rightholder (or a proprietary licensee) may demand that the other trademark rightholder (or a licensee) affix an indication in connection with the other's products or services that sufficiently mitigates any confusion between the goods and services of both parties.[69]

3. Marks that represent the collective goodwill of multiple suppliers

21.58 In practice, unaffiliated parties – such as multiple suppliers of products or services of a similar kind that meet certain quality standards – may each use the same mark in connection with their own goods and services. In such cases, the marks may often represent consumer goodwill acquired by the suppliers collectively.

21.59 It may be the case that only one of these suppliers holds the trademark rights to the mark which is used by all. Moreover, this trademark rights holder may try to enforce its exclusive rights in the mark against any of the other suppliers.

21.60 For example, the masters of Japanese schools of martial arts (*budo*), classical dance (*buyo*), flower arrangement arts (*kado*), tea ceremonial arts (*sado* or *chado*), and so on may each utilize school names that represent their collective goodwill – for example, '*Kyokushin*' for a school of *Karate*, '*Hanayagi-ryu*' for *buyo*, '*Ikenobo*' for *kado*, '*Urasenke*' for *sado*. Suppose that only one of the masters of a certain school owns the trademark rights to the name of the school. If the relationship between the master (the trademark owner) and other masters deteriorates, the trademark owner may use his exclusionary rights to prevent other masters from using the same name for their schools. In one such dispute over the use of a *Karate* school name, the court rejected the trademark rightholder's attempt to exercise his exclusive rights.[70] In the court's opinion, because the school name represented the collective goodwill of all the school masters, the trademark rightholder's exercise of his exclusive right would amount to an abuse of trademark rights, unless the school masters collectively authorized the rightholder to exercise such right.

---

69 *See id.* at art. 24–4.
70 Ōsaka Kōtō Saibansho [Osaka High Ct.] 29 September 2004, Heisei 14 (ne) no. 3283, *available 24 September 2015 at* http://www.courts.go.jp.

4. Non-assignability of regional collective trademark rights

21.61 Regional collective trademarks – the JPO registration of which under the Trademark Act began in 2006 – allow associations of suppliers to register the trademark rights for marks they all use uniformly.[71] The member suppliers of these associations collectively hold the consumer goodwill of their marks. The four Chinese characters shown in Figure 21.7, pronounced '*Dogo Onsen*', is an example of a regional collective trademark.[72] The association of Japanese style hotels with hot-spring spas in the Dogo area, Dogo Onsen Ryokan Cooperatives,[73] owns these trademark rights. The member hotels provide their services to consumers and hold the collective consumer goodwill.

Figure 21.7 The shape of Dogo Onsen (hot-spring spa in the Dogo area) and the trademark in Chinese characters pronounced as 'dogo onsen'

21.62 The ownership of the rights to such regional collective trademarks by associations is useful in preventing disputes among multiple suppliers, as illustrated by the *Karate* school case. However, if such rights were assignable to one or more of the members or to a third party, the risks of such disputes may be realized. In order to prevent such problems, the rights to regional collective trademarks are not assignable.[74]

---

71   *See* Trademark Act, *supra* note 3, at art. 7–2.
72   *See* Class 44, *Provision of the facilities of hot-spring spas in the Dogo area of Matsuyama, Ehime Prefecture of Japan*, Registration No. 5,071,495; Class 43, *Provision of accommodations with the facilities of hot-spring spas in the Dogo area of Matsuyama, Ehime Prefecture of Japan*, Registration No. 5,435,121.
73   *See* DOGO ONSEN, *available 24 September 2015 at* http://www.dogo.or.jp/pc (last visited 15 February 2015).
74   *See* Trademark Act, *supra* note 3, at art. 24–2, para. 4.

5. Security interests in trademark rights

21.63 Because marks are assignable, it is not surprising that creditors who recognize the value of their debtors' marks seek to hold security interests in these marks. However, from the viewpoint of creditors, it is nearly essential that they obtain legal assurances for their security rights against any third party assignees of the marks and for their priority over any other creditors. Under the Japanese regulations concerning the protection of marks, it is difficult to ensure such rights and priority of security interests when dealing with unregistered marks.

21.64 The Trademark Act provides that a pledge may be established on a registered trademark right.[75] Such a pledge becomes effective only when registered with the JPO.

21.65 However, it is common in Japanese business practice to use 'an assignment for the purpose of a security interest' (*Joto-tanpo*). In order to establish *Joto-tanpo*, debtors assign their ownership of assets to their creditors in order to secure the creditors' right. This assignment of ownership is made only for granting a security interest to the creditor, and it is not intended to transfer the actual ownership of the relevant assets to the creditor. Upon the default of the debtor's payment obligation to the creditor, the creditor may take complete ownership of such assets or may sell such assets to any third party. However, if the value obtained by the creditor through such an acquisition of the whole ownership or sale of such assets exceeds the amount of the secured debt, the excess amount must be returned to the debtor.

21.66 *Joto-tanpo* can be established for a registered trademark right only to the extent that the right is assignable. When debtors agree to grant a *Joto-tanpo* on their registered trademark rights for the benefit of their creditors, the creditors may demand that the debtors register the transfers of such trademark rights with the JPO.[76] Since the assignment of a registered trademark right is not effective until its registration with the JPO, such registration is essential.

---

[75] Article 98, Paragraph 1, Items 1 and 3 of the Patent Act applied *mutatis mutandis* by Article 34, Paragraph 3 of the Trademark Act.
[76] *See, e.g.*, Ōsaka Chihō Saibansho [Osaka Dist. Ct.] Sept. 12, 2013, Heisei 24 (wa) no. 12967, *available 24 September 2015 at* http://www.courts.go.jp.

E. CONCLUSION

21.67 This chapter has offered a description of the laws applicable to trademark transactions in Japan including the latest legislative developments. This chapter, however, does not attempt to represent an exhaustive description of all the relevant legal aspects applicable to trademark transactions to date. Those who research or practice in the area of trademark transactions for Japanese marks should refer to the latest information and possibly consult with lawyers licensed under Japanese law. Additionally, it should be noted that the business and registration practice for the newly introduced types of trademarks is still a work in progress. Moreover, it is important to keep in mind that the legal principles applicable to trademark transactions carry over to those marks that are not registrable under the Trademark Act.

22

TRADEMARK TRANSACTIONS IN ASEAN: CONVERGENCES AND DIVERGENCES IN EMERGING MARKETS

Susanna H. S. Leong[*]

A. INTRODUCTION	22.01	4. Philippines	22.45
		5. Cambodia	22.46
B. TRADEMARKS AS PROPERTY	22.05	6. Myanmar	22.47
		7. Brunei	22.48
C. ASSIGNMENT OF REGISTERED TRADEMARKS	22.12	8. Malaysia	22.50
		9. Laos	22.53
1. Assignment of registered trademarks with or without goodwill/business	22.14	10. Indonesia	22.55
		E. REGISTRATION OF TRANSACTIONS	22.57
2. Assignment of an application for registration of a trademark	22.21	1. Singapore	22.58
		2. Vietnam	22.60
3. Formalities: assignments must be in writing	22.22	3. Thailand	22.62
		4. Philippines	22.64
4. Assignment of unregistered trademarks	22.23	5. Cambodia	22.65
		6. Myanmar	22.67
		7. Brunei	22.68
D. LICENSING OF REGISTERED TRADEMARKS	22.27	8. Malaysia	22.69
		9. Laos	22.72
1. Singapore	22.30	10. Indonesia	22.73
2. Vietnam	22.35		
3. Thailand	22.38	F. CONCLUSION	22.74

A. INTRODUCTION

Trademarks play an important function as indicators of origin and as guarantees of quality. Increasingly, trademarks are also seen as important tools for advertising and building brand equity. Businesses are always seeking new signs to promote and to sell their goods and services. As would be expected, the list of signs that can constitute a trademark has also expanded greatly and ranges from the traditional signs of words, logos and two-dimensional graphical representations to the non-conventional ones such as colours; shapes of goods

22.01

---

[*] Associate Professor and Vice Dean (Graduate Studies), NUS Business School, National University of Singapore.

Chapter 22 TRADEMARK TRANSACTIONS IN ASEAN

and aspects of packaging; smells; sounds; gestures or moving signs; position signs and interior décor of shops.

22.02 Trademarks, therefore, form an important part of a firm's intellectual property portfolio and, in many small and medium sized firms, trademarks are probably the most common intellectual property created that is of great value to the firms. As these firms grow in their sales and revenues, the trademarks that are applied to their goods or services also rise in tandem with their value and become important company assets. Examples of such firms in Asia include Samsung (South Korea); Huawei (China); Toyota (Japan); and SingTel (Singapore), just to name a few.

22.03 Transactions dealing in trademarks have grown in volume and they are featured with increasing significance in a firm's overall corporate strategies. Commercial exploitation of a trademark may take many different forms: using the trademark to better protect the trader's market share (that is, his profits) by barring others from using an identical or similar mark in relation to identical or similar goods or services; licensing the trademark for use by third parties for commercial returns (for example, through a franchise); selling his trademark outright for a specified value (for example, in a company acquisition); and using the trademark to obtain credit for his business undertakings (for example, as collateral in a loan). Amongst all these means, perhaps the most common form of commercial dealing in a trademark is either an assignment or a license of the use of the mark by the trademark proprietor.

22.04 This chapter considers trademark transactions (in particular assignment and licensing) and the laws governing them from the perspectives of Member countries of The Association of Southeast Asian Nations (ASEAN),[1] with particular reference to Singapore. In ASEAN, Member countries have differing legal systems and traditions, and are at different stages of economic development. To date, all Members in ASEAN have acceded to the World Trade Organization Agreement (WTO) and are signatories to the Agreement on Trade-Related Aspects of Intellectual Property Rights (TRIPS). Thus, in terms of intellectual property (IP) legal infrastructure, convergence in the laws is expected amongst ASEAN Members. However, subtle differences still remain within ASEAN and IP laws in the region are far from being harmonized. The writing of this chapter is based on information obtained from primary sources of law, namely trademark statutes and subsidiary

---

1 The Member countries of ASEAN include Brunei Darussalam; Cambodia; Indonesia; Laos PDR; Malaysia; Myanmar; Philippines; Singapore; Thailand; and Vietnam.

regulations of Member countries in ASEAN as well as case authorities wherever they are available.

B. TRADEMARKS AS PROPERTY

22.05 Whilst businesses may pride themselves in creating innovative signs to promote and sell their goods and services, it should be noted that there is no property in a sign as such.[2] Property rights accrue to a sign only when it carries *goodwill* with it or when it has been *registered* as a trademark.

22.06 In Singapore, a registered trademark is personal property.[3] An application for registration of a trademark is also a property right under Section 41 of the Singapore Trade Marks Act[4] and may be dealt with in the same way, with the necessary modifications wherever applicable, as a registered trademark. The property right in an unregistered trademark resides in the goodwill of the business to which the unregistered trademark is used and applied.

22.07 Elsewhere in ASEAN, we see trademarks being explicitly treated as conferring property rights upon successful and valid registrations in some jurisdictions whilst others refer to the exclusive right of a trademark proprietor or owner to use a registered mark.

22.08 Besides Singapore, Vietnam and Brunei are two other Member countries of ASEAN in which the trademark laws explicitly provide that a registered trademark is property.

22.09 In Vietnam,[5] trademarks are classified in the category of 'industrial property rights' which means 'rights of organizations and individuals to inventions, industrial designs, layout-designs of semiconductor integrated circuits, trade secrets, marks, trade names and geographical indications they have created or own, and right to repression of unfair competition'. The basis for establishment of property rights in the form of industrial property rights in a mark lies in the grant of protection of title according to registration procedures as

---

2   Guy Neale and others v. Ku de Ta SG Pte Ltd [2013] SGHC 250 at [51].
3   *See* Singapore Trade Marks Act (Cap 332, 2005 Rev Ed) at § 36 [hereinafter Singapore TMA].
4   *Id.* at § 41.
5   Law No. 50/205/QH11, of 29 November 2005, on Intellectual Property Law (promulgated by the Order No. 28/2005/L-CTN of 12 December 2005, of the President of the Socialist Republic of Vietnam) (VN003) [hereinafter Vietnam Law on Intellectual Property]. This law was amended in 2009 by Law No. 36/2009/QH12 on June 19, 2009, amending and supplementing a Number of Articles of the Law on Intellectual Property (promulgated by the Order No. 12/2009/L-CTN on June 29, 2009 of the President of the Socialist Republic of Vietnam), June 19, 2009, WIPO Lex. No. VN047 (Viet.).

stipulated by law or the recognition of international registration under treaties to which the government of Vietnam is a contracting party.[6] It is interesting to note that in the case of a well-known mark, property rights will be established on the basis of a 'process of use' instead of through the 'process of registration'. The conferment of property rights on trademarks, as with all the other industrial property rights, is limited and conditional. Specifically, the property rights enjoyed by a trademark proprietor in Vietnam must not be exercised in a manner that is prejudicial to the government's interests, public interests, legitimate rights and interests of other organizations and individuals and cannot violate other relevant provision of law.[7]

22.10   In Brunei, the governing law on trademarks is the Trade Marks Act[8] and a registered trademark is property within the definition of 'property'[9] found in Chapter 4 of the Interpretation and General Clauses Act. Similarly, an application for registration of a trademark is also treated as property.

22.11   On the other hand, trademark laws in Member countries such as Thailand,[10] Cambodia,[11] Malaysia[12] and Philippines[13] confer an exclusive right to use a

---

6   *Id.* at art. 6(3)(a).
7   *Id.* at art. 7(2).
8   Trade Marks Act (Chapter 98, Laws of Brunei, Revised Edition 2000) (BN008) [hereinafter Brunei TMA].
9   Interpretation and General Clauses Act, Laws of Brunei, Chapter 4, s 3(1) defines 'property' to include: *(a)* money, goods, choses in action, land and every description of property, whether movable or immovable; and *(b)* obligations, easements and every description of estate, interest and profit, present or future, vested or contingent, arising out of, or incident to, any property as defined in paragraph *(a)*.
10 Trademark Act, B.E. 2543, s 44 (1991) (consolidated as of 2000) (TH004) [hereinafter Thailand TMA]. Under Thailand's Trade Mark Act, the successful registration of a trademark shall confer on the owner of the trademark the exclusive right to use it for the goods for which it is registered.
11 The Law concerning Marks, Trade Names and Acts of Unfair Competition of the Kingdom of Cambodia, NS/RKM/0202/006 (2002) (KH001) [hereinafter Cambodia TMA]. The Law was approved by the National Assembly on 6 December 2001, at the 7th plenary session, 2nd legislature and approved wholly the formality and legality by Senate on 9 January 2002 at 6th plenary session, 1st legislature. Article 11 of Cambodia TMA confers on a registered trademark owner the exclusive right to use the registered mark in relation to any goods or services for which it has been registered. Article 11 further provides that anyone who uses a registered trademark without the consent of the registered trademark owner infringes the mark and the registered trademark owner shall have the rights to institute court proceeding against that person.
12 Trade Marks Act (Act 175 of 1976, as last amended by Act A1138 of 2002) (MY044) [hereinafter Malaysia TMA]. A registered trademark confers on the registered proprietor of a trademark the exclusive right to use the trademark in relation to the goods or services for which the mark is registered. Under Section 36 of the Malaysia TMA, the fact that a person is registered as proprietor of a trademark shall be prima facie evidence of the validity of the original registration of the trademark and of all subsequent assignments and transmissions thereof. *Id.*, s 36 at [36].
13 Intellectual Property Code of the Philippines (Republic Act No. 8293)(1997)(PH001) *as amended* Implementing Rules and Regulations of the Republic Act No. 9502 of 2008, July 4, 2008, WIPO Lex. No. PH048 (Phil.) *as amended* Republic Act No. 10372, entitled 'An Act Amending Certain Provisions of Republic Act No. 8293, otherwise known as the Intellectual Property Code of the Philippines', and for other purposes, Feb. 28, 2013, WIPO Lex. No. PH100 (Phil.) [hereinafter IPC Philippines]. The IPC Philippines prescribes the intellectual property code and establishes the intellectual property office, providing for its powers and

registered trademark on the trademark proprietor without express reference to a registered trademark as property.

C. ASSIGNMENT OF REGISTERED TRADEMARKS

22.12 An assignment of a trademark involves an outright sale under which there is a 'one-off' transfer of the personal property in the trademark to the new owner. Thereafter, the original trademark proprietor (the assignor) ceases to have any rights over the trademark. An assignment of a registered trademark is essentially a contract under which property rights in the trademark are transferred from the trademark proprietor (assignor) to the new owner (assignee) and contract law applies to issues, such as formation of contract, terms and conditions, discharge of contractual obligations and remedies for breach.

22.13 In some ASEAN Member countries, including Singapore, an assignment of a registered trademark may be total or partial (limited so as to apply in respect of some but not all of the goods or services for which the trademark is registered).[14]

1. Assignment of registered trademarks with or without goodwill/business

22.14 In Singapore,[15] a registered trademark is assignable and transmissible in the same way as other personal or movable property, and is so assignable or transmissible either in connection with the goodwill of a business or independently.[16] This is a significant change from the early days when it was thought that trademarks did not exist independently of the goodwill they represented. Consequently, trademarks could not be assigned (or licensed) separately from the business in which they were used. Common law has traditionally characterized the nature of a trademark right at common law as one 'to restrain other persons from using the mark. But it was an adjunct of the

---

functions, and for other purposes. Part III of the IPC Philippines is devoted to trademarks. Part III, Section 138 of the IPC Philippines states that a certificate of registration of a mark shall be prima facie evidence of the validity of registration, the registrant's ownership of the mark, and of the registrant's exclusive right to use the mark in connection with the goods or services for which the mark is registered.

14 For Singapore, see Singapore TMA, supra note 3, at § 38(2). For Brunei, see BTMA, supra note 8, at § 25(2). For Malaysia, see Malaysia TMA, supra note 12, at § 55(1). For Indonesia, see Law No. 15 of 1 August 2001, regarding Marks, article 1(13) (ID046) [hereinafter Indonesia LM].

15 For a detailed discussion on assignment of trademarks in Singapore, see SUSANNA H.S. LEONG, INTELLECTUAL PROPERTY LAW OF SINGAPORE at ¶¶ 32.011 to 32.014 (2013).

16 See Singapore TMA, supra note 3, at § 38(1).

goodwill of a business and incapable of separate existence disassociated from that goodwill.'[17] The underlying concern is that of consumer confusion. However, the law has since moved on and it is generally accepted that the concept that a trademark could be applied only to goods actually manufactured or selected by the trademark proprietor no longer represented commercial reality. The public is increasingly familiar with merchandising as a business model and they recognize that a mark could relate to goods that had been manufactured by others under the proprietor's control. The law has to evolve to keep up with changing business practices and public perceptions.

22.15 Singapore has followed the practices of other jurisdictions such as the United Kingdom in the liberalization of the rules on assignment and licensing of trademarks. So far as the other Member countries of ASEAN are concerned, we see similar trends in their trademark laws. Several Member countries of ASEAN such as Thailand,[18] Philippines,[19] Brunei,[20] Indonesia,[21] and Malaysia[22] allow assignments of registered trademarks with or without the goodwill of the business.

22.16 However, concerns of public confusion exist particularly when the assignment was unaccompanied by the goodwill of the assignor's business and Member countries in ASEAN respond to this issue differently.

22.17 Singapore has taken a liberal approach as far as this issue is concerned. It used to be a legal obligation under the old law to advertise an assignment of a trademark when the assignment was unaccompanied by the goodwill of the assignor's business, but this requirement has since been abolished. In cases where the assignment of the mark is not accompanied by the acquisition of the assignor's business, the responsibility lies on the assignee to make the necessary arrangements with the assignor to ensure that the mark will continue to be

---

17 GE Trade Mark, [1972] 1 W.L.R. 729 at 742 (Eng.).
18 Thailand TMA, *supra* note 10, at § 49. Under Thai law, the right to registered trademark may be assigned or transferred by succession with or without the business concerned in the goods for which the trademark is registered.
19 *See* IPC Philippines, *supra* note 13, at § 149.1. In Philippines, a trademark registration or an application for registration of a mark may be assigned or transferred with or without the transfer of the business using the mark.
20 *See* Brunei TMA, *supra* note 8, at § 25. In Brunei, a registered trademark is transmissible by assignment or transfer in the same way as other property. It may be assigned either in connection with the goodwill of a business or independently.
21 *See* Indonesia LM, *supra* note 14, at art. 41(1). In Indonesia, a transfer of rights to a registered mark may be accompanied by the transfer of goodwill, reputation or other things related to the mark.
22 *See* Malaysia TMA, *supra* note 12, § 55(1).

C. ASSIGNMENT OF REGISTERED TRADEMARKS

exclusively indicative of one trade origin or source (namely, the assignee) after the assignment. Failure to take the necessary precautionary steps by the assignee in a split assignment to ensure distinctiveness may risk the registration being revoked on the grounds that the mark has become deceptive as to the trade source it denotes. A possible solution is the incorporation of restrictive covenants in the assignment, but enforceability may be an issue as they are considered restraint of trade clauses and are subject to the courts' review in light of test of reasonableness. The assignee is thus forewarned.

22.18 Elsewhere, such as in Malaysia, the legal obligation to advertise an assignment of a trademark when the assignment was unaccompanied by the goodwill of the assignor's business is preserved.[23] It should also be noted that a trademark shall be deemed not to be assignable or transmissible if, as a result of the assignment or transmission whether under common law or by registration, more than one of the persons concerned would have exclusive rights to the use of an identical trademark or to the use of trademarks so nearly resembling each other as are likely to deceive or cause confusion.

22.19 In the Philippines, if the assignment or transfer is liable to mislead the public – in particular the nature, source, manufacturing process, characteristics or suitability for their purpose, of the goods or services to which the mark is applied – the assignment or transfer shall be null and void.[24]

22.20 In Vietnam, it is specifically stated that assignment of rights must not cause confusion as to properties or origins of goods or services bearing such marks.[25] Important terms which must be incorporated in an industrial property right assignment contract include the full names and addresses of the assignor and assignee; assignment bases; the price; and the rights and obligations of the parties.

2. Assignment of an application for registration of a trademark

22.21 An application for registration of a trademark is treated as property and may constitute the subject of an assignment. In Singapore, an application for the registration of a trademark is assignable in the same way as a registered

---

23   *Id.* at § 55(5).
24   IPC Philippines, *supra* note 13, at § Section 149.2.
25   Vietnam Law on Intellectual Property, *supra* note 5, at art. 139.

trademark. This is also the position in most of the other Member countries in ASEAN such as Vietnam,[26] Thailand,[27] Philippines[28] and Brunei.[29]

3. Formalities: assignments must be in writing

22.22 In Singapore, to be legally effective, trademark assignments must be in writing signed by or on behalf of the assignor or his personal representative.[30] Similarly, ASEAN Member countries such as Vietnam,[31] Philippines, Cambodia, Brunei, Malaysia and Indonesia also require assignments of registered trademarks to be in writing to be effective.[32]

4. Assignment of unregistered trademarks

22.23 In general, it may be said that property rights in a sign accrued through lawful and valid registrations in Member countries of ASEAN and unregistered trademarks are therefore not treated as property as such. The protection of unregistered trademarks often falls within the realms of unfair competition laws or the tort of 'passing off'. Thus, it may be concluded that unregistered trademarks are assignable only if accompanied by the goodwill of the business.

22.24 In Singapore, it is expressly stated in the Trade Marks Act that nothing shall be construed as affecting the assignment or transmission of an unregistered

---

26 *Id.* at art. 87(6). Under Vietnam Law on Intellectual Property, a trademark proprietor who is conferred industrial property rights in a registered mark (including an application for registration) may assign the registration right to organizations or individuals in the form of contracts, bequeathal or inheritance.
27 An application for registration of a trademark is assignable and transferable by succession under art. 48 of the Thailand TMA.
28 IPC Philippines, *supra* note 13, § 149.1. In the Philippines, a trademark registration or an application for registration of a mark may be assigned or transferred with or without the transfer of the business using the mark.
29 Brunei TMA, *supra* note 8, at § 28(1).
30 *See* Singapore TMA, *supra* note 3, at § 38(3).
31 Under Vietnamese law, an assignment of industrial property rights must be established in the form of written contracts. It is specifically stated in Article 139 of the *Law on Intellectual Property* that assignment of rights must not cause confusion as to properties or origins of goods or services bearing such marks. Important terms which must be incorporated in an industrial property right assignment contracts include the full names and addresses of the assignor and assignee; assignment bases; the price and the rights and obligations of the parties. *See* Vietnam Law on Intellectual Property, *supra* note 5, at § 138(2).
32 *See* IPC Philippines § 149.3 which states 'the assignment of the application for registration of a mark, or of its registration, shall be in writing and require the signatures of the contracting parties'. See Art. 48 of the Cambodia TMA that states '[a]ny change in the ownership of the registration of a mark or collective mark, shall be in writing and shall, at the request of any interested party, to the Registrar, be recorded and, published by the Registrar. Such change shall have no effect against third parties until such recording is effected.' *See* § 25(3) of Brunei TMA that states '[a]n assignment of a registered trade mark is not effective unless it is in writing and signed by or on behalf of the assignor'. *See also* § 35 and § 47 Malaysia TMA and art. 40 and 41 Indonesia LM.

trademark as part of the goodwill of a business.[33] So, the position of assignments of unregistered trademarks reverts to common law. As explained before, at common law, there is no right of property in a trademark other than as an adjunct of the goodwill of the business in which the mark is used. Therefore, an unregistered trademark is not assignable in Singapore unless it is accompanied by the goodwill of the business in which it is used.

22.25 The position of assignment of unregistered trademarks in Brunei is similar to that in Singapore. Section 25(6) of the Brunei Trade Marks Act provides that an unregistered trademark is assigned or transferred as part of the goodwill of a business.[34]

22.26 In Malaysia, both a registered and an unregistered trademark may be assigned with or without the goodwill of the business, provided that the trademark is used in good faith in Malaysia.[35]

D. LICENSING OF REGISTERED TRADEMARKS

22.27 A license of a trademark involves only a granting of a limited right to use the mark (duration of use and geographical restrictions) by the trademark proprietor to a particular person or persons. There are several different types of trademark license and the more common ones include: (a) an exclusive license;[36] (b) a sole license;[37] (c) a bare license;[38] and (d) a sub-license.[39]

---

33 *See* Singapore TMA, *supra* note 3, at § 38(7).
34 Brunei TMA, *supra* note 8, at § 25(6).
35 Malaysia TMA, *supra* note 12, at § 55(1A).
36 Generally, an exclusive license means a license (whether general or limited) authorizing the licensee to the exclusion of all other persons, including the person granting the license, to use a registered trademark in the manner authorized by the license. For example, see Singapore TMA at § 43. Accordingly, an exclusive licensee is the only person authorized to use the mark within a stipulated territory. The licensor is not permitted to grant licenses to any others within the territory and he is also not allowed to compete with the licensee in the specified geographical location. It is however possible for the licensor to grant exclusive licenses to different individuals in different territories.
37 Under a sole license, the licensor grants to the licensee the right to use the trademark for a limited period of time to the exclusion of others but not the licensor himself. This means that the licensor may still use the trademark and compete with the licensee. *See* explanation in Kickapoo (Malaysia) Sdn Bhd v. The Monarch Beverage Co (Europe) Ltd [2010] 1 SLR 1212, at [49].
38 A bare license is a license under which the licensor (proprietor of the trademark) has no power to control the quality of the goods sold under the license. *See* explanation in Kickapoo (Malaysia) Sdn Bhd v The Monarch Beverage Co (Europe) Ltd [2010] 1 SLR 1212, at [42].
39 A sub-license is a license granted by a licensee to a third party in accordance with the terms and conditions of the original license. For example see Vietnam Law on Intellectual Property at art. 143.

22.28 The laws governing licensing of trademarks may differ across Member countries in ASEAN but in general, we see an over-arching concern by the governments in most Member countries of the impact of licensing of trademarks in causing public confusion. As such, trademark laws in most Member countries of ASEAN require the licensor to exercise some form of effective control of the quality of the goods or services of the licensee in connection with which the mark is used. Failure to provide for such quality control in the license contract will in general render the license contract invalid in most Member countries.

22.29 Aspects of the laws governing licensing of trademarks in Member countries of ASEAN, with the exception of Myanmar, are discussed as follows.

1. Singapore

22.30 In Singapore, it should be noted that there are no explicit restrictions on the powers of trademark proprietors to grant trademark licenses under the Trade Marks Act.[40]

22.31 However, courts in Singapore continue to require trademark proprietors to exercise '*some* control or supervision of the use of the trademark by the purported licensee'[41] in order to establish the requisite trade connection for a valid trademark license.

22.32 The absence of control on the part of the trademark proprietor of the use of the registered trademark by the licensee may render the mark deceptive and liable to be revoked under Section 22(1)(*d*) of the current Trade Marks Act.[42] In this regard, the courts in Singapore[43] have expressed reservations over the views postulated in *Scandecor Developments AB v. Scandecor Marketing AB*,[44] in particular Lord Nicholls' proposed notion of an evolving or changing trade source in a licensed trademark and its applicability in Singapore laws. Therefore, it is advisable for the trademark proprietor to ensure that *a trade connection* is maintained between him and the goods sold or services rendered under the licensed trademark in the form of some quality control or supervision over the use of the mark by his licensee. The onus is on the parties, in

---

[40] For a detailed discussion on trademark licensing in Singapore, see LEONG, *supra* note 15, at ¶¶ 32.014 to 32.027.
[41] *See* Weir Warman Ltd v. Research & Development Pty Ltd [2007] 2 SINGAPORE LAW REPORTS 1073 at [65].
[42] Singapore TMA, *supra* note 3, at § 22(1)(d).
[43] *See* Kickapoo (Malaysia) Sdn Bhd v. The Monarch Beverage Co (Europe) Ltd [2009] SGCA 63 at [44]–[53].
[44] Scandecor Developments AB v. Scandecor Marketing AB [2001] UKHL 21 (Eng.).

D. LICENSING OF REGISTERED TRADEMARKS

particular the trademark proprietor, to take the necessary steps to make sure the licensed mark does not become deceptive and revocable on the ground that the use of the mark by the licensee is liable to mislead the public, particularly as to the nature, quality, or geographical origin of the goods or services in question under Section 22(1)(*d*) of the Singapore Trade Marks Act.

Trademark licenses may be general or limited[45] and they may be exclusive or non-exclusive. A limited trademark license is one that applies in relation to some, but not all, of the goods or services for which the trademark is registered.[46] An exclusive license means 'a license (whether general or limited) authorising the licensee to the exclusion of all other persons, including the person granting the license, to use a registered trademark in the manner authorised by the license'.[47] A license must be in writing signed by or on behalf of the grantor otherwise it is 'not effective'.[48] 22.33

Sub-licensing is also allowed under the current Trade Marks Act if the license so provides.[49] 22.34

2. Vietnam

Article 141 of 'Law on Intellectual Property' defines licensing of an industrial object as 'the permission by the owner of such industrial property object for another organization or individual to use the industrial property object within the scope of his/her use right'.[50] Just as in the case of an assignment, the law in Vietnam also requires that a license of industrial property objects are to be made in written contracts. A number of restrictions are imposed on licensing of industrial property objects. For example, sub-licenses with a third party are not permitted unless they are made with the consent of the licensor. Trademark licensees are obliged to indicate on goods and goods packages that such goods have been manufactured under trademark license contracts. 22.35

In Vietnam, the law recognizes the following types of licenses:[51] 22.36

(a) Exclusive license. Under an exclusive license, the licensee shall have an exclusive right to use the licensed industrial property object while the

---

45 *See* Singapore TMA, *supra* note 3, at § 42(1).
46 *See id.* at § 42(2).
47 *See id.* at § 43(1).
48 *See id.* at § 42(3).
49 *See id.* at § 42(8).
50 Vietnam Law on Intellectual Property, *supra* note 5, at art. 141.
51 *Id.* at art. 143.

licensor may neither enter into any industrial property object license contract with any third party nor, without permission of the licensee, use such industrial property object.

(b) Non-exclusive license. Under a non-exclusive license, the licensor shall still have the rights to use the industrial property object and to enter into non-exclusive industrial property object license contracts with others.

(c) Sub-license. For this category, the licensor is a licensee of the right to use an industrial property object under another contract.

22.37 It is interesting to note that the 'Law on Intellectual Property'[52] expressly provides that an industrial property object license contract must not have provisions which unreasonably restrict the right of the licensee in particular anti-competitive practices such as:

(1) prohibiting the licensee to improve the industrial property object except in the case of trademarks;
(2) compelling the licensee to transfer free of charge to the licensor improvements of the industrial property object made by the licensee or the right of industrial property registration or industrial property rights to such improvements;
(3) restricting the licensee directly or indirectly to export goods produced or services provided under the industrial property object license contract to the territories where the licensor neither holds the respective industrial property rights nor has the exclusive right to import such goods;
(4) compelling the licensee to buy all or a certain percentage of raw materials, components or equipment from the licensor or a third party designated by the licensor not for the purpose of ensuring the quality of goods produced or services provided by the licensee;
(5) forbidding the licensee to complain about or initiate lawsuits with regard to the validity of the industrial property rights or the licensor's right to license.

3. Thailand

22.38 Part 5 of Trade Mark Act is devoted to trademark licensing.[53] The owner of a registered trademark may license the right to use the trademark to another person in respect of all or some of the goods for which the trademark is registered.

---

52 *Id.* at art. 144.
53 Thailand TMA, *supra* note 10, at arts 68 to 79.

D. LICENSING OF REGISTERED TRADEMARKS

22.39 Under Thai law, a trademark license must be in writing and must be registered with the Registrar. In order to be registered, the application for registration of the license must contain the following important particulars:

(a) Conditions or terms between the registered trademark owner and licensee to ensure that the trademark owner exercises effective control over the quality of the goods of the licensee.
(b) The goods for which the trademark is to be used.[54]

22.40 If the Registrar of Trade Marks is satisfied that the licensing agreement of a trademark would not cause the public to be confused or misled and that it is not contrary to public order or morality, the Registrar shall order the registration of the licensing agreement and may impose conditions or restrictions as he considered necessary.[55] In the event that the Registrar finds that license agreement will confuse or mislead the public or is contrary to public order or morality, the Registrar shall refuse to register the license.

22.41 The decision of the Registrar to impose conditions or restrictions in the licensing agreement or to refuse the registration of the licensing agreement shall be communicated to the trademark owner and licensees. The law provides for an avenue for appeal of the Registrar's decision to the Trade Mark Board.

22.42 The trademark owner together with the licensees may apply to the Registrar to amend the conditions and restrictions of a trademark license as well as the goods covered by the license.[56] The trademark owner together with the licensees may also apply to the Registrar to cancel the registration of a license agreement. In cases where the trademark license has expired, either the trademark owner or the licensee may apply to the Registrar to cancel the registration of the license.

22.43 It should be noted that any interested person or the Registrar may petition to the Trade Mark Board to cancel the registration of a trademark license if any of the following conditions are satisfied:

(a) the use of the trademark by the licensee has confused or misled the public or is contrary to public order or morality or to public policy; or

---

[54] *Id.*, at § 68.
[55] *Id.* at § 69.
[56] *Id.* at § 71.

(b) the trademark owner can no longer exercise effective control over the quality of the goods under the license.[57]

In the event that the registration of a trademark is cancelled, the licensing of the mark shall also cease to have effect.[58]

22.44 A trademark owner shall have the right to use the trademark himself and to license to persons other than the designated licensee unless the licensing agreement provides otherwise.[59] A licensee shall have the right to use the trademark throughout the country for all the goods for which the trademark registered and for the entire term of the trademark registration and its renewal unless the licensing agreement provides otherwise.[60] Furthermore, unless expressly provided for in the trademark licensing agreement, a licensee may not sublicense his right to use the registered trademark in a trademark licensing agreement.[61]

4. Philippines

22.45 It is mandated by law that any license of a registered trademark or an application of registration shall provide for effective control by the licensor of the quality of the goods or services of the licensee in connection with which the mark is used. Failure to provide for such quality control in the license contract or if such quality control is not effectively carried out will render the license contract invalid.

5. Cambodia

22.46 Under Cambodian law, both the registration of a trademark as well as the application for registration may be the subject of a licensing contract. Article 19 of The Law concerning Marks, Trade Names and Acts of Unfair Competition provides that any trademark licensing contract shall provide for effective control by the licensor of the quality of the goods or services of the licensee in connection with which the mark is used.[62] If the trademark licensing contract does not provide for such quality control or if such quality control is not effectively carried out, it shall not be valid.

---

57   *Id.* at § 72.
58   *Id.* at § 76.
59   *Id.* at § 77.
60   *Id.* at § 78.
61   *Id.* at § 79.
62   Cambodia TMA, *supra* note 11, at art. 19.

6. Myanmar

There is no relevant law available for Myanmar at this time. However, government efforts are underway to draft Myanmar's new Trade Mark Law.[63] The Myanmar Intellectual Property Office will also be established to accept and register applications for trademark registration.

22.47

7. Brunei

A license to use a registered trademark must be in writing; otherwise, it is not effective.[64] It may be a 'general' or a 'limited' license. A 'limited' license is one that applies only in relation to some, but not all, of the goods or services for which the trademark is registered or in relation to use of the trademark in a particular manner or a particular locality.

22.48

An 'exclusive' license means a license (whether general or limited) authorizing the licensee to the exclusion of all other persons, including the person granting the license, to use a registered trademark in the manner authorized by the license. An 'exclusive' licensee has the same rights against a successor in title that is bound by the license as he has against the person granting the license. An 'exclusive' licensee is entitled to bring infringement proceedings against any person other than the proprietor in his own name.

In contrast, a mere licensee must call on the proprietor of the registered trademark to take infringement proceedings in respect of any matter that affects his interests. In the event that the proprietor refuses to do so or fails to do so within two months after being called upon, the licensee may bring the proceedings in his own name as if he were the proprietor.

22.49

8. Malaysia

Under the Trademark Act, trademark proprietors in Malaysia are able to grant licenses to others for the use their trademarks under a system whereby, at the Registrar's discretion, a person could be registered as a 'registered user'.[65]

22.50

---

63 See Darani Vanchanavuttivong, *Trademarks in Myanmar: An Emerging IP Regime*, available 24 September 2015 at http://www.tilleke.com/sites/default/files/2014_Jan_Trademarks_in_Myanmar_AMCHAM.pdf.
64 In the case of a body corporate, the requirement of writing is satisfied by affixing the corporate's seal. See Brunei TMA, *supra* note 8, at § 29(2).
65 Malaysia TMA, *supra* note 12, at § 48.

22.51 The use of the registered trademark by the 'registered user' was regarded as 'permitted use'[66] and such use was deemed to be use by the proprietor.[67] The proprietor was obliged by law to maintain control over the use of the trademark and the quality of the goods or services provided by the 'registered user'[68] and this control in turn ensured that there continued to be a *trade connection* between the trademark proprietor and the goods ultimately sold to the consumers by the 'registered user'.

22.52 Under the system of 'registered users', the trade source, as denoted by the registered trademark after the grant of a license, continued to be with the trademark proprietor. Registration as a 'registered user' is not automatic and has to comply with the conditions set out under the Trademark Act.[69] The Registrar is required to scrutinize the license and satisfy himself that the use of the registered trademark by the 'registered user' would not be contrary to the public interest.

9. Laos

22.53 No specific provisions on assignment or licensing of registered trademarks are available in Laos intellectual property laws.[70] However, it may be gleaned from the rights conferred on an industrial property owner that assignment and licensing of a registered trademark are permitted under Laotian law.

22.54 A registered trademark is classified as industrial property under Laotian law and an industrial property owner is conferred the following rights:

(a) to enjoy the benefits derived from the exploitation of the industrial property;
(b) to transfer all or part of the owner's rights to another person by sale, exchange, rent or assignment;
(c) to permit another person to exploit all or part of the owner's rights to the industrial property;
(d) to inherit industrial property and to pass ownership of the industrial property by inheritance;

---

66   *See id.* at § 3(1). Permitted use in relation to a registered trademark means the use of the trademark by a registered user thereof in relation to goods or services with which he is connected in the course of trade and in respect of which the trademark remains registered and he is registered as a registered user, being use which complies with any conditions or restrictions to which his registration is subject.
67   *See id.* at § 48(5).
68   *See id.* at § 48(1).
69   *See id.* at § 48(1).
70   *See* Law No. 01/NA of 20 December 2011, on Intellectual Property (LA025).

(e) to take legal action to protect its industrial property from violation by other parties.[71]

10. Indonesia

22.55 A license to use a registered trademark may apply to all or parts of the goods or service for which the mark is registered. Unless provided in the licensing agreement, it shall be valid for the entire territory of the Republic of Indonesia and for a period not exceeding the period of protection of the registered mark concerned. A license to use a registered trademark must be recorded in the General Register of Marks. Sub-licenses are permissible under Indonesian law.

22.56 It is interesting to note that Article 47(1)[72] expressly provides that a licensing agreement shall not contain any provisions, which may directly or indirectly damage the Indonesian economy or to contain restrictions that obstruct the ability of the Indonesian people to master and develop the technology in general. If a licensing agreement contains such restrictions, the Directorate General must reject the request to record the licensing agreement in the General Register of Marks.

E. REGISTRATION OF TRANSACTIONS

22.57 Assignments and licenses of trademarks are registrable transactions in all Member countries of ASEAN, with the exception of Laos (there are no specific provisions on assignments and licensing) and Myanmar (there is no specific law on intellectual property or trademarks).

1. Singapore

22.58 Under the Singapore Trade Marks Act, it is mandatory for assignees and licensees to record their interests. Every person is deemed to have notice of a license if the prescribed particulars of the grant of the license are entered in the Trade Mark Register under section 39(1) of the current Trade Mark Act.[73]

22.59 Failure to record their interests will render:

---

71 *Id.* at Part 4, art. 47 (revised).
72 Indonesia LM, *supra* note 14, at art. 47(1).
73 Singapore TMA, *supra* note 3, at 39(1). *See also id.* § 42(6).

(a) the transaction ineffective as against a person acquiring a conflicting interest in or under the registered trademark in ignorance of the transaction;[74]

(b) a person (who becomes the proprietor of a registered trademark by virtue of any registrable transaction) not being entitled to damages, an account of profits or statutory damages in respect of any infringement of the registered trademark occurring after the date of the transaction and before the date of the application for the registration of the prescribed particulars of the transaction.[75]

2. Vietnam

22.60 Under Vietnamese law, an assignment of an industrial property object such as trademarks shall be valid upon its registration with the state management agency in charge of industrial property rights.[76]

22.61 In the case of a license of an industrial property object, the legal effectiveness of the license vis-à-vis a third party is dependent upon registration of the license with the state management agency in charge of industrial property rights.

3. Thailand

22.62 Any assignment or transfer by succession of a registered trademark shall be registered with the Registrar.[77] Similarly, a trademark licensing contract must also be registered according to Thai law. However, as the Trade Mark Act[78] does not define the term 'trademark license', this has given rise to queries as to the types of agreements that may be considered to be trademark licenses and, thus, have to be registered with the Registrar at the Department of Intellectual Property.

22.63 Very often, questions are raised in regards to whether distributorship agreements that involve the use of a trademark constitute a trademark license and are, thus, registrable. In *Bangchak Petroleum v. Sanpatong SR Petroleum*,[79] a decision by the Thai Supreme Court in 2010, it was held that an agreement

---

74 *See id.* at § 39(3).
75 *See id.* at § 39(4).
76 *See* Vietnam Law on Intellectual Property, *supra* note 5, at art. 220.
77 Thailand TMA, *supra* note 10, at § 51.
78 *See generally* Thailand TMA, *supra* note 10.
79 Thai Supreme Court Dika. No. 10207/2553, Bangchak Petroleum Public Company Limited v. Sanpatong SR Petroleum Limited Partnership et al. (2010).

wherein one party only acts as a middleman to distribute or sell the other party's products to consumers is not a trademark license, even if there was an element of use of the mark BANGCHAK with the products. The important point to note in this case is that the mark was in fact used by its owner and must be distinguished from the situation where the third party sought to obtain their own supply source and then apply the trademark owner's trademark (with consent obtained in an agreement) onto the supplied products. The agreement in the latter situation would be considered a trademark license and registrable under Thai Laws whereas the agreement in the former situation would be considered a simple distributorship that is not registrable.

4. Philippines

Assignments and transfers must also be recorded at the Intellectual Property Office and they shall have no effect against third parties until they are so recorded.[80] Similarly, a trademark license must be recorded with the Intellectual Property Office; otherwise, it shall have no effect against third parties. **22.64**

5. Cambodia

In Cambodia, any change in the ownership of the registration of a mark shall be in writing and shall be recorded and published by the Registrar.[81] A change in ownership of the registration of a mark that is not recorded with the Registrar shall have no effect against third parties.[82] **22.65**

Similarly, any license contract concerning a registered mark or an application of the registration must be recorded with the Registrar, failing which it is invalid against third parties.[83] **22.66**

6. Myanmar

There is no relevant law available at this time.[84] **22.67**

---

[80] IPC Philippines, *supra* note 13, at § 106.1.
[81] Cambodia TMA, *supra* note 11, at art. 48.
[82] *Id.*
[83] *Id.* at art. 52.
[84] *See supra* Part D(6).

7. Brunei

22.68 An assignment of a registered trademark or any right in it is a registrable transaction within the Brunei Trade Marks Act and must be registered with the Registrar.[85] Failure of registration of an assignment of registered trademark will render the transaction ineffective as against a person acquiring a conflicting interest in or under the registered trademark in ignorance of it.

8. Malaysia

22.69 A registered trademark confers on the registered proprietor of a trademark the exclusive right to use the trademark in relation to the goods or services for which the mark is registered.

22.70 Under section 36 of the Trademark Act, the fact that a person is registered as proprietor of a trademark shall be prima facie evidence of the validity of the original registration of the trademark and of all subsequent assignments and transmissions thereof.[86]

22.71 Where a person becomes entitled by assignment or transmission to a registered trademark, he shall make application to the Registrar to register his title and the Registrar shall on receipt of the application and proof of title to his satisfaction, register that person as the proprietor of the trademark in respect of the goods or services in respect of which the assignment or transmission has effect and cause particulars of the assignment or transmission to be entered in the Register.[87]

9. Laos

22.72 As explained above, there are no specific provisions on assignment or licensing of registered trademarks in Laos intellectual property laws.[88]

10. Indonesia

22.73 The rights to a registered mark may be transferred by (a) inheritance; (b) testament; (c) donation; (d) agreement; or (e) other reasons recognized by

---

[85] Brunei TMA, *supra* note 8, at § 25.
[86] Malaysia TMA, *supra* note 12, at § 36.
[87] *See generally id.* at § 26.
[88] *See supra* Part D(9).

law.[89] The transfer of rights to a registered mark must be recorded in the General Register of Marks and be accompanied by supporting documents.[90] The transfer of rights to a registered mark that is not recorded in the General Register of Marks shall not have legal consequences to any other party.[91]

F. CONCLUSION

22.74 Globalization of economic activity has increased the movement of people, culture, goods and services, and capital and investments, as well as information and technology, across countries and in the process, it has prompted trademark owners to take their brands to markets beyond their own. With Asia's billions marching towards modernity, the economic centre will shift from the West to the East.[92]

22.75 The commercial practice of taking or granting a license/assignment of trademarks is expected to become of increasing economic significance as the emerging economies in Asia develop and grow. In this context, it is heartening to observe that governments in ASEAN are paying attention to the needs of businesses in the commercialization of intellectual property rights such as trademarks and have quickened their legislative processes to put in place the necessary legal infrastructure to encourage and support licensing/assignment activities in this region. Whilst the laws in many Member countries of ASEAN are perhaps still in their early stages of development, the legal framework already in place provides the necessary foundation upon which other future initiatives such as gradual harmonization in the intellectual property laws of Member countries can take place.

---

89 Indonesia LM, *supra* note 14, at § 40(1).
90 *Id.* at §§ 40(1)–40(2).
91 *Id.* at § 40(5).
92 *See discussion in* KISHORE MAHBUBANI, THE NEW ASIAN HEMISPHERE: THE IRRESISTIBLE SHIFT OF GLOBAL POWER TO THE EAST (PublicAffairs, 2008).

23

TRADEMARK TRANSACTIONS IN INDIA: EXPLORING THE GENRE, SCOPE AND CONSEQUENCE

Raman Mittal[*]

A. INTRODUCTION	23.01
B. LICENSING OF REGISTERED TRADEMARKS UNDER THE TRADE MARKS ACT OF 1999	23.04
1. Scope of trademark licensing	23.05
2. Term and territorial scope of license	23.11
3. Conditions for and extent of use of mark by licensee	23.13
4. Procedure for registration, variation, and cancellation of registration	23.18
5. Rights and obligations of licensor	23.23
(a) Liability for acts of licensee	23.25
(b) Right to sue infringers and right to be impleaded	23.26
(c) Right to keep licensing details secret	23.27
(d) Obligation to furnish information to the Registrar	23.28
6. Rights and obligations of licensee	23.29
(a) Use of mark under accompanying legend	23.30
(b) Assignment and sublicensing by licensee	23.31
(c) Right to initiate infringement proceedings	23.32
(d) Right to be impleaded	23.35
(e) Right to be notified in case of new license or cancellation	23.36
(f) Right over goodwill generated	23.37
(g) Proprietorship over the mark	23.38
(h) Right to challenge the mark	23.39
7. Quality control over the use of the licensed trademark	23.40
8. Trafficking under Trade and Merchandise Marks Act of 1958	23.43
9. Character merchandising and trademark licensing	23.46
10. Licensing and hybridization of trademarks	23.48
C. LICENSING OF UNREGISTERED TRADEMARKS	23.49
D. BREACH OF TRADEMARK LICENSE AND CONSEQUENCES	23.51
E. ASSIGNMENT OF TRADEMARKS	23.55
1. Relation between trademark assignment and assignment of goodwill	23.59
2. Restrictions on assignment	23.60
3. Assignment resulting in splitting of trademark on territorial basis	23.62
4. Registration of the assignee of a registered trademark	23.63
5. Assignment of unregistered trademarks	23.69
6. Assignment of certification and associated trademarks and discretion of registrar	23.70
F. ROYALTY FOR TRADEMARK TRANSACTIONS AND TREATMENT UNDER TAXATION LAWS	23.71
G. CONCLUSION	23.73

---

[*] Associate Professor, Faculty of Law, University of Delhi.

A. INTRODUCTION

Trademark transactions have become indispensable for doing business in India in its domestic and international dimensions while being crucial for growing business practices such as franchising, merchandising and technology transfer. A trademark indicates the source or origin of a product or service and hence allows consumers to make generalisations regarding its quality. In the process a trademark serves as a business identifier and becomes a valuable property of the owner. This dual function of trademarks as an indicator of source and as a valuable property goes to define the structure of trademark transactions in India.

23.01

Trademark transactions in India are regulated by both the major sources of law, that is, statutory law and common law. For contractual transactions related to registered trademarks it is the Trade Marks Act, 1999[1] together with the Contract Act, 1872[2] that provide the bulk of governing law, while common law is additionally relevant for unregistered trademarks. Apart from this, the Specific Relief Act, 1963[3] and taxation statutes[4] also inform various aspects of trademark transactions in India.

23.02

This chapter presents an exposition and analysis of legal provisions and judicial precedents regulating trademark transactions in India together with related business practices. While license and assignment are the two forms in which trademark transactions manifest themselves, this chapter delves into various aspects of these contracts, such as form, type, term, extent and registration. Rights and liabilities of the parties that emanate from such contracts have been elaborated. The chapter also discusses the treatment of royalties under taxation laws together with the concepts of trafficking and merchandising of trademarks.

23.03

B. LICENSING OF REGISTERED TRADEMARKS UNDER THE TRADE MARKS ACT OF 1999

Licensing of registered trademarks has two aspects – one where the license contract is registered under the Trade Marks Act and the other where the license contract is not so registered. The Act defines the expression 'permitted

23.04

---

1 The Trade Marks Act, No. 47 of 1999 [hereinafter Trade Marks Act].
2 Indian Contract Act, No. 9 of 1872.
3 The Specific Relief Act, No. 47 of 1963.
4 Income Tax Act, No. 43 of 1961.

use'[5] which includes use of a trademark by both registered and unregistered licensees. Where the license contract is registered under the Trade Marks Act, the licensee is known as the 'registered user'. Registration of a licensee as a registered user is not compulsory under the Act and the licensing of a registered trademark without registering the licensee as registered user is governed by the provisions of the Trade Marks Act as well as common law.[6] The position (as shown in Figure 23.1) can be described as:

- All registered users are permitted users but all permitted users are not registered users.
- All permitted users are licensees but all licensees are not permitted users.
- All registered users are licensees but all licensees are not registered users.

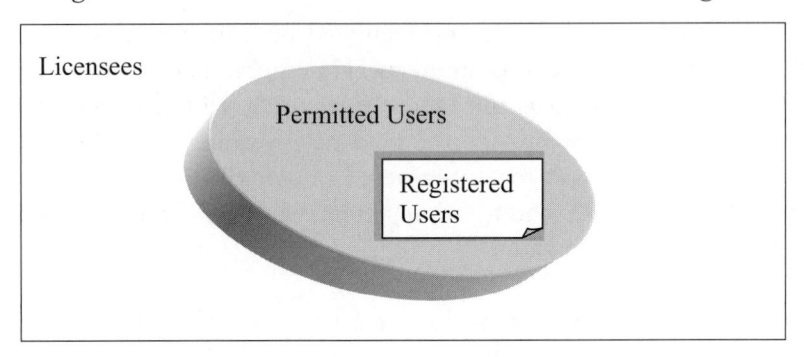

Figure 23.1   Licensees of trademarks

The recordation of a license in this manner is permissive rather than mandatory. But significant advantages stem out of such recordal of the license.

1. Scope of trademark licensing

23.05 A licensee may be registered as registered user for the whole or part of goods/services for which the licensed trademark had been registered.[7] There are certain conditions which the Trade Marks Act has laid down for the purpose of licensing. India is a member of the World Trade Organization (WTO) and these conditions are in accordance with Article 21 of the Agreement on Trade-Related Aspects of Intellectual Property Rights (TRIPS).[8]

---

5   Trade Marks Act, *supra* note 1, § 2(1)(r).
6   *See* Thukral Mechanical Works v. Nitin Machine Tools, (1998) P.T.C. 18 (Del) (stating that licensing of registered trademarks without registration of licensee is quite common and it will not affect the validity of registration of trademark).
7   Trade Marks Act, *supra* note 1, at § 48(1).
8   Agreement on Trade-Related Aspects of Intellectual Property Rights, 15 April 1994, Marrakesh Agreement Establishing the World Trade Organization, Annex 1C, 1869 U.N.T.S. 299, 33 I.L.M. 1197 (1994) [hereinafter TRIPS Agreement].

B. LICENSING OF REGISTERED TRADEMARKS UNDER THE TRADE MARKS ACT OF 1999

23.06 Licensing is the result of a contract and the contract has to be in writing.[9] Though a contract of trademark license has to be in writing, the law prescribes no specific form for making such a contract, which is, therefore, left to be decided by the parties.

23.07 A trademark license may be limited to one person or may be granted to a number of persons.[10] A license could be designed to be exclusive or non-exclusive. An exclusive license divests the licensor of the rights to grant further licenses of the rights licensed while a non-exclusive license is a mere promise not to sue. However, registration as registered user is not permitted in respect of part only of the registered trademark or of the mark from which something has been deleted.

23.08 The primary purpose of such registration is to put third parties on notice of the existence of license. The other purpose is to give rights to the licensee to sue in case of infringement of the trademark by third parties. Therefore, public interest is served if the license is recorded. Though such registration is not compulsory, there are various advantages that stem from it:

- The registered user could take action against the infringer.[11]
- The registration is valid against an assignee of the registered proprietor.
- A sole registered user is protected against the appointment of additional registered users and a non-sole registered user is protected against the subsequent appointment of a sole registered user.
- An applicant for registration of a trademark could base the application on the intended use of the registered user.
- Disputes as to priority of rights between the licensor and licensee or between licensees *inter se* could arise because of a grant of conflicting exclusive rights. Such disputes can be more easily resolved when the contract has been registered.

23.09 Registration of a trademark license is not compulsory and there is no specific bar to being an unregistered licensee of the registered proprietor of a trademark.[12] In *Cycle Corporation of India Ltd. v. T.I. Raleigh Industries Pvt. Ltd.*,[13] it was observed that there was no specific bar to being an unregistered licensee so

---

9 Trade Marks Act, *supra* note 1, at § 49(1)(a).
10 *Id.* at § 49(1)(b)(i).
11 *Id.* at § 52(1).
12 Prestige Housewares India Ltd. and Anr. v. Gupta Light House and Anr., MANU/IC/5032/2007: 2007 (35) PTC 876 (IPAB).
13 Cycle Corporation of India Ltd. v. T.I. Raleigh Industries Pvt. Ltd., 1995 A.I.R. (Cal.) 73 at 77. *See also* In re, American Greetings Corporation's Application [1984] 1 W.L.R. 189.

long as there is a connection in the course of trade between the licensor and licensee's goods.

23.10 The Act, in principle, does not bar the registration of more than one person as registered user for the same trademark in respect of the same goods or services.[14] But the grant of registered user should not be contrary to any other law in force. For example, in the case of drugs, not more than one person can be a registered user for the same trademark in respect of the same goods (drug) because of the provisions of section 17B of the Drugs and Cosmetics Act, 1940.[15] In this case even the registered proprietor of the licensed trademark will himself lose the right to use the trademark for the same goods.[16]

2. Term and territorial scope of license

23.11 There is no fixed term for the grant of license under the Trade Marks Act and the same is dependent on the terms of contract entered into between the licensor and the licensee. So, licensing may be for a particular period of time or it may be forever.[17] Nevertheless, the Registrar of Trade Marks may ask for confirmation, at any time, from the registered proprietor of the trademark as to whether the registered user arrangement still subsists.[18]

23.12 The territorial limits within which the licensed trademark must be used by the licensee have to be determined by the parties to the license contract.[19] The territorial scope is, however, limited to the territorial scope of the registered trademark. So, it cannot be broader than the territorial scope of the trademark but it could be narrower. However, the proprietor of a trademark can expand his trademark rights by virtue of use by a licensee.[20]

3. Conditions for and extent of use of mark by licensee

23.13 The use by a licensee must comply with any conditions or restrictions to which the registration of licensed trademark is subject. Otherwise, the Registrar has the power to cancel the registration of license on an application by any

---

14 Trade Marks Act, *supra* note 1, § 49(1)(b)(i). *See also* Texmo Industries, Coimbatore and others v. Aqua Pump Industries and others, MANU/IC/0072/2004: (2005) (31) P.T.C. 335 (where the Intellectual Property Appellate Board held that the same trademark could be split up, owned and used by different entities in respect of different products).
15 The Drugs and Cosmetics Act, No. 23 of 1940.
16 Antox v. State Drug Controller of Tamil Nadu, MANU/TN/0067/1990: 1991 IPRL 264.
17 Trade Marks Act, *supra* note 1, § 49(1)(b)(iv).
18 *Id.*, § 51.
19 *Id.*, § 49(1)(b)(iii).
20 *See infra* Part B.8–10.

B. LICENSING OF REGISTERED TRADEMARKS UNDER THE TRADE MARKS ACT OF 1999

person.[21] Further, the use by the licensee is subject to the license contract which may include such conditions as manufacturing processes, marketing methodology, branding style, promotional expenditure, advertising domains, after-sale services, policing the mark, and so on.

23.14 In *Baker Hughes Limited and Another v. Hiroo Khushalani and Another*,[22] a clause in the 'Basic Agreement' provided that if the shareholding of the licensor in the licensee fell below 40 per cent, the licensee would lose the right to use the trademark of the licensor in its corporate name.[23] Another clause postulated that the text of the agreement should be incorporated as part of the Articles of Association of the licensee.[24] The motion to include these provisions in the Articles of Association stood defeated and the licensee allowed the shareholding of the licensor to fall below 40 per cent but continued to use the licensor's trademark in its corporate name. There was another contract between the parties, described as the 'Technology Transfer Agreement', which was executed on the same day; one of its clauses stated: 'This agreement as signed and executed, shall constitute the only valid and binding agreement between the parties hereto in relation to the subject matter hereof and all previous understanding or arrangements whether written or oral shall stand expressly cancelled and superseded by this agreement.'[25]

23.15 The scope of Technology Transfer Agreement was different from the 'Basic Agreement'. A plea that the technology transfer contract supersedes the other contract was rejected by the court. It was argued by the defendants that in the presence of the Technology Transfer Agreement they are not bound to follow the 'Basic Agreement'.[26] The court held that the 'Basic Agreement' was adopted and acted upon by the defendant licensee and after having taken the benefit of the 'Basic Agreement' the licensee could not be heard to say that the same was not adopted by it and if the same was not adopted by it, the question that arises is as to how it was using the trade name 'BAKER' as part of its corporate name.[27]

23.16 In addition, a licensee has no right to continue using the licensed trademark beyond the term of license or after the license has been cancelled or revoked. An injunction was granted where the licensee continued to use a registered

---

21 Trade Marks Act, *supra* note 1, § 50(1)(c)(i).
22 Baker Hughes Limited and Another v. Hiroo Khushalani and Another, MANU/DE/0411/1998: I.L.R. 1999 (Del.) 41.
23 *Id.* at para. 4.
24 *Id.* at para. 4 & para. 6.
25 *Id.* at para. 7.
26 *Id.* at para. 69.
27 *Id.* at para. 25.

trademark and claimed proprietorship after the termination of the license by notice. The goods involved in *Synthes A.G. Chur v. Rob Mathys India* were surgical instruments and implants, so public interest was also involved.[28] Upon such prolonged use of the licensee, the licensor obtains a right to sue the licensee for infringement and also for breach of contract.

23.17 Finally, licensing should not result in causing confusion or deception among the public. Otherwise, the Registrar has the power to cancel the registration of license on an application by any person.[29] The use of a registered trademark in relation to goods/services will not be deemed to be likely to cause deception or confusion to the public merely because the form of connection in the course of trade undergoes a change from what previously existed between the goods and the registered proprietor.[30]

4. Procedure for registration, variation, and cancellation of registration

23.18 The procedure for registration as registered user under a trademark license is provided under section 49(1) of Trade Marks Act.[31] The provision typically requires:

- a joint application by the registered proprietor and the proposed licensee;
- a written contract entered into between the parties specifying the conditions under which the registered proprietor proposes to permit the use of the mark; and
- an affidavit by or on behalf of the registered proprietor providing details as to:
    - the relationship subsisting or proposed between the parties;
    - the degree of control to be exercised by the proprietor over permitted use;
    - the fact of sole registered user or multiple registered users;
    - the goods/services in respect of which the use of the trademark is being permitted; and
    - the term of the license.

23.19 The Registrar is the final authority for granting the status of registered users. Once the conditions prescribed under section 49(1) have been complied with, the Registrar is duty bound to register the licensee as registered user. It is not a matter of discretion for the Registrar. The Registrar, then, shall issue a notice

---

28 Synthes A.G. Chur v. Rob Mathys India, 1996 MANU/DE/1103/1996: PTC 401 (Del).
29 *See* Trade Marks Act, *supra* note 1, §50(1)(c)(i).
30 *Id.*, § 56(2).
31 *Id.*, § 49(1).

B. LICENSING OF REGISTERED TRADEMARKS UNDER THE TRADE MARKS ACT OF 1999

in the prescribed manner of the registration of a person as a registered user, to other registered users of the trademark, if any.[32]

On an application by the registered proprietor, the Registrar can vary the registration of the registered user in respect of the goods/services or in respect of any condition subject to which the registration has been granted. Such conditions of use would also include the duration or term of use which can be varied by the Registrar thereby bringing about a renewal of the license. Cancellation of the registration as registered user can be effected by the Registrar on an application by the registered user or the registered proprietor or by any other person or on his own motion in accordance with section 50 of the Trade Marks Act.[33]

23.20

Before cancelling the registration, the registered proprietor shall be given a reasonable opportunity of being heard.[34] But no provision has been made for giving a hearing to registered users. If the right of being heard has been extended to the registered proprietor then the same could and should have been extended to the registered user as well. However, the registered user should get a right of hearing by virtue of principles of natural justice independent of the statutory provisions.

23.21

What would be the consequence if a registered user ceases to be one under section 50? Would the license contract terminate upon cancellation? Would the registered user cease to be a licensee when he ceases to be a registered user? It seems that he would continue to be a common law licensee even when he is no longer a registered user. The reason is that in the first place registration as registered user is not compulsory under the Act; the licensee remains a licensee even without registration. So, how can the cancellation of status 2 have a bearing on status 1 when status 2 was not a necessary requirement for status 1? The only consequence of such cancellation is that the licensee will no longer be a registered user and hence will not be entitled to the privileges that flow from the status of a registered user.

23.22

5. Rights and obligations of licensor

Trademark licensing is based on the legal fiction that use of a trademark by a licensee will be a deemed use by the trademark owner and inure to the owner's

23.23

---

32 *Id.*, § 49(3).
33 *Id.*, § 50.
34 *Id.*, § 50(3).

sole benefit.[35] Therefore, no application can be filed by anyone for revocation of the trademark on the grounds of non-use, if the licensee has used the trademark in that period. In *Cycle Corporation of India v. Raleigh Industries*,[36] it was held that the bona fide use of a registered trademark by an authorised user, not registered as registered user, will be treated as use by the registered proprietor for the purposes of section 47(1)(b). In another case, *J.K. Jain v. Ziff Davies Inc.*,[37] it was held that the licensee having accepted and recognised the proprietary right of the licensor cannot deny subsequently the ownership of the licensor in the impugned trademark. The court held that use of all the trademarks or any other trademark owned by a licensor or its affiliates, at any time during or after the term of the contract will accrue solely to the benefit of the licensor.

23.24 In particular, the rights and obligations of licensors under Indian law can be summarized as follows.

(a) Liability for acts of licensee

23.25 The benefit of licensee's acts, no doubt, inures to the licensor. But, conversely speaking, could the licensor be held liable for the acts of the licensee? A trademark license does not create any agency relationship between the licensor and the licensee. Therefore, the licensor is not directly responsible for the acts of the licensee. But if a licensor has authorised the licensee to carry out an infringement, he could be held liable. It is the implied duty of the licensor to take such measures as he is capable of in order to prevent the licensee from infringing a third party's rights. Moreover, looking from another angle, the licensor should not be allowed to achieve through the licensee what he could not achieve himself. In addition to this, the licensor's liability on account of the use of the mark by the licensee could arise where the licensor fails to exercise proper quality control over the licensee's use of the mark.

(b) Right to sue infringers and right to be impleaded

23.26 The registered proprietor of a trademark who has licensed out his trademark, whether with or without registering the licensee as a registered user, would be able to prevent others from using the mark by an action of infringement or

---

35 *Id.*, § 48(2).
36 Cycle Corporation of India v. Raleigh Industries, 1995 A.I.R. (Cal.) 73 at 77. *See also* Fatima Tile Works v. Sudarsan Trading Company Ltd., 1992 A.I.R. (Mad.) 12.
37 J.K. Jain v. Ziff Davies Inc., MANU/DE/1334/2000: 2000 PTC 244 (Del).

B. LICENSING OF REGISTERED TRADEMARKS UNDER THE TRADE MARKS ACT OF 1999

passing off.[38] He also has a right to be impleaded as a defendant in an action of infringement brought by the registered user.[39]

(c) Right to keep licensing details secret

If the parties should so desire, the Registrar shall take steps to keep the information provided by the applicant secret so that it is not divulged to the business rivals of the licensor or licensee.[40]

23.27

(d) Obligation to furnish information to the Registrar

The registered proprietor of a trademark has an obligation to confirm to the Registrar as to whether the license contract filed and registered continues to be in force. The Registrar may, at any time during the continuance of the registration of the registered user, by notice in writing, require the registered proprietor to confirm to him within one month that the agreement filed under section 49(1)(a) continues to be in force. If the registered proprietor fails to furnish the confirmation, the registered user shall cease to be the registered user on the day immediately after the expiry of the said period and the Registrar shall notify the same.[41] This seems to be quite unreasonable a provision. If the registered proprietor wants to get rid of the registered user, he may not respond to the notice of the Registrar. This could amount to punishing the licensee when the fault is that of the licensor. What would be the consequence if a registered user ceases to be one under section 51? He would not cease to be a licensee, though he will not have the advantages that come with the status of a registered user. It is submitted that if this provision is required to be kept in the statute at all, it should be amended to obligate both the registered proprietor and the registered user simultaneously to furnish information to the Registrar. Then it should suffice even if one of them responds to the notice of the Registrar. The law is concerned with the supply of information – from whichever source it may emanate. This amendment would obviate the possibility of harassment of a registered user and also serve the purpose better.

23.28

6. Rights and obligations of licensee

The rights of a licensee are contractual in nature to the extent that they emanate only from the contract formed between him and the licensor. But once the contract is entered into the scope of licensee's rights is to be

23.29

---

38 JMA Industries v. Union of India, 1980 A.I.R. (Del.) 200.
39 Trade Marks Act, *supra* note 1, § 52.
40 *Id.*, § 49(4).
41 *Id.*, § 51.

determined by the terms of the contract as well as the Trade Marks Act. In particular, the rights and obligations of licensees can be summarized as follows.

(a) Use of mark under accompanying legend

23.30 Under Indian law use of an accompanying legend along with the mark indicating that the mark is reproduced under a license is not required. But the licensor may impose such condition on the licensee by inserting a term to that effect in the license agreement. The inclusion of such a license legend may reduce the chances of the licensor being held liable for product liability claims.

(b) Assignment and sublicensing by licensee

23.31 The licensee cannot further assign or transmit the use of the trademark that has been licensed to him because the right to use granted by registration is not an assignable or transmissible right. Where the registered user is an individual and is also a member of a partnership firm, in that case the partnership firm can continue the use of the licensed trademark so long as the registered user continues to be a member. If the registered user is a partnership firm and after the registration of license it is reconstituted, then the reconstituted partnership firm may continue to use the licensed trademark so long as the reconstituted firm has a partner who was a partner of the original firm at the time of the registration of the license contract.[42] The Trade Marks Act is silent on the aspect of sublicensing. Therefore, if it is not prohibited by the statute, it can be permitted by the licensor.

(c) Right to initiate infringement proceedings

23.32 Subject to a contract to the contrary, the registered user obtains a right to initiate infringement proceedings against a third party in the same manner as the registered proprietor. He is, however, in all such cases required to implead the registered proprietor as defendant.[43] This is so because then the proprietor of the trademark will have a right to project his opinion in the matter of infringement. So, the right of the registered proprietor and registered user are concurrent in this matter. However, if a registered proprietor himself is not entitled to take action, a licensee is certainly not entitled to take action, for such action is always on behalf of and for the proprietor and the right to such action emanates from the proprietor.[44] It is to be noted here that the Trade

---

42 Trade Marks Act, *supra* note 1, § 54.
43 *Id.*, § 52.
44 Babul Products Private Ltd. v. Zen Products, MANU/GJ/0346/2005: 2005 (31) PTC 135.

B. LICENSING OF REGISTERED TRADEMARKS UNDER THE TRADE MARKS ACT OF 1999

Marks Act makes no distinction between the exclusive and non-exclusive licensee vis-à-vis the right to sue.

However, a licensee who is not a registered user has no right to institute infringement proceedings against a third party.[45] Here, the licensee has to assert his rights only through the licensed proprietor of trademark. In *Himalaya Drug Co. v. Arya Aushadhi Pharmaceutical Works*,[46] the appellants filed an infringement proceedings against the respondent for using a mark, 'peptilin', for drugs to treat peptic ulcers. The appellant was using the marks 'saptlin' and 'septiline' for drugs for treating tonsillitis under an unregistered license. The court held that the appellant had no right to sue.

23.33

In *Babul Products Private Ltd. v. Zen Products*,[47] license contract authorised the licensee (who was a permitted user and not a registered user) to discover and prosecute infringement or passing off in relation to the licensed trademarks. The court held that such an agreement cannot confer a right on the plaintiff to take action. The court reasoned that even if such agreement is treated as conferring a power of attorney to the plaintiff to take action, such action can only be initiated in the name and on behalf of the proprietor and not in the name of the licensee. The court did not agree with the argument of the plaintiff, that since the application for registered user was pending and because the registration would relate back to the date of the application, the plaintiff should be entitled to initiate infringement action to avoid advantage being taken by unscrupulous persons.

23.34

(d) Right to be impleaded

A registered user has a right to be impleaded in all proceedings relating to the rectification of the register and appeal against the decision of the Registrar affecting a registered trademark. A registered user so made a party to the proceedings shall also not be liable for any costs unless he enters an appearance and takes part in the proceedings.[48]

23.35

(e) Right to be notified in case of new license or cancellation

A registered user has a right to be notified by the Registrar in the event of any application for cancellation of the license under section 50.[49] If a new contract has been entered into between the licensor and a third party as a registered

23.36

---

45 Trade Marks Act, *supra* note 1, § 53.
46 Himalaya Drug Co. v. Arya Aushadhi Pharmaceutical Works, 1999 A.I.R.(M.P.) 110.
47 Babul Products Private Ltd. v. Zen Products, *supra* note 44.
48 Trade Marks Act, *supra* note 1, at § 136.
49 *Id.*, § 50(2).

user in respect of the same trademark covering the same goods or services, the earlier registered user has a right to be notified to that effect.[50]

(f) Right over goodwill generated

23.37 Generally, during the use of a trademark by a registered user under a trademark license, a lot of money and effort will be expended to popularise the mark and for promotion of the products/services under that mark, which in turn leads to the generation of goodwill around the licensed trademark. Since the use of the mark by the registered user is attributed to the registered proprietor, the registered user has no right over the goodwill generated by the use of the licensed trademark during the whole term of the license.[51] So, upon the termination of the license contract, all goodwill generated by the licensee around the licensed trademark belongs to the registered proprietor. In *Velcro Industries v. Velcro India Ltd.*,[52] it was contended by the defendant licensee that it was entitled to continue the use of the trademark 'Velcro' as a part of their corporate name because it had independently developed a reputation in India. Moreover, the license contract between the parties did not provide that on termination of the license, the licensee would cease to use the licensed mark as a part of their trade name. The court held that even if the license between the parties did not provide that on termination of the license, the licensee would cease to use 'Velcro' as a part of its trade name, that would make no difference, since 'Velcro' was a registered trademark of the licensor and to allow the licensee to use it as a part of its corporate name is to permit it to give an impression to the public that it was still connected with or had a license from the licensor.

(g) Proprietorship over the mark

23.38 The use of the licensed trademark by the licensee does not create any proprietary rights in favour of the licensee. Use by a licensee is always use by the owner and the licensee cannot claim any independent proprietorship on the marks. The moment the license expires the ex-licensee is estopped from using the licensed mark. In *Ziff-Davies Inc. v. Dr. J.K. Jain and Others*,[53] it was held: 'The source of authority to use the trademark was only the license in view of the correspondence and the agreement. The moment license ceases the defendants being just a licensee could not claim ownership of the trade

---

50 *Id.*, § 49(3).
51 *Id.*, § 48(2). *See also* Babul Products Private Ltd. v. Zen Products, MANU/GJ/0346/2005: 2005 (31) PTC 135.
52 Velcro Industries v. Velcro India Ltd., 1992 Indlaw Mum 6333: 1993(1) Arb.LR 465.
53 Ziff-Davies Inc. v. Dr. J.K. Jain and Others, MANU/DE/0215/1998: 1998 PTC (18) 739.

B. LICENSING OF REGISTERED TRADEMARKS UNDER THE TRADE MARKS ACT OF 1999

mark.'[54] In *Eaton Corporation v. BCH Electric Limited*[55] the defendant licensee claimed to be a 'concurrent user' of the licensed trademark and thereby staked claim over proprietorship over the mark. The court held that claiming to be a concurrent user of the trademark by virtue of the use during the licensing period is fraudulent and dishonest while the status of 'concurrent user' under section 12 of the Trade Marks Act is predicated on honesty.

(h) Right to challenge the mark

23.39 Many trademark licenses contain a clause whereby the licensee is restricted from challenging the licensed mark. However, such a clause could have competition law issues. Since such a clause may fall foul of the Competition Act, an alternate or additional clause could be inserted in the license whereby the licensor is given the right to terminate the license should the mark be challenged by the licensee.[56]

7. Quality control over the use of the licensed trademark

23.40 Quality control by the proprietor of a trademark over the use of the licensed mark is an independent requirement both under statutory and common law as to trademarks. It is also contrary to a proprietor's self-interest to allow the quality of the goods sold under his mark to decline. Therefore, the requirement of quality control by the proprietor of a trademark is a function of legal necessity and commercial expediency. There is no definition of quality control in the Trade Marks Act. However, as per general practice of trade, quality control could be achieved in the following ways:

- by specification of formulae, standards, methods, directions, instructions, and so on, to be followed by the licensee;
- by inspection of manufacturing processes, facilities, products, packagings, services, advertising, and so on, of the licensee;
- by analysing the samples of the licensee's products.

23.41 The Trade Marks Act has two kinds of provisions as to quality control; first, direct provisions found in sections 49(1)(b) and 50(1)(d) which mandate a registered proprietor to exercise quality control over the registered user;

---

54 *Id.* at para 15.
55 MANU/DE/1836/2013: 2013 (55) PTC 417 (Del).
56 *See* Competition Act, 2002; Act No. 12 of 2003. *See also*, RAMAN MITTAL, LICENSING INTELLECTUAL PROPERTY: LAW & MANAGEMENT, 598–600 (2011).

Chapter 23 TRADEMARK TRANSACTIONS IN INDIA

second, the provisions mandating quality control are implicit in other provisions such as section 57 read with section 9.[57] The absence of quality control would turn a license into a naked license and could result in the following consequences:

- Without a provision as to quality control, the license contract cannot be registered.[58] The relationship subsisting or proposed between the licensor and the registered user and the degree of control supposed to be exercised by the licensor has to be furnished to the Registrar at the time of registration of the licensing contract.
- It is not enough to simply write such terms into the contract and leave it at that. It is incumbent upon the proprietor to *enforce* proper quality control as per the contract. If the proprietor fails to do so, the Registrar, either on his own motion or on an application by any person, may cancel the registration of the license.[59] In *PioneerHi-Bred International Inc USA v. Pioneer Seed Co. Ltd.*,[60] the plaintiff successfully sought an injunction against the use of the licensed mark by the defendant licensee because the defendant had not allowed the licensor to test the quality of seeds produced by the licensee.
- The absence of quality control could bring into question the very validity of the trademark. This is because in the absence of quality control the trademark ceases to perform its essential function as an identifier of source of goods. The trademark then could be said to be deceptive, misleading or generic.[61]
- Lack of exercise of quality control can be equated with allowing misuse of one's mark and if the proprietor fails to check such misuse, he risks being deemed to have abandoned the mark and thus may lose his rights to the mark.
- If the proprietor does not exercise the required quality control and allows the quality of products under the licensee's mark to decline, he may be made liable under product liability claims.

23.42 It is submitted that the Trade Marks Act should be amended so as to do away with the direct provisions as to quality control contained in sections 49(1)(b) and 50(1)(d).[62] This change will not adversely affect consumers, for the courts have alternative and better tools to protect the consuming public. Additionally,

---

57 Trade Marks Act, *supra* note 1, §§ 9, 49(1)(b), 50(1)(d), 57.
58 *Id.*, § 49(1)(b).
59 *Id.*, § 50(1)(d).
60 Pioneer Hi-Bred International Inc USA v. Pioneer Seed Co. Ltd, LAWS (DLH) 1988 (5) 36: 1988 (2) ArbLR 340: 1988 (1) Del Law 136.
61 Trade Marks Act, *supra* note 1, § 57(1).
62 *Id.*, §§ 49(1)(b), 50(1)(d).

it will prevent superfluous legal actions initiated by competitors whose ultimate goal is not to safeguard consumers, but to control the course of trade. Trademark proprietors will also enjoy more flexibility and variety in conducting their licensing activities and they will not be burdened by unfounded claims of naked licensing in response to their legitimate claims of infringement. The proposed amendment will make the validity of licensing directly dependent on whether the consuming public have been deceived or not. This will provide a much clearer guideline for trademark proprietors compared to the non-uniform interpretation of quality control by the courts and the Registrar under the present provisions.[63]

8. Trafficking under Trade and Merchandise Marks Act of 1958

Trafficking in trademarks had been explicitly mentioned as something prohibited under the Trade and Merchandise Marks Act, 1958.[64] The policy of the old statute was that instead of removing confusion, trademarks should not themselves become a source of it through trafficking so as to play a fraud on the public. The old law of course permitted licensing of trademarks but at the same time sought to avoid that licensing which could amount to trafficking by obligating the Central Government to examine whether the proprietor had registered the mark without any intention of using it himself or solely for the purpose of licensing out.

23.43

But the present Trade Marks Act of 1999, which repealed the Act of 1958, has done away with any requirements as to the approval of the Central Government or any other authority in matters of licensing.[65] The Act of 1999 has removed any explicit reference to a prohibition against trafficking also.[66] The licensor and licensee are absolutely free to enter into a license contract and if it satisfies the form, even the Registrar has no discretion – he has to register it. What do we infer from this change in law? Do we infer that the Trade Marks Act, 1999 marks a shift in the policy behind trademark licensing? Does it mean that trafficking has now become acceptable? The underlying tenor of the

23.44

---

63 For detailed reasons as to why direct quality control provisions are no longer required, see Raman Mittal, *Analysis of the Mysterious Element of Quality Control in Trade Mark Licensing*, 15 J. INTELL. PROP. RTS. 285 (July 2010).
64 *See* The Trade and Merchandise Marks Act, No. 43 of 1958, § 48 (the old trademark statute in India). *See also* Vishnudas Trading v. Vazir Sultan Tobacco Co. Ltd. (1997) 4 S.C.C. 201 (where the Supreme Court of India disallowed the practice of registering multiple marks without any intention of using them since it would allow the trader to enjoy the mischief of trafficking in trademarks).
65 *See* Trade and Merchandise Marks Act, 1958, at § 48(1) and compare it with the amended provision in the Trade Marks Act, *supra* note 1, at § 48(1). *See also* Rule 85 in the Trade Mark Rules, 1959 and the absence of such a provision in the Trade Mark Rules, 2002.
66 *Id.*

1999 Act is that trademarks may be dealt with as commodities in their own right. The upshot of the analysis is that the owner of a trademark can license the same to the extent to which it could sustain the mark itself.

23.45 Theoretically, why should there be a problem with trafficking? This issue can be approached from four angles. First, many unused trademarks, in which there is no question of any reputation, are granted registration. Second, when goods are marketed featuring the name or pictures of a popular fictional character, they are of interest to the purchasers because of the character. It is not necessary that the purchasers believe that there is a connection in the course of trade. Third, it is virtually impossible to construct a legal framework which would distinguish between straightforward character merchandising (using for example a popular cartoon character having no independent existence as a trademark), the practice of decorating goods such as T-shirts or mugs with a trademark having a reputation in connection with quite different goods, and cases where a trademark simultaneously decorates and distinguishes their source. Fourth, every character such as name, title, and so on is not a trademark. So, there is nothing wrong if the owner of the character wishes to merchandise it by licensing and on the basis of such licensing he could in future stake claims of acquiring a trademark by virtue of user.

9. Character merchandising and trademark licensing

23.46 Character merchandising potentially involves the licenses relating to copyright, trademarks and designs; however, trademark is perhaps the most important form of intellectual property implicated in it and is also the most controversial. Commercially, character merchandising has become a successful practice but there are arguments that it should not be a trademark matter, since the characters are not trademarks in the first place, nor are they used as trademarks; instead they serve merely to enhance the eye-appeal of the goods. True, every instance of character merchandising may not involve trademark licensing; only when a 'trademark' is subjected to merchandising does it involve licensing of trademarks. Another difficulty is that in traditional trademark licensing a trademark is licensed for use by the licensee on the goods or services with which the licensor has some relationship. But in the case of character merchandising, the trademark is usually licensed for goods or services from which the licensor is far removed, thereby the trademark itself becomes a commodity to be traded.

In *D.M. Entertainment Pvt. Ltd. v. Baby Gift House and Ors.*,[67] an Indian celebrity, Daler Mehndi, had assigned all rights in his persona including his trademark to the plaintiff company for the purpose of merchandising. The defendant was, without permission, selling dolls named 'Daler Mehndi Dolls' that were able to sing a few lines from the celebrity's famous song.[68] The court held it to be a violation of the celebrity's right to control the commercial exploitation of his persona and accordingly injuncted the defendant under the theory of passing off.[69] In *Chorion Rights Ltd. v. Ishan Apparel & Others*,[70] the plaintiffs were carrying on merchandising activities in the trademark 'Noddy'. But the plaintiffs were unable to injunct the defendants because when they chose to bring their case under the Trade Marks Act, they could not establish a prior user and a claim of dilution could not be sustained as the defendants had registered and used the same trademark 'Noddy' in respect of apparel prior to the plaintiffs.[71] Therefore, it is important that the owner of a trademark who wishes to indulge in merchandising adequately protects his trademark for the *relevant goods or services* in order to provide an additional layer of protection.

23.47

10. Licensing and hybridization of trademarks

From 1958 the Government of India did not allow foreign trademarks to operate in India. Therefore, industry came up with the idea of hybrid trademarks. Hybrid trademarks such as 'Maruti Suzuki', 'Lehar Pepsi', 'Hero Honda', and so on were treated as single trademarks in India. In the absence of foreign trademarks, foreign firms did operate through these hybrid marks and they flourished in the Indian market for about three decades. With liberalisation gaining ground in the 1990s, the government of India allowed the use of foreign trademarks which resulted in the end of the era of hybrid trademarks in India. It is significant to note that Article 20 of TRIPS does not allow member states to impose hybridization or encumbering of trademarks. But there can be no objection to hybridization which is at the instance of the parties.

23.48

C. LICENSING OF UNREGISTERED TRADEMARKS

Unregistered trademarks are subjected to licensing on the same scale as registered ones. Such licensing is regulated mostly under the Indian Contract

23.49

---

67   D.M. Entertainment Pvt. Ltd. v. Baby Gift House and Ors, MANU/DE/2043/2010.
68   *Id.* at para. 9.
69   *Id.* at paras. 16–18.
70   Chorion Rights Ltd. v. Ishan Apparel & Others, MANU/DE/1071/2010.
71   *Id.* at para. 18.

Act and the common law as to unregistered trademarks. The concepts underlying the licensing of unregistered trademarks are similar to those underlying the law contained in the Trade Marks Act. Thus, many of the issues discussed above in the context of registered trademarks, apply similarly to licensing of unregistered trademarks. Through licensing an unregistered trademark the owner may expand the geographic scope of its protection as the use of the mark by the licensee is deemed to be use by the owner. In *Rob Mathys India Pvt. Ltd. v. Synthes Ag Chur*,[72] it was observed:

> It is well settled that use of an unregistered trademark under a license granted by the proprietor bona fide under its control and supervision is use of the unregistered mark by the proprietor. Under no principle or precedent can it be held that at common law use by the licensee of an unregistered mark is not use by the licensor or that such use will invalidate a passing off action or disentitle the licensor to protection of its trademark.[73]

23.50 Since the use of the mark by the licensee inures to the benefit of the licensor, therefore, for the purposes of obtaining a registration, the owner of a mark may rely on use of the mark solely by a licensee, provided there is adequate quality control. Accordingly, many trademark licenses usually contain a provision requiring the licensee to assist the owner of the mark in obtaining and maintaining trademark registrations. On the issue of writing, in *Riverdale School Society v. Riverdale High School and Ors*,[74] where the franchisee disowned the written contract, the Intellectual Property Appellate Board held an oral arrangement in respect of an unregistered trademark to constitute a license.

D. BREACH OF TRADEMARK LICENSE AND CONSEQUENCES

23.51 A breach of license would naturally result in a breach of contract. But apart from a simple breach of contract, it could also result in infringement of trademark or passing off.[75] Breach of a trademark license could be caused by the licensor or the licensee. Where the licensee is the breaching party, the remedies could be for breach of contract as well as for infringement of trademark/passing off. These remedies are to be found in the Indian Contract Act, the Specific Relief Act and the Trade Marks Act/law of passing off. Thus, all kinds of remedies could be claimed by a licensor as against a licensee. Where the breaching party is the licensor, the licensee's remedies are restricted

---

72 Rob Mathys India Pvt. Ltd. v. Synthes Ag Chur, MANU/DE/0308/1997.
73 *Id.* at para. 13.
74 Riverdale School Society v. Riverdale High School and Ors, MANU/IC/5034/2007: 2008 (36) PTC 131.
75 Fedders North American v. Show Line and Ors. MANU/DE/1938/2006: 2006 (32) PTC 573.

D. BREACH OF TRADEMARK LICENSE AND CONSEQUENCES

to claims of breach of contract, which are to be found in the Indian Contract Act and the Specific Relief Act.

23.52 'Damages' is the only remedy under the Contract Act. The other remedies of specific performance and injunction are afforded by the Specific Relief Act. Infringement of trademark attracts both tortious and criminal remedies. Therefore, depending on various circumstances, a breach of a trademark license could attract contractual, tortious, criminal and equity remedies. So, for a single act law may afford multiple and overlapping remedies. In such a situation, are these independent wrongs worthy of attracting independent remedies or is it the choice of the victim to choose any one of them? Second, is it a matter of choice for the victim or should one remedy take precedence over the other?

23.53 Licensing is a basic right of the licensor under the Trade Marks Act and it gets operationalised when it is carried through the vehicle of a contract. There is no reason to limit the application of only one set of remedies. Where the licensee fails to pay the stipulated royalty, the license contract stands terminated on account of the breach of a material term. This leads to a contractual claim for damages. But where the licensee continues to use the mark without payment of royalty, he infringes the proprietary rights of the licensor and is liable accordingly. The licensor could recover under both the laws and there is no overlap between the rights as they are cumulative.

23.54 In *Pioneer Hi-Bred International v. Pioneer Seed*,[76] the defendants were registered users of the trademark 'pioneer' for seeds. They were alleged to have violated the terms of the license contract. When the plaintiff applied for interim injunction, it was pleaded by the defendant that the right procedure for the plaintiff was to approach the Registrar under section 50 of the Trade Marks Act for cancellation of the license. But the court overruled this objection and an interim injunction restraining the use of the mark was granted. The court stated that the Trade Marks Act does not in any way expressly bar or oust the jurisdiction of the civil court to grant the relief of injunction if a legal right of the plaintiff is being violated. The court said that having eaten the fruits of the contract, the licensee is estopped from contending that the contract itself is void.[77] This is a case drawing a balance between the law of contract and trademark law. The court here interprets the breach of a provision of license contract to be an infringement of trademark rights of the

---

[76] Pioneer Hi-Bred International v. Pioneer Seed, LAWS (DLH) 1988 (5) 36: 1988 (2) ArbLR 340: 1988 (1) Del Law 136.
[77] *Id.* at para. 3. *See also* Motilal Padampat Sugar Mills v. State of UP (1979) 2 S.C.R. 641; Baker Hughes Limited and Another v. Hiroo Khushalani and Another, MANU/DE/0411/1998: I.L.R. 1999 (Del.) 41.

proprietor. The court granted an injunction even though another remedy under the contract was available.

E. ASSIGNMENT OF TRADEMARKS

23.55 Assignment of trademarks may be discussed in relation to registered trademarks and unregistered trademarks. An assignment of a trademark has to be in writing in respect of both registered and unregistered trademarks.[78] Though a contract of assignment has to be in writing, the law prescribes no specific form for making such a contract. Assignment need not be for the whole of the goods/services covered by the assigned trademark, it can be for a part of such goods/services.[79]

23.56 In *Riverdale School Society v. Riverdale High School and Ors.*[80] the applicant franchisor was the prior user and unregistered proprietor of the trademark 'Riverdale' and had been using the mark in the name of its school since 1979. The franchisor's school admitted students from class Lower KG to class V. In 1994 the franchisor permitted the respondents franchisees to use the mark 'Riverdale' for schools that admitted students from class VI onwards. The royalty was paid till the year 2000 but was discontinued thereafter. A further cause for the dispute between the parties was stated to be an advertisement released in newspapers by the franchisees to the effect that they were going to extend their activities from the Class 'Lower KG to Standard V' under the name 'Riverdale'. The franchisees had also obtained registration of the mark 'Riverdale' with the Trade Mark Registry.[81]

23.57 It was argued by the franchisor that the franchisees could not claim proprietary rights over the mark 'Riverdale' as they were the licensees and the registration had been obtained by withholding the material facts from the Registry. On the other hand, it was contended by the franchisees that the use of the mark 'Riverdale' with the knowledge and consent of the applicants, amounts to assignment. The franchisees denied having signed any document as to franchising and stated that they had started using the mark 'Riverdale' on an oral understanding only. Since the case of the franchisees rested on oral understanding or oral contract, the only question to be decided was whether there could be an oral assignment of a trademark. Relying on sections 39 and

---

78 Trade Marks Act, *supra* note 1, § 2(1)(b).
79 *Id.*, § 38.
80 Riverdale School Society v. Riverdale High School and Ors., MANU/IC/5034/2007.
81 *Id.* at para. 2.

E. ASSIGNMENT OF TRADEMARKS

2(1)(b) of the Trade Marks Act the Intellectual Property Appellate Board held that although it is possible for an unregistered trademark to be assigned, the assignment has to be in writing. Since the franchisees could not produce any written instrument conveying an assignment, the arrangement was held to have been only permissive and hence merely a license.

The simplest kind of assignment is that of the whole of a trademark and all interests in it, but it is not the only possibility. The Trade Marks Act allows for partial assignments as well, which may be limited so as to apply to only some of the goods or services for which the mark is registered. It is also possible to split up the mark and assign it territorially with some restrictions. 23.58

1. Relation between trademark assignment and assignment of goodwill

As per the Trade Marks Act, 1999 the trademark and goodwill of a business need not necessarily be assigned simultaneously.[82] This statutory provision marks a departure from the earlier principle of common law where a trademark could only be transferred along with the goodwill of the business in the goods/services in respect of which the trademark was used because it had been recognised in the common law that trademark and goodwill are inseparable.[83] However, the vast majority of assignments include the transfer of goodwill. There is usually a specific reason if goodwill is omitted: frequently taxation or price. This position is in consonance with Article 21 of the TRIPS Agreement which states that: '… the owner of a registered trademark shall have the right to assign the trademark with or without the transfer of the business to which the trademark belongs'.[84] 23.59

2. Restrictions on assignment

It is not possible to assign a trademark if the assignment would result in the creation of exclusive rights in more than one person to use the same or similar trademark for the same or similar goods/services, or for goods/services of the same description, if it is likely to deceive or cause confusion in the minds of consumers. This provision is intended to prevent the concurrent and simultaneous use by more than one person of the same or similar trademark in relation to the same or similar goods/services in the same territorial area either within India or outside India, if such use is likely to cause confusion or 23.60

---

82 Trade Marks Act, *supra* note 1, §§ 38 & 39.
83 Reuter v. Mulhens, (1953) 70 RPC 235 at 250.
84 TRIPS Agreement, *supra* note 8, Art. 21 (providing the international framework for the regulation of trademark licensing and assignment at the international and multilateral level).

deception in the minds of consumers. If the exclusive rights created by the assignment are such that two persons will not have the same rights for sale of the same or similar goods/services in India or in the same market outside India then an assignment that creates multiple exclusive rights is valid under the Act.[85]

23.61 It is necessary for the assignee to advertise the assignment in accordance with the directions of the Registrar.[86] The objective of imposing this condition of advertisement on the assignor is to give notice of assignment to the public, thereby safeguarding their interests. This is because when a mark which has become distinctive of one origin is assigned for goods/services of a different origin, it could deceive the public or cause confusion. An advertisement indicating the change of origin consequent upon assignment will mitigate such potential deception or confusion. The assignee has to apply to the Registrar within six months of the assignment for directions with respect to advertisement. An extension of up to three months is permissible in this regard. It is then within the discretion of the registrar to prescribe the form, manner and timing of such advertisement. In *Nico Quality Products v. N.C. Arya Snuff and Cigar Co.*[87] it was held that section 42 of Act was a condition precedent to apply for registration of trademarks in cases wherein assignment of trademarks was made without goodwill[88] of business, therefore, assignment will not take effect unless such advertisement was made.

3. Assignment resulting in splitting of trademark on territorial basis

23.62 The assignment of a trademark which results in the creation of multiple exclusive rights in more than one person operating in different parts of India in respect of the same or similar goods/services is prohibited under section 40 only if it is likely to deceive or cause confusion.[89] Where the goods/services covered under the assigned trademark are dissimilar, territorial assignment of the same trademark within India is permissible.[90] As a general rule, splitting of the same trademark on a territorial basis for the same/similar goods/services

---

85 Trade Marks Act, *supra* note 1, § 40.
86 *Id.*, §42.
87 Nico Quality Products v. N.C. Arya Snuff and Cigar Co, MANU/TN/2680/2013.
88 In the case of assigning the trademarks with goodwill of business, the entire business of the transferor goes to the hands of the transferee.
89 Trade Marks Act, *supra* note 1, at § 40.
90 *Id.*

within India is not permissible. But the Registrar may approve such assignment if he is satisfied that the future use of the trademark resultant on assignment would not be contrary to public interest.[91]

4. Registration of the assignee of a registered trademark

According to the Trade Marks Act:[92] **23.63**

> Where a person becomes entitled by assignment or transmission to a registered trademark, he shall apply in the prescribed manner to the Registrar to register his title, and the Registrar shall, on receipt of the application and on proof of title to his satisfaction, register him as the proprietor of the trademark ... Provided that where the validity of an assignment or transmission is in dispute between the parties, the Registrar may refuse to register the assignment or transmission until the rights of the parties have been determined by a competent court.[93]

An application for registration of assignment was treated as abated as the applicant did not respond to the Registrar's objections.[94] The Registrar has a duty to appreciate the evidence furnished by the assignee in support of his title and if in doubt, the Registrar must hear the affected parties before deciding the matter in the interest of natural justice.[95] Where the Registrar had registered a disputed assignment without notice to the affected parties, his order of registration was set aside.[96]

Such registration by the assignee is compulsory in the light of section 45(2) **23.64** which is as follows:

> Except for the purpose of an application before the Registrar under sub-section (1) or an appeal from an order thereon, or an application under section 57 or an appeal from an order thereon, a document or instrument in respect of which no entry has been made in the register in accordance with sub-section (1), shall not be admitted in evidence by the Registrar or the Appellate Board or any court in proof of title to the trademark by assignment or transmission unless the Registrar or the Appellate Board or the court, as the case may be, otherwise directs.[97]

---

91 *Id.* at § 41.
92 *Id.* at § 45.
93 *Id.*
94 Forward Auto Industries v. Brakes International, 1999 PTC 787 (Del).
95 Brakes International v. Tilak Raj Bagga, 1998 A.I.R.(Del.) 146.
96 Kohinoor Paints v. Paramveer Singh, MANU/DE/0713/1995: 1996 PTC 69. *See also* Bawa Jagmohan Singh v. Registrar of Trade Marks, MANU/DE/2053/2001: 2002 (24) PTC 417 (Del).
97 Trade Marks Act, *supra* note 1, § 45(2).

The bar to receiving a document of the nature referred to in section 45(2) does not operate at the interlocutory stage. It would operate only at the final hearing of the suit. This is evident from the fact that the question of admitting a document in evidence does not arise at the interlocutory stage but only at the final hearing.

23.65 In *Sun Pharmaceuticals Industries Limited v. Cipla Limited*,[98] the defendant countered a suit for infringement on the ground that the plaintiff had no right to institute said suit as the plaintiff was not yet the registered owner of the trademark; proceedings in relation to assignment of the impugned trademark were still pending. It was held that as per the language of section 45(1) the assignee acquires title to the registered trademark on assignment and not by registration.

23.66 In *SKOL Breweries Ltd. v. Som Distilleries and Breweries Ltd. and Anr.*,[99] under an action for infringement and passing off it was contended by the defendant that the plaintiff had no *locus-standi* to maintain the suit. It was not the registered proprietor of the trademark because on the date of the suit the assignment had not been recorded. It was held that where the court is satisfied that the assignment is valid and an application for registering it is made or an application will in all probability be made shortly and only the formality of the procedure under section 45 remains to be completed there can be no difficulty whatsoever in entertaining not merely the interlocutory applications but deciding the suit itself. Therefore, a person who has acquired title to a trademark by assignment cannot be non-suited for want of title *per se* on the ground that the assignment is not entered on the register. Section 45, thus, confers discretion upon the Registrar to admit in evidence a document or instrument in respect of which no entry has been made in the register.

23.67 Such an interpretation is necessitated as the rights of a bona fide assignee could be set at naught not merely by a dishonest assignor, but even by an honest assignor who, not surprisingly, may lose all interest in defending the trademark against infringement upon assigning the trademark and receiving the consideration for the same. The field would thereby be left wide open for infringement of the trademark pending the assignee being brought onto the register as the proprietor of the mark assigned to him. In any event the process in an application under section 45 is bound to take some time. If a contrary interpretation is followed, then it would entitle the world at large in the

---

98   Sun Pharmaceuticals Industries Limited v. Cipla Limited, MANU/DE/1527/2008: 2009 (39) PTC 347 (Del).
99   SKOL Breweries Ltd. v. Som Distilleries and Breweries Ltd. and Anr., MANU/MH/1194/2009: 2009 Indlaw Mum 1764.

meantime to infringe the trademark at will. There would be nothing to prevent them from doing so although their act would be in violation of law.[100]

23.68 In *Classic Equipments (P) Ltd. v. Johnson Enterprises*,[101] the respondent filed for recordal of the assignment on the basis of the assignment deed. However, after such application, but before the recordal, the petitioner sent a notice to the Registrar informing the Registrar about the revocation of the assignment and alleging that the consideration in respect of the contract of assignment had failed, thereby requesting the Registrar not to record the assignment. Nevertheless, the Registrar proceeded to put the deed of assignment on record. It was held that under section 45 it is not for the Registrar to adjudicate upon a dispute between the assignor and the assignee. The Registrar is to register the title on receipt of the application and on proof of the title. If the assignment does not violate any principles of Trade Marks Act and documents have not been executed by misrepresentation or fraud, the Registrar has to register the same. The court held:[102]

> Once an Assignment Deed has been executed, the assignor ceases to have any right, title or interest in the property assigned. It is not open to the assignor to cancel the assignment by means of a communication. The Deed of assignment can only be cancelled under the provisions of Specific Relief Act ... It is not open for the Registrar to go behind the terms of the assignment and he is only required to satisfy himself about the construction of the assignment deed and whether there is in fact an assignment.

Further, the court held that in order to rely on the proviso of section 45(1), it is incumbent on the petitioner to show that *prima facie* a dispute exists between the assignor and the assignee and secondly, the assignor must place on record sufficient material to show that the assignor has taken steps to get the disputes resolved through a court or is likely to take such steps within a reasonable time.

5. Assignment of unregistered trademarks

23.69 An unregistered trademark can be assigned with or without the goodwill of the firm.[103] But if an unregistered trademark is assigned without goodwill, the assignee will get no rights to enforce it without either building his goodwill

---

100 SKOL Breweries 2009 Indlaw Mum at para. 26, *See also* M/s. Modi Threads Ltd. v. M/s. Som Soot Gola Factory and Anr., 1992A.I.R. (Del.) 4; Sun Pharmaceuticals Industries Ltd. v. Cipla, MANU/DE/1527/2008: 2009 (39) PTC 347.
101 Classic Equipments (P) Ltd. v. Johnson Enterprises, MANU/DE/4819/2009: 2009 (41) PTC 385 (Del).
102 Classic Equipments, at paras. 29 and 30.
103 Trade Marks Act, *supra* note 1, § 39.

around the mark or registering the mark. This is because in the absence of goodwill no action for passing off will lie. The assignment of an unregistered trademark is subject to the same restrictions as those for a registered trademark in order to avoid the creation of multiple exclusive rights.[104]

6. Assignment of certification and associated trademarks and discretion of registrar

23.70 A 'certification trademark'[105] shall not be assignable otherwise than with the consent of the Registrar, for which application shall be made in writing in the prescribed manner.[106] Here, discretion has been given to the Registrar and this provision is to be seen in contradistinction to other provisions whereby the Registrar has no discretion in allowing or refusing assignment in case of trademarks other than certification trademarks. Further, the restrictions for registration of trademarks in general as mentioned in sections 41 and 42 of the Act do not apply in the case of certification trademarks.[107] Associated trademarks shall be assignable only as a whole and not separately but, subject to the provisions of this Act, they shall, for all other purposes, be deemed to have been registered as separate trademarks.[108]

F. ROYALTY FOR TRADEMARK TRANSACTIONS AND TREATMENT UNDER TAXATION LAWS

23.71 The licensor and the assignor both get compensation/royalty in return for the grant. However, there will be a difference in their treatment under taxation laws. As a general rule, payments made for an assignment of intellectual property must be capitalized by the assignee and may be taxed as capital gains to the assignor. Whereas royalties paid under a license are deductible business expenses of the licensee and comprise ordinary business income for the licensor.[109] However, many complicated questions do arise as to the treatment of such payment under the taxation laws.

---

104 *Id.* at § 40–1.
105 For definition of certification trademark *see id.* at § 2(1)(e).
106 *Id.* at § 43.
107 *Id.* at § 69(c).
108 *Id.* at § 44.
109 *See* J.L. Morison (India) Ltd. v. Deputy Commissioner of Income Tax, MANU/IK/0181/2014; CIT v. Ciba of India Ltd., MANU/SC/0125/1967.

23.72 In *ITO v. Sylvania and Laxaman (P) Ltd.*[110] because of labour problems the respondent's factory was sealed by the government and hence no production could take place for about a decade. In order to keep its brand name alive/popular the respondent licensed its trademark to various parties under strict quality control specifications and earned royalties on it. The royalty income was held not to be a passive income and was allowed to be treated as business income. Further, business expenses were also allowed to be set-off against this income. In *Pepsi Foods Ltd. v. Collector of Central Excise*,[111] the appellant was selling soft drink concentrate to the licensee and had also licensed his trademark to be put on the soft drink bottles by the licensee under two different contracts. A royalty was to be paid based on the retail price of the number of bottles sold. The appellant did not include the royalty received from the licensee in the sale price of the soft drink concentrate. The Supreme Court of India held that the sale of the concentrate was interlinked with the royalty charges inasmuch as the concentrate is sold only to those who agree to pay for the brand name and held that the royalty received from the trademark licensee should form part of the sale price of the concentrate.

G. CONCLUSION

23.73 Transacting in trademarks through licenses and assignment is a basic right of the proprietor of a trademark and it becomes operational when it is carried through the vehicle of a contract. The law in India has implemented a registered user system whereby the recordation of the license is permissive rather than mandatory. However, significant advantages stem out of such recordal. The primary purpose of such registration is to put third parties on notice of the existence of the license. Another important purpose is to give rights to the licensee to sue in case of infringement of the trademark by third parties. Therefore, public interest is served if the license is recorded. The use by a licensee must comply with any conditions or restrictions to which the registration of the licensed trademark is subject. Otherwise, the Registrar has the power to cancel the registration of the license on an application by any person. The licensee cannot further assign or transmit the use of the trademark that has been licensed to him because the right to use granted by registration is not an assignable or transmissible right.

23.74 A breach of a trademark license would result in a breach of contract and it could also result in infringement of the trademark or passing off. Breach of a

---

110 ITO v. Sylvania and Laxaman (P) Ltd,, MANU/ID/5047/2007.
111 Pepsi Foods Ltd. v. Collector of Central Excise, 2004 (28) PTC 186 (SC).

trademark license could be caused by the licensor or the licensee. Where the licensee is the breaching party, the remedies can be for breach of contract as well as for infringement of trademark/passing off. These remedies are to be found in the Indian Contract Act, the Specific Relief Act and the Trade Marks Act/law of passing off. Thus, all kinds of remedies could be claimed by a licensor as against a licensee. Where the breaching party is the licensor, the licensee's remedies are restricted to claims of breach of contract, which are to be found in the Indian Contract Act and the Specific Relief Act. Therefore, depending on various circumstances, a breach of a trademark license could attract contractual, tortious, criminal and equity remedies. So, for a single act, law may afford multiple and overlapping remedies.

23.75 Quality control by the proprietor of a trademark over the use of the licensed mark is an independent requirement both under statutory and common law as to trademarks. Moreover, it is also contrary to a proprietor's self-interest to allow the quality of the goods sold under his mark to decline. Therefore, the requirement of quality control by the proprietor of a trademark is a function of legal necessity and commercial expediency. The Trade Marks Act of 1999 has done away with any requirements as to the approval of the Central Government or any other authority in matters of licensing, while also removing any explicit reference to a prohibition against trafficking. The underlying tenor of the 1999 Act is that trademarks may be dealt with as commodities in their own right, meaning thereby that the owner of a trademark can license the same to the extent to which it could sustain the mark itself. Hence, the dynamics of commercial forces have shaped the legal landscape of trademark licensing and the law continues to develop in response to changes in the way in which trademarks are used to sell goods and services in the market.

INDEX

Abuse Decree (1962) 8.23, 8.25
acquisitions *see* mergers and acquisitions (M&As)
ADR *see* alternative dispute resolution (ADR)
Agreement on Trade-Related Aspects of Intellectual Property Rights (TRIPS) *see* TRIPS (Agreement on Trade-Related Aspects of Intellectual Property Rights)
agreements
  asset purchase 7.39
  coexistence 5.03, 15.03
    and consent agreements 11.11, 11.22, 11.23, 11.24
    definitions 11.11, 17.09
  consent *see* consent agreements, trademarks
  delimitation 11.23
  distribution 11.05
  domain name transactions, agreements on use
    general principles 4.26–4.29
    situations of joint use 4.30
  licensing *see* licensing agreements, trademarks
  prior-rights 11.23
  purchase (Germany) 16.33–16.35
  trademark portfolio splitting transactions 5.39–5.56
    co-existence, non-compete and mutual support provisions 5.03, 5.51
    conflict resolution, governing law and jurisdiction 5.56
    duration and termination 5.55
    implementation of the allocation 5.46–5.50
    maintenance of trademark 5.53–5.54
    scope of agreement 5.52

    trademark delimitation and allocation 5.42–5.45
alternative dispute resolution (ADR) 13.01
  see also trademark dispute resolution mechanisms
  EU Policy 13.03, 13.14, 13.19, 13.21–13.25, 13.64, 13.65
  methods for solving trademark disputes 13.02–13.26
  mediation 13.03–13.05
  UDRP 13.06–13.11
American Law Institute (ALI) Principles
  choice-of-court clauses 12.10, 12.14, 12.16, 12.24
  choice-of-law clauses 12.36
animation characters and commercial value 3.02, 3.17, 3.19
  copyright-expired characters, adopting 3.19, 3.21, 3.22, 3.23
  examples
    Buster Brown 3.22, 3.23
    Mickey Mouse/Steamboat Willie 3.02, 3.10–3.15, 3.17
    Superman 3.26–3.29
    Yellow Kid 3.19, 3.21, 3.22
  reversion of copyright in a trademarked character 3.26–3.29
  trademark and copyright, whether inseparable 3.10–3.15
anti-abuse rules, double tax treaties 8.22–8.26
antitrust law
  German trademark agreements
    coexistence agreements 16.51–16.52
    license agreements 16.40–16.45
  intellectual property and trademarks 6.24, 6.26
  tying arrangements 6.72
  United States 6.11

INDEX

Apple Corps (UK), action against Apple Inc. (US) 10.01, 10.02
Apple trademark 7.46, 10.01
applicable law
   coexistence agreements, Germany 16.53–16.57
   trademark portfolio splitting transactions 5.05–5.08
arbitration of international intellectual property disputes 13.27–13.68
   arbitration clauses
      and choice-of-court clauses 12.07
      covering contractual and non-contractual claims 13.35–13.46
      intellectual property carve-out clauses 13.47–13.60
      scope 13.34–13.60
   clauses covering contractual and non-contractual claims 13.35–13.46
   conditions and features 13.29–13.60
   consent of parties to submit to arbitration 13.34–13.60
   decisions *erga omnes* 13.33
   emergency arbitrators 13.68
   governing law 13.61–13.65
   intellectual property carve-out clauses 13.47–13.60
   New York Convention 13.58
   objective arbitrability of intellectual property disputes 13.30–13.33
   provisional measures 13.66–13.68
arm's length price, related party transactions 8.47–8.53
arm's length principle, related party transactions 8.43–8.46
ASEAN (Association of Southeast Asian Nations)
   assignment of registered trademarks 22.12–22.26
      application for registration 22.21
      formalities 22.22
      with or without goodwill/business 22.14–22.20
      unregistered trademarks 22.23–22.26
      in writing 22.22
   licensing of registered trademarks 22.27–22.56
   registration of transactions
      Brunei 22.68
      Cambodia 22.65–22.66
      Indonesia 22.73
      Laos 22.72
      Malaysia 22.69–22.71
      Myanmar (Burma) 22.67
      Philippines 22.64
      Singapore 22.58–22.59
      Thailand 22.62–22.63
      Vietnam 22.60–22.61
   trademarks as property in 22.05–22.11
Asia, trademark transactions in *see* ASEAN (Association of Southeast Asian Nations); Brunei; Cambodia; China, trademark transactions in; India; Indonesia; Japan, trademark transactions in; Laos; Malaysia; Myanmar (Burma); Philippines; Singapore; Thailand; Vietnam
Assembly of the Paris Union 2.08, 2.31, 2.39
assets
   asset purchase agreements containing trademarks 7.39
   intangible 7.01, 7.02, 8.68
   sale of, and trademark use
      within acquired division (*Chain v. Tropodyne*) 10.21–10.23, 10.32, 10.73
      restricted to field of use and geographical territory (*Seattle Brewing & Malting Co v. Commission*) 10.24–10.32, 10.76
   substance of and capital gains/royalties distinction 8.28
   trademark license as 17.52–17.53
assignment of licenses, United Kingdom 15.77–15.80
assignment of trademarks
   in ASEAN
      application for registration 22.21
      formalities 22.22
      with or without goodwill/business 22.14–22.20
      registered trademarks 22.12–22.26

unregistered trademarks 22.23–22.26
in writing 22.22
in Brazil 19.46–19.62
in China
  concept and formalities 20.26–20.33
  procedures and regulations 20.34–20.36
confirmatory assignments, in United Kingdom 15.37–15.39
and consent agreements 11.03, 11.06
defined 11.03
equitable, in United Kingdom
  requirements 15.35–15.36
  and trusts 15.32–15.34
in France 17.08–17.12
free assignability as international standard 5.10–5.11
in gross 18.10, 18.12, 18.19, 18.20
in India 23.55–23.70
  assignment of certification and associated trademarks at discretion of Registrar 23.70
  and assignment of goodwill 23.59
  assignment of unregistered trademark 23.69
  by licensee 23.31
  registration of assignee of a registered trademark 23.63–23.68
  restrictions on assignment 23.60–23.61
  resulting in splitting of trademark on territorial basis 23.62
in Japan
  general principles 21.53–21.55
  non-assignability of regional collective trademarks 21.61–21.62
  trademarks representing collective goodwill of multiple suppliers 21.58–21.60
  trademarks simultaneously representing the goodwill of diversified suppliers 21.56–21.57
language 15.21
and license-back 18.39–18.41
partial 5.12–5.22
  actual, under Swiss law 5.19, 5.20
  effect 5.14–5.15
  license grant compared 5.31–5.38
  limitations 5.16–5.18

overview 5.12–5.13
restrictions on 5.36
Swiss law, technicalities under 5.19–5.22
in United Kingdom 15.16–15.18
regional collective trademarks, non-assignability (Japan) 21.61–21.62
restrictions on, in India 23.60–23.61
resulting in splitting of trademark on territorial basis, in India 23.62
right to sue prior infringers, in United Kingdom 15.24
Singapore Treaty on the Law of Trademarks (2006) 2.17
strategic, in United States 18.39–18.41
taxation 8.27–8.37
  capital gains, tax treatment 8.33–8.35
  double tax treaties, impact in international context 8.36–8.37
  royalties/capital gains distinction 8.27–8.32
trademark rights in different fields of use (concurrent use) 10.79–10.94
  co-existence separately 10.91–10.93
  doctrine of concurrent use 10.80–10.90
  imperfect co-existence (with license untouched) 10.94
and TRIPS Agreement (Article 21) 2.13
in United Kingdom 15.11–15.39
  assignment of right to sue prior infringers 15.24
  confirmatory assignments 15.37–15.39
  consideration 15.23
  identification of IPRs being assigned 15.22
  language 15.21
  part assignment 15.16–15.18
  registration 15.30–15.31
  requirements for equitable assignment 15.35–15.36
  title, implied covenants as to 15.25–15.29
  trusts and equitable assignments 15.32–15.34
  unregistered trademarks 15.19
  valid assignment requirements 15.20

INDEX

in United States (current rule)
18.06–18.20
origin of rule 18.12–18.15
rationale for rule 18.10–18.11
shifting towards assignment 'in gross'
18.19–18.20
validity 15.20
Association of Southeast Asian Nations *see*
ASEAN (Association of Southeast Asian Nations)
auctions, private 4.07
Australia
Personal Property Securities Register (PPS Register) 9.01, 9.15, 9.18, 9.24
PPSA (Personal Property Securities Act, Cth), 2009
introduction of 9.01
PPSA systems and trademarks 9.14–9.31
pre-PPSA position 9.03–9.07
reforms 9.08–9.13
reforms
options 9.32–9.37
PPSA (Personal Property Securities Act, Cth), 2009 9.08–9.13
Register of Company Charges 9.06, 9.07, 9.36
Registrar of Trade Marks 9.04, 9.05, 9.23, 9.24, 9.27, 9.28
registration of security interests over trademarks in
new PPS Register 9.10, 9.11
PPSA reforms 9.08–9.13
PPSA systems and trademarks 9.14–9.31
pre-PPSA position 9.03–9.07
reform options 9.32–9.37
Securities and Investments Commission 9.04
Trade Marks Act 1995 (Cth), (TMA) 9.03, 9.05, 9.06, 9.19, 9.24, 9.28, 9.29
Trade Marks Office 9.23, 9.25, 9.33, 9.36
Trade Marks Office Manual of Practice and Procedure 9.34, 9.35
Trade Marks Register

advantages of registration 9.01
discretion to record security interests in 9.04
ongoing role of recording claims in 9.23–9.24
PPSA reforms 9.12
PPSA systems and trademarks 9.14, 9.15, 9.17, 9.22–9.31, 9.33
pre-PPSA position 9.04, 9.07
reform options 9.33, 9.34
trademarks and PPSA systems 9.14–9.31
imperfect information and transition costs 9.16–9.22
problems caused when title in property passes to secured party 9.25–9.31
Trade Marks Register, ongoing role of recording claims in 9.23–9.24
authorship works and *Dastar Corp* case
copyright-expired characters, adopting 3.06
works distinguished from trademark goodwill 3.07–3.10
auxiliary tax status, intellectual property companies 8.70–8.75

bankruptcy and trademark licenses, law intersecting in United States
concurrent use (assignment of trademark rights in different fields of use) 10.79–10.94
co-existence separately 10.91–10.93
doctrine of concurrent use 10.80–10.90
imperfect co-existence (with license untouched) 10.94
corporate transactions, trademarks in (case law) 10.18–10.67
Exide Technologies decision (corporate division sale of assets and trademark use) 10.09, 10.33–10.67, 10.71, 10.79, 10.93, 10.94
sale of assets and trademark use restricted to field of use/geographical territory (*Seattle Brewing & Malting Co. v Commission*) 10.24–10.32, 10.76

sale of assets and trademark use within acquired division (*Chain v. Tropodyne*) 10.21–10.23, 10.32, 10.73
ending of uncertainties 10.68–10.94
  concurrent use (assignment of trademark rights in different fields of use) 10.79–10.94
  looking beyond the form/facing the substance 10.68–10.74
  sales, vs. licenses 10.75–10.78
hypothetical case 10.05–10.07
uncertainties 10.02, 10.03
  adding 10.57–10.67
  causing 10.44–10.67
  ending 10.68–10.94
  Exide Technologies decision 10.44–10.67
  Interstate Bakeries decision 10.58, 10.67
  Lakewood decision 10.61–10.67
Belgium, licence box regime 8.76
BEPS (*Base Erosion and Profit Shifting*)
  report and Action Plan (2013), OECD 8.02, 8.05–8.09, 8.84
  Action Plan reports 8.07, 8.08
  member country preferential schemes 8.07
  transparency goals 8.07, 8.09
brands
  asset purchase agreements containing trademarks 7.39
  brand management principles 7.06–7.08
  brand strength score (BSS) 7.07
  distressed vs. going concern (brand-only vs. business enterprise with brand) scenarios 7.23–7.36
    distressed business enterprise (liquidation/brand only) 7.24, 7.25–7.30
    going concern business enterprise 7.31, 7.32–7.36
  dual nature of competition, over branded goods 6.23
  historical transactions involving 7.22–7.39
    asset purchase agreements containing trademarks 7.39
    distressed vs. going concern scenarios 7.23–7.36
    underlying circumstances 7.38

valuation of brands transacted 7.37–7.38
Income Approach to valuing 7.09, 7.10–7.19
  Excess Earnings methodology 7.18–7.19
  Relief from Royalty methodology 7.13–7.17, 7.45
industry, importance of 7.41–7.44
key transactions
  distressed enterprise 7.25–7.30
  going concern business enterprise 7.32–7.36
Market Approach to valuing 7.09, 7.20–7.21
most valuable 7.46
public goods 6.22
Purchase Price Allocation 7.40, 7.41, 7.44
rebranding 5.61
switching 6.60
SWOT analysis of brand positioning 7.06
trademarks and products 6.07
valuation of
  additional methods 7.45
  common approaches 7.09–7.21
  Comparable Transaction method 7.20, 7.21
  Income Approach 7.10–7.19
  Market Approach 7.20–7.21
  strategic vs. financial target 7.37
  transacted brands 7.37–7.38
Brazil
  assignment of application and/or registration 19.46–19.62
  Civil Code 19.08, 19.27, 19.41, 19.42, 19.46, 19.58, 19.59
  Consulate 19.19, 19.21, 19.34
  Federal Constitution 19.08
  franchising and trademarks in 19.22–19.34
  Industrial Property Law 19.08, 19.09, 19.11, 19.12, 19.27, 19.36, 19.38, 19.52, 19.54, 19.57
  legal nature of trademarks 19.06–19.12
  licensing 19.13–19.21
  master licenses 19.14
  non-exclusive licenses 19.14

INDEX

sole licenses 19.14
Theory of Property Rights, Civil Code 19.08
trademark as collateral and security interest 19.35–19.45
Brazilian National Institute of Industrial Property (INPI) 19.01, 19.02, 19.11, 19.15, 19.17, 19.18, 19.20, 19.26, 19.30, 19.32, 19.47, 19.50, 19.55, 19.61
Brunei
  assignment of trademarks 22.15, 22.21, 22.22, 22.25
  governing law on trademarks 22.10
  licensing of registered trademarks 22.48–22.49
  registration of trademark transactions 22.68
  Trade Mark Act 22.68
  trademarks as property in 22.08, 22.10

Cambodia
  assignment of trademarks 22.22
  licensing of registered trademarks 22.46
  registration of trademark transactions 22.65–22.66
  and trademarks as property 22.11
capacity, transfers of domain names transactions 4.20–4.21
capital gains
  royalties/capital gains distinction 8.27–8.32
  tax treatment 8.33–8.35
cash flow streams, brand valuation 7.11, 7.12
characters
  see also copyright
  cartoon 3.02, 3.17, 3.19
    copyright-expired characters, adopting 3.21, 3.22, 3.23
    reversion of copyright in a trademarked character 3.26–3.29
    trademark and copyright, whether inseparable 3.10–3.15
  copyright-expired 3.06, 3.19–3.24
  derivative works 3.39
  exploiting when trademark claimant not copyright owner 3.19–3.29

keeping out of copyright public domain, impact on trademarks 3.16–3.18
legally-privileged copying 3.35
merchandising of and trademark licensing, in India 23.46–23.47
reversion of copyright in a trademarked character 3.25–3.29
trademark symbols as 3.03
visual, overlapping of copyright and trademarks 3.01, 3.39
China
  access to WTO 20.08, 20.67
  Anti-Unfair Competition Law 20.25
  application for registration 20.13–20.15
    examination of 20.16–20.19
  assignment of trademarks
    concept and formalities 20.26–20.33
    procedures and regulations 20.34–20.36
  Classification of Goods and Services 20.15
  Contract Law of PRC 20.48
  distinctiveness of trademark 20.17
  establishment of rights 20.12–20.25
  evolution of trademark law 20.03–20.11
  founding of PRC (1949) 20.05
  General Principles of the Civil Law 20.51
  goodwill, ownership 20.50
  Guaranty Law of the PRC 20.54, 20.55, 20.60, 20.65
  licensing of trademarks 20.37–20.52
    exclusive licenses 20.40
    legal responsibilities following termination of a trademark license contract 20.51–20.52
    maintenance of trademark rights 20.48–20.49
    non-exclusive licenses 20.40
    obligations of owners and licensees 20.42–20.49
    sole licenses 20.40
    supervision of quality of marked goods 20.43–20.47
    types of licenses 20.40–20.41
  National People's Congress, Standing Committee 20.06
  and Paris Convention 20.21, 20.31

pledge of trademarks
    definition and legal basis 20.53–20.59
    effects of pledge contract of rights
        20.65–20.66
    procedural requirements 20.60–20.64
Product Quality Law of PRC 20.44
Property Law of the PRC 20.54, 20.55,
    20.60, 20.65
Qing government 20.04
registered trademarks 20.13–20.19
signs, detrimental to public order, social
    morals or customs 20.18
Trademark Law of PRC
    assignment of trademarks 20.30, 20.34
    establishment of rights 20.12, 20.15,
        20.18, 20.19, 20.20, 20.21, 20.22,
        20.24
    evolution of trademark law 20.06,
        20.07, 20.08, 20.09, 20.10, 20.11
    trademark licensing 20.39, 20.43, 20.45,
        20.52
Trademark Office of State Administration
    for Industry and Commerce 20.33,
    20.39, 20.47, 20.62
    establishment of rights 20.13, 20.15,
        20.16, 20.19
and TRIPS Agreement 20.08, 20.31
unregistered trademarks 20.20–20.25
choice-of-court clauses 12.01, 12.04–12.30
    and arbitration clauses 12.07
    country court chosen 12.05
    exclusivity considerations 12.06
    foreseeability, assuring 12.09
    Hague Convention 12.10, 12.13, 12.16,
        12.19, 12.21, 12.24, 12.28
    how country court chosen 12.05
    legal certainty, assuring 12.09
    legal issues 12.09–12.28
        issues difficult and easy to harmonize
            12.28
        limitation 12.20–12.24
        special treatment of international
            trademark licensing agreements
            12.26–12.27
        validity 12.13–12.19
    practice 12.05–12.08
choice-of-law clauses 12.01, 12.31–12.40

legal issues 12.34–12.40
practice 12.32–12.33
scope 12.39–12.40
validity 12.35–12.38
civil law systems
    see also common law systems
    and common law systems, in TRIPS
        Agreement 1.03–1.07
    ex ante approach in role of government
        1.12
    function of trademarks 1.19
    and geographical indications 1.06
CLIP (European Max-Planck Group on
    Conflict of Laws in Intellectual
    Property)
    Principles for Conflict of Laws in
        Intellectual Property
    choice-of-court clauses 12.10, 12.13,
        12.16, 12.19, 12.21
    choice-of-law clauses 12.37, 12.38,
        12.40
    and validity 12.36
coexistence
    and absence of likelihood of confusion
        11.31
    agreements 5.03, 15.03, 17.09
        and consent agreements 11.11, 11.22,
            11.23, 11.24
    in Germany 16.50, 16.51–16.52,
        16.53–16.57
    and concurrent use 10.94
    imperfect, with license untouched 10.94
    sales and not licences 10.91–10.93
    trademark portfolio splitting transactions
        5.03, 5.51
commercial value, licensing
    characters, exploiting when trademark
        claimant not copyright owner
        adopting copyright-expired characters
            3.19–3.24
        reversion of copyright in a trademarked
            character 3.25–3.29
        overlapping of copyright and trademarks
            3.01, 3.39
        trademark owner no longer a copyright
            owner

593

INDEX

characters, keeping out of copyright public domain 3.16–3.18
Dastar Corp (US) case and trademark licensing 3.05–3.18
   trademark and copyright, whether inseparable 3.11–3.15
   trademark goodwill distinguished from authorship works 3.07–3.10
   trademarks as copyrighted works 3.30–3.38
common law systems
   see also civil law systems
   adaptation of TRIPS Agreement 1.27
   and civil law systems, in TRIPS Agreement 1.03–1.07
   ex post approach in role of government 1.12
   function of trademarks 1.19
   unregistered trademarks protected at 1.09
Common Regulations under the Madrid Agreement and Protocol
   disposal right, restrictions of 2.48, 2.49, 2.50, 2.51, 2.52
   licensing of trademarks 2.44, 2.46
   and WIPO, normative framework 2.05, 2.09
Community Trade Mark Regulation (CTMR)
   see also European Union (EU)
   and consent agreements 11.09
   Draft CTMR 14.11
   and German law 16.03, 16.14, 16.29, 16.47, 16.49
   overview of harmonized rules 14.04, 14.05, 14.06, 14.09, 14.10, 14.12
   relevant Articles 14.01
   trademark portfolio splitting transactions 5.08
Community Trade Marks (CTMs) 5.10, 14.01
   see also European Union (EU)
   CTM Register 14.09
   and French law 17.36
   and German law 16.14, 16.15, 16.18
   overview of harmonized rules 14.03, 14.04, 14.05, 14.06, 14.08, 14.09

Comparable Transaction method, brand valuation 7.20, 7.21
comparative advertising 6.62
competition
   arenas outside a market 6.29
   as basis for institutional and social change 6.33
   concepts, models and trademark law 6.38–6.70
   trade secrets 6.56, 6.57, 6.58
   see also exit, voice and loyalty framework
   dual nature of, over branded goods 6.23
   EU law 11.37, 11.38, 15.92
   forms 6.41
   and GATT Panels 1.67
   images 6.15
   and innovation 6.06
   intellectual property and competition law 6.39, 6.40
   intellectual property and trademarks 6.15–6.37
      analysis of Lemley and McKenna 6.23–6.27, 6.36, 6.37
      antitrust law 6.24, 6.26
      market definition 6.25–6.28
      public goods 6.16, 6.18, 6.19, 6.22
   monopolies 6.05, 6.09, 11.38
   non-price *see* non-price competition
   norms 6.30
   perfect competition 6.32
   and product differentiation 6.42
   and trademark law 6.11, 6.12, 6.13
   TRIPS Agreement and trademark transactions 1.62–1.69
   unfair competition
      complete harmonization 14.48–14.51
      function theory 14.48, 14.52–14.56
      Martin Y Paz/Depuydt case 14.43–14.47, 14.49, 14.52, 14.57
      national 14.43–14.58
      Paris Convention 1.16
      United Kingdom law 15.91–15.92
Competition and Markets Authority (CMA), United Kingdom 15.91
concurrent use (assignment of trademark rights in different fields of use) 10.79–10.94

see also bankruptcy and trademark licenses, law intersecting in United States
co-existence separately 10.91–10.93
doctrine of concurrent use 10.80–10.90
imperfect co-existence (with license untouched) 10.94
confirmatory assignments, United Kingdom 15.37–15.39
conflict of laws rules, Germany 16.54, 16.56
conflict resolution 5.56
consent agreements, trademarks
  and assignment of trademarks 11.03, 11.06
  circumstances in which may arise 11.13–11.19
  confusion, likelihood of 11.31–11.34
  and cross-license agreements 11.07
  definitions 11.11, 11.26
  and Israel Trademarks Ordinance 11.10
  legal foundation 11.02–11.12
  and licensing 11.04–11.05, 11.06
  provisions 11.20, 11.21, 11.22
  public and private considerations 11.35–11.41
  and TRIPS Agreement 11.08
  types 11.20–11.24
  undertakings in, impact on the parties 11.25–11.30
consideration, assignment (United Kingdom) 15.23
consumer sovereignty 6.08
contract law
  arbitration claims 13.35–13.46
  China
    legal responsibilities following termination of a trademark license contract 20.51–20.52
    maintenance of trademark rights 20.48
    pledge contract of rights, effects 20.65–20.66
  contractual rights, vs. ownership 5.31–5.32
  executory contracts 10.43
  France
    assignment 17.08–17.12
    contractual freedom in 17.06–17.31
    general principles of contract law 17.07–17.22
    licensing of trademarks 17.13–17.22
    and national laws 17.03
    specific dispositions 17.23–17.31
  trademark portfolio splitting transactions 5.31–5.32
  and UDRP 13.10
copyright
  authorship works, distinguished from trademark goodwill 3.07–3.10
  in cartoon characters 3.02, 3.17, 3.19
    copyright-expired characters, adopting 3.21, 3.22, 3.23
    reversion of copyright in a trademarked character 3.26–3.29
    trademark and copyright, whether inseparable 3.10–3.15
  characters, exploiting when trademark claimant not copyright owner
    adopting copyright-expired characters 3.19–3.24
    reversion of copyright in a trademarked character 3.25–3.29
  copyright-expired characters, adopting 3.19–3.24
  fair use doctrine 3.35, 6.63
  infringement of 3.32, 3.36
  owner of
    trademark owner becoming 3.30–3.38
    trademark owner no longer a copyright owner 3.07–3.18
  reversion of, in a trademarked character 3.25–3.29
  as right 'in gross' 3.01, 3.32, 3.34
  trademark owner no longer a copyright owner
    characters, keeping out of copyright public domain 3.16–3.18
    trademark and copyright, whether inseparable 3.11–3.15
    trademark goodwill distinguished from authorship works 3.07–3.10
  and trademarks 3.30–3.38, 6.63
  whether inseparable 3.11–3.15
corporate transactions, trademarks in 10.18–10.32

INDEX

Exide Technologies decision (corporate division sale of assets and trademark use) 10.09, 10.33–10.67, 10.71, 10.93, 10.94
    causing uncertainties 10.44–10.56
    details of case 10.34–10.43, 10.59, 10.67, 10.79
    procedures 10.18–10.19
    sale of assets and trademark use
        within acquired division (*Chain v. Tropodyne*) 10.21–10.23, 10.32, 10.73
        restricted to field of use and geographical territory (*Seattle Brewing & Malting Co v. Commission*) 10.24–10.32, 10.76
Court of Cassation, France 17.10, 17.44
Court of Justice of the European Union (CJEU) 14.02, 14.06, 14.16, 14.17, 14.59–14.62
    see also European Union (EU)
    and French law 17.01, 17.15
    and German law 16.16, 16.17
    unfair competition 14.47, 14.48, 14.52, 14.55
covenants not to sue 6.75
cross-license agreements 11.07
CTMR *see* Community Trade Mark Regulation (CTMR)
CTMs *see* Community Trade Marks (CTMs)

damages, infringement of trademarks 3.37, 3.38
deception 3.34
delimitation agreements 11.23
developing countries, failures of market-driven policies in 6.69
dilution notion
    'blurring' 3.23, 3.37
    overlapping of copyright and trademarks 3.01
    trademarks as copyrighted works 3.36, 3.37
    in United States 1.11
Diplomatic Conference, Singapore (2006) 2.24

disposal of registration of marks, restrictions on right of 2.47–2.52
dispute resolution mechanisms *see* trademark dispute resolution mechanisms
distinguishing function of trademarks 1.20, 1.23, 1.50
distressed business enterprise (liquidation/brand only scenario) 7.23, 7.24
    see also brands
    key transactions
        Borders 7.28
        Circuit City 7.29
        Hostess Brands 7.25
        Linens 'n Things 7.30
        Polaroid 7.26
        Sharper Image 7.27
distribution agreements 11.05
distribution networks, selective (EU law)
    Copad/Dior case 14.02, 14.14–14.16, 14.17, 14.21, 14.30, 14.35, 14.37
    exhaustion of rights, impact on 14.19–14.22
    licensee, rights against 14.29–14.36
    more nuanced approach, adopting 14.40–14.42
    open questions 14.23–14.28
    outside traders, rights against 14.37–14.39
    product quality concept, expansion 14.17–14.18
domain name transactions
    economic life of domain name following registration 4.04
    geographical restrictions 4.15
    holders or users of name 4.18–4.30
        agreements on use, case of 4.26–4.30
        eligibility 4.19
        transfer, case of 4.26–4.30
    license of domain name 4.32
    location of use of name 4.14–4.17
    management 4.03
    nature of 4.31–4.32
    resales 4.01
    sale of domain name 4.08, 4.31
    second level domain 4.13
    secondary markets 4.01, 4.33

specification of object for the transaction 4.06–4.13
third level domain 4.10–4.12
top level domain
  blocking of 4.16
  country code (ccTLDs) 4.09, 4.22, 4.23, 13.12
  generic (tTLDs) 13.06
  lease of 4.09
  private auctions 4.07
  sale of 4.08
  and second level domain 4.13
  UDRP (Uniform Domain Name Dispute Resolution Policy) 13.06–13.11
  as model for other ADR systems for trademark-related domain name disputes 13.12–13.26
WordPress platform 4.02
domestic restructuring, related party transactions 8.54–8.56
double tax treaties, impact in international context
  anti-abuse rules 8.22–8.26
  assignment 8.36–8.37
  licensing 8.18–8.26

enforcement of trademarks 1.54–1.61, 1.69
equitable assignments, United Kingdom
  requirements 15.35–15.36
  and trusts 15.32–15.34
EU law *see* European Union (EU)
European Max-Planck Group on Conflict of Laws in Intellectual Property *see* CLIP (European Max-Planck Group on Conflict of Laws in Intellectual Property)
European Union (EU)
  see also specific European countries
  acquis (best practice) 13.22
  competition law 11.37, 11.38, 15.92
  and consent agreements 11.09
  Court of Justice of the European Union (CJEU) *see* Court of Justice of the European Union (CJEU)
  dispute resolution mechanisms 13.03, 13.14, 13.16, 13.19, 13.21–13.25, 13.64, 13.65

geographical indications, protection 1.07
  and German law 16.09, 16.11–16.18
harmonization 17.02
  complete 14.48–14.51
  overview of harmonized rules 14.03–14.13
  see also Office for Harmonization in the Internal Market (OHIM)
national doctrines, no pre-emption of 14.57–14.58
overview of harmonized rules 14.03–14.13
  Community Trade Mark Regulation 14.03–14.09
  reform plans 14.11–14.13
  Trade Mark Directive 14.10
Savings Agreement with 8.20, 8.21
selective distribution networks
  Copad/Dior case 14.02, 14.14–14.16, 14.17, 14.21, 14.30, 14.35, 14.37
  exhaustion of rights, impact on 14.19–14.22
  licensee, rights against 14.29–14.36
  more nuanced approach, adopting 14.40–14.42
  open questions 14.23–14.28
  outside traders, rights against 14.37–14.39
  product quality concept, expansion 14.17–14.18
unfair competition law, national
  complete harmonization 14.48–14.51
  function theory 14.48, 14.52–14.56
  Martin Y Paz/Depuydt case 14.43–14.47, 14.49, 14.52, 14.57, 14.58, 14.59
Excess Earnings methodology, Income Approach (brand valuation) 7.18–7.19
exclusivity considerations
  choice-of-court clauses 12.06
  exclusive jurisdiction 12.20–12.21
  license grants, United Kingdom 15.50–15.51
  scope of exclusive right 6.10
  trademark and copyright, whether inseparable 3.15
  trademark portfolio splitting transactions 5.24, 5.27

597

INDEX

executory contracts 10.43
exhaustion of rights, EU 14.19–14.22
Exide Technologies decision (corporate division sale of assets and trademark use) *see* bankruptcy and trademark licenses, law intersecting in United States; sale of assets and trademark use
exit, voice and loyalty framework (Hirschman) 6.39, 6.43, 6.45, 6.59
  see also competition
  comparative advertising and voice 6.62
  competition, intellectual property and trademarks 6.33, 6.34, 6.35, 6.36
  concept of exit 6.46, 6.47, 6.50
  concept of loyalty 6.36, 6.51, 6.52, 6.53, 6.60, 6.64, 6.73, 6.74
  concept of voice 6.48, 6.49, 6.50, 6.61, 6.62, 6.65
  and covenants not to sue 6.75
  criticisms 6.68
  developed and developing countries 6.69, 6.70
  non-price competition 6.43, 6.53, 6.56, 6.60, 6.65
  shifts in emphasis 6.57, 6.58
  and trade secrets 6.56
  and trademark law/transactions 6.59, 6.75, 6.76
expenses, tax treatment 8.38–8.40

fair use doctrine, copyright 3.35, 6.63
fair value, intangible assets 7.01
fonds de commerce see France, trademark as element of the *fonds de commerce*
France
  Civil Code 17.12, 17.13, 17.18, 17.20, 17.35
  contractual freedom 17.06–17.31
    assignment 17.08–17.12
    general principles of contract law 17.07–17.22
    licensing 17.13–17.22
    specific dispositions 17.23–17.31
  Council of State (*Conseil d'Etat*) 17.52, 17.53
  Court of Cassation 17.10, 17.44
  domain name transactions 4.11
  intuitus personae (personal obligations) 17.18
  Monetary and Financial Code 17.40
  National Industrial Property Institute (INPI) 17.25, 17.28, 17.30, 17.31, 17.35
  tax considerations
    apport partiel d'actifs (tax qualification) 17.54, 17.55
    influence on a merger and acquisition qualification 17.54–17.56
    qualification of a trademark license as an asset 17.52–17.53
    trademark operations for free 17.49–17.51
  trademark as element of the *fonds de commerce* 17.04, 17.32–17.45, 17.57
  trademarks and securities 17.33–17.41
  transfers of trademarks 17.42–17.45
  warranties, licence agreement 17.17
franchising, in Brazil 19.22–19.34
  Brazilian Franchise Law 19.25
  Business Format Franchising 19.24
  Franchise Agreement 19.32, 19.33
  Franchise Disclosure Document (FDD) 19.31, 19.32
function theory, unfair competition 14.48, 14.57–14.58

General Agreement on Tariffs and Trade (GATT) Panels 1.67
Generally Accepted Accounting Principles (GAAP), US 7.40
geographical indications 1.06, 1.07, 1.52
Germany
  Civil Code (BGB) 16.05, 16.06, 16.07, 16.22, 16.34, 16.47
  coexistence agreements
    antitrust law, restrictions imposed by 16.51–16.52
    applicable law 16.53–16.57
    in general 16.50
  Commercial Law Code 16.04
  conflict of laws rules 16.54, 16.56
  existing rules
    and EU law 16.09, 16.11–16.18
    legal framework, overview 16.02–16.10

MarkenG (German Trademark Act), sections 27–31 16.19–16.25
legal framework 16.03
license agreements 16.36–16.49
   antitrust law, restrictions imposed by 16.40–16.45
   in general 16.36–16.39
   infringement of trademarks 16.47–16.48
   and insolvency proceedings 16.46
   registration of license 16.49
MarkenG (German Trademark Act)
   legal framework 16.03
   license agreements 16.36, 16.37, 16.38
   securities, trademarks as 16.61, 16.63
   sections 27–31 16.19–16.25
mergers and acquisitions 16.58–16.60
Patent and Trademark Office 16.49
practical considerations 16.33–16.63
purchase agreements 16.33–16.35
registered trademarks, company symbols and titles of works 16.26–16.32
representations and warranties 16.59
and Rome I Regulation 16.54, 16.57
securities, trademarks as 16.61–16.63
Stock Corporation Act 16.04
territoriality principle and trademark law 16.11
Trademark Register 16.62
and TTBER (Technology Transfer Block Exemption Regulation) 16.41, 16.43, 16.44
going concern business enterprise 7.23, 7.31
see also brands
key transactions
   American Airlines merger with US Airways 7.33
   Jarden Corporation, acquisition of Yankee Candle Company 7.32
   Liberty Global acquisition of Virgin Media 7.34
   Swatch Group acquisition of HW Holdings Inc 7.36
   T-Mobile acquisition of MetroPCS 7.35
goods and services
see also public goods

branded goods, dual nature of competition over 6.23
detachment of mark from particular goods or services 3.33
partial assignment vs. license grant 5.33–5.34
private or public 6.16, 6.17, 6.18, 6.22
products and trademarks 6.07
supervision of quality of marked goods, China 20.43–20.47
goodwill, trademark
   assignment of
     in India 23.59
     in United Kingdom 15.12
     in United States 18.06–18.15
   collective, of multiple suppliers (Japan) 21.58–21.60
   distinguishing from authorship works 3.07–3.10
   in India 23.37, 23.59
   intangible 18.15
   in Japan 21.56–21.60
   overlapping of copyright and trademarks 3.01
   ownership, in China 20.50
   registered trademarks, assignment in ASEAN 22.14–22.20
   rights over, in India 23.37
   trademark portfolio splitting transactions 5.11
   trademarks simultaneously representing the goodwill of diversified suppliers (Japan) 21.56–21.57
   and TRIPS Agreement 1.60, 1.61
   in United Kingdom 15.12
governing law
   arbitration of international intellectual property disputes 13.61–13.65
   in Brunei 22.10
   licensing agreements, Japan 21.38
   trademark portfolio splitting transaction agreements 5.56

ICANN *see* Internet Corporation for Assigned Names and Numbers (ICANN)
illegality, tying arrangements 6.73

impleaded, right to be (in India) 23.26, 23.35
Income Approach, brand valuation 7.09, 7.10–7.19
    Excess Earnings methodology 7.18–7.19
    Relief from Royalty methodology 7.13–7.17, 7.45
indemnities, UK licensing 15.62–15.64
India
    assignment of trademarks 23.55–23.70
        and assignment of goodwill 23.59
        of certification and associated trademarks at discretion of Registrar 23.70
        by licensee 23.31
        registration of assignee of a registered trademark 23.63–23.68
        restrictions on 23.60–23.61
        resulting in splitting of trademark on territorial basis 23.62
        of unregistered trademarks 23.69
    impleaded, right to be 23.26, 23.35
    licensing of trademarks
        assignment and sublicensing by licensee 23.31
        Basic Agreement 23.15
        breach of license and consequences 23.51–23.54
        character merchandising and trademark licensing 23.46–23.47
        conditions for and extent of use of mark by licensee 23.13–23.17
        by licensee 23.31
        licensing and hybridization of trademarks 23.48
        obligation to furnish information to the Registrar 23.28
        procedure for registration, variation and cancellation of registration 23.18–23.22
        proprietorship over the mark 23.38
        quality control over use of licensed mark 23.40–23.42
        right over goodwill generated 23.37
        right to be impleaded 23.35
        right to be notified in case of new license or cancellation 23.36
        right to challenge the mark 23.39
        right to initiate infringement proceedings 23.32–23.34
        right to keep licensing details secret 23.27
        rights and obligations of licensee 23.29–23.39
        rights and obligations of licensor 23.23–23.28
        scope of trademark licensing 23.05–23.10
        Technology Transfer Agreement 23.15
        term and territorial scope of license 23.11–23.12
        Trade Mark Act (1999), under 23.04–23.48
        trafficking under Trade and Merchandise Marks Act 1958 23.43–23.45
        unregistered trademarks 23.49–23.50
        use of mark under accompanying legend 23.30
    Registrar of Trade Marks 23.11, 23.13, 23.17, 23.19, 23.20, 23.27, 23.28, 23.61, 23.62, 23.63, 23.70
    regulation of trademark transactions 23.02
    rights and obligations of licensor 23.23–23.28
        liability for acts of licensee 23.25
        right to sue infringers/right to be impleaded 23.26
    royalties, tax treatment 23.71–23.72
    and TRIPS Agreement 23.05
    WTO membership 23.05
Indonesia
    assignment of trademarks 22.15, 22.22
    General Register of Marks 22.55, 22.56, 22.73
    licensing of registered trademarks 22.55–22.56
    registration of trademark transactions 22.73
industry
    importance of 7.41–7.44
    industrial applicability, patentability criteria 1.05

INDEX

infringement of trademarks
  and copyright 3.32
  Germany 16.47–16.48
  India 23.26, 23.32–23.34
  remedies 3.36, 3.37, 3.38
  right to initiate infringement proceedings 23.32–23.34
  United Kingdom
    assignment of right to sue prior infringers 15.24
    rights of licensees to bring infringement proceedings 15.65–15.70
injunctions, trademark infringement 3.36
innovation and competition law 6.06
INPI (Brazilian National Institute of Industrial Property) 19.01, 19.02, 19.11, 19.15, 19.17, 19.18, 19.20, 19.26, 19.30, 19.32, 19.47, 19.50, 19.55, 19.61
insolvency proceedings
  see also bankruptcy and trademark licenses, law intersecting in United States
  brand valuation 7.24–7.30
  and license agreements, in Germany 16.46
intangible assets 7.01, 7.02, 8.68
intellectual property (IP)
  see also competition; copyright; patents; trademark transactions; trademarks
  carve-out clauses 13.47–13.60
  and competition law 6.39, 6.40, 6.55
  objective arbitrability of intellectual property disputes 13.30–13.33
  and trademarks 6.15–6.37
    analysis of Lemley and McKenna 6.23–6.27, 6.36, 6.37
    antitrust law 6.24, 6.26
    market definition 6.25–6.28
    public goods 6.16, 6.18, 6.19, 6.22
    trademark law 6.01, 6.02
Intellectual Property Office, Myanmar (Burma) 22.47
Intellectual Property Office, United Kingdom 13.04, 15.31, 15.90
intellectual property rights (IPRs), assignment 15.22
intent-to-use (ITU) trademark applications, United States 18.07

International Bar Association Guidelines for Drafting International Arbitration Clauses 13.57
International Centre for Dispute Resolution (ICDR) 13.53
International Law Association (ILA) 12.10, 12.29
International Trademark Association (INTA) 11.11, 11.26
international trademark transactions
  see also trademark transactions
  choice-of-court clauses 12.01, 12.04–12.30
    and arbitration clauses 12.07
    exclusivity considerations 12.06
    how country court chosen 12.05
    legal issues 12.09–12.28
    practice 12.05–12.08
  choice-of-law clauses 12.01, 12.31–12.40
    legal issues 12.34–12.40
    practice 12.32–12.33
    scope 12.39–12.40
    validity 12.35–12.38
  legal issues
    choice-of-court clauses 12.09–12.28
    choice-of-law clauses 12.34–12.40
    issues difficult and easy to harmonize 12.28
    limitation 12.20–12.24
    special treatment of international trademark licensing agreements 12.26–12.27
    validity 12.13–12.19
  limitation
    exclusive jurisdiction 12.20–12.21
    public policy 12.24
    weak party 12.22–12.23
  validity
    capacity 12.18–12.19
    choice-of-court clauses 12.13–12.28
    choice-of-law clauses 12.35–12.38
    formal 12.13–12.14, 12.37
    substantive 12.15–12.17
Internet Corporation for Assigned Names and Numbers (ICANN)

see also alternative dispute resolution (ADR); domain name transactions; trademark dispute resolution
    Application Guidelines 4.07
    location of use of domain name 4.16
    and Top Level Domains 4.07, 4.08
    and UDRP 13.06, 13.10, 13.14
inventive step, patentability criteria 1.05
IP *see* intellectual property (IP)
IPRs *see* intellectual property rights (IPRs), assignment

Japan
    assignment of trademarks
        general principles 21.53–21.55
        non-assignability of regional collective trademarks 21.61–21.62
        trademarks representing collective goodwill of multiple suppliers 21.58–21.60
        trademarks simultaneously representing the goodwill of diversified suppliers 21.56–21.57
    choice-of-court clauses 12.10
    Civil Code 21.09, 21.12, 21.32
    concept of trademark under Japanese law
        changes in legal definition of trademarks 21.07–21.10
        laws to consider when negotiating trademark transactions 21.11
        scope of 'trademarks' in context of trademark transactions 21.03–21.04, 21.07
        Trademark Act 21.05–21.06
    licenses
        Anti-Monopoly Act, application 21.51–21.52
        definitions 21.12
        governing laws of licensing agreements 21.38
        licensing agreements for marks not registered under the Trademark Act 21.29–21.37
        non-exclusive right to use 21.17–21.23
        proprietary right to use 21.24–21.28
        'right to use' trademarks provided under Trademark Act 21.13–21.16

    royalties, Japanese taxes imposed on 21.39–21.47
    termination of licensing agreements 21.48–21.50
    Patent Office (JPO) 21.14, 21.15, 21.18, 21.19, 21.20, 21.24–21.27, 21.44, 21.54, 21.61
    right to use trademarks
        non-exclusive 21.17–21.23
        proprietary 21.24–21.28
        Trademark Act 21.13–21.16, 21.18
    security interests 21.63–21.66
    Trademark Act
        Amendment of 2014 21.37
        concept of trademark 21.05–21.06
        marks not registered under, licensing agreements 21.29–21.37
        'right to use' trademarks 21.13–21.16, 21.18
        and TRIPS Agreement 21.10
Joint Recommendation Concerning Trademark Licenses (2000)
    function of trademarks 1.31
    and Singapore Treaty 2.30–2.43
    as soft law instrument 2.08
    and WIPO, normative framework 2.08
joint registration, domain names transactions 4.25
joint ventures 5.60
jurisdictions
    exclusive, choice-of-court clauses 12.20–12.21
    licensing of trademarks 11.04
    trademark portfolio splitting transaction agreements 5.56

ktMINE database service 7.16, 7.17, 7.39

Laos
    licensing of registered trademarks 22.53–22.54
    registration of trademark transactions 22.72
leases, domain name transactions 4.09
lex contractus principle 12.40
lex loci protectionis principle 5.06, 12.37, 12.39, 12.40
licence box regime, taxation 8.76–8.86

licensee estoppel 6.65
licensing agreements, trademarks
   and consent agreements 11.06
   cross-license agreements 11.07
   defined 8.12
   in Germany 16.36–16.49
      agreements and insolvency proceedings 16.46
      antitrust law, restrictions imposed by 16.40–16.45
      in general 16.36–16.39
      infringements of trademarks 16.47–16.48
      registration 16.49
   international, special treatment 12.26–12.27
   in Japan
      governing laws 21.38
      marks not registered under the Trademark Act 21.29–21.37
      termination of agreements 21.48–21.50
   oral 10.13
   in writing 10.13
licensing of trademarks 5.23–5.30
   agreements *see* licensing agreements, trademarks
   in ASEAN 22.27–22.56
      Brunei 22.48–22.49
      Cambodia 22.46
      Indonesia 22.55–22.56
      Laos 22.53–22.54
      Malaysia 22.50–22.52
      Myanmar (Burma) 22.47
      Philippines 22.45
      Singapore 22.30–22.34
      Thailand 22.38–22.44
      Vietnam 22.35–22.37
   asset, trademark license as 17.52–17.53
   assignment of licenses, United Kingdom 15.77–15.80
   and bankruptcy *see* bankruptcy and trademark licenses, law intersecting in United States
   in Brazil 19.13–19.21
   breach of license and consequences, India 23.51–23.54
   character merchandising and trademark licensing, India 23.46–23.47
   in China 20.37–20.52
      exclusive licenses 20.40
      legal responsibilities following termination of a trademark license contract 20.51–20.52
      maintenance of trademark rights 20.48–20.49
      non-exclusive licenses 20.40
      obligations of owners and licensees 20.42–20.49
      sole licenses 20.40
      supervision of quality of marked goods 20.43–20.47
      types of licenses 20.40–20.41
   commercial value, licensing of *see* commercial value, licensing
   compulsory, under TRIPS Agreement 1.49–1.53
   conditions for and extent of use of mark by licensee
      in India 23.13–23.17
   conditions on transfers and licenses, and enforcement of marks 1.54–1.61, 1.69
   and consent agreements 11.04–11.05, 11.06
   and copyright licensing 3.01
   definitions 21.12
   domain name transactions 4.32
   flexibility of license grants 5.36
   in France 17.13–17.22
   in Germany *see* licensing agreements, trademarks
   governing laws 21.38
   in India
      assignment and sublicensing by licensee 23.31
      Basic Agreement 23.15
      breach of license and consequences 23.51–23.54
      character merchandising and trademark licensing 23.46–23.47
      conditions for and extent of use of mark by licensee 23.13–23.17
      hybridization 23.48

licensing and hybridization of
    trademarks 23.48
obligation to furnish information to the
    Registrar 23.28
procedure for registration, variation and
    cancellation of registration
    23.18–23.22
proprietorship over the mark 23.38
quality control over use of licensed
    mark 23.40–23.42
right over goodwill generated 23.37
right to be impleaded 23.35
right to be notified in case of new
    license or cancellation 23.36
right to challenge the mark 23.39
right to initiate infringement
    proceedings 23.32–23.34
right to keep licensing details secret
    23.27
rights and obligations of licensee
    23.29–23.39
rights and obligations of licensor
    23.23–23.28
scope of trademark licensing
    23.05–23.10
Technology Transfer Agreement 23.15
term and territorial scope of license
    23.11–23.12
under Trade Mark Act (1999)
    23.04–23.48
trafficking under Trade and
    Merchandise Marks Act 1958
    23.43–23.45
unregistered trademarks 23.49–23.50
use of mark under accompanying legend
    23.30
in Japan
    Anti-Monopoly Act, application
        21.51–21.52
    definitions 21.12
    governing laws of licensing agreements
        21.38
    licensing agreements for marks not
        registered under the Trademark
        Act 21.29–21.37
    non-exclusive right to use 21.17–21.23
    proprietary right to use 21.24–21.28

right to use trademarks 21.13–21.28
royalties, Japanese taxes imposed on
    21.39–21.47
termination of licensing agreements
    21.48–21.50
Trademark Act 21.13–21.16,
    21.29–21.37
Joint Recommendation Concerning
    Trademark Licenses 1.31, 2.08,
    2.30–2.43
license grant compared to partial
    assignment
    affected goods and services 5.33–5.34
    flexibility of license grants vs.
        restrictions on partial assignments
        5.36
    license to register new trademarks
        5.37–5.38
    ownership v. contractual rights
        5.31–5.32
    post-transactional arrangement,
        duration 5.35
licensee estoppel 6.49, 6.65, 18.37
and loyalty 6.35
Madrid System 2.44–2.46
'naked licenses' 1.22
obligation to furnish information to the
    Registrar
    in India 23.28
ordinary licenses 10.12–10.17
quality control
    in India 23.40–23.42
    licenses without 1.22
    purpose 10.13
    in United Kingdom 15.54–15.61
recordal of licenses under Article 19.2 of
    TRIPS 1.02, 1.29–1.34, 1.54, 2.41
right to be notified in case of new license
    or cancellation, in India 23.36
right to keep secret, in India 23.27
right to use, in Japan
    non-exclusive 21.17–21.23
    proprietary 21.24–21.28
    Trademark Act 21.13–21.16
rights against licensee 14.29–14.36
rights and obligations of licensee, in India
    23.29–23.39

rights of licensees to bring infringement
    proceedings 15.65–15.70
sales vs. licenses 10.75–10.78
scope, in India 23.05–23.10
Singapore Treaty 2.30–2.43
sublicensing, United Kingdom
    15.52–15.53
Swiss law, technicalities under 5.28–5.30
term and territorial scope of license, in
    India 23.11–23.12
termination of licensing agreement, in
    Japan 21.48–21.50
trademark portfolio splitting transactions
    license grant compared to partial
        assignment 5.31–5.38
    limitations 5.26–5.27
    overview 5.23–5.25
trademark transactions between third
    parties 8.12–8.26
    double tax treaties, impact in
        international context 8.18–8.26
    royalties, tax treatment 8.14–8.17
tying arrangements 6.73
United Kingdom 15.40–15.85
    assignment of licenses 15.77–15.80
    Contracts (Rights of Third Parties) Act
        (COTPA), 1999 15.81–15.82
    formalities 15.44–15.46
    grant and exclusivity 15.50–15.51
    key terms 15.47–15.49
    liabilities and indemnity 15.62–15.64
    nature of a license 15.42–15.43
    quality control 15.54–15.61
    registration 15.83–15.84
    rights of licensees to bring infringement
        proceedings 15.65–15.70
    sublicensing 15.52–15.53
    term and termination 15.72–15.76
    unregistered trademarks 15.85
    warranties 15.71
in United States (current rule)
    18.21–18.37
    origin of rule 18.29–18.31
    rationale for rule 18.27–18.28
unregistered trademarks
    in India 23.49–23.50

in United Kingdom 15.85
use of mark under accompanying legend,
    in India 23.30
limitation, international trademark
    transactions 12.20–12.24
    exclusive jurisdiction 12.20–12.21
    public policy 12.24
    weak party 12.22–12.23
Lisbon Agreement on the Protection of
    Appellations of Origins 1.06
Lisbon Conference (International Patent and
    Trademark Conference), 1958 1.30
Lisbon Revision Conference (1958) 1.30,
    2.10
loyalty *see* exit, voice and loyalty framework
    (Hirschman)
Luxembourg, licence box regime 8.76, 8.77,
    8.81

Madrid Agreement Concerning the
    International Registration of Marks
    (1891)
    ownership, change in 2.25
    trademark portfolio splitting transactions
        5.08
    and WIPO, normative framework 2.05,
        2.09
Madrid Protocol (Protocol Relating to the
    Madrid Agreement Concerning the
    International Registration of Marks),
    1989
    ownership, change in 2.25
    trademark portfolio splitting transactions
        5.08
    and WIPO, normative framework 2.09
Madrid System Concerning the
    International Registration of Marks
    licenses 2.44–2.46
    and Madrid Protocol 2.09
    ownership, change in 2.25–2.29
    rules 2.56
Malaysia
    assignment of trademarks 22.15, 22.18,
        22.22, 22.26
    licensing of registered trademarks
        22.50–22.52

INDEX

registered users 22.51, 22.52
registration of trademark transactions 22.69–22.71
  Trademark Act 22.70
and trademarks as property 22.11
Market Approach, brand valuation 7.09, 7.20–7.21
markets
  developing countries, failures of market-driven policies in 6.69
  market definition 6.25–6.28
  models 6.42
  public goods 6.19, 6.20
  structure 6.31
Max-Planck-Institute, Germany 16.17
mediation 13.03–13.05
mergers and acquisitions (M&As) 5.01
  see also brands
  bankruptcy filings 7.24
  distressed business enterprise (liquidation/brand only scenario) 7.23, 7.24
    key transactions 7.25–7.30
  France 17.54–17.56
  Germany 16.58–16.60
  going concern business enterprise 7.23, 7.31
    key transactions 7.32–7.36
  ownership, change in 2.18
  sale of assets and trademark use within acquired division 10.21–10.23
  trademark portfolio splitting transactions 5.01, 5.40, 5.55
  transfers of trademarks and brand valuation 7.22–7.39
monopolies
  competition 6.05, 6.09, 11.38
  and property 6.09
  trademarks as 6.03, 6.05, 6.09
Myanmar (Burma)
  Intellectual Property Office 22.47
  licensing of registered trademarks 22.47
  registration of trademark transactions 22.67

naked licensing (licensing without quality control) 1.22

National Industrial Property Institute (INPI), France 17.25, 17.28, 17.30, 17.31, 17.35
National People's Congress, Standing Committee (PRC)
  Trademark Law of PRC 20.06, 20.07
Netherlands, the 8.76, 8.77
new trademarks, license to register 5.37–5.38
non-obviousness, TRIPS Agreement 1.05
non-price competition 6.09
  concepts, models and trademark law 6.42, 6.54, 6.55, 6.66
  exit, voice and loyalty framework (Hirschman) 6.43, 6.53, 6.56, 6.60, 6.65
  and intellectual property 6.55, 6.67
  invention/innovation 6.54
  Stigler on 6.32, 6.33
numerus clausus doctrine 17.10

OECD (Organization for Economic Cooperation and Development)
  BEPS report and Action Plan (2013) 8.02, 8.05–8.09, 8.84
  Commentary 8.61
  Model Tax Convention 8.04, 8.18, 8.19, 8.21, 8.29, 8.44, 8.61
  Transfer Pricing Guidelines for Multinational Enterprises and Tax Administrations 8.07, 8.42
Office for Harmonization in the Internal Market (OHIM) 13.03, 14.01, 14.05
  see also European Union (EU)
open questions, selective distribution networks 14.23–14.28
Organization for Economic Cooperation and Development (OECD) *see* OECD (Organization for Economic Cooperation and Development)
ownership of trademarks
  see also assignment of trademarks; transfers of trademarks
  changes in
    'blacklisting' of documents or information 2.16, 2.20
    'capping' of inventory of allowed requirements 2.16, 2.20

dependence of international registration 2.10
documentary evidence 2.16, 2.18, 2.19, 2.22
under Madrid System 2.25–2.29
mergers 2.18
notarization or certification of legal documents 2.23
under Paris Convention 2.10–2.13
under Trademark Law Treaty and Singapore Treaty 2.14–2.24
and TRIPS Agreement 2.13
vs. contractual rights 5.31–5.32
goodwill, China 20.50
intellectual property owner as price-setter 6.41
international tax strategies 8.64–8.68
obligations of Chinese owners 20.42–20.49
  maintenance of trademark rights 20.48–20.49
  supervision of quality of marked goods 20.43–20.47
shared 5.57–5.59
six-month priority period for trademark owners (Paris Convention) 1.15
trademark owner becoming a copyright owner 3.30–3.38
trademark owner no longer a copyright owner
  trademark goodwill distinguished from authorship works 3.07–3.10
  trademarks and copyright 3.11–3.15
and UDRP 13.19

Paris Convention for the Protection of Industrial Property of 1883, as revised and amended
and China 20.21, 20.31
and European Union 14.05
ownership, change in 2.10–2.13
and Paris Union 2.10, 2.11, 2.12
registrability of trademarks 1.25
six-month priority period for trademark owners 1.15
and TRIPS Agreement 1.14–1.16, 1.25, 1.26, 1.40, 1.59, 1.61, 2.06

unfair competition, protection against 1.16
and WIPO 2.06
Paris Union
  Assembly 2.08, 2.31, 2.39
  and Paris Convention 2.10, 2.11, 2.12
partial assignment
  actual, under Swiss law 5.19, 5.20
  effect 5.14–5.15
  license grant compared (portfolio splitting transactions)
    affected goods and services 5.33–5.34
    flexibility of license grants vs. restrictions on partial assignments 5.36
  license to register new trademarks 5.37–5.38
  ownership v. contractual rights 5.31–5.32
  post-transactional arrangement, duration 5.35
  limitations 5.16–5.18
  Swiss law focus, technicalities under 5.19–5.22
  trademark portfolio splitting transactions 5.12–5.22, 5.14–5.15
    limitations 5.16–5.18
    overview 5.12–5.13
    restrictions on partial assignment 5.36
  in United Kingdom 15.16–15.18
passing off tort
  reverse passing off, in United States 3.05
  and TRIPS Agreement 1.09, 1.10, 1.27
  in United Kingdom 15.08, 15.19, 15.85
patents
  and loyalty 6.64, 6.65
  and trademarks 6.63
  and TRIPS Agreement 1.05
People's Republic of China (PRC) see China
perfect competition 6.32
Personal Property Securities Register (PPS Register), Australia 9.01, 9.15, 9.18, 9.24
Philippines
  assignment of trademarks 22.15, 22.19, 22.21, 22.22
  licensing of registered trademarks 22.45

INDEX

registration of trademark transactions 22.64
and trademarks as property 22.11
portfolio splitting transactions, trademarks *see* trademark portfolio splitting transactions
PRC (People's Republic of China) *see* China
pre-right (coexistence) agreements *see* coexistence
price discrimination 6.20
prior-rights agreements 11.23
private goods
  see also public goods
  allocation 6.17
  definitions 6.16
  markets 6.21
Private International Law Association of Japan and Korea
  Joint Proposal (Principles of Private International Law on Intellectual Property Rights)
    choice-of-court clauses 12.10, 12.13, 12.21
    choice-of-law clauses 12.36
product quality concept, expansion 14.17–14.18
property
  see also intellectual property (IP); intellectual property rights (IPRs)
  labelling of 6.10
  legal definition of property rights 6.18
  and monopolies 6.09
  rights 'in gross' 3.34
  title in passing to secured party in Australia 9.25–9.31
  trademarks as 15.07, 22.05–22.11
    competition law 6.03, 6.05, 6.09
public goods
  see also goods and services
  as brands 6.22
  categorisation as 6.16
  markets 6.19, 6.20
  problem of 6.18
  third party effects 6.17
purchase agreements, Germany 16.33–16.35
Purchase Price Allocation (PPA) 7.40, 7.41, 7.44

quality control, licensing
  India 23.40–23.42
  licenses without 1.22
  purpose 10.13
  United Kingdom 15.54–15.61
rebranding 5.61
Register of Company Charges, Australia 9.06, 9.07, 9.36
Registrar of Trade Marks, Australia 9.04, 9.05, 9.23, 9.24, 9.27, 9.28
Registrar of Trade Marks, India 23.11, 23.13, 23.17, 23.19, 23.20, 23.27, 23.28, 23.61, 23.62, 23.63, 23.70
Registrar of Trade Marks, Thailand 22.40
registration of trademarks and licenses
  see also Madrid System Concerning the International Registration of Marks; Protocol Relating to the Madrid Agreement Concerning the International Registration of Marks (1989); unregistered trademarks
  ASEAN countries, application for registration 22.21
  Brazil, assignment of registration 19.46–19.62
  Brunei 22.68
  Cambodia 22.65–22.66
  China 20.13–20.19
    examination of application, in China 20.16–20.19
    new trademarks, license to register 5.37–5.38
  filing of application for 1.25
  France, *Droit d'enregistrement* 17.44
  Germany 16.49
  India 23.18–23.22
  Indonesia 22.73
  joint registration 4.25
  Laos 22.72
  Malaysia 22.69–22.71
  Myanmar (Burma) 22.67
  in the nineteenth century 1.14
  Philippines 22.64
  registrability dependent on use 1.25
  Singapore 22.58–22.59
  Thailand 22.62–22.63

United Kingdom 15.30–15.31, 15.83–15.84
Vietnam 22.60–22.61
related parties, trademark transactions between 8.41–8.56
  arm's length price 8.47–8.53
  arm's length principle 8.43–8.46
  domestic restructuring 8.54–8.56
Relief from Royalty methodology, Income Approach (brand valuation) 7.13–7.17, 7.45
residence of companies, international tax strategies 8.59–8.63
royalties
  failure to pay as breach of license agreement 10.16
  licensing 8.13
  Relief from Royalty methodology 7.13–7.17, 7.45
  royalty base 7.14
  royalty rate 7.15, 7.16, 7.17
  tax treatment
    in India 23.71–23.72
    in Japan 21.39–21.47
    from point of view of beneficiary 8.14–8.15
    from point of view of debtor 8.16–8.17

sale of assets and trademark use
  within acquired division (*Chain v. Tropodyne*) 10.21–10.23, 10.32, 10.73
  Exide Technologies decision (corporate division sale of assets and trademark use) 10.09, 10.33–10.67, 10.71, 10.93, 10.94
  causing uncertainties 10.44–10.56
  details of case 10.34–10.43, 10.59, 10.67, 10.79
  restricted to field of use and geographical territory (*Seattle Brewing & Malting Co v. Commission*) 10.24–10.32, 10.76
second level domain 4.13
securities/security interests
  Australia, registration of security interests over trademarks
    PPSA reforms 9.08–9.13
    PPSA systems and trademarks 9.14–9.31
    pre-PPSA position 9.03–9.07
    reform options 9.32–9.37
  in Brazil (trademark as collateral) 19.35–19.45
  in France 17.33–17.41
  in Germany 16.61–16.63
  in Japan 21.63–21.66
  in United Kingdom 15.86–15.90
  in United States 18.42–18.44
Security and Exchange Commission (SEC) filings, United States 7.15
shared ownership 5.57–5.59
Singapore
  assignment of trademarks 22.13, 22.14, 22.17, 22.21
  licensing of registered trademarks 22.30–22.34
  registration of trademark transactions 22.58–22.59
  Trade Marks Act 22.06
  trademarks as property in 22.08
Singapore Diplomatic Conference (2006), Records 2.24
Singapore Treaty on the Law of Trademarks (STLT), 2006
  licenses 2.30–2.43
  ownership, change in 2.14–2.24
  and Trademark Law Treaty 2.07, 2.14–2.24
  trademark portfolio splitting transactions 5.08, 5.10
  and WIPO, normative framework 2.05, 2.07
Spain, licence box regime 8.76
Standing Committee on the Law of Trademarks, Industrial Designs and Geographical Indications (SCT) 2.01
STLT *see* Singapore Treaty on the Law of Trademarks (STLT), 2006
sublicensing 15.52–15.53, 23.31
Switzerland
  arbitration of international intellectual property disputes 13.39–13.41, 13.43

INDEX

Federal Trademark Protection Act (TPA) 5.08, 5.10, 5.28, 5.58
Free Exchange Agreement (1972) with EU 8.73
legal technicalities
  licensing 5.28–5.30
  partial assignment 5.19–5.22
Swiss Institute of Intellectual Property (IIP) 5.22
taxation issues
  arm's length price 8.48
  arm's length principle 8.45
  company residence 8.59, 8.60, 8.62
  Controlled Foreign Company rules (CFC rules) 8.85
  Corporate Tax Reform III 8.74, 8.85
  domestic restructuring 8.55
  exemptions 8.33
  expenses 8.39
  licence box regime 8.79
  royalties 8.14
  tax status 8.69, 8.70

taxation and trademark transactions
see also trademark transactions
anti-abuse rules, double tax treaties 8.22–8.26
assignment 8.27–8.37
  capital gains, tax treatment 8.33–8.35
  double tax treaties, impact in international context 8.36–8.37
  royalties/capital gains distinction 8.27–8.32
BEPS report and Action Plan (2013) 8.02, 8.05–8.09, 8.84
capital gains
  royalties/capital gains distinction 8.27–8.32
  tax treatment 8.33–8.35
double tax treaties, impact in international context 8.18–8.26
  assignment 8.36–8.37
expenses 8.38–8.40
in France 17.46–17.56
  apport partiel d'actifs (tax qualification) 17.54, 17.55
  qualification of a trademark license as an asset 17.52–17.53
  tax influence on merger and acquisition qualification 17.54–17.56
  trademark operations for free 17.49–17.51
international tax strategies 8.57–8.86
  ownership 8.64–8.68
  residence of companies 8.59–8.63
  tax status 8.69–8.86
licensing 8.12–8.26
  double tax treaties, impact in international context 8.18–8.26
  royalties, tax treatment 8.14–8.17
Model Tax Convention (OECD) 8.04, 8.18, 8.19, 8.21, 8.29, 8.44, 8.61
related parties, trademark transactions between 8.41–8.56
  arm's length price 8.47–8.53
  arm's length principle 8.43–8.46
  domestic restructuring 8.54–8.56
royalties, tax treatment
  assignment 8.27–8.32
  Japan 21.39–21.47
  from point of view of beneficiary 8.14–8.15
  from point of view of debtor 8.16–8.17
tax status 8.69–8.86
  auxiliary status 8.70–8.75
  licence box regime 8.76–8.86
third parties, trademark transactions between 8.10–8.40
  assignment 8.27–8.37
  expenses, tax treatment 8.38–8.40
  licensing 8.12–8.26
TD *see* Trade Marks Directive (TMD)
territoriality principle, German trademark law 16.11
Thailand
  assignment of trademarks 22.15, 22.21
  licensing of registered trademarks 22.38–22.44
  Registrar of Trade Marks 22.40
  registration of trademark transactions 22.62–22.63
  Trade Mark Act 22.38, 22.62

Trade Mark Board 22.41, 22.43
and trademarks as property 22.11
Theory of Property Rights, Brazilian Civil
    Code 19.08
third level domain 4.10–4.12
third parties
    and consent agreements 11.36
    third party effects 6.17
    trademark transactions between 8.10–8.40
        assignment 8.27–8.37
        capital gains 8.27–8.35
        double tax treaties, impact in
            international context 8.18–8.26,
            8.36–8.37
        expenses, tax treatment 8.38–8.40
        licensing 8.12–8.26
        royalties, tax treatment 8.14–8.17,
            8.27–8.32
title
    full title guarantee, United Kingdom
        15.25, 15.26, 15.27
    implied covenants as to (United Kingdom)
        15.25–15.29
    limited title guarantee, United Kingdom
        15.25, 15.26, 15.27
    passing to secured party (Australia)
        9.25–9.31
TLDs *see* Top Level Domains (TLDs)
TMD *see* Trade Marks Directive (TMD)
Top Level Domains (TLDs)
    blocking of 4.16
    country code (ccTLDs) 4.09, 4.22, 4.23,
        13.12
    generic (tTLDs) 13.06
    lease of 4.09
    private auctions 4.07
    sale of 4.08
    and second level domain 4.13
Trade Marks Directive (TMD)
    and consent agreements 11.09
    Draft TMD 14.11, 14.13
    and German law 16.15, 16.20
    and licensing of UK trademarks 15.41
    overview of harmonized rules 14.02, 14.10
    relevant Articles 14.01
    selective distribution networks
        14.16–14.23, 14.25–14.42

trademark portfolio splitting transactions
    5.08
unfair competition 14.47–14.53
Trade Marks Office, Australia 9.23, 9.25,
    9.33, 9.36
Trade Marks Register, Australia
    advantages of registration 9.01
    discretion to record security interests in
        9.04
    ongoing role of recording claims in
        9.23–9.24
    PPSA reforms 9.12
    PPSA systems and trademarks 9.14, 9.15,
        9.17, 9.22–9.31, 9.33
    pre-PPSA position 9.04, 9.07
    reform options 9.33, 9.34
Trade Marks Registry, United Kingdom
    15.01, 15.06, 15.16, 15.32, 15.37, 15.65
trade secrets 6.30
    concepts, models and trademark law 6.56,
        6.57, 6.58
    and trademarks 6.02, 6.03
trademark dispute resolution mechanisms
    13.02–13.26
    ADR methods for solving trademark
        disputes 13.01, 13.02–13.26
    and EU law 13.03, 13.14, 13.16, 13.19
    EU Policy 13.03, 13.14, 13.21–13.25
    mediation 13.03–13.05
    asymmetrical 13.11
    and EU law 13.64, 13.65
    UDRP (Uniform Domain Name Dispute
        Resolution Policy) 13.06–13.11
    as model for other ADR systems
        13.12–13.26
    World Trade Organization dispute
        settlement system 1.01
    WTO Dispute–Settlement Panel 1.37,
        1.39, 1.42
trademark enforcement 1.54–1.61, 1.69
trademark law
    and competition law 6.11, 6.12, 6.13
    and concepts/models 6.38–6.70
    exit, voice and loyalty framework
        (Hirschman) 6.59
    and intellectual property 6.01, 6.02
    and policy 6.08

Trademark Law Treaty (TLT), 1994
  conditions on transfers and licenses, and enforcement of marks 1.61
  ownership, change in 2.14–2.24
  and Singapore Treaty 2.07, 2.14–2.24
  trademark portfolio splitting transactions 5.08, 5.10
  and United States 18.13
Trademark Manual of Examining Procedure (TMEP), US 11.40, 11.41, 18.08
trademark portfolio splitting transactions
  agreements 5.39–5.56
    co-existence, non-compete and mutual support provisions 5.03, 5.51
    conflict resolution, governing law and jurisdiction 5.56
    duration and termination 5.55
    implementation of the allocation 5.46–5.50
    maintenance of trademark 5.53–5.54
    scope 5.52
    trademark delimitation and allocation 5.42–5.45
  allocation
    and delimitation 5.42–5.45
    implementation of 5.46–5.50
  applicable law 5.05–5.08
  assignability
    free, as international standard 5.10–5.11
    partial 5.12–5.22, 5.31–5.35
  building blocks 5.03, 5.09–5.38
  cross-border trademark portfolio splits 5.06, 5.07
  exclusivity considerations 5.24, 5.27
  joint ventures 5.60
  key issues 5.62
  lex loci protectionis principle 5.06
  license 5.23–5.30
    limitations 5.26–5.27
    overview 5.23–5.25
    Swiss law focus, technicalities under 5.28–5.30
  maintenance of trademark 5.53–5.54
  mergers and acquisitions (M&As) 5.01, 5.40, 5.55
  partial assignment 5.12–5.22
    actual, under Swiss law 5.19, 5.20

    effect 5.14–5.15
    license grant compared to 5.31–5.38
    limitations 5.16–5.18
    overview 5.12–5.13
    Swiss law, technicalities under 5.19–5.22
  rebranding 5.61
  shared ownership 5.57–5.59
  and Singapore Treaty 5.08, 5.10
  and Trademark Law Treaty 5.08, 5.10
  and TRIPS Agreement 5.08, 5.10
  typical provisions 5.42–5.56
trademark transactions 6.71–6.76
  see also assignment, trademark transactions; domain name transactions; licensing of trademarks; OECD (Organization for Economic Cooperation and Development)
  and competition 6.63
  copyright and patent compared 6.63
  corporate 10.18–10.32
    Exide Technologies decision (corporate division sale of assets and trademark use) 10.09, 10.33–10.67, 10.71, 10.79, 10.93, 10.94
    sale of assets and trademark use restricted to field of use/geographical territory (*Seattle Brewing & Malting Co. v Commission*) 10.24–10.32, 10.76
    sale of assets and trademark use within acquired division (*Chain v. Tropodyne*) 10.21–10.23, 10.32, 10.73
  covenants not to sue 6.75, 6.76
  disposal, restrictions on right of 2.47–2.52
  domain name transactions *see* domain name transactions
  in EU law *see* European Union (EU)
  in France *see* France
  in Germany *see* Germany
  importance of 2.03
  international *see* international trademark transactions
  normative framework of WIPO 2.04–2.09
    Joint Recommendation Concerning Trademark Licenses 2.08

and Madrid Protocol 2.09
Paris Convention 2.06
and Singapore Treaty 2.05, 2.07
ownership, change in 2.10–2.29
   'blacklisting' of documents or information 2.16, 2.20
   'capping' of inventory of allowed requirements 2.16, 2.20
   dependence of international registration 2.10
   documentary evidence 2.16, 2.18, 2.19, 2.22
   under Madrid System 2.25–2.29
   mergers 2.18
   notarization or certification of legal documents 2.23
   under Paris Convention 2.10–2.13
   under Trademark Law Treaty and Singapore Treaty 2.14–2.24
   and TRIPS Agreement 2.13
portfolio splitting transactions *see* trademark portfolio splitting transactions
related parties, between 8.41–8.56
   arm's length price 8.47–8.53
   arm's length principle 8.43–8.46
   domestic restructuring 8.54–8.56
Singapore Treaty and Joint Recommendations 2.30–2.43
taxation strategies *see* taxation and trademark transactions
third parties, between 8.10–8.40
   assignment of transactions 8.27–8.37
   double tax treaties, impact in international context 8.18–8.26, 8.36–8.37
   expenses, tax treatment 8.38–8.40
   licensing 8.12–8.26
   royalties, tax treatment 8.14–8.17, 8.27–8.32
transfer of trademarks *see* transfer of trademarks
transfers in gross 6.74
and TRIPS Agreement (Article 21) 1.02, 1.43–1.69, 2.13
tying arrangements 6.72, 6.73
in United Kingdom *see* United Kingdom
in United States *see* United States
trademarks
   asset purchase agreements containing 7.39
   in Australia *see* Australia
   and bankruptcy *see* bankruptcy and trademark licenses, law intersecting in United States
   as copyrighted works 3.30–3.38
   definition of signs constituting (TRIPS Agreement) 1.16
   detachment from particular goods or services 3.33
   foreign, controlling use of 1.33
   functions of
      distinguishing function 1.20, 1.23, 1.50
      information transmission 3.33
      origin-indicating 1.52
      and TRIPS Agreement 1.19, 1.20–1.28, 1.52
      trust function 1.23
   in gross
      commercial value, licensing 3.24, 3.30, 3.34
      competition 6.71, 6.74
      rule against, in United States 18.01, 18.03, 18.10
      shifting towards, in United States 18.19–18.20
      United States 18.01, 18.03, 18.10, 18.12, 18.19, 18.20
   impact on of keeping characters out of copyright public domain 3.16–3.18
   infringement *see* infringement of trademarks
   legal nature (Brazil) 19.06–19.12
   maintenance 5.53–5.54
   in major legal systems, and TRIPS Agreement 1.08–1.13
   as monopolies 6.03, 6.05, 6.09
   new *see* new trademarks
   and patents 6.63
   pledge of, in China
      definition and legal basis 20.53–20.59
      effects of pledge contract of rights 20.65–20.66
      procedural requirements 20.60–20.64
   and products 6.07

as property 15.07, 22.05–22.11
  competition law 6.03, 6.05, 6.09
quality control over use of licensed mark
    23.40–23.42
regional collective, non-assignability
    (Japan) 21.61–21.62
right to challenge, in India 23.39
'right to use' in Japan, licensing of
  non-exclusive 21.17–21.23
  proprietary 21.24–21.28
  under Trademark Act 21.13–21.16
as securities, in Germany 16.61–16.63
symbols as characters or artistic works
    3.03
and trade secrets 6.02, 6.03
transactions *see* trademark transactions
transfers *see* transfers of trademarks
use of under accompanying legend, in
    India 23.30
Trademarks Directive *see* Trade Marks
    Directive (TMD)
Transfer Pricing Guidelines for
    Multinational Enterprises and Tax
    Administrations, OECD 8.07, 8.42
transfers of trademarks
  see also assignment of trademarks;
      ownership of trademarks
  brand valuation 7.22–7.39
  domain names, holders or users 4.19–4.25
    capacity 4.20–4.21
    contact information 4.24
    eligibility 4.19
    establishment conditions 4.22–4.23
    joint registration 4.25
  in France 17.42–17.45
  multiple jurisdictions 2.23
  transfers in gross 6.74
  TRIPS Agreement
    conditions on transfers, and
        enforcement of marks 1.54–1.61
    recordal under Article 19.2 1.02,
        1.29–1.34, 1.54, 2.41
Transparency Proposal, Transparency of
    Japanese Law Project 12.10, 12.13,
    12.21
TRIPS (Agreement on Trade-Related
    Aspects of Intellectual property Rights)

adaptation in common law systems
    1.27
battle between common and civil law
    1.03–1.07
and China 20.08, 20.31
and consent agreements 11.08
consultations 1.67
and dispute resolution 13.61
drafting history of Article 21 1.44–1.48
flexibility of 1.69
foreign trademarks, controlling use of 1.33
and goodwill 1.60, 1.61
and India 23.05
and Japan 21.10
and Lisbon Conference (1958) 1.30
origin of trademark provisions in
    1.03–1.16
and Paris Convention 1.14–1.16, 1.25,
    1.26, 1.40, 1.59, 1.61, 2.06
and passing off tort 1.09, 1.10, 1.27
patent section 1.05
signature at Marrakesh (1994) 1.04
trademark portfolio splitting transactions
    5.08, 5.10
trademark provisions in 1.17–1.42
  Article 15 1.02, 1.18–1.19
  Article 20 1.36–1.42
  function of trademarks 1.19, 1.20–1.28
  recordal of transfers and licenses under
      Article 19.2 1.02, 1.29–1.34, 1.54,
      2.41
trademark transactions provisions (Article
    21) 1.02, 1.43–1.69
  assignment of trademarks 2.13
  compulsory licenses of trademarks
      1.49–1.53
  conditions on transfers and licenses, and
      enforcement of marks 1.54–1.61,
      1.69
  drafting history 1.44–1.48
  role for competition law 1.62–1.69
and trademarks in major legal systems
    1.08–1.13
and United States 18.15
use requirement 1.25, 1.27, 1.28
and Vienna Convention on the Law of
    Treaties (VCLT) 1.13, 1.64

trusts
  and equitable assignments, in United Kingdom 15.32–15.34
  trust function of trademarks 1.23
tying arrangements, trademark transactions 6.72, 6.73

UDRP (Uniform Domain Name Dispute Resolution Policy) 13.06–13.11
  see also domain name transactions
  adoption (1999) 13.06
  domain name transactions 4.12
  and ICANN 13.06, 13.10, 13.14
  as model for other ADR systems for trademark-related domain name disputes 13.12–13.26
undertakings, consent agreements 11.25–11.30
unfair competition
  complete harmonization 14.48–14.51
  function theory 14.48, 14.52–14.56
  Martin Y Paz/Depuydt case 14.43–14.47, 14.49, 14.52, 14.57, 14.58, 14.59
  national 14.43–14.58
  Paris Convention 1.16
Uniform Commercial Code (UCC) 18.42
Uniform Domain Name Dispute Resolution Policy *see* UDRP (Uniform Domain Name Dispute Resolution Policy)
Uniform Resource Identifier (URL) 4.02
United Kingdom
  assignment of trademarks 15.11–15.39
    confirmatory assignments 15.37–15.39
    consideration 15.23
    identification of IPRs being assigned 15.22
    language 15.21
    part assignment 15.16–15.18
    registration 15.30–15.31
    requirements for equitable assignment 15.35–15.36
    right to sue prior infringers 15.24
    title, implied covenants as to 15.25–15.29
    trusts and equitable assignments 15.32–15.34
    unregistered trademarks 15.19

  valid assignment requirements 15.20
  Companies House, charges over trademarks registered at 15.90
  Competition and Markets Authority 15.91
  competition law 15.91–15.92
  Intellectual Property Office 13.04, 15.31, 15.90
  law and trademarks 15.05–15.10
  licence box regime 8.76
  licensing of trademarks 15.40–15.85
    assignment of licenses 15.77–15.80
    Contracts (Rights of Third Parties) Act (COTPA), 1999 15.81–15.82
    formalities 15.44–15.46
    grant and exclusivity 15.50–15.51
    key terms 15.47–15.49
    liabilities and indemnity 15.62–15.64
    nature of a license 15.42–15.43
    quality control 15.54–15.61
    registration 15.83–15.84
    rights of licensees to bring infringement proceedings 15.65–15.70
    sublicensing 15.52–15.53
    term and termination 15.72–15.76
    unregistered trademarks 15.85
    warranties 15.71
  passing off tort 15.08, 15.19, 15.85
  reasonable notice, termination of trademark licence arrangement on 15.73
  security interests 15.86–15.90
  Trade Marks Registry 15.01, 15.06, 15.16, 15.32, 15.37, 15.65
United Nations Commission on International Trade Law (UNCITRAL) Arbitration Rules 13.54
United States
  see also American Law Institute (ALI)
  antitrust law 6.11
  assignment, current rule ('with goodwill') 18.06–18.15
    origin of rule 18.12–18.15
    rationale for rule 18.10–18.11
    shifting towards assignment 'in gross' 18.19–18.20

INDEX

assignment and license-back 11.03, 18.39–18.41
Copyright Office, registration with 3.38, 3.39
Dastar Corp case and trademark licensing 3.05–3.18
dilution notion 1.11
domain name transactions 4.12
function of trademarks 1.21
Generally Accepted Accounting Principles 7.40
Hy-Cross principle 18.18
intent-to-use (ITU) trademark applications 18.07
intersection of trademark and bankruptcy laws *see* bankruptcy and trademark licenses, law intersecting in United States
judicial developments 18.16–18.20, 18.32–18.37
   assignment 'in gross' 18.19–18.20
   early (conservative) decisions 18.17–18.18
   evolution of the standard 18.32–18.35
   recent developments 18.36–18.37
Lanham (Trademark) Act 1.21, 1.22, 3.05, 18.04, 18.05, 18.45
   trademark assignment 18.12, 18.15, 18.17
   trademark licensing 18.21, 18.22, 18.25, 18.29, 18.30, 18.32, 18.33
licensing of trademarks, current rule ('with control') 18.21–18.37
   origin of rule 18.29–18.31
   rationale for rule 18.27–18.28
Patent and Trademark Office *see* USPTO (United States Patent and Trademark Office)
reverse passing off 3.05
and Security and Exchange Commission (SEC) filings 7.15
security interests 18.42–18.44
strategic transactions 18.38–18.44
   assignment and license-back 11.03, 18.39–18.41
   security interests in trademarks 18.42–18.44

Supplemental Register, use of 1.15
trademark law 18.03–18.05
Trademark Manual of Examining Procedure (TMEP) 11.40, 11.41, 18.08
Uniform Commercial Code 18.42
unregistered trademarks
   see also registration of trademarks and licenses
   in ASEAN 22.23–22.26
   India 23.49–23.50, 23.69
   licensing
      in India 23.49–23.50
      in United Kingdom 15.85
   protected at common law 1.09
   in United Kingdom 15.19, 15.85
USPTO (United States Patent and Trademark Office) 11.40, 18.08, 18.26, 18.42, 18.43
   Assignment Recordation Branch 18.09

validity of assignment, UK 15.20
validity of international trademark transactions
   capacity 12.18–12.19
   choice-of-law clauses 12.35–12.38
   formal 12.13–12.14, 12.37
   substantive 12.15–12.17, 12.38
Vienna Convention on the Law of Treaties (VCLT)
   double taxation 8.26
   and TRIPS Agreement 1.13, 1.64
Vietnam
   assignment of trademarks 22.20, 22.21, 22.22
   Law on Intellectual Property 22.35, 22.37
   licensing of registered trademarks 22.35–22.37
   registration of trademark transactions 22.60–22.61
   trademarks as property in 22.08, 22.09
voice *see* exit, voice and loyalty framework (Hirschman)

warranties
   France 17.17
   Germany 16.59
   United Kingdom 15.71

weak party, choice-of-court clauses 12.22–12.23
weighted average cost of capital (WACC) 7.08
Whois database, domain name transactions 4.24, 4.29
WIPO (World Intellectual Property Organization) *see* World Intellectual Property Organization (WIPO)
WordPress platform, domain name transactions 4.02
World Intellectual Property Organization (WIPO)
  dispute resolution mechanisms 13.06, 13.14
  General Assembly 2.08
  global function 2.01
  International Bureau 2.27, 2.29, 2.44, 2.50
  Lisbon Agreement 1.06
  normative framework 2.04–2.09
  Common Regulations 2.05, 2.09
  Joint Recommendation Concerning Trademark Licenses 2.08
  Madrid Protocol 2.09
  Paris Convention 2.06
  Singapore Treaty 2.05, 2.07
  Report of 2013 (*Brands – Reputation and Image in the Global Marketplace*) 2.03, 2.53
  technical Committees 2.55
World Trade Organization (WTO)
  Chinese accession to 20.08, 20.67
  dispute settlement system 1.01
    WTO Dispute–Settlement Panel 1.37, 1.39, 1.42
  Indian membership 23.05
  naked licensing 1.22
  TRIPS Agreement *see* TRIPS (Agreement on Trade-Related Aspects of Intellectual property Rights)